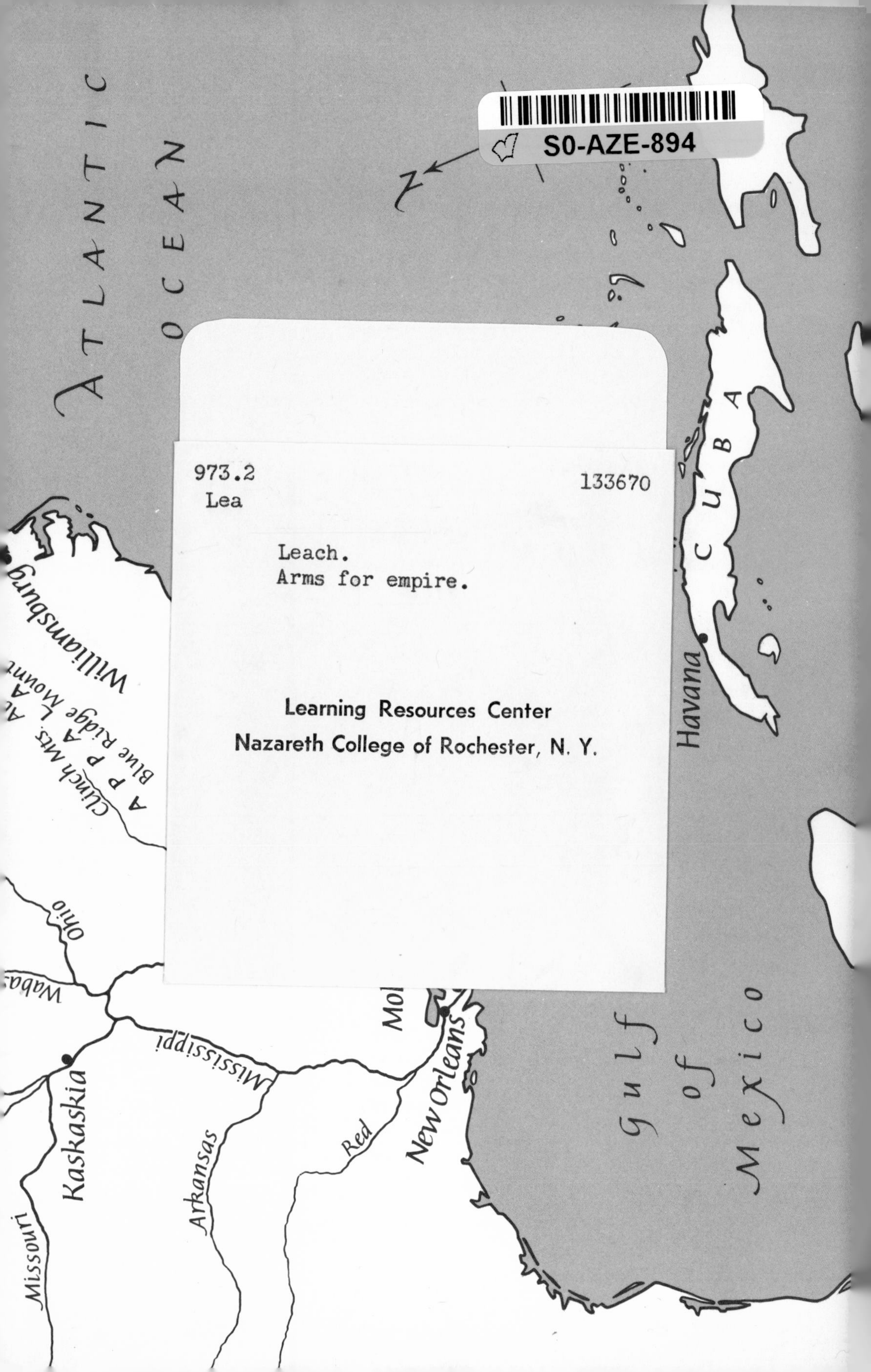

ATLANTIC

OCEAN

N

CUBA

Havana

Williamsburg

Blue Ridge Mount.

Clinch Mts.

A P P A L A

Ohio

Wabash

Mississippi

Kaskaskia

Missouri

Arkansas

Red

New Orleans

Mol

Gulf

of

Mexico

THE MACMILLAN WARS OF THE UNITED STATES

Louis Morton, *General Editor*

DARTMOUTH COLLEGE

———◆———

VOLUMES PUBLISHED

HISTORY OF THE UNITED STATES ARMY
Russell F. Weigley
TEMPLE UNIVERSITY

FRONTIERSMEN IN BLUE
The United States Army and the Indian, 1848–1865
Robert M. Utley
NATIONAL PARK SERVICE

PRESIDENT WILSON FIGHTS HIS WAR
World War I and the American Intervention
Harvey A. DeWeerd
THE RAND CORPORATION

THE SWORD OF THE REPUBLIC
The United States Army on the Frontier, 1783–1846
Francis Paul Prucha
MARQUETTE UNIVERSITY

BLOOD ON THE BORDER
The United States Army and the Mexican Irregulars
Clarence C. Clendenen
HOOVER INSTITUTION ON WAR, REVOLUTION, AND PEACE

THE WAR OF AMERICAN INDEPENDENCE
Military Attitudes, Policies, and Practice, 1763–1789
Don Higginbotham
UNIVERSITY OF NORTH CAROLINA

ARMS FOR EMPIRE
A Military History of the British Colonies in North America, 1607–1763
Douglas E. Leach
VANDERBILT UNIVERSITY

THE AMERICAN WAY OF WAR
A History of Military Strategy and Policy
Russell F. Weigley
TEMPLE UNIVERSITY

VOLUMES IN PREPARATION

THE MEXICAN WAR
K. J. Bauer
RENSSELAER POLYTECHNIC INSTITUTE

SHERMAN'S FRONTIER REGULARS
The United States Army and the Indian, 1866–1890
Robert M. Utley
NATIONAL PARK SERVICE

HISTORY OF THE UNITED STATES AIR FORCE
Alfred F. Hurley
UNITED STATES AIR FORCE ACADEMY

THE CIVIL WAR
Thomas L. Connelly
ALLEGHENY COLLEGE

THE WAR OF 1812
R. A. Preston
ROYAL MILITARY COLLEGE OF CANADA
and
S. F. Wise
QUEENS UNIVERSITY (CANADA)

WORLD WAR II (PACIFIC)
Louis Morton
DARTMOUTH COLLEGE

AMERICAN MILITARY INTERVENTION IN LATIN AMERICA
Annette Baker Fox
INSTITUTE OF WAR AND PEACE STUDIES, COLUMBIA UNIVERSITY

HISTORY OF THE UNITED STATES ARMY
Raymond G. O'Connor
TEMPLE UNIVERSITY

THE SPANISH-AMERICAN WAR
J. A. S. Grenville
UNIVERSITY OF LEEDS
and
David Trask
STATE UNIVERSITY OF NEW YORK (STONYBROOK)

WORLD WAR II (EUROPE AND AFRICA)
Hugh M. Cole
RESEARCH ANALYSIS CORPORATION

THE KOREAN WAR
Martin Blumenson

Arms for Empire

A MILITARY HISTORY OF THE BRITISH COLONIES
IN NORTH AMERICA, 1607–1763

ARMS
FOR EMPIRE

A MILITARY HISTORY
OF THE BRITISH COLONIES
IN NORTH AMERICA, 1607-1763

★

Douglas Edward Leach

The Macmillan Company, New York, New York

Collier-Macmillan Publishers, London

The Macmillan Company
866 Third Avenue, New York, N.Y. 10022
Collier-Macmillan Canada Ltd., Toronto, Ontario

Library of Congress Catalog Card Number: 72-81078

Permission from the Eastern National Park and Monument Association to reprint the map of Fort Necessity
and Vicinity, 1754, which originally appeared in *New
Light on Washington's Fort Necessity: A Report on the
Archeological Explorations at Fort Necessity National
Battlefield Site* by J. C. Harrington, is gratefully
acknowledged.

FIRST PRINTING

Printed in the United States of America

FOR CAROL AND BRADFORD

*May their generation find the
good peace that somehow
has eluded mine.*

Contents

Maps

Preface

THE TIME IS long past when armed conflict may be presented to serious, sensitive readers as a kind of glorious adventure. Our tragic, degrading experiences with war in the twentieth century should have purged us of any such delusion. Now we know war for what it really is—one of humanity's most monstrous failures. But the history of armed conflict should not be ignored, for it has been a tremendously determinative part of human experience. Some of our natural interest in the subject derives from the fact that people involved in war do respond to extraordinary forms of challenge; dramatic confrontations, dangerous ventures, personal heroism are intrinsic. It is fascinating to see how human beings conduct themselves in such circumstances. But far deeper are the lessons to be learned, lessons that may prove valuable in the search for international peace. By studying the tragedy of war we may acquire, with God's help, some of the wisdom that is essential if man is to banish armed conflict from this planet which is, after all, every man's home.

Europeans migrating to North America in the seventeenth and eighteenth centuries to establish homes in a new land did not escape the scourge of war, nor did the Indians who were confronted with that extraordinary migration. Of the 156 years between the founding of Jamestown and the Treaty of Paris, more than one-third were

years of warfare somewhere in the colonies. At first there were
sporadic outbreaks of hostility between whites and Indians. Soon
rival European colonies were vying with each other for territorial
and commercial advantage, often involving allied Indians in the
process. The Indians, having their own intertribal enmities and
needing both the trade and the military support of one group or
another of the Europeans, inevitably became enmeshed in the expanding web of diplomacy and war. Starting in 1689, the English
colonies were involved in a fateful series of four great wars against
the French, with the Spaniards more often than not participating
as allies of the latter. From this series of wars the English emerged
triumphant in 1763, having defeated their European enemies and
opened the entire area east of the Mississippi River to future British
expansion. The French and Spaniards suffered significant territorial
losses, but the Indians lost even more—their own future. Henceforth they were to be a scorned, rejected, and exploited people.

This book tells the story of these momentous developments. Its
title, *Arms for Empire: A Military History of the British Colonies
in North America, 1607–1763*, has been chosen to define the scope
of the study. Emphasis has been placed upon the experiences of the
British colonies in mainland America, although developments are
interpreted within the larger context of European colonization and
the concerns of the European nations contending for predominance
in the New World. Thus defined, it is a very large subject. I have
tried to present a balanced and fair account of the principal developments, accurate in detail and constructive in interpretation.

My usual practice in quoting directly from primary sources has
been to make certain minor changes of form where that has seemed
advisable in the interest of clarity, without altering in any way the
wording of the original. Ancient forms of *i*, *j*, *u*, and *v* have been
replaced with their modern equivalents, as has the old character
thorn. Raised letters have been brought down to the line, and
various abbreviations including the ampersand have been spelled
out. In the matter of dates, I have not converted from the Julian
calendar which was in general use throughout the English-speaking
world until 1752.

No man can finish a project such as this without feeling grateful
to many institutions and individuals who have made valuable contributions to the finished product. On several occasions the Research
Council of Vanderbilt University provided funds to aid research

and writing. My files of notes testify to the excellent work done by my former research assistant Chester R. Young, now Professor of History at Cumberland College. Advice, technical help, and courtesies have been graciously rendered by Professors Paul H. Hardacre and Carl R. Phillips, and Mr. Herbert J. Peck, Jr., all of Vanderbilt University, Professor Charles H. Morgan of Amherst College, Professor Rand Burnette of MacMurray College, Colonel Edward P. Hamilton and Mrs. Thomas V. Lape of the Fort Ticonderoga Museum, Dr. David A. Armour of the Mackinac Island State Park Commission, Mr. Robert K. Krick of the Fort Necessity National Battlefield, and Mr. Howard P. Brokaw. My typists, Mrs. James A. Luton and Mrs. V. Jacque Voegeli, performed their essential tasks with helpful efficiency. Working space away from interruptions was most kindly provided at one crucial stage by Mrs. Fred M. Downey, Jr. I also am grateful for the patient counsel of Professor Louis Morton of Dartmouth College, general editor of the growing series in which this volume now takes its place, and for the assistance rendered by the editorial staff of the Macmillan Company.

Finally, and here I have difficulty finding words adequate for my thought, I am deeply grateful to my wife Brenda for her invaluable support through the years. This has been of two kinds: practical, which includes typing, collating, and checking; and moral, which goes far beyond all else. *Proverbs* 31: 10-31.

Douglas Edward Leach

Vanderbilt University
May, 1972

ABBREVIATIONS USED IN NOTES

AHR   *American Historical Review*

CHR   *Canadian Historical Review*

CSP   *Calendar of State Papers, Colonial Series, America and West Indies* (42 vols. to date; London, 1880–   )

JSH   *Journal of Southern History*

MCR   Nathaniel B. Shurtleff, ed., *Records of the Governor and Company of the Massachusetts Bay in New England* (5 vols.; Boston, 1853–1854)

MHC   Massachusetts Historical Society *Collections* (The digit preceding the abbreviation is the number of the series.)

MVHR   *Mississippi Valley Historical Review*

NEQ   *New England Quarterly*

NYCD   E. B. O'Callaghan and Berthold Fernow, eds., *Documents Relative to the Colonial History of the State of New-York* (15 vols.; Albany, 1856–1887)

WMQ   *William and Mary Quarterly,* Third Series

Arms for Empire

A MILITARY HISTORY OF THE BRITISH COLONIES
IN NORTH AMERICA, 1607–1763

☆   ☆   ☆   ☆   ☆

CHAPTER 1

The Genesis of the American Military Tradition

No ONE KNOWS when organized fighting, or warfare, first began occurring among the peoples of the world, but one may safely assume that when a band of migrating Mongolians made the first human footprints on North American soil more than 20,000 years ago they already were acquainted with the phenomenon. Their many descendants undoubtedly continued fighting among themselves, generation after generation, with club and spear. Early in the eleventh century A.D. blond Scandinavians arrived on the east coast of the continent, and before long, as the sagas relate, Norsemen and Indians were spilling each other's blood. Five centuries later other Europeans began exploring the mysterious shores of what is now the eastern portion of the United States. Although they hoped to establish peaceful relations with the native peoples, they came fully armed and expecting trouble not only from the Indians but from European rivals as well. So the tragic pattern of conflict continued to evolve.

Probably at that time there were fewer than 300,000 Indians east of the Mississippi River, none of whom could have had any conception of the overwhelming wave of European migration that was to begin rolling into their territories. On numerous occasions these Indians received the first European arrivals with cautious hospitality. Unfortunately, early friendliness soon was abused by one people or

1

the other, with the consequence that suspicion and hostility quickly took the place of amiability. The Europeans marked down the native Americans as primitive and even savage, a heathen people whose penchant for wickedness was unrestrained by true religion. Even the sympathetic Roger Williams asserted that "all Indians are extremely treacherous. . . ." [1] What the Indians were saying about the Europeans at the same time has not been recorded.

Certainly the first reception given the Jamestown colonists in 1607 was anything but hospitable. As one member of the expedition recalled, "there came the Savages creeping upon all foure, from the Hills, like Beares, with their Bowes in their mouthes, charged us very desperately in the faces, hurt Captaine Gabrill Archer in both his hands, and a sayler in two places of the body very dangerous." [2] In similar fashion a landing party of Pilgrims, while camped just above a Cape Cod beach in 1620, were given a taste of Indian hostility. It was a cold dawn, and the men were busy about breakfast, yawning, and stamping their feet, when there came a great yelling from the nearby woods, followed by the sinister whirr of incoming arrows. Grabbing their muskets, the English returned the greeting with gusto until the Indians broke off and fled. At this, some of the party, with more courage than prudence, "followed them about a quarter of a mile . . . and shot off two or three pieces . . ." to let the Indians know "they were not afraid of them or any way discouraged." [3] These Europeans, like many others in similar circumstances, considered it essential to impress unmistakably upon the "inferior" native people that white men were in full command of the situation. Like a horse, they believed, an Indian was "safe" only after he had been mastered.

Although the individual Indian was as strong and brave as any man on earth, in general the Indians were not very far advanced in the science of organized warfare. A typical war party consisted of volunteers who had rallied to the call of some fellow tribesman or tribal chief seeking vengeance against a foe. [4] The individual warrior, his face carefully patterned with colorful pigments, and armed with bow and arrows, club, or tomahawk, seemed a terrifying figure. Able to subsist for many days on a minimal supply of parched corn carried in a small leather pouch at his belt, highly skilled in woods lore and tracking, an Indian warrior could cover great distances through the wilderness either in stealthy advance or swift retreat. Once in contact with the enemy, the war party would seek favorable ground and then either advance or make a stand. If both sides wanted action, they eventually came to grips, first discharging their arrows and then falling to in hand-to-hand combat. Apparently little attention was given to formal tactics except for the ambush, and in that particular form of attack the Indians were truly skilled. The Europeans, schooled in the highly developed tactics of the Old World and saturated with the feudal concept of honor, quickly developed an attitude of contempt for the skulking, evasive mode of fighting practiced by the Indians. They quickly learned, also, to fear it.

If the Indians had been the only potential foe, however, the English colonists would have been much less concerned with the problem of defense and less willing to make the personal sacrifices required to maintain a high level of preparedness. But to the south were the Spaniards, already more than a hundred years into the game of colonization and firmly established in much of the vast area from Florida and Mexico down to Santiago and Buenos Aires. Ever since 1565, there had been a small Spanish base at St. Augustine on the east coast of Florida, guarding the important sea route from the Caribbean to the ports of Spain. Originally the Spanish government had denied that any other nation, with the exception of Portugal, had any right to colonize or even trade in the New World, an exclusive claim based upon the papal decree of 1493 and the subsequent Treaty of Tordesillas. All intruders were subject to attack by Spanish forces, as the French learned to their grief when they tried to settle in northern Florida. Neither France nor England, of course, ever accepted Spain's restriction. Both of these countries established colonies of their own during the first half of the seventeenth century, and circumstances gradually compelled Spain to modify its extreme claim. By 1670 the Spanish government was forced to recognize that England was in effective occupation of the east coast from New England down almost to the mouth of the Savannah River; but prior to that time, and even later in the disputed region close to northern Florida, English settlements had to reckon with the possibility of Spanish attack.[5]

After establishing themselves in Acadia and at Quebec in the valley of the St. Lawrence River, the French too were a possible menace to English settlement. From such bases French influence among the Indians and consequent Franco-Indian power began to spread in an expanding arc, challenging English aspirations in neighboring areas. The fact that the English were Protestants while the Spanish and French remained loyal to Rome of course intensified the rivalry and lent an element of crusading zeal to the endeavors of the various rivals. Other nations too were involved, especially in the early years. The mercantile-minded Dutch, and the Swedes as well, tried their hand at colonization, principally in the region between the Connecticut River and Chesapeake Bay. Under these circumstances, in a world where governments and organized groups of ambitious investors so readily resorted to force as a way of achieving their objectives, every English colonist had reason to take stock of his military capability, weighing well the possibility of armed interference by Indians and European rivals alike.

Defense meant weapons, organization, and training. In the early days of English colonization, troops frequently were outfitted with metal helmets known as "pikeman's pots" and various pieces of body armor, including breastplates and backplates. But plate armor proved restrictive and fatiguing in the swamps and woods of eastern America as the colonists, made clumsy by such apparatus, struggled to cope with the lightly clad, elusive Indians. When the natives began to acquire guns in considerable quantities, an inevitable development, the colonists began exchanging their body armor for more practical garments, such as padded jack coats and thick leather buff coats. In similar fashion they readily replaced their sharp-pointed pikes with flintlock muskets, while cumbersome swords sometimes gave way to knives and even hatchets. Later the bayonet was to become one of the chief auxiliary weapons of the musketeer. Pike and sword faced toward the receding past; gunpowder and its brood of utilizing weapons claimed the future.

By the beginning of English colonization in America, firearms ranging in size from pistols to ponderous cannon were familiar weapons.[6] He who would understand the colonial wars must begin with the flintlock musket, which was the basic weapon of the early colonist. This was a smooth-bore gun whose barrel, with an interior diameter of about three-quarters of an inch, ranged in length from about $3\frac{1}{2}$ feet to as much as $4\frac{1}{2}$ feet. Its total weight was some 14 or 15 pounds, light enough for a man to handle and fire without using a supporting stake. Ammunition for the musket usually was in the form of cartridges, especially during the eighteenth century. Each cartridge consisted of one charge of granulated powder and a lead ball rolled in a piece of brown paper, which was folded or tied together at both ends. When loading his weapon, the musketeer simply extracted a cartridge from a special box worn on his waistbelt or suspended from his shoulder, bit open the lower end of the cartridge, poured about a thimbleful of the powder into the pan of the flintlock mechanism and the remainder down the barrel, and then with a special rod known as a rammer drove the ball and paper firmly down upon the powder. It was even possible, though tricky, to avoid the ramming entirely by "making up of the Cartridges to such an Exactness, that, after they are placed in the Muzzle, one Thump with the Butt-end on the Ground will make them run down to the Breech of the Barrel." [7]

The flintlock mechanism consisted of a steel plate located at the rear end of the barrel on the right side and nearly perpendicular to it; a small receptacle or pan just below the plate with a touch hole leading into the interior of the barrel; a cock whose upper end contained a small vise operated by a thumb screw; and a spring which, when activated by the trigger, would cause the head of the cock to dart forward toward the steel plate. Usually the musketeer carried with him about a dozen fairly flat pieces of flint, each about $1\frac{1}{4}$ inches square with a beveled striking edge. One of these flints was kept firmly held in the vise on the cock. After priming the pan and loading his weapon, the soldier drew the cock back to the half-cock, or safety position, or, if intending to fire immediately, all the way back. Then, resting the barrel in his left hand, he took aim and pulled the trigger. Instantly the spring was released, the cock darted forward causing the flint to strike against the steel plate, while at the same time the pan was automatically exposed. The sparks created by flint striking against steel dropped into the priming powder, the resulting flash raced through the touch hole into the barrel, and the gun fired.

The soft lead bullet, moving at a relatively low velocity (as compared with a modern rifle bullet), had great knockdown power. As soon as it struck any resistant object, such as human flesh, it began to spread, causing large wounds as it plowed on. The effective range was short. A well-trained musketeer could hit a stationary man at a distance of perhaps 80 to 100 yards; while the extreme effective range in volley fire, where the target was not an individual but a massed formation of troops, probably was not much more than 150 or 200 yards. Obviously this gun was at its best when used in close fighting. One contemporary military expert insisted that

> a soldier must be very unfortunate indeed who shall be wounded by a common musket at 150 yards, provided his antagonist aims at him; and as to firing at a man at 200 yards with a common musket, you may just as well fire at the moon and have the same hopes of hitting your object. I do maintain and will prove, whenever called on, that no man was ever killed at 200 yards, by a common soldier's musket, by the person who aimed at him.[8]

Some troops carried flintlock weapons of smaller size than the conventional infantry musket. Pistols, for example, operated on the same principle as the musket and were especially useful in the hands of mounted soldiers or troopers. In range and accuracy, of course, they did not begin to match the musket, but they could be conveniently carried in leather holsters, ready for quick use. A "bastard musket" was a gun that deviated from the ordinary or usual size of the musket, probably having a somewhat smaller bore. Lighter still was the "caliver," a shoulder weapon that developed into what eighteenth-century soldiers called a "fusil." Also fairly common in the colonies was the "carbine," a flintlock gun only about 3 or 4 feet long, well suited for use by mounted troops.[9]

Artillery entered the military scene in America at an early date. A cannon was essentially a heavy, rather thick iron tube closed at its rear end and mounted on some kind of wooden platform or wheeled carriage. Near the closed end was a touch hole through which fire could be introduced. Loading was done through the muzzle, either by ladling the appropriate quantity of gunpowder directly from a bucket and then inserting the wad and projectile, or else by using a prepared cartridge containing both powder and ball. The wadding might consist of straw, rags, or indeed almost any similar material. When the cannon was loaded, the gunner elevated the barrel to achieve the proper range and then fired by applying a length of burning match to the priming powder in the touch hole or vent. As soon as the piece was fired, the crew rushed forward to prepare it for another shot. One of the men pressed his finger over the touch hole to stifle any lingering flame within, while another swabbed out the barrel with a cylindrical "sponge" on the end of a long pole. Then it was powder, wad (rammed down), and shot all over again. A good crew could get off a shot about every four minutes.[10]

There were many types of artillery projectiles, including a flimsy container packed with small metal balls whose spreading mass in flight could be devastating to exposed personnel, and a pair of metal weights coupled by a length of chain especially effective in tearing down ships' rigging. Most commonly used, however, were the iron cannonballs, either solid, for battering, or explosive, for widespread destruction by blast and fragmentation. The latter type, known as bombs, consisted of a hollow shell packed with explosive powder. A fuse leading in through the casing was ignited automatically by the firing of the propelling charge in the gun, and the shell itself subsequently exploded after a predetermined period in flight. Also sometimes used, especially for setting targets afire, was solid shot that had been heated red hot just before being inserted in the gun. For this, a special technique was required. After the propelling charge had been inserted, it was protected by a dry wad and then a wadding of green turf or wet straw. The bore then was swabbed with a wet sponge. Next, the glowing red ball was lifted from the nearby fire by means of a special tool and carefully inserted in the barrel. Hopefully, the wet wadding prevented premature ignition of the propelling charge. When the gunner applied his match to the touch hole, the fiery shot sailed across the sky like a malignant comet.[11]

In the seventeenth century, various types and sizes of artillery were distinguished by such picturesque designations as "falcon," "minion," "saker," and "culverin," but later it became common practice to identify a cannon by the weight of its projectile. Thus, one spoke of "6-pounders," "12-pounders," and "24-pounders." In addition, besieging armies made good use of the mortar, a squat, short-barreled piece mounted on a heavy wooden base and elevated for high-angle fire. This was used chiefly to drop explosive bombs into fortifications or entrenchments. Some artillery in the eighteenth century had an effective range of 1,000 yards or more, but cannon generally were employed against targets considerably closer than that.

During the early years of English settlement, the colonies were left largely to their own resources in the matter of defense, for England had little support to offer at such a great distance. Colonial charters issued by the crown usually included specific authorization for the proprietor or governor to maintain and employ military forces. For example, the grant of Maryland to Lord Baltimore in 1632 stated that because

> in so remote a region, placed among so many barbarous nations, the incursions as well of the barbarians themselves, as of other enemies, pirates and ravagers, probably will be feared; therefore we have given, and for us, our heirs, and successors, do give by these presents, as full and unrestrained power as any captain-general of an army ever hath had, unto the aforesaid now baron of Baltimore, and to his heirs and assigns, by themselves, or by their captains, or other officers, to summon to their standards, and to array all men, of whatsoever condition, or wheresoever born, for the time being, in the said province of Maryland, to wage war, and to pursue, even beyond the limits of their province, the enemies and ravagers aforesaid, infesting those parts by land and by sea, and (if God shall grant it) to vanquish and captivate them, and the captives to put to death, or, according to their discretion, to save, and to do all other and singular the things which appertain, or have been accustomed to appertain unto the authority and office of a captain-general of an army.[12]

Article 13 of the same charter empowered the proprietor, in case of insurrection, to impose martial law, and gave him authority to punish any of his colonists who refused to bear arms.

Implicit in these charter provisions was the assumption that the colonists themselves would be ready and able to serve as soldiers, an assumption resting mainly upon the English tradition and practice of a compulsory military obligation distributed through all ranks of the population. When Machiavelli early in the sixteenth century remarked that "never did anybody establish a republic or a kingdom who did not suppose that the same persons who inhabited it would need with their weapons to defend it," he was expressing a view that had long been commonplace in England and would later take deep root in America as an important part of the English heritage.[13] Toward the end of the colonial period, the tradition was as strong as ever. The opening words of a Massachusetts publication of 1758 could hardly be more explicit:

> As it is the essential Property of a free Government to depend on no other Soldiery but it's own Citizens for it's Defence; so in all such free Governments, every Freeman and every Freeholder should be a Soldier. . . . Every Man therefore that wishes to secure his own Freedom, and thinks it his Duty to defend that of his Country, should, as he

prides himself in being a Free Citizen, think it his truest Honour to be a Soldier Citizen.[14]

The English system of compulsory military training through the agency of a citizen militia was readily transplanted in American soil. In all of the early colonies such as Virginia, Plymouth, and Massachusetts Bay, a large proportion of the first settlers must have had some previous experience with the English militia. They remembered that the obligation was seldom popular among the common people of England and often was evaded. Nevertheless, the system as developed under the Tudor monarchs and continued under the early Stuarts did provide the majority of able-bodied males between the ages of sixteen and sixty with some knowledge of weapons and tactics. Required maintenance of arms, obligatory enrollment, forced contribution of horses or equipment, compulsory service—these were longstanding practices accepted as normal by the people of England. Quite naturally, when men began to consider the prospects for establishing colonies in America and when they contemplated the potential dangers from Indians and hostile Europeans, they readily incorporated their previous experience into their thinking about colonial defense. Equally important is the fact that of the hundreds and thousands of Englishmen who began migrating to the new colonies, a large percentage had received some basic training in the militia or at least knew how to handle a gun, while some could even boast of charging to the cannon's mouth during the campaigns in the Low Countries.

Stand now, an invisible spectator, at the edge of an English field and watch the village trainband, or company, perform its ragged drill. The unkempt ranks tramp by, battered old muskets shouldered at a dozen different angles, feet casting an overwhelming vote for rugged individualism. Laughable, yes, but in those ranks march young men who one day will sail across the wide ocean and make homes for themselves in the English colonies of the New World. There, facing hostile Indians and Europeans, some of them at least may begin to value the militia system of old England and be thankful for the training they have received.

The so-called "iron rule" period during the second decade of the Virgina Colony's desperate struggle for survival meant, first of all, the introduction of stern military discipline for the colonists.[15] Of the three principal men who governed Virginia during that crucial interval—Sir Thomas Dale, Sir Thomas Gates, and Lord De La Warr—all were veteran soldiers with a record of active service either in Ireland or on the Continent.

Constructive labor was demanded of every colonist; teamwork was the order of the day. The men were divided into labor companies of about fifty men each, commanded by captains. Significant work projects were undertaken, including the construction of a system of palisades to protect the main settlement at Jamestown and the building of a fort at Henrico some 40 miles farther up the river. Even though the military regime continued for several years, there was little or no further development of military organization until the following decade when a sudden unexpected Indian attack nearly wrecked the colony in 1622. After Virginia came under royal control in 1624, the outlines of a definite militia organization began to emerge. Military obligation commenced at the age of seventeen and continued until the age of sixty. All men within that age range, with a few exceptions, were expected to belong to a unit, and as the area of settlement expanded, new units were formed.[16]

In the meantime, England's second colony in America had been established at Plymouth in 1620. Intending to settle by themselves in a remote place, the Pilgrim leaders foresaw the need for military preparedness even though they themselves were quite out of touch with martial affairs. They gathered a good supply of weapons, including a few small cannon; equally important, they acquired the services of a professional consultant. Miles Standish, a veteran soldier, agreed to accompany the Pilgrims to America, to advise them in matters military, and if necessary to lead them in battle. His presence probably saved the courageous but inexperienced Pilgrim company from obliteration. It was Standish who trained the Pilgrim men in the use of firearms, instructed them in the proper performance of military duties, led them in their first skirmish with the Indians, and laid the foundations for a system of militia in the young colony.[17]

The Pilgrims did not intend to be surprised and overwhelmed if they could prevent it. Early in 1621, with the advice of Standish, they organized a rudimentary system of defense and adopted a few basic military regulations. This was the foundation upon which the colony began to build a militia, at first in the original settlement at Plymouth and later, as the colony expanded, in the new villages as well. A law enacted in 1634 made every colonist "subject to such military order for trayning and exercise of armes as shall be thought meet, agreed on, and prescribed by the Governor and Assistants." [18] Two years later, authority spoke emphatically by specifying a fine of three shillings for unauthorized absence from a training session. Nor was any man allowed to establish his own household until he had acquired the arms and ammunition that all heads of households were required to maintain. Thus, from the earliest days, Plymouth Colony stood armed against its potential foes.

The Puritan colony of Massachusetts Bay, with its principal settlement at Boston, was equally concerned with military preparedness. Of some twenty men identifiable as leaders during the first three years of the Bay Colony, at least four had brought with them some experience of military command. John Underhill probably was most highly qualified of all, having received professional training and having seen active service in the Netherlands; much of the responsibility for developing military preparedness in Massachusetts rested upon the firm shoulders of this hard-bitten veteran. In April 1631, the Court of Assistants ordered the captains of militia to drill their men every Saturday, a stringent requirement in a pioneering community with so many urgent demands upon the people's time and strength. All musketeers were expected to have on hand a pound of powder, twenty bullets, and two fathoms of match. But the ineffectiveness of the system soon became all too apparent. A test alarm produced almost instant confusion. The hastily assembled militiamen, "like men amazed, knew not how to behave themselves, so as the officers could not draw them into any order." [19] If some of the lads in the ranks had trouble smothering their snickers and guffaws, the authorities were not at all amused. They doubled the watch and took steps to make sure that such dangerous confusion could never happen again.

By 1635, in each of the three well-established, well-organized English colonies—Virginia, Plymouth, and Massachusetts—there had evolved a system of militia training on a more or less regular basis. This was largely derived from the old system in the mother country, modified according to the needs and capabilities of infant states in a distant wilderness land. The principle of universal compulsory service, that every citizen may be required to assist in the defense of the state, was firmly rooted in past experience and for the most part went unchallenged. Indeed, the majority of the colonists, being themselves irrevocably committed to the venture of founding new states in the wilderness and seeing all about them the perils of the New World environment, seemed to feel a true sense of obligation in the matter of military service. Onerous as it might be to maintain the required paraphernalia and periodically to quit the planting field for the drill field, most men fulfilled their obligation with little protest. As new colonies were formed they created their own militias, drawing upon the experience of the older colonies as well as their English heritage. The usual age range for compulsory military training was sixteen to sixty, which meant that a large proportion of the adult males had a long if not always regular or' intensive experience with martial affairs.[20] Indeed, the callused hand of the pioneering settler cradled a musket as easily as a pitchfork, and military training of a sort was nearly as much a part of his diet as salt pork and corn mush.

The rules and regulations governing the militia in each colony were frequently modified or changed to meet new needs and circumstances. Three factors were of great influence in this evolutionary process: local conditions and needs in particular colonies, the nature of the American environment in general, and the continuing development of military science in Europe.

Adaptation to the local situation is most easily demonstrated in those colonies which came to have large numbers of slaves among their population. There the militia often considered its prime responsibility to be the tracking down of fugitive slaves and the repression of slave revolts. South Carolina is a notable example, especially after the passage of the Militia Act of 1721.[21] Such duties inevitably affected the organization and operation of the militia, as shown by Georgia's Militia Act of 1755. Recognizing that a major emergency, such as invasion by a foreign foe, would provide the slaves with their best opportunity for insurrection, an apprehensive legislature required that in time of invasion when the entire militia was called into active service each company leave behind one-quarter of its personnel to be formed into local patrols for suppressing any slave uprisings.[22]

The nature of the New World environment—vast extents of terrain, much of it wilderness—and the presence of the forest-dwelling Indians gradually but firmly dictated changes in the organization and operation of the militia. Such changes did not come easily to tradition-bound colonists, but the instinct to survive will have its effect sooner or later upon even the most glacial of attitudes. Forest warfare was not battlefield warfare in the usual European sense of the term. The enemy would appear and disappear with disconcerting rapidity, while heavily encumbered troops struggled to maintain their formations and bring their weapons to bear. Under such conditions, nearly every aspect of accepted military practice, including tactical formations and the weapons employed, was subject to review and possible modification.

The seventeenth century was a period of significant development in European military science. Major improvements were made in equipment, munitions, weapons, organization, and above all in tactics. One need only call to mind such great innovators as Gustavus Adolphus, Oliver Cromwell, and the two Le Telliers to be aware of the scope of the changes being made in European armies. Weaponry was being made to catch up with forward-moving technology, and tactics with weaponry. By the early decades of the next century, the science of warfare had reached a sort of plateau beyond which it would make little significant progress until about the time of the Napoleonic Wars. American leaders who legislated for and led the militia inevitably became aware of the advances being made, and so whatever improvements were deemed appropriate for American conditions sooner or later found their way into the colonial units.

Most of the colonies required all freemen of military age to own and maintain certain specified weapons, ammunition, and other military equipment. This could be a fairly expensive obligation for the individual householder. In South Carolina, for example, every soldier was required to appear for training with "a good sufficient gun, well fixed, a good cover for their lock, one good cartridge box, with at least twenty cartridges of good powder and ball, and one good belt or girdle, one ball of wax sticking at the end of the cartridge box, to defend the arms in rain, one worm, one wier and four good spare flints, also a sword, bayonet or hatchet." [23] The reiteration of the word "good" suggests that all too many colonists of modest means sought to fulfill their obligation year after year with worn and broken equipment.

Arms requirements were enforced by a periodic "view of arms," or by a house-to-house visitation. A Puritan officer in Massachusetts reported that the men were "very observant to keep their armes in good order," but the experience of most colonies showed the need for careful inspections.[24] There seems to have been a considerable

amount of evasion, with the same guns showing up in different
hands as the inspectors arrived. At an outlying settlement in Maine
the local officer, complaining of the inhabitants, stated that although
"they generly apeered on Training days under arms yet I find
severol of them was borrowed. . . ."[25] The problem was a common
one, causing a flurry only in times of sudden emergency. A surviving record in the hand of a company clerk depicts the usual
situation:

> By vertue of A verbal order from Leift nathaniel Willyams to veiw
> the arms of our company: I with sergeant gibson, serjeant hawkins
> and corporal paine. did Acordingly go through the company and found
> the souldiers most of them furnished acording to Law with arms and
> amunition and thos that weer not so furnished I gave acount of in
> writeing to the Leftenant aforsaid

March 1st 168$\frac{8}{9}$:   Daniel fairfeild clerk[26]

In addition to the arms and ammunition owned by individuals,
the colonies generally tried to maintain a public supply in conveniently located depositories. The Duke of York's Laws, for example, required that every town in New York have a storehouse
containing at least one barrel of powder, 150 pounds of bullets,
and 30 pounds of match, all in good condition. In Massachusetts,
a colony official known as the surveyor-general was responsible for
seeing that the public supplies of powder and bullets were maintained ready for use.[27] The cost of these reserve supplies was met
by public taxation and constituted for the colonists a further burden
in the interests of defense.

Compulsory-service legislation in all the colonies generally provided for some occupational exemptions. A composite list of such
exemptions garnered from the laws of various colonies would include members of the legislature, magistrates and judges, clerks of
court, sheriffs and constables, ministers and deacons, physicians and
surgeons, college professors and their students, schoolmasters, mill-
ers, mariners, overseers supervising four or more slaves, and constant herdsmen. As a special encouragement to an infant industry,
Virginia in 1730 exempted all men laboring in ironworks.[28] In some
colonies, certain high officials could obtain exemption for one of
their personal servants. Edward Johnson of Massachusetts, commenting on the situation in his colony, observed wryly that "there
are none exempt, unless it be a few timerous persons that are apt

to plead infirmity, if the Church chuse them not for Deacons, or they cannot get to serve some Magistrate or Minister." [29] Where loopholes exist, they are ever sought. On the other hand, some men who might have been willing to serve were deliberately excluded. Many colonies barred Indians and Negroes from the militia. The General Assembly of Virginia in 1723 conceded that free Negroes and Indians might be employed as drummers and trumpeters, and even required that in time of actual emergency all such persons must march with the militia, but only in the capacity of laborers.[30] The dread of putting death-dealing weapons in the hands of black (and sometimes even white) servants was often great.

Within the militia organization the trainband, or company, consisting of local men under local leaders, was the basic unit. Companies varied greatly in size. A Massachusetts law of 1652 specified sixty-four men plus the commissioned officers, which would be little more than half the size of an average on-paper company in Cromwell's New Model Army.[31] Many companies far exceeded that number, athough it was not unusual to divide companies to make new ones as the population grew. A full-size company was commanded by a captain assisted by a lieutenant and an ensign, the latter being charged with the honor and responsibility of bearing and guarding the company's colors. Noncommissioned officers included two or more sergeants and several corporals. In addition there was a company clerk, generally considered a noncombatant, whose duty it was to call the roll, note deficiencies, and keep all records. Every self-respecting company also tried to retain one or two drummers and perhaps even some trumpeters. In most cases these musicians, if one may use the term loosely, were hired under special arrangements, often at the company's own expense.

The need for rapid reconnaissance over wide areas early led to the formation of special groups of mounted men and subsequently their organization into troops of cavalry. It was a form of service that proved attractive to young men who considered themselves gentlemen and who scorned the prospect of tramping through the dust with the infantry. Compared with the lowly foot soldier in the trainband, the trooper was an imposing figure. Straight in the saddle, he was the very picture of quiet self-assurance and aristocratic courage. At his side hung his sword, ready to hand. Just forward of his saddle was a brace of flintlock pistols in leather holsters, or else a flintlock carbine. Heavy jack boots protected his legs against brush and other low growth through which he might have to charge. Under wilderness conditions the mounted units were especially useful in ranging the frontier, scouting in advance of the slow-moving foot soldiers, and pursuing bands of fleeing Indians.

Commissioned and noncommissioned officers of the militia occupied positions of considerable responsibility, especially in times of danger when the very survival of the community might depend upon their skill and judgment. In colonies where the aristocratic tradition was strong, as in Virginia and South Carolina, military commissions were monopolized by the upper class.[32] Generally it was the governor who made the appointments, and he naturally gave preference to the men who dominated the political, economic, and social life of the colony. Commissioned officers in these colonies customarily selected their own noncommissioned officers. They could make and they could break.

Elsewhere, the conditions of frontier living and the communal emphasis of separatist groups produced some interesting experiments in the democratization of military command. In the early formative period of the militia, such colonies as Plymouth, Massachusetts, Connecticut, Rhode Island, and even New York permitted the soldiers of a unit, or sometimes the freemen of the community in which the unit was established, to elect the commissioned officers, usually subject to the approval of some higher authority such as the county court or the colony legislature. In time, however, the practice proved somewhat unsettling to the order and discipline of the military units themselves and to the communities as a whole.[33] To overcome this problem, the governmental authorities began to withdraw from the people the right to choose their military leaders. In 1668, the General Court of Massachusetts reserved to itself the appointment of all commissioned officers in the troops, companies, and regiments. A few years later, the court formally adopted the sensible practice of encouraging the local committees of militia in the various towns to make nominations for these positions, although still insisting that "the allowing and appointing of all commission[ed] military officers in this jurisdiction belongs propperly and only to this Court by lawe. . . ."[34] The government of Rhode Island became concerned about "the irregular proceedings of the soldiers in their election of military officers" with "several abuses and inconveniences arising therein," and in 1713 ordained that "for the future, all and every the commissioned officers, for the militia of this colony, shall be nominated, appointed, chosen and elected by the Governor, general council and Assembly. . . ." [35] For many years this issue continued to agitate the colony.

The very close relationship between the method of selecting military officers and the state of discipline in the military units is obvious, and the decline of the elective method in colony after colony is a clear indication of the hardening of military practice under the mounting threat of external enemies and internal disorder. In general, the power and prestige of the rising aristocracy became the controlling element in the militia of virtually every colony.[36] Yet it would be a mistake to assume that the spirit of democracy was entirely stifled. All the personnel were still part-time soldiers, and the leaders continued to be chosen from among civilian neighbors. Especially in New England, where the town-meeting tradition was so strong, did the trainbands retain an atmosphere of tempered democracy that would have shocked and offended a true aristocrat or a professional martinet. George Washington finally managed to stamp some of it out at Cambridge in 1775.

Normally the governor of a colony performed the functions of a commander in chief for the militia of his colony. Sometimes in addition special councils of war or military committees were set up to supervise the militia, make decisions, and issue necessary orders. Such councils usually included the governor, some members of his council, and the top commanders of the militia. In a time of sudden emergency, a committee of this kind could meet hastily and send out orders to the militia without waiting for the full council to assemble. At the county level there usually was a commander of militia, known sometimes as the lieutenant and sometimes as the sergeant major, who had authority to call out the entire militia of the county in a time of emergency without waiting for orders from above. Likewise, a local commander such as the captain of a trainband or a troop might assemble his men to meet a sudden threat, at the same time sending word to his superiors. Thus, there was a chain of command extending from the governor down to the lowliest private, and a means of sending the militia into action at every level according to circumstances and without undue delay.

Worth noting is the way in which civil authority permeated and dominated the military structure. Always the military commanders were kept aware of their dependence upon the approval of civilian

leaders at every level, a condition made relatively easy by the fact
that the military men themselves were essentially civilians. The
point emerges clearly in the wording of the commissions issued to
officers of the trainbands in Rhode Island:

> To A. B., apoynted _____, of the Traine Band of the towne of
> _____. By vertue of these presents in his Majesties name, you are
> impowered and fully authorized to exercise and disciplyne the Com-
> pany and Trayne Band of the sayd towne in the use and exercise of
> armes, in the art millitary, and in the orderly posture of disciplyninge,
> on such daies and at such times as the lawes of this Collony have
> apoynted; and in that respect to observe the rules of the lawes as to
> fines and pennaltyes; thereby willing and commanding all infeariour
> officers and companys in the sayd Traine Band, to be respectively
> obedient to your legall commands therein. And that in case or cases
> of extreme necessity, by the approach or assault of an enemy, any waies
> to disturb the peace of the sayd towne or any part of this Collony;
> you, with the aforesayd company, are duly to observe and follow such
> orders, instructions or directions, as shall from time to time be given
> to you by the Generall Assembly of this Collony, the Governor, or
> Governor and Councill; and if need require, the Councill of Warr in
> the sayd towne, the commands and directions of either as aforesayd
> you are to observe; and the performance of the premises at all times
> and occasions shall be your suffitient warrant.[37]

This tradition and practice of subordinating the arm of defense
to civil authority is undoubtedly one of the great legacies of our
early history, nowhere more firmly expressed than in the Virginia
Bill of Rights: ". . . in all cases the military should be under strict
subordination to, and governed by, the civil power." [38]

The rapid spread of settlement in all the colonies not only complicated the problem of military administration, but also increased
the difficulty of raising and concentrating military force in a time
of emergency. Rapid communication could mean the difference
between survival and obliteration. Virtually every community or
plantation was a potential target for enemy attack, either by seaborne forces or by Indian raiders; and in such a situation, it was
essential that ways be found to spread the alarm over a large area
with great rapidity. Old England had relied for many centuries
upon a system of beacons. On prominent hilltops across the land,
fagots were kept in position ready to be ignited. The community
that first sighted an enemy would quickly fire its beacon, others
would then see the sudden blaze and ignite their own, and so the

alarm would spread from hilltop to hilltop while the men of the trainbands caught up their weapons and began to assemble under their leaders. This system was carried over to the American colonies, as Boston's famous Beacon Hill still testifies. But it was unsafe to rely upon only one method, and so the colonies generally specified several forms of alarm. The authorities in Rhode Island, for example, ordered "that this form be observed, Vidg't: Three Muskets distinctly discharged, and a Herauld appointed to go speedilie threw the Towne, and crie, Alarum! Alarum!! and the Drum to beate incessantly; upon which, all to repair . . . unto the Town House, ther to receive information of the Town Councill what is farther to be done." [39]

Anyone who has served with the armed forces in a combat zone knows well the galvanizing effect of a sudden alarm in the dead of night. In colonial times it was the dull thud of a cannon, or a series of spaced musket shots, or the sharp relentless roll of a drum, or the rapid clumping of hoofs and a hoarse cry of "Arm! Arm!" that would send the men leaping from their beds to throw on some clothing, seize weapons, and peer anxiously out of doors. The leaping light of the beacon on a nearby hilltop would serve as confirmation, while ever more distant shots and flaring fires told of the spreading alarm. Then the men in arms would hasten to the appointed rendezvous, report to their officers, and await further orders.

Fortunately, emergency calls were not frequent. Far more often than not, the assembling of the militia was an event planned in advance and carried out as a matter of routine. Units were required by law to muster periodically. These occasions really fulfilled three purposes: to ascertain the availability of personnel, to view arms, and to train the men for combat. As the General Court of Plymouth stated in 1643, it was important that "all postures of pike and muskett, motions, rankes and files, etc, messengers, skirmishes, seiges, batteries, watches, sentinells, etc, bee alwayes performed according to true millitary discipline." [40] Thus the occasional days of training were intended primarily to afford civilian soldiers the opportunity to achieve proficiency in the practice of war.

In most of the colonies, laws were passed from time to time specifying the number of training days required each year. During the early period of settlement when danger seemed ever threatening, the authorities demanded frequent sessions, in the case of Mas-

sachusetts Bay one a week. As time went on, however, the tendency
was to reduce the frequency until the annual number reached four
or even two. As early as September 1636, the General Court of
Connecticut decreed that the men in every settlement "shall traine
once in every moneth," and then went on to make special provision
for the lubberly by providing that if there are "divers very unskil-
full" they may be required to drill more frequently.[41] Here, perhaps, was born the "awkward squad" of later American armies. To
an overworked farmer struggling to keep his land in maximum
production, the obligation of periodic training could be a burdensome form of taxation. That the problem did not go unrecognized
by the authorities is shown by the numerous enactments by which
the months of heaviest work for the farmer were kept free from
training.[42]

With the coming of regimental organization, the colonies began
to make provisions for occasional musters of the larger units in
order to accustom officers and men to the problems involved in
large-scale operations. Mock skirmishes now became more feasible,
while regimental reviews afforded a spectacle far surpassing the
show provided by the thin lines of a single village trainband. A
typical arrangement was to have all the companies composing a
regiment assemble at some central place once each year for a day
of training and ceremonial. If it was not convenient to assemble
an entire regiment, several companies might be brought together
for joint training and mock combat.

As soon as the men began to convene, whether for a regimental
muster or merely a company training day, control and discipline
became a matter of concern. In theory, once the hour had struck
and the men came together on the field, every member as though
by the waving of a magic wand was temporarily transformed from
a civilian into a soldier and came under military command and discipline. Forbidden was "all talking, and not keepeing sylence, during the tyme of the exercise, jereing, quarrelling, fighting, departing
collers without lycence, or dismission, etc. . . ."[43] Offenses, including
unauthorized absence from training as well as disorderly conduct
on the training ground, usually were punished with fines collected
by the constable or company clerk. If necessary, the coercive power
of the courts might be utilized to force payment, even to the distraint of property. In most colonies, the proceeds might be used by
the company itself for its various needs, including the purchase of

drums and colors. Occasionally more ingenious arrangements were made. One Massachusetts company "was willing upon Samuell Cartors desier to free him from paying any fin[e]s for Neglecting to trayn provided he give them a barrell of Sider yerely and to bring it in to the fe[ild] or where they may Conveniently drinke it. . . ." [44] When monetary penalties were found ineffective, other kinds of military punishments might be applied. The militia laws of the colonies authorized company officers to punish offenders by such diverse methods as stocks, bilboes, riding the wooden horse, lying neck and heels, and running the gauntlet.[45] Occasionally, it seems, even more direct and expeditious action was taken: One commander in Virginia boasted that when a certain militiaman "was drunk and rude to his captain . . . I broke his head in two places." [46]

Always the principal purpose of the organization, training, and discipline was to have a large pool of competent soldiers available and ready for active service whenever needed. The militia was both a training school and a reservoir of manpower. In case of a sudden threat to a local area, such as an Indian raid or an invasion of pirates, the militia in that vicinity might be called up *in toto,* and would go into action just as constituted. There was no time for further training or reorganization. But for extended operations, such as a major expedition against some distant fort, the militia units themselves were not called into active service. Instead, the usual practice was to use the militia as a pool from which trained soldiers could be drawn in whatever numbers needed for the particular purpose. Those selected would be organized into new units under officers assigned by higher authority, given additional training if time permitted, and then sent on the mission. Troops performing active duty of this kind were paid regular wages, usually in accordance with a scale established by law. In the meantime, the militia organization was left intact, able to carry on the usual training of civilians, while standing ready as the immediate arm of defense in local areas.

Individuals were selected for active service by a variety of methods; indeed, sometimes in ways so haphazard as to suggest that the weighty responsibility of sending a man out to risk his life for the community was taken rather lightly. Most colonies set up some system of assigned quotas for military units or towns or counties based upon a formula related to population. But how were individuals chosen to fill the quota? In New England, where the basic political unit was the town, the choice often was made by the town committee of militia or perhaps the selectmen. The individuals chosen then were notified in person by the constable.[47] That this method could be grossly unfair is perfectly obvious, yet there is no reason to believe that serious abuses of the system were frequent. The more informal method of allowing the captain of the trainband to raise the required number of men by his own devices also was quite common, especially when the quotas were small and the contemplated service relatively brief.

In the Manuscript Room of the New York Public Library there is an interesting old memorandum book used during the period from 1696 to 1719 by Henry True, captain of militia in the town of Salisbury, Massachusetts, as a personal record book for the company which he commanded. For us it is a microscope through which we may view various aspects of military administration, including the procedures used in selecting men for active duty. When Captain True received an order from his superiors to raise a certain number of men, his practice was to announce a muster of the company. The men being assembled, True would call for volunteers. If the quota was not filled by this means, he would impress the necessary number of men. One variation sometimes employed was to impress more men than required. From that group the necessary number were then chosen, the actual selectees being compensated in some fashion by the impressed men who did not go. Some of the men in True's company were called into temporary service as guards for some frontier outpost or as scouts in the woods. When it was time to relieve a man from such duty, another member of the company would be impressed to take his place. Apparently it was the captain's responsibility to administer this program of rotating service, and sometimes it was necessary for him to find weapons and equipment for the designated individuals. One of the entries in True's book refers to

> an order From Colonol Saltonstall baring date the 9th of Feb, 1705/6 for the pressing of a man to relese John maxfild: which was accordingly done: Robert Stockman was prest and Sent up to haverhill the 12th of Feb. Curent for the Ende aforesaid: and was fitted out by myself with a gunn flints bullits and a paire of good Snow shoose which he ingaged to returne to me againe or to pay for them or what damage he did them etc.

On 23 June 1711 the Salisbury company assembled and True

announced that he had orders to provide ten men for an impending operation. Calling for volunteers, True saw seven of his men step forward. Thereupon he impressed three more, one of whom secured a substitute for £8, after which the ten men—seven volunteers, two draftees, and one mercenary—marched off to war. In the spring of 1714, True had to impress one man from his company to replace a deserter who had run away from the fort at Casco. He impressed a group of men, some five in all, whereupon together they raised enough money to hire a single substitute—the one man required. It is impossible to escape the conclusion that the captain knew in advance that this would be done, and that in effect the whole deal was "managed." There was no stigma whatsoever attached to this arrangement. Later the substitute decided that he wanted to come home, and so he in turn hired one of the original impressed men to be his replacement.

Use of the militia for offensive operations was not unlimited. The old English tradition that the trainbands might not be employed outside their own counties except in a case of actual invasion readily took root in the American colonies. As interpreted on this side of the ocean, the tradition meant that militiamen were not to be sent beyond the colony's borders without their own consent, a restriction which sometimes became enshrined in actual legislation.[48] So there developed among the people in early America a strong, living tradition that in a free society compulsory military service in distant areas must not be imposed solely by the will of the executive.

Training day, however, was another matter. Probably most American colonists, despite their aversion to taxes and other obligatory contributions, were in general agreement with the advocate of military preparedness who poetized,

> *That Countrey sure will best be kept from harmes,*
> *Whose Subjects pleasure take to practise Armes.*[49]

Indeed, if the truth were known, it is likely that most young men in the colonies did rather enjoy the routine military training required by the militia system, although custom and fashion may have dictated a certain amount of formulary grumbling. Training day was a community activity that provided a break in the usual routine of farm or village life, an opportunity to show off before the girls, and even some excitement.

On the day appointed, young William Osgood was up early, as usual. Lifting the heavy bar of the house door, he thrust his head outside and was relieved to see that the glow of the rising sun was just appearing over the eastern hills and that the weather would be fair. Far down the rutted road that led to the village green he heard the optimistic crowing of a rooster. By now his wife and children were dressing, also in expectation of a temporary break in routine. Osgood pulled his shirt on over his head, drew on a pair of dark woolen stockings, stepped into his everyday leather breeches, and thrust his feet into a well-worn but comfortable pair of black leather shoes which he fastened with a buckle. While his wife and children were busy preparing breakfast, Osgood went outside to feed the stock and do all the other chores that were necessary before he could be gone for as long as a day. Then it was back to the house for a hearty breakfast of bacon and eggs, cornbread with butter, and a mug of milk. The family agreed that wife and children would walk down to the village at noon, bringing a lunch for all of them, and would remain to visit with friends and watch the afternoon's activities. All would return home together at the end of the day after the trainband was dismissed.

Osgood's military equipment stood ready, having been assembled and checked the previous evening. The 5-foot flintlock musket, inherited from his father, was in excellent operating condition, one of the best in the company. His leather cartridge box held twenty carefully prepared cartridges. In addition, he had a large leather haversack that he wore slung over his shoulder, in which he could carry any extra clothing or gear he might need.

Breakfast completed, Osgood donned a jacket, clapped his only hat on his head, and began to pick up his equipment. As he did so there came a knock on the door, and two friends from up the road, similarly equipped and attired, stood waiting. Osgood said good-bye to the family, and the three men shouldered their guns and started down the road together. As they disappeared over the rise, there suddenly came from the direction of the village the insistent drubbing of a drum. Other figures could be seen hurrying along the crest, muskets in hand.

Captain Thomas Bradbury, a leader in the local church and owner of one of the best farms in the county, was already at the edge of the green. Having tethered his mount in the shade of a large tree, the captain stood conferring with his two subordinate officers and the company clerk. Bradbury wore his next-to-best outfit, including a well-tailored coat with turned-back cuffs, waistcoat, breeches, and knit worsted stockings. The costume was completed by a pair of riding boots showing just a trace of early morning dust, a carefully arranged cravat, and a three-cornered cocked hat perched squarely on the head. At his left side, suspended from a waist belt, hung his sword, a cherished possession obtained some years ago from England.

Whatever Captain Bradbury knew about war and military affairs had been learned in part from his own experience as a militiaman in the ranks during his younger days, when he had even seen some action against hostile Indians, but mainly from his reading and rereading of three military texts that stood on a shelf in his parlor alongside a dozen assorted volumes of law, medicine, literature, and theology. The first was a book that had been well thumbed by his father before him—Richard Elton's *The Compleat Body of the Art Military,* reprinted in London in 1659. Here he had found explicit instructions on the various postures of pike and musket, military formations, and the duties of military personnel. The twenty-sixth chapter had proved especially useful when Bradbury was first selected to be a commissioned officer; it was entitled *"Directions to all such as shall desire to exercise a Foot-Company, with some admonitions to the Souldiers, as shall be exercised by them."* Here could be found some good, practical advice, useful to an inexperienced and rather nervous young officer. In fact, throughout the second half of the seventeenth century a considerable proportion of the militia leaders in the colonies chewed and digested the well-seasoned admonitions of Elton. A good captain, Elton insisted, must himself be thoroughly familiar with the prescribed drill so that he can teach it to his men. He must be attentive to their welfare without becoming overly familiar. And in battle the captain must be valiant, "casting off all appearances of fear or danger whatsoever, cheerfully animating his Souldiers to fall on. . . ." [50] Elton also had words of advice for the men in the ranks:

> A Private *Souldier* ought to be very active, not slothfull and idle, informing himself of his duty, learning from his Corporall, or other Officers the true use, and well handling of his armes, always keeping them neat, clean, and well fixed. . . .

> A private souldier ought to avoyd all quarrelling, mutinies, swear-

ing, cursing, or lying, and to be content with his wages, and likewise to be a good husband in the well managing of his means, keeping himselfe neat and handsome in his apparell, avoyding drunkenness, and all manner of gaming, truly to serve and feare God, and to be obedient unto all the commands of his superiours, cheerfully going on upon all duties, and to be loving, kind, and courteous, unto all his fellow souldiers. . . .

A Sentinel must be very vigilant, carefully casting his eyes about him, and harkning whether he heare the noyse or approach of any drawing neer him; which if he perceive, he is presently to command them to stand, presenting his Musket or Pike to their brest, and . . . calling his Corporal for to take the word, unlesse he should be commanded to come in silently.[51]

Even more useful to a man such as Captain Bradbury, faced as he was with the problem of building military efficiency in a company of occasional soldiers, was a small pocket manual published in Boston in 1701: Nicholas Boone's *Military Discipline. The Compleat Souldier, or Expert Artillery-Man.* Here were pieced together the most immediately practical and useful portions of Elton; the Duke of Monmouth's *Abridgment of the English Military Discipline,* which had been published in Boston in 1690; and a rather pompous and windy but much-esteemed earlier work, William Barriffe's *Military Discipline: or The Young Artillery-Man.* Equally helpful was Bradbury's third book, William Breton's recently published *Militia Discipline. The Words of Command, and Directions for Exercising the Musket, Bayonet, & Carthridge* (Boston, 1733). This compact little volume included instructions on facings, doublings, countermarchings, and wheelings, together with an abstract of important military legislation. Captain Bradbury always carried his copy of Breton's little manual in his coat pocket on training days, in case he ever encountered a problem for which he was not prepared, a precaution he preferred not to reveal to his lieutenant and ensign.

Although Captain Bradbury cherished his three military books and sometimes perused still others that he borrowed from his major, he always remembered as a sort of personal warning a paragraph he had read once in a book dating back to Queen Elizabeth's time. It was a stinging satire on the militia captain whose only knowledge of military matters is derived from books. Such an officer coming onto the training field with his company, the author remarked with contempt,

> will ranke them three and three, but at every third ranke he must call to his boy, *hola sirra, where is my Booke?* and having all ranked them, then marcheth he on faire, and farre wyde from a souldiers march: then commeth he to cast them into a ring, about, about, about, till he hath inclosed himselfe in the Center; now there is he puzzelled, *hola maister stand still untill I have looked in my Booke:* by this time there is a faire ring broken.[52]

Bradbury was not that kind of a captain, and he knew his job well enough to retain the respect of his neighbors who marched under his command. He remembered, too, the earnest admonition delivered by the Reverend Oliver Peabody on the occasion of the Artillery election in 1732. After deploring an apparent decline of martial spirit among the people, Mr. Peabody had urged the officers

> to attend with dure [*sic*] Care, and in the proper Seasons, on Military Exercises on Days of Troopings, Trainings, etc. and this for the true and noble End thereof; not for *Sport* and *Mirth,* nor to give magnificent *Treats* to your Soldiers, which is so destructive to Martial Skill and Valour, and so often frustrates the great Ends of Trainings; but for the advancement of Military Art and Skill, and to fit your Soldiers for *Actual Service.*

Nor should the men of the militia

> slight, nor carelessly neglect to attend, much less designedly avoid the Exercises prescribed by Law, for their Education in this manly and necessary Art. They are not to come to the Field to mock and deride their officers, nor meerly for Sport and Diversion; but with hearty desires and sincere endeavours to acquaint themselves with all the Exercises, and every part of the Art of War.[53]

Captain Bradbury glanced at the little groups of armed men now beginning to cluster along the edges of the green, bantering and laughing together, and wondered whether those men and boys really would prove themselves soldiers in a day of combat. The drummer had stopped his beating. The captain drew out his watch—eight o'clock of a bright day, with the sun now well above the eastern hills. He signaled to the drummer, who responded with a martial roll, and the sergeants began forming up the company on the green.

William Osgood took his place in the second rank, and for a
moment there was much shuffling as the sixty-odd men sought to
straighten their lines under the supervision of the sergeants. When
all was in order, the company clerk strode forward, a little man
looking as though he bore the responsibility of the world on his
shoulders. Record book in hand, he proceeded to call the roll,
noting down the names of any members not present. One puffing
latecomer slid into position just in time to answer to his name.
When satisfied that his tally was accurate, the clerk reported to
the captain, after which the company officers, accompanied by the
clerk with his ever-present record book, proceeded to the view of
arms. Every musket was inspected to see that it was actually in
working order; every cartridge box was opened to make sure that
the proper number of charges were in readiness. All defects were
duly noted. During this rather prolonged business, the small
gathering of spectators along the edges of the green, mostly children and older men, shifted positions restlessly or chatted in small
groups.

Things livened up considerably when the company at last was
called to attention for the morning drill. The oldsters off to one
side, themselves veterans of many a training day, were always
hoping to see some atrocious blunder on the part of the officers
or men that would result in glorious turmoil and make the day
memorable. Elton himself had anticipated such a possibility, cau-
tioning the officer that if he did make a mistake and throw the
company into confusion "he ought not to be daunted, but to pull
up the Spirit of a Souldier as well as he can, and endeavour . . .
again." [54] But Captain Bradbury was determined to give no one the
satisfaction of a laugh, and he began the morning's work with the
cool assurance of a professional. According to Monmouth, "The
Words of Command are to be given leisurely, that the Soldiers may
have time to perform the Exercise without confusion. And above
all, *Silence* is to be kept very strictly. And the first Word of Command before you begin the Exercise, is, *Silence.*" [55] Bradbury also
remembered the instruction of Elton that a commander, in exercising his company, must "*stretch* out his voice so, as he may conveniently be heard, and understood by the inferiour Officers, and
Souldiers. . . . He must likewise order all his Words of Command
so, as that they may be proper, and cleerly pronounced forth unto
the Souldier, without any faltering." [56]

Bradbury ordered the company divided into groups for instruction. Then the bawling of commands began, ringing across the green and bouncing off the wall of the meeting house, as the officers and noncommissioned officers put the men through the standard exercises. Boys who had recently come of military age were closely watched by the instructors to make sure that they performed the fundamental movements correctly. They were shown how to stand at attention with feet planted firmly, heels about 10 inches apart, toes turned slightly out, left arm hanging straight at the side, musket grounded at the outside of the right foot. "A Soldier having his Firelock shoulder'd, must stand with a strait Body, holding up his Head without moving, and always looking towards the Commanding Officer, or he who exercises the Battalion; nor must he use any Motion but what the Word of Command, when given, directs." [57] Novices were warned to "carry their Firelocks firm on their Shoulders, and raise their Muzzels high, that they may not clash in their Facings." [58] Should the next word of command be "Face to the right about!" a long-barreled musket, incorrectly sloped on the shoulder, could easily unstraighten the nose of the man next in line.

The instructions given by the company's noncommissioned officers were short and to the point for, as Elton remarked, the instructor in explaining the procedure should not be long-winded lest he bore his men, "who rather would be pleased with more actings, then by too much talkings." [59] But of course some of the soldiers had to be reminded repeatedly that in doing facings at the word of command ("Face to the Right! Face to the Left! Face to the Right About! Face to the Left About!") they must pivot on the ball of the *left* foot and step with the *right*, the left foot being "the keeper of *Rank* and *File*." [60] Upon hearing the word of command they must perform the first motion immediately, and then count to themselves deliberately, *"One—Two,"* performing the second motion on the count of *Two*.[61] Presumably the sergeants found ways to make their meaning more clear to the men than the actual words of old Barriffe: *"Facing is a particular turning of the Aspect from one part to another, whereby the Front proper becomes a Front accidentall: And a Front accidental, may bee reduced to his proper Front."* [62]

Much time was spent on the complicated procedure of handling the musket, or manual of arms. This, of course, was essential if the men were to achieve a high rate of directed fire in action. "In practising the Exercise," advised one guidebook, "the Men should be taught to do all the Motions with great Briskness, and as it were with a Spring, which not only helps to mark the Time, and distinguish the Motions, but gives Spirit to the Men themselves." [63] The exercise for the firelock, as prescribed by Monmouth, included the following sequence of commands:

Musketiers, have a Care to the Exercise, and carry your arms well. Lay your Right hands on your Muskets.

Poize your Muskets.
Rest your Muskets.
Cock your Muskets.
Guard your Muskets.
Present.
Fire.
Recover your arms.
Half-bend your Muskets.
Clean your Pans.
Handle your Primers.
Prime.
Shut your Pans.
Blow off your loose Corns.

(Be sure to blow all together at one strong blast, bringing your pan up to your mouth. . . .)

Cast about to Charge.
Handle your Chargers.
Open them with your Teeth.
Charge with Powder.
Draw forth your Scowrers.
Shorten them to an Inch.
Charge with Bullet.
Ram down powder and Ball.
Withdraw your Scowrers.
Shorten them to a Handful.
Return your Scowrer.
Poise your Muskets.
Shoulder your Muskets.
Poise your Muskets.
Order your Muskets.

(In the loading process, after the cartridge has been bitten open, the open end is covered with the ball of the thumb. Then the powder is shaken into the barrel, after which the ball is retained in the teeth while the rest of the cartridge is dropped down the barrel after the powder. The ball is then taken from the teeth and inserted. Finally the entire charge is rammed down with the scourer.)

(. . . being set down to the ground all together that it seem but one thump.) [64]

Captain Bradbury watched all this activity with a keen eye, intervening here and there to give special help to Jacob, or Henry, or John, or young Abraham Brown. "Now hold your gun almost level in your left hand, close to your body—that's it. When you bite the cartridge, do it a good way down, and then place your thumb over it. Use your forefinger to poke the ball into the muzzle, and when you reach for your rammer do it with your thumb and forefinger—so. In ramming, be sure to do it briskly and with enough force. See here, men, quick firing depends chiefly upon quick loading, and that depends chiefly upon your dexterity in drawing your rammer, ramming down, and then replacing the rammer through the pipes. Look to it, George, and see if you can't be as brisk as the corporal there." [65] Fortunately, these men were better pupils than those in a certain company of militia which, it is said, stood

> Considering wether the right or left Shoulder
> Was the most proper to Cary the Arms of a Souldier
> And after an hour was Spent and near
> To Learn right from Left and the front from the rear
> And often Questioning how and which way
> They were drawn up at last into battle array.[66]

Now the entire company was brought back into formation, so that all might go through the manual of arms two or three times together, with the captain himself shouting out the sequence of commands. Young Osgood snapped through the motions with a mounting sense of pride in himself and his companions, and sneaked a look to see if the spectators were watching with approval. They were. When the captain was satisfied with this phase of the training he gave the men a brief rest and then took up the marching and field evolutions.

The company was drawn up with the men precisely spaced in ranks and files, the ensign carrying the colors, and the drummer on a line with the front rank ready to drum the beat. "Face to the Right!" (*One—Two*). "When the word is given to march, both Front and Rere step all at a time with their left Feet, setting them down all together, so that they may be heard. . . ." [67] To the steady drubbing of the drum, the company tramped up and down and around the green, muskets carried on left shoulders, feet rising and falling together. Bradbury could make the drill as complicated as

his own skill and that of his soldiers would allow, for the military
literature was replete with formations and evolutions. All of this
was supposed to train the company for maneuvering as a unit on
the battlefield—now marching through a narrow defile, now advancing to meet the enemy, now wheeling to repel an attack on
the flank. There were brief moments of disorder as one man or another misunderstood a command or forgot which way was *left,* and
at one point a dog very nearly threw the entire company into
confusion when it suddenly discovered its master in the third file
and raced in after him. But on the whole things went well, and one
octogenarian on the sidelines was heard to remark that the company looked the best he had seen it since old Cap'n Morse had
died (when the old-timer himself was a file leader).

The climax of the morning's activity came when Captain Bradbury turned to the drill for volley fire, a drill that was supposed
to transform sixty or more individual musketeers into a single
multibarreled weapon of mass destruction. For a European company
of infantry, volley fire was very nearly its supreme act, indeed, its
raison d'être. When performed by highly trained regulars, the procedure was a superb demonstration of disciplined coordination,
wonderful to observe, fearful to face. The crashing volleys of such
a company sent wave after wave of leaden balls tearing through
the ranks of any unit directly opposite. Military theorists valued
such disciplined delivery not only for its immense power of destruction, but also because it greatly diminished one of the hazards inherent in permitting soldiers to fire at random—the danger of hitting
one's own comrades.[68] Virtually all experts (in Europe at least)
agreed that the wild melee, with each soldier fighting and firing as
an individual, was not a proper form of battle.

In the American colonies the trainbands respected volley fire
and strove for the same degree of skill as the regulars, but they
usually had to compromise with a reasonably accurate facsimile.
Just a few drills per year were not enough; therefore, as one
authority wisely remarked, one should first consider "what is absolutely necessary to be done; and next, what Militia can be brought
to do. For a little and well is better than a great deal that is stark
naught." [69] In open battle, a company of militia seldom proved
able to slug it out, volley for volley, with an opposing company
of regulars—and the regulars knew it.

Captain Bradbury begins by drawing the company up in its usual formation with six ranks, that is, each file consisting of six men. Upon command, every other man steps up beside the man ahead of him, thereby reducing the six ranks to three. At another command, the second and third ranks move up to half-distance, close behind the first rank. Bradbury makes sure that his intention is clearly understood: No powder is to be actually inserted, even in the pan. Then comes the command "Make Ready!" Muskets swing down together, and there is a clatter of clicking as the cocks are drawn back. At once

> the Men of the Front Rank . . . kneel down on their right Knees, placing the Butt-end of their Firelocks on the Ground, keeping their Thumbs on the Cocks, and their Fingers on the Trickers. The Center and Rear-Ranks Close forward at the same time with recover'd Arms, the Men of the Center Rank placing their left Feet on the Inside of the right Feet of their File-Leaders, bringing their right Feet to the Right, but not in a Line with their Left, only in the same Position as when they Rest. The Men in the Rear-Rank place their left Feet on the Inside of the Right Feet of those in the Center Rank, bringing their right Feet to the Right as those in the Center Rank did.[70]

Placing the feet in this manner is called "locking," and it enables the men in the rear ranks to level their muskets just to the right of the men in front. Everyone has a clear aim ahead. "Present!" Up come the muskets to the horizontal aiming position. As William Osgood sights along his barrel he wonders how he would feel if facing him, just 50 yards away, was a massed unit of enemy soldiers also preparing to fire. Instead of Frenchmen or Spaniards or Indians, however, he sees his wife and children strolling down the hill into the village, with the noonday meal in a large basket. "Fire!" The hammers snap forward almost as one, and the mock volley is delivered. Immediately the men recover their muskets, the front rank rising up, while the center and rear ranks fall back to half-distance. Then they half-cock, prime, load, and shoulder their guns, ready to repeat the evolution as ordered. The drill showed that this company, under optimum conditions, would be able to deliver a volley approximately every thirty seconds. When satisfied that his men were performing the evolution with reasonable proficiency, Captain Bradbury had them deliver a couple of volleys with their muskets primed but not loaded, firing in the pan only. This, of course, made for a somewhat greater degree of realism.

By now the sun was at its zenith, and Osgood's face was shining

with perspiration. Most of the men had long since tossed their
jackets or vests off to one side. The captain wiped his face with a
kerchief, took a look at his watch, and dismissed the company for
an hour. The men scattered in all directions, some hurrying home,
others meeting with families and friends in shady places to enjoy
the food they had brought in their baskets or knapsacks. A nearby
well afforded good cool water, but most of the men drowned their
thirst with cider or beer. The commissioned officers and the clerk
looked after their own horses, and then strolled over to the nearby
inn for a cooked meal.

Conspicuously present on the green was the constable, for training day could easily degenerate into a tumult, especially if liquor
flowed freely. Most of the men and boys of Captain Bradbury's
company behaved themselves well, although engaging in a certain
amount of good-natured horseplay. The older family men sat
around munching their food and exchanging views on the weather,
crops, and politics.

In due time, the rolling of the drum called the company together
once more. Before resuming the day's training, Captain Bradbury,
with the clerk at his elbow, called the men's attention to several
items of business. The collection of fines from delinquents had
created a surplus in the company treasury; would the company
approve using the money for the purchase of a new drum? After
some discussion, the proposal was adopted. As a benefactor had
recently donated a set of new colors, the old were now brought
forward and "solde at an out Cry at the head of the Company." [71]
The sergeant who bought them agreed to give the company a barrel
of cider or else pay 5s. 7d. After this, the business meeting was
speedily brought to a conclusion and the company resumed its
training.

Captain Bradbury led the men across the road to a field beyond
which rose the steep side of a hill. Trailing along behind the
company went the crowd of spectators, the Osgood family among
them. At the far edge of the field, just at the foot of the hillside,
stood a wooden target crudely shaped to represent the figure of a
man. The soldiers were to try their skill at shooting, for Captain
Bradbury firmly endorsed the old admonition that "the fierie shot,
either on horsebacke, or foote, being not in hands of the skilfull,
may do unto themselves more hurt than good: wherefore the same
is often to be practised, that men may grow perfect and skilfull

therein." [72] Or, as Monmouth put it, "Tis very necessary for all captains and Commanders of Companies . . . to practise their men to shoot at a Mark which is extream useful." [73] Useful indeed. Although Captain Bradbury retained a great respect for volley fire, at least in theory, he knew enough about forest warfare to set a high value on individual marksmanship.

One of the sergeants drove a small stake into the ground about 50 paces from the target to mark the firing line, and the shooting began. For more than an hour the men, firing as individuals, tested their aim until the wooden target was splintered from top to toe and several trees behind the target and on either side were well pocked. The occasional misfire brought roars of laughter from soldiers and spectators alike, first at the embarrassingly feeble "click" when the trigger was pulled, and again at the look of surprise and chagrin that spread across the face of the unlucky marksman. By the time the practice was concluded, a veil of acrid smoke hovered over the field, giving a slight foretaste of the atmosphere of battle.

Not all such sessions went so smoothly. Accidents were always a possibility. Many years ago, the captain recalled, a corporal had been shot through the arm when a musket went off unexpectedly. And there was the time that old Daniel Wade lost his right hand when his gun blew apart. More recently, the company had done a little experimenting with tin grenades, following carefully the prescribed exercise outlined in one of the manuals. Suddenly there was an explosion followed by an outcry. As a result of that episode, Corporal Thomas Oakes lost three of his fingers and had to be dropped from the company roster.[74]

In some parts of the colonies, the militia training was sweetened by occasional athletic competition among the men, with prizes being offered by the commanders.[75] But for Bradbury's company the high point of the day was the mock battle or practice skirmish. Sometimes the company would be divided in two, with one half assigned to defend a portion of the training field or a fortified works while the other half tried to capture it. Occasionally one or two neighboring companies and the regimental troop of horse would participate and a more elaborate skirmish would be arranged. This was the event that drew the largest audience, the men being urged on in their efforts with rousing cheers from the sidelines. Such practice gave all the members of the company, officers especially, the chance to improve their proficiency in battlefield techniques and

evolutions.[76] Bradbury's men set to with a will, following carefully
the instructions of their leaders, and carried on the mock combat
until the sun began to drop in the west. William Osgood's wife
noted the lateness of the hour, called the children, and started up
the road toward home to begin supper.

The drum rolled again, and the weary militiamen formed up in
rank and file. Captain Bradbury spoke a few words of praise and
reproof as needed and reminded the men of their duty in case of
an alarm. Then the village pastor stepped forward from the sidelines to conclude the session with a prayer.[77] Ten minutes after
the "Amen" not a soldier or spectator was to be seen on the training
ground. Most, like William Osgood and Thomas Bradbury, ate a
hearty supper and went to bed early, thinking about the coming
day's work among cattle and crops.

Occasionally the entire regiment of the county, foot and horse,
assembled at some appointed place for a period of regimental
training under the direction of the colonel. Then more than ever
the various companies were on their mettle, none wanting to be
found backward in training or skill. At such affairs, the mock
combat was much more realistic because of the larger numbers
involved. As early as 1639, the colony of Massachusetts had been
able to hold a training session for two regiments lasting the whole
day, with the soldiers proving themselves "very skilful and ready
in divers sorts of skirmishes and other military actions. . . ." [78] On
another occasion "about 1200 men were exercised in most sorts of
land service; yet it was observed that there was no man drunk,
though there was plenty of wine and strong beer in the town, not
an oath sworn, no quarrel, nor any hurt done." [79] That was cause
for rejoicing.

Regimental training customarily included a full-scale regimental
review, with all the units drawn up in formation on the field, the
ranks 4 paces apart and the files at arm-length distance. The specific instructions given in William Brattle's *Sundry Rules and Directions for Drawing up a Regiment* suggest the ceremonial polish
to which every self-respecting regiment aspired. "Immediately upon
notice given that the *General* is a coming," says Brattle,

> the *Major* is to order the Soldiers to Shoulder their Arms, from which
> Position they are always to Rest their Arms when the Compliment is
> to be paid, and as soon as He approaches near the Right Flank, the

Major is to order the Soldiers to Rest their Arms, by the following Word of Command

To the Front Present your Arms.

At the performing the last Motion of the above command, all the *Drummers* are to beat a March, and the *Major* is immediately *to take his Post on the Right of the Battalion,* and the *Adjutant* on *the Left of the Battalion, dressing in a Line with the Rank of Officers.* As the *General* passes along the Front, the *Officers* are *to Salute* Him with their Half Pikes or Partisans, and to time it in such a manner, that each may just finish his Salute and pull off his Hat, when the *General* comes opposite to him.

The *Ensigns* are to drop their Colours, bringing the spear pretty near the Ground just when the Colonel drops the point of his Half Pike, pulling off their Hats at the same time, and not to raise the Colours till the *General* has passed them. . . .

The *Serjeants* in the Rear are to pull off their Hats without bowing their Heads when the *General* passes them, holding their Halberd in their Hand, as the Officers do their Half Pikes without bowing their Heads. . . .

As soon as the Ceremony of Viewing the Regiment is over, the General then acquaints the Colonel what he would have performed. And the General for the most part orders the Manual Exercise to be performed; then to go thro' some part of the Firings, and lastly to March by Him either in grand division, sub-divisions or single Company's.[80]

Regimental trainings being as infrequent as they were, any attempt at such ceremony must have fallen far short of the precision implied above; militia seldom if ever achieved the drillfield polish of the regulars. One suspects that at times the regimental trainings, like the dress rehearsal of a school pageant, revealed far more confusion and disorder than skill and precision. In such cases, we may wonder which suffered more, the self-confidence of the soldiers or the assurance of the spectators. "Exercise Regimentally in the Afternoon;" noted Samuel Sewall in his diary, "when concluded, Mr. Mather prayd." [81]

Whatever the ordinary American colonist knew about the art of war was learned as a member of the militia organization. The system, with all its inadequacies, provided the only military training in the colonies and sometimes served as the only form of defense immediately available. Such training, ladled out in small doses at fairly regular intervals over a period of years, did endow the average citizen with at least a rudimentary knowledge of military practice. Many a colonial soldier went into combat with nothing more, for expeditions sometimes were hastily assembled and organized; the men had to rely upon whatever they already knew and could do.

Just as the proof of any pudding is in the eating, so the real test of militia training occurred in the crucible of combat. The Elizabethan military expert Robert Barret was speaking with the wisdom of an old veteran when he said that "to have a souldier to be very perfect, and a good executioner indeede, it is needfull to have bin in some good peeces of service, and to have seene men to fall on both sides, which doth flesh and harden a souldier very much." [82] In general the colonial militia, when thrown into actual combat, performed reasonably well provided the conditions were not bewildering or the opposition overwhelming. There can be no doubt that the existence of the militia system as a traditional form of community service provided the necessary foundation for eventual military success, first against the hostile Indians, then against France and Spain, and finally against England herself.

NOTES

1. Letters of Roger Williams, 1632–1682, J. R. Bartlett, ed. (Providence, 1874), p. 276.
2. Lyon G. Tyler, ed., Narratives of Early Virginia, 1606–1625 (New York, 1907), p. 10.
3. William Bradford, Of Plymouth Plantation, 1620–1647, Samuel Eliot Morison, ed. (New York, 1952), p. 70.
4. Harold E. Driver, Indians of North America (Chicago, 1961), pp. 370–371.
5. Max Savelle, The Origins of American Diplomacy: The International History of Angloamerica, 1492–1763 (New York, 1967), pp. 199–201.
6. A list of weapons and other military equipment considered appropriate for a body of one hundred men venturing in America is given in MCR, I, 26.
7. [William Breton], Militia Discipline. The Words of Command, and Directions for Exercising the Musket, Bayonet, & Carthridge (Boston, 1733), p. 72.
8. Quoted in Harold L. Peterson, Arms and Armor in Colonial America, 1526–1783 (New York, 1956), p. 163.
9. Peterson, Arms and Armor in Colonial America, pp. 40–41, 68.
10. Albert Manucy, Artillery through the Ages: A Short Illustrated History of Cannon, Emphasizing Types Used in America (Washington, 1962), passim.

11. *The Gentleman's Compleat Military Dictionary. Containing The Military Art; Explaining the Terms and Phrases Us'd in the Field or Garrison* (18th ed.; Boston, 1759).

12. Merrill Jensen, ed., *English Historical Documents: American Colonial Documents to 1776* (New York, 1955), p. 89.

13. Niccolò Machiavelli, *The Chief Works and Others*, Allan Gilbert, trans. (3 vols.; Durham, 1965), II, 585–586.

14. *The Exercise for the Militia of the Province of the Massachusetts-Bay* (Boston, 1758), p. 3.

15. Darrett B. Rutman, "The Virginia Company and Its Military Regime," in Darrett B. Rutman, ed., *The Old Dominion: Essays for Thomas Perkins Abernethy* (Charlottesville, Va., 1964), pp. 1–20.

16. Philip A. Bruce, *Institutional History of Virginia in the Seventeenth Century* (2 vols.; New York, 1910), II, 4, 15–20, 64.

17. Douglas Edward Leach, "The Military System of Plymouth Colony," *NEQ*, XXIV (September, 1951), 343–345, 347–348.

18. Nathaniel B. Shurtleff, ed., *Records of the Colony of New Plymouth in New England* (12 vols.; Boston, 1855–1861), I, 22.

19. John Winthrop, *Winthrop's Journal "History of New England," 1630–1649*, J. K. Hosmer, ed. (2 vols.; New York, 1908), I, 92.

20. In a time of public danger, Massachusetts once provided for the training of boys from ten to sixteen years of age in the use of small guns, half-pikes, and bows. Parental permission was a prerequisite. If boys then were like boys now, there could have been scenes of earnest pleading in some Puritan homes. (See *MCR*, II, 99.)

21. David William Cole, " The Organization and Administration of the South Carolina Militia System, 1670–1783" (Unpublished Ph.D. dissertation, University of South Carolina, 1953), p. 139. The Act of 1721 may be found in Thomas Cooper and D. J. McCord, eds., *Statutes at Large of South Carolina* (10 vols.; Columbia, 1836–1841), IX, 631–641, and also in the Selective Service System's *Backgrounds of Selective Service*, II, Part 13, pp. 23–33.

22. Allen D. Candler, ed., *The Colonial Records of the State of Georgia* (26 vols.; Atlanta, 1904–1916), XVIII, 26–29.

23. Cooper and McCord, *Statutes at Large of South Carolina*, IX, 618; *Backgrounds of Selective Service*, II, Part 13, p. 9.

24. [Edward Johnson], *Johnson's Wonder-Working Providence, 1628–1651*, J. Franklin Jameson, ed. (New York, 1910), p. 231.

25. Thomas Procter(?) to Samuel Waldo, 26 May 1744, Samuel Waldo Papers (Massachusetts Historical Society).

26. John Marshall, Diary (Massachusetts Historical Society).

27. *The Colonial Laws of New York from the Year 1664 to the Revolution* (5 vols.; Albany, 1894–1896), I, 50; Herbert L. Osgood, *The American Colonies in the Seventeenth Century* (3 vols.; New York, 1904–1907), I, 513–514.

28. William Waller Hening, ed., *The Statutes at Large; Being a Collection of All the Laws of Virginia. . . .* (13 vols.; Richmond, New York, 1810–1823), IV, 298–299.

29. *Johnson's Wonder-Working Providence,* p. 228.

30. Hening, *Statutes at Large,* IV, 119.

31. *MCR,* III, 267; Charles Harding Firth, *Cromwell's Army: A History of the English Soldier during the Civil Wars, the Commonwealth and the Protectorate* (Reprint of 3d ed., London and New York, 1962), p. 43.

32. W. Roy Smith, *South Carolina as a Royal Province, 1719–1776* (New York, 1903), p. 174; Bruce, *Institutional History of Virginia,* II, 24–27.

33. A contested militia election in Hingham, Massachusetts, in 1645 revealed the possible consequences of mixing politics with defense. (See Winthrop, *Journal,* II, 229–245.) The government of Rhode Island asserted in 1741 that the act empowering freemen and soldiers to select their own officers had been found to be "vastly prejudicial to this colony" (John Russell Bartlett, ed., *Records of the Colony of Rhode Island, and Providence Plantations, in New England* [10 vols.; Providence, 1856–1865], V, 3).

34. *MCR,* V, 30.

35. Bartlett, *Records of the Colony of Rhode Island,* IV, 149, 155.

36. Anne Kusener Nelsen, "The Colonial Militia: Aristocratic or Democratic?" (Unpublished essay, Vanderbilt University, 1966).

37. Bartlett, *Records of the Colony of Rhode Island,* II, 211–212.

38. Henry Steele Commager, ed., *Documents of American History* (5th ed.; New York, 1949), p. 104.

39. Bartlett, *Records of the Colony of Rhode Island,* I, 154–155.

40. Shurtleff, *Records of the Colony of New Plymouth,* II, 62.

41. J. H. Trumbull and C. J. Hoadly, eds., *The Public Records of the Colony of Connecticut* (15 vols.; Hartford, Conn., 1850–1890), I, 4.

42. See, for example, Trumbull and Hoadly, *Public Records of the Colony of Connecticut,* I, 15.

43. Shurtleff, *Records of the Colony of New Plymouth,* II, 61.

44. Henry True, Memorandum and Account Book, 1696–1719 (New York Public Library).

45. See, for example, *MCR,* II, 223; *The Colonial Laws of New York from the Year 1664 to the Revolution,* I, 52; *Backgrounds of Selective Service,* II, Part 9, p. 7, Part 12, p. 44, Part 13, pp. 9–10.

46. William Byrd, *The Secret Diary of William Byrd of Westover, 1709–1712,* Louis B. Wright and Marion Tinling, eds. (Richmond, 1941), p. 414.

47. *MCR,* III, 321; Shurtleff, *Records of the Colony of New Plymouth,* II, 63–64; Douglas Edward Leach, "The Causes and Effects of King Philip's War" (Unpublished Ph.D. dissertation, Harvard University, 1952), pp. 328–330.

48. *The Colonial Laws of New York from the Year 1664 to the Revolution,* I, 53; *The Acts and Resolves, Public and Private, of the Province of the Massachusetts Bay* (21 vols.; Boston, 1869–1922), I, 18; Candler, *Colonial Records of the State of Georgia,* XVIII, 10; *Backgrounds of Selective Service,* II, Part 11, p. 21; Cole, "Organization and Administration of the South Carolina Militia System," pp. 39–40.

49. William Barriffe, *Military Discipline: or The Young Artillery-Man* (3d ed.; London, 1643), p. 152.

50. Richard Elton, *The Compleat Body of the Art Military* (London, 1659), p. 184.

51. Elton, *The Compleat Body of the Art Military,* p. 176.

52. Robert Barret, *The Theorike and Practike of Moderne Warres, Discoursed in Dialogue Wise* (London, 1598), p. 6.

53. Oliver Peabody, *An Essay to Revive and Encourage Military Exercises, Skills and Valour among the Sons of God's People in New-England* (Boston, 1732), pp. 24–25.

54. *Compleat Body of the Art Military,* p. 21.

55. [James Fitzroy Scott (Duke of Monmouth)], *An Abridgment of the English Military Discipline* (Boston, 1690), p. 6.

56. *Compleat Body of the Art Military,* p. 21.

57. Humphrey Bland, *An Abstract of Military Discipline; More Particularly with Regard to the Manual Exercise, Evolutions, and Firings of the Foot, from Col. Bland* (Boston, 1743).

58. Bland, *Abstract of Military Discipline.*

59. *Compleat Body of the Art Military,* p. 21.

60. Barriffe, *Military Discipline,* p. 33.

61. Bland, *Abstract of Military Discipline.*

62. *Military Discipline,* p. 32.

63. *The Exercise for the Militia of the Province of the Massachusetts-Bay,* p. 12.

64. [Scott], *Abridgment of the English Military Discipline,* pp. 10–11, 28–30, 32. The second portion in parentheses is paraphrased.

65. These instructions are not an exact quotation, but are derived from specific instructions in *The Exercise for the Militia of the Province of the Massachusetts-Bay,* pp. 9–12.

66. Quoted in Isabel M. Calder, ed., *Colonial Captivities, Marches, and Journeys* (New York, 1935), p. 56.

67. [Scott], *Abridgment of the English Military Discipline,* p. 76.

68. *The Exercise for the Militia of the Province of the Massachusetts-Bay,* pp. 4–5.

69. *The Exercise for the Militia of the Province of the Massachusetts-Bay,* p. 4.

70. [Breton], *Militia Discipline,* p. 70.

71. True, Memorandum and Account Book (New York Public Library).

72. Barret, *Theorike and Practike of Moderne Warres,* p. 3.

73. [Scott], *Abridgment of the English Military Discipline,* p. 163.

74. For an actual case see Samuel Sewall's Diary, in 5 *MHC,* VI, 88.

75. See, for example, Byrd, *Secret Diary,* pp. 415–417.

76. See, for example, Samuel Sewall's Diary, in 5 *MHC,* V, 100, 349.

77. Samuel Sewall's Diary, in 5 *MHC,* VI, 55.

78. Winthrop, *Journal,* I, 300.

79. Winthrop, *Journal,* II, 42.

80. Brattle, *Sundry Rules and Directions for Drawing up a Regiment* (Boston, 1733).

81. 5 *MHC,* V, 350.

82. Barret, *Theorike and Practike of Moderne Warres,* p. 37.

CHAPTER 2

The Opening Stages of Armed Conflict, 1622-1689

THE PERIOD BEFORE 1689 was one of beginning, growth, testing, and revision of the colonial military systems. Actual experiences of partial mobilization and occasional combat, mostly with groups of Indians reacting against European intrusion, enabled colonial leaders to spot some of the weaknesses in the systems they had contrived and, if possible, make appropriate adjustments. This process of learning by experience often proved unpleasant—some of the lessons came hard—but the test of deadly combat was compelling, and the colonists did begin to modify their military practices to fit the conditions of warfare in the American wilderness.

Of course, when measured on the scale of world history, the Indian wars of the seventeenth century were relatively minor affairs. Active participants were numbered in the hundreds or, at the most, a few thousands. What is of lasting significance, however, is the extent to which these sporadic conflicts, often bloody and demoralizing for one side or both, created a pattern of attitudes and actions that was to dominate the problem of Indian-white relations until the end of the nineteenth century, if not to the present day. This tragic pattern became evident very early, as a review of the chief factors will indicate.

From the very beginning of English colonization, Indians and whites attracted and repelled each other in an increasingly complex pattern of relationships. We must remember that the Indians never were a united people, but instead were divided among themselves, with tribal animosities leading frequently to open warfare. This condition was discovered by the Europeans when they first began to arrive. Typically thereafter, a tribe which was being threatened by its enemies would seek support from a nearby group of colonists, who at first possessed the great advantage of firearms. Often the colonists would welcome such an overture, especially if the real motive was not immediately apparent. Indeed, the colonists themselves sometimes hoped for just such a relationship for their own security or some other advantage. Almost inevitably, however, an alliance of this kind carried with it the animosity of the rival Indians. These, in turn, often felt impelled to counteract the new alliance by seeking for themselves the support of some other group of Europeans, especially those already in contention with the first group. In this fashion most tribes within the reach of European influence sooner or later became loosely attached to one of the rival imperial systems—French, Spanish, or English. Colonial leaders found it advantageous to build and maintain a strong network of Indian relationships in order to have native allies; they likewise saw the advantage in undermining the comparable networks of their enemies. Indian diplomacy was a major responsibility and concern of nearly all the colonial governors, whether in Quebec, Boston, Charleston, or St. Augustine. The result, of course, was to keep the Indians divided.

When dealing with a strong, independent tribe, colonial leaders usually maintained protocol and behaved much as they would if negotiating with representatives of a European state. But once a tribe had entered into treaty relations with the whites, involving an obligation of fidelity and possibly even subordination, colonial authorities glided easily into the assumption that the natives were subjects. There was a tendency to treat them like children who must be disciplined and kept docile by fear of punishment. In fact, if there was one dominant principle that characterized the Indian policy of most colonial governments, it was the importance of responding to the first serious outbreak of insubordination with the utmost rigor. Let there be no mistake as to who was master! This policy was considered essential for English security in a wilderness land where Indians outnumbered the white population, and few colonists had any serious doubts that God and justice were on their side.

Trouble usually began as the result of friction between the two races dwelling in close proximity along an expanding frontier. Potential causes were numerous, some of the more common being trespass, theft, physical abuse, and the attempt to impose the ways of one race upon members of the other. Indian resentment of white expansionism and domination often found its earliest outlet in random acts of vandalism and violence by impulsive young men acting without official tribal sanction. White retaliation also might be unofficial, but it was almost certain to be severe and sometimes indiscriminate, so that escalation into full-scale war came all too easily. Colonial governments naturally were prone to believe their own people who complained about Indian violence, and gave them military backing when it seemed desirable.

The frightful Indian uprising in Virginia in 1622, which in a matter of hours reduced the colony's population by about 25 percent, a massacre that seemed to have occurred without any immediate provocation, made a deep and lasting impression on the colonial mind. For the remainder of the seventeenth century, especially in times of interracial tension, frontier folk and even colonial governments seemed obsessed with the fear of secret plots among the Indians. Whenever the colonists heard rumors of unusual movements, extraordinary assemblages, or secret conferences attended by sachems from far and near, they were quick to suspect a budding conspiracy designed to wipe out the whites in a sudden, concerted attack. Racial identity convinced many colonists that all Indians, in spite of any apparent animosities among themselves, were basically hostile and would readily unite when the right opportunity came along. This unpleasant thought had an equally disturbing corollary—that even those tribes which had attached themselves to the English as friends and allies were not to be trusted; indeed, they might even be carrying on an elaborate deception for the purpose of lulling the colonists into a fatal complacency.

Puritan New England's first serious conflict with Indians occurred in 1637 when Massachusetts and Connecticut set out to chastise the Pequot tribe. Some years earlier, the Pequots had migrated from the upper Hudson Valley to Connecticut, coming as rough-handed, aggressive intruders who forced their way in among the more docile tribes of the area. Naturally, they were feared and hated by the local Indians, who understood only too well the meaning of the appellation Pequot—"destroyer." In 1635 the situation was further complicated by the beginning of Puritan migration from Massachusetts Bay into the attractive valley of the lower Connecticut River, where several new English villages were planted, among them Hartford. The local Indians seemed receptive, probably anticipating a profitable trade with the English, but the Pequots appeared to be a distinct threat to the peaceful expansion of the new colony. From the point of view of the colonizers, nothing would clear the air better than a wholesome chastisement that would reduce the arrogant Pequots to a state of respectful pacifism, but as yet no adequate provocation had been offered.

Then in 1636, an English trader was murdered by Indians who lived on Block Island. Fearing Puritan vengeance, the culprits fled to the mainland and found sanctuary among the Pequots of southeastern Connecticut. Here was an opportunity for Massachusetts to test the mettle of its militia and cow the Indians. Late in the summer of 1636, Captain John Endicott and a party of ninety well-armed volunteers appeared at Block Island and proceeded to ravage the Indian villages there, killing all the Indian males who came within reach. After this, they proceeded to the Pequot country to demand the surrender of the fugitive murderers. The Pequots procrastinated until Endicott lost his patience and unleashed his men for a second orgy of destruction.

After this bitter experience, the Pequots thought only of revenge. They coveted the assistance of the Narragansett tribe of Rhode Island, but the Narragansetts preferred to see the Pequots humbled and agreed to lend their support to the Puritan authorities. Consequently, the Pequots found themselves standing alone. Already, under their sachem, Sassacus, they were harassing the English settlements in the lower Connecticut Valley, defying the power of Puritan New England. Such a challenge did not go unanswered, for the English were convinced that until the Pequots were tamed there would be no peace, no security for the infant colony of Connecticut. A decision for war was made in the spring of 1637.[1]

The English knew that Sassacus' people were concentrated in two fortified villages east of the Thames River, and these became the target for an expedition of some ninety Connecticut and Massachusetts soldiers together with a contingent of Mohegan warriors, all under the command of Captain John Mason. Instead of attacking from the direction of the settlements in Connecticut, however, the expedition sailed along the coast and into Narragansett Bay, preparatory to launching a surprise overland attack from the east. Landing in the Narragansett country on the western shore of the bay, Mason acquired further Indian support, and then headed west toward the two Pequot villages. Lugging heavy muskets and other equipment through the woods, the men tramped some 30 miles or more to reach the nearest enemy village, located just beyond the Mystic River. They arrived on 25 May 1637 undetected by the careless Pequots inside the palisade.

At dawn the next day Mason attacked, breaking through the feeble defenses and setting fire to the huddle of huts within. Then the soldiers and their Indian allies formed an unbroken ring all around the flaming village in order to prevent the escape of any Pequots fleeing from the holocaust. The words of the Puritan chronicler Nathaniel Morton complete the tale without a trace of pity or remorse:

> Those that escaped the Fire were slain with the Sword . . . so as they were quickly dispatched, and very few escaped: The Number they thus destroyed, was conceived to be above Four hundred [a large proportion of whom were women and children]. At this time is [sic] was a fearful sight to see them thus frying in the Fire, and the streams of Blood quenching the same; and horrible was the stink and scent thereof; but the Victory seemed a sweet Sacrifice, and they [the English] gave the praise thereof to God, who had wrought so wonderfully for them, thus to enclose their Enemies in their hands, and give them so speedy Victory over so proud, insulting, and blasphemous an Enemy.[2]

Said one participant, with cool assurance, "We had sufficient light from the word of God for our proceedings." [3]

Captain Mason's successful attack upon the Pequot stronghold was decisive. Within a few weeks, troops from Massachusetts and Connecticut completed the destruction of the enemy tribe. Sassacus, now a fugitive, was slain by Mohawk Indians. A remnant of the Pequots survived, but only as an enfeebled, subjected minority group under the domination of the colonial government. In retrospect, what seems most striking about the whole "war," if it may be thus exaggerated, is the frightful intensity of English vengeance. There can be no doubt that Mason's ruthless destruction of a whole community of Indians, an act of vengeance out of all proportion to the provocation and devoid of either justice or humanity, was an important precedent in Anglo-Indian warfare. What the Puritan governments were saying to all the other tribes of New England, whether friendly or otherwise, was "Behave, or else!"

Much the same warning, in Dutch, soon was echoing in the valley of the Hudson River. The situation, as it developed, paralleled rather closely the one in Connecticut. One day an Indian murdered an elderly Dutchman with an ax. The murderer found sanctuary with his own people, and in 1642 a punitive expedition sent against the tribe failed to apprehend the fugitive. Therefore, when opportunity presented itself, the Dutch fell upon the unsuspecting natives with a steely cruelty scarcely exceeded in the long and bloody history of Indian warfare. Reprisals followed, other groups of Indians became involved, and for the next two years Kieft's War, as this senseless conflict has been called, raged in the colony on the Hudson. It staggered the colony, indeed almost ruined it, but the superior firepower of the whites finally prevailed, and a treaty was concluded in 1645.[4]

In the meantime, there was further trouble in Virginia. Following the terrible massacre of 1622, the colony had managed to strike down Indian opposition and subdue the neighboring tribes, so that white expansion could be resumed. Early in the 1640s, however, the elderly chief Opechancanough, an implacable enemy of the English, became convinced that a second chance to smash the intruders was at hand. He noticed the unrest and confusion resulting from the unpopular authoritarianism of Governor Sir John Harvey; perhaps, too, he became aware of turbulence in England which would prevent the mother country from sending aid to Virginia. So Opechancanough began to lay his plans and make his preparations. The sudden widespread attack that he launched on 18 April 1644 caught the English by surprise, just as in 1622, and the hostile Indians managed to kill about 500 settlers at a stroke.[5] Fortunately for the colony, Opechancanough's warriors, despite the staggering effect of their first blow, were not able to carry the offensive deep into the heart of the long-settled plantation region along the James River, but instead withdrew in expectation of the inevitable counterattack. Under the aggressive leadership of a new governor, Sir William Berkeley, the military force of Virginia was brought to bear upon the Indians, destroying their crops and burning their villages. Eventually Opechancanough himself, "that bloody monster" as one contemporary labeled him, was taken prisoner, after which the uprising collapsed.[6]

More than ever, as new English settlements were established on an expanding frontier, the colonial leaders were faced with the difficult problem of providing an adequate defense for life and property against the possibility of sudden surprise attacks by a foe who seemingly could appear and just as quickly disappear in a trackless wilderness. Indian warfare had no "front line" of combat; rather, the vast extent of the wilderness was a sort of no-man's-land with here and there a lonely island of defense. For the English the great problem was how to enable such a community, cut off from immediate outside assistance and defended only by local man-power, to withstand the assault. Under these circumstances, the old European concept of the stronghold was quickly adapted to Ameri-can conditions. One form of the American adaptation was the wooden fort, or blockhouse, with loopholes through which the de-fenders could fire upon the surrounding enemy. In a time of danger, the entire white population in the vicinity was expected to congre-gate within the fort. When the last person was safely inside, the massive door would be barred shut, the men would take their stations at the loopholes, and the community would defend itself until the attackers became discouraged or reinforcements arrived.

New England favored another kind of stronghold known as the garrison house, which had one great advantage over the fort: It was owned and maintained by a private family, who used it as a dwelling. Many of these structures were specially designed to afford protection, having walls sufficiently thick to stop arrows and bullets, a very heavy door secured with a great crossbar, and windows pro-tected by wooden shutters. Some communities designated several dwellings, conveniently located in various sections of the town, to serve as garrison houses, and every family knew to which garrison house it must fly when the alarm was given.[7]

The stronghold concept of local defense helped to solve an im-mediate problem in a practical way, but there were certain diffi-culties inherent in the arrangement. One was the problem of sub-sisting and sustaining the large group of people—men, women, and children—who crowded into the fort or garrison house. Prudence required that some forethought be given to the provision of food and water, together with reserve supplies of weapons, ammunition, and other military necessities. Most forts and garrison houses had a spring or well nearby, often within the area enclosed by a palisade of vertical stakes. Ready access to water was essential not only for drinking but also to douse any fires that might be started by the attackers.

Another problem was the obvious vulnerability of all other property in the community—dwellings, outbuildings, crops, live-stock, and boats—once the populace had congregated in the common center of defense. Marauders were enabled to ravage at will, virtually unmolested, which meant that all the remainder of the community might be destroyed as the defenders watched helplessly from their stronghold. Such was the fate of Brookfield, Massachusetts, in 1675, and the town had to be abandoned even though the Indians were unsuccessful in their attempts to overwhelm the defenders.[8] Such had been the fate, too, of peasant communities in Europe during the age of feudal warfare, when the fortified manor house or castle was the center of defense and the refuge for the local populace. This was understood by the people of the American frontier; although they occasionally complained and sought to find a better solution, for the most part they accepted the situation as one of the normal hazards of frontier life.

In addition, there was the clear danger of being effectively surrounded and cut off from outside assistance. The stealthy movement of Indian raiding parties enabled them to invest a stronghold before word of the situation could be sent out. So it might be many hours, perhaps days, before the authorities elsewhere would become aware of the emergency. More time would pass before reinforcements from the militia could be gathered and dispatched; and if the enemy were present in great strength, the rescue force might have difficulty reaching the beleaguered stronghold.

The disadvantages of the stronghold defense emphasized the importance of adequate advance preparations for strong local defense conducted by the members of the local militia or garrison. The geography of some areas, notably peninsulas, suggested the possibility of excluding hostile intruders by erecting a barrier wall, much as Hadrian had done in Roman Britain. In America, the abundance of trees dictated the use of wooden stakes set upright in the ground to form a palisade, more than 5,000 stakes for every mile of wall. This was a prodigious task to accomplish. By 1634 Virginia had erected a palisade some 6 miles long, extending from Martin's Hundred on the James River to Cheskiack on the York, protecting at least 300,000 acres of territory including Jamestown.[9] Unfortunately, such barriers deteriorated rapidly and were not difficult to breach, so that few communities were willing to make the heavy investment required. Experience with wilderness warfare soon made it obvious that the European concept of an extensive wall to protect large areas was quite impractical.[10] This is not to say that fixed defenses, properly located and designed, were of no value. Forts were indeed useful in defending harbors, river mouths, and individual towns. Experience also taught the English that the Indians were not very skillful or persistent in siege warfare. Relatively simple fortified structures, if amply garrisoned and supplied, became little islands of security in the wilderness, bases from which military expeditions could venture forth when they wished to go on the offensive and to which they could retire for safety.

In a much larger sense also, during the seventeenth century, the English colonists faced a problem of military self-sufficiency. The mother country was in no position to extend much naval or military assistance across 3,000 miles of ocean, especially during the period of the civil war in the 1640s when Parliament was largely pre-occupied with domestic affairs. Recognizing this fact, as well as the continuing menace of French, Dutch, Spanish, and Indian enemies, some of the colonies sought mutual cooperation for mutual defense. The most elaborate, albeit only temporarily successful, attempt of this kind began in 1643 when the New England Puritan colonies, excepting Rhode Island, established an intercolonial league known as the United Colonies, or the New England Confederation. Commissioners from the participating states met together periodically to concert policy in dealing with the Indians or other potential foes. This organization continued to function, with varying degrees of success, until 1684.

When in 1654 England, at that time engaged in a war with Holland, sent Major Robert Sedgwick to New England with four ships for the purpose of leading the colonies in an attack upon New Netherland, the experience of intercolonial cooperation already was eleven years old. Before Sedgwick could get the offensive fully underway, however, news of peace arrived and the operation had to be canceled. Not wishing to return home empty-handed, Sedgwick headed north and, exceeding his orders, during the summer of 1654 captured the French posts at St. John, Port Royal, and Penobscot. (These forts were retained until 1667, when they were exchanged for a clear title to the Caribbean islands of Montserrat, Antigua, and part of St. Kitts.[11]) However, such active naval intervention by England in support of her American colonies was a rarity during most of the seventeenth century.

In 1660, England restored the Stuart king Charles II to his throne, and in France the following year the young, ambitious Louis XIV assumed the full powers of divine-right monarchy. Both nations, along with Spain and the Netherlands, were committed to the mercantilistic concept of empire, in which the race for colonies was a race for economic self-sufficiency and always at the expense of international competitors. France more than England, however, became partially diverted by closer ambitions on the continent of Europe, requiring the development of a great modern army. Drawing upon the French population of some 20 million, Louis and his able minister of war, the Marquis de Louvois, fashioned a standing army that was to become the dread of weaker neighboring states. These potential victims of Louis' territorial ambitions, none of whom alone could match the power of the new French Army, came to realize that their only hope lay in coalition.

Spain, exhausted by war and the extravagance of incompetent rulers, was far into a long period of decline and decay. Its present monarch, the unhappy and unhealthy Charles II, could never be expected to reverse the trend, and did not. Only the continuing inflow of precious metals from Spain's colonies in the New World gave the temporary appearance of prosperity. The Dutch states were not so far beyond their peak of glory as was Spain, but before them too stretched a long, gradual downgrade. Their one mainland colony in North America, centered on the Hudson Valley, fell to the English in 1664. After that they were scarcely to be considered an American power, although they did retain several small stations in the Caribbean, and their highly efficient merchant marine continued to carry on a profitable trade in many parts of the world. As for England, she was just beginning to lay claim to her heritage as a well-endowed island kingdom. England's age of greatness lay just ahead. Her population of about 4 million was only one-fifth that of France, her future principal rival; but the English people were becoming aware of their own attractive prospects and were quite unwilling to concede the race at the beginning. Moreover, England was now wedded to the sea and eager for the advantages of an overseas empire.

By 1675 England's mainland colonies in North America, extending along the coast from New England to South Carolina, contained a population estimated at more than 125,000.[12] Far to the north, on the island of Newfoundland and at Hudson Bay, were a few British fishing and fur-trading posts; while in the opposite direction, gracing the blue waters of the Caribbean, was a valuable necklace of tropical islands also under the flag of England. This conglomeration of American territories was now busy developing a varied economy in which the export of staple foodstuffs, furs and hides, lumber, naval stores, and fish played a major part. There was a flourishing intercolonial trade, together with a fair amount of small-scale manufacturing. Even more important was the fact that the colonists had insisted on taking out to America with them, as part of their prized possessions, the basic legal and political rights of Englishmen; and during the early stages of colonial development, they had managed to utilize those rights in the building of a free society with representative government.

Spain's territory in the New World stretched from the Florida peninsula around the shores of the Gulf of Mexico to the Isthmus of Panama, and beyond as far south as the cold and boisterous sea that lashes Cape Horn. This area included all of present Mexico and Central America, as well as the greater part of South America. In addition, important islands of the West Indies, most notably Cuba, were embraced within the Spanish imperial system. But the vast extent of the Spanish Empire in America was deceiving; scope did not mean strength. Unlike the English, Spaniards did not migrate to the colonies in large numbers. Those who did go, whether for short-term ventures or otherwise, formed a dominant minority, while the greater part of the population consisted of Indians, Negroes, and persons of mixed blood, few of whom had any real stake in the success of Spanish imperialism.

Florida, the Spanish territory nearest to the area being settled by the English, never developed into a strong, healthy colony. The Spaniard who was so unfortunate as to be governor of Florida had his residence in the sleepy little garrison town of St. Augustine on the east coast, headquarters for a semitropical colony whose total European population probably numbered less than 2,000. Normally fewer than 300 soldiers were available for the defense of the entire colony.[13] A few scattered forts and mission stations, feeble at best, stood between St. Augustine and the English territory to the north, their officers and priests desperately trying to counteract the growing influence of English traders among the Indians. In 1670, the very year when English settlement began at Charleston, Spain found it expedient to sign the Treaty of Madrid, which recognized England's right to east coast territory as far south as Carolina.

Governors and other officials of the Spanish empire in America worked under a severe handicap that was not always appreciated by their English counterparts. In theory, the governmental system of the empire was highly centralized under the supreme authority of the crown as exercised through the Council of the Indies in Spain. It was this council that appointed the colonial administrators, gave them their instructions, and issued the laws which they were to administer. In practice, of course, the distance across the ocean and the vastness of the empire itself precluded complete conformity with such a rigid system of control. Colonial administrators were under constant tension, being obliged by circumstances to take initiative when the system theoretically demanded otherwise. They often found it necessary to make decisions and issue orders, knowing only too well that what they did might later be repudiated by the Council of the Indies, with resulting rebuke or other penalty. The alternative was indecision and consequent stagnation. Most of the more intelligent and courageous Spanish colonial officials tried to find a reasonably safe middle course between the two extremes, getting done that which was absolutely necessary and little more. So the empire wobbled on, looking considerably more powerful than it really was.

One of Spain's major imperial rivals was France, who by 1675 could boast of a growing colony stretching in a long crescent from Acadia through the St. Lawrence Valley and on into the region of the Great Lakes. Actual settlements of any considerable size, however, were few. The two principal communities were Quebec, the center of government, and Montreal, the emporium for the far-reaching fur trade. Along both shores of the St. Lawrence River, and to a lesser extent in Acadia, were small farming communities and fishing villages where dwelt the greater part of New France's sturdy Roman Catholic population of *habitants*. Outposts and mission stations helped extend French influence widely among the Indians of many tribes who were linked with the French through the fur trade and, to a lesser degree, through the activity of missionary priests. The entire white population of New France, mostly concentrated along the upper reaches of the St. Lawrence River from the vicinity of Quebec to the vicinity of Montreal, was less than 10,000.[14] This means that in 1675 the population of New France and Florida combined was less than 10 percent of the total population of the English mainland colonies lying between them.

Since 1663, and even more completely since 1674, New France had been a royal colony under the direct control of the crown. As in the Spanish Empire, administration tended to be authoritarian in nature, affording little opportunity for the colonists themselves to practice self-government. At the top stood three high officials— the governor, the bishop, and the intendant. The governor, appointed by the crown, usually was a military man. He was the commander in chief of the colony's armed forces, and was principally responsible for the conduct of military affairs and Indian relations. There were some regular troops permanently stationed in New France, the so-called *troupes de la marine*. But equally important for the immediate security of the colony was the militia, in which nearly all the able-bodied male colonists were enrolled. As in the English colonies, the militia consisted of local companies, each under the command of a local *capitaine de milice*.[15] Religious affairs, broadly interpreted, were under the authoritative supervision of the bishop. As for the intendant, he was supreme in the civil administration of the colony, including matters of justice and finance. With authority thus divided somewhat ambiguously among three top officials, all fearful of offending a distant royal master, one is not surprised to discover, as in the Spanish colonies, a notable lack of efficiency and confidence in the government of New France.

The economy of New France rested rather uneasily upon the profits of the fur trade, an uncertain enterprise subject to fluctuating conditions not only in European markets but in the American hinterland as well. An upset in the field of Indian relations could be disastrous, for it was the natives who controlled the sources of peltry. The ability of the French traders to consort amicably with the Indians was an important asset, but was more than offset by the higher prices that the English were able to offer. New France also was developing a fairly sound agricultural base, providing most of the food and much of the clothing required by the population. In addition, there was some lumbering and even a little shipbuilding and small-scale industry, but not enough to reduce appreciably the colony's very heavy dependence upon Europe.

Increasing colonial populations and expanding zones of interest and influence made it ever more clear that Spain, England, and France were engaged in a race for predominance in America, with the richness of the prize scarcely yet discernible. The fact that no clear and mutually accepted boundaries had ever been drawn or were likely to be drawn separating the territories of one nation from those of another pointed toward an era of friction and violence along wilderness frontiers that were advancing into ever closer proximity.

Of all the many Indian tribes scattered along these expanding frontiers and therefore affected by the imperial conflict, five in particular were destined to play a crucial role. These were the so-called Five Nations of the Iroquois Confederacy, whose home territory extended through New York from the upper Hudson River west to the Genesee. The geographical location of this loose confederation athwart the crossroads of the western fur routes and the lines of communication from both Albany and Montreal to the Great Lakes gave the Iroquois a remarkable opportunity. Both the English and the French could profit tremendously from their friendship and support; both feared their hostility. However, the French and their Indian allies had long since earned the enmity of the Five Nations, while the English of New York were so fortunate as to inherit from their Dutch predecessors a mutually advantageous trade relationship with them. This meant that during most of the colonial period, the Five Nations, sometimes singly and sometimes in concert, tended to support the British and oppose the French in order to protect their own vital interests.

Considered fierce and aggressive by Europeans and Indians alike, the Iroquois were proving to be a real menace to the French and several other tribes within the orbit of French influence on the northern frontier. So threatening had they become by the early 1660s that a Canadian expedition was sent down into the Iroquois country in 1666 to chastise the Mohawks, easternmost of the Five Nations. After destroying a number of Mohawk villages, the expedition retired without carrying the offensive any farther. At this particular time England was involved in a war with France, and conceivably the bold intrusion from Canada into territory claimed by New York could have provoked colonial retaliation. Fortunately, New York preferred to let the affront pass, and the two mother countries made peace the following year. More serious was the warfare that had erupted in the West Indies as a part of the same international conflict. "This war," as one modern historian has noted, "marked the real beginning of the confrontation of France and England over colonial mastery in America." [16] The Peace of Breda in 1667, followed by the Anglo-Spanish Treaty of Madrid in 1670, brought only a temporary respite from what was to be a century of intense international imperial rivalry studded with armed clashes and full-scale warfare on land and sea.

Conflict with the Indians in the English colonies at last mounted to a fearsome climax in 1675, both in New England and Virginia. In the latter colony, open hostilities grew out of a long intensification of Indian-white friction during the 1660s and early 1670s, culminating in a series of retaliatory atrocities. A group of Doeg Indians, claiming that a prominent frontier planter named Thomas Mathew had failed to pay them for some goods, raided his plantation and made off with a number of hogs. Thereupon, a party of armed colonists went after the raiders, slaying several. Soon after this affray, in July 1675, the Doegs murdered Mathew's herdsman. Again the Virginians retaliated. A strong force crossed over into Maryland in pursuit of the Indians, and unfortunately exacted blood not only from the Doegs but also, by mistake, from some friendly Susquehannocks who happened to be in the vicinity. Now the fighting between Indians and whites spread rapidly along the exposed Virginia frontier. Settlers in the back country were terrorized by destructive Indian raids upon isolated communities and habitations. By the time the House of Burgesses had convened the following March, nearly 300 colonists had been slaughtered.[17]

Governor William Berkeley, for reasons not entirely clear, was strongly averse to the kind of all-out offensive warfare demanded by the embittered frontiersmen. Instead, he preferred to establish a string of wilderness forts that would serve as bases for parties of armed rangers and in this way hopefully prevent further incursions. The hope proved futile, for of course the Indians "quickly found out where about these Mouse traps were sett, and for what purpose, and so resalved to keepe out of there danger; which they might easely ennough do, with out any detriment to there designes." [18] Sad experience soon demonstrated that forest-wise and determined warriors were easily able to avoid the clumsy patrols and slip around the isolated outposts to continue their bloody work. Yet Berkeley remained unmoved; and so the frontiersmen, grumbling about this and other longstanding grievances, began to assemble under arms. For leadership they turned to an outraged, ambitious young planter named Nathaniel Bacon who, although a resident of the colony for less than two years, was already rising high in the councils of Virginia's government. Bacon agreed to lead them forth against the Indians, with or without the governor's blessing. What Bacon had to work with was his own sheer audacity and the eager aptitude of a sizable body of Virginians who had been trained in the militia and toughened by frontier living. These men were suspicious of nice distinctions between friendly Indians and bloody-handed hostiles. They wanted only to clear the Virginia frontier of the Indian menace once and for all.

The campaigning and skirmishing that filled the next six months were a confusing mixture of Indian fighting and civil conflict, Bacon lashing out at the redskins with one hand and clawing at the enraged Governor Berkeley with the other. Virginians at that time apparently fought better than they wrote, for the surviving records do little to clarify the confused swirl of events. That Bacon was a bold and clever leader, as well as an opportunist, seems sufficiently clear. Never in the several forays which he made against the Indians did his troops number more than a few hundred. On more than one occasion he demonstrated his ability to inspire his followers with a resounding harangue, but his skill as a military tactician is less certain. Bacon's army, if it may be called that, fought more by instinct than by formal rules, a fact attributable to its unofficial status, the nature of its dual opposition, and the conditions of the American wilderness.

On his first campaign, in May of 1676, Bacon went looking for a band of hostile Susquehannocks known to be in the vicinity of the Roanoke River. Friendly Occaneechee Indians, who lived on an island in the river, afforded hospitality to the army and even brought in some enemy prisoners, but Bacon, whose supplies were now dangerously low, demanded still more provisions. This led to a quarrel and then a fight. Later, when the smoke had cleared, the surviving Indians were gone, their village ruined. The frontiersmen helped themselves to what they needed, and went on their way.[19]

Again in August, Bacon rallied his followers and set forth on a

new adventure against the Indians. This time he chose as his target
a group known as the Pamunkeys, who formerly had been numbered among the tame tribes, but now were suspected of treachery.
Advancing to the vicinity of the upper York River, the army came
upon an Indian path which might lead to the elusive foe. In order
to follow this woodland trail the men broke formation and moved
ahead as best they could, subordinating military habit to frontier
conditions.[20] The path led to a small Pamunkey village which had
already been alarmed, so that most of the Indians escaped. Doggedly,
Bacon continued his search with little success until at last he
located a sizable group holed up in a thicket. As the colonists attacked, the Indians fled. What followed resembled a mass hunt for
wild deer. Indians were killed from behind or seized as prisoners,
while a considerable amount of plunder was scooped up. This action
was typical of the kind of warfare in which this motley little army
excelled. Although at least partially trained as militiamen in the
drillbook formations and tactics of European armies, Bacon's men
were quick to forget all but the forward thrust. Eager for blood
and plunder, familiar with the forest, scornful of refinements, they
relied upon a fluid but hard-hitting kind of attack requiring a
minimum of coordination and a great deal of individual initiative.
The terrified Indians seemed unable to cope with such audacity.

In the meantime, the civil uprising against the Berkeley regime
had gained such force that the heavy-handed old governor and his
leading supporters fled from Jamestown to the Eastern Shore,
thereby placing the waters of Chesapeake Bay between them and
the aroused Baconians. Then, when Bacon became involved in the
campaign against the Pamunkeys, Berkeley rallied his loyal following and led them back across the bay to reoccupy the capital. Thereupon Bacon returned to confront his chief antagonist. With the
Berkeleyites in full possession of Jamestown, the rebels hurriedly
constructed a simple earthwork commanding the narrow exit from
the low peninsula on which the town was situated. Now all was
ready for what promised to be the climactic showdown.

After some exchanges of fire, on 15 September Berkeley ordered
his troops to attack Bacon's position. Unfortunately for the governor, the force available for this sally included many men who served
only out of fear, secretly hoping for nothing more than a peaceful
accommodation and the security of their skins. The assault force
burst from the town "with horse and Foote in the Van, the Forlorne

being made up of such men as they had compell'd to serve." They advanced toward the rebels "with a narrow Front, and pressing very close upon one anothers shoulders that the Forlorne might be their shelter." [21] One contemporary wit likened the attacking party to "scholers goeing to schoole," for they "went out with hevie harts, but returnd hom with light heeles." [22] In plain language, Bacon's men defended their position so effectively that the governor's troops quickly faltered, came to a halt, and then broke into a rapid retreat to regain the shelter of the town. Subsequently, Governor Berkeley again withdrew from Jamestown, whereupon Bacon entered the capital and destroyed it by fire lest it once more become available as a base for the opposition.

In a little over a month, however, Bacon was dead of dysentery, and with him died the resistance movement. Both the royal authority and the uneasy peace of the frontier were soon restored. Bacon's campaigning against the Indians, together with his brief show of force against the governor, hardly deserve the name of war, and can offer little of value to the student of military history. Perhaps the most that can be said is that Bacon's Rebellion, as it came to be called, served as a test for the system of training established in the Virginia militia, at the same time providing further evidence of the necessity for modifying European battle formations and tactics in the American wilderness. Indian opposition in this brief struggle was never massive or well organized; consequently, the English forces were not fully challenged. They were able to function successfully without serious attention to method, and little was learned.

Of all the Indian-white conflicts prior to 1687, the one that most thoroughly embodies all the trends and problems of American warfare in the seventeenth century is King Philip's War, which started in 1675 and raged through much of New England for several years. This desperate struggle is an outstanding case of Indian warfare instigated by the Indians themselves for the purpose of rolling back the tide of white expansion. It began rather feebly in the western corner of Plymouth Colony on 20 June 1675 when Wampanoag Indians appeared in the frontier settlement of Swansea and proceeded to loot and burn a few abandoned dwellings. This ominous vandalism triggered a sequence of events that led quickly into full-scale warfare involving the three allied Puritan colonies of Plymouth, Massachusetts Bay, and Connecticut.

Philip, sachem of the Wampanoags, was the son of the late chief
Massasoit, who during his lifetime had faithfully remained at peace
with Plymouth ever since agreeing to a treaty in 1621. Since Massasoit's death, his son had become increasingly resentful both over
the loss of tribal land (although he himself had sold much of it
to the English) and over the tendency of the colonial authorities to treat him like a naughty child. Philip was proud, and repeated humiliations only increased his resentment. There is some
evidence to suggest that in the years before 1675 he began attempting to weave together a widespread intertribal conspiracy against
the English.[23] At least his influence among neighboring tribes seems
to have been growing, while actual Indian preparations for war
became evident to the colonists. Taking all available evidence into
consideration, and in view of subsequent developments during 1675
and 1676, the best supposition is that several of the New England
tribes, with Philip prodding them on, had recently been discussing
and considering the possibility of a unified uprising against the
colonies, but that Wampanoag anger boiled over before the conspiracy was complete and before the tribes were ready for the
supreme effort. The outbreak was clearly premature, with the result
that the Wampanoags found themselves irrevocably at war with the
combined power of the Puritan colonies, while the old rivalries and
divisions among the other tribes remained as yet unresolved. Some
tribes, caught up in the enthusiasm of Philip's bold enterprise and
excited by the prospect of striking at the English, joined the
Wampanoag uprising, but other tribes, no less important, hung
back or even gave their active support to the colonies.

After the Nipmucks of central Massachusetts and the river Indians
of the upper Connecticut Valley had joined the uprising during the
summer, the harvest moon looked down upon a widening arc of
terror stretching all the way from Cape Cod to the upper Connecticut River. Few towns, even the well-established ones along the coast,
now could feel secure. Frontier villages and lone farmsteads were in
the grip of a chilling fear, for the enemy had already shown himself
to be cruel and ruthless in his warfare. The isolation of such places
made it relatively easy for the marauding Indians to strike without
warning; local defense against such attacks proved to be in practice
a bewildering problem.

Garrison and expeditionary forces were raised from the colonial
militia and placed under the leadership of amateur officers whose

main qualifications were public spirit, manly courage, and a text-book knowledge of tactics. Such forces shouldered muskets bravely and marched into the wilderness in search of Indians. Almost immediately they began to learn some bitter lessons—occasionally too late to be of any use. The Indians proved extremely competent in moving through the forest quietly and swiftly. They took maximum advantage of their intimate knowledge of terrain and demonstrated their skill in the art of ambush. Sometimes the Indians would lie in concealment along both sides of the path, at a place where the advancing English force would find itself at a disadvantage. The first intimation of trouble might be a crashing volley from Indian guns and the whirr of feathered arrows. When that happened, it took a steady company and a bold commander to avoid disastrous defeat. At other times the Indians would lure some unit of colonial soldiers into a trap by confronting them at first with a relatively weak party that soon began to retreat before them. Then, as the eager colonial force pursued, the main body of the Indians would move around the flanks, surrounding the English and overwhelming them with superior numbers.

On 4 September 1675 more than half a company of Massachusetts men were killed when they marched into an Indian trap unaware. Two weeks later, another company was surprised and mangled in much the same way. A contemporary historian recalled that day as "the Saddest that ever befel *New-England*," bringing as it did "the Ruine of a choice Company of young Men, the very Flower of the County of *Essex*." [24] Worst of all was the stunning defeat administered to a company of Plymouth Colony men the following March. On the prowl for Indians, this company rashly pursued an apparently weak group only to find itself suddenly beset on both flanks by great numbers of the enemy. A bare handful of survivors escaped from that deadly embrace. The Reverend William Hubbard, preaching in Boston a few weeks later, was moved to remark ruefully that "it is one thing to drill a Company in a plain Champagne and another to drive an enemy through the desert woods." [25] This was exactly the kind of lesson the English had to learn well if they were going to survive in the American wilderness.

Despite widespread colonial suspicion of all Indians, even those who professed friendship, English forces came to rely more and more upon friendly Indians as scouts. This growing practice could not guarantee immunity from ambush—indeed, there was always the possibility that such scouts intended to betray the colonial troops—but it did increase the chance of getting some advance warning of the enemy's presence. Indians had an almost uncanny ability to discover and follow any signs of human presence in the woods, and every sensible commander learned to value their services, especially when attempting to locate and pursue an elusive enemy band.

When the Wampanoags first began hostilities against Plymouth Colony in the summer of 1675, everybody wondered what the powerful Narragansett tribe would do. Since the days of the Pequot War, when the Narragansetts had sided with the English, these Indians had become increasingly truculent as white settlement continued to press upon their homeland in Rhode Island. If the Narragansetts should rise up and give active aid to Philip, New England's peril would be greatly increased. In order to prevent such an eventuality Puritan emissaries, backed by a strong military force, approached the Narragansetts and induced some of the lesser tribal leaders to sign a treaty of fidelity. One of the terms required the Narragansetts to yield up any Wampanoags who came into their custody.[26] During the ensuing months, the Narragansetts not only avoided compliance, but even gave reason to suspect that they were in sympathy with Philip's attempt to smash the colonies. In October, however, one of the Narragansett sachems formally reaffirmed the obligation and pledged that all enemy Indians residing with his people would be turned over to the English within ten days. The tenth day came and went without the surrender of a single Wampanoag.

Early in November the Commissioners of the United Colonies decided to adopt a policy of strong coercion, preferring to have the Narragansetts as open enemies than false friends.[27] A major expedition was organized and sent into the Narragansett country in December with orders to force compliance or, that failing, to attack. By this time, most of the tribe was holed up for the winter in a fortified village located in a remote swamp near the present West Kingston, Rhode Island. The English knew of this Indian stronghold, and after waiting in vain for a further opportunity to confer with the sachems, they decided to proceed with the second part of their instructions and make a killing thrust. A Narragansett defector agreed to lead them to the place.

The intercolonial force, consisting of two companies from Plymouth Colony, five from Connecticut, six from Massachusetts, a troop of horse, and a large number of Indian auxiliaries, some 1,100 men in all, assembled at a place known as Pettaquamscutt, about 6 miles due east of the objective. On the nineteenth of December they trudged westward through a fresh fall of snow toward the Indian village. Their defector-guide, true to his word, brought them to the edge of the swamp. Here they encountered a party of Narragansetts, and shots were exchanged, whereupon the Indians quickly withdrew into the depths of the swamp with the colonial troops in full cry. Soon the pursuers could see their objective ahead of them through the frozen swamp—a heavily defended, palisaded Indian village. Within the bristling perimeter of stakes and brush waited hundreds of Indian men, women, and children. Some of them were old enough to remember well the merciless slaughter of Indians at the Pequot fort in 1637. They were determined to fight like wildcats for their lives.

The first troops to arrive, finding a gap in the defenses, rushed impetuously into the village but soon were forced out again with heavy losses. Other companies quickly arrived on the scene, and once again the attackers pushed their way into the fortified area. Here the fight raged with unchecked fury at close quarters, as the English struggled to overwhelm the desperate Narragansetts. Men were falling on all sides, while the terrified noncombatants huddled in the wigwams. Eventually Indian resistance began to weaken; the colonial troops "by degrees made up higher, first into the Middle, and then into the upper End of the Fort, till at last they made the Enemy all retire from their Sconces and fortified Places, leaving Multitudes of their dead Bodies upon the Place." [28] Some of the Narragansetts managed to escape from their village through gaps in the English lines; the condition of these survivors, many probably wounded, must have been pitiable as they wandered through the swampland on that stormy winter night.

In the meantime, the victorious English had set fire to the Indian village and burned it to the ground, destroying the tribe's winter stores of corn. Estimates of the number of enemy Indians killed in the Great Swamp Fight vary greatly. The total number may have exceeded 500 men, women, and children. Exact figures are not needed in this case; more important is the undoubted fact that the colonial expedition had dealt a crushing blow to one of New England's major tribes. The Narragansetts still had some fighting strength left, as they were able to demonstrate later in the war, but not enough to prevent their ultimate defeat and humiliation.

Colonial forces also found an effective way to deal with hostile Indians even when they were unable to meet and defeat them in open battle. They sought out Indian villages or other places where the natives were known to congregate and, after chasing them away, proceeded systematically to destroy their crops and their caches of food. During the winter of 1675–76, the fugitive enemy came close to starvation, and when the English resumed this scorched-earth policy in the spring, Philip's cause began to enter its last decline.[29]

At the same time, increasingly effective use was being made of Indian auxiliaries to track down the dwindling enemy bands. An outstanding innovator in this regard was Captain Benjamin Church of Plymouth Colony, who had been wounded in the Great Swamp Fight, and who later was given command of an independent company of volunteer whites with some friendly Indians attached. The English volunteers were bold, aggressive men, attracted to this dangerous service by the prospect of booty, including Indian slaves; the friendly Indians were trusted hunters and woodsmen known to be loyal to the English.[30]

Church had learned much about Indian fighting during the earlier part of the war, and from this experience he developed a mode of operation that proved highly effective. He used his Indian auxiliaries for scouting and tracking and treated them as fellow soldiers. When advancing through wooded country, Church kept his men in a rather loose formation which offered no mass target to a hidden enemy but which enabled them to deploy quickly when the enemy was detected.

> . . . His manner of Marching thro' the Woods was such, as if he were discovered, they appeared to be more than they were. For he always Marched at a wide distance one from another, partly for their safety: and this was an *Indian* custom, to March thin and scatter. Capt. *Church* inquired of some of the *Indians* that were become his Souldiers, *How they got such advantage often of the English in their Marches thro' the Woods?* They told him, That the *Indians* gain'd great advantage of the *English* by two things; the *Indians* always took care in their Marches and Fights, not to come too thick together. But the *English* always kept in a heap together, that it was as easy to hit them as to hit an House. The other was, that if at any time they discovered a company of *English* Souldiers in the Woods, they

knew that there was all, for the *English* never scattered; but the *Indians* always divided and scattered.[31]

Clearly Church was an improvisor, the kind of commander who is willing and able to adapt old ways to new conditions. He was one of the first American military leaders to develop a style of fighting based upon Indian experience as well as English practice, shaped to the demands of the wilderness environment. Beyond this, Church showed remarkable audacity in his practice of recruiting additional strength from among the very prisoners taken by his fast-moving company. He

> would pick out some that he took a fancy to, and would tell them, *He took a particular fancy to them, and had chose them for himself to make Souldiers of; and if any would behave themselves well, he would do well by them, and they should be his men and not Sold out of the Country.*

That in itself was sufficient inducement for many. But

> If he perceived they look'd surly, and his *Indian* Souldiers call'd them treacherous Dogs, as some of them would sometimes do, all the notice he would take of it, would only be to clap them on the back, and tell them, *Come, come, you look wild and surly, and mutter, but that signifies nothing, these my best Souldiers were a little while a go as wild and surly as you are now; by that time you have been but one day along with me, you'l love me too, and be as brisk as any of them.* And it prov'd so.[32]

Philip was trapped and killed in August 1676 by Captain Church and a mixed party of colonists and Indians. This virtually put an end to the war in southern New England, and a year later the northern tribes were reduced to submission. New England had survived the worst Indian war of the seventeenth century, but only at terrific cost. Under the pressure of Indian attack the whole outer line of English settlement had crumbled. Entire villages and towns lay in utter ruin, while many others had been severely damaged by fire. The people of these and other communities were scattered far and wide, perhaps never again to reassemble as neighbors. Voices familiar in town meeting or at militia muster were to be heard no more. Probably about 500 colonial soldiers had been killed in action or had died of wounds, and the toll among civilians doubtless brought the total figure to well over a thousand. The Puritan colonies estimated their war expenses at about £100,000, which of course dramatically increased the tax burden on the people. In addition, the whole economy had been rocked to its foundations. Both the fishing industry and agriculture felt keenly the shortage of manpower, while the fur trade of the frontier suffered a blow from which it never fully recovered. Clearly King Philip's War, the first really extensive military conflict in American history, was a staggering experience for young New England. As for the Indian tribes of the area, at least in southern New England, they were tragically broken forever.

Looking back over the history of these early conflicts between Indians and colonists, we can begin to see certain trends and characteristics that were emerging to form the tragic pattern of the future. One very significant development already touched upon was the modification of European military techniques. Wilderness conditions and the nature of Indian warfare presented a difficult challenge to a young society accustomed to a professionalized style of warfare on familiar terrain. From the very outset it was necessary for the colonists to come to grips with every new condition, every new problem, on its own terms. Their endeavors, sometimes tragically clumsy, sometimes highly effective, began shaping a new military tradition founded upon the best of the old. Occasionally there appeared a leader such as Benjamin Church, imaginative, resourceful, daring, to show the way in adapting European methods to wilderness conditions. Colonial America was a laboratory of forest warfare where new techniques and tactics, new weapons and ways, were developed and tested. In the long run, success was gained through a fortunate combination of well-tested fundamentals and imaginative improvisation.

One tactic that was found to be highly effective in Indian fighting, under certain conditions, was encirclement. Captain Mason used this tactic with almost total success in his attack on the Pequot fort in 1637. The effectiveness of the encircling tactic usually depended upon two factors—superior strength and complete surprise. If either or both were lacking, the Indians had opportunity to throw the attackers off balance and defeat them, or else to break through the lines and escape. Complete surprise sometimes became possible for the English because their Indian enemies proved incorrigibly careless when in camp, neglecting to maintain alert sentries. Captain Church demonstrated with perfect precision how encirclement should be employed as a field tactic. On one occasion his native scouts discovered an encampment of Narragansetts,

> and well observing their fires, and postures, Returned with the intelligence to their Captain, who gave such directions for the surrounding of them, as had the direct effect; surprizing them from every side so unexpectedly, that they were all taken, not so much as one escaped.[33]

Indian warfare proved to be a brutalizing business. The colonists had come to America prepared to believe the worst about the "wild" natives; their experiences with these people of the forest sometimes confirmed their apprehensions. Early optimism about peace and brotherhood, even the possibility of converting the Indians to Christianity, melted rather quickly in the flames of violence and war, producing a new attitude that was a combination of contempt, fear, and hatred. The ill-considered boast of one early colonist, that "we neither feare them nor trust them, for fourtie of our Musketeeres will drive five hundred of them out of the Field," was seldom heard after 1637 as the Indians obtained firearms and demonstrated their growing ability to use them with deadly effect.[34]

Both sides killed indiscriminately; both also took prisoners and then abused them cruelly. Indians who fell into the hands of colonial forces might be interrogated under torture or the threat of torture to extract whatever information they could give about the location, condition, and plans of the enemy. After yielding up this intelligence, they might then be put to death or perhaps forced to lead the English to their compatriots. Male prisoners who were recognized as participants in former acts of violence were likely to be considered criminals and given short shrift. The hangman's noose and the firing squad disposed of many such, especially in the last weeks of King Philip's War, when the Indian cause was rapidly crumbling.

Whenever a tribe was brought to final defeat, the victorious English imposed terms of peace that were clearly formulated in their own best interests, with special regard to future security and expansion. Commonly, the beaten tribe was looked upon as collectively guilty of some crime, possibly even treason, which justified a thoroughgoing severity. The English had little regard for Indian promises and feared that if the tribe were allowed to regain its strength it would once again threaten their settlements and exact a terrible price for the earlier defeat. So the terms of peace imposed were characteristically stringent and thorough, with a strong emphasis on complete submission. Usually included was some form of continuing supervision by colonial authorities.

The idea that the best long-range solution to the problem of Indian-white relations was to confine the Indians to clearly designated reservations began to emerge quite early. In view of the long and sometimes tragic history of this concept after it had hardened into policy, its early emergence in the colonies is of no little significance. The year 1646 marks an identifiable beginning. In Massachusetts the General Court appointed a committee to see about purchasing some land "for the incuragment of the Indians to live in an orderly way amongst us," and to establish rules "for their improveing and enjoying thereof." [35] Under the sponsorship of the Reverend John Eliot, the Christian Indians of Massachusetts later acquired a township of their own at Natick, where they had the opportunity to develop a community in accord with the ways of the English, while enjoying English encouragement and protection.

It was also in 1646, following the Indian uprising of 1644, that the colony of Virginia adopted a reservation policy. As part of the agreement made with Necotowance, Opechancanough's successor, most of the area lying north of the York River was designated as an Indian reservation, supposedly in perpetuity.[36] Part of the trouble with the reservation policy—and this has been true throughout most of our history—is that the integrity of the agreement has seldom been able to survive the insistent pressure of pioneer land greed. Ruin by gnawing and nibbling, if not by sudden obliteration, has been the fate of many a reservation tribe. But in colonial times the reservation policy seemed a good solution, one that protected the future of both races. And so, in the years after 1676 more and more Indians found themselves trying to carry on their way of life on special tracts designated for them by the increasingly dominant colonial authorities. This, in turn, helped free other land for white settlement and exploitation, following its purchase or its conquest.

The sporadic warfare of the seventeenth-century frontier—in New England, New York, Virginia, and Carolina—generally resulted in the defeat and degradation of the Indians who set themselves in opposition to the white advance. It was not "civilized" warfare, as between equals, but rather a warfare of deliberate cruelty, bloody reprisals, indiscriminate destruction. Treachery was commonplace and expected. Thus, a tragic pattern for such wars was early set; and once set, it tended to perpetuate itself through more than two centuries. The reiterated crushing of Indian resistance, accompanied by the overbearing imposition of penalties and controls, gradually broke the fierce, independent spirit of the tribes, a spirit already tragically weakened by the Indians' growing dependence upon European trade goods and intoxicating liquors.[37]

The English, on the other hand, although they sometimes suffered serious setbacks at the hands of the fighting Indians, always managed to recover from their defeats, regain lost ground, and then forge ahead. Superior technology, a great depth of resources, the ability to learn from experience, and a constantly growing population, all contributed to the increasing margin of strength that made for colonial success against the Indians. And in the last analysis much credit must be given to the system of compulsory military training that provided the colonies with an ever-available reservoir of manpower. The fundamental soundness of the old militia system, one of England's important legacies to America, was tested and proved in the Indian wars of the seventeenth century.

Rival ambitions of Spaniards, Frenchmen, and Englishmen on the continent of North America and the islands of the West Indies in the years before 1689 began to break out into occasional violence. In most instances the home governments were not directly involved; seldom did they instigate or openly encourage action that subsequently might prove embarrassing and even jeopardize the peace. Yet when an episode did occur, the respective mother countries felt obliged to uphold their own. It was almost as though several mutually antagonistic families had sent their children out to play together in an enclosed yard. Soon there was competition for the toys, competition for space in which to play, competition for dominance in the games. Black looks led to name-calling, name-calling to pulling and shoving, and that to the exchange of blows and wild yells of rage. The parents cannot be said to have sent their children out to fight, but that was what happened, and the parents were kept busy arguing with each other over their children's behavior.

Anglo-Spanish rivalry centered in the region which is now the state of Georgia and which became an international arena soon after the founding of Charleston, South Carolina, in 1670. The new English colonists entered upon the Indian trade with an enthusiasm that promised no good for the feeble Spanish colony in Florida, and soon the Spanish influence among the Indians north of the Alta-maha River began to weaken. Superior English inducements, ma-terial rather than spiritual, were having their effect. In almost helpless dismay the Spanish missionary priests watched the tribes loosen the ties that until now had attached them to the imperial system of Spain, and become eager suppliers of the English traders from Charleston in return for English liquor and other trade goods. The trade was not only in deerskins. Some of the English trafficked in captured Indians, buying these prisoners from tribes which had taken them in war and selling them in Charleston or other sett'e-ments as far north as New England.[38]

As if the disruption of Spanish influence among the Indians were not sufficient, English pirates and freebooters continued to prey upon Spanish shipping in the Bahama Channel, and even attacked the Spaniards on land, despite the fact that England and Spain were officially at peace. In 1680, a large party of Indians under English leadership besieged the Spanish mission of Santa Catalina on St. Catherine's Island about 100 miles south of Charleston. This was well below the line claimed by Spain in the Treaty of Madrid. Al-though the inhabitants were able to hold their position until the attackers withdrew, the episode was a dire warning of a dark future, revealing only too clearly the power and aggressive intent of Spain's antagonists in that part of America. Three years later, English raid-ers attacked and burned a Spanish outpost at Matanzas Inlet, the southern approach to St. Augustine.[39] Such provocations, although unofficial, in Spanish eyes seemed to be undeniable proof of English hostility and desire to undermine the already shaky Spanish colony in Florida.

When a settlement of Scots was begun at Port Royal near if not actually below the border claimed by Spain, St. Augustine reacted with alarm and anger. In 1686, a small Spanish raiding force pounced upon the Scotch settlement and destroyed it, burned some other dwellings and carried off plunder at Edisto Island still farther north, and then began moving on Charleston itself. Had not a violent storm intervened, causing the raiders to withdraw, the very capital of Carolina might have come under attack. Yet England and Spain remained at peace.[40]

If not as weak numerically as the Spanish population of Florida, the French population of Canada nevertheless seemed hardly equal to the task of expanding and at the same time defending the frontiers of New France in the face of determined opposition by the much more numerous English colonists. New France's enemies were active not only in New England and the colonies farther south but also, to a much lesser degree, in Newfoundland and along the bleak, windswept shores of Hudson Bay. Canada, apparently threatened from both north and south, could take comfort only from the fact that the English monarchy was, at the moment, well inclined toward Louis XIV and that there seemed to be little or no effective co-ordination among the various English groups in North America. At Hudson Bay, the tough, enterprising English fur traders held a number of important sites and were busily engaged in extending their trade with the willing natives. In fact, it appeared that these isolated little groups in a cold and lonely land were getting themselves in a position to dominate the fur trade of the vast northern area. Then suddenly in 1686 the French struck boldly. A raiding party from Montreal surprised the English posts, gained control at each one, and seized a great store of booty that included some 50,-000 beaver pelts.[41] Who could doubt that the English would try to regain their lost positions when opportunity presented itself?

Meanwhile along the St. Lawrence, in council chamber and humble cottage, there was mounting apprehension over the growing threat from the south, a threat that combined English expansion north and west toward the zone of French influence with the attendant animosity of the Iroquois tribes. In combination they seemed to carry mortal peril for New France. As early as 1673, the French had constructed Fort Frontenac on the north shore of Lake Ontario near the exit into the upper St. Lawrence. One important purpose of this new fur-trading outpost was to prevent the aggressive warriors of the Five Nations from crossing the St. Lawrence and poaching in the hunting grounds of the French-allied Indians north of Lake Ontario. The Iroquois soon proved repeatedly that they could skirt Fort Frontenac and continue their activities with little difficulty.

When La Salle began his ambitious program for turning the Mississippi Valley into a vast French fur-trading emporium, the Five Nations recognized the danger of being economically isolated and cut out of the western fur trade. Their response was a new drive to extend their own power in the West, beginning with a direct attack upon the Illinois Indians in 1680. This challenge to the future growth of New France was unmistakable; the vital interests of the Iroquois Confederacy were clashing head-on with the equally compelling interests of Canada, while the English viewed with obvious satisfaction the discomfiture of their northern rivals. Already, in fact, Iroquois-French hostility was coming to be recognized and counted upon as an ace-in-hand for the future security and prosperity of the English colonies.

New York had acquired a new governor in 1683, the imperial-minded, aggressive Irishman, Thomas Dongan. This man saw in full perspective the now rapidly emerging picture of Anglo-French rivalry in North America, with domination of the expanding western fur trade as the key to Indian alliances; Indian alliances, the key to control of the continent; and the Anglo-Iroquois alliance, the kingpin of the entire structure. At all costs, Dongan realized, New York must hold the loyalty of the Five Nations. Against French claims and actions to the contrary, Dongan continued to insist that English territory extended all the way to the south bank of the St. Lawrence River and the shores of the Great Lakes. And he encouraged English traders to extend their activity far out in the West in order to undercut the French position there.[42]

At Quebec, the Marquis de Denonville, Governor of New France, stoutly denied Dongan's extreme claims and, indeed, would not even recognize the right of Englishmen to come and trade in the West. Nor would he admit the validity of New York's special relationship with the Iroquois Confederacy. As a matter of fact, courageous French missionaries had been active for some time in certain parts of the Iroquois country, converting the Indians to the Catholic faith and a new regard for the French as brothers. Some of the converts had even been persuaded to migrate to the region just south of the St. Lawrence, where they now lived in their own villages under French supervision and instruction. These transplanted Iroquois became known as the Caughnawaga Indians, a name derived from their principal settlement. To Dongan, of course, this French activity among the Iroquois represented a highly dangerous subversion, threatening the very existence of New York and New England. Clearly, then, both sides were coming to believe themselves seriously endangered by the expansion of the opposition.

Both were in a mood conducive to the outbreak of violence, perhaps even war.

In 1686 and again in 1687, the kings of England and France reached an agreement designed to prevent open hostilities between their respective American colonies, even in a time of war between the two mother countries. The idea was to shield the infant states in the New World from the consequences of Europe's everlasting quarrels. But the rival ambitions of colonists and their governors rendered such a solution ineffective. Those men actually on the scene in America saw much more clearly than their superiors in London or Paris the importance and richness of the prize at stake.[43]

The truth is that neither England nor France had a clear title to the vast region drained by the Mississippi River. Although the French were more active in preliminary exploration, they certainly held no monopoly; English explorers had penetrated the Appalachian barrier at a fairly early date. If French explorers such as Joliet and La Salle were the first to traverse the area, establishing contact with the natives, New France did not have the capacity to follow exploration with effective occupation. As one modern scholar has well pointed out, the French "could not be said to have occupied the west, anymore than the seamen of New England occupied the Atlantic ocean in their voyages to Europe, Africa, and the West Indies." [44] The West must be thought of as a huge no-man's wilderness, or rather, Indian's wilderness, in which assertive, ambitious Englishmen and Frenchmen, sometimes with and sometimes without the backing of their respective governments, were maneuvering for advantage.

In Quebec, Governor Denonville's patience was sorely tested by the reiterated outrages committed by parties of Iroquois against the French fur traders and allied Indians, outrages which if not actually encouraged by New York's Dongan were scarcely discouraged by him either. Again the overextended network of Montreal's fur trade and Indian alliances seemed in danger of destruction. Denonville decided to act before the proportions of the threat grew larger. In July 1687 he assembled a punitive expedition of some 3,000 French militia, regular soldiers, and Indians, at Irondequoit Bay on the south side of Lake Ontario, with the intention of invading the land of the Senecas, westernmost of the Five Nations. The purpose was to convince these Indians, by the ruthless application of force, that they had better leave the French in peace.[45] After pausing to construct a palisaded base camp on the shore of the lake, Denonville began to advance upriver toward the principal villages of the tribe. The Iroquois had been aware that the French were approaching in force and so were not taken completely by surprise. Seneca warriors lying concealed at the edge of a swamp suddenly opened fire on Denonville's army, and a sharp skirmish ensued. The French, suffering heavy losses, began to show signs of panic, but Denonville was able to rally his men and turn a near defeat into victory. A little later, some of the French troops got their first real taste of savagery when they saw their Indian allies cutting the throats of Seneca corpses found on the battleground, sucking out the blood, and then cutting up the flesh for the stewpots.

During the next nine days, Denonville's force tramped through the Seneca country while the Indians lay low. Systematically, the French destroyed the deserted villages and the crops of corn and beans in the adjacent fields. Then, having accomplished this destruction and after asserting French sovereignty over the area, they withdrew. An avenging band of Iroquois warriors finally arrived at the shore of Irondequoit Bay only to find the base camp already burned and the last of the French flotilla just disappearing from view far out on the lake. Denonville next proceeded to Niagara, where he built a small fort and left a garrison to hold that strategic location. Then he and the rest of the army returned to Montreal, well satisfied with what had been accomplished.[46] Now Iroquois hatred of the French, being nourished by Dongan, was deeper than ever before. Shortly after the Senecas had been chastised in this fashion, King James accorded the Iroquois the status of English subjects and instructed Dongan to give them his protection.[47]

For a period of about five months, starting in October 1687, the governor of New York and the governor of New France engaged in an acrimonious exchange of correspondence. The sting was scarcely lessened by the fact that it was all couched in the polite verbiage of international diplomacy. Each accused the other of aggression and breach of treaty, while asserting his own rectitude. Dongan insisted that the French fort at Niagara was on English soil, and disposed of all French claims in the West by sarcastically denying that "a few loose fellowes rambling amongst Indians to keep themselves from starving gives the French a right to the Country." [48] The Iroquois resorted to action rather than debate. During the winter, they besieged both the French outpost at Niagara and Fort Frontenac, squeezing them so tightly that the garrisons were unable to hunt and fish, and had to subsist on salt pork and flour. Disease crept in where the Indians could not. Of a total of 240 men in these two forts, 180 failed to survive.[49] Denonville, unable to rally sufficient strength to smash back the Iroquois threat to New France, finally achieved a truce with several of the Five Nations. Both sides needed time to prepare for the impending showdown. Not long after this the garrison at Niagara was withdrawn and the post was left to the wilderness and the Indians.

In 1688 there existed one other condition affecting to a large degree the mounting tension between the English and the French in North America. Since the accession of James to the English throne, all the New England colonies, together with New York and New Jersey, had been combined under one government administered by the royally appointed governor, Sir Edmund Andros. All the representative legislatures were abolished while the militia organizations, hitherto an important pillar in the structure of self-government, became instead an arm of royal authority. The new superstate, known as the Dominion of New England, was governed by decree. This profound reorganization reflected the new king's belief that consolidation meant efficiency and, even more important, due subordination to royal prerogative. It is not surprising, then, to discover that the affected colonial populations were unhappy and restive, especially when it became apparent that Governor Andros was inclined to be arbitrary in his rule.

These were the years when the English world was uneasy about the apparent upsurge of Roman Catholic power in Europe. In the popular mind, "popery" was deplorable not only for its qualities as a form of religion, but also because it seemed to have a marked affinity with political absolutism. From this viewpoint, priest and tyrant stalked hand in hand through the history of a thousand years. The culmination was seen in the person of Louis XIV of France, Roman Catholic, absolutist monarch, enemy of Protestantism and freedom, terror of the independent states of Europe. Of particular concern to the English was the fact that their own king, James II, was an avowed Roman Catholic who seemed determined to lift his religion to a dominant position in his own country against the clear wish of his subjects. Was England to survive the tyranny of Charles I only to fall under the tyranny of his son?

Recently England had trembled at the prospect of a sinister Franco-Roman plot to overthrow Protestantism and political rights. In the colonies there existed the same fear, augmented by the presence of the Indians. The French Catholics of Canada, it was said, were contriving a deep conspiracy with the savages for the sudden conquest of the English colonies. This diabolical project would be aided by treason within, for there were believed to be Catholic sympathizers in high places. The autocratic rule of Governor Andros in the Dominion of New England caused some fearful colonists to suspect that even he was an active participant in the plot.

Against such a dark background of suspicion and unrest we must view the outbreak of Indian trouble in northern New England during the fall of 1688. This alarming development was coincidental with the beginning of the Glorious Revolution in England, but the slowness of communications across the ocean kept the definite news of James's overthrow from the ears of the American colonists until the following March. Andros managed to repress the offending Indians temporarily during the winter, but while he was away from Boston on that mission the discontents of the Puritans were coming to a head. Andros returned to Boston only to be confronted with a popular uprising that swept him and his regime out of power in April 1689. A similar upheaval occurred in New York within a few weeks, elevating to power in that town a captain of militia named Jacob Leisler. These turbulent events were in part legitimized by the success of the Glorious Revolution in England, which installed on the throne the Dutch Protestant hero, William of Orange, and his wife Mary, the Protestant daughter of the deposed James. While awaiting instructions from the new monarchs, the component colonies of the now defunct Dominion of New England resumed their separate identities and reestablished the old forms of representative government.

The repercussions of the Glorious Revolution were felt in all the colonies. French power, Catholic intrigue, Indian malevolence —these were real issues and ever-present dangers in the minds of most English colonists. The peril was felt everywhere, as though it were in the very air, but its principal source lay toward the north, in French Canada. There was the enemy. French exploration, French relations with the Indians, French claims to territory, all seemed to support the reality of an intention to outflank the English in America and deny them the fruits of their endeavors. This was the condition of the colonial mind when word arrived that William and Mary on 7 May 1689 had proclaimed the existence of a state of war between England and France.

NOTES

1. In my discussion of the Pequot War I have relied heavily upon the authoritative works of Professor Alden T. Vaughan: "Soldiers and Savages: A History of the Pequot War" (Unpublished M.A. thesis, Columbia University, 1958); "New England Puritans and the American Indian, 1620–1675" (Ph.D. dissertation, Columbia University, 1964); "Pequots and Puritans: The Causes of the War of 1637," *WMQ*, XXI (April, 1964), 256–269; *New England Frontier: Puritans and Indians, 1620–1675* (Boston, 1965).

2. *New Englands Memoriall*, Howard J. Hall, ed. (Facsimile ed., New York, 1937), p. 101.

3. John Underhill, *Newes from America; A New and Experimentall Discoverie of New England,* in Charles Orr, ed., *History of the Pequot War* (Cleveland, 1897), p. 81.

4. J. Franklin Jameson, ed., *Narratives of New Netherland, 1609–1664* (New York, 1909), pp. 213, 274–275; Allen W. Trelease, *Indian Affairs in Colonial New York: The Seventeenth Century* (Ithaca, 1960), pp. 67, 82–83.

5. Robert Beverley, *The History and Present State of Virginia,* Louis B. Wright, ed. (Chapel Hill, 1947), p. 60; Richard L. Morton, *Colonial Virginia* (2 vols.; Chapel Hill, 1960), I, 153.

6. *A Perfect Description of Virginia,* in *The Virginia Historical Register, and Literary Advertiser,* II (April, 1849), 67.

7. Thomas Hutchinson, *The History of the Colony and Province of Massachusetts-Bay,* Lawrence Shaw Mayo, ed. (3 vols.; Cambridge, Mass., 1936), II, 50n.; Thomas Tileston Waterman, *The Dwellings of Colonial America* (Chapel Hill, 1950), pp. 239–243; Hugh Morrison, *Early American Architecture* (New York, 1952), pp. 76–79.

8. Douglas Edward Leach, *Flintlock and Tomahawk: New England in King Philip's War* (New York, 1958), pp. 81–84.

9. Philip A. Bruce, *Institutional History of Virginia in the Seventeenth Century* (2 vols.; New York, 1910), II, 98–99; Morton, *Colonial Virginia,* I, 122–124; Wesley Frank Craven, "Indian Policy in Early Virginia," *WMQ,* I (January, 1944), 74.

10. Leach, *Flintlock and Tomahawk,* pp. 165–166.

11. Keith Grahame Feiling, *British Foreign Policy, 1660–1672* (London, 1930), p. 226.

12. U.S. Bureau of the Census, *Historical Statistics of the United States: Colonial Times to 1957* (Washington, D.C., 1960), p. 756.

13. Verne E. Chatelain, *The Defenses of Spanish Florida, 1565 to 1763* (Washington, D.C., 1941), p. 35; John Jay TePaske, *The Governorship of Spanish Florida, 1700–1763* (Durham, 1964), pp. 77–78; John R. Dunkle, "Popula-

tion Change as an Element in the Historical Geography of St. Augustine,"
Florida Historical Quarterly, XXXVII (July, 1958), 3–10. There was only a
small scattering of Spaniards living in Florida away from St. Augustine.

14. W. J. Eccles, *Frontenac: The Courtier Governor* (Toronto, 1959), p. 268.

15. Eccles, *Frontenac*, pp. 214–215.

16. Max Savelle, *The Origins of American Diplomacy: The International History of Angloamerica, 1492–1763* (New York, 1967), p. 93.

17. Charles M. Andrews, ed., *Narratives of the Insurrections, 1675–1690* (New York, 1915), pp. 16–18, 105–108; Thomas J. Wertenbaker, *Torchbearer of the Revolution: The Story of Bacon's Rebellion and Its Leader* (Princeton, 1940), pp. 74–78; Wilcomb E. Washburn, *The Governor and the Rebel: A History of Bacon's Rebellion in Virginia* (Chapel Hill, 1957), pp. 20–21; Morton, *Colonial Virginia*, I, 231–232.

18. Andrews, *Narratives of the Insurrections*, p. 50.

19. Wilcomb E. Washburn has charged that Bacon's successful forays against the Indians were instigated largely for the purpose of plunder, and that it was not the enemy Indians who suffered most heavily in these raids but nonbelligerent tribes which had long been subservient to Virginia. (See Washburn, *The Governor and the Rebel*, pp. 29, 36–38, 42–46.)

20. Andrews, *Narratives of the Insurrections*, p. 124.

21. Andrews, *Narratives of the Insurrections*, p. 133. A "forlorn" or "forlorn hope" was a special group, sometimes consisting of volunteers, designated to lead an attack. A modern equivalent might be "shock troops."

22. Andrews, *Narratives of the Insurrections*, p. 70.

23. Leach, *Flintlock and Tomahawk*, pp. 48–49.

24. William Hubbard, *The History of the Indian Wars in New England from the First Settlement to the Termination of the War with King Philip, in 1677*, Samuel G. Drake, ed. (Roxbury, Mass., 1865), p. 113.

25. *The Happiness of a People in the Wisdome of Their Rulers Directing and in the Obedience of Their Brethren Attending unto What Israel Ought to Do* (Boston, 1676), p. 60.

26. A copy of the treaty is in the Connecticut Archives (Hartford), War I, 9. Printed texts appear in Hubbard, *History of the Indian Wars*, pp. 76–79, and Richard LeBaron Bowen, *Early Rehoboth* (4 vols.; Rehoboth, Mass., 1945–1950), III, 66–68.

27. Douglas Edward Leach, "A New View of the Declaration of War against the Narragansetts, November, 1675," *Rhode Island History*, XV (April, 1956), 33–41.

28. Hubbard, *History of the Indian Wars*, p. 147.

29. William Harris, *A Rhode Islander Reports on King Philip's War: The Second William Harris Letter of August, 1676*, Douglas Edward Leach, ed. (Providence, 1963), p. 22.

30. Leach, *Flintlock and Tomahawk*, chap. 8. A more detailed discussion of this topic may be found in Douglas Edward Leach, "The Causes and Effects of King Philip's War" (Unpublished Ph.D. dissertation, Harvard University, 1952), chap. 11.

31. Thomas Church, *The History of King Philip's War,* Henry Martyn Dexter, ed. (Boston, 1865), pp. 122–123.

32. Church, *History of King Philip's War,* pp. 121–122.

33. Church, *History of King Philip's War,* p. 102.

34. [Francis Higginson], *New-Englands Plantation* (3d ed.; London, 1630).

35. *MCR,* II, 166, III, 85.

36. Morton, *Colonial Virginia,* I, 156; Craven, "Indian Policy in Early Virginia," p. 76.

37. Douglas Edward Leach, *The Northern Colonial Frontier, 1607–1763* (New York, 1966), pp. 91–92, 100–103, 146–147.

38. Almon Wheeler Lauber, *Indian Slavery in Colonial Times within the Present Limits of the United States* (New York, 1913), pp. 105–106, 119, 169–170.

39. Verner W. Crane, *The Southern Frontier, 1670–1732* (Durham, 1928), pp. 24–25; Chatelain, *Defenses of Spanish Florida,* p. 78.

40. Alexander S. Salley, Jr., ed., *Narratives of Early Carolina, 1650–1708* (New York, 1911), p. 205; Herbert E. Bolton, ed., *Arredondo's Historical Proof of Spain's Title to Georgia* (Berkeley, 1925), pp. 41–43; David Duncan Wallace, *South Carolina, A Short History, 1520–1948* (Chapel Hill, 1951), p. 41.

41. W. J. Eccles, *Canada under Louis XIV, 1663–1701* (New York, 1964), pp. 147–148.

42. Ruth L. Higgins, *Expansion in New York, with Especial Reference to the Eighteenth Century* (Columbus, Ohio, 1931), p. 36; Leach, *Northern Colonial Frontier,* pp. 106–108; Arthur H. Buffinton, "The Policy of Albany and English Westward Expansion," *MVHR,* VIII (March, 1922), 343–346.

43. Gustave Lanctot, *A History of Canada. Volume II: From the Royal Régime to the Treaty of Utrecht, 1663–1713,* M. M. Cameron, trans. (Cambridge, Mass., 1964), pp. 95, 107.

44. Eccles, *Canada under Louis XIV,* p. 67.

45. Denonville's campaign against the Senecas is thoroughly examined in George B. Selden, Jr., "The Expedition of the Marquis de Denonville against the Seneca Indians: 1687," in Rochester Historical Society Publication Fund Series, IV (1925), 1–82.

46. Eccles, *Frontenac,* p. 185; Eccles, *Canada under Louis XIV,* pp. 150–154; Lanctot, *History of Canada,* II, 106.

47. *NYCD,* III, 503–504. Earlier a Mohawk orator had exclaimed, "Lett the Governor of Cannida doe what hee will and pull as hard as hee can hee shall not break the chain that is betwen us and Corlaer [traditional Iroquois term for the governor of New York], wee will hold fast, and let us all hold the chaine of friendship verry fast, and that will be the only means to make the Governor of Canida fall upon his left side" (*ibid.,* p. 483).

48. *NYCD,* III, 528.

49. Eccles, *Canada under Louis XIV,* pp. 157–158.

☆　　　☆　　　☆　　　☆　　　☆

CHAPTER 3

The Anglo-French Struggle Begins:
King William's War, 1689-1697

ARDENT PROTESTANTS in the colonies received news of the declaration of war in 1689 if not with outward joy at least with some sense of satisfaction, knowing as they did the past record of their new king. William of Orange had made his reputation in Europe as the heroic Protestant leader of the Dutch people in their tenacious resistance to the aggressive territorial ambitions of Louis XIV. Now, having mounted the English throne, thereby linking England with Holland in matters of foreign policy and defense, William was ready to hurl defiance at his old enemy. For the moment France was very nearly isolated; even Catholic Spain stood hostile, eager to profit by Louis' predicament. In Europe the military conflict now getting underway in the spring of 1689 became known as the War of the League of Augsburg; in the English colonies, the people called it simply King William's War.[1]

Looking back over the years, we have no difficulty seeing that 1689 was indeed the year of the great divide, marking as it does the beginning of a series of four major wars whose outcome would shape the whole future of North America. In a sense, all before 1689 was preparation; all after, a part of the fateful contention to decide if the continent north of Mexico was to be French and Catholic or British and Protestant. After seven decades of bitter rivalry and struggle, the issue was settled. But that was not the end, for the outcome actually cleared the way for the American Revolution and, subsequently, the birth of a new nation undreamed of in 1689 when, with Parliament's promise to support him, William declared war on France.

Ordinary colonists, learning of this momentous declaration in June, were in no position to view the beginning conflict in such broad perspective. They thought mainly of immediate and largely personal concerns. For men of military age, trained in the militia, there was the sobering prospect of a call to arms which might mean prolonged and dangerous service terminated, perhaps, by a fatal musket ball in some remote corner of the wilderness or a mortal fever in some distant encampment. Merchants and seafarers foresaw greatly increased risks to vessels and valuable cargoes on the high seas, for the navies and privateers of the warring powers were now unleashed. Businessmen in general predicted steeply rising costs, possibly counterbalanced by wartime inflation and extraordinary opportunities for combining patriotism with profits. To pioneering farmers and traders far out on the extended frontiers where civilization had only a precarious fingergrip, the outbreak of war meant simply the fearsome likelihood of Indian raids, cruelly destructive to both property and human life. Only those colonists who had lived through the terror of the widespread Indian warfare in New England or Virginia a scant thirteen years earlier could understand fully the meaning of renewed conflict in this pattern.

Neither France nor England was willing to commit much in the way of men and materiel to the colonial theater of the war, which really was little more than a sideshow of the great international conflict in Europe. As a consequence, the colonies carried on their quarrel largely on their own and with their own very limited resources. By European standards, therefore, the war in America really wasn't much of a war at all. In fact, during the eight years of colonial conflict, only two campaigns of major strategic importance were seriously projected; and of those, only one was actually attempted. It ended in complete failure. The war in the colonies produced only two men whose military exploits make them in any sense outstanding, and one of those is remembered mostly for his dismal failure—Sir William Phips. The other was the self-inflated governor of New France, Count Frontenac, an elderly veteran.

If the war in the colonies had any lasting importance, it resided in the fact that this first major encounter between the rival empires served as a test for their systems of defense, while at the same time establishing certain patterns of military operations that were to persist and be further refined during the later conflicts. Certainly, King William's War was a test for the colonial militias in the various colonies, especially in areas directly threatened by the enemy. Nearly all troops raised in these colonies during the war had received most of their training as members of the local trainbands. The speed with which such troops could be mobilized and organized into new battle-ready units revealed both the value and the limitations of militia training. Another important revelation of the war was the serious lack of any real sense of unity and mutual obligation among the dozen English colonies. Any colony directly threatened by the enemy of course demanded support and assistance from its neighbors; but more often than not, the other colonies managed to find excuses to explain why they could not provide such aid. Cooperation usually was minimal and grudging, which meant that the English advantage of a colonial population eighteen times greater than the population of New France was largely negated.

Except for sporadic outbursts of activity on the part of the colonists, much of the actual fighting and ravaging during this first war was carried on by groups of Indians allied with one side or the other. In general, Indian-style warfare prevailed along the exposed frontiers of Canada and the northern colonies of England. Indian raids on isolated communities often came with little or no warning because the warriors were so skillful in advancing through the wilderness swiftly and silently. As a consequence, the colonial authorities had great difficulty organizing any effective form of defense. Whenever possible, Indian raiders struck suddenly in overwhelming force, destroyed as much property as they could, took what prisoners they wanted, and then swiftly disappeared. If a relief force was gathered together and dispatched to the site of the attack, it usually arrived too late to do anything more useful than inter the mangled corpses found scattered over the ground and among the charred ruins. The sardonic comment of Edward Randolph was simply truth exaggerated: "After Advice given to *Boston* of a Town or Settlement being burn'd and destroyed," he said, "in about a Fortnights time an Army or Party of about two or three hundred Men would be sent to the Place to see if it were true or not, and whether the *Indians* did not stay for their coming; which Army of ours usually abide thereabouts till they have eaten and consumed what stock of Cattle or Sheep the Indians had left, and then return home again." [2]

As the Eastern Indians of New England were emboldened by the expectation of French support, so the Five Nations of the Iroquois Confederacy counted upon English backing in their longstanding feud with Canada. Soon after the news of war reached the English colonies, but before the 12,000 *habitants* of New France had learned of this ominous development, the Iroquois went on the offensive. Toward the end of July in 1689 a war party of some 1,500 Iroquois warriors made an undetected approach to the outlying French village of Lachine, a peaceful farming community only 7 miles from Montreal. Shielded from observation by a storm, they made their way into the unsuspecting village during the night of 25–26 July. By the first light of dawn they struck, and when their work was finished fifty-six out of seventy-seven dwellings had been destroyed and two dozen *habitants* lay dead.[3]

The Lachine massacre of 26 July was followed by a series of lesser but nonetheless demoralizing Indian raids on outlying French settlements, disrupting the routine of agricultural production. French access to the West and its treasure of furs was becoming extremely precarious because of Iroquois fury; in September, the governor ordered that even Fort Frontenac, guardian of Canada's gateway to the Great Lakes, be abandoned. But then came a dramatic change of leadership. On 2 October a newly appointed governor from France, Count Frontenac, stepped ashore at Quebec and prepared to take command of the faltering colony. Now in his early seventies, Frontenac was coming back to a post he previously had held for ten years starting in 1672. He knew the Canadians well, and he understood the great importance of the West. Above all, Frontenac was determined to advance the long-range interests of New France at the expense of the hateful Iroquois and the English of New England and New York.

The new governor brought with him a detailed, royally approved plan for the conquest of New York, a plan which if successful would result in the expulsion or subordination of the English inhabitants there. This would mean French domination of the extensive fur trade presently enjoyed by the New Yorkers through their special relationship with the Five Nations, geographical separation of New England from the other English colonies to the south, and the acquisition by France of an ice-free port at the mouth of the Hudson River. Here indeed was a dazzling opportunity for a soldier-governor to win the gratitude of his sovereign and with it undoubted honors and favors. Well might Louis be grateful, for the conquest of New York would tilt the balance of colonial power away from England and toward France in what might well prove to be the first decisive step leading to the ultimate extinction of England's colonies in North America.[4]

A man less self-assured than Frontenac might have boggled at the assignment. Could a mere 12,000 Canadian men, women, and children provide enough military power to split the English colonies asunder? Frontenac was counting heavily upon a number of factors in his favor, including the professional troops already stationed in Canada, timely support by units of the French Navy, the strength of many Algonquin tribes hostile to both the Iroquois and the English, and possibly, too, the disunity of the English colonies themselves. Above all, he was confident in his own leadership.

However, once Frontenac had arrived at Montreal he became for the first time fully aware of how weak and discouraged his people really were. Soon the disappointed but still determined governor was forced to acknowledge that with winter fast approaching there was neither time nor will for an immediate offensive, and so he reluctantly shifted away from his plotted course and took another tack. This was an audacious attempt to entice the Iroquois into a treaty of peace which would give Canada time to regain its equilibrium and make careful preparations for a later offensive against the English. Frontenac's wooing was unsuccessful; the Iroquois mistrusted the French and spurned the proffer of peace. "This warr with the French is never to be laid aside," they promised the English. "Wee will never give the French a Smile, nay wee will never be Reconsiled with them So long as there is a frenchman alive."[5] Confronted by such stubborn belligerency, Frontenac returned to his plans for offensive action.

Up to this time the English colonies had done little more than talk rather wildly about the French Catholic–Indian threat to their security. Deeply involved as they were in the internal tension and strife accompanying the Glorious Revolution, including the Leislerian upheaval in New York, they themselves were far too distracted and divided to undertake anything resembling offensive action against New France. Had Frontenac known more fully the extent of these divisions and distractions he might have had the wisdom to let them go on festering, uninterrupted by French intervention. Instead, apparently feeling that he must have some kind of victory, he inaugurated a strangely vicious offensive campaign against the northern frontier, a campaign not powerful enough to break English morale and yet sufficiently destructive and extensive to arouse widespread resentment and opposition.

The form of warfare was barbaric, with Frenchmen joining Indians in the ruthless destruction of livestock, dwellings, and other property, and in the slaughter of innocent civilians. Active participation by white personnel in this kind of raid, under white leadership, helped to establish a new and terrible pattern for the ensuing colonial wars, a pattern that was to be imitated by the English but most consistently and successfully followed by the French. As for the French participants themselves, drawn largely from the ranks of the *coureurs de bois* and the Canadian militia, they demonstrated a fortitude that commands admiration in spite of the deplorable methods employed. Accustomed to the ways of the wilderness, they were tough and aggressive and seemingly contemptuous of hardship or danger. Before them lay long, cold days of plodding on snowshoes through seemingly endless forests. Soaked and chilled by icy rain or sleet, they would make their bed for the night in a bough-lined hole dug in the snow. Here they would huddle together to share what little warmth they had and to escape the freezing blast of the winter wind. As one colonist remarked with obvious awe, "Europeans will hardly think it possible that Men could make such a March through the Wilderness in the severest Frosts, without any Covering from the Heavens, or any Provision, except what they carried on their Backs." [6] Apparently, these hardy men accepted their mission in a spirit of adventure, as an outlet for patriotism, ambition, greed, or simply resentment against the English.

During the early weeks of 1690, three distinct raiding parties of Canadians and Indians were organized to strike at the English frontier. The first, at Montreal, was commanded by Jacques Lemoyne de Sainte-Hélène and Nicolas D'Ailleboust de Mantet, and consisted of approximately 160 Canadians, many of them rough and ready *coureurs de bois,* together with about 100 converted Iroquois

and other Indians. Their assignment was to proceed south along
the frozen Lake Champlain–Lake George waterway to the upper
Hudson, where they were to attack the important fur-trading
center of Albany or, if that proved impracticable, some other
English settlement. The second party, led by François Hertel de
Rouville, was organized at Trois Rivières on the St. Lawrence
River. It was much smaller than the first, only about fifty French
and Indians, the latter mostly Abnakis from northern New England. This group was to advance south through the New Hampshire
wilderness and strike at targets of opportunity east of the Merrimack River. The third force, consisting of fifty Canadians and
sixty Abnakis under the command of the Sieur de Portneuf, was
to advance from Quebec up the Chaudière River to the Kennebec
and descend upon the area of settlement along the coast of Maine
south of the Androscoggin River.[7] Presumably the overall purpose
of this triple offensive was to demoralize the frontier inhabitants,
drive them from their advance positions, and stall any impending
offensive against New France. Success also would impress the
Indians, both pro-French and uncommitted, with the determination and strength of Frontenac's colony.

The wide separation of the three groups and the varied conditions under which they advanced prevented any close coordination. It was the Montreal group that struck first, after a wilderness
trek of such great difficulty that some of the weaker members had
to turn back. Not many more than 200 of Sainte-Hélène's men
finally arrived in the valley of the upper Hudson during the first
week of February. The preferred target, Albany, was at odds with
the new provincial government headed by Jacob Leisler and consequently lacked the advantage of military support from the lower
parts of the colony. Garrisoned by a small force of English regulars
and an even smaller number of Connecticut militiamen, Albany
sat stolidly and stubbornly on its own Dutch bottom, apparently
unaware of the enemy's approach.[8]

Fearing the strength of the Albany garrison, the Indians of
Sainte-Hélène's group persuaded their French comrades to turn
upon the village of Schenectady instead. This small community
was situated on the south bank of the Mohawk River 15 miles
northwest of Albany. Most of the dwellings were closely grouped
within a sheltering palisade of vertical stakes a short distance
above the edge of the frozen river. Only a narrow cart path through

the woods provided a line of communication between Schenectady and Albany, and in the wintertime that was seldom traveled.[9] Adding to Schenectady's dangerous isolation was a record of rivalry and hostility with Albany that kept the two frontier communities at arm's length. If Albany was against Leisler, Schenectady was inclined to be for him. Under these circumstances it had proved impossible to organize any kind of coordinated defense for the New York frontier.[10] However, winter being what it was in this northern country, few people seriously expected any large body of the enemy to be abroad until after the spring thaw.

On the night of 8 February, when Sainte-Hélène's group was making its final approach, the inhabitants of Schenectady were crawling into their beds and blowing out their candles with little concern for what the next few hours might bring. Worse yet, the small detachment of garrison soldiers stationed in the village was anything but alert; no one had even bothered to close the gate of the palisade! [11] Arriving within sight of the slumbering village, the well-armed but nearly exhausted French and Indians, breathing white vapor into the icy air, stood silent in the knee-deep snow, contemplating their objective and resolving to warm themselves speedily at a bonfire of blazing houses. Quietly they slipped into the village and formed a complete ring around the cluster of dwellings. Then suddenly they began their attack. The startled inhabitants first learned of their desperate plight by the chilling sound of the war whoop and the pounding of hatchets and gunbutts on shutters and doors. Breaking in wherever they could, the excited raiders, fierce from their long ordeal in the wilderness, slaughtered many of the terror-stricken villagers and roughly herded the others as prisoners. In all, they killed about five dozen persons outright, and burned down nearly every house.[12] Thanks to the total surprise, they themselves lost in the action only two of their number. By noon the raiders were ready to depart, anticipating a hot pursuit after news of the attack had reached Albany. Accordingly they released all their prisoners except twenty-seven males, threw a last glance at the still-smoking ruins of the village, and plunged again into the wilderness. They were assisted in their retreat by a number of horses taken at Schenectady and now employed to draw toboggans loaded with plunder and supplies. Later these same animals were to provide roast meat for the weary French and Indians struggling toward Montreal.

Albany had news of the attack about seven hours before the intruders finally withdrew from Schenectady but was hesitant to send out any large force of its own for fear that an even larger body of the enemy might be preparing for an attack on Albany itself. A band of Mohawks who did go in pursuit of the retreating French and Indians managed to kill or capture more than a dozen stragglers, but total losses suffered by the Montreal group from start to finish were reckoned at only seventeen Canadians and four Indians.[13] It took more than two weeks for the news of Schenectady's fate to reach Boston. The militia was at once placed on alert, and patriotic citizens began subscribing to a fund for the furtherance of action against the enemy. "I thought 'twas time to doe something, now we're thus destroy'd by Land too," remarked one prominent Bostonian in recording his donation.[14] Interrogation of French prisoners at Albany early in March uncovered Frontenac's intention to attack the New England frontier as well, this being the assignment of the second and third assault forces. Yet at the New Hampshire frontier settlement of Salmon Falls, 13 miles above Portsmouth on the Salmon Falls River, there was a negligence nearly matching that of Schenectady. Hertel's party arrived there on 17 March, divided into three groups, and at dawn the next morning made simultaneous attacks upon the town's three fortified structures. As at Schenectady, the surprise was complete, and the French had it all their own way. They and their Indian allies killed about thirty-four of the English, and captured another fifty-four. Spreading to the outlying farms, they burned the buildings and slaughtered the livestock, so that only devastation was left behind. During their withdrawal, Hertel's men were slowed by the weakness of their prisoners and eventually were overtaken by a hastily organized party of militia from Portsmouth. The pursuit proved futile, however, and the French made a clean escape, losing not a single prisoner.[15]

In the meantime, the third assault force under Portneuf had been making its way slowly southward toward the coast of Maine, its members sustaining themselves in the wilderness by hunting. Not until mid-May did they appear in the vicinity of the small English fort at Falmouth, on Casco Bay. By this time Portneuf had been reinforced by Hertel and a number of his men after the destruction of Salmon Falls, as well as by considerable numbers of Abnaki warriors who were only too happy to have such an opportunity for prisoners and plunder. Captain Sylvanus Davis, the commander of the garrison at Falmouth, later estimated the size of the attacking force at 400 to 500 men.[16]

The English first discovered the presence of such unwelcome visitors when Portneuf's undisciplined Indians fell upon a lone colonist outside the settlement and split the air with their scalp-cries. Upon hearing this, a party of about thirty volunteers of Davis's garrison rashly left the protecting walls to hunt down what they assumed to be a weak group of marauding Indians. They found instead a wildcat with many claws; only four of the volunteers regained the fort alive. This blow was an ominous beginning to a siege that lasted about four days. Captain Davis and the remaining men, backed by a number of women and children, stoutly held off the enemy until 20 May. Then, with the greater part of his men either dead or wounded and the French preparing to plant explosives or an incendiary device at the base of the palisade, Davis bargained for terms in order to prevent the indiscriminate slaughter of the civilians. A surrender was accordingly arranged.[17] Davis understood it to mean that the English would be allowed to withdraw from the site without molestation, but the enemy Indians had other ideas. They murdered some of the wounded, and seized a number of captives. Davis himself was retained by the French, who took him back with them to Quebec.

Frontenac's three-pronged offensive in the early months of 1690 had indeed struck terror along the New York–New England frontier for now every isolated community considered itself a potential target with no reliable defense available against such sudden and devastating blows. Many a family in the vicinity of Albany or southern New Hampshire or coastal Maine packed up its portable belongings, abandoned its hard-won homestead, and hurried off to safer sites. Just as in the earlier days of Indian warfare, the frontier began to curl and crack like an edge of paper exposed to the flames, and as this happened men who held sizable speculative investments in frontier land saw their hopes withering too. But all was not loss, and this was where Frontenac's miscalculation is perhaps most apparent. Some of the English, at least, began to gain a new awareness of their common problem and to realize the urgent need for intercolonial cooperation. Although longstanding points of jealousy and enmity were not quickly forgotten, there did begin to emerge at this time some evidence of a common will to join strength to

strength for the purpose of throwing back the French and their
Indian allies. It was almost a reincarnation of the spirit of 1588,
born of undisguised fear, hatred of autocracy, and a fervent antipathy toward the Roman Church.

Weeks before the Franco-Indian attack on Salmon Falls, the
leaders of Massachusetts had been contemplating the prospects for
an offensive against French Acadia, that is, the region east of the
Penobscot River including the present Nova Scotia. This territory
in French hands constituted a serious menace not only to the
frontier of settlement in Maine and New Hampshire, but also
to the fishing and trading interests of Massachusetts in the Bay of
Fundy and the North Atlantic. New Englanders were convinced
that Acadia was being used by the French as a breeding ground
for Indian hostility against the English colonies. The Abnakis in
particular were being brought more deeply under French influence
and incited, it was thought, to harass the settlements between the
Merrimack and the Kennebec rivers in order to weaken the English
hold on that area.[18]

Why not strike at the source of the trouble? On 25 March, exactly
one week after the disaster at Salmon Falls, Governor Simon Bradstreet of Massachusetts informed acting Governor Jacob Leisler of
New York that "We are at present forwarding an Expedition
against the French at Nova Scotia and L'Acadie. . . ." Success in
this endeavor, he continued, "will Encourage to an Attempt upon
Canada wherein we must desire the joint concurrance and Assistance
of all the Governments in these their Majesties Colonys. . . ."[19]
Accordingly, an intercolonial meeting of commissioners was scheduled for the last Monday of the following month.

Sometime during the next few weeks there stepped forward in
Boston to lead the proposed expedition a "local boy who had made
good," thirty-nine-year-old Sir William Phips. Born into a humble
family in frontier Maine, Phips had made his way up in the world
as carpenter, contractor, and adventurer. He was not of the usual
Puritan mold. The title before his name was a recently acquired
reward from the crown for salvaging treasure from a sunken ship
off the coast of Hispaniola. Subsequently, Phips had returned to
Boston and begun the life of an honored citizen, joining the North
Church and qualifying as a freeman. Puritan leaders, the Reverend
Increase Mather among them, lauded him for his previous efforts
when visiting England to have the old charter restored. Such a

man, offering his services as commander of the expedition against
Acadia, was gladly accepted.

In 1690 fewer than a thousand French *habitants* and soldiers
were holding all of Acadia. The principal settlement was at Port
Royal on the west coast of Nova Scotia, where there was little more
than a small cluster of buildings guarded by an ill-kept fort. Falmouth had not yet been attacked by Portneuf and Hertel when
Phips and his little army boarded a small fleet and headed north
toward the Bay of Fundy. They reconnoitered the area of Penobscot Bay and the coast farther north, plundered a few isolated
French habitations, and then moved along to their principal objective, where they arrived on the evening of 9 May. The fort was
weakly held by 72 French soldiers and a handful of local inhabitants when it was confronted by Phips' seven armed vessels and
736 New Englanders, eager for spoil.

Phips sent in a demand for surrender, and the necessary arrangements were speedily made. On 11 May the French commander and
his officers handed over their swords; Port Royal came under English
control.[20] Without further ado the New Englanders joyfully turned
to the congenial task of despoiling the church and gathering up
plunder, while their commander dealt with the problem of future
government in the area. Compliant French inhabitants, possibly
indifferent to the swirl of international contention, solemnly ac-
quiesced as Phips proffered the oath of loyalty:

> You and every one of you do swear by the dreadful Name of the
> everliving God, That you will bear true Faith and Allegiance to
> Their most Excellent Majesties *William* and *Mary,* of *England, Scot-
> land, France* and *Ireland* King and Queen: *so help you God in our
> Lord Jesus Christ!* [21]

A French sergeant was installed as "president" of the subdued and
subservient community. On 16 May (as the siege of Falmouth was
beginning) the fort at Port Royal was demolished by Phips' men,
and a few days later the triumphant armada, laden with captured
guns, prisoners, and booty, headed for Boston where it arrived on
30 May amidst salutes and general acclaim.

The conquest of Port Royal was a piddling victory of little
strategic importance, and as might have been expected, the French
were back in full control of the area the following year. But what
Phips had accomplished was to give a great boost to New England's

sagging morale, counteracting, at least in part, the impact of the defeat at Falmouth. Phips now was widely admired as a successful commander, his men esteemed themselves as proven soldiers, and the plunder from the stricken French settlement was gladly accepted as some slight recompense for New England's own suffering at the hands of its enemies.

The intercolonial conference previously announced by Bradstreet had been held in New York during the last week of April. All the colonies as far south as Virginia had been invited to send delegates, but only seven men from New York, Connecticut, Plymouth, and Massachusetts actually attended. Despite this disappointing response, the conference adopted Leisler's bold proposal for a two-pronged drive against the very heart of French Canada: the fortified town of Quebec on the upper St. Lawrence River. This major operation was planned without the prior knowledge of the English government and would be carried on without English support. If successful, it could mean the ruin of French interests in North America, the gaining of the entire fur trade for England, and possibly even a final end to the old Indian menace, or so the New Englanders fondly thought. "It was *Canada* that was the chief Source of *New-England's* Miseries," said Cotton Mather later. *"There* was the main Strength of the *French*; *there* the *Indians* were mostly supplied with Ammunition; *thence* Issued Parties of Men, who uniting with the Salvages, barbarously murdered many Innocent *New-Englanders. . . ."* [22] Much the same consideration motivated the New Yorkers as well.

The plan of operation laid out in the spring of 1690 is of great interest as the first rough draft of what was to become for the remainder of the colonial wars the standard English pattern for the conquest of Canada. Two principal thrusts were to converge simultaneously upon the upper valley of the St. Lawrence, crushing the heartland of New France as in a vise. The first, or interior, thrust was to be made by an army advancing north from Albany and down the Champlain Valley toward Montreal. Such an advance through 150 miles of wilderness was heavily dependent upon two factors—the cooperation of the Iroquois and effective arrangements for the transport of necessary supplies. If successful, this effort would present a serious threat to Montreal, causing Frontenac to retain a large proportion of his available troop strength in that area. The second, or seaborne, thrust was to be made by a fleet and army advancing from Boston to the St. Lawrence River and up the river to Quebec. By forcing the French to divide their strength between Montreal and Quebec, one of the English forces presumably would be able to capture its objective, join with the other, and complete the downfall of Canada. This ambitious project, planned and conducted entirely by colonists who were amateurs in war, was the largest, the most complex, and in many ways the most difficult military campaign ever attempted in English America up to that time. Each wing depended upon the other, and in the last analysis everything depended upon the efficacy of the militia system and upon the acquired skills as well as the courage of a pioneering and seafaring people.

Leisler naturally considered the interior thrust as a particular responsibility of his province and wanted the commander to be a New Yorker. However, he was persuaded to let the post go to Fitz-John Winthrop, scion of Connecticut's most prominent family, who would bring to the endeavor a sizable contingent of Connecticut militia.[23] In addition, the Iroquois promised to provide 1,800 warriors. The man chosen to command the seaborne thrust from New England was the dauntless conqueror of Port Royal, Sir William Phips. His task was as difficult and dangerous as the other, involving an amphibious landing against a defended stronghold. This would require a high degree of skill, not only in the actual landing and assault but in the crucial matter of supply and support from the ships. Timing and close coordination at every stage were needed to ensure the victory. During the first part of the summer, while preparations were underway, the planners had to cope with a host of problems and the usual delays that seemed to plague all major military efforts in the colonies. Finally, in the early days of August, Winthrop's army marched north from Albany toward Lake George, and on the twenty-first of the month Phips' fleet of thirty-four nondescript vessels sailed from Boston for the Gulf of St. Lawrence.

If at the outset of this great venture there was high optimism, it began to be eroded by circumstances over which the leaders had little or no control. Smallpox made an unwelcome appearance both in Winthrop's plodding ranks and on board the wallowing ships of the invasion fleet, seriously reducing the available manpower. Winthrop encountered another disappointment when he finally arrived at Wood Creek near Lake Champlain, where he was to be joined by several hundred Iroquois. Instead of several hundred ready warriors, however, he found fewer than six dozen, who hastened to explain that "the Great God had stopt their way" by spreading smallpox through the tribes.[24] Equally serious was the shortage of canoes available at Wood Creek to transport the army down Lake Champlain and no possibility of obtaining more in sufficient time. After discussing these discouraging circumstances with his officers, Winthrop decided that it would be foolish to push on with what now appeared to be a hopeless mission.

Captain John Schuyler with a raiding force consisting of the available Indians, now numbering about 120, together with 29 white troops was sent north to harass the outskirts of Montreal. This was a feeble substitute for what should have been a hard-driving army, but at least it might draw some French attention away from what Phips was about to attempt at Quebec. On 23 August, Schuyler managed to launch a sharp attack upon the village of La Prairie, just across the river from Montreal, killing a number of inhabitants, slaughtering cattle, and burning some dwellings. During the subsequent withdrawal, Schuyler's Indians murdered two French prisoners who because of their wounds were unable to keep up with the party.[25] Winthrop, in the meantime, led the remainder of his army back down to Albany. News of this unhappy retreat arrived in Boston on 28 August, exactly a week after the fleet had taken its departure. The New Englanders were understandably depressed, for now the task of Phips and his 2,200 men was made much more dangerous, and victory less certain.[26]

Happily ignorant of Winthrop's failure, Phips and his motley fleet continued their leisurely approach to the mouth of the St. Lawrence as though time were a matter of little consequence. Their objective, on the north bank of that treacherous river, lay some 400 miles upstream in a position fitted by nature for defense. Quebec was built on a great, rocky, prowlike wedge of terrain in the angle formed by the St. Charles River as it emptied into the much larger St. Lawrence. The town itself was divided, part of it perched high above the river on the heights of the promontory, the remainder nestled uneasily below at the water's edge. An enemy intending to assault Quebec from the St. Lawrence River had three choices: to pass upriver beyond the town and land above it, to land directly at or near the lower town, or to land below the town on the far side of the St. Charles. The first choice was rendered difficult by the steep cliffs that ran parallel to the river's edge for a considerable distance above Quebec. A landing at the town itself was likely to be repulsed by the concentrated firepower of the defenders, who would have the advantage of the high ground. This left only the third choice as a good possibility, but even this posed major difficulties. About 2 miles downriver from Quebec was an area of thicketed lowland along the shore. Here landings could be made if tide and weather were favorable, but then in order to reach Quebec the invaders would have to advance to the St. Charles, fight their way across that stream under heavy fire, and storm the heights that still lay before them. Upon what, then, might Phips base his hope of success? It was largely a matter of numerical strength. The New England force greatly outnumbered the defending garrison, and unless Quebec were strongly reinforced with large numbers of additional troops it could hardly expect to hold off such an army indefinitely.

Toward the end of September, as the nights were growing crisp, definite word reached Quebec of a large fleet of English ships in the lower St. Lawrence. Quickly the news was passed along to Frontenac, who still was at Montreal with the bulk of the colony's available troops; the elderly governor immediately embarked for Quebec to take charge of the defense. Next day, upon intercepting more positive information, Frontenac set in motion a decisive shift of troop strength from Montreal to Quebec, for by this time he was confident that all serious danger to Montreal from the direction of Lake Champlain was over for the year. By the evening of 5 October, Frontenac's command at the threatened capital included more than 2,000 determined troops, far exceeding the force which Phips could hope to put ashore.[27]

Phips had been making painfully slow progress upriver, coping with adverse winds, contending with treacherous currents, and pausing on occasion to raid minor settlements along the way. His ascent of the St. Lawrence actually occupied about three weeks of precious time, during which Frontenac was able to complete his preparations. At last, on 6 October, the anxious sentries stationed on the heights of Quebec sighted the vanguard of the invasion fleet moving up past the Île d'Orléans, sails taut with a fresh easterly breeze. The ships came to anchor impudently just below the town— four heavy-gunned warships together with thirty transports and auxiliary vessels crammed with New England militiamen, all peer-

ing at the high ramparts of Quebec as though it were the citadel
of the devil himself. Soon a boat bearing a white flag put off from
one of the warships and made toward the town. Four canoes were
sent out to meet her, and returned escorting a blindfolded English
emissary who, when conducted into the presence of Frontenac and
his officers, delivered a presumptuous demand that Quebec be surrendered forthwith. The French governor, old soldier that he was
and fully confident in the heavily reinforced army now present
under his command, was ready with his response. Stoutly denouncing King William of Orange as a mere usurper and the New
Englanders as rebels against their rightful sovereign James Stuart,
Frontenac rejected the demand with scorn. If Phips wanted Quebec
he would have to take it by force of arms.[28]

A council of war on board the flagship finished putting together
a plan of attack. The fact that such a plan had not been completed
earlier seems strange, but may be explained by the New Englanders'
inexact knowledge of the terrain in the vicinity of Quebec, as well
as their overoptimistic expectation that the mere sight of their
armada would produce a surrender. According to the plan now
adopted, the landing force under Major John Walley, after being
ferried to the shore about 2 miles downriver from Quebec, was to
wheel to the south until it had reached the ford near the mouth
of the St. Charles. Then, when the troops were ready to drive across
the St. Charles, the smaller vessels of the fleet would move into the
mouth of that stream to assist the crossing with their guns and,
if necessary, their boats. Once the crossing was made, the warships
would begin battering the town itself and, at the right moment,
land an assault party of 200 men at the foot of the promontory
while Walley's men fought their way through the defenses on the
opposite side. In this way it was hoped that French resistance
would crumble and Quebec would fall.[29] The landing would be
risky, for Frontenac had deployed some of his troops beyond the
St. Charles to resist just such an attempt. Furthermore, the English
lacked any exact knowledge of the tides along the shore and the
condition of the beach.

On 7 October, Phips ordered the operation to begin, despite
adverse weather with violent gusts of wind. Disaster was barely
averted. A bark carrying sixty men of the landing force ran aground
in an exposed position and came under heavy enemy fire from the
shore. After a very tense time, the craft finally was floated on the

rising tide and brought back safely out of range. By this time, though, prudent counsel had effected the cancellation of any further attempts for that day. On the evening of this first failure, at about six o'clock, 800 more French reinforcements tramped into Quebec.[30]

The next morning all was once again in readiness, and the operation was resumed. According to a French observer, "From 11 o'clock until noon nothing was done on board the ships but crying God save King William, beating drums, sounding trumpets and playing hautboys. Half an hour afterwards all their boats, full of people, made towards the shore between the village called Beauport and the town [of Quebec.]"[31] Because of losses caused by disease Walley's landing force consisted of not much more than 1,200 men; the French naturally tended to exaggerate its size, and thought that nearly 2,000 troops were coming against them. The New Englanders stormed ashore successfully after wading in from their boats through icy water, guns held high and dry. They immediately found themselves engaged by a small force of French, who peppered them with musket fire from a nearby swamp. Charging forward, the invaders drove the enemy away, suffering only light casualties in this first skirmish. So far all seemed well.

The remainder of the operation during the next few days is wrapped in controversy, with conflicting evidence coming from various witnesses. Officers of the landing force maintained that their men fought the French courageously over difficult terrain but that they were seriously handicapped by an almost complete breakdown of the supply service from ship to shore.[32] The weather was bitter cold as it can be at Quebec in mid-October and many of the soldiers, inadequately sheltered during the long nights in the open, suffered greatly. There were numerous cases of frostbite.

During the evening of the eighth, with the army now ashore to the north of the St. Charles, Phips moved the four warships to a position within gun range of Quebec, and came to anchor. This was in preparation for the bombardment and secondary landing which was scheduled to begin as soon as the main force had crossed the St. Charles. The French were not willing to wait upon plan, however, and began firing at the anchored vessels. This goaded Phips into returning the fire, with the consequence that in the mounting excitement of action he expended most of his available ammunition in a furious but futile cannonading of the town, regardless of the fact that Walley's men were as yet in no position to take advantage of the diversion. Frontenac, in contrast, was playing his cards with the coolness of a veteran. He had just enough men north of the St. Charles to keep Walley's miserable troops apprehensive and occupied, while retaining the bulk of his forces in and around the town to oppose the main thrust when it came. Under these circumstances, it never did come. Somehow, after the first night ashore all the spirit seemed to have drained out of the New England army, although up to that point less than thirty lives had been lost.

On 10 and 11 October, the English continued skirmishing over the uneven ground without any great success, until Phips aboard his flagship came to the realization that Quebec was beyond his grasp. Indeed, there was a growing possibility that his ill-supplied troops on shore would stumble into a major disaster. Therefore the commander sent word for the army to reembark. The shivering, discouraged militiamen were more than ready to quit the place; and when the order to withdraw was received, the rush to the boats was precipitate. Walley later admitted that his men scrambled for places in disorderly haste, every man for himself. Appropriately, a drenching rain added to the discomfort and confusion. Five large field pieces could not be taken off with the men and had to be abandoned to the enemy, causing one Frenchman to remark wryly that the English "must have supposed we had need of artillery." [33] By midnight, after four difficult days ashore, the weary New Englanders found themselves safe on board the vessels of the fleet.

Phips called a council of war which agreed that there was no further hope of taking Quebec. Happily, there was an exchange of prisoners, Captain Sylvanus Davis, late of Falmouth, being one of those returned to the English. Then the frustrated armada headed downriver toward home. Even yet for many of the men the suffering was not over. Violent weather separated the ships and drove them far off their course, while smallpox and "camp fever" continued to take a deadly toll. Several of the vessels were wrecked. One by one the returning ships straggled in to Boston and disgorged their burdens of men whose eyes revealed an inner conflict between chagrin and stubborn pride. Some of those eyes burned with fever, too, and before long the disease was sweeping through the town.

Boston received the bad news of Phips' failure with deep groans and much wringing of hands.[34] The failure of an enterprise that had begun with such high hopes inevitably became a matter of political controversy in a society still sharply divided over the issues of the Glorious Revolution. Violent partisanship quickly became evident as men grasped for a satisfying explanation of the disaster, and of course either Phips or Walley was made to bear a major part of the blame. Was it Phips who ordered the reembarkation, or did the army simply panic and begin a precipitate withdrawal that could not be checked? One prominent officer stated unequivocally that the order came from the fleet, and Cotton Mather, who was not present at Quebec, later made the same assertion.[35] A more hostile critic depicted a cowardly withdrawal on impulse. The troops, he said, "began to talk of returning, which notion noe sooner catcht their Crowns but (as a Suddain Thaw in the Mountains causes the Water to tumble downe the Rivers) soe did they hurry on board and happy Commander Could seize his boat first. . . ."[36]

Cotton Mather thought he saw the punishing hand of God in the defeat, with special reference to the toleration of Anglican worship in the Puritan capital; but more mundane explanations seem closer to the mark. The detrimental effect of Winthrop's failure to attack Montreal is sufficiently obvious. There is good reason to believe that the heart was taken out of Walley's army when the men ashore heard reports of the large numbers of French troops confronting them. This would also, perhaps, explain why, as the *Paris Gazette* so smugly remarked, *"ils se rembarquerent avec precipitation."* [37] The rapid shift of French troops from Montreal to Quebec during Phips' extremely slow advance up the St. Lawrence River was decisive. In addition, the English were handicapped by slipshod planning, inadequate training, epidemic disease, a faulty service of supply, and astonishingly poor coordination between naval and land forces.[38] Under the circumstances a campaign against Quebec was no game for amateurs, especially when effective leadership was so notably lacking. An abler commander than Phips might have been able to override the handicaps if he had made his moves with dispatch and determination, but such was not New England's fortune. Quebec was to remain for many years yet the fountainhead of Franco-Indian resistance to English ambitions on the northern frontier.

After Phips' spectacular failure, the French and the English in

North America continued to exchange blows across the wide wilderness frontier with little or no effect upon the larger war raging abroad. Minor stings provoked retaliation in kind, but this activity was generally sporadic and uncoordinated. Apparently, both sides in North America had thrown their hardest punches early in the conflict; now they had neither the means nor the determination to conquer, only the sullen impulse to keep lashing out. To this kind of warfare there was no foreseeable end, and the discouragement in the exposed English frontier communities was epidemic. There simply was no way to protect and preserve all the scattered villages and farms throughout the wilderness area. For Canada, the year following Phips' failure at Quebec was a time of sore trial, as Frontenac struggled to stave off destruction and disaster. Not only was the country desperately short of supplies, but the dreaded Iroquois once again were on the prowl. At that time, it was said, "No man stirred the least Distance from a Fort, but he was in danger of losing his Scalp," and the very gutters of the buildings were stripped off and melted for bullets.[39]

On the first day of August 1691 a mixed force of several hundred English and Indians, led by Major Peter Schuyler, the Albany merchant and commissioner of Indian affairs, appeared at La Prairie and began to attack the settlement. Schuyler's own account provides a vivid picture of the fighting that followed:

We fell in with 420 Men lying without the Fort ready to receive us, they charged us so hard to force a retreat of 150 yards, where there happened a ditch, which our Men posessed themselves of, the French advancing so farr in their full body were well received, and lost many of their Men, we drove them back but they rallied and advanced a second time towards the ditch and fired upon us, but did us noe damage, instantly our people rose up and discharged upon their whole body, and killed a great many; neverthelesse they ralyed the third time, but to avoid the ditch, they drove their Men towards the East and thought to divide our people, then we left the ditch fell into their reer and then in a full body, ingaged them in the plain ground and faught them fairly, until we drove them into their Fort in great disorder and took three French prisoners.[40]

Finding the French resistance so strong, Schuyler completed what damage he could and then began to withdraw to the place where he had left his canoes. Before long he ran into another French force deployed across his route. In the hard, close fighting that now took place, Schuyler's group suffered fairly heavy losses. Although they were able to open the way to their vital means of transport, they had to abandon a considerable quantity of luggage and supplies. The English who survived these hot firefights in and below La Prairie finally arrived back at Albany with little cause for elation except for the mere fact of having returned at all. Again it had been proved that Canada, with all its weaknesses, was no easy prize; the Canadian militia, joined with regulars from France, proved a foe worthy of respectful regard.[41]

French-inspired Indians continued to harass the New England frontier, and on 25 January 1691/92 virtually destroyed the community of York on the coast of Maine. According to the best-informed of the New England colonial historians, the minister at York was killed while mounting his horse at his own door.[42] Altogether some fifty of the inhabitants were slaughtered and nearly twice that many taken captive, while four garrisons managed to hold out and survive. This kind of experience, with all its terror and horror, its noise of savage ferocity and raging flames, its smoke of destruction and stench of death, summarized King William's War for many American colonists who knew little of the affairs of state abroad and hardly more of the real issues in the colonies.

Quite naturally the suffering frontier folk were inclined to blame an indecisive and rather bewildered government for failing to protect them more effectively; but as the colonial historian Thomas Hutchinson later pointed out,

> The settlement of a new country could never be effected, if the inhabitants should confine themselves to cities or walled towns. A frontier there must be, and nothing less than making every house a fort, and furnishing every traveller with a strong guard, could have been an effectual security against an enemy, as greedy after their prey as a wolf, and to whom the woods were equally natural and familiar.[43]

The general state of defense became only too apparent to John Usher in 1692 when he made a tour of inspection shortly after assuming his post as governor of New Hampshire. He found in his province only 754 men of military age. The various fortifications for the protection of the populace consisted, in the main, of palisaded dwellings.[44] Edward Randolph observed at about the same time that the "inhabitants of New Hampshire have most of them left their dwelling houses destitute, and crowd 7 or 8 families into One little house inclosed with Stoccadoes." [45]

A great pall of fear hung over the northern frontier. Isolated villages learned to be on the alert for telltale signs of lurking Indians—startled cows loping for home, mysterious animal calls or cries.[46] Inhabitants of Maine asserted plaintively that

> there are no Towns in the Province that do tast so deeply of the Cupp As Wells, York, Barwick alias Newitchawannick, Who have our Hands much taken from Our Labours by Watching, Warding, Frequent Alarms. Many of Us are driven from Our Homes. . . . And Wee daily grow more and more feeble and deplorable: daily Walking and working with fear, Trembling and Jeopardy of life.[47]

In New York, Robert Livingston reported that two men out haying were surprised by French Indians who

> kills the one and takes off his skull, and what is become of the other we know not. . . . The other people that were a mowing . . . heard 3 gunns goe off, went to the river side see noe body but the cannoe that they went over in cutt and sunk in the water. We sent a party of horse thither who found one of the men lying in the water at the shoare side, who was buryed here in towne [Albany] yesterday.[48]

The insidious, creeping infection of terror sometimes broke to the surface in strange ways. In Boston, a three-year-old boy suddenly announced from his cradle, "News from Heaven, the French were come." His Puritan father was inclined to accept this awful pronouncement as a warning from on high, for, as he solemnly remarked, "No body has been tampering with him as I could learn." [49] Poor child, he had been listening too intently to the daily conversation of his elders. Even as far south as Virginia, the colonists felt themselves threatened by a bewildering, terrifying kind of warfare which could loosen their hold on the valuable lands of the interior and conceivably make the French virtual masters of the continent.

After the fiasco of the Dominion of New England, the English government was understandably wary of attempting to herd the colonies, but the war against French Canada did place a premium on effective coordination. Some of the most strategically important locations were the most vulnerable and needed more protection than could be provided by the colony within whose jurisdiction they fell. Albany is a case in point. It was argued that Albany was "the only bulwark and safe guard of all Their Majestys plantations on the main of America," for the Albany fur trade was the very cement of the Anglo-Iroquois alliance, and on the maintenance of that alliance, it was thought, depended the whole future of the northern frontier.[50] Relying on this argument, Governor Henry Sloughter of New York in 1691 proposed to the neighboring colonies that a common defense fund be established "for the raising and paying of men dureing this warr, that if possible the memory of the French might be rooted out of America."[51] If the idea of erasing French culture was appealing, the thought of meeting financial quotas was not, and consequently little or nothing came of Sloughter's proposal. A year later, the Iroquois were loudly complaining not only of New York's failure to provide adequate defenses for the frontier, but of colonial lethargy in general. "What is it that our neighbours of n:[ew] England and the Rest of the English that are in Covenant with us doe," inquired one disgruntled sachem, and then went on to answer his own question, "they all Stay att home and Sett us on to doe the worke. . . ."[52]

The crown tried to make a fresh start toward solving the problem of intercolonial coordination by granting special military authority to New York's new governor, Benjamin Fletcher. In the fall of 1692, the royal governors of neighboring colonies were instructed to establish a system of quotas as a contribution to the defense of New York when needed; and the following spring Fletcher was given command of the Connecticut militia, with authority to summon quotas of men from other colonies as well. This arrangement proved so leaky as to be virtually useless. Connecticut refused to recognize Fletcher as commander and withheld its men, arguing loudly that other colonies were not contributing proportionally to the common defense. Even within New York itself there was no unity, and the assembly balked stubbornly whenever the governor requested more funds for military purposes.[53]

Early in 1693 a French expedition of about 625 regulars, militiamen, and Indians headed for the Mohawk country beyond Schenectady with the intention of demoralizing the Iroquois and then doing what harm they could to the English and Dutch in the vicinity of Albany. Among the French Indians was a Dutch prisoner who had been taken at Schenectady three years before. Seizing his opportunity, this man made a break for freedom when he knew the expedition was passing by his old village, and arrived safely among his former neighbors. His warning that the enemy was near was passed along to Albany, but apparently no one took the risk of trying to alert the Mohawk villages toward which the raiders were actually heading.[54] Most of the Mohawk warriors were absent on the hunt, and the French, encountering little or no resistance, burned three of the Indian towns. Then, deciding not to tempt fate by approaching Albany, where the aroused colonists were mobilizing to strike back, the raiders began their withdrawal toward Montreal.

Peter Schuyler with a hastily assembled pursuit force of New Yorkers and Indians gave the French such a vigorous chase that the retreating enemy had to abandon some of their weak and wounded in order to escape at all. At one time during the pursuit, when the English and Indians had stopped to cook their rations and catch a few hours of sleep, Schuyler visited among his Indians and was invited to share their repast. They brought him a bowl of broth steaming hot from the stewpot. As Schuyler later recalled, the broth went down well until the Indians, "putting the Ladle into the Kettle to take out more, brought out a French Man's Hand, which put an End to his Appetite." [55]

Most of the French troops, nearly exhausted from their long, hard march through the wilderness, did finally get back to Canada and safety. Their daring exploit had brought them close to disaster; but although they had not been able to attack Albany, their ravaging of the Mohawk villages was a punishing blow against the Iroquois tribe most closely attached to the English interest. No wonder that the Five Nations were expressing their dismay at the apparent inertia and disunity among the English colonies, and even beginning to give serious consideration to the possible advantages of neutrality in the Anglo-French conflict. A spokesman for the Onondagas put it bluntly when he declared that New York and the Five Nations were "tyred and stiff with holding fast the chain alone while the rest of Our neighbours sit still and smoake it. . . ." [56]

One example may serve to illustrate the point. In Massachusetts Sir William Phips, apparently quite undaunted after his failure at Quebec, now occupied the governor's chair. Feeble, frontier New Hampshire, little more than a thin scattering of wilderness outposts to the north of the powerful Bay Colony, at this time was under the governorship of John Usher, who sensed a certain coolness and perhaps arrogance on the part of his Massachusetts colleague. As it happened, the Bay Colony was interested in the possibility of annexing its weak neighbor, and indeed many of New Hampshire's own residents likewise favored this solution to their problems, but Governor Usher remained firmly opposed. When hostile Indians began attacking New Hampshire settlements in the summer of 1694, Usher called his men to arms and sent a hurried appeal to Massachusetts for additional troops. That was on 18 July. At once the Massachusetts governor began a strange game of duck the responsibility and pass the buck. On 19 July Phips informed Usher that he lacked power under the royal charter to send the militia outside his colony without legislative consent, but he promised to seek volunteers. From New Hampshire's governor came an even more urgent appeal, almost desperate in tone: Loss of life and property was heavy; the frontier was crumbling. This was followed by another letter, dated 23 July, suggesting that even if the royal charter did contain the prohibition cited by Phips, his commission as governor conveyed ample authority.

In the meantime Phips had gone to Maine, leaving affairs at Boston in the hands of Lieutenant Governor William Stoughton. Upon consultation with members of the council, Stoughton ordered a hundred Massachusetts soldiers into New Hampshire, but unaccountably these orders "faild in the Execution" and had to be renewed.[57] This time the men, only sixty in number, were ordered to Kittery in Maine, within the Bay Colony's own jurisdiction. On 30 July Usher renewed his appeal to Phips, chiding him for his inaction. Then came a strange statement from Stoughton, who perhaps saw more clearly than either Usher or Phips the true nature of the problem. After deploring the narrow interpretation being placed on the Massachusetts charter by Phips and stating his belief that the governor did in fact have ample instructions permitting him to send aid to neighboring colonies in distress, Stoughton hinted that the real problem was in the militia itself, many officers and men being reluctant to risk their lives in the wilderness of New Hampshire. Shortly after this, in a petition addressed to the crown, the government of Massachusetts begged to be excused from helping defend New York, justifying its reluctance on the grounds of heavy internal expenses and "the frequent succours we are obliged to yeild our Neighbours in the Province of New Hampshire."[58]

Frontenac's policy was to incite the Indians of northern New

England against the English in order to keep that frontier ablaze, while at the same time either walloping or wooing the Five Nations, according to circumstances. After the chastisement of the Mohawks in 1693, Frontenac actively sought an accommodation with the Iroquois Confederacy, hoping to capitalize on the Indians' disillusionment with their English allies. New York, however, was able to avert that disaster, and even persuaded the tribes to resume hostilities against the French. His peace offensive having failed, Frontenac then resorted once more to the big stick.

Fort Frontenac, having been reoccupied and repaired since its abandonment in 1689, provided a good advance base for a major offensive against the Iroquois country, especially the villages of the hostile Oneidas and Onondagas. In the early summer of 1696, a striking force of more than 2,000 soldiers and Indians assembled at Montreal; and when this army began moving upriver toward Lake Ontario, the crusty old governor, whose sheer determination had somehow managed to raise New France out of the lowest depths of despair, was in personal command. Final preparations were made at Fort Frontenac; and then the army proceeded by boat and canoe to the south shore of Lake Ontario, where they entered the Iroquois country, roughly 125 miles west of Albany. Lacking the physical endurance to stride along rough wilderness trails, Frontenac had himself carried in a sort of armchair on poles, like an Oriental potentate.

As before, the Indians were taken at a disadvantage and offered little or no resistance. Most of them fled out of reach, leaving their fields and villages to be ravaged by the French, who systematically and ruthlessly destroyed crops and dwellings in order to impose famine. After accomplishing this destruction and feeling well satisfied with their effective demonstration of French power, Frontenac and his men returned to Montreal. Cadwallader Colden, a New Yorker, contemptuously labeled the whole affair "a kind of heroick Dotage," and depreciated the severity of the punishment inflicted upon the Onondagas and Oneidas.[59] It seems more reasonable to assume that for these Indians as for any others the loss of a summer's harvest and the burning of entire villages was a great blow both to morale and to the Indians' ability to resume the offensive. Three of the five tribes now had suffered heavily at the hands of Frontenac, and the lesson was not lost upon the leaders of the Iroquois Confederacy. Of what use had the English been to them in their time of disaster?

While the governor of New France was thus engaged against the Iroquois in New York, others of his men were inflicting a humiliating defeat upon the soldiers of Massachusetts. On 15 July the fort at Pemaquid, on the coast of Maine, was surrendered by its commander to a mixed force of French and Indians. This fort actually was of dubious value in the present war, but as a symbol of English jurisdiction and power along the sparsely occupied coast of Maine its fall echoed heavily in Boston. The French made sure that the structure was left in ruins, a monument to the futility of English aspirations east of the Kennebec River.[60]

By this time the Anglo-French war in New England was degenerating into what was little more than a feud carried on at the encouragement of the belligerent colonial governments by shifting bands of irregulars. No further official expeditions of major proportions were undertaken, but the sporadic killing continued. Massachusetts tried to stimulate aggressive raiding activity on the part of volunteer bands by holding out the lure of substantial bounties for enemy scalps. The prices ranged from £10 for the scalp of an Indian child under ten years of age up to £50 for the scalp of an Indian man or woman.[61] Even though penalties were provided for making fraudulent claims, a policy such as this—so clearly reflecting the brutalizing influence of wilderness warfare—represented a serious threat not only to the actual enemy but to neutral and even friendly Indians as well. The remarkable exploit of the formidable female from Haverhill, Hannah Dustin, should be viewed in the light of this very policy. Held captive by a band of hostile Indians, Mrs. Dustin and two other prisoners under her influence, a woman and a boy, awaited their opportunity to escape. One night when all members of the Indian family with whom they were housed had gone fast asleep, the three captives saw their chance. Seizing hatchets, they swiftly brained four adults and six children. Then before heading back toward home, Mrs. Dustin and her companions crouched over the corpses and calmly peeled off the scalps! These bloody trophies they carried off with them, intending of course to collect the bounty offered by the government.[62]

Not only along the New England frontier, but nearly everywhere that groups of hostile nationals confronted each other in the New World, there was the threat of violent conflict. If one side seemed weak, the other was almost certain sooner or later to take advantage of the weakness. Both the fisheries and the fur trade were important and profitable enterprises, tempting as targets. Fishing boats ventured near enemy-held shores at their own risk, and traders operating in remote wilderness posts had need to care for their defenses. In the far north, at Newfoundland and Hudson Bay, English and French stations were likely prizes for raiders whose objectives were clearly more economic than military. Some of these places changed hands more than once during the course of the war; it was a warfare of grab and hold, with the French scoring highest. By the latter part of 1697, they had wrested most of Newfoundland and the key posts at Hudson Bay from their English rivals.[63]

Clearly neither Britain nor France attached much importance to the wilderness skirmishing in North America. Whenever the great powers did consider the American theater in some fashion related to the European conflict, it usually was in terms of naval warfare. In fact, mercantile investments provided almost the sole incentive for expending military and naval resources in America, and that consideration directed attention largely to the islands of the West Indies. From time to time, naval reinforcements were sent out to augment the vessels on West Indian duty, but such additional commitments seldom produced results commensurate with the costs. More often, ship rot and tropical disease undermined the effectiveness of vessels and crews. The Caribbean proved to be a watery graveyard of maritime ambitions.[64]

After the naval battle of La Hogue, fought off the coast of France in 1692, the French Navy had to recognize the futility of trying to match English and Dutch sea power, fleet to fleet. So the course of French naval activity began to lead in another direction, with a growing emphasis on *guerre de course,* the attempt to undermine England's strength by preying upon her seaborne commerce.[65] This was an expanded form of privateering, with swift, heavily armed naval vessels operating as lone raiders. For England, the safeguarding of her lines of mercantile trade was essential. English and colonial ships often found it advantageous to sail in groups or convoys, but this meant delays while such convoys were organized. At the same time, the hazards of sea travel in wartime sharply increased the costs of insuring ships and cargoes. During this struggle along the sea lanes, both sides managed to seize or destroy large numbers of enemy vessels, from warships to fishing shallops, and many a brisk lad who sought adventure and fortune before the mast found instead only a grave in the deep.

The war in Europe was proving indecisive; neither side seemed capable of forcing matters to an advantageous conclusion. In the meantime, business and trade were suffering under the handicaps of war, citizens were in despair at the increasing burden of taxation, and governments were watching the level of public indebtedness rise at an alarming rate. France's debt had nearly doubled since 1688; England's was already above £50 million.[66] Both sides needed time to rest, replenish, and reorganize.

The first significant break came in 1696 when the Duchy of Savoy made an accommodation with France and withdrew from the Grand Alliance. After this, nearly all the belligerents began the active pursuit of peace, with an understanding that there was no real victor in the war. The Treaty of Ryswick, concluded on 20 September 1697, marked the formal cessation of Anglo-French hostilities.[67] Louis XIV now recognized William of Orange as the true king of England, thereby officially abandoning the cause of James Stuart and the Jacobites. The treaty further provided for the mutual relinquishment of all colonial territory seized during the course of the war and the release of all prisoners. These terms left no doubt that the war was a stand-off. It was on the ninth of December that several ships from England reached Boston Harbor with news that peace had been concluded.[68] From Boston the welcome word spread rapidly across the countryside, while other vessels from abroad were carrying the same information to seaports up and down the coast.

When spring came, the governor of New York sent Peter Schuyler, accompanied by released French prisoners, to Canada with the terms of the treaty. Schuyler's mission was to make whatever arrangements were necessary for obtaining the release of English prisoners, many of them civilians taken in the various border raids and still in Canadian or Indian hands. This proved to be a slow and uncertain business, but eventually most of those yet alive were returned to English territory to be welcomed by their rejoicing families and friends.[69]

King William's War was the preface to the greater conflicts of the next century, introducing in dim outline some of the conditions and problems of the coming decades in English America. Colonial leaders were beginning to appreciate the fundamental importance of wilderness geography—forest, mountains, waterways, and the very vastness of the area—as a determinant of tactics. Some experience had been gained in the difficult art of moving and supplying large expeditionary forces over great distances in the wilderness. But the most impressive development was the use of mixed raiding parties of Europeans and Indians, as pioneered by the French. Utilizing Indian techniques in the woods, and matching Indian stamina with that of tough *coureurs de bois,* the French had discovered a weapon that could terrorize whole frontiers. It was not the savage brutality that was new—after all, the English had amply demonstrated their own capacity for ruthless violence against the Pequots in 1637, and the Iroquois against Lachine in 1689—but the effective joining of Indians and Europeans in a planned, deliberate use of savagery to achieve a definite military objective. This was a deplorable development at the very beginning of the Anglo-French colonial wars; its effect was to create terror and build hatred, assuring that the animosity between Europeans and Indians and between English and French would persist and fester throughout the period.

The Franco-Indian raiding parties clearly demonstrated again what the Algonquin Indians had already shown in earlier wars, that isolated frontier settlements were extremely vulnerable to surprise attack. Successful assaults in which whole villages were ruined and dozens of civilians either slaughtered or taken captive quickly cooled the colonial enthusiasm for frontier expansion. The westward movement was either stopped altogether or else thrown into reverse during years when Anglo-French and Indian warfare raged along the frontiers. Even in years of relative tranquillity, the potential danger of Franco-Indian raids was an inhibiting factor for land speculators and pioneering farmers.

The Five Nations of the Iroquois Confederacy emerged from King William's War greatly weakened by their losses and sadly disillusioned with their English allies. Their losses had been suffered in waging vigorous offensive warfare against the Canadian frontier and the tribes allied with the French, as well as at the hands of the expeditions sent by Frontenac to ravage their villages.[70] Still valuing their important economic relationship with New York in the fur trade, the Iroquois deeply resented the English colonies' failure to unite and carry the war to the enemy's country. If, as the Iroquois were prone to believe, they had been pushed into the forefront as an expendable shield for the English, it was a role they did not relish. So it is not surprising that the more astute of their tribal leaders already were beginning to reexamine their traditional assumptions and the concomitant policy of alignment with the English. For the future security of the New York frontier, indeed for the very survival of an English hope of continuing westward expansion, this reassessment on the part of the Iroquois was an ominous sign.

But at least for the moment there was cause for general rejoicing in the conclusion of peace. That the terms of the Treaty of Ryswick offered little prospect of a true accommodation among the contending powers could easily be overlooked in the joy of finding at last an end to the dangers and deprivations of the past eight years. Colonial life began to resume its normal course, with fathers and brothers at home, goods passing easily along the usual routes of commerce, traders and pioneers following the trails and rivers of the deep forest, and the ambitious schemers, both French and English, dreaming their grandiose, expansionist dreams of the future.

NOTES

1. A good general discussion of the causes and character of the War of the League of Augsburg may be found in John B. Wolf, *The Emergence of the Great Powers, 1685–1715* (New York, 1951), chap. 2. It is to be noted that hostilities first began in Europe in 1683 when Turkish armies advanced on Vienna. France invaded the Rhineland in 1688, and England declared war in May of 1689. Spain entered the conflict in 1690.

2. *Edward Randolph; Including His Letters and Official Papers from the New England, Middle, and Southern Colonies in America.* . . . (Publications of the Prince Society, XXVIII [Boston, 1899]), 64. See also Thomas Hutchinson, *The History of the Colony and Province of Massachusetts-Bay*, Lawrence Shaw Mayo, ed. (3 vols.; Cambridge, Mass., 1936), I, 335.

3. W. J. Eccles, *Frontenac: The Courtier Governor* (Toronto, 1959), pp. 192–194; W. J. Eccles, *Canada under Louis XIV, 1663–1701* (New York, 1964), pp. 164–165; Gustave Lanctot, *A History of Canada. Volume II: From the Royal Régime to the Treaty of Utrecht, 1663–1713*, M. M. Cameron, trans. (Cambridge, Mass., 1964), p. 110.

4. Eccles, *Frontenac*, pp. 200–201; Lanctot, *History of Canada*, II, 114; H. P. Biggar, "Frontenac's Projected Attempt on New York in 1689," *New York State Historical Association Quarterly Journal*, V (April, 1924), 139–147.

The plan had been conceived and developed by others; Frontenac was the man selected to carry it through to completion.

5. Lawrence H. Leder, ed., *The Livingston Indian Records, 1666–1723* (Gettysburg, Pa., 1956), p. 155. See also Cadwallader Colden, *The History of the Five Indian Nations Depending on the Province of New-York in America* (Ithaca, 1958), Part 2, chaps. 2–3.

6. Colden, *History of the Five Indian Nations*, p. 102.

7. Leder, *Livingston Indian Records*, pp. 158–159; Eccles, *Frontenac*, pp. 224–226; Lanctot, *History of Canada*, II, 115–116; G. M. Wrong, *The Rise and Fall of New France* (2 vols.; New York, 1928), II, 515; Nellis M. Crouse, *Lemoyne d'Iberville: Soldier of New France* (Ithaca, 1954), pp. 55–56.

8. Jerome R. Reich, *Leisler's Rebellion: A Study of Democracy in New York, 1664–1720* (Chicago, 1953), pp. 81–82.

9. Jasper Danckaerts, *Journal of Jasper Danckaerts, 1679–1680*, Bartlett B. James and J. Franklin Jameson, eds. (New York, 1913), pp. 201, 212–213.

10. Some shafts of light on this situation are provided by the sources published in Edmund B. O'Callaghan, ed., *The Documentary History of the State of New-York* (4 vols.; Albany, 1849–1851), I, 297–312.

11. According to one source, a delegation of Albany men had been at Schenectady only a few days before, suggesting in vain that the village maintain a more effective watch (O'Callaghan, *Documentary History of the State of New-York*, I, 306).

12. Of the sixty persons known to have been killed during the assault, six may be identified as garrison troops and another eleven as Negroes (O'Callaghan, *Documentary History of the State of New-York*, I, 304–305). The fortified dwelling of John Alexander Glen, across the river from Schenectady, was spared, apparently because the Glen family had on former occasions shown kindness toward French prisoners. (See Colden, *History of the Five Indian Nations*, pp. 102–103; Francis Parkman, *Count Frontenac and New France under Louis XIV* [Boston, 1877], pp. 215–216.)

13. O'Callaghan, *Documentary History of the State of New-York*, I, 302. Numerous details of the operation against Schenectady were obtained by the English from three Canadian participants who were among those captured by the Mohawks during the withdrawal. (See Leder, *Livingston Indian Records*, pp. 158–162.)

14. Samuel Sewall's Diary, in 5 *MHC*, V, 311.

15. Eccles, *Frontenac*, pp. 225–226; Lanctot, *History of Canada*, II, 116.

16. 3 *MHC*, I, 104.

17. 3 *MHC*, I, 104–105; O'Callaghan, *Documentary History of the State of New-York*, II, 259–260; Eccles, *Frontenac*, p. 226.

18. Cotton Mather was not the only Bostonian to lay primary blame upon the French when he lamented that *"New-England was miserably Briar'd in the Perplexities of an Indian War"* (*The Life of Sir William Phips*, Mark Van Doren, ed. [New York, 1929], p. 62). George F. Sensabaugh has called attention to the way in which Mather compared New England's Indian warfare to the heavenly warfare of *Paradise Lost*. The English, according to Mather,

were on God's side; the Indians were being incited by satanic Frenchmen (*Milton in Early America* [Princeton, 1964], p. 39).

19. James P. Baxter, ed., *Documentary History of the State of Maine,* V (Portland, Me., 1897), 66.
20. *A Journal of the Proceedings in the Late Expedition to Port-Royal* (Boston, 1690), pp. 3–6; Lanctot, *History of Canada,* II, 173–174.
21. *Journal of the Proceedings in the Late Expedition to Port-Royal,* p. 11.
22. *Life of Sir William Phips,* p. 67.
23. Reich, *Leisler's Rebellion,* pp. 95–97.
24. Major General Winthrop's Journal, Gay Transcripts, State Papers, VII, 105–114 (Massachusetts Historical Society). Leisler, at this time suffering from serious loss of public support, later charged that Winthrop himself was responsible for the failure of the Iroquois, but this seems unlikely. See Reich, *Leisler's Rebellion,* pp. 103–104. There is no reason to doubt that disease was an actual factor in the Iroquois failure, while a growth of French influence among the tribes also may have been working to the disadvantage of the English.
25. 6 *MHC,* III, 12–13. Schuyler's account of his mission has been published in O'Callaghan, *Documentary History of the State of New-York,* II, 285–288.
26. 5 *MHC,* V, 329.
27. See the account by a contemporary French observer in *NYCD,* IX, 455. An interesting inside view of conditions at Quebec during this period was given by Captain Sylvanus Davis, who still was a prisoner there (3 *MHC,* I, 110–112). See also Eccles, *Frontenac,* pp. 234–235.
28. *NYCD,* IX, 455–457.
29. Thomas Savage, *An Account of the Late Action of the New-Englanders, under the Command of Sir William Phips, against the French at Canada* (London, 1691); John Walley, "Major Walley's Journal in the Expedition against Canada in 1690," in Hutchinson, *History of the Colony and Province of Massachusetts-Bay,* I, 460. Unfortunately, Phips' original journal of the expedition was accidentally destroyed before being brought into print. See Gerald S. Graham, ed., *The Walker Expedition to Quebec, 1711* (Toronto, 1953), p. 114n.
30. *NYCD,* IX, 457; Mather, *Life of Sir William Phips,* pp. 76–77.
31. *NYCD,* IX, 457.
32. Major Thomas Savage was especially emphatic in criticizing the failure of supplies, and testified that when the assault troops made their landing they carried with them on the average only about three-quarters of a pound of powder, some fifteen to eighteen bullets, and two biscuits apiece. Savage, *Account of the Late Action of the New-Englanders.*
33. *NYCD,* IX, 458.
34. 5 *MHC,* V, 334.
35. Savage, *Account of the Late Action of the New-Englanders;* Mather, *Life of Sir William Phips,* p. 81.
36. Abstract of a letter from James Lloyd, 8 January 1690/91, Gay Transcripts, Phips Papers, I, 82–86 (Massachusetts Historical Society).

37. *Ibid.,* p. 92.

38. An able assessment of Frontenac's strategy at Quebec, emphasizing the factor of the tide at the ford of the St. Charles, is to be found in Eccles, *Frontenac,* pp. 237–243.

39. Colden, *History of the Five Indian Nations,* p. 121; Eccles, *Frontenac,* p. 246; Lanctot, *History of Canada,* II, 123.

40. *NYCD,* III, 804.

41. Schuyler's journal of the expedition has been published in *NYCD,* III, 800–805. See also Colden, *History of the Five Indian Nations,* pp. 114–115; Parkman, *Count Frontenac,* pp. 289–293; Eccles, *Frontenac,* pp. 248–249; Lanctot, *History of Canada,* II, 124.

42. Hutchinson, *History of the Colony and Province of Massachusetts-Bay,* I, 343. Out of gratitude for mercy previously shown by Colonel Benjamin Church to some captive Indian women and children, it was said, the Indians released two aged English women and five children taken by them from York. This tradition is related in a letter from Ebenezer Hazard, dated 1779, in the Sir William Pepperrell Papers, II, 213 (Massachusetts Historical Society).

43. *History of the Colony and Province of Massachusetts-Bay,* II, 75.

44. John Usher to the Board of Trade, 29 October 1692, Gay Transcripts, Phips Papers, II, 34–38 (Massachusetts Historical Society). An abstract of this letter appears in *CSP* (1689–1692), pp. 727–728.

45. *Edward Randolph; Including His Letters and Official Papers from the New England, Middle, and Southern Colonies in America. . . .* (Publications of the Prince Society, XXXI [Boston, 1909]), 411.

46. Letter of 3 September 1696, Massachusetts Archives, LXX, 296–297.

47. Petition from Kittery, August 1695, Massachusetts Archives, CXIII, 124.

48. *NYCD,* III, 783–784.

49. Samuel Sewall's Diary, in 5 *MHC,* V, 348.

50. *NYCD,* III, 785.

51. *NYCD,* III, 785. See also *Edward Randolph; Including His Letters and Official Papers,* XXXI, 413–414.

52. Leder, *Livingston Indian Records,* p. 165; Colden, *History of the Five Indian Nations,* pp. 110–113.

53. 6 *MHC,* III, 22–24, 28; John F. Burns, *Controversies between Royal Governors and Their Assemblies in the Northern American Colonies* (Boston, 1923), p. 293; James S. Leamon, "Governor Fletcher's Recall," *WMQ,* XX (October, 1963), 527–542.

54. Colden, *History of the Five Indian Nations,* pp. 128–129.

55. Colden, *History of the Five Indian Nations,* p. 132.

56. Record of a conference with the Indians at Albany, 15–22 August 1694, Penn Manuscripts, Indian Affairs, I (1687–1753), 14 (Historical Society of Pennsylvania).

57. Stoughton to Usher, 26 July 1694, Gay Transcripts, Phips Papers, IV, 54–55 (Massachusetts Historical Society).

58. Draft of petition from the General Court, 14 October 1694 (*ibid.,* pp. 70–72).

59. Colden, *History of the Five Indian Nations,* p. 172; Parkman, *Count Frontenac,* pp. 410-414; Eccles, *Frontenac,* pp. 265–266; Lanctot, *History of Canada,* II, 130–131.

60. Hutchinson, *History of the Colony and Province of Massachusetts-Bay,* II, 69–71.

61. Massachusetts Archives, XXX, 435–436.

62. Parkman, *Count Frontenac,* pp. 385–387.

63. Gerald S. Graham, *Empire of the North Atlantic: The Maritime Struggle for North America* (Toronto, 1950), pp. 76–81.

64. Aspects of naval warfare in the Caribbean are discussed in William Laird Clowes, *The Royal Navy: A History from the Earliest Times to the Present* (7 vols.; London, 1897–1903), II, *passim;* John Ehrman, *The Navy in the War of William III, 1689–1697: Its State and Direction* (Cambridge, 1953), pp. 609–611; Herbert Richmond, *The Navy as an Instrument of Policy, 1558–1727,* E. A. Hughes, ed. (Cambridge and New York, 1953), *passim.*

65. Graham, *Empire of the North Atlantic,* pp. 61–64.

66. Wolf, *Emergence of the Great Powers,* p. 171.

67. For the text of the treaty consult Frances Gardiner Davenport, ed., *European Treaties Bearing on the History of the United States and Its Dependencies* (4 vols.; Washington, D.C., 1917–1937), II, 360–365; and Fred L. Israel, ed., *Major Peace Treaties of Modern History, 1648–1967* (4 vols.; New York, 1967), I, 145–152.

68. John Marshall, Diary, 1689–1711 (Massachusetts Historical Society).

69. In the Massachusetts Archives, LXX, 398–399, are listed sixteen captives received aboard a Massachusetts vessel on 17 January 1698/99, and twenty-one believed still in the hands of the Indians on 24 January 1698/99.

70. *NYCD,* IV, 337–338; *CSP* (1700), pp. 542–543.

CHAPTER 4

The Struggle Resumes: Queen Anne's War, 1702-1713

THE TWENTY-FOURTH of April 1701 was observed in Massachusetts as a public fast. On that occasion Cotton Mather preached a special sermon in which he remarked, with more than usual perspicacity, that in the Peace of Ryswick "the Wind came not about the right way; there must be another Storm, and War, before all clear up, according to our Desires." Mather did not make that pronouncement without serious consideration of recent developments in both Europe and America, developments which gave little cause for optimism. Like most New Englanders who had lived through the recent war, he had a deep-seated dread of French aggression combined with an exaggerated notion of French capabilities, all of which led him to conclude that "the Plantations are in a very Hazardous Condition." [1]

It is true that Louis XIV, now in his sixties and well past the peak of his career, still was obsessed with the concept of French supremacy in Europe, a concept which he was inclined to identify with the prestige and power of his own name. Other national rulers were equally concerned with protecting and, if possible, advancing their own particular interests at the expense of contending rivals. It was an age of intensive international competition, and in that sense no different from our own. The virtual stalemate of the recent war showed how difficult it was for any single power to gain predominance so long as the many states, great and small, were aligned in blocs or alliances of approximately equal strength. But if there should occur some significant rearrangement of the pattern, resulting in a major addition of strength to one side and a corresponding weakening of the other, the precarious balance of power would be destroyed, and Europe then might fall under the sway of a master state. With this in view, the one nation most feared was France; the rearrangement most dreaded, especially by England, was a dynastic union combining the worldwide territories and resources of France and Spain. In 1701 such a combination was a distinct possibility.

Charles II, the Hapsburg king of Spain, had died the previous year without issue, which meant that in all likelihood his throne soon would be gained by an ambitious relative from some other branch of the family. Among the eager contenders, even before the king's death, was Louis XIV, grandson of Philip III of Spain and husband of Charles's sister. Louis contended not for himself directly but for his own grandson, Philip of Anjou, in the expectation that Philip's accession to the Spanish throne would give France the full advantage of Spain's friendly support without actually provoking England to open resistance. Shortly before his death, Charles had been persuaded to change his will in Philip's favor, after which he quickly expired and left the nations to straighten out the ensuing mess. The unsuccessful candidates grumbled and plotted revenge, while the fortunate *designé*, with the hearty blessing of his royal grandfather, assumed his new dignity as Philip V of Spain.

At first England seemed inclined to accept this ominous development with reasonable good grace, on the understanding that France and Spain would not engage in any concerted interference with British commerce and especially that there would be no actual union of the two crowns.[2] But Louis XIV unwisely began to push his advantage by sending French troops into the Spanish Netherlands and also by building up French trade with Spain and the Spanish Empire to the detriment of English and Dutch merchants. When France capped its success by arranging a formal alliance with Spain, the disappointed Austrian Hapsburg contender for the Spanish inheritance, Leopold I, hastened to join a counterbalancing Grand Alliance with England and Holland in 1701. Then, after the former James II of England died that same year, Louis XIV compounded his villainy in English eyes by recognizing James's son as the rightful king of Great Britain and Ireland. In Europe, the stage was now set for a new war.

American developments were scarcely less ominous. Indian relations seemed like a vast uncharted quagmire of shifting quicksand, atremble under every passing tread. Each tribe was watching its own advantage, more careless than ever of traditional alignments and previous commitments, anxious to recoup earlier losses without running the risk of disaster. This often meant assessing the relative strength of rival European colonies and gravitating toward the stronger. New Englanders in particular were painfully aware that the Peace of Ryswick had not solved the problem of Indian hostility along the blood-stained frontier in Maine, New Hampshire, and western Massachusetts. Sullen groups of Indians, only momentarily pacified, still thought in terms of revenge for past losses and all the humiliations inflicted upon them by the white expansionists. Only one consideration now inclined them toward an accommodation— their yearning for the advantages of English trade. The recent war had wiped out the few English communities east of the Kennebec River, leaving the area from the Kennebec to Acadia a sort of no-man's-land. This condition was favorable not only to the Eastern Indians, as they were collectively known, but also to the French, who hoped to establish the Kennebec as their southern boundary.[3] Although the government of Massachusetts had managed to hammer together a treaty with the Eastern Indians in 1699, and the sachems openly expressed their intention to remain neutral in any future Anglo-French conflict, it was obvious that French influence among these volatile tribes remained strong. Indeed, there was no good reason to suppose that whenever the lightning flashes of war once again were seen along New England's wilderness frontier these Indians would long resist the temptation to raid any English settlements that might be left exposed.[4]

In New York the Indian problem was equally confusing and disturbing. As early as July of 1698 the Five Nations, traditionally staunch allies of the English, had begun to show definite signs of diplomatic bifurcation. At a conference with Governor Bellomont during that month, they paraded their worries and their grievances: the high prices of English trading goods, continued attacks by French Indians, the reoccupation of Fort Frontenac by the French, and perhaps most important of all, large-scale loss of Iroquois land to greedy, scheming English speculators. Of what use to the Five Nations was their traditional alliance with New York if the government of that province would not protect them against English land-jobbers and French imperialists? All too fresh in Indian memory was the chastisement inflicted upon the Iroquois by Frontenac in 1696. With the French still firmly based on Fort Frontenac, the New York Indians felt themselves constantly intimidated. "A greater evil could not have attended all of us in the five Nations . . ." they complained, "than the suffering the French to resettle Candarque [Fort Frontenac] which will always be as a thorn in our sides and keep us in such a continual alarm and watchfulness that we shall never be able to hunt freely whilst such a power and fortress is so near not only to annoy but in a capacity to destroy us."[5]

Already badly disillusioned by the obvious indecisiveness of the English colonies in the last war and greatly weakened by their own losses, the Iroquois no longer felt any real enthusiasm for leading the attack upon New France as they formerly had done. Yet they still valued highly their economic relationship with Albany in the fur trade and saw the great advantage of maintaining this role. At the same time, they were coming under increasing French influence and pressure which laid down for them the alternative of making their peace with Quebec or else suffering continued attacks from the north and west. Some of the Iroquois, deeply impressed by the teachings or the proffered inducements of French missionary priests, actually were migrating northward to take up residence in the Catholic Indian community of Caughnawaga near Montreal. And even among those who remained in New York there was forming a pro-French faction to challenge the old policy of unswerving attachment to the English.[6]

By midsummer of 1700, the government of New York was seriously alarmed by the increasing evidence of French success in swaying the Five Nations. Yet within the province there was no agreement as to what should be done. The legislature made a futile gesture when it passed a law aimed against French priests "who by their wicked and Subtle Insinuations Industriously Labour to Debauch Seduce and withdraw the Indians from their due obedience unto his most Sacred majesty. . . ."[7] This act contained more sonorous syllables than teeth. Some New Yorkers urged that a fort be constructed somewhere in the territory of the Onondagas to bolster the English position, but this proposal immediately became a political issue. Opponents could point to the decrepit condition of the fortifications at Schenectady and Albany, arguing that here was a deficiency far more immediate and serious. And once again was heard the old argument that New York was the very keystone of the English colonies, that its security was vital to all of them, and that therefore the cost of fortifying New York's exposed frontier should be shared by neighboring governments. This argument, so popular in New York, was accorded little respect elsewhere, and nothing was accomplished.[8]

Versailles and London were satisfied to leave the thorny question of Iroquois political allegiance in the hands of a binational commission as a means of fending off a crisis that might lead to war. But the Iroquois themselves preferred to work out their own destiny as best they could, and proceeded to do so by taking a long step in the direction of an advantageous neutrality which would free them from the menace of French harassment yet enable them to continue their profitable economic relationship with New York. In 1701 they signed two treaties, one with the French and one with the English. In the first they made their peace with Canada and gained the assurance that in any future Anglo-French conflict if they remained neutral the French would respect their neutrality. As the pro-French western tribes of the Great Lakes region also were parties to this treaty, the old hostility and rivalry over the fur trade in the West seemed at last put aside, to the great advantage of New France. "With the signing of this treaty an epoch had come to an end," is the well-founded judgment of one modern authority on early Canadian history. "The Iroquois had finally accepted defeat in their century-long struggle to wrest control of the western fur trade from the French." [9] In the second treaty, with the English, the Five Nations sought to protect their future in another way by deeding their hunting grounds to the English crown, of which they formally acknowledged themselves subjects. Presumably now the crown would stand as guarantor of these lands against any, whether French or English, who tried to intrude upon them. With these two treaties neatly concluded the Iroquois were able to enjoy, at least for a time, the advantages of neutrality even as the opposing pro-French and pro-English factions within the tribes continued to struggle for predominance. On balance, the Iroquois treaties of 1701 constituted a serious diplomatic defeat for the English, while spurring the French to increase their endeavors, through the influence of traders and missionaries, to win the full trust and support of the New York Indians.

Farther south, in the vast interior region stretching from Pennsylvania to the Gulf of Mexico, English traders were busy developing their profitable contacts with the various tribes, while becoming increasingly concerned over French advances in the Mississippi Valley. When Pierre Lemoyne, Sieur d'Iberville, planted the French flag on the lower Mississippi in 1699, he provided his country with a strategically located base from which to challenge the English advance into the Southeast. This became evident when groups of Indians who had been alienated from the English because of harsh treatment at the hands of traders began attaching themselves to the newly arrived French regime. Iberville's first major triumph of Indian diplomacy occurred in 1700, when the populous Choctaw nation allied itself with the French of Louisiana. Subsequently, the Choctaws and the Chickasaws were persuaded to end their longstanding enmity, so that by 1702 the French, through favorable relations with the Indians of the area, seemed well on the way toward consolidating their grasp on the lower Mississippi and along the Gulf coast.[10] In this way, the tribes of the Southeast fell into the same fatal mold that so ruthlessly had been shaping the destiny of the northern tribes—alignments and alliances marking some tribes as pro-English and their enemies as pro-French. The consequence could be a dangerous, possibly fatal involvement in future Anglo-French wars.

Some Americans looked west from Charleston or Philadelphia or Boston and thought they saw a clear pattern of French advance beyond the Appalachian Mountains. It seemed that the French must be following a planned program of expansion designed to bring the entire Mississippi Valley under the white lilies of Louis XIV. This would mean an unbroken belt of French territory stretching from Acadia and the St. Lawrence to the Gulf of Mexico, like a great iron chain confining the English colonies to the narrow coastal strip east of the mountains. English traders would be prevented from going among the Indians of the interior, and English pioneers would be denied access to the rich lands of the transmontane West. Under these conditions, it was feared, the English colonies ultimately would wither and die for lack of expansion.

Actually, there is good reason to doubt that the French government at this time had either the vision or the resources to formulate

such an elaborate plan, to say nothing of pursuing it to its conclusion; but apprehensive Englishmen were impressed by the evidence they saw. The ambitious explorations of La Salle in the
1680s seemed like a grand overture. With the founding of Biloxi
and the activity of Iberville in Louisiana after 1699, it appeared
that the French had been able to provide a firm anchor for the
southern end of their chain. In 1701, Antoine de la Mothe Cadillac
established a military post at Detroit on the strategic water link
between Lake Erie and Lake Huron. By this time, too, there was a
French mission station on the upper Mississippi River at Cahokia
more than 400 miles southwest of Detroit and some 700 miles above
the Gulf. Although the peppery Governor Frontenac had died in
1698 after having humbled the Iroquois, other French leaders,
including the new governor, Louis Hector de Callières, seemed to
be carrying forward the French banner in much the same spirit.

To top it all, there was the gloomy prospect of a confrontation
with the united French and Spanish empires. This not only would
increase the hazards of American seaborne commerce, but also
would pose a direct threat to the southern frontier in Virginia and
especially Carolina. Traders from those colonies had long been
crossing the Appalachians or skirting around their southern end to
trade with the tribes as far west as the lower Mississippi. It was these
men who felt themselves most directly threatened by Iberville's
colony and by the possibility of Franco-Spanish union which would
align Spanish Florida with French Louisiana.

So it was that many of the English colonists, whether backwoods
farmers or town-dwelling men of affairs, were more than a little
uneasy about the future. They viewed with dismay the ample
evidence of instability among the Indians and expansion of French
control in the transappalachian West, while the English colonial
governments seemed characterized by apathy and ineptitude. Who
would stop the French and tame the Indians and hold open the
West for future English expansion? There appeared to be no clear,
consistent English policy for coming to grips with the dangerously
swelling problem. Was there not to be one last opportunity for an
aroused empire to make good the western claims that lay buried in
most of the colonial charters, claims to the great resource-filled territory beyond the ridges of the Appalachians?

To men pondering the future of America in this mood of
apprehension and pessimism there came at last an answer. In the

spring of 1702, England and Holland declared war on France and Spain in order to prevent Louis XIV from gaining effective control of Spain and the Spanish Empire, dominating the continent of Europe, and gathering the lion's share of Atlantic commerce. King William III, Louis' archfoe, had died less than two months before the fateful decision was made, but his successor, Queen Anne, stood ready to prosecute the new war with all the strength and will of her nation. The outbreak of a new international conflict in 1702 was not the kind of solution most Americans desired, but for the few ardent imperialists and aggressive expansionists, it created the kind of situation in which they could find an outlet for their frustrations and ambitions. One of these men was Governor James Moore of South Carolina, an ambitious, autocratic politician whose record as an Indian trader marked him as one of the hard and determined breed. Moore's idea was for South Carolina to organize and conduct a vigorous offensive against Spanish Florida, with the principal objective of capturing St. Augustine. Rousing the people of his colony early in the autumn of 1702, Moore recruited an expedition of some 800 whites and Indians, rounded up a few pieces of artillery and fourteen small vessels, and headed south in high expectation of humbling the Dons.[11]

It was mid-October when the Spanish governor, Joseph de Zúñiga y Cerda, a man of long and distinguished military service, first learned that an armed force from Carolina was approaching his colony. At once he began preparations to repel the attack, knowing full well how meager were the resources available. Florida was a feeble outpost of the Spanish Empire, poorly supported and weakly defended. Other than St. Augustine, the only settlements were a scattered handful of military outposts and Catholic missions, including the recently founded Pensacola on the Gulf. With a colonial population totaling only about 1,600, mostly concentrated at St. Augustine, the colony was defended by an army able to muster no more than 400 effective soldiers.[12] The principal defensive work guarding St. Augustine was the Castillo de San Marcos, a waterside fortress whose walls and bastions, constructed of resilient coquina, were virtually impervious to solid shot. This great fortress, brooding over the sunbaked little garrison town, would have to be taken by Moore and his Carolinians if they wanted to control St. Augustine and its anchorage.

The invasion force divided in order to approach St. Augustine

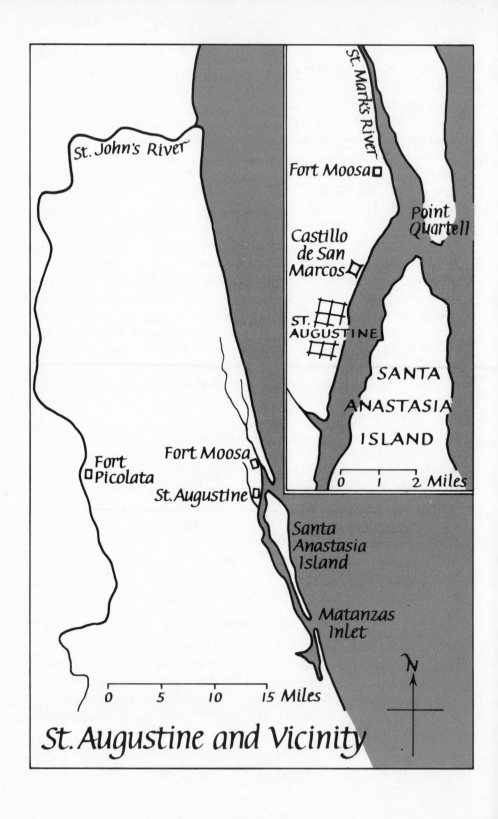

St. John's River

St. Marks River

Fort Moosa

Point
Quartell

Castillo
de San
Marcos

ST.
AUGUSTINE

SANTA

ANASTASIA

ISLAND

0   1   2 Miles

Fort
Picolata

Fort Moosa

St. Augustine

Santa
Anastasia
Island

Matanzas
Inlet

0   5   10   15 Miles

N

St. Augustine and Vicinity

from two directions. One group, commanded by Colonel Robert Daniel, took to canoes at the mouth of the St. Johns River 35 miles above St. Augustine and began advancing upriver, while the remainder of the army, under Moore himself, continued on down the coast to confront the objective from the sea side. Going upstream on the St. Johns (southward), Daniel and his men were able to reach a point of debarkation due west of St. Augustine, and thus approach the town from the rear. The two forces converged during the last week of October and found the town itself deserted; Zúñiga and his people had wisely withdrawn into the sheltering walls of the *castillo*. The defenders, knowing their own weakness, sent an urgent appeal to the Spanish base at Havana by a frigate that made its way out into the open sea through the Matanzas Inlet 13 miles below St. Augustine. Cheered by the hope of powerful reinforcements, the Spaniards then steeled themselves to meet the anticipated assault.

Moore, thirsting for a glorious victory, established his headquarters in the Spanish friary as his men drew their siege lines before the *castillo*. Then began the long days and weeks of siege activity, with the English cannon hurling their 9- and 12-pound solid shot into the coquina walls, while sweating sappers labored under the return fire of Zúñiga's guns to push their trenches closer and closer to the looming target. Inside the fortress were far too many people to be adequately sheltered under cover; many of them had no place to remain but on the open parade. If the English gunners ever began dropping explosive shells within the enclosure, the effect would be horrible. Fortunately for the Spaniards and Indians huddled within the *castillo*, Moore had not brought any shells with him, only solid shot, and few if any mortars. Recognizing his need, the Carolina governor dispatched one of his ships to obtain mortars and explosive shells from the English base at Jamaica more than 1,000 miles to the south by sea routes under Spanish surveillance. It was a chancy mission, but apparently essential for the success of the Carolinian enterprise. The Spaniards knew on what errand the English ship had gone, and they dreaded its return. With equal fervor they longed for the arrival of reinforcements from Havana to lift the siege. Which would first appear? Under these conditions, any sighting of a sail on the far horizon would cause tremendous excitement, combining fear and hope, until the nationality of the new arrival was clearly established.

December succeeded November, and the siege continued without
any sign of a break, the guns on both sides booming their mutual
defiance. At last, on the thirteenth of December, sentries on the
walls excitedly reported sails on the horizon; these proved to be
English, but they were not bringing shells from Jamaica. Two days
later sails were again sighted, and to the vast relief of the besieged
they were identified as Spanish. Help from Havana had arrived.

By this time Moore was beginning to realize that his chance of
breaking into the fortress or forcing Zúñiga to surrender was gone.
The siege had been underway for nearly seven weeks, the English
really were no closer to victory than at the start, and the army was
becoming restless. To linger much longer in the face of the enemy's
obvious determination to hold on was to invite disaster. So it was
that the frustrated Carolinians had to prepare for their withdrawal.
Leaving much of St. Augustine in ruins, they also burned their own
ships, for with Spanish sea power now in the vicinity Moore considered it safer for his men to withdraw northward on foot along the
beach. This gave the Spaniards an excellent opportunity to send a
force by sea to waylay the weary English at the mouth of the St.
Johns, but the commander of the Spanish relief fleet was cautious
and declined to seize the opportunity. Thus Moore's little army
was able to make its escape and report its failure at Charleston.[13]

South Carolina's reaction to Moore's return was of gale force.
Many of the vessels used for the expedition and now lying as blackened hulks at St. Augustine had been pressed into the government
service. Their owners, whose anguish is not difficult to imagine,
loudly demanded compensation. Indeed, the whole venture had
been extremely costly, if not in lives then certainly in money. The
assembly, torn with dissension, began issuing bills of credit as legal
tender in an attempt to cover the debt, a fateful precedent that led
inevitably to inflation and depreciation.[14]

In 1703 the irrepressible Moore, who by this time had been
replaced as governor, proposed an overland expedition to ravage
the Apalache country east of Pensacola. The assembly would not
give official governmental backing to the venture, so Moore proceeded on his own, raising a large force composed mostly of friendly
Indians. Late in 1703 this predatory host, hungering for plunder,
slaves, and revenge, began its devastating sweep through the Spanish
mission country. What Moore and his men did there during subsequent months adds up to one of the blackest chapters of the colonial

wars. They sacked villages, gathered booty, exacted tribute, tortured and killed both Indians and Spaniards, and in general left the Apalache mission system a smouldering wreck. Moore boasted that "Apalatchia is now reduced to so feeble and low a condition, that it can neither support St. Augustine with provisions, nor distrust [*sic*], endamage or frighten us: our Indians living between the Apalatchia and the French. In short, we have made Carolina as safe as the conquest of Apalatchia can make it." [15] The army of free-booters brought back with them, in addition to inanimate plunder, more than a thousand mission Indians, some of whom were held as slaves. The remainder were permitted to settle along the Savannah River below Augusta.[16] The effect of all this on the Spanish position in Florida was tremendous. Impressed by Carolina's obvious striking power and hoping, no doubt, for an accommodation that would enable them to enjoy the advantages of English trade under favorable conditions, the Indians of the region began loosening their old attachments to the Spaniards. Those Indians who feared the English too much to approach them either retreated to the immediate vicinity of St. Augustine or migrated to French-dominated territory in Alabama.[17]

In retrospect it is clear that if the Carolina expedition of 1702 had been better planned and better supplied, the Castillo de San Marcos could have been taken. That, in turn, almost certainly would have led to the speedy collapse of all Florida, as demonstrated by the developments of 1703–04. Moore's failure at St. Augustine, therefore, was a matter of great consequence, a lost opportunity to win Florida for the British Empire. Even though the subtropical colony was now left nearly crippled, it remained in Spanish hands as a base from which trouble for the English later could emerge, possibly with the participation of the French.[18]

Indeed, the French in Louisiana had great cause to be concerned about the spreading influence and power of the Carolinians, whose ambitions clearly reached as far as the Gulf coast and the lower Mississippi Valley. Already the weak Spanish garrison at Pensacola and the tiny French contingent stationed at Mobile near the mouth of the Alabama River were hard pressed to retain the loyalty of the local Indians and ward off the hostility of those Creeks and other southeastern Indians now giving their support to the English. Iberville had been succeeded by his younger brother, the Sieur de Bienville, upon whose shoulders fell the growing weight of English

and Indian hostility. Available to Bienville for the defense of
France's claims along the Gulf coast and up the lower Mississippi
River were less than 200 soldiers, a force obviously far too small.[19]

In 1703 a small party of Frenchmen journeyed upriver from Mobile to buy grain from the Alabama Indians, probably in the hope
of furthering better relations. Their hope was rudely shattered as
the Alabamas fell upon them and killed all but one, who made his
escape and brought the news back to Bienville. This distressing
episode marked the beginning of open hostilities between the
French and the Alabama Indians. Bienville, in response, offered his
Indian allies a bounty of ten crowns for each Alabama scalp they
brought in. Indians and French together made several raids northward into the Alabama country, burning the Indian dwellings and
trying to force the natives into submission. They were only partially
successful.[20] Always the small French garrison was severely handicapped by lack of adequate support from France and the peculiar
hardships imposed by a hostile environment. "In these times of
famine," wrote Bienville to the home government in 1708, "one
hears nothing but grumbling every day especially about a thousand
little things that the soldiers need and lack such as blankets and
coats." [21]

English traders, with their cheaper goods and their well-developed
system of transport, held a clear advantage over the French in the
contest for Indian allies. The important Creek nation was brought
into closer alignment with Carolinian policy in 1705, and a year
later English influence began to prevail even among the remote
Chickasaws.[22] Such favorable connections with various tribes of the
Southeast enabled the English to keep their French and Spanish
rivals constantly off balance, while at the same time reaping the
profits of an expanding Indian trade. War policy and commercial
policy went hand in hand.

The northern frontier also was an arena of active strife, as in the
previous war, with this notable difference—New York now enjoyed
virtual immunity thanks to the stance of neutrality adopted by the
Five Nations in 1701. With the Iroquois neutral, the French of
Canada had no compelling reason for invading the territory of New
York and were careful not to engage in any overt action that might
disturb the favorable situation. Most New Yorkers, to say the least,
were quite happy to be spared the pains of conflict, not only for
reasons of personal security but also for the financial advantages of

an uninterrupted fur trade. Even the exchange of trading goods and peltry between Albany and Montreal, carried on largely by means of the Catholic Indians of Caughnawaga, continued during the war.[23]

New England bore the brunt of Canada's offensive effort while bitterly resenting New York's profitable neutrality. By the time of Queen Anne's War, the New England colonies had further increased their population advantage over New France, the former counting now nearly 100,000 inhabitants as against New France's 15,000. This huge discrepancy, together with a comparable difference in material resources, limited the French to little more than a campaign of harassment along the frontier. Never was there any real possibility of a sustained French offensive to overwhelm and conquer the New England colonies. In fact, as a modern Canadian historian has noted, the French border raids of Queen Anne's War,

> galling as they were to the English colonists, were from the Canadian standpoint essentially defensive in character. They cloaked the inability of Canada to undertake a major offensive against New York or Boston. They were designed to keep the English colonies absorbed in the immediate problems of frontier defence and if possible forestall any serious invasion of Canada.[24]

At first there was a possibility that the usually pro-French Abnaki Indians of eastern Maine might cling to an Iroquois-like neutrality, but French agents were able to incite these Indians, and once the warriors had begun to harass English settlements the old deadly enmity between New England and the Abnakis was fully renewed.[25] Again the northern frontier lived in almost constant dread of surprise attack. "There was no safety to him that went out, nor him that came in, but dreadful calamity on every side," wrote a contemporary historian.[26] The inhabitants of Lancaster, a town located less than 40 miles west of Boston, tabulating the dwellings that had been burned and the livestock killed in their community, complained of being "forced to get our bread with the perill of our Lives which hang In Doubt Continually and but Little peace day nor Night." [27]

Out of this kind of warfare emerged numerous tales of terror and heroism, exaggerated no doubt, but conveying nevertheless a vivid impression of life and death on a frontier beset by hostile warriors. At Amesbury, it was said, two unarmed men were chased

by Indians and took shelter in a deserted house. There they found
a pair of old guns without any ammunition. With the Indians now
upon them, the desperate fugitives made their stand with the two
useless weapons in hand, poking the muzzles through loopholes and
bluffing their enemies by shouting to each other, "Here they are,
but do not fire till they come nearer." [28] If the story is true, the
bluff worked and the men were saved. The colonial historian
Thomas Hutchinson recorded a somewhat similar tale. At Oyster
River, New Hampshire, a group of women were congregated
in a garrison house while their husbands were away at work. When
the house was suddenly attacked by a band of marauding Indians,
"the women put on their husbands hats and jackets, and let their
hair loose, to make the appearance of men; and firing briskly from
the flankarts, saved the house and caused the enemy to retreat." [29]
But perhaps a little closer to the reality of frontier agony was the
elaborately contrived comment of Cotton Mather: "Ever now and
then, we hear of some, who in Planting their *Corn*, alas, have their
Fields water'd with their Blood: Some, who while *Mowing their
Grass*, are Cut down by the *Scythe* of a *Bloody Death*: Some, who
stepping forth to look their *Cattel*, have themselves become *Sheep
for the Slaughter*." [30]

Stealthy raiding activity by woods-wise Indians still baffled the
frontier communities after nearly a century of hard experience. The
Indians were swift and silent in approach and elusive in retreat;
woe to those pursuers who let their zeal lead them into an ambush.
Under such conditions, the public mood sometimes sank to a state
of near despair, especially in the more exposed villages such as
Northampton and Deerfield. Even the men of God minced no words
when speaking of the hostile Indians. "They are to be looked upon
as theives and murderers," said one. "They doe acts of hostility,
without proclaiming war . they don't appear openly in the feild to
bid us battle, they use those cruelly that fall into their hands.
they act like wolves and are to be dealt withall as wolves." [31]

The Marquis de Vaudreuil, governor of Canada since 1703, well
realized the importance of keeping the Indians enflamed against the
English by encouraging them to engage in actual hostilities along
the frontier. His main objective was to keep the English so busy
trying to defend their scattered settlements that they would have
no energy or resources remaining to wage an offensive against
Canada. Hopefully, too, the frontier settlers would eventually

become totally discouraged and abandon their precarious holdings, allowing the whole line of advance settlements to crumble. Then the French, with the help of their loyal Indians, would be able to move in and exploit their advantage to the full, no longer threatened by the power of English expansionism.

The Franco-Indian attack on Deerfield, Massachusetts, in the late winter of 1704 illustrates most dramatically the nature of this frontier warfare.[32] Deerfield, a village of about 270 inhabitants, marked the farthest reach of Massachusetts' northwestern frontier, being situated a short distance west of the Connecticut River, not far below the present Vermont line. Occasional warnings from New York that hostile Indians were known to be plotting an assault on the town enhanced the sense of isolation and danger. In the autumn of 1703, the inhabitants were living in a state of almost constant apprehension, as graphically described by their pastor in a letter to Governor Joseph Dudley at Boston:

> We have been driven from our houses and home lots into the fort [a palisaded area containing the meeting house and about fifteen dwellings]. . . . we have in the alarms several times been wholey taken off from any business, the whole town kept in our children of 12 or 13 years and under we have been afraid to improve in the feild for fear of the enemy. . . . We have been crowded to gather into houses to the preventing indoor affairs being carryed on to any advantage . . . the fronteir difficulties of a place so remote from others and so exposed as ours are more than can be known if not felt.[33]

But time and the advent of winter seemed to soften the fear, and the watch became less alert.[34] The bitter cold and deep snow of midwinter, the inhabitants thought, was the best protection they could have. However, in the early morning of 29 February 1703/4 a daring band of about fifty Canadians together with some 200 Abnakis and Caughnawagas, all under the command of Hertel de Rouville, scrambled over the unguarded palisade. Hastily spreading out to envelope the dwellings within, they battered down doors and overwhelmed the startled inhabitants, killing some and sparing others for captivity. Once in control, the raiders turned to looting and burning, so that the compact little farming village was left a shambles. Altogether, approximately forty of the settlers, including women and children, lay dead under a cold winter sky. Later, when the French and Indians began their withdrawal toward Canada, they forced 111 miserable captives to go with them, ill-prepared for such a difficult journey.[35]

New England's imperfect defense against this cruel form of warfare was the product of experience gained during and since the time of King Philip's War. To stem panic and prevent the abandonment of exposed settlements, the government designated certain communities as frontier towns; householders in such places were forbidden to withdraw under pain of losing title to their property.[36] Towns considered to be in peril often were reinforced with garrison troops impressed through the militia system. By the summer of 1704, Massachusetts was able to report that it was maintaining no less than 1,900 armed men along the frontiers, many of them regularly quartered in frontier towns.[37] The garrison house, privately owned and occupied but always available as a public refuge, remained the core of the defensive system. Its bulletproof walls and heavily shuttered windows provided a haven whenever hostile Indians were thought to be near.

Of course, the mere maintenance of public havens was not a satisfactory solution to the problem of continuing Indian raids; somehow the intruders had to be hunted down whenever possible. Gradually, the embittered English frontiersmen were becoming more adept at conducting these "search-and-destroy" missions; indeed, for some bold and enterprising spirits, the tracking down of hostile Indians developed into a sort of specialty. As an encouragement, the colonial governments again offered bounties for scalps. During Queen Anne's War, the government of Massachusetts, for example, would pay £10 per scalp to an impressed soldier in regular service, £20 to a volunteer, and £50 to a volunteer serving without pay (a real freebooter).[38] Scalp bounties emphasize the inhumanity of frontier warfare and in particular the callous attitude of more and more colonists toward all Indians. One of the great evils associated with the bounty system was the peculiar temptation it created for the scalp-hunters. If an Indian were taken alive, was it worth while to run the risk of trying to get him back to the authorities and claim a reward, when an amount almost as large could be obtained for his scalp? And why be overzealous in attempting to distinguish between enemy Indians and those who were neutral or perhaps even friendly? A scalp was a scalp when flung on the bounty table. It is not suggested that English colonists abandoned all scruples; but in the intense heat of frontier warfare there was ample scope for the upsurge of brutality.[39]

New England also attempted a somewhat more ambitious form of offensive warfare by once again enlisting the services of the old Indian-fighter of Plymouth Colony, Benjamin Church. This daunt-less veteran led a waterborne expedition north along the coast of Maine in the late spring of 1704, picking off occasional unlucky hostiles as he went. Part of the time Church and his men operated independently of the warships in the flotilla, skirting along the shore and advancing up the rivers in ships' boats. "Their custom," wrote an early New England historian, "was to rest in the day, and row in the night; and never to fire at an Indian if they could reach him with a hatchet, for fear of alarming them." [40] Arriving at last before the French settlement of Minas, on the eastern arm of the Bay of Fundy, the English seized control of the village and burned the greater part of it to the ground. Church sent off a message to the governor of New France, threatening that "if he did not prevent his French and Indians from committing such barbarities upon poor helpless women and children, as the people of Deerfield had suf-fered the last year, he would return with a thousand Indians and let them loose upon the frontiers of Canada to commit the like bar-barities there." [41] The expedition indulged in some additional ravaging and then returned to the Bay Colony without attacking the principal French settlement at Port Royal.

By this time the martial ardor of both New France and New England was beginning to flag. The respective mother countries had given little real assistance to their contending colonies, for this war like the last was essentially a European and oceanic conflict, with the North American theater of no more than tertiary concern to the major powers. Therefore, both New France and New England began to consider the possibility of establishing between themselves the kind of unofficial neutrality that already prevailed in New York. The quest began quite simply with an exchange of letters and then an exchange of emissaries by Governor Vaudreuil and Governor Dudley in an effort to effect an exchange of prisoners. Out of this emerged concrete proposals for a truce. Altogether, fifty-seven French and forty-three English captives gained freedom through these hopeful negotiations; but Vaudreuil's terms for a general ces-sation of hostilities in 1706 proved unacceptable to Dudley and the

Massachusetts General Court.[42]   Thus, after more than a year of relative quiet, the guns were readied once again for further combat.

From the perspective of the exposed frontier of New England, French-inspired and French-led Indian raids were the major menace, but New England fishing and mercantile interests were more immediately concerned with the problem of Port Royal, France's principal outpost in Acadia. As a base for armed vessels, Port Royal stood as a potential threat to the sea lanes between Massachusetts Bay, the Grand Banks, and England. In addition, Acadia was viewed as a sanctuary and recruiting ground for hostile Indians being used by the French in their campaign to expand their power as far south as the Kennebec. The reduction of Port Royal, then, was a logical first step toward the elimination of the Franco-Indian menace in northern New England. Furthermore, previous experience suggested that Port Royal was a target well within New England's own capability. At this time the French population in all Acadia numbered only about 1,500.[43] Yet despite these considerations, not all New Englanders looked forward with equanimity to the conquest of Acadia. There were some traders in Massachusetts, men of considerable prominence and influence, "topping men" as one observer called them, who were profiting by a surreptitious commerce with the French, a trade that would be destroyed by an English conquest.[44] Such men were satisfied to leave Acadia in its present condition, a relatively weak French outpost partially dependent on New England. Twice in 1707, a numerically strong New England expeditionary force descended upon Port Royal and went through the motions of besieging the settlement. The French governor, Daniel Auger de Subercase, offered determined resistance, and the English never pressed their advantage very hard. So Port Royal continued to stand as a symbol of French sovereignty in the maritime region north and east of Massachusetts.

The failure to conquer Port Royal in 1707 produced immediate political repercussions in Boston. Governor Dudley's unpopularity increased even more as his enemies, including Cotton Mather, sought to place the blame on him. They dredged up the history of the abortive peace negotiations with Governor Vaudreuil in 1705, charging that Dudley and certain of his cohorts, most notably the aggressive and somewhat devious trader Samuel Vetch, had used these negotiations as a screen for their illegal and traitorous commerce with the enemy. Dudley was called "our Criminal Gov-

ernour," unscrupulous as an executive and especially damnable for
making available to the hostile savages in Maine weapons later used
in the slaughter of English settlers.[45] His detractors charged, moreover, that when Church made his foray into Acadia he was under
orders from Dudley to preserve the fort at Port Royal, so that the
scheming governor might appropriate it for his own use and profit.
The more recent failure of 1707 simply lent strength to the accusation. "It was the Universal Opinion," sneered the accusers, "That if
the Army had only staid, and Plaid at *Coits* in their Camp (far
enough from the Fort) at *Port-royal,* the Fort would have been
within a few Days Surrendered to them." [46] There is little doubt
that Dudley did carry on some of his affairs in a way that is open to
question, but such admission does not concede the truth of the extreme charges made by his political enemies. That such charges were
either false or misleading was not obvious at the time, and Dudley
continued to bear the heavy burden of a difficult wartime governorship under the lash of his implacable opponents. Of significance here
is not the governor's guilt or innocence, but the persistence of bitter
division among New Englanders in their time of sore trial.

That New England had better look to its own defenses was demonstrated on 29 August 1708 when French and Indian raiders, after
a rendezvous on the shore of Lake Winnipesaukee in New Hampshire, made a predawn attack on the town of Haverhill, just 30 miles
north of Boston. It was Deerfield all over again. Later, from the
surviving inhabitants who still remained in the stricken town came
the usual pathetic petition to the general court, citing their heavy
losses and pleading for an abatement of taxes.[47] Attacks such as the
ones on Deerfield and Haverhill had an important side effect—they
further embittered relations between New England and New York.
The latter's neutrality and consequent immunity from attack was
interpreted in Massachusetts as cold, calculated self-interest, enabling New York to rake in its usual profits from the fur trade. It
was said that New York readily permitted the passage of war parties
on their way to attack the New England frontier, that the blood-
thirsty savages killed their human prey with weapons obtained from
New York, and even that "sometimes the plunder, made in the
county of Hampshire [in Massachusetts], became merchandize in
Albany." [48] If further evidence were needed to prove perfidy, argued
the embittered New Englanders, there was New York's official encouragement of Iroquois noninvolvement, when those fierce war-

riors might well be employed for the chastisement of New France and her Eastern Indian allies.

A strong infusion of English naval power could have produced rather readily the surrender of Port Royal or St. Augustine or both, thereby easing the two extreme flanks of the English mainland colonies. But such aid was not made available prior to 1711, as most of England's warships sent to American waters spent their time cruising in or near the Caribbean, an area of great economic importance as well as a cockpit of territorial rivalries and a focal point of vital sea lanes. Both England and France tried to maintain adequate numbers of fighting ships in West Indian waters, which in turn necessitated the maintenance of base facilities on one or more of the islands. Probably the most important single objective of naval operations in the Caribbean during this war was the capture or, conversely, the safeguarding of the vessels employed in carrying bullion from the Spanish colonies to Spain. The English believed, not unreasonably, that Spanish gold and silver were essential for sustaining the entire war effort of Spain and her allies. French and Spanish warships had the responsibility of protecting the treasure fleets and ensuring their safe arrival in Europe; English warships hoped to pounce upon the richly laden vessels and sever this important line of supply. Although enjoying some success, especially in the spring of 1708, the British never were able to cut off the flow entirely.[49]

The French were particularly successful in American waters in the use of privateers, which played havoc with Anglo-American commerce. Sometimes, as in the French attack on the Caribbean island of Nevis in 1706, privateers acted directly in support of regular military-naval operations, but mostly they cruised as lone raiders, pouncing on slower-sailing merchant ships or plunging into weakly defended bays and harbors to destroy fishing vessels and coasters. The island of Martinique in the French West Indies served as a major haven for these raiders of the sea. It was reported that one English colony, Massachusetts, had lost 140 of its ships by the middle of 1705, and English officials in the West Indies complained of "the privateers as thick as bees about and among these islands."[50] For England, there were three possible answers to the menace: well-guarded convoys; search-and-destroy missions by fast, well-armed warships; and crippling attacks upon the bases where privateers rested and refitted. All three methods required heavy commitments of naval resources at a time when England had little to spare for use in American waters.

So long as the Spaniards retained St. Augustine as a base, there was the additional danger of an amphibious attack upon nearby English coastal settlements, especially Charleston. During the summer of 1706, a small French naval force commanded by Jacques Lefebvre put into the harbor of St. Augustine and began preparations for just such an attack. A few small Spanish vessels and a modest number of Spanish soldiers were added to the force, and on 20 August the expedition set forth. En route, *La Brilliante*, carrying General Arbousset, the commander of the land forces, and some two hundred of his troops, was engaged by a Dutch warship and became separated from the convoy. Greatly weakened by this unforeseen loss, the rest of the flotilla arrived safely in the vicinity of Charleston on 27 August, whereupon the English watch on Sullivan's Island sent up a smoke signal to summon the militia, and the authorities in the port proclaimed a state of martial law. Here was the first major test of South Carolina's defenses, especially the militia; the men responded with alacrity. Lefebvre demanded a capitulation, a demand which the Carolinians rejected out of hand. Then, on the morning of 29 August, the French commander unleashed his landing force. The invading troops, organized in two main parties, managed to inflict some damage to outlying property, until one of the parties, feasting greedily on captured fowl, was surprised and defeated by a detachment of the militia. After this embarrassing setback, the intruders gave up their enterprise and sailed away toward St. Augustine.[51]

The greatest misstep was yet to be taken, however. Soon after Lefebvre's departure, Arbousset arrived in *La Brilliante* and put his men ashore at Seewee Bay, east of Charleston. The invaders, seemingly unconcerned about the absence of Lefebvre and his ships, advanced toward Charleston as though they intended to take the town by direct assault. But the English, made ten feet tall by their previous victory, fell upon the French with a will. While one group of the defenders met and completely defeated the French landing force, another boldly boarded the anchored *La Brilliante* and gained control of the vessel. No victory could be more complete. Since the first arrival of the enemy more than 30 of them had been killed by the Carolinians, and some 320 French, Spanish, and Indian prisoners were in English hands.[52] This affair very nearly freed South Carolina from danger of attack by sea, for neither the French nor the Spaniards had naval power to spare in further attempts of such dubious benefit, when more profitable opportunities still existed in the Caribbean.

The successful defense of Charleston in 1706 also contributed to a marked upsurge in the aggressive, expansionist spirit of the Carolinians, producing in turn a significant alteration in their frontier policy. No longer was it enough to intimidate and dominate groups of Indians hitherto aligned with the French. Interest now began to center upon a program to culminate in the actual conquest of the principal French and Spanish outposts.[53] Twice in 1707 a large force of Indians stiffened with a core of English troops besieged and attacked Pensacola, but failed to capture the prize. On the second occasion, Bienville himself came to the aid of his Spanish allies with a contingent of French and Indians. Most of the attackers had already withdrawn before this relief force arrived, but the French gesture helped strengthen a feeling of Franco-Spanish solidarity.[54]

At this time, the man who emerges as the most imaginative and ambitious of the Carolina imperialists was the provincial Indian agent, Thomas Nairne. A frontier planter, Nairne had captained one of the companies in the unsuccessful siege of St. Augustine in 1702 and had further proved his prowess in the subsequent ravaging of the Indian country. Now, in 1707, he put together a grand scheme for English military conquest in the Southeast, domination of all the important tribes as far west as the Mississippi River, and a corresponding expansion of English trade beyond the mountains. Nairne himself and others, aided by a liberal purse provided by the Carolina assembly, began to intrigue with the Choctaws and other tribes upon whom the French depended for support. Bienville moved quickly to counter this influence and was able to prevent Nairne from realizing his ambitions.[55] Later, in 1711, the British sent the Creeks to ravage the Choctaw country, and the following year the Alabamas appeared to be on the verge of moving against Mobile itself; but again Bienville demonstrated his skill in forest diplomacy and managed to forestall the potential disaster. The Carolina–Gulf–Mississippi frontier remained a vast arena of contending ambitions throughout the period of Queen Anne's War, with tribal affiliations the key to victory. No one had yet proved able to gain complete control of that key.

For many years New Englanders had been convinced that the one sure way to drive the French out of North America was to cut the very heart out of Canada—by seizing and holding Quebec. But ever since the embarrassing failure of Phips in 1690, they had been reluctant to repeat such an attempt without material assistance from England in the form of warships and possibly regular troops as well. Such dependence was rather distasteful to the independent-minded colonial leaders, but hard experience offered no alternative. This, then, explains why New England did not proceed against Quebec in the early years of Queen Anne's War—there was no guarantee of English backing.

One prominent colonist who now became convinced that a concerted attack on Canada was a logical next move was the controversial merchant Samuel Vetch. His previous activity as a far-ranging trader had brought him not only an unwelcome public pelting for his alleged dealings with the enemy, but also a fair knowledge of conditions in New France. Once convinced, Vetch was a man to act. In England he used his personal contacts to open official doors, and in due time was able to lay before the Board of Trade a clearly expressed proposal. How absurd it is, argued Vetch, that a wealthy and powerful land such as Britain's American colonies

> shou'd so tamely allow such a troublesome neighbour as the French, not only to sitt down peaceably beside them, but with a handfull of people vastly dispersed to possess a country of above 4,000 miles extent, quite encompassing and hemming in betwixt them and the sea, all the Brittish Empire upon the said Continent of America, by which they have already so mightily obstructed the Brittish trade, all America over, and must in time totally ruin the same, unless seasonably prevented. . . .[56]

Surely the time had come to take decisive counteraction. What Vetch had in mind was a campaign rather closely resembling that of 1690, with an army advancing from Albany to Montreal through the Champlain Valley and a powerful amphibious force sailing up the St. Lawrence River to seize Quebec. The essential difference was that this time competent, professional leadership and adequate resources would be provided.

After careful consideration, the board recommended the proposal to the secretary of state and the Privy Council in December 1708, and two months later Vetch had the great satisfaction of seeing his plan translated into positive orders from the crown. For the first time, regular British forces in great strength would be sent across the Atlantic to participate alongside American colonials and Indians in a concerted attempt to smash down the French menace. Vetch and his fellow colonists had reason to interpret this new development as Britain's awakening, at last, to the great importance of the American theater of war.[57] Colonel Francis Nicholson, former governor of Virginia and an ardent advocate of united colonial action against the French, offered to help in the preparations.

It was near the end of April 1709 when H.M.S. *Dragon,* bringing Vetch, Nicholson, and the plans for the "Glorious Enterprise," dropped anchor in Boston Harbor.[58] Once ashore, Vetch plunged into the complex task of rallying the northern colonies and getting them started on the preparations necessary for a major military operation. As this was an official project endorsed by the crown, New York now had little choice but to abandon its neutral stance and cooperate alongside New England. The Albany force was to include the four independent companies of regulars already stationed in New York, plus contingents of colonial troops from Connecticut, New York, New Jersey, and Pennsylvania, some 1,500 men in all. Hopefully, this intercolonial army would enjoy the invaluable assistance of the Iroquois, who were asked to provide a sizable contingent of warriors. The other New England colonies were to raise a force of 1,200 men. Then, when the expected British fleet with an army of 4,000 regulars arrived at Boston, the New England force would embark and approach Quebec from the sea, while the Albany force advanced down the Champlain Valley to complete the conquest. The operation as a whole was to be under the command of a senior British officer arriving with the fleet; but Nicholson, despite his rather limited military experience, agreed to assume command of the Albany force.

The colonies undertook the project with notable enthusiasm, raising their contingents and accumulating the necessary stocks of supplies. Indian scouts were hired to learn as much as possible about the state of the French defenses in the vicinity of Montreal and Quebec, supplementing the valuable knowledge already possessed by Vetch from his own previous observations.[59] In June 1709 an advance detachment of troops secured the southern end of the

Champlain Valley, and the hard labor necessary to maintain an effective base in that area began. Roads, storehouses, and fortifications were built during the summer. The army at Albany grew as more troops from Connecticut joined those of New York. Soon the total number exceeded the contemplated 1,500. In addition, Vetch noted with satisfaction, four of the Iroquois tribes gave up their neutrality as New York had done and contributed several hundred warriors to bolster Nicholson's force.[60]

At Boston, too, an army larger than originally anticipated was assembling to go forth against "the Idolaters of *Canada*," as Cotton Mather labeled the enemy.[61] Here in this former stronghold of Puritanism, the impending campaign was again taking on the coloring of a crusade. Troops were being drilled, ships prepared in the harbor. But how long could such enthusiasm be sustained? July passed slowly without any glimpse of a British fleet on the horizon. By August men were beginning to wonder why the Royal Navy had not yet appeared. On 29 August more than fifty companies assembled for training at Boston; and still no sign of the British. "We had our army in pay all this month nothing done by them only eat and drink and Run the Country in debt," scribbled one disgusted colonist in his diary.[62]

Above Albany, Nicholson's men were struggling to build and maintain a pipeline of transport and supply that was continually breaking down under the difficulties imposed by terrain and distance. The bulk of the Albany force was now encamped at Wood Creek, south of Lake Champlain, at the far end of a string of wilderness posts and routes stretching back to Albany. Keeping this line of communication and supply open and functioning week after week was more than the army could well manage. Somebody reckoned that it cost as much to transport the army's supplies from Albany to the advance base as the supplies themselves originally cost. To make matters worse, it was now the "sikly time of the year," and disease was becoming a ravager among the troops.[63] Both at Boston and Wood Creek, the anxious leaders still waited for the arrival of the fleet from England and the expected signal to start the operation. By mid-September, Vetch and Nicholson realized that the game was up. The approach of the Canadian autumn with its freezing weather made the operation against the French settlements on the St. Lawrence impracticable. Nevertheless,

the forces were held in a state of readiness pending further word
from England, for there still remained the possibility of using
them against a closer, easier objective.

It was not until October that Boston received official notification
from England that the entire operation had been canceled. The
probable reason for the cancellation is not difficult to discover.
Already the warring powers were exploring the prospects for a
settlement of their quarrel, and it seemed likely that one of the
requirements would be the mutual restoration of captured territory
in America. This prospect naturally caused the authorities in
London to take a second look at such an expensive, dangerous, and
possibly futile endeavor as the projected invasion of Canada. Why
go to all the expense and trouble only to hand the country back
to France at the peace table? [64] News of the cancellation hit Boston
like a sudden, soaking flood of ice water; work, worry, and expense
were all for nothing. What was especially hard to accept was the
fact that the British government had reached the decision as early
as the first of July, but with incredible carelessness had neglected
to speed the news on to America. Now nothing further could be
done; all that remained was to disband the colonial armies. At
Wood Creek and all the way down to Albany, the disgusted soldiers
destroyed the structures they had built and abandoned their corridor
to the wolves. So ended a hopeful enterprise, at least for the present.
Significantly, Americans began asking themselves why and how
the mother country could be so careless of their aspirations and
sacrifices. Even the hopes for peace proved illusory.

The following year Britain tried again, this time actually sending
to Boston a squadron of six warships, including three of fifty guns
each, and a regiment of marines. Other regiments were to follow,
but the usual delays intervened, and it was decided to limit the
campaign to an easier target—the old French thorn-in-the-side,
Port Royal. In terms of size and strength, Port Royal was no Quebec.
Easily accessible from the Bay of Fundy, it was situated on·relatively
level terrain which presented no serious obstacles to an attacking
army. Governor Subercase, whom Vetch considered a "very brave
and experienced officer," had available for the defense of Port
Royal an undependable population, including less than 300 soldiers
and militiamen.[65] Against this pathetic little garrison, the British
sent in September a force consisting of the six warships, numerous
transports, and an army of nearly 3,500, mostly New England

militiamen from Massachusetts, Connecticut, New Hampshire, and Rhode Island, reinforced with the regiment of marines. Commanding this determined army was Colonel Nicholson, assisted by Vetch.[66]

On 24 September the fleet arrived off Port Royal, and the next day began disembarking the troops. So overwhelming was the British force that Subercase, watching from his ill-equipped and decaying fort as the invaders prepared their siege lines during the next few days, readily saw the futility of prolonged resistance. Accordingly, when British batteries opened on him at close range, he hastened to sign the proffered articles of capitulation.[67] The jubilant Nicholson, now partially compensated for the frustration and disappointment of the preceding year, gave a new name to the old French settlement—Annapolis Royal, in honor of the queen. Acadia became a British province under the governorship of the fast-rising imperialist Samuel Vetch.

In other ways, too, 1710 was a significant year for the war effort in America. Queen Anne's concern for the needs and aspirations of her American subjects was appreciably sharpened when four New York Indians, escorted by Peter Schuyler, paid a visit to the Court of St. James. These dignified emissaries assured the queen that it was not only the British colonists who longed to see French Canada removed forever as a threat over their heads—the Five Nations as well would welcome such a happy solution to their problems.[68] Equally effective in stimulating more British aid for the colonies was the change of ministries that occurred in 1710, with Tories replacing Whigs in the seats of power. Whig policy had been characterized by a marked reluctance to divert military and naval forces from the European theater, but now Henry St. John, the new secretary of state for the Northern Department, apparently saw great potential advantages both to England and to himself in the reduction of Canada, and gave his endorsement to a renewal of the "Glorious Enterprise." An official document issued over the queen's name early in 1711 provided justification. The French, it was argued, had long demonstrated their belligerent, aggressive intentions in America and, as a result,

> enjoy almost the whole trade of furrs and peltry . . . they have also the trade of whale oyle and finns,—and the cod fishery which is the great nursery of their seamen, and is so necessary and advantageous to them in all their commerce . . . they encircle all our plantations on the

continent of North America, by which (if not prevented) they may in
time dispossess us thereof, and annex the great Empire of North
America to the Crown of France . . . they will also by their plantations
on the River Mississippi, be able to possess themselves of severall of
the rich mines of Mexico, and of the trade of great part of that
country.[69]

Exaggerated as these statements were, they reflected clearly the
uneasy mind of Anglo-American imperialism at the time, and provided a rationale upon which to rest the economic ambitions of the
colonial imperialists. To destroy Canada seemed a clear and necessary imperative, "a consummation devoutly to be wished."

So the fateful decision was made, and a powerful fleet with
a strong force of regulars was detailed for the job. Overall command
was given to Rear Admiral Sir Hovenden Walker, whose naval
experience included combat command in the previous war and a
tour of duty in the West Indies early in the present conflict.
Walker was an officer of rather modest qualities, which unfortunately did not include determination, tenacity, and bulldog
courage; but he was considered suitable for the task of leading an
overwhelming force against the defenses of Quebec. Under Walker,
as commander of the land forces, was Brigadier General John Hill,
who also had the advantage of combat experience, and carried a
wound from the siege of Mons. More important in his selection,
perhaps, was the fact that he was the brother of Abigail Masham,
the queen's close friend. For carrying out this important mission,
Hill was given an army consisting of seven regiments and a battalion of marines, with a total strength of more than 5,000 men.
The northern colonies were expected to make heavy contributions
of additional men, supplies, and ships for the expedition.

Francis Nicholson, who again was designated to command the
western arm of the now-traditional pincer, was sent from England
in advance of the fleet to notify the colonies and get them started
on the necessary preparations. It was unfortunate that Nicholson
was delayed by adverse weather, for there was much to be accomplished before the operation could actually begin. Not until 8 June
did Nicholson arrive at Boston. Late that afternoon he strode into
the council chamber and revealed the royal plan to Governor
Dudley and his council.[70] By this time Walker and the main body
of the fleet were already on their way across the Atlantic; no time
must be lost. A general embargo was clamped upon the seaports

to prevent news of the undertaking from reaching the French. On 21 June a meeting of leaders from the various participating colonies convened at New London for the purpose of planning and concerting their preparations.[71] As in 1709, the northern colonies, still feeling the sting of Franco-Indian raids and encouraged by the prospect of substantial military aid from England, showed a spirit of mutual cooperation all too rare in their previous experience. Apparently the novelty of ample British aid in a popular colonial cause was a powerful stimulant whose possible after-effects had not yet been contemplated in the colonies. With remarkable zeal the various governments began raising their quotas of men and gathering supplies for the expeditions. Even Quaker Pennsylvania, which in 1709 had refused to make any contribution to the operation against Canada, now voted £2,000 for the enterprise, although still declining to send any troops.[72]

The fleet of warships and transports bearing Walker, Hill, and the British army appeared off Boston and processed into the harbor during the last week of June. Nantasket Road, 10 miles below the town, was adopted as the fleet anchorage, while the army established a large camp on Noddles Island where the troops could be exercised and otherwise prepared for the coming campaign. Immediately upon arrival, Walker set about discovering what kind of support he was going to get from the colonists, for this was a matter of vital concern. To be successful he needed a large force of colonial troops, Indian auxiliaries (especially for the Albany wing), additional supplies of various kinds, more seamen to man the ships, and experienced pilots to lead the expedition up the St. Lawrence River to Quebec. What he soon began to find was that the original spirit of cooperation and obedience concealed a strong residual reluctance on the part of the people, in Boston if not all of New England, to make any great sacrifices even in such a popular cause as the reduction of Canada. Colonial cooperation proved qualified and partial at best. Day after day through the month of July, Walker had to wrestle with administrative problems that seemed peculiarly aggravated by the incomprehensible stubbornness of the New Englanders.

The matter of food and other supplies for the expedition was very much on the admiral's mind, for he anticipated the possibility of becoming winterbound at frozen Quebec, in which case he must have a large reserve stock if his men were not to starve. To his disgust he found the New Englanders unwilling or, as they insisted, unable to meet his demands. Producers of bread and other foodstuffs seemed strangely reluctant to commit themselves to Walker's requisitions, while the merchants of Boston were equally hesitant. Soon, too, it became apparent that the local community was taking advantage of the army's need by raising the level of prices. More specifically, the merchants tried to establish a rate of exchange between English currency and colonial currency that would be to their advantage. All this was strongly resented, of course, by the British commanders. At one point Walker went so far as to fire at Governor Dudley and his council a threat to remove his entire command elsewhere; it was an idle blast and nothing more, for the season was advancing rapidly and there was need to get on with the campaign.[73] Obviously the extraordinary demand for supplies in support of the thousands of men, English and American, now encamped around Boston was creating a highly inflationary condition, with consequent friction and tension both between the colony and its visitors and among the colonists themselves. As for the merchants, they were simply following their own highly developed instincts in seeking to profit from the abnormal situation.

New England pilots who had had some experience navigating the difficult waters of the St. Lawrence River were hard to find, and those who were known to qualify preferred not to serve. No doubt they had honest reservations about their ability to take a large warship through the unknown currents and thick fogs for which the lower part of the great river was notorious; this reluctance on the part of New England's ablest mariners only served to enlarge Walker's own apprehensive fear of the river. "The Bay, and River of St. *Lawrence*," he later wrote, "from the frequency of Fogs, unfathomable Depths of the Water, Rapidity and Uncertainty of the Currents, were enough to elude and baffle the skill, and confound the Care, Diligence, and Watchfulness of the most expert and able Pilots. . . ."[74] In the upshot, Walker was forced to rely upon mariners serving under compulsion, men who had loudly professed their own inadequacy. Moreover, there is good reason to believe that Walker had partly convinced himself, even while still at Boston, that he would not be able to bring his fleet safely into position before the walls of Quebec.

Such doubts were infectious. Soon after Walker's ships arrived at Boston some of his sea-weary men, sailors and soldiers alike, began to slip away from their commands and disappear into the narrow alleys of Boston or the fields and woods of the surrounding countryside. Colonial seamen, too, impressed into service on board the vessels of the expedition, took every opportunity to escape. These men could laugh off the ordinary hazards of seafaring in the merchant marine, but considered an involuntary voyage up the treacherous St. Lawrence in the teeth of French resistance no laughing matter. Sympathetic relatives and friends ashore made it easy for them to disappear and stay out of sight until after the fleet had gone. Walker, confronted with this epidemic of desertion, placed much of the blame on the colonial population, and complained bitterly to the local authorities. The impact of the problem may be gauged not only by the admiral's vociferous complaints, but also by the strong terms of a special order issued by the Massachusetts legislature in response: Constables and other civil officers in pursuit of deserters were authorized to commandeer the assistance of other persons and, under certain circumstances, "with Force to enter any Houses, or Places of which the said Officer shall have Information, or just Suspicion that any such Deserter or Deserters are entertained and concealed, . . ." [75] Colonists harboring deserters were made liable to a fine of £50 or imprisonment for twelve months. This stern enactment was published by beat of drum in various towns of the colony toward the end of July, but by this time most of the damage had been done. One of Walker's officers reckoned that more than 250 men deserted while the forces were at Boston.[76]

In the eyes of British military authorities striving to maintain discipline and prepare for a major campaign while coping with such problems, the Bostonians appeared to be ill-natured and sour, stubborn and disobedient. Angry British complaints coupled with stringent countermeasures on the part of the colony government only served to increase the general public's disdain for the military. The result was a form of Anglo-American tension in Boston between civilians and British regulars that boded ill for the future. Indeed, the sun of History in its relentless march across the heavens of time was beginning to throw a shadow toward Lexington Green.

Governor Dudley's task, in these circumstances, was not an easy one. His people, whose regard he valued, were suspicious of royal officers and fearful of royal power. At this very time their sentiments may have been honed to a new sharpness by the presence in Boston of a French emissary, the Sieur de la Ronde Denis, whose purpose ostensibly was to negotiate for the release of prisoners. In actuality, he was a spy and *agent provocateur,* with instructions to observe military preparations. Beyond that, insofar as possible, he was to sow among the Bostonians the idea that once Britain had conquered Canada she then would proceed to impose a royal, authoritarian form of government on all the continental colonies.[77] If La Ronde Denis was successful in spreading this idea among the local leaders, it would account for some of the uncooperative behavior that was such a baffling, infuriating puzzle to Walker and his military colleagues. Yet on the other hand, most New Englanders lived in dread of the French and Indians, and would like nothing better than to see them crushed in their nest by the heel of the British Army. Apparently, the Bostonians were being torn by two opposing considerations of self-interest, which would explain their ambivalent behavior toward the expedition. At the same time, there can be no doubt that some of Walker's trouble stemmed from nothing more than a rising tide of self-assertive Yankee individualism, reluctance to make sacrifices for a distant crown, and plain, old-fashioned greed for gain. It all added up to a most unhappy summer for the queen's officers.

In spite of many difficulties, however, the plans and preparations for the attack on Canada did move forward during the month of July. At Albany, the western wing was beginning to assemble under Nicholson's command, with contingents from Connecticut, various parts of New York, and New Jersey making their way toward the staging area on the upper Hudson. The efforts of Governor Robert Hunter and Peter Schuyler of New York produced encouraging signs of active support from the Five Nations and other friendly tribes, who were beginning to sense an English victory. Iroquois sachems, anxious to know whether this time the British really were in earnest in their designs against Canada, journeyed all the way to Boston as honored guests to view the impressive fleet and army assembled there. Walker and Hill, having already been apprised of the importance of Iroquois support, went to great lengths to create in the minds of these Indian leaders an awareness of British determination and might. They "shew'd them our troups and fleet, and did all they could to imprint in them great ideas of the Queen and make them long to be under her government and to be fellow subjects with those men that they saw command armys and fleets so vastly superior to any ideas they ever had before of either," wrote one of the British officers with obvious satisfaction.[78] One easily imagines the stolid sachems resplendent in their wilderness regalia approaching the long, ordered ranks of redcoats, the sudden hoarse bellow of command from the officer in charge, the measured *slap-slap* of the "Present Arms." Walker himself recorded that, on this occasion,

> I entertained them . . . with Wine, Musick, and the Seamen dancing, and they appeared very much delighted therewith . . . one of them in the Name of the five Nations, made a long Speech to me . . . to this Effect; *viz.* "That they had long expected what they now saw, and were much rejoiced that the Queen had taken such care of them, of which they had almost despaired; that at this Time they would exert themselves in a most extraordinary manner, and hoped that the *French* in *America*, would now be reduced." [79]

Yes, it was an impressive show that the British put on, and the Indians assured their hosts that Iroquois warriors in large numbers would be ready to serve with Nicholson's army. This helped to counterbalance the bad news that had come from Governor Vetch in Acadia, where the hostile Indians had ambushed part of the garrison and even laid siege to Annapolis Royal itself before again retreating into the wilderness.[80] There could be no doubt of a strong continuing French influence in that area, despite the British occupation. But if Walker could only succeed against Canada, the source of such trouble would be dried up, and Britain's future in America would be assured.

Of course the French knew that a major operation against them was being prepared, and by mid-July they had clear indications that Canada itself was the target.[81] Governor Vaudreuil had cause to be uneasy. The total field strength available to him consisted of only about 2,300 men, and although the Hurons and some of the western tribes might provide valuable assistance, this was hardly adequate for repelling the thousands of British coming against him.[82] When Walker sailed from Nantasket Road on the morning of 30 July, he commanded an armada consisting of nine warships and two bomb ketches, together with some sixty transports and auxiliary vessels carrying 12,000 soldiers, sailors, and Indians. The landing force alone consisted of nearly 7,500 troops. To these impressive numbers must be added the more than 2,000 soldiers and Indians under Nicholson's command at Albany who were preparing to drive on Montreal by way of the Champlain Valley.[83] Now there was every reason to believe that Quebec, and with it all Canada, was doomed.

Walker himself, however, enjoyed no such feeling of confidence. It is bad enough when a commander is overconfident, but his under-confidence at the outset of an operation is far worse. The com-mander's own doubts inevitably filter down through his officers to the lowest ranks, and the contagion eats away both courage and morale. A soldier facing combat needs to believe that he is partici-pating in a well-conceived, well-prepared operation with sufficient strength to afford at least a fighting chance for success. That sense of quiet self-assurance was lacking in Walker. Although he was carrying with him supplies of food sufficient for about three months, he dreaded a prolonged operation that would lead him on into the season of freezing weather when his army might face starvation. "I must confess, the melancholy Contemplation of this . . . strikes me with Horrour," confessed Walker, unhappily probing his turgid imagination. "For how dismal must it have been to have beheld the Seas and Earth lock'd up by Adamantine Frosts, and swoln with high Mountains of Snow, in a barren and uncultivated Region, great numbers of brave Men famishing with Hunger, and drawing Lots who should die first to feed the rest, without the least appear-ance of Relief?" [84] Such was the specter-haunted mood of this com-mander on his way to challenge Vaudreuil and French Canada.

The fleet made its way past Cape Breton Island and into the Gulf of St. Lawrence before the bulk of Colonel Nicholson's army of colonial militia and Indians, 2,300 strong, was well on its way from Albany to Lake Champlain. Nicholson's men soon found them-selves slapping at insects and sweating in the August sun as they applied themselves to the hard labor of building roads, poling boats, manhandling bulky supplies along wilderness trails, and setting up fortified bases. Much excitement was generated when some of the Indians with the army brought in an old leather moccasin they had found under a bush. It contained a note specifying the size, composition, and assignment of several parties of French and Indians, some 180 men in all, presumably operating in the area.[85] Possibly it was a deliberate "plant," designed to entice the British into an ambush. If so, it failed of its purpose. By the middle of September, Nicholson was firmly established at

Wood Creek and preparing for the push down the Champlain Valley to Montreal.

It was on the twenty-first of August that Walker's fleet entered the St. Lawrence River, and the vague fears with which Walker so long had tormented himself now began to appear as grim realities. The weather was foggy; no land at all could be seen. Gingerly, the swarm of vessels under sail groped their way upriver together, trying to maintain contact yet avoid collision. Soon the notorious currents were beginning to nudge the ships off their intended course, making it difficult for them to keep close track of their position. By the evening of 23 August, after hours of difficult progress, Walker was well past Anticosti Island, in a stretch of the river 70 miles wide from shore to shore. A hundred miles upriver from the island the north shore of the St. Lawrence bends sharply southward as the river abruptly narrows from 70 to about 30 miles in width. With a fresh wind blowing in from the Atlantic and the whole of the lower river enshrouded in fog, Walker's fleet now was advancing steadily toward that rugged, inhospitable "west" shore.[86] Late on the evening of the twenty-third, some time after Walker had retired to his cabin, lookouts on the admiral's ship gave a cry of "Land!" and then, "Breakers!" Aroused by the sudden commotion, Walker hastily donned his robe, stuffed his feet into a pair of slippers, and went on deck. There he encountered a scene of consternation. The fleet was about to pile up on the rocks of the north shore! Desperate shifting of sails and rapid maneuvering saved most of the ships, but seven of the loaded transports and one small supply vessel foundered near the rocky Île aux Oeufs. In all, nearly 900 persons—740 of the British troops (including 35 female camp followers) and about 150 sailors—perished in those cold waters. Their bodies were strewn along the beach like sodden driftwood. Of the hundreds of colonial troops in the expedition, none were lost.[87]

When the fleet had been regathered, Walker found that he still had more than 11,000 men, or better than 90 percent of the original force under his command; but Quebec still lay many miles farther up the narrowing river and summer was approaching its end. Badly shaken by the disaster and recalling all his previous doubts and fears, the admiral now summoned a council of war which, predictably, was persuaded that the risk of continuing

on up the St. Lawrence that late in the year, with dwindling
supplies, was too great. A decision then was made to turn the fleet's
strength against the French post at Placentia, Newfoundland, but
a short time later even this secondary mission was dropped. Accordingly, the colonial troops were sent off toward home in their transports, while Walker and Hill took the remainder of the armada
back across the Atlantic to explain their monumental failure.[88]

American historians ever since have been inclined to heap blame
upon a timid and vacillating British admiral. In hindsight, it is
easy to compare Walker's powerful armada and landing force with
the known weakness of the defenses at Quebec and conclude that
if only the fleet had continued upriver, Canada would have fallen
to the British in 1711. Possibly this assessment is correct. Although
Walker cited the lateness of the season and the inadequacy of his
supplies, the terrible accident at Île aux Oeufs need not have
delayed his advance more than a few days at the most. By making
judicious use of the pilots available, Walker should have been able
to continue a cautious approach to Quebec, while Nicholson
pushed on past Lake Champlain to Montreal. Together the two
armies had more than enough strength to overwhelm the defenders
of New France before the cold winds became severe and ice began
to form in the river. A bold and determined commander would
have kept his eye steadily on his goal and pushed on to victory—or
catastrophe.

It was the distinct possibility of catastrophe that made Walker
decide to turn back from a mission in which he had largely lost
faith even before the tragic night of 23 August. To the badly
shaken admiral it seemed clear that too many factors were against
him—the unfortunate delays both in England and New England
that caused him to come so late to the St. Lawrence, the dubious
quality of his pilots in a strange river famed for its treachery, the
advantages of terrain possessed by the French at Quebec as shown
by the experience of Sir William Phips in the previous war, and
the fearsome prospect of becoming winterbound in Canada without
sufficient food. In their appraisement of the situation, the admiral
and his officers weighed the factors as they understood them. They
did not minimize the serious consequences of giving up the great
venture; they simply concluded that the risk was far too great for
the possible gain. Therefore they decided to withdraw.[89]

And what of Nicholson and his army, soon to be poised in the

Cut a piece of brown wrapping paper into a right-angle triangle. Snip off the small end.

Place a wooden dowel (*former*) 6 inches long, as round as a musket ball and hollowed at one end to receive the musket ball, along the edge of the paper. Insert the ball and begin to roll.

Roll the paper around the *former*. With the musket ball, press a corner of the paper over the end of the *former* and, while holding the ball firmly in place atop the paper, continue wrapping the *former*. Wrap a single loop of twine below the ball. Thrust a finger in the paper roll until it touches the ball. Pull the loop of string tight and, with the *former*, make a neck of paper below the ball so that it may be tied to hold the ball in place.

The result is a paper tube.

Pour black powder in the top.

Twist the end of the paper tightly. The cartridge is now complete and may be placed in the cartridge box to be carried into battle.

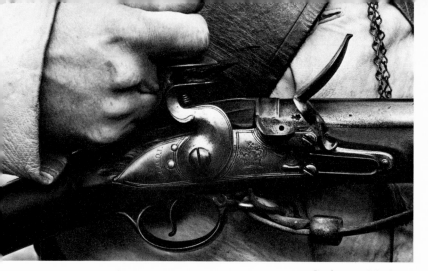

Cock your Muskets!

Handle your Chargers!

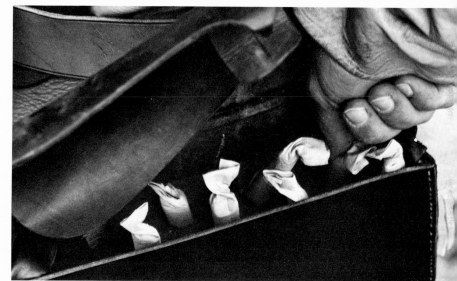

Loading and firing the musket. *From* America's First Army, *by Burke Davis (The Colonial Williamsburg Foundation)*

Open them with your Teeth!

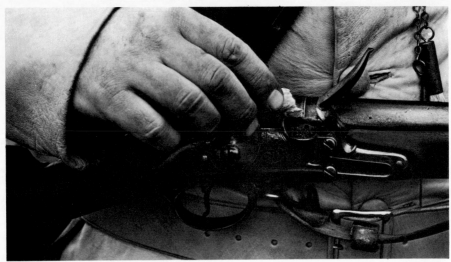

Prime!

Charge with Powder!

Fire!

Dutch Soldier, 17th century. *Courtesy of Howard P. Brokaw*

The burning of Jamestown, 1676, by Howard Pyle. *Courtesy of Howard P. Brokaw*

Sir William Phips, Governor of Massachusetts, by Harry Sutton. *The Commonwealth of Massachusetts, courtesy of Secretary of State John F. X. Davoren*

Samuel Vetch, ca. 1751. *Courtesy of the Museum of the City of New York*

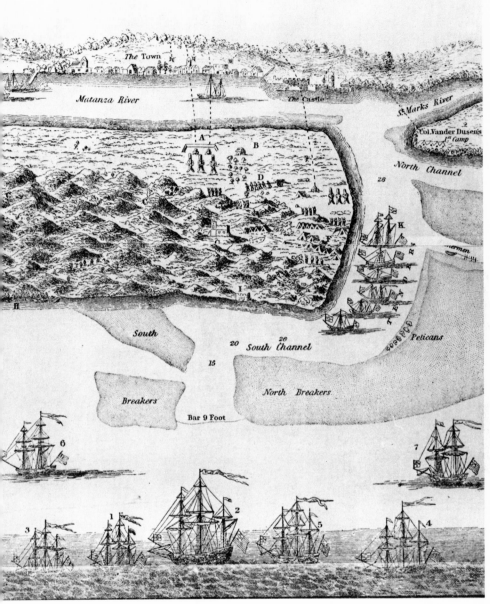

A view of the town and castle of St. Augustine and the English camp before it, 20 June 1740, by Thomas Silver.

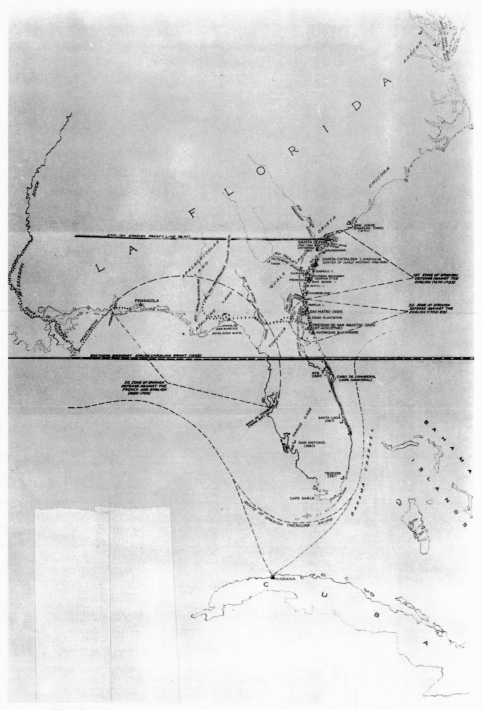

The frontier of Spanish Florida, 1565-1763. *Courtesy of the Carnegie Institution*

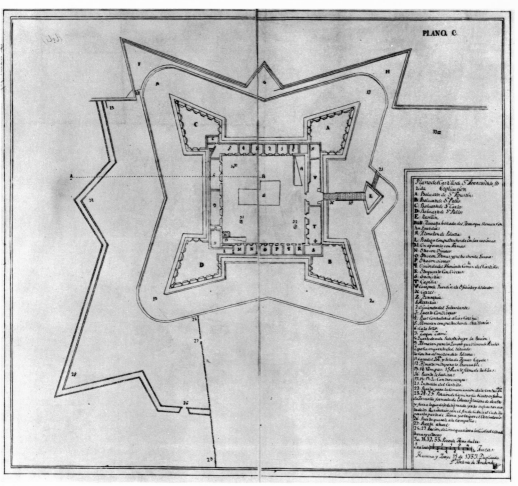

Plan of the Castillo de San Marcos, St. Augustine. *Collections of the Geography and Map Division, Library of Congress*

Sir William Pepperrell, the Victor of Louisbourg, by John Smibert.
Courtesy of the Essex Institute, Salem, Massachusetts

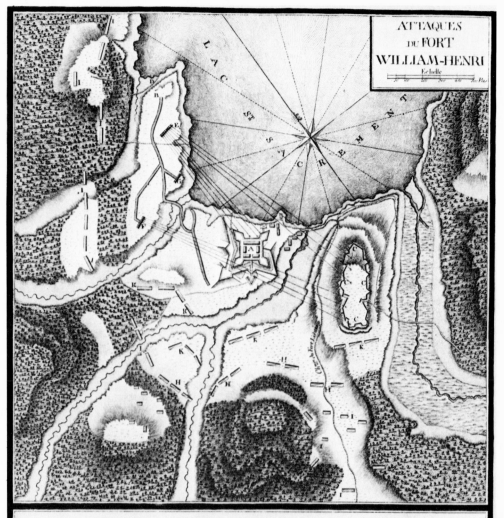

Plan of Montcalm's attack on Fort William Henry, August 1757. *Courtesy of The Public Archives of Canada, Manoir Richelieu Collection*

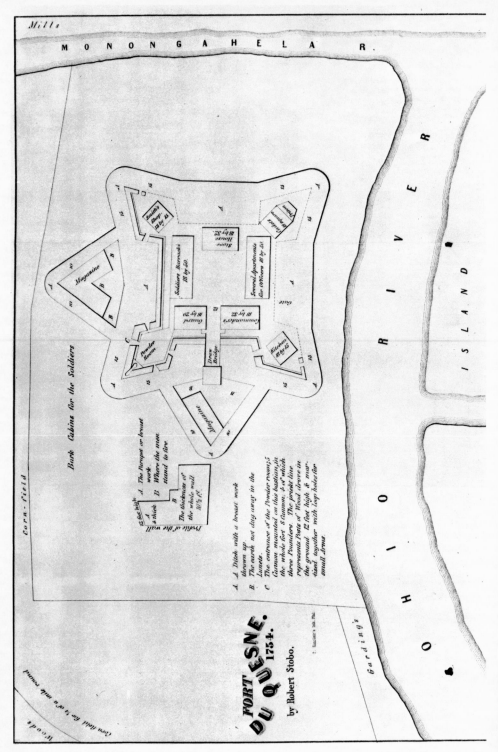

Robert Stobo's plan of Fort Duquesne, 1754. *Courtesy of The Public Archives of Canada*

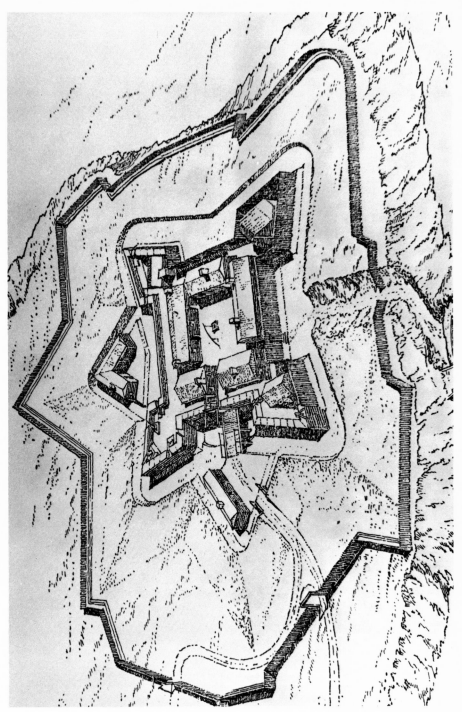

Conjectural view of Fort Duquesne. *Courtesy of the Historical Society of Western Pennsylvania*

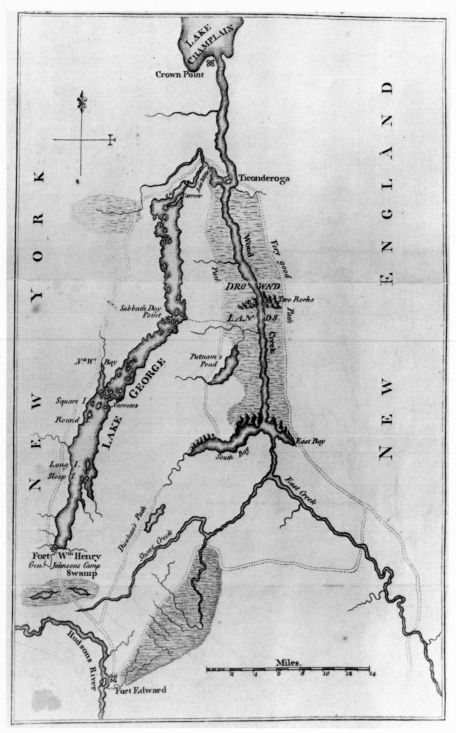

Map of the area from Fort Edward to Crown Point. *Courtesy of the Massachusetts Historical Society*

Chippewa Warrior, 1763, by Dirk Gringhuis. *Courtesy of the Mackinac Island State Park Commission*

British Regular (Royal Americans), 1763, by Dirk Gringhuis. *Courtesy of the Mackinac Island State Park Commission*

Canadian Militiaman, 1752, by Dirk Gringhuis. *Courtesy of the Mackinac Island State Park Commission*

Troupes de la Marine, 1756, by Dirk Gringhuis. *Courtesy of the Mackinac Island State Park Commission*

One of Rogers' Rangers on the attack, by C. E. Hawley. *Courtesy of Fort Ticonderoga Museum and the Holiday Inn of Lake George, New York*

English Soldier, by Howard Pyle *Courtesy of Howard P. Brokaw*

vicinity of Wood Creek, ready for the advance down the Champlain Valley? News, even of disaster, traveled slowly. The troops in the western wilderness toiled on until about the nineteenth of September when an express brought to Nicholson intelligence of the disaster in the St. Lawrence and Walker's decision to terminate the operation. For Nicholson, who had taken one such blow in 1709, this was the last straw. Flying into a rage, he tore his wig from his head, hurled it to the ground, and stamped on it.[90] Later, after regaining his composure, Nicholson set about preparing to liquidate his own portion of the grand enterprise. By the first week in October the army was back at Albany. There the regiments were mustered for a last general review, after which a happy afternoon was spent in field sports with the men competing for monetary prizes offered by their disappointed commander.[91] Then the army was disbanded.

Nicholson's reaction to the great failure was scarcely more volatile than that of the northern colonies as a whole. Victory had seemed so sure when the fleet sailed away from Boston and the western army tramped toward the lakes. Now Quebec, the vital spring of French dominion in North America, was again secure, and the northern frontier remained gloomily under the dread threat. At the same time, Canadian reaction was predictable—a transport of relief and joy. It was 1690 all over again. In that earlier period of rejoicing after Phips' withdrawal, the pious French at Quebec had named their waterfront church "Notre Dame de la Victoire" and had listened to a sermon of thanksgiving preached by the Reverend Joseph Séré de Colombière. Now in 1711 the same church was renamed "Notre Dame des Victoires," and the same priest was able to preach the same sermon once more.[92]

Among the English, the shock of failure was quickly succeeded by a wave of recriminations. The colonists naturally heaped most of the blame on Admiral Walker, a verdict warmly endorsed by Nicholson and Governor Dudley.[93] In England there was some tendency to make political capital of the affair, to the disadvantage of the Tory ministry, accompanied by the charge that New England had not given wholehearted support to the expedition. Walker's complaints of profiteering and the encouragement of desertion in Boston now fell into fertile soil, discrediting the colonies and to some extent obscuring their actual sacrifices in the aborted campaign. Some men, eager to find the worst in the situation, went so far as to suggest darkly that the operation against Canada had been sabotaged deliberately by "a few smuggling Traders" in order to preserve their illegal traffic with the enemy. Jeremiah Dummer, the Massachusetts agent in London, took considerable pains to answer these charges, while again urging that Canada be conquered and retained.[94] As for the Five Nations, who once again had bet their future security on British determination and might, their sentiments after the fiasco of 1711 may readily be imagined. It is sufficient to note that in the spring of 1712 the Iroquois resurrected their treaty of neutrality, with the full approval of Governor Vaudreuil.[95]

In the South, too, there was bad news for the British. The Tuscarora Indians of North Carolina, a tribe distantly related to the Iroquois of New York, had been growing increasingly impatient in their relations with the whites. Not without reason they grumbled over the highhanded tactics of the Carolina traders, who operated in the Indian country without adequate governmental supervision. And worse yet, these same traders sometimes dealt in human commodities, sending a stream of anguished Tuscaroras into slavery. As always, too, there was the problem of territorial expansion, with the British relentlessly pushing their settlements ever deeper into the forested lands of the interior. When in 1711 prospectors began surveying land for a group of Swiss colonists who planned to settle at what was to become New Bern, the Tuscaroras retaliated with a deadly blow. Striking without warning in September 1711, they massacred dozens of frontier inhabitants and opened a conflict known as the Tuscarora War. At that time North Carolina was only thinly settled and hardly able to defend itself against the Indians; the reaction of Virginia to the north and South Carolina to the south would be decisive. Virginia, rent by political squabbling among its own leaders, was in no position to play the hero's role, but she did manage to neutralize the northern Tuscaroras.[96] South Carolina responded with a military offensive intended to stamp out the Indian uprising.

Toward the end of 1711, Colonel John Barnwell, an Irish colonist who had risen to prominence in South Carolina during Queen Anne's War, marched north with a force of some thirty Carolinians and nearly 500 allied Indians. Arriving on the upper Neuse early in 1712, Barnwell proceeded to despoil the Tuscarora villages in that area and constructed a fort at the mouth of

Cotechney Creek as an anchor for British authority. His success caused such alarm among the hostile Indians that in April he was able to arrange a peace. Not for long did the Tuscaroras remain submissive, however, and so a second expedition, commanded by the son of former Governor James Moore of South Carolina, struck at the offending tribe early the following year. Moore, who had about as many colonial soldiers under his command as Barnwell, enjoyed the support of a much larger number of Indians and was able to strike an even harder blow. In March he hurled his men against the principal Indian stronghold of Nohoroca, located about 40 miles northwest of New Bern, near the present town of Snow Hill. This vicious fight lasted three days, during which time hundreds of Tuscaroras were slain by Moore's men. The British burned down the Indian fort and forced the survivors to make peace. After this, there was no more trouble from the Tuscaroras. The greater part of the tribe soon began migrating northward to seek the protection of the Iroquois Confederacy, which accepted them as kinsmen who had fallen upon bad days. Henceforth the Iroquois were known no longer as the Five Nations, but rather the Six Nations, even though the Tuscaroras remained a subordinate member of the family. The breaking of Tuscarora strength on the North Carolina frontier in 1713 was like the trampling down of a barrier; white expansionists hastened to take advantage of the new situation and the westward movement gained additional momentum.

In the meantime, the larger war both in the New World and the Old had been dragging on toward a conclusion. To a considerable extent the political overturn of 1710 in England, which had brought the Tories into power, was symptomatic of a growing popular yearning for an end to the long, expensive war. France too was nearing a state of exhaustion, and was, indeed, in a far more precarious condition than most of her enemies. Spain, France's ally, continued to flounder. Thus, although the armies in Europe still grappled wearily with each other, and the ships of war coursed the gray seas as they had been doing for years, neither side was able to force a clear decision. By 1711 or 1712, the belligerent powers were ready to accept a peace if appropriate terms could be arranged. Certainly neither side was in a position to dictate terms to the other; there was no question of a surrender. Yet on balance, the Bourbon courts found themselves under the greater compulsion to achieve a settlement, and that gave a definite advantage to the British.

Early in 1712 negotiations began at the Dutch town of Utrecht, primarily involving Britain and France, but with other powers also participating. There were many issues to be settled, some of them exceedingly complex. By April of 1713, however, the two principal governments had reached agreement, and in the following summer Spain too made her peace with Britain. These agreements or treaties comprise the Peace of Utrecht, which brought to a conclusion the War of the Spanish Succession.[97] In world perspective, undoubtedly the most important provision was that the French and Spanish crowns must remain separate and distinct. This, along with the official recognition by Louis XIV and Philip V of the legitimacy of the Protestant succession in Britain, dissolved the principal reason for England's participation in the war. With great reluctance Spain ceded to England Gibraltar and the island of Minorca in the Mediterranean, both strategically located. Possession of these bases would contribute immeasurably to British naval dominance east of Gibraltar. An important commercial advantage also was gained by the British when Spain granted them the *asiento*, a thirty-year monopoly for the annual importation of 4,800 African slaves into the Spanish colonies. As part of this lucrative arrangement, the British investors providing the slaves would have the additional privilege of sending one trading vessel each year to Spanish America for the purpose of selling British goods in that otherwise closed market.

The Peace of Utrecht likewise produced major territorial gains for Britain in the Western Hemisphere at the expense of France. In the West Indies, the island of St. Kitts came under full British control, ending a long history of division between the two nations. France retained Canada, the strategically located Île Royale (Cape Breton Island) at the southern entrance to the Gulf of St. Lawrence, and Île St. Jean (Prince Edward Island), but turned over to British control the territory along the shores of Hudson Bay, the great island of Newfoundland, and the territory of Acadia. The Hudson Bay territory greatly strengthened the British as competitors in the northern fur trade. Newfoundland not only dominated the northern approaches to the Gulf of St. Lawrence, but also served as the major western Atlantic base for the fisheries. Of the two principal islands guarding the wide mouth of New France's major river and vital line of communication, Britain now held one and France the other. Acadia, ambiguously defined in the treaty of 1713, certainly included at the very least the greater part of the peninsula of Nova Scotia, and possibly much more. This territory was now open for British development, and no longer could serve the French as a base from which to launch Indian attacks upon the settlements of northern New England or privateering attacks upon New England shipping. On the southern frontier, France and Spain retained their respective holdings, largely because of Bienville's success during the war in holding firm against great Anglo-Indian pressure. In 1712 the adroit French colonizer even had managed to arrange a peace with the pro-English Alabamas.

Unfortunately, the provisions concerning America in the Peace of Utrecht included a number of ambiguities that later would arise like specters to haunt the relations between France and Britain during the next few decades. The uncertain boundaries of Acadia have already been mentioned. Similarly, the treaty provided no clear definition of the actual territory around Hudson Bay ceded to the British, nor did it spell out in unmistakable terms the respective rights of Britain and France in the fisheries near Newfoundland. Such crucial matters were shunted off to be decided later by a binational commission. Equally portentous was the paragraph regulating future relations between each of the two nations and those groups of Indians having special relationships with the other. Here an attempt was made to define the actual status of the Iroquois Confederacy, the key group in future westward expansion. France agreed not to molest in the future these Indians *"soumis a la Grande Bretagne. . . ."* [98] Did this mean that the Iroquois now were officially recognized as subjects of the British crown and therefore under British jurisdiction? It was an important question wide open to later dispute.

Despite such weaknesses, however, the Peace of Utrecht constituted an extremely important international settlement, marking a definite turning point in the developing struggle for dominance in North America. To the British colonists, it meant a happy end to Queen Anne's War, with excellent prospects for future expansion and development. Britons could almost forget for the moment that Louisiana and Canada as well as Florida remained unconquered, or that the Indians were still present in their far-flung villages, a restive, unhappy third force. Compared with the years since 1689, with their deep tragedies and bitter losses, the period lying just ahead seemed bright with promise. Whether these hopeful prospects meant future greatness for the British world, or only further struggle, would become more clear during the next half-century.

NOTES

1. 7 *MHC*, VII, 397–398.
2. John B. Wolf, *The Emergence of the Great Powers, 1685–1715* (New York, 1951), pp. 61–62.
3. Memorial from John Nelson to the Board of Trade, 2 November 1697, Lansdowne Manuscripts 849, f. 61 (British Museum); Extract from a letter from Lieut. Gov. Stoughton of Massachusetts to the Board of Trade, 24 October 1698, Lansdowne Manuscripts 849, f. 45 (British Museum). A published version of the former may be found in *CSP* (1697–1698), pp. 53–55, and of the latter in *ibid.*, pp. 500–501.
4. Massachusetts' attempts to establish a satisfactory relationship with the Eastern Indians during the period 1699–1702 are revealed in Massachusetts Archives, XXX, 439–441, 447–449, 461–462, 464–471, 476–477.
5. Henry F. DePuy, comp., *A Bibliography of the English Colonial Treaties with the American Indians, Including a Synopsis of Each Treaty* (New York, 1917), p. 5.
6. Important documents relating to these matters are found in the Lansdowne Manuscripts 849, ff. 88–90 (British Museum). Published versions are given in *CSP* (1700), pp. 431–441.
7. *The Colonial Laws of New York from the Year 1664 to the Revolution* (5 vols.; Albany, 1894-1896), I, 429.
8. Important documents relating to these matters are found in the Lansdowne Manuscripts 849, ff. 29, 78, 80 (British Museum). Published versions are given in *CSP* (1700), pp. 542–549, 568–600.
9. W. J. Eccles, *Frontenac: The Courtier Governor* (Toronto, 1959), p. 333.
10. Verner W. Crane, *The Southern Frontier, 1670–1732* (Durham, 1928), pp. 68–69.
11. Crane, *Southern Frontier*, pp. 75-76.
12. Charles W. Arnade, *The Siege of St. Augustine in 1702* (Gainesville, Fla., 1959), pp. 9–10; John Jay TePaske, *The Governorship of Spanish Florida, 1700–1763* (Durham, 1964), pp. 108–109; John R. Dunkle, "Population Change as an Element in the Historical Geography of St. Augustine," *Florida Historical Quarterly*, XXXVII (July, 1958), 8–10. An English visitor to St. Augustine reported that the town was defended by 150 poorly trained, poorly equipped men and boys. *Edward Randolph; Including His Letters and Official Papers from the New England, Middle, and Southern Colonies in America. . . .* (Publications of the Prince Society, XXXI [Boston, 1909]), 562.
13. Arnade, *Siege of St. Augustine in 1702*, pp. 57–59; TePaske, *Governorship of Spanish Florida*, p. 112.
14. "A New Description of That Fertile and Pleasant Province of Carolina, by

John Archdale, 1707," in Alexander S. Salley, Jr., ed., *Narratives of Early Carolina, 1650–1708* (New York, 1911), p. 303; David Duncan Wallace, *South Carolina, A Short History, 1520–1948* (Chapel Hill, 1951), pp. 69, 134.

15. James Moore, "An Account of What the Army Did under the Command of Colonel Moore in His Expedition Last Winter, against the Spaniards and Spanish Indians. In a Letter from the Said Col. Moore to the Governor of Carolina," in B. R. Carroll, comp., *Historical Collections of South Carolina* (2 vols.; New York, 1836), II, 576.

16. Moore, "Account of What the Army Did under the Command of Colonel Moore," p. 576; Herbert E. Bolton, ed., *Arredondo's Historical Proof of Spain's Title to Georgia* (Berkeley, 1925), pp. 61–62; Wallace, *South Carolina*, p. 71.

17. Bienville to Pontchartrain, 6 September 1704, in Dunbar Rowland and Albert Godfrey Sanders, eds., *Mississippi Provincial Archives, 1704–1743: French Dominion* (Jackson, Miss., 1932), pp. 26–27; TePaske, *Governorship of Spanish Florida*, p. 115.

18. Crane presents evidence to show that Moore and other leading Carolinians already considered the French in Louisiana the principal enemy, and thought of Florida as a potential French base of operations. The French government concurred in regarding Florida as "the first line of defense for Louisiana" (Crane, *Southern Frontier*, p. 78).

19. Rowland and Sanders, *Mississippi Provincial Archives, 1704–1743: French Dominion*, p. 490; Crane, *Southern Frontier*, pp. 83–84.

20. Richebourg Gaillard McWilliams, ed., *Fleur de Lys and Calumet, Being the Pénicaut Narrative of French Adventure in Louisiana* (Baton Rouge, 1953), pp. 65–69, 72; Bienville to Pontchartrain, 25 February 1708, in Rowland and Sanders, *Mississippi Provincial Archives, 1704–1743: French Dominion*, p. 113.

21. Bienville to Pontchartrain, 25 February 1708, in Rowland and Sanders, *Mississippi Provincial Archives, 1704–1743: French Dominion*, p. 112.

22. Crane, *Southern Frontier*, pp. 82–86.

23. For a revisionist view of New York's policy of neutrality, see G. M. Waller, "New York's Role in Queen Anne's War, 1702–1713," *New York History*, XXXIII (January, 1952), 40–53. See also Arthur H. Buffinton, "The Policy of the Northern Colonies towards the French to the Peace of Utrecht" (Unpublished Ph.D. dissertation, Harvard University, 1925), pp. 361–372.

24. George F. G. Stanley, *Canada's Soldiers, 1604–1954: The Military History of an Unmilitary People* (Toronto, 1954), p. 47.

25. Gustave Lanctot, *A History of Canada. Volume II: From the Royal Régime to the Treaty of Utrecht, 1663–1713*, M. M. Cameron, trans. (Cambridge, Mass., 1964), p. 154.

26. Samuel Penhallow, *The History of the Wars of New-England with the Eastern Indians* (Collections of the New Hampshire Historical Society, I [Concord, 1824]), 27.

27. Massachusetts Archives, CXIII, 365.

28. Penhallow, *History of the Wars of New-England*, p. 49.

29. Thomas Hutchinson, *The History of the Colony and Province of Massachusetts-Bay*, Lawrence Shaw Mayo, ed. (3 vols.; Cambridge, Mass., 1936), II, 121.

30. *Frontiers Well-Defended. An Essay, to Direct the Frontiers of a Countrey Exposed unto the Incursions of a Barbarous Enemy, How to Behave Themselves in Their Uneasy Station?* (Boston, 1707), p. 4.

31. Rev. Solomon Stoddard to Gov. Dudley, 22 October 1703, in 4 *MHC*, II, 236–237.

32. An exemplary first-hand account of the entire affair, our most complete source, has been left by the minister of the town, the Reverend John Williams, under the title *The Redeemed Captive Returning to Zion* (Boston, 1707). The clearest, most vivid secondary account is that by Francis Parkman in *A Half-Century of Conflict* (2 vols.; Boston, 1892), I, chap. 4.

33. Rev. John Williams to Gov. Dudley, 21 October 1703, Massachusetts Archives, CXIII, 350.

34. Penhallow, *History of the Wars of New-England*, p. 29; Hutchinson, *History of the Colony and Province of Massachusetts-Bay*, II, 102.

35. Deerfield itself was not abandoned after its ordeal. A number of houses, especially those located some distance south of the palisaded area, remained intact, and additional garrison troops were brought in to guard the town. But for a long time afterward, the going was hard in Deerfield. Successive petitions to the Massachusetts General Court from the remaining residents speak of their "Broken Condition," and plead for financial aid (Massachusets Archives, CXIII, 362, 412).

36. See, for example, J. H. Trumbull and C. J. Hoadly, eds., *The Public Records of the Colony of Connecticut* (15 vols.; Hartford, Conn., 1850–1890), IV, 462–463.

37. 5 *MHC*, VI, 91–93.

38. Penhallow, *History of the Wars of New-England*, p. 52. For an example of such legislation in Connecticut, see Trumbull and Hoadly, *Public Records of the Colony of Connecticut*, IV, 464.

39. Friendly Indians were well aware of the peril to them in this situation. See, for example, Connecticut Archives, Indians, I, 52, where some Connecticut Indians complain to the authorities concerning English threats to get their scalps and sell them in Massachusetts.

40. Penhallow, *History of the Wars of New-England*, p. 34. Church's exploits are described in Thomas Church, *The History of the Eastern Expeditions of 1689, 1690, 1692, 1696, and 1704 against the Indians and French*, Henry Martyn Dexter, ed. (Boston, 1867), pp. 128–181.

41. Hutchinson, *History of the Colony and Province of Massachusetts-Bay*, II, 108.

42. Lanctot, *History of Canada*, II, 155; G. M. Waller, *Samuel Vetch: Colonial Enterpriser* (Chapel Hill, 1960), pp. 79–82.

43. John Bartlet Brebner, *New England's Outpost: Acadia before the Conquest of Canada* (New York, 1927), p. 46.

44. Quoted in Gerald S. Graham, *Empire of the North Atlantic: The Maritime Struggle for North America* (Toronto, 1950), p. 86.

45. "A Memorial of the Present Deplorable State of New-England . . . ," in 5 *MHC,* VI, 43. See also Waller, *Samuel Vetch,* pp. 79–93.

46. "The Deplorable State of New-England, by Reason of a Covetous and Treacherous Governour and Pusillanimous Counsellors," in 5 *MHC,* VI, 128.

47. Massachusetts Archives, CXIII, 456. See also Samuel Sewall's Diary, in 5 *MHC,* VI, 234; Parkman, *Half-Century of Conflict,* I, 92–94; Lanctot, *History of Canada,* II, 158.

48. Hutchinson, *History of the Colony and Province of Massachusetts-Bay,* II, 106. These charges persisted for many years. Although there was some justi-fication for New England's resentment, a more balanced view is presented in Waller, "New York's Role in Queen Anne's War, 1702–1713."

49. William Laird Clowes, *The Royal Navy: A History from the Earliest Times to the Present* (7 vols.; London, 1897–1903), II, 374–376; Herbert Richmond, *The Navy as an Instrument of Policy, 1558–1727,* E. A. Hughes, ed. (Cam-bridge and New York, 1953), pp. 341–342, 352.

50. Quoted in Richmond, *Navy as an Instrument of Policy,* p. 352. See also *ibid.,* p. 310n. For contemporary mention of the problem see Sewall's Diary, in 5 *MHC,* VI, 71, and John Marshall's Diary, 1689–1711 (Massachusetts Historical Society), during April, 1704. The latter notes also that in De-cember, 1704, some French prisoners escaped from custody in Massachusetts and made their getaway by seizing a sloop that they found ready for sea.

51. Wallace, *South Carolina,* p. 75; TePaske, *Governorship of Spanish Florida,* pp. 118–119.

52. "An Impartial Narrative of the Late Invasion of S. Carolina by the French and Spaniards, Aug. 1706," in *CSP* (1706–1708), pp. 248–254; Wallace, *South Carolina,* p. 75; TePaske, *Governorship of Spanish Florida,* pp. 119–120.

53. Crane, *Southern Frontier,* p. 88.

54. Rowland and Sanders, *Mississippi Provincial Archives, 1704–1743: French Dominion,* pp. 113–115, 490.

55. Bienville to Pontchartrain, 12 October 1708, in Dunbar Rowland and Albert Godfrey Sanders, eds., *Mississippi Provincial Archives, 1701–1729: French Dominion* (Jackson, Miss., 1929), pp. 39–41. See also Crane, *Southern Frontier,* pp. 90–91.

56. "Canada Surveyed," in *CSP* (1708–1709), p. 42. A supplementary document is given in *ibid.,* pp. 147–150.

57. "H.M. Instructions to Colonel Vetch," in *CSP* (1708–1709), pp. 230–232. See also Waller, *Samuel Vetch,* pp. 100–119.

58. Gay Transcripts, State Papers, X, 19–39 (Massachusetts Historical Society); Sewall's Diary, in 5 *MHC,* VI, 254.

59. Lawrence H. Leder, ed., *The Livingston Indian Records, 1666–1723* (Gettys-burg, Pa., 1956), pp. 202–206; Waller, *Samuel Vetch,* pp. 126, 142.

60. Bruce T. McCully, "Catastrophe in the Wilderness: New Light on the Canada Expedition of 1709," *WMQ,* XI (July, 1954), 442.

61. Cotton Mather's Diary, in 7 *MHC,* VIII, 30.

62. John Marshall, Diary, 1689–1711 (Massachusetts Historical Society).

63. Quoted in McCully, "Catastrophe in the Wilderness," p. 455. See also

Vetch's letters of 2 and 12 August 1709, in Gay Transcripts, State Papers, X, 40–48 (Massachusetts Historical Society).

64. Waller, *Samuel Vetch,* p. 156.

65. "Canada Surveyed," in *CSP* (1708–1709), p. 42. See also Brebner, *New England's Outpost,* p. 55; Lanctot, *History of Canada,* II, 184.

66. Clowes, *Royal Navy,* II, 526–527; Graham, *Empire of the North Atlantic,* pp. 90–91.

67. Penhallow, *History of the Wars of New-England,* pp. 63–67; Hutchinson, *History of the Colony and Province of Massachusetts-Bay,* II, 136–137.

68. William Thomas Morgan, "The Five Nations and Queen Anne," *MVHR,* XIII (September, 1926), 169–189; Waller, *Samuel Vetch,* pp. 171–174.

69. Instructions for Gov. Robert Hunter, 6 February 1710/11, in Gerald S. Graham, ed., *The Walker Expedition to Quebec, 1711* (Toronto, 1953), p. 269. William T. Morgan has made valuable estimates of the economic motivation underlying the effort to seize Canada. See his "Queen Anne's Canadian Expedition of 1711," Queen's University *Bulletin,* No. 56 (1928), p. 8, and "The South Sea Company and the Canadian Expedition in the Reign of Queen Anne," *Hispanic American Historical Review,* VIII (May, 1928), 143–166.

70. Sewall's Diary, in 5 *MHC,* VI, 313–314.

71. "Minutes of a Council of War held at New London by H.M. commands," in Graham, *Walker Expedition,* pp. 302–307.

72. *Minutes of the Provincial Council of Pennsylvania, from the Organization to the Termination of the Proprietary Government* (10 vols.; Philadelphia and Harrisburg, 1851–1852), II, 534–539; Morgan, "Queen Anne's Canadian Expedition of 1711," pp. 18–19.

73. Sewall's Diary, in 5 *MHC,* VI, 317; Graham, *Walker Expedition,* pp. 64–65, 101, 104–114, 119, 121, 319–322, 335–344, 379.

74. Graham, *Walker Expedition,* p. 77. See also *ibid.,* pp. 196–200, 372–374, 378, 380.

75. Graham, *Walker Expedition,* p. 207. See also *ibid.,* pp. 118, 120–122, 124, 130–131, 203–208, 344–346, 348, 357; Hill to Lord Dartmouth, 31 July 1711, in Gay Transcripts, State Papers, X, 179–187 (Massachusetts Historical Society).

76. Richard King to St. John, 25 July 1711, in Graham, *Walker Expedition,* p. 317.

77. Graham, *Walker Expedition,* pp. 25, 100, 146, 240, 249, 296, 325, 332, 340, 358–359, 379. The idea was not a mere phantom. St. John, in a letter to Governor Hunter dated 6 February 1710/11, had stated without equivocation that "if we succeed in the great design, it will certainly become the wisdom of Her Majesty's councills to think of proper means for taking away of usurpations, for buying out private property [proprietaries], and thereby putting the whole Empire of North America on one uniform plan of government" (Graham, *Walker Expedition,* p. 278).

78. Colonel King's Journal, in Graham, *Walker Expedition,* p. 325.

79. Admiral Walker's Journal, in Graham, *Walker Expedition,* p. 125.

80. Colonel King's Journal, in Graham, *Walker Expedition,* pp. 319, 323–324. See also *ibid.,* pp. 246–247; Waller, *Samuel Vetch,* pp. 202–203.

81. M. de Costebelle to Pontchartrain, 24 July 1711, in Graham, *Walker Expedition,* pp. 245–246.

82. Lanctot, *History of Canada,* II, 161.

83. Clowes, *Royal Navy,* II, 527; Graham, *Walker Expedition,* p. 30; Morgan, "Queen Anne's Canadian Expedition of 1711," pp. 24–25. There are some apparent discrepancies in the statistics concerning ships and men. In general, preference has been given to Graham.

84. Admiral Walker's Journal, in Graham, *Walker Expedition,* p. 74.

85. Thomas Buckingham, *The Private Journals Kept by Rev. John [i.e., Thomas] Buckingham, of the Expedition against Canada, in the Years 1710 & 1711* (New York, 1825), p. 120.

86. Graham, *Walker Expedition,* pp. 33–34.

87. Graham, *Walker Expedition,* pp. 34–35, 44n., 138–140, 330, 333–334, 350, 352; Clowes, *Royal Navy,* II, 529; Waller, *Samuel Vetch,* p. 225.

88. The story of mishap was not yet finished. After arriving in England, Walker's flagship *Edgar* was destroyed by an internal explosion, with the loss of all hands then on board, along with the admiral's own papers. Walker himself, fortunately, was on shore at the time.

89. According to Vetch, the general and his regimental commanders were inclined to get on with the mission, confident that they could take Quebec. Walker and his captains were the strong doubters, and their view prevailed. (See Graham, *Walker Expedition,* pp. 365–366.)

90. The story of Nicholson's rage was told by an eyewitness many years after the event. See Peter Kalm, *Peter Kalm's Travels in North America,* Adolph B. Benson, ed. (2 vols.; New York, 1937), I, 366. See also Buckingham, *Private Journals,* pp. 122–123.

91. Buckingham, *Private Journals,* p. 128.

92. Graham, *Walker Expedition,* pp. 42, 396–399.

93. Graham, *Walker Expedition,* p. 40. Likewise, Governor Spotswood of Virginia, as William Byrd noted in his diary under date of 23 October 1711, considered the great failure to be "the fault of the Admiral" (*The Secret Diary of William Byrd of Westover, 1709–1712,* Louis B. Wright and Marion Tinling, eds. [Richmond, Va., 1941], p. 426).

94. Jeremiah Dummer, *A Letter to a Noble Lord, Concerning the Late Expedition to Canada* (London, 1712).

95. Lanctot, *History of Canada,* II, 162.

96. William L. Saunders, ed., *The Colonial Records of North Carolina* (10 vols.; Raleigh, N.C., 1886–1890), I, 810–813, 815–818; Byrd, *Secret Diary,* pp. 447–448, 450–452.

97. Texts of the various treaties are given in Charles Jenkinson, comp., *A Collection of All the Treaties of Peace, Alliance, and Commerce, between Great-Britain and Other Powers, from the Treaty Signed at Munster in 1648, to the Treaties Signed at Paris in 1783* (3 vols.; London, 1785), I, 375–399, II, 5–144; Frances Gardiner Davenport, ed., *European Treaties*

Bearing on the History of the United States and Its Dependencies (4 vols.; Washington, D.C., 1917–1937), III, 152–251; and Fred L. Israel, ed., *Major Peace Treaties of Modern History, 1648–1967* (4 vols.; New York, 1967), I, 177–239.

98. Davenport, *European Treaties*, III, 213.

CHAPTER 5

"Cold War" Eighteenth-Century Style, 1713-1738

THE PEACE OF UTRECHT in 1713 was the first in a sequence of international treaties that finally restored peace in the Western world after more than two decades of warfare. By 1721 the guns were silent all over Europe, and men at last were able to resume their lives in relative peace. This did not mean that security had been achieved by individuals or by nations, for indeed the years after Utrecht proved to be a time of uneasy, uncertain peace broken sporadically by minor conflicts among the greater and smaller powers. But major war, at least, was successfully avoided until 1739.

England's Queen Anne, having outlived all of her seventeen children, died in 1714 and was succeeded by George I, ruler of the small German state of Hanover. In the following year, the late King William's archfoe Louis XIV, whose ambition had led his country into four wasteful wars over a period of nearly half a century, likewise proved his own mortality. His successor at Versailles was a boy of five, and the reins of government came to rest slackly in the hands of a regency. France was left financially weak and quite uncertain of its future; not for many years would Britain again have to dread the military power of a marching France, as she once had dreaded the marching regiments of Louis XIV. The crown of Spain continued to be worn by Louis' grandson, Philip V, but Spain also was weak and fully divorced from France by the terms of the recent peace. In the 1720s, both England and France came under the control of administrations intent upon economic rebuilding and development, for which the disruption of war was especially to be avoided, and peace became the cornerstone for the national policy of both England's Robert Walpole and France's Cardinal Fleury. For all these major powers and ancient rivals, a long period of international security appeared far preferable to further military adventures.

In America, too, the colonies were content to resume normal activity. For most of England's mainland colonies from Nova Scotia to the Carolinas this meant economic growth and territorial expansion, inspired by enterprising merchants, fur traders, and land speculators. Together these colonies comprised a zone of settlement more than 1,200 miles in length, containing in 1713 a population, black and white, estimated to be about 375,000. Their governments, whether royal, proprietary, or corporate, were strong and vigorous, with elected assemblies in most of the colonies becoming increasingly insistent upon gaining and holding parliamentary rights even at the expense of royal governors.

The French in North America, far less numerous than their British rivals, were equally intent on pursuing their own ambitions. Having lost the Hudson Bay territory, Newfoundland, and Nova Scotia, they concentrated their limited resources and apparently vast energy elsewhere, including the area of the Great Lakes and the Mississippi Valley. Already firmly anchored not only in the valley of the St. Lawrence River but also along the Gulf coast, the French continued developing outposts and small settlements along the strategic water routes of the vast interior valley. Naturally, France already claimed this vast territory as her own.[1]

At first, the rival national settlements were separated on every frontier—north, west, or south—by a wilderness buffer zone occupied only by Indians. But as exploration proceeded and the activities of fur traders and pioneers expanded, these wilderness buffer zones were shrinking. This was a dangerous situation, breeding trouble for the future, especially as the rival powers could come to no agreement defining the boundaries of their expanding territories. Britain refused to accept the Appalachian Mountains as the western boundary of her coastal colonies, and continued to claim territory all the way across the Mississippi Valley and on to the

Pacific Ocean. On the southern frontier, where both France and Spain confronted the Carolinians, there was similar disagreement. Spain claimed the area as far north as Port Royal in South Carolina, well above the mouth of the Savannah River, while Britain stubbornly maintained its right to jurisdiction as far south as the 29th parallel, some 60 miles below St. Augustine.[2]

With the existence of such boundary disputes and the conditions of competitive expansionism that prevailed in North America during the first half of the eighteenth century, it is not surprising that the years following the Peace of Utrecht were characterized by what the twentieth century has labeled a "cold war." While it is true that the period was free from major international conflicts in America, the constant state of tension between the rival colonial systems did occasionally flame into open violence. Military preparedness was considered essential, but in fact was seldom able to be maintained at a level deemed satisfactory by the colonial authorities. Many settlers—English, French, Spanish—continued to live in apprehension, for the day of true peace had not yet arrived.

The Indians, as always, were caught in the midst of these intense rivalries, often being used by the contending colonial powers for their own ambitious purposes. More and more, the balance of power between Indians and whites continued to shift in favor of the more numerous, technologically advanced Europeans. By 1713 most of the local tribes in New England had been either subdued in war or peacefully domesticated, leaving only the outer, more remote groups as a cause for continuing concern to the frontier colonists. French influence was extremely strong among some of these Indians, especially the Abnakis and other groups in Maine, who collectively were known to the New Englanders as the Eastern Indians. Protestant missionaries who ventured to exert a counterinfluence made little headway. One governor wrote pessimistically that these missionaries entertained only "very distant views of success, so bigotted are the natives to anti-christian idolatry, thro' the unwearied application of the Jesuits and those sent by them. . . ." Indeed, if only the Indians still were "in their first state of gross heathenism the missionaries think they might more reasonably expect to see of the fruit of their labours."[3] This being the case, the French were able to maintain the Eastern Indians as a constant potential threat against further English expansion in the direction of Canada.

Inhabiting a great arc of territory stretching from Nova Scotia across northern New England to Lake Champlain and beyond to the Great Lakes, many tribes were resentful of white expansionism and therefore inclined to support the French interest, which appeared to offer little or no threat to their territories. This amicability toward the French existed even though some Indians still found it advantageous to continue trade relations with the British colonies. Even the Iroquois Confederacy was ambivalent in its policy, despite its traditional "chain of friendship" with New York. Of major importance in the Albany fur trade, this powerful confederation of six tribes had managed to extend its sway over a large extent of territory reaching as far west as the Maumee and Wabash rivers. Both the British and French clearly recognized the key role of the Iroquois on the northern frontier, the British struggling to hold these Indians firmly within their traditional orbit, the French working diligently to entice them away. If the French somehow should succeed in gaining the allegiance of the Iroquois tribes, exclaimed one New Yorker with deep foreboding, "then I Conceive they are Masters of North America (Which God forbid)." [4]

Below Pennsylvania, the problem of Indian relations was equally crucial for the rival imperial powers, and here the struggle was triangular, involving Spain as well as Britain and France. The area of principal concern extended from the Tennessee River down to the Gulf coast, and as far west as the Mississippi River. Various tribes, dwelling in this area, found themselves being courted and pressured by the British in Carolina, the Spaniards in Florida, and the French in Louisiana. The Europeans were competing not only for trade, but also for military support; everyone knew that the loss of Indian alliances could be fatal in the tough competition for empire.

A brief review of the six principal tribes in the South will help to make the picture clear. In the northern part of South Carolina, along the upper reaches of the Wateree, Broad, and Saluda rivers, were located the Catawbas, a small Siouan nation noted for its bravery in war.[5] Although no longer numerous and powerful, these Indians occupied territory close enough to the white settlements of South Carolina to be a cause for concern should they become hostile. To the south of Charleston, principally in the area between Beaufort Sound and the Savannah River, lived the Indians known as Yamassees, a people related to the Creek nation. They had moved up into this region with the consent of the Carolinians, who now carried on a profitable trade in the Yamassee villages.[6] Having formerly dwelled much farther south in the vicinity of St. Augustine, the Yamassees recently had resumed contact with the Spaniards, while also being influenced by their kinsmen the Creeks. The Creek nation was both influential and powerful, with a population totaling probably between 7,000 and 9,000 in some sixty villages.[7] Their home territory lay between the upper Suwannee and the Alabama rivers, in the broad, sloping region below the southern termination of the Appalachian Mountains. Here the rivers flowed south to the Gulf, while trading paths crossed from east to west. The strategic location of the Creek nation athwart the rivers and trails of the far South, and between the three European contestants for the area, destined them for a major role in the years after 1713.

Above the Creeks, in the mountainous area east of the Tennessee River, were the many villages of the Cherokees, an Iroquoian people numbering perhaps 11,000. This nation, too, was well located for trade, especially with the British colonists of Virginia and the Carolinas.[8] There was intense rivalry between the Cherokees and their neighbors to the south, the Creeks, a factor of considerable importance in the international competition for Indian alliances. Likewise, the two remaining tribes, the Choctaws and the Chickasaws, were mutually hostile. The former, occupying the area between the Tombigbee and the Pearl rivers, had come under strong French influence since the founding of Louisiana. The Chickasaws, on the other hand, were more independent and quite open to the advances of far-ranging Carolina traders. Located to the north of the Choctaws, the Chickasaw villages were found primarily between the Tennessee River and the Mississippi, more than 500 miles west of Charleston.

Cold-war tensions built up quickly on the southern frontier after Utrecht, and exploded into open violence in the spring of 1715. At dawn on 15 April, Good Friday, the Yamassees suddenly attacked a group of Carolina agents and traders sojourning in one of their villages, thereby precipitating a war with South Carolina that was to continue, with some interruption, until 1728. The surprise massacre set an example for other Indians, Creeks and Catawbas in particular, who joined in the spreading warfare first against the British wilderness traders and then against the prosperous plantations around Charleston. As fierce groups of warriors swept across the countryside killing white families and setting fire to plantation

homes, refugees began pouring into Charleston with whatever possessions they could bring.[9] Two months after the outbreak, the chief
justice of the colony called the war "one of the greatest Afflictions
that could well be brought upon this Province," and went on to
tell how

> the barbarous heathen Indians that are round about us from North to
> South and Five times our Number have all united themselves together
> and made War upon us Beginning with the Murder of our Traders
> and Several of the Inhabitants in the out Settlements And have since
> made further Incursions into the Settlements Killing all they meet
> destroying and laying wast the Plantations where they came plundering
> and then burning the Houses Lying Sculking in the Bushes and
> Swamps that we know not where to find them nor could follow them
> if we did So that we may as well goe to War with the Wolfs and
> Bears.[10]

"The whole Country is in Armes and nothing in it but hurry and
Confusion," he added.

What had caused this staggering crisis in the affairs of an apparently prosperous, growing colony? Contemporaries jumped to
the conclusion that the Yamassees had been incited by the Spaniards,
and there may be some truth in this interpretation. After the end of
Queen Anne's War, the Spanish officials at St. Augustine did make
a deliberate effort to regain influence with the Creeks and the
Yamassees by entertaining them and distributing presents. Shortly
after the Indian war broke out in 1715, Governor Charles Craven
of South Carolina expressed the view that it was St. Augustine
from which "Our Yamasee Indians who first began this warr upon
us have received their principal incouragement to Attack us." [11] If
so, this would indicate a notable success for Spanish diplomacy,
since the Yamassees had previously shown great hostility toward the
Spaniards and their Indian allies. It is also quite possible, indeed
likely, that the French at Mobile were partly responsible for the
outbreak of the Yamassee War, although they flatly denied it.[12]
Certainly Governor Bienville felt directly threatened by British
attempts to establish trade relations with the Choctaws, and he saw
that an effective countermeasure would be to promote a war between the Creeks, who controlled the trade routes leading toward
the Choctaw country, and the Carolinians. Thus, Bienville may
have used the Creeks as *agents provocateurs* among the Yamassees,
with the result that both these tribes went to war against the English

in the spring of 1715. According to one recent assessment, the Yamassee War was "as much Bienville's dark work as anybody's." [13] Although the evidence is slight, the theory is not unreasonable in the light of conditions at that time. Indeed, both the French and Spaniards, independently, may have had a hand in arousing the Indians.

It is not likely, however, that either Louisiana or Florida would have had much influence with the Yamassees had these Indians not been feeling a growing sense of resentment against the British who lived nearby and came often among them. The principal cause of the outbreak was the constant abuse of the Yamassees by the Carolina traders. Charges against these rough backwoods business-men are numerous, varied, and quite well documented. In addition to the usual problems of verbal and physical abuse, cheating, liquor, and debauchery associated with the fur trade nearly everywhere, it is evident that the traders, with complete disregard for the Indians' welfare, were leading them deeper and deeper into debt. One con-temporary estimated that by the spring of 1715 this debt had climbed to a total of more than £50,000, far beyond the capacity of the Yamassees to repay.[14] Even if we postulate a lower figure such as £10,000, which probably is much closer to the actual debt, the situation still was poisonous. To make matters worse, some of the traders had begun to exact repayment forcibly by seizing as slaves the wives and children of their Yamassee debtors. It was this kind of callous mistreatment more than anything else that finally brought about the explosion of 1715.

The colony government went on a war footing as the militia rallied to the defense of the settlements. Militiamen fought vigor-ously in defense of their own homes and communities, but showed great reluctance to go and defend other settlements, even when the need was great, so the assembly called for a standing army of 1,200 men, 500 of whom were to be Negroes and another hundred to be friendly Indians. This force presumably would be available to serve anywhere within the colony.[15] That South Carolina would consider putting weapons into the hands of its blacks is a clear indi-cation of how great the Indian peril seemed to be.

In June the Catawbas and other hostile Indians launched an assault upon the Santee area above Charleston, but were met and defeated by Captain George Chicken and a small force of militia-men. Soon afterward, the Catawbas began to seek an accommodation

with the British and ceased to participate actively in the war. This
encouraging development was accompanied by a general lull on all
sides, as the Yamassees and Creeks regathered and prepared themselves for a campaign of obliteration. The storm broke swiftly again.
Crossing the Edisto River, the warriors began attacking and burning plantations in the area of the Stono River just to the west of
Charleston, and were not finally repulsed until they had ventured
to within 12 miles of the town.[16] Had this attack occurred during a
time of war with France or Spain, and been synchronized with a
seaborne assault by European troops, Britain might have suffered
a major defeat in the South. As it was, however, the Indians alone
were not able to sustain the attack for long, and the whites began to
apply enough pressure to drive them beyond the Savannah River.
The tide of Yamassee-Creek power now was definitely on the ebb,
leaving ruin in its wake. On 13 October 1715 a clergyman in the
colony stated:

> the Southern parts which include a fifth of the Province are entirely
> depopulated, and the whole must have undoubtedly [been] a Sacrifice
> to their Barbarity had not the Honorable the Governour by meeting
> them with invincible Courage and bravery with the divine blessing,
> put a Stop to their Career and pursued his Conquest with such un-
> wearied Diligence as hath given us occasion to hope that we shall
> become an overmatch for them and the Province restor'd to its former
> tranquillity.[17]

In the meantime, the Creeks were endeavoring to draw wavering
Cherokees into the struggle against the British, which would greatly
enhance the power of the warring Indians and complicate the problem of defense for the colonists. The Cherokees, however, were
watching closely for indications as to which side was likely to emerge
victorious. Seeking to influence their decision, South Carolina made
a show of force in the Cherokee country, and the matter was finally
settled when the Cherokees treacherously murdered some Creek
emissaries. With the powerful mountain tribe coming to the support of the British in the winter of 1715–16, the Creeks found
themselves isolated. They, in turn, attached themselves to the
Spaniards, who already were providing sanctuary for the Yamassees.
In 1717 the Creeks, like their former allies the Catawbas, withdrew
from the war altogether.
    It was after this disillusioning experience that the Creek nation

came to formulate a new policy in its dealings with the various European colonies of the Southeast. This was a policy of neutrality which, although often difficult to maintain because of the divergent attachments of certain factions among the Creeks, gave the nation a chance to pursue its own best interests amidst the strong cross-currents of rival colonial expansionism. The game was to play off one European power against another, always if possible avoiding a firm commitment to any, but of course accepting readily all the material benefits to be derived from such a competitive situation. It was much like the game the Iroquois were attempting to play on the northern frontier, but even more complex because three nations rather than two were competing for the trade and goodwill of the Indians. With diplomacy being their only tool for survival, the Creeks learned how to play the diplomatic game with great skill. In the meantime, their war with the Cherokees continued until 1727, when the British arranged for an intertribal meeting at Charleston that finally brought hostilities to an end.[18]

For South Carolina the war with the Yamassees and Creeks had been devastating. A colony of only a few thousand settlers does not have to lose very many lives or a vast amount of property before it finds itself in serious straits. Plantation agriculture, the newly developed cattle industry, and the Indian trade all were hard hit by the war. The colony's indebtedness increased greatly. To these discouraging conditions was added a mounting dissatisfaction with proprietary control, resulting in the political overturn of 1719 and the subsequent establishment of royal government. Moreover, an unpleasant pattern, all too familiar in colonial history, had re-emerged as intercolonial relations felt the strain of emergency conditions during 1715 and 1716. Behind this strain lay a growing rivalry between South Carolina and Virginia traders, with the latter attempting to break in on the peltry trade of the Cherokees and other southeastern tribes. After the outbreak of hostilities in the spring of 1715, some Carolinians were convinced that the enemy tribes were being supplied by traders from Virginia. Here in a southern setting was New England's old charge against New York.[19] When South Carolina appealed to Virginia for material support against the Indians, there was at first a prompt response and a shipment of much-needed military hardware. But later, when the two colonies worked out an arrangement for the sending of soldiers from Virginia, the terms and their interpretation provided fuel for mutual recrim-

ination. Each colony accused the other of bad faith, while many
Carolinians bearing the brunt of the war continued to believe
that the Chesapeake colony was in part responsible for their suffering. This animosity lingered on long after the crisis had passed.[20]

One other major consequence of the Yamassee War was that
the British government became more aware of the imperial challenge
now developing so strongly in North America. The rather casual
colonial rivalry between England, Spain, and France in the
seventeenth century always had been regarded as a minor sideshow
against the larger backdrop of European affairs. Now, however, this
rivalry was intensified, taking on significant dimensions of its own
and threatening serious consequences for any power who proved
negligent in forwarding its own interests. King William's War and
Queen Anne's War had contributed greatly to this growing awareness; and the developments in the Southeast, coming hard on the
heels of Utrecht, served to underline the lesson. French expansionism in particular was causing increasing concern among British
colonial leaders, including some of the governors. From their
vantage point in America, it now seemed abundantly evident that
a single-minded, determined French regime was reaching around
behind the British coastal colonies to claim and occupy a solid
belt of territory extending from the St. Lawrence River through
the region of the Great Lakes and down the Mississippi Valley to
the Gulf coast. This was interpreted as a master plan which, when
completed, would enable the French to block all westward expansion of the British colonies beyond the Appalachians, confining
them to the narrow coastal strip east of the mountains. Here they
would ultimately wither and die while France, swollen with territory
and power, would enjoy the limitless resources, the millions of
acres of virgin soil, and the lucrative fur trade of the vast interior.[21]

Alarmed at this prospect which from the American viewpoint
was coming to seem terribly imminent, such men as Governor
Alexander Spotswood of Virginia, Governor William Keith of
Pennsylvania, Governor Robert Hunter of New York, and Richard
Berresford, the agent for Carolina, began to bombard the Board of
Trade in London with detailed warnings and appeals. There was
increasing talk of the need for better intercolonial cooperation
and mutual support, as well as countermeasures on the part of the
British government. Colonel Caleb Heathcote, a prominent New
York land speculator, jurist, and member of the governor's council,

expressed the view of a small but increasing circle of colonial imperialists when he urged that the separate colonies pull together in the face of the French menace. "For as every part of North America is struck at," wrote Heathcote in 1715,

> so all our interests are the same, and what number [member?] soever is wounded or hurt, the whole ought to reckon themselves agreived, and not carelessly suffer the French to angle us away, province by province, till at last all will be gon; and as it is impossible that we and the French can both inhabit this Continent in peace but that one nation must at last give way to the other, so 'tis very necessary that without sleeping away our time, all precautions imaginable should be taken to prevent its falling to our lotts to remove.[22]

Greater force was lent to the argument when in 1717 the French advanced 200 miles up the Alabama River from Mobile to construct Fort Toulouse near the junction of the Coosa and Tallapoosa rivers. From this new base they began to exert an increasing influence over the neighboring Indians, to the obvious disadvantage of the British. Here was a post, as one Frenchman correctly observed, "quite advanced in the direction of Carolina and very important in preventing the English from entering Louisiana. . . ." [23] The following year a settlement was begun at New Orleans on the east bank of the lower Mississippi, strengthening the French hold on the greatest river of North America. Not to be outdone entirely, the Spaniards in 1718 made their bid for a greater share in the destiny of the Southeast by building Fort San Marcos at the head of Apalachee Bay. As yet the British had not a single base west of the Appalachians.

The warnings from British colonial leaders began to make an impression on the Board of Trade. In 1720 the king ordered South Carolina to secure its claim as far south as the Altamaha by building a fort near the mouth of that river. Colonel John Barnwell proceeded to carry out these instructions, and in 1721 Fort King George stood on the north bank as a symbol of British defiance of both Spain and France in that area. The Spaniards, who continued to claim all territory to the Savannah River and beyond, repeatedly protested this incursion, but without effect. Apparently Britain at last had decided to drive in stakes on the far southern frontier.[24]

Eight years after the signing of the Treaty of Utrecht, the Board

of Trade, drawing heavily upon advice from America, presented
to the king a lengthy report on conditions in the colonies, including
the mounting threat of French and Spanish imperialism.[25] This
highly significant document clearly reflects the American fear of
French encirclement. New York, it was suggested,

> by reason of its situation, being almost in the middle of the British
> Colonies on the Continent, and the nearest of any to the French set-
> tlements on the River [of] Canada, and to their Indians, as well as for
> the immediate influence or command it has over the five Nations of
> Indians, might most properly be made the seat of Government for a
> Captain General . . . and a barrier to the Neighbouring Colonies.[26]

For this reason, the forts of New York should be repaired and new
ones built "in such places, where they may best serve to secure
and enlarge our Trade and Interest with the Indians, and break
the designs of the French in these parts." Priority should be given
to the construction of a fort near Lake Ontario. The report went
on to point out how the French, in order to make good their
vast claims, had constructed numerous small forts at strategic
locations throughout the interior, from the upper reaches of the
St. Lawrence to the mouth of the Mississippi. This progress had
been supplemented by French success in attracting a number of
important Indian tribes into their system and to their support.

Having drawn a fairly grim picture of French advance, the
Board of Trade then put forward some additional recommendations. Both the northern and the southern extremities of the British
colonial area should be more thoroughly fortified and defended.
As for the western frontier, although the Appalachian Mountains

> may serve at present for a very good frontier, we should not propose
> them for the boundary of your Majestys Empire in America. On the
> contrary, it were to be wished, that the British Settlements might be
> extended beyond them, and some small forts erected on the great
> Lakes, in proper places, by permission of the Indian proprietors; and
> we would particularly recommend the building of a fort on the Lake
> Erie, . . . whereby the french communications from Quebec to the
> River Mississippi, might be interrupted, a new trade opened with some
> of the Indian nations, and more of the natives engaged in your
> Majesty's interest.[27]

Here, as Professor Richard W. Van Alstyne has pointed out, the
British were flouting the intent of the Utrecht settlement and
recommending a policy of aggressive expansion.[28] It must be reit-

erated, however, that the Treaty of Utrecht did not establish clearly defined boundaries. The expansionists in America, both French and British, were operating in a very fluid situation, where the temptation to grab and hold was almost too strong to be resisted.

With obvious concern, the Board of Trade referred to the extremely complex problem of relations with the various tribes of Indians and the pursuit of the economically important trade in furs and peltry. All the major contenders for American territory realized the importance of maintaining friendly relations with the neighboring tribes for purposes of commercial intercourse and mutual support. But the Indians were fickle (or so it often seemed to the colonists) and inclined to shift allegiance for their own immediate advantage. Indian diplomacy, with its traditional giving of gifts and formalized exchange of sentiments and opinions, was an expensive and often frustrating concern of colonial governors and other officials. Their success, or lack of it, might make the difference between victory and defeat in the continuing struggle for the riches of America.

There is no doubt that the single most important factor influencing the shifting pattern of Indian alignments was the fur trade, on which the Indians had come to depend for firearms and ammunition, liquor, and a variety of European manufactured goods ranging from knives and needles to stockings and woolen blankets.[29] The French enjoyed a certain advantage in dealing with Indians because they had the facility to fraternize with them in a way that seemed abhorrent to most Englishmen. As one colonist complained, the French traders "live and marry among them, in short are as one people which last is not Comendable but gains their affection . . . but our Nation is quite the Reverse notion, and will be baffeld out of this trade."[30] Moreover, the Indians had long been aware that the French were interested primarily in the exchange of goods rather than the transfer of large areas of land for purposes of settlement; whereas the British often came as potential farmers, which meant the ultimate destruction of the forest and the Indians' way of life. But in the last analysis, Indian affiliation was shaped largely by the need for an ample and sure supply of trading goods at reasonable prices, and it was exactly here that the British, with their superior manufacturing industry and their more efficient system of distribution, could outbid the French for Indian support.

All in all, it was a hard-fisted game played for extremely high stakes. Individuals were involved for their own profit, and governments for security and advantage. The trade had become an economic necessity for the Indians, while at the same time corroding their culture and undermining their character through disease, drunkenness, and debt. Many traders were unscrupulous in their dealings with the Indians, cheating them in business and abusing them at pleasure. Government regulation of the trade was often attempted but seldom effective in preventing the degradation of the Indians, who kept coming back for more simply because there was no longer a real alternative. The hard cynicism and callous inhumanity of Anglo-Indian relations is well demonstrated in the words of one colonial governor: "It is always the maxim of our Government upon the Continent to promote war between Indians of different Nations with whom we Trade and are at peace with ourselves for in that consists our safety, being at War with one another prevents their uniting against us." [31]

After their defeat at the hands of the British during the conflict of 1715–16, the Yamassees took refuge with the Spaniards in Florida. From there they carried on sporadic raiding activity against the Carolina frontier with at least the tacit consent of the Spanish authorities, and sometimes, apparently, with the active support of some of the Creeks. Thus, the situation remained unstable for a number of years. Shortly after the Cherokee-Creek treaty of 1727, in which the Creeks promised not to give any more support to the Yamassee marauders, a number of Lower Creeks took part in a renewed outburst of Yamassee raiding that took the lives of five Carolinians on the Altamaha.[32] During the winter of 1727–28 the government of South Carolina, aroused and angered by these bold incursions, organized a punitive expedition to settle scores with the Yamassees once and for all. Command was given to an experienced Indian fighter, Colonel John Palmer. With an expeditionary force of about 100 militiamen and some friendly Indians, Palmer left Charleston and proceeded by boat down the coastal channel toward St. Augustine, where the remaining villages of the Yamassees were to be found. At the mouth of the St. Johns River the men took to the land and continued southward. Their approach was soon discovered, which gave the Indians time to assemble at their principal fortified village, Nombre de Dios, virtually under the guns of the Castillo de San Marcos.

Late in February the Carolinians launched their attack, during which they killed some thirty of the Indians and took about fifteen prisoners. The surviving Yamassees fled in dismay to the sheltering walls of the nearby Spanish fort. For three more days Palmer lingered in the vicinity, hoping for another chance at the Indians. During this time the Spaniards made no move against the British intruders other than keeping them at a distance by gunfire. When there was nothing more to be accomplished by staying, Palmer put the torch to Nombre de Dios and headed home. The fact that the Spaniards, even at their point of greatest strength, had not dared intervene was a revelation not lost upon the chastened Yamassees and more distant Indians who learned of the affair. British prestige increased among the larger tribes, and for the time being, at least, the Carolina frontier began to experience an unaccustomed feeling of security.[33]

New England, too, had had its troubles with frontier Indians who enjoyed the unofficial backing of the French. The years after 1713 witnessed a strong revival of British expansionism in New Hampshire and Maine, with groups of land speculators encouraging newly arrived Scotch-Irish immigrants to push forward beyond Casco Bay to the lower Androscoggin and Kennebec rivers. Merry-meeting Bay, the junction of these two rivers, quickly became the threshold for a new zone of pioneer settlement.[34] Beyond the Kennebec, to the east, lay wilderness territory claimed by both the British and the French. The latter viewed the advance of the New Englanders as an immediate threat to their claim when Canada had no large mobile population available to pour into the disputed area. Only one factor was working to the advantage of the French, and that was the strong influence being exerted over the Eastern Indians by Catholic missionary priests. At St. Francis, near the place where the river of the same name flows into the St. Lawrence, and at Bécancour, on the south side of the St. Lawrence a short distance east of Trois Rivières, were important French mission stations ministering effectively to groups of Abnaki Indians who migrated easily up the rivers from Maine to enjoy these advantages. More primitive stations deep in the wilderness of New England were located at Panawamské on the upper Penobscot River near the present Passadumkeag, and at Norridgewock on the upper Kennebec in what is now the township of Madison. The French influence radiating from these bases was widespread among the Eastern Indians who, although they had made their peace with Massachusetts in 1713, remained highly suspicious of British intentions and deeply resentful of the advancing tide of British settlement.

Actually, these frontier Indians were being subjected to strong pulls from opposite directions, which made them constantly uncomfortable and irritable. The influence from Quebec via the various mission stations was primarily emotional, providing the Indians with a ritualistic and mystical form of religion together with a satisfying sense of being supported by a militant regime that seemed to respect and not threaten their way of life. The pull from Boston, on the other hand, was mostly economic, for the New Englanders were better able to provide the Indians with trading goods in exchange for furs.[35] These opposite pulls forced the Indians into an ambivalence that was both puzzling and infuriating to the rival colonial governments.

The New England colonial historian Thomas Hutchinson, generally an intelligent and well-informed observer of Indian affairs, once offered a possible reason for the apparent discrepancies in European interpretations of the Indian position. When the natives were at their villages, he said,

> the priests were continually exciting them to act vigorously and drive all the English to the westward of Kennebec, and such was their influence over them that they would often set out from home, with great resolution to persist in their demands, and in their parleys, with the commanders of [English] forts, as well as at more public treaties, would appear, at first, to be very sturdy, but were soon softened down to a better temper and to agree that the English should hold the lands without molestation. When they returned home, they gave their father [the French priest] an account of great firmness they had shewn in refusing to make any concessions, and to this we are to impute the erroneous relation of these treaties [by certain French authors].[36]

At best this explanation could have been little more than an educated guess by Hutchinson, but it may be a valuable clue to the mystery of Indian vacillation in dealing with the French and the British during this period of New England history. One wonders how the Indian diplomats "were soon softened down to a better temper." Perhaps the strong New England rum was part of the answer. Probably, too, the British negotiators would bring to bear an intimidating sternness of manner that the Indians, already so obviously the underdogs in past encounters, found difficult to outface. Whatever the reason, the Eastern Indians proved again and again to be as fickle as the wind of their own country, saying one thing to the French and another to the British, and seldom holding fast to one policy or position for very long.

From time to time the Indians appeared openly insolent toward the white settlers in Maine and committed acts of vandalism and violence. When this sort of behavior occurred, the British were inclined to believe that the French missionaries were encouraging their wild charges to commit such depredations in order to undermine the advancing line of settlement. Indian outrages began to occur farther and farther south, well below Casco Bay and even the Saco River. Families began to evacuate the exposed areas for fear of greater trouble to come, and that in turn frightened the great land speculators of Boston.[37] Finally, in September 1721, the legislature forbade all trade with the offending Indians, hoping that deprivation would bring them to their senses.[38] It didn't, and the trouble expanded.

In June 1722 the Indians descended the Kennebec in their canoes and began vandalizing the British settlements in the vicinity of Brunswick. They attacked ships, fired on the king's colors at the fort, burned down houses, and made off with a few captives.[39] That they did not kill indiscriminately is significant; apparently their intention was to show their resentment at a recent British attempt to arrest the French missionary at Norridgewock and the detention and questioning of the half-breed trader Saint-Castin, as well as to discourage further British advances. Whatever the cause of this latest eruption, the government of Massachusetts responded in dead earnest. Governor Samuel Shute, a veteran of Marlborough's campaigns, issued an official proclamation dated 25 July 1722, in which he denounced the Eastern Indians as rebels and traitors.[40] Shute's pointed proclamation virtually constituted a declaration of war. As it happened, Governor Shute soon returned to England, leaving William Dummer to carry on the war as acting governor, and so the conflict has come to be known as Dummer's War.

The initial outbreak at Brunswick was followed by a spreading wave of depredations that soon lapped as far west as the upper Connecticut Valley. Indian frustration and resentment of previous defeats and humiliations once again found an outlet in the opportunity to terrorize British frontier folk and vandalize their property. Violence rapidly escalated. New Englanders were convinced that the French were inciting and supporting the Indian raiders, and there is no reason to doubt that this was so. To some extent, all the contending powers in America had become accustomed to utilizing Indians in this way when they found it advantageous. From the French point of view, the Eastern Indians were useful tools for convincing the British that it was better not to intrude into the Kennebec Valley, a strategic wilderness route leading directly toward the Chaudière River and Quebec.

As the war continued, attention came to focus on the mission village of Norridgewock on the east bank of the Kennebec River, where the dedicated Jesuit priest Sebastien Rasles had for many years been working among the Abnakis. New Englanders looked upon Rasles as "a constant and Notorious Fomenter and Incendiary to the Indians to kill, burn, and destroy . . . ," and therefore the principal author of their miseries.[41] The character and role of this lone missionary have been a matter of dispute ever since. Careful research in the last hundred years has shown that Rasles was indeed active in promoting Indian resistance to the British, whom he considered heretical intruders, and that he himself was a man of action as well as contemplation. He carried out his difficult task with great skill, combining the role of Christian missionary with that of political agent for Quebec, yet never able to overcome completely the creeping influence of the British traders even among his immediate charges. The Indians at Norridgewock were wavering in their attachments, and that was a serious concern for Father Rasles.[42]

In the summer of 1724, the British decided to pay a call on Rasles and his Indians, with the express intention of arresting the priest. A force commanded by Captain Johnson Harmon of York, Maine, with Captain Jeremiah Moulton as second-in-command, moved up the Kennebec and approached the village on 12 August. Harmon divided his force, which in itself suggests that he had good information on the fighting strength available to defend Rasles. He himself took about half the men, or nearly eighty, to destroy the cornfields along the nearby riverbanks, while Moulton led a company of equal size against the village itself. Arriving at his objective about three o'clock in the afternoon, Moulton posted some of his men on the north and south sides of the village, and then with the remainder approached from the east, leaving the fourth, or river, side unguarded. Rasles and the Indians apparently did not detect this approach until the British were almost upon them. Bursting into the midst of the village, the eager New Englanders quickly engaged the startled defenders. There was a brief but fierce fight in which Rasles himself took part. Many of the Indians tried to escape across the river, which must have been anticipated by Moulton, for his men killed a number of the enemy there. When the smoke had cleared, it was found that among the corpses sprawled here and there in the village were those of several leading Indian warriors, notorious to the British, and the dead body of Father Rasles. The attacking force spent the night at the scene of this easy victory. On the next day, after burning Norridgewock to the ground, they started back downriver with the scalps of their enemies.[43] The New England historian Penhallow called the affair "the greatest victory we have obtained in the three or four last wars," revealing through his unconscious exaggeration the intense emotionalism of those who had felt themselves constantly menaced by the existence of Norridgewock.[44]

There is no doubt that the destruction of Rasles and his wilderness base was the major turning point of the war. After this, the Indians were noticeably less aggressive and well organized, the British patrols increasingly bold and successful. To encourage the frontier fighters in their tracking down of hostile Indian prowlers or fugitives, the government again offered a sizable bounty for enemy scalps.[45] Men who considered themselves good woodsmen and handy with a gun—and in need of money—formed private companies to go off into the wilderness and exploit this opportunity. The scalp-hunters, as Parkman said, were "much like hunters of wolves, catamounts, or other dangerous beasts, except that the chase of this fierce and wily human game demanded far more hardihood and skill." [46] One such group was led by Captain John Lovewell of Dunstable. The experience of Lovewell's company is worth following rather closely, for it reveals much about the character, the techniques, and the difficulties of Indian fighting in the eighteenth century.

About the middle of April 1725, Lovewell and his men tramped out of Dunstable and headed north toward Lake Winnipesaukee in New Hampshire, probably with a fairly clear notion of where Indians might be found. Passing by the large lake with its many wooded islands, they continued on to the western shore of Lake

Ossippee, where they paused to construct a crude fortification. Here they left one of their number sick, under the care of their surgeon and with a guard of eight men. The remainder, numbering about thirty-five, continued northward toward the upper portion of the Saco River where they thought they might find some Pequawket Indians. Nearing what is now known as Lovewell's Pond in Fryeburg, Maine, the company bivouacked in the woods, and that night became aware of the possible presence of Indians lurking around their campsite. Next morning, 8 May, they heard a gunshot nearby and soon discovered a lone Indian apparently shooting ducks. Was this a decoy planted to lead them into an ambush? Divesting themselves of their packs, which they left on the ground unguarded, the scalp-hunters cautiously advanced behind their leader and soon encountered an Indian who raised his gun and fired, wounding Lovewell and one other. For this, the Indian quickly paid with his life; and the company's chaplain, a twenty-one-year-old student of theology, helped to peel off the scalp. When the men returned to the place where they had left their packs, they found them gone, and soon discovered why. A band of warriors suddenly burst from cover, yelling and firing at the startled British. Again Lovewell was hit, and others with him. A contemporary account, obviously derived from an eyewitness, reads like a military citation:

> Capt. *Lovewell* and Ensign *Robins* were mortally wounded by the Indians first shot from their Ambushments, who (notwithstanding supporting themselves by such Trees as they could lay hold on) kept firing on the Enemy, and encouraging their Companions, they both had their Guns in hands, *Lovewell*'s being cock'd and presented when he was past speaking.[47]

Staunchly, the outnumbered frontiersmen stood their ground, firing and firing again as fast as they could reload. One man, though, lost his nerve and made a break for it, heading for the little fortification at Lake Ossippee some 20 miles to the rear. When able, the rest of the company drew back in good order to the nearby shore of Lovewell's Pond where, with the water at their backs, they intended to make a last stand.[48]

It was about 10:00 A.M. when the Indians resumed the fight, hemming in the little company of desperate men, pouring in their shot at every opportunity through choking clouds of gunsmoke. Parkman, as usual, paints the scene with remarkable vividness:

The Indians had the greater agility and skill in hiding and sheltering themselves, and the whites the greater steadiness and coolness in using their guns. They fought in the shade; for the forest was dense, and all alike covered themselves as they best could behind trees, bushes, or fallen trunks, where each man crouched with eyes and mind intent, firing whenever he saw, or thought he saw, the head, limbs, or body of an enemy exposed to sight for an instant. The Indians howled like wolves, yelled like enraged cougars, and made the forest ring with their whoops; while the whites replied with shouts and cheers.[49]

Hour after hour the fight went on, with fewer and fewer of the British left unscathed. The young chaplain now lay seriously wounded, faintly praying while Indian bullets continued to cut the air above him. It is not known how many Indians were engaged, probably not many more than the whites or the result would have been different. As it was, the Abnakis themselves must have taken heavy losses, for shortly after the sun went down they withdrew and the fight was over. More than two-thirds of the British were either dead or seriously wounded; Lovewell himself had not survived that fierce encounter. It seems certain that had the Indians returned after dark and burst into the little circle of defenders, they would have made the bloody work complete; but they did not, and during the night the haggard survivors began their painful withdrawal to the south. One man who was unable to go with the others because of his injury asked his companions to leave a loaded gun with him so that he might kill one more Indian when they came to scalp him in the morning. When some of the men finally did reach Lake Ossippee they found the fortification abandoned, for the one man who had run from the fight had arrived there earlier with a tale of disaster. Fortunately, they did discover some food left behind, which gave them a little more strength to continue their hasty retreat. Eventually, scattered remnants of Lovewell's old company, footsore and hollow-eyed, came straggling into Berwick or Biddeford or Dunstable. A party of men subsequently sent by Governor Dummer to the scene of action at Lovewell's Pond found and buried a dozen British corpses. For a time the scalp-hunting business seemed to have lost some of its attraction.

By now, however, the Eastern Indians saw how little tangible aid they were going to get from the French, and were rendered considerably more tractable not only by their own heavy losses in combat, but also by their need for British trading goods. At Boston on 15 December 1725, four leaders of the Eastern Indians placed their marks at the bottom of an official document, committing their people to a course of peace and due submission to British law. The following summer a conference between the Massachusetts authorities and the various tribes of northern New England was planned at Falmouth to ratify the agreement. To the great chagrin of the British, only the Penobscots appeared, but despite some disagreements and tension the leaders of that tribe gave their endorsement to the peace, supposedly in the name of all. A year later other tribes of the Eastern Indians, including the Norridgewocks, came to the table and made their marks.[50] So ended Dummer's War on the New England frontier.

In the meantime, New Englanders, continuing to look toward the north, had been discovering that the acquisition of Nova Scotia was no panacea. For one thing, the French inhabitants there, the Acadians, remained firmly attached to their land, their religion, and their way of life. Even though French authority had been officially excluded since 1713, French influence continued to reach across the border, principally through the agency of the Catholic priests among the Acadian people. British authorities in Nova Scotia chafed because the Acadians, most of whom wanted nothing more than to be left in peace to work their farms, would not accept the full obligation of British subjects, especially the obligation to fight for British interests. Understandably, it was feared that these stubborn folk, when war broke out between Britain and France, would rise up in support of the French and Indian enemy.

France had decided to minimize the strategic effect of the loss of Nova Scotia by developing a strong military and naval base on Cape Breton Island. Accordingly, at the entrance to a sizable, well-sheltered harbor on the east coast of the island, French engineers and laborers had been constructing at great cost the walled fortress of Louisbourg, embracing a garrison town which also developed into a center of trade. Here at Louisbourg, important elements of the French Navy could be sheltered and serviced behind the protecting guns of the fortifications and, when needed, could readily issue forth to defend the Gulf of St. Lawrence against any intruders. In these years of relative peace, however, the harbor at Louisbourg was a mercantile magnet, drawing merchant vessels from France, the St. Lawrence Valley, the West Indies, and New

England. At Louisbourg a bustling community of merchants was engaged in the profitable exchange of a great variety of products, some of which remained for the sustenance of the local population, including garrison troops, traders, and fishermen, while the greater part continued on through the channels of national and international trade. As an important center of French military and commercial interests, Louisbourg was in an excellent position to exert a continuing influence among the Acadians in Nova Scotia, and did so during this period of cold war.

On the southern frontier, the smashing of the Yamassees by Palmer in 1728, together with a treaty of friendship signed by seven leading Cherokees while on a visit to London in 1730, contributed greatly to the security of South Carolina. The immediate native enemy had been rendered impotent, and the greatest nearby native tribe had been won to friendship.[51] At about this time also, a few imperialist-minded Englishmen were developing a plan to create a new proprietary colony in the "debatable land" lying between Spanish Florida and the settlements of South Carolina. Two principal ideas fused in this ambitious project: The first was to provide a place of opportunity for British people of good character who were victims of economic disability at home; the second was to create a buffer state, well defended by its own free inhabitants, to serve as a protection for South Carolina against Indians and other potential enemies. To these two purposes was naturally added a third—the further promotion of the economic prosperity of the British Empire. The royal charter granted in 1732 to *The Trustees for establishing the Colony of Georgia in America* clearly announced these three objectives.[52]

Actually, Georgia was carved out of territory originally appertaining to Carolina. The new colony, bounded on the north by the Savannah River and on the south by the Altamaha River, was to extend from the sources of those two streams westward across the continent in happy disregard of all French and Spanish claims and settlements. As a military buffer state, Georgia was to be inhabited by a free population consisting mainly of small yeoman farmers, ready and able to fight in time of danger. In terms closely resembling those of earlier colonial charters, Georgia's royal charter provided for the maintenance of a ready militia, the backbone of colonial defense. Officers appointed by the trustees were authorized to

train, instruct, exercise and govern a militia . . . , to assemble in
martial array the inhabitants . . . , and to lead and conduct them, and
with them to encounter, expulse, repel, resist and pursue . . . , and
conquer by all fitting ways, enterprises and means whatsoever, all and
every such person or persons as shall at any time hereafter, in any
hostile manner, attempt or enterprise the destruction, invasion, detriment or annoyance of our said colony.[53]

In addition, the trustees were authorized to "erect forts and fortify
any place or places within our said colony, and the same to furnish
with all necessary ammunition, provisions, and stores of war, for
offence and defence. . . ." Here was further evidence that the many
warnings and pleas emanating from colonial leaders ever since the
Treaty of Utrecht had been heeded in London. Georgia was in
part a direct outgrowth of the Board of Trade's report of 1721,
and has been well described as "an English spear poised to prick
the lordly domain of the Spanish sovereign and to warn the Bourbon
monarchy of France that the English penetration in to the Mississippi Valley, long a matter of dispute between Carolina traders and
French outposts, was but a premonition of what was to come." [54]
Imperialistic motives were becoming stronger in British overseas
planning, even as Walpole sought earnestly to preserve the peace
of Europe.

Among the twenty prominent men named in the charter as
original trustees of Georgia was a thirty-six-year-old member of
Parliament named James Oglethorpe. A former army officer,
Oglethorpe had served in 1717, apparently with some distinction,
as aide-de-camp to Prince Eugene of Savoy.[55] More recently, he
had been one of the prime movers in the scheme for Georgia,
combining a desire to help the deserving poor with a strong imperialistic urge to challenge Spain in North America. Georgia
offered him a chance to do both. Early in 1733, Oglethorpe arrived
in Georgia with the first group of selected settlers and founded the
town of Savannah on the south bank of the Savannah River a
short distance from the sea. Demonstrating his ability to deal
effectively with the natives, he managed to win the goodwill of
the local Indians, a subgroup of the Creek nation. These Indians
readily conveyed to the new colony virtually the entire tidewater
region lying between the Savannah and the Altamaha rivers.[56]

South Carolina viewed the new project with favor, even though
it meant an end to her own expansion toward the south, for the

potential value of Georgia as a buffer was obvious to a people who well remembered the terror of the Yamassee War. The French and Spanish immediately recognized the founding of Georgia as a distinct threat to their own interests, and Spain in particular challenged the legality of the grant. As soon as possible, Governor Francisco del Moral Sánchez of Florida took steps to strengthen his defenses against renewed British incursions, but his resources were pathetically small. Pressure exerted through the channels of international diplomacy seemed the only feasible way of forcing the British to back away from Florida's northern frontier.[57]

Oglethorpe, in the meantime, was acting like a man who had come to stay regardless of who might cry "Trespass." Looking south beyond the Altamaha, he concluded that the St. Johns River, just 30 miles above St. Augustine, was the proper limit for Georgia jurisdiction, and accordingly began a program of fort building that left no doubt of his determination to hold fast against any opposition. In 1736 Oglethorpe founded a garrison town, Frederica, on the west side of St. Simons Island to stand guard over the inner water route leading north toward Savannah and South Carolina. He obtained from Britain a contingent of combative Scottish highlanders and their families who began the border settlement of New Inverness on the north bank of the Altamaha near its mouth. Here, too, was erected a military outpost. Then, with giant steps, Oglethorpe began to build other strongpoints on the direct line to St. Augustine—Fort St. Simons at the southern end of St. Simons Island, Fort St. Andrews at the northern end of Cumberland Island, Fort William at the opposite end of the same island, and Fort St. George close to the very mouth of the St. Johns River itself. This new line of military posts was like the barrel of a gun aimed directly at the principal Spanish base.[58]

Even as Oglethorpe's engineers and workmen were hard at their tasks, negotiations between Spanish officials and the government of Georgia were getting underway. In the fall of 1736 Oglethorpe and Governor Moral Sánchez of Florida agreed that the British should pull back from their southernmost position near the St. Johns River, after which the situation was to remain *in statu quo* pending a decision on boundaries by Britain and Spain. Such a slight concession on the part of Oglethorpe only aroused the anger of the Spanish crown. For his imprudence in agreeing to that arrangement, the unhappy governor of Florida was recalled to

Spain in disgrace, and the so-called Treaty of Frederica became a dead document.[59]

The next three years gave abundant proof of the tensions being generated along the southern frontier. Some were of long standing, but many are to be attributed largely to the founding of Georgia. Negro slaves escaping from the plantations of South Carolina almost invariably headed southward, for the authorities in Florida had let it be known that blacks escaping from the British colonies would be given sanctuary and freedom. This official policy was intensified in the decade of the 1730s, as Anglo-Spanish tensions rose. The existence of Georgia as a buffer colony inhabited almost solely by whites made successful escape more difficult, for any black man seen in Georgia would arouse immediate suspicion. Nevertheless, some fugitives did get through to Florida, and their reception by the Spaniards only served to aggravate the enmity between the hostile colonies.[60]

Until about 1738 the British on the southern frontier seemed to be making good progress with the Indians, to the great anguish of the Spaniards and French, who generally were unable to match the tangible rewards dangled by Charleston and Savannah. An officer at New Orleans reported in 1733 that "twelve Englishmen had arrived at the Chickasaws with sixty horses loaded with merchandise and munitions which they were selling very cheaply, and they are directing all their efforts toward trying to reconcile these two nations [Chickasaws and Choctaws] with a view to entering the country of the Choctaws, offering to trade with them . . . at a very advantageous price. It appears in all their movements," he concluded, "that they are neglecting nothing to attempt to lead our good allies astray." [61] Bienville echoed this dismal theme when he wrote about that time that the British had made infinite progress in gaining the minds of the Indians. The Creeks seemed to be leaning toward the British, the Chickasaws were entirely theirs, and even some of the Choctaws were wavering, he said. And, as if that were not enough, the Illinois Indians to the north also were showing the malignant effects of their influence.[62] Part of the British strategy was to promote an alliance between the Chickasaws and Choctaws, while at the same time gaining ground with the Creeks and maintaining good relations with the Cherokees. In 1738 the Choctaws actually began exploring the possibility not only of a regular trade with the British but even an alliance. Furthermore, by the beginning of 1739 only about nine Indian villages, most of them in the vicinity of St. Augustine, were still thoroughly loyal to the Spanish regime.[63] Yet the British did not have it all their own way, and toward the end of the 1730s there were signs of trouble. Much of this may be attributed to the misbehavior of British traders, rough men who had an eye only for profit and pleasure, and whose acquaintance with the gentle art of diplomacy was of the slimmest. Tribes which had been led to believe in British friendship sometimes discovered that in a time of danger from enemies their supposed friends were too far away to be of much help. This was true, certainly, in the case of the Chickasaws. As for the Choctaws, they were far too close to the base of French power to shake themselves free of that influence even for the apparent advantages of British trade. So the situation remained fluid and a constant worry to all parties concerned.

On the military side, Britain moved in 1737 to bolster its defensive strength on the southern frontier by placing all forces in South Carolina and Georgia under the supreme command of Oglethorpe, who now was given a general's commission. This and other measures taken, including the strengthening of the militia, were in response to a growing danger of imminent military action. As early as 1736 the Spanish government had been contemplating an offensive against Georgia, and during the winter of 1737–38 preparations for such a move were in full swing at Havana, the principal Spanish base. The operation was scheduled for the spring of 1738. On the day before the troop-laden transports were to sail, the authorities at Havana received royal orders canceling the expedition. Had it proceeded as planned, Georgia in its feeble condition might well have crumbled and the whole British position in the Southeast been greatly weakened. But within a few months Oglethorpe, who had been in England since 1737, arrived in Georgia with a regiment of newly raised regulars, South Carolina was further improving its defenses, and the opportunity for an easy conquest was gone.[64]

During the long period of uneasy peace after 1713, Britain had allowed her navy and army to hibernate so as to avoid the constant heavy expense of maintaining them in a vigorous, active condition. Units were cut down to minimal size; ships were kept at their moorings; officers were turned off on half-pay. The navy leveled off at about 16,000 officers and men, and the army at only about 2,000 more. Even so, the two services, the navy in particular, were a constant and heavy drain on the treasury and, therefore, an important factor in British politics. The senior service, the navy, was more popular with the general public, which liked to think of those ships of oak as Britain's primary line of defense and the cement of empire. The standing army, still less than a hundred years old and therefore relatively new in British tradition, was rather suspect as the potential tool of tyranny. Both services were governed and administered separately by a complex hierarchy of boards, offices, and officials, which contributed heavily to the notorious slowness and inefficiency of nearly all military affairs. One modern historian, after examining this administrative structure, was led to remark that "it is something of a mystery how, with so much overlapping and inefficiency, Britain ever put an army in the field." [65]

The commissioned officers were mostly from the upper class, many of them younger sons of prominent families. Often such young men, self-centered and snobbish, looked upon a military career only as a step toward fame and wealth. There were no established academies for the training of career officers, and the usual entrée was personal influence or money. A young gentleman might begin his army career, for example, by purchasing an ensign's commission in a selected regiment. Later, when a vacancy occurred at a higher rank, he could buy his own promotion, and so continue climbing the ladder of command. In time of war he might even apply his financial resources to the recruiting of a new regiment; if successful, he would then be entitled to the colonelcy. This could be a sound financial investment, for once commissioned a colonel he would begin to receive substantial monetary returns over and above his salary, in the form of perquisites derived from regimental income.[66] A young gentleman might begin a naval career by persuading some captain to take him to sea with him in the character of a personal servant or aide. If his service proved satisfactory, a commission would become available in due time. The introduction to life on board a man-of-war was likely to be a disillusioning experience for anyone accustomed to a fair degree of luxury. "At once resign a good table for no table, and a good bed for your length and breadth," wrote one who knew.

Nay, it will be thought an indulgence, too, to let you sleep where day ne'er enters, and where fresh air only comes when forced. . . . Your light for day and night is a small candle, which is often stuck at the side of your platter at meals, for want of a better convenience; your victuals are salt, and often bad; and, if you vary the mode of dressing them, you must cook yourself.[67]

Clawing their way upward from these circumstances, young officers often became obsessed with the lure of personal advancement, ingratiating with superiors and contemptuous of those below.

Since promotion in both services ordinarily came through means not directly related to actual ability, and in the higher ranks by a rather rigid system of seniority, it is no wonder that Britain's military leadership not infrequently was characterized by mediocrity and even incompetence. Especially in the army, it was difficult, perhaps impossible, to maintain any really significant standards of competence for commissioned officers. The idea still lingered that blue blood was fighting blood, and all too often England found to her cost that this was a fallacy. As explained by one military historian,

the eighteenth-century officer corps subordinated the military values of expertise, discipline, and responsibility to the aristocratic values of luxury, courage, and individualism. The aristocrat was an amateur at officership; it was not for him a vocation with ends and standards of its own, but an incidental attribute of his station in society.[68]

The snobbish attitude of British army officers often included an ill-concealed disdain for colonists in general, which began at an early date to worsen relations between army units stationed in America and the local populace.

The enlisted personnel were entirely from the lower classes, and all too often from the very dregs of that society. There was in navy or army life at that time little to attract and much to repel the ordinary honest citizen. Yet somehow the ships had to be manned and the ranks filled. Because voluntary enlistment brought few recruits, recourse was constantly had to the courts and the press-gang. Magistrates often spared convicted criminals on condition that they join one of the military services. Sir John William Fortescue, the leading historian of the British Army, asserted flatly that "the ranks were filled in great measure by professional criminals, who passed from regiment to regiment, spreading everywhere the infection of discontent, debauchery, and insubordination." Is it any wonder that military personnel were held in such low regard? "The most honest man in England had but to don the red coat to be dubbed a lewd profligate wretch." [69] And what of the ordinary seamen in the king's ships? They were mostly tough and experienced sailors, trained on the decks and in the rigging of merchant vessels, and brought into the Royal Navy against their will by the hated press-gangs. They knew what to expect—lower pay and a harder life.

Discipline in Britain's armed forces was notably harsh. This seemed necessary if rough, conniving, unruly men of dubious character were to be transformed into well-regulated sailors and soldiers. Insubordination, neglect of duty, disobedience, and other breaches of the regulations were inexorably punished by hanging, shooting, flogging, picketing, and other grievous penalties designed more to terrorize the offender's comrades than to reform the culprit himself. Desertion was fairly common, as men made desperate by hard conditions sought to escape to freedom; apparently no punishment, no matter how severe, could snuff out this manifestation of hope.

The British private served king and country for 20 shillings per month, actually seeing very little of that thanks to various deductions, authorized and otherwise.[70] It is fairly safe to surmise that the ordinary soldier had little need for a pocket in his uniform. Like his counterpart afloat, he subsisted on a coarse and monotonous diet notably deficient in fresh meat and vegetables but probably not substandard for the common people of that day. Food was distributed from army supplies by officials known as commissaries. The usual practice in barracks or camp was for small groups of soldiers to draw their rations as a unit and then cook them as they desired. Sometimes on troop transports after many weeks at sea soldiers and sailors alike shared a diet whose only virtue was that it kept a man alive until the fleet arrived in port. The description given in Smollett's *Adventures of Roderick Random* conveys an impression sufficiently distinct:

> Our provision consisted of putrid salt beef, to which the sailors gave the name of Irish horse; salt pork of New England, which, though neither fish nor flesh, savoured of both; bread from the same country, every biscuit whereof, like a piece of clock-work, moved by its own

internal impulse, occasioned by the myriads of insects that dwelt within it; and butter served out by the gill, that tasted like train-oil thickened with salt.[71]

In spite of peacetime economies, by 1739 the British Navy was the most powerful sea force afloat, although both France and Spain still could offer a respectable challenge, especially if they acted in concert. It is probably true that French and Spanish men-of-war were better designed and better constructed than the ships of the Royal Navy, but Britain enjoyed a greater number of ships and to some extent a detectable superiority in their use.

Pass the British fleet in review to appraise its power. First there are the seven monstrous first-rates, the backbone of the line, great looming wooden fortresses with tier upon tier of guns gaping through the gunports along each side. Such ships carry as many as a hundred cannon, some weighing as much as 7,000 pounds and hurling an iron ball of more than 40 pounds. Next come a dozen second-rates of about ninety guns each, nearly as formidable as the great ships of the first group and beautiful with their many sails stretched taut across the sky. Lesser ships follow: forty third-rates of seventy to eighty guns, sixty-two fourth-rates of fifty to sixty guns, and finally a swarm of even smaller fighting ships and auxiliary vessels.[72] All but the very last are primarily floating platforms for cannon which are used to slash down the rigging and puncture the hulls of enemy ships or to pound enemy earthworks and fortified positions ashore. The ships' guns can be used effectively only at fairly close range, for they are not instruments of great accuracy nor are the heaving decks of warships at sea a very stable base from which to take aim. But at close range their power of destruction can be tremendous.[73] Now send off these men-of-war to near and distant stations around the world—to the ports of Britain, to the blue Mediterranean, to the steaming coast of tropical Africa, to the fever-breeding harbors of the Caribbean, to the icy seas off the coast of Nova Scotia. There they are capable of cruising for weeks on end, protecting Britain's sea lanes, attacking enemy shipping and shore bases, supporting Britain's army in its overseas campaigning, even, if necessary, holding restless colonists in awe.

However, maintenance of a large, battle-ready navy was difficult and costly. Such ships required a constant supply of mast and spar timber, hemp for the manufacture of rope, and naval stores derived from the pine tree—resin, tar, pitch, and turpentine. England herself could not produce these items in sufficient quantities and had depended heavily upon the Baltic area for their supply. More recently, however, she had been seeking to develop more secure sources within her own empire. New England was well known for its tall straight pines, eminently suited for masts. The best of these were reserved for the king's use. Bounties were offered for the raising of hemp and for the production of naval stores. Under this encouragement, hemp was being grown in a number of colonies, while the extraction of resinous products from the pine had become an important industry, especially in the Carolinas. The navy's increasing reliance on American sources increased the strategic importance of the colonies, while the accompanying regulations and subsidies created political and economic issues of considerable consequence.[74]

Another aspect of the difficult problem of naval maintenance was the great vulnerability of wooden-hulled ships to dry rot and the relentless gnawing of the tropical worm *teredo navalis*. Britain's warships were prone to rapid deterioration, especially in the tropics, unless given the benefit of careful maintenance, not always possible under the existing conditions of active service and governmental economy.[75]

Naval efficiency, however, is not determined only by the physical condition of men and ships. When war did come, the Royal Navy found itself handicapped in carrying out its vast assignment by two other conditions. The first was the frozen rigidity of prescribed tactics, or what Professor Michael Lewis has aptly labeled "the blight of the Permanent Instructions." [76] These official rules governing combat formations and their use were binding on naval commanders, committing them all too rigidly to the traditional tactics of the time-honored line of battle. Although basically sound and often appropriate, the rules tended to stifle individual initiative and bold innovation in the face of unforeseen conditions and opportunities. It was a rare and bold commander who dared to digress, and woe to him if his digression produced less than a magnificent victory. The second handicap was the great political influence of England's merchants. Such men, having their investments in ships and cargoes, were inclined to consider the navy an instrument designed primarily for their protection. In wartime they made demands upon the Admiralty that were not always in accord with more important strategic considerations. As a consequence, the navy had to devote too much of its strength to guarding convoys, chasing after enemy privateers, and otherwise protecting and promoting British commerce. Important as these tasks might be, their priority was not justified by the total demands of an imperial struggle across half the world.[77]

The army sometimes was transported by the navy, but its proper element was *terra firma* where it could spread itself out in battle array and maneuver to bring its firepower most effectively to bear upon enemy formations and positions. At that time, it may be said, there were only two combat branches of the army—the cavalry and the infantry, for both the Royal Regiment of Artillery and the loosely organized engineers served under the Board of Ordnance, a governmental organization that provided cannon and munitions to the armed forces. If a particular campaign, operation, or expedition required a "siege train," then units of artillery and groups of engineers, along with a variety of civilian technicians, would be assigned or recruited for that purpose. Once in being, the siege train came under the authority of the senior army commander in the field, to be employed as he directed.

Cavalry and infantry were usually organized in regiments, although smaller units existed for special kinds of service, most notably the so-called independent companies sometimes stationed in the colonies. A regiment of foot was commanded by a colonel. Serving under the colonel's command were his lieutenant colonel, major, adjutant, chaplain, quartermaster, surgeon, and surgeon's mate. A typical regiment was divided into twelve companies, at least one of which usually consisted of specially equipped troops known as grenadiers, whose specialty was hurling small, fused, hand bombs. Another company might be comprised of light infantry, agile men with relatively lightweight equipment, capable of rapid movement on difficult terrain. The remaining companies were ordinary infantry who carried the usual long-barreled musket. Contrary to modern practice, the colonel himself commanded one of the companies, while the lieutenant colonel led another, and the major a third. This left nine companies each under the command of a captain. Every company commander usually was assisted by a lieutenant, an ensign, two sergeants, and several corporals. One or two drummers marched with the company, providing a beat for

tramping feet and in battle conveying the captain's orders. The
remainder of the men, perhaps forty in all, were privates. In time
of war the number of privates in each company might be increased
to sixty or more, so that the numerical strength of a line regiment
would stand at about 850.[78]

Under the influence of the Hanoverian kings, especially George
II, the British Army had entered the age of "spit and polish." Although the sailor's uniform remained loose, practical, and comfortable, that of the soldier became tight, stiff, and showy, better
suited to the parade ground than the battlefield. It consisted of a
tricornered hat; shirt and stock; close-fitting waistcoat; red outer
coat with brass buttons, fancy facing, and tails; tight breeches;
gaiters; and shoes.[79] Close-order drill, an important part of training for combat, was a matter of automated precision that was
achieved only through frequent and lengthy practice. Marching
was a large part of the soldier's life. Wherever he went on land,
he carried himself on his own two legs, often lugging a great
weight on back and shoulders. Fortescue gives us an itemized account of what a grenadier carried on the march:[80]

	lb.	oz.
Coat	5	2
Firelock with sling, etc.	11	0
Knapsack with contents, viz.:		
2 shirts, 2 stocks,		
2 pair stockings, 1 pair		
summer breeches, 1 pair		
shoes, brushes, and blackball	7	10
	23	12
Other items, and 6 days' provisions	39	7
Total	63	3

This would make the miles long indeed, especially in wild, hilly
country where the way was rough. Regiments in the field had to
make their own arrangements for auxiliary transport. This sometimes was accomplished through a contractor, who would undertake to provide a specified number of horses and wagons; at other
times, simply by impressing the necessary carts and animals from
the local populace. An army moving overland on campaign often
stretched along the road for miles, a long column of marching
men directed by officers on horseback. With the column was the
train of horse-drawn artillery, munition carts, and heavy farm

wagons heaped high with casks of salted or pickled meat and other foodstuffs, officers' chests, and tents. Rumbling and creaking, the heavy-laden vehicles raised a choking cloud of dust that settled slowly upon the troops behind; the hoarse shouts of the wagoners together with the cracking of whips provided an erratic accompaniment to the more regular sound of tramping feet.

The weapons of the individual foot soldier had changed little since the latter part of the seventeenth century. These included the smooth-bore firelock musket, short of range and inaccurate but deadly at close quarters, and the long slender bayonet which had long since replaced the pike in most European armies. Battle tactics remained correspondingly tradition-bound, centered upon the defense or reduction of fortified positions in accordance with well-defined procedures, and upon the confrontation of opposed armies in the open field. Units entering battle were maneuvered by their officers in tight, disciplined formations, company by company in straight rank and file. The climax came when the two armies were brought face to face in line of battle, separated by only a few yards of open ground. In these positions, the infantry would commence firing in volleys, while units of cavalry attempted to turn the enemy's flank. If the opposition began to waver and show signs of breaking, the commander would order a bayonet charge to win the field and complete the destruction of the enemy force. This kind of fighting required a high level of proficiency and discipline, which of course placed civilian militia at a distinct disadvantage. It is worth noting, however, that the procedures and practices of the regular army provided a pattern for imitation by the commanders of colonial forces raised to fight in the colonial wars.

In the use of artillery, especially against stationary targets, the army had a somewhat greater opportunity than the navy to employ the science of ballistics. Theoretically, gunners were supposed to take into consideration a variety of controlling factors when aiming their cannon; but in actual combat, gunnery was largely a matter of eye and estimate. Given the relatively short ranges of the guns used in the field, well-trained artillerymen often were able to deliver effective fire upon enemy positions, providing significant support for the infantry. Artillery was most important in siege operations against fortified positions, to breach walls and demoralize the enemy garrison.

Medical services available to the troops were woefully inadequate, although it must be remembered that the medical care received by most civilians in that age was perhaps no better. There was no organized medical corps in the army nor were field hospitals regularly maintained. A severe epidemic among the troops or heavy casualties in battle might result in the establishment of a temporary hospital. At other times, sick or injured soldiers were kept in their barracks or tents to recuperate, or else deposited in some civilian household. Epidemic disease, especially in the tropics, periodically swept through the ranks, filling not only the regimental hospital but the graveyard as well. Conditions of comfort and sanitation in these military hospitals left much to be desired. A chaplain who went to visit the patients in one such hospital found the stench there "so Nauseous, that I could not tarry. . . ." [81] Regimental surgeons, assisted by surgeon's mates, carried the entire burden of medical care in the field, and at times they must have found the work overwhelming. Few of the soldiers could have had much faith in the powers of these men, their instruments, or their remedies.

Such were the armed forces maintained by Britain during the early decades of the eighteenth century, some 35,000 men with their ships and guns, to protect and preserve an empire in an age of cold war. The challenge of "hot war," so soon to confront them, would be the real test of quality. When that test came in 1739, it marked the beginning of a renewed international struggle extending over a period of more than twenty years. At stake were the future growth and prosperity—perhaps even the very survival—of three great world empires.

NOTES

1. "A Map of the English and French Possessions on the Continent of North America. 1727, H. Popple," indicates the major water routes followed by the French. Popple was an employee of the Board of Trade. His map is in Additional Manuscripts 23615, f. 72 (British Museum).

2. John Tate Lanning, *The Diplomatic History of Georgia: A Study of the Epoch of Jenkins' Ear* (Chapel Hill, 1936), pp. 92–93, 106–107.

3. Gov. Jonathan Belcher to Mr. Grant, 8 February 1733/34, in 6 *MHC*, VII, 12.

4. [Philip Livingston] to Samuel Storke, 13 March 1734, Manuscripts Miscellaneous, V (New York State Library). See also Livingston's letters of

24 August 1736 and November 1736 in the same volume. On 31 July 1738 Livingston complained that "the french are suffered to surround us on all sides and we quietly must Submitt to their Incroachments, it's what ought to be Redressed but I see no prospect of it"; he went on to emphasize the importance of holding the Six Nations firmly in the British interest.

5. Douglas (Summers) Brown, *The Catawba Indians: The People of the River* (Columbia, S.C., 1966), pp. 133–134.

6. Verner W. Crane, *The Southern Frontier, 1670–1732* (Durham, 1928), pp. 162–164; David H. Corkran, *The Creek Frontier, 1540–1783* (Norman, Okla., 1967), p. 57.

7. Robert L. Meriwether, *The Expansion of South Carolina, 1729–1765* (Kingsport, Tenn., 1940), p. 14; Corkran, *Creek Frontier*, p. 4.

8. Meriwether, *Expansion of South Carolina*, p. 13.

9. Crane, *Southern Frontier*, pp. 168–169.

10. Quoted in Richard P. Sherman, *Robert Johnson: Proprietary & Royal Governor of South Carolina* (Columbia, S.C., 1966), p. 19.

11. William L. Saunders, ed., *The Colonial Records of North Carolina* (10 vols.; Raleigh, N.C., 1886–1890), II, 177. See also B. R. Carroll, comp., *Historical Collections of South Carolina* (2 vols.; New York, 1836), I, 192; John Jay TePaske, *The Governorship of Spanish Florida, 1700–1763* (Durham, 1964), pp. 198–204; Crane, *Southern Frontier*, p. 167.

12. Richebourg Gaillard McWilliams, ed., *Fleur de Lys and Calumet, Being the Pénicaut Narrative of French Adventure in Louisiana* (Baton Rouge, 1953), p. 164.

13. Corkran, *Creek Frontier*, p. 58.

14. Frank J. Klingberg, ed., *The Carolina Chronicle of Dr. Francis Le Jau, 1706–1717* (Berkeley and Los Angeles, 1956), p. 159; Brown, *Catawba Indians*, pp. 135–138; Corkran, *Creek Frontier*, pp. 57–58; Edgar Legaré Pennington, "The South Carolina Indian War of 1715, as Seen by the Clergymen," *South Carolina Historical and Genealogical Magazine*, XXXII (October, 1931), 252. I am indebted to Professor Paul H. Bergeron of the University of Tennessee for the use of his unpublished essay on the causes of the Yamassee War.

15. David William Cole, "The Organization and Administration of the South Carolina Militia System, 1670–1783" (Unpublished Ph.D. dissertation, University of South Carolina, 1953), pp. 48–49.

16. Crane, *Southern Frontier*, p. 173.

17. Frank J. Klingberg, ed., *Carolina Chronicle: The Papers of Commissary Gideon Johnston, 1707–1716* (Berkeley and Los Angeles, 1946), p. 147.

18. David Duncan Wallace, *South Carolina, A Short History, 1520–1948* (Chapel Hill, 1951), pp. 127–128; M. Eugene Sirmans, *Colonial South Carolina: A Political History, 1663–1763* (Chapel Hill, 1966), pp. 134–136; Corkran, *Creek Frontier*, pp. 74, 76–77.

19. Crane, *Southern Frontier*, p. 177.

20. Leonidas Dodson, *Alexander Spotswood, Governor of Colonial Virginia, 1710–1722* (Philadelphia, 1932), pp. 34–37; Cole, "Organization and Administration of the South Carolina Militia System, 1670–1783," p. 49.

21. Emmett Francis O'Neil, "English Fear of French Encirclement in North America, 1680–1763" (Unpublished Ph.D. dissertation, University of Michigan, 1941), chap. 4; Richard W. Van Alstyne, *The American Empire: Its Historical Pattern and Evolution* ([London], 1960), pp. 4–5.

22. Heathcote to Governor Hunter, 8 July 1715, *NYCD*, V, 430.

23. McWilliams, *Fleur de Lys and Calumet*, p. 246. See also *ibid.*, p. 165; Daniel H. Thomas, "Fort Toulouse: The French Outpost at the Alibamos on the Coosa," *Alabama Historical Quarterly*, XXII (Fall, 1960), 135–230; Daniel H. Thomas, "Fort Toulouse—in Tradition and Fact," *Alabama Review*, XIII (October, 1960), 243–257.

24. Lanning calls the building of Fort King George a "flagrant intrusion into Spanish territory" *(Diplomatic History of Georgia*, p. 11). See also TePaske, *Governorship of Spanish Florida*, pp. 125–130; Wallace, *South Carolina*, pp. 126–127; Sirmans, *Colonial South Carolina*, p. 135.

25. The report of 8 September 1721 may be consulted in Colonial Office 324, X, 296–431 (Public Record Office, London), and in Additional Manuscripts 23615 (British Museum). It has been published in *NYCD*, V, 591–630, and (with minor deletions) in *CSP* (1720–1721), pp. 408–449.

26. *NYCD*, V, 602.

27. *NYCD*, V, 624–625.

28. *American Empire*, p. 4.

29. For a review of this subject see Crane, *Southern Frontier*, chap. 5; and Douglas Edward Leach, *The Northern Colonial Frontier, 1607–1763* (New York, 1966), chap. 9.

30. Philip Livingston to Storke and Gainsborough, 31 October 1734, Manuscripts Miscellaneous, V (New York State Library).

31. Quoted in Sherman, *Robert Johnson*, p. 98.

32. Crane, *Southern Frontier*, p. 248; Sirmans, *Colonial South Carolina*, pp. 156–157; Corkran, *Creek Frontier*, pp. 76–77.

33. Crane, *Southern Frontier*, pp. 249–251; TePaske, *Governorship of Spanish Florida*, pp. 131–132, 208–209; Sirmans, *Colonial South Carolina*, p. 157.

34. Leach, *Northern Colonial Frontier*, p. 131.

35. *Ibid.*, pp. 147–149.

36. Thomas Hutchinson, *The History of the Colony and Province of Massachusetts-Bay*, Lawrence Shaw Mayo, ed. (3 vols.; Cambridge, Mass., 1936), II, 197. Francis Parkman quotes from a letter apparently written by the French missionary Rasles about 1720 in which the priest claims that any treaty made by the Abnakis with the English "is null and void if I do not approve it, for I give them so many reasons against it that they absolutely condemn what they have done." Then Parkman goes on to show how the situation sometimes was reversed: When Rasles was present, his Indians "would denounce the heretics and boast of the brave deeds they would do against them, yet after a meeting with English officials, they would change their minds and accuse their spiritual father of lying" (*A Half-Century of Conflict* [2 vols.; Boston, 1892], I, 222, 224).

37. Letter dated 30 December 1723, in William B. Trask, ed., *Letters of Colonel*

Thomas Westbrook and Others Relative to Indian Affairs in Maine, 1722–1726 (Boston, 1901), pp. 42–43.

38. *The Acts and Resolves, Public and Private, of the Province of the Massachusetts Bay* (21 vols.; Boston, 1869–1922), II, 228.

39. Trask, *Letters of Colonel Thomas Westbrook and Others*, pp. 42–43; Samuel Penhallow, *The History of the Wars of New-England with the Eastern Indians* (Collections of the New Hampshire Historical Society, I [Concord, 1824]), 91; Parkman, *Half-Century of Conflict*, I, 229–230.

40. Massachusetts Archives, XXXI, 106–108. This has been published in Penhallow, *History of the Wars of New-England*, pp. 94–95.

41. Trask, *Letters of Colonel Thomas Westbrook and Others*, pp. 88–91.

42. Fannie Hardy Eckstorm, "The Attack on Norridgewock: 1724," *NEQ*, VII (September, 1934), 541–578. The English were familiar with Norridgewock through personal contact. Hutchinson tells us that the chapel there had been built by carpenters from New England (*History of the Colony and Province of Massachusetts-Bay*, II, 237).

43. Trask, *Letters of Colonel Thomas Westbrook and Others*, pp. 70–71; *Boston Gazette* for 17 to 24 and 24 to 31 August 1724; Hutchinson, *History of the Colony and Province of Massachusetts-Bay*, II, 234–238; Eckstorm, "Attack on Norridgewock: 1724," pp. 568–570.

44. *History of the Wars of New-England*, p. 108. When Harmon with his grisly trophies arrived at Boston just ten days after the victory, he was greeted with "great Shouting and Triumph" by the assembled multitude (Samuel Sewall's Diary, in 5 *MHC*, VII, 343).

45. *The Acts and Resolves, Public and Private, of the Province of the Massachusetts Bay*, II, 258–259; Hutchinson, *History of the Colony and Province of Massachusetts-Bay*, II, 238.

46. *Half-Century of Conflict*, I, 250.

47. *Boston Gazette* for 10 to 17 May 1725.

48. Thomas Symmes, *Historical Memoirs of the Late Fight at Piggwacket, with a Sermon Occasion'd by the Fall of the Brave Capt John Lovewell and Several of His Valiant Company, . . .* (2d ed.; Boston, 1725), gives a good contemporary account of the action.

49. *Half-Century of Conflict*, I, 254.

50. Penhallow, *History of the Wars of New-England*, pp. 123–132; Henry F. DePuy, comp., *A Bibliography of the English Colonial Treaties with the American Indians, Including a Synopsis of Each Treaty* (New York, 1917), pp. 11–12.

51. John Pitts Corry, *Indian Affairs in Georgia, 1732–1756* (Philadelphia, 1936), p. 108; Wallace, *South Carolina*, pp. 129–130; Sirmans, *Colonial South Carolina*, p. 161.

52. The charter has been published in Allen D. Candler, ed., *The Colonial Records of the State of Georgia* (26 vols.; Atlanta, 1904–1916), I, 11–26.

53. Candler, *Colonial Records of the State of Georgia*, I, 24–25.

54. Clarence L. Ver Steeg, Introduction to Pat[rick] Tailfer *et al.*, *A True and Historical Narrative of the Colony of Georgia. . . .* (Athens, Ga., 1960), p. ix.

55. Amos A. Ettinger, *James Edward Oglethorpe, Imperial Idealist* (Oxford and New York, 1936), pp. 67–68.

56. *Ibid.*, p. 134; E. Merton Coulter, *Georgia: A Short History* (Rev. ed.; Chapel Hill, 1947), p. 26.

57. TePaske, *Governorship of Spanish Florida*, pp. 134–136.

58. Robert G. McPherson, ed., *The Journal of the Earl of Egmont: Abstract of the Trustees Proceedings for Establishing the Colony of Georgia, 1732–1738* (Athens, Ga., 1962), pp. 143–144, 146–147; Ettinger, *James Edward Oglethorpe*, p. 169; Coulter, *Georgia*, pp. 30–31, 36–37.

59. Ettinger, *James Edward Oglethorpe*, pp. 175–177; Corry, *Indian Affairs in Georgia*, pp. 117–118; Coulter, *Georgia*, pp. 40–41.

60. McPherson, *Journal of the Earl of Egmont*, p. 349; Corry, *Indian Affairs in Georgia*, pp. 119–120; Meriwether, *Expansion of South Carolina*, p. 26; Sirmans, *Colonial South Carolina*, pp. 207–208.

61. Chevalier de Loubois to Maurepas, 8 May 1733, in Dunbar Rowland and Albert Godfrey Sanders, eds., *Mississippi Provincial Archives, 1729–1740: French Dominion* (Jackson, Miss., 1927), p. 217.

62. Rowland and Sanders, *Mississippi Provincial Archives, 1729–1740: French Dominion*, p. 193.

63. Corkran, *Creek Frontier*, pp. 98–99; Sirmans, *Colonial South Carolina*, p. 197; TePaske, *Governorship of Spanish Florida*, pp. 209–213.

64. Tailfer *et al.*, *True and Historical Narrative of the Colony of Georgia*, pp. 66–67, 82–83; McPherson, *Journal of the Earl of Egmont*, pp. 296–298, 301–306, 314–315, 334, 347–349; Lanning, *Diplomatic History of Georgia*, chap. 4; Meriwether, *Expansion of South Carolina*, p. 188; Ettinger, *James Edward Oglethorpe*, pp. 190–200; TePaske, *Governorship of Spanish Florida*, pp. 137–138; Sirmans, *Colonial South Carolina*, pp. 195–196.

65. Dorothy Marshall, *Eighteenth Century England* (New York, 1962), pp. 47–48.

66. R. E. Scouller states that an ensign's commission usually cost £200 or more, while that of a colonel seldom went for less than £400 (*The Armies of Queen Anne* [Oxford, 1966], p. 138). Later the crown attempted to apply a form of price control to these transactions (John W. Fortescue, *A History of the British Army* [13 vols. and 6 atlases; London, 1889–1930], II, 30). See also the comment in Samuel P. Huntington, *The Soldier and the State: The Theory and Politics of Civil-Military Relations* (Cambridge, Mass., 1957), p. 23.

67. Quoted in William Laird Clowes, *The Royal Navy: A History from the Earliest Times to the Present* (7 vols.; London, 1897–1903), III, 21.

68. Huntington, *Soldier and the State*, pp. 26–27. Much the same idea is expressed by Scouller: "Officers were, in the main, gentlemen of substance who would view themselves as subordinate to their army superiors only for strictly limited purposes. Social rank, for example, could often outweigh army rank" (*Armies of Queen Anne*, p. 265).

69. Fortescue, *History of the British Army*, II, 32.

70. Fortescue, *History of the British Army*, I, 318–319, 570; Charles M. Andrews, *Guide to the Materials for American History, to 1783, in the Public Record*

Office of Great Britain (2 vols.; Washington, D.C., 1912–1914), II, 273–274; Scouller, *Armies of Queen Anne,* pp. 127, 220, 240, 279, 287.

71. Chap. 33.

72. Daniel A. Baugh, *British Naval Administration in the Age of Walpole* (Princeton, 1965), pp. 245–246.

73. For data on the various types of guns in service with the British Navy at this time see Clowes, *Royal Navy,* III, 11.

74. The standard treatment of one major aspect of this problem is Robert G. Albion, *Forests and Sea Power: The Timber Problem of the Royal Navy, 1652–1862* (Cambridge, Mass., 1926).

75. Baugh, *British Naval Administration in the Age of Walpole,* pp. 241–243.

76. Michael Lewis, *The Navy of Britain, a Historical Portrait* (London, 1948), p. 483.

77. Baugh, *British Naval Administration in the Age of Walpole,* pp. 18–21; Gerald S. Graham, "The Naval Defence of British North America, 1739–1763," in Transactions of the Royal Historical Society, Ser. 4, XXX (1948), 100–103.

78. Scouller, *Armies of Queen Anne,* pp. 99–101.

79. An excellent idea of grenadier uniforms may be obtained by studying Plates 55–72 in A. E. Haswell Miller and N. P. Dawnay, *Military Drawings and Paintings in the Collection of Her Majesty the Queen* (London, 1966).

80. Fortescue, *History of the British Army,* II, 592n.

81. Stephen Williams' Journal, in Louis Effingham De Forest, ed., *Louisbourg Journals, 1745* (New York, 1932), p. 147.

☆   ☆   ☆   ☆   ☆

CHAPTER 6

The War of the 1740s

THE LONG INTERVAL of cold war since the Peace of Utrecht was broken in 1739 with the outbreak of a new conflict among the powers of western Europe, a conflict in which the American colonies were to play a subsidiary but nonetheless significant role. This war was not a single or a simple one, but rather a shifting complex of wars with multiple causes and multiple objectives. Its earliest phase was a maritime war between Britain and Spain which began in 1739. This struggle had barely gotten underway when certain governments in Europe, especially that of Prussia, challenged the status of the female Hapsburg, Maria Theresa, thereby precipitating what has become known as the War of the Austrian Succession, with Spain, France, and Prussia the principal opponents of Austria, the Netherlands, and Britain. Actually Britain's entry into this continental struggle was gradual and almost surreptitious; not until March 1744, by mutual declarations of war, did Britain and France officially renew their old enmity. When they did, it meant that once more the Bourbon monarchies were linked as allies against the British, a matter of great moment for Britain's American colonies. In British America this new conflict became known as King George's War. Because these various international struggles, all so closely interrelated, occupied the greater part of the decade from 1739 to 1749 we may for the sake of convenience lump them together under the simple term, "The War of the 1740s." [1] While it is true that by this time the importance of colonial empire was becoming more fully appreciated, most European statesmen continued to give priority to European affairs. Only a small minority of younger leaders such as William Pitt were beginning to realize the great importance of worldwide empire. Strategic considerations emphasizing Europe rather than the wider world prevailed, which is why military and naval resources were husbanded so carefully at home and seldom shared in significant quantities with the struggling colonies.

By the decade of the 1740s, France again was able to deploy impressive forces on land and sea as a threat to her British rival. In Europe, Britain's major concern was to guard her own territory against the threat of a cross-Channel invasion by the powerful army of Louis XV, possibly coordinated with a domestic uprising in support of the Stuart pretender. In addition, she was anxious to prevent the Bourbon powers, especially France, from gaining overwhelming strength on the Continent. A cornerstone of this longstanding, one may even say traditional, British policy was the military and financial support given by England to allied states on France's borders, most notably the Netherlands, as a means of checking French territorial ambitions. Britain herself could not hope to match the armies of Louis XV in the field, but her deficiency in this regard was counterbalanced by the combined land forces of her allies and, most important of all, by the strength of the Royal Navy. It was the navy, with its majestic oaken ships of the line and coursing frigates, that would keep open the long sea lanes to Britain's colonies and deny the free use of the ocean to Britain's enemies. This meant, among other things, that France could not expect to move her superior army as she might wish against England itself, or England's most distant colonies. It has well been said that at this epoch the real defense of British America was in the English Channel.[2]

Within the American theater were two major zones of activity: The first, which included the entire eastern part of North America from Newfoundland to the southern tip of the Florida peninsula, has already been examined; its problems of the fur trade, territorial expansion, border disputes, Indian relations, and military strategy are familiar. The other major zone was the region of the Caribbean

Sea with its surrounding frame of islands and main. Spain, France, and Britain all had strategic and territorial interests in this area, making it truly a cockpit of international rivalries. Heavily fortified Spanish bases at Porto Bello on the Isthmus of Panama, Cartagena on the north coast of South America, and Havana on the island of Cuba, still served as points of assembly for Spanish treasure fleets laden for the homeward voyage. French territory included the important sugar islands of Guadeloupe and Martinique which also could provide bases for naval squadrons and privateers. The British owned several islands in the Leeward and Windward groups, besides the island of Jamaica. On the latter, just across the bay from Kingston, was located the important naval base at Port Royal, providing the Royal Navy a haven and repair facility within easy striking range of French and Spanish territory.

At many places and in many ways, bold and enterprising British traders and entrepreneurs were inserting little taps to drain the riches from Spain's great empire, all of which were clear violations of the Spanish mercantile system and extremely annoying to Madrid. From Jamaica, for example, British vessels carried on a flourishing clandestine trade with Spanish ports in the area, despite official attempts to prevent it. Spanish patrol vessels, the energetic and often privately owned *guardacostas*, prowled the trade routes and hovered ominously wherever British ships were to be expected, but they never managed to stamp out the traffic. Their questionable interference with lawful commerce on the high seas verged on piracy, while the rough handling they gave to suspected smugglers only served to rub salt into old wounds. Britons especially objected to the Spanish practice of stopping and searching any vessel whose behavior seemed at all suspicious, even on the high seas. When such a search raised some doubt about the legitimacy of the vessel's affairs, the usual procedure was to take the ship into custody until the matter could be settled in the Spanish courts. This meant a tedious wait, loss of profits, and often the ultimate condemnation of the vessel and its cargo. In response, British mercantilists and imperialists raised the cry of "No search!" and "Freedom of the seas!" A wave of patriotic fervor began to surge in England, deliberately fostered by the interested merchant class of Britain's great seaports. While the king's first minister, Robert Walpole, remained committed to a policy of peaceful accommodation if at all possible, his political opposition, preferring drastic countermeasures against

Spain, took every opportunity to fuel the fires of patriotic indignation. The most famous example of their endeavors is the interrogation of the one-eared mariner Robert Jenkins in the House of Commons in 1738. According to this man's testimony, the ship of which he was master had been stopped and searched seven years earlier by a Spanish patrol vessel. The Spaniards had then plundered the English ship and, before letting Captain Jenkins go, had brutally sliced off one of his ears. As tangible evidence of the outrage, he could point to the ugly stump on the side of his head, and lo, the missing appendage held forth in his hand for all the members of the House to see. According to time-honored tradition, Jenkins then stoutly declaimed: "I committed my soul to God," adding pointedly, "and my cause to my country." [3]

Spain was willing to continue the search for a peaceful solution of the Caribbean problem, but the British mercantile patriots would accept nothing less than unconditional "freedom of the seas." Walpole finally was forced to insist that Spain forego the searching of suspected vessels, a concession that would have made it virtually impossible for the Spanish authorities to control the illicit trade. This concession the royal government at Madrid would not make. Accordingly, to the great regret and misgiving of Walpole, the British government issued a declaration against Spain in October 1739, precipitating the so-called "War of Jenkins' Ear." [4] Although Britain did have some genuine grievances against Spain, especially in the excesses of the *guardacostas*, there was no necessity for war in 1739. This new international conflict was largely the product of British politics combined with the ambitions of aggressive commercial imperialism; Britain was giving vent to its old lust for spoiling the Spanish Empire. Some British leaders thought in terms of new territory that might be acquired—Florida, for example, as well as tropical lands farther south, which would strengthen the British mercantile empire. Others hoped that the tightly regulated Spanish mercantile system might be cracked open, permitting British merchants to trade more brazenly than ever within that system, much as Hawkins had done two centuries before. Still others laid emphasis on the rich plunder that might be gained by raiding the Spanish Empire, especially the fabulous cargoes of bullion that regularly accumulated at American terminals, such as Porto Bello and Cartagena, awaiting shipment across the Atlantic. Even ordinary seamen and soldiers might expect to share in booty wrested from the Dons; it seemed as though there was something for nearly everybody in a war against decadent Spain.[5]

Months before the actual declaration of war, the British ministry had authorized colonial governors in America to issue letters of marque and reprisal to enterprising sea captains yearning to sink their claws into Spanish commerce. Even more significant and provocative were the orders handed to Vice Admiral Edward Vernon some three months prior to his government's declaration of war. Vernon was directed to proceed to the West Indies with a small but powerful fleet and begin ravishing Spanish ships and colonies.[6] For the next nine years, various kinds of armed ships—Spanish, British, and, after 1743, French—hovered off the coasts and along the ocean routes, doing what damage they could to the enemy for their own personal gain. The War of the 1740s was, indeed, a great breeder of privateers if not always of patriots. No less an authority than Admiral Vernon, referring to the breed of sea dogs who sailed as privateers, testified that "serving the public is the least part of either their thoughts or inclinations. The attaining plunder from merchant ships they hope to make an easy prey of, being the principal motive, and they little care who it is from, and are many of them as ready for making it on their own nation as any other."[7] In other words, the line separating privateering from piracy was easily blurred. But whatever their motives, thousands of hardy young men of the warring nations, Americans as well as Europeans, seized the opportunity of an expanding war to go adventuring on the high seas at the expense of oceanic commerce.

Admiral Vernon and his fleet arrived at Port Royal in Jamaica at about the time that the British government announced its declaration of war in October 1739. He needed only to reprovision before commencing operations against the Spaniards. The first major objective that Vernon selected for his small but ready fleet was the town of Porto Bello, located near the northernmost point of the Isthmus of Panama. This well-fortified base was a notorious nest of the *guardacostas*, and even more important, a terminus on the treasure route. Arriving with six ships of the line on the afternoon of 20 November 1739, Vernon commenced his attack the next day. The little fleet sailed boldly into the narrow entrance to the harbor, which was guarded by the formidable Iron Castle on the left and the Gloria Castle on the right. As the ships came within close range of the guns of the Iron Castle, the wind unexpectedly dropped, leav-

ing them becalmed like sitting ducks. This could have been fatal if
the Spanish defenses had been maintained at a high level of readiness. Fortunately for the British, however, the forts had been badly
neglected, many of their guns were not in position to fire, the supply
of ammunition was low, and the garrison force inadequate. Vernon's
men turned to with a will, pouring in a hot fire from gun decks and
tops that drove the Spaniards from their stations. Then the landing
party was sent ashore in boats. Advancing briskly to the foot of the
walls, the agile sailors boldly scrambled through the embrasures,
then turned to haul up the marines. By day's end, the fort was under
the British flag, and the next day the other forts and the town itself
were surrendered.[8]

Vernon's quick conquest netted less wealth than had been hoped,
but there was special satisfaction for the British in seizing the three
guardacostas found in the harbor. After systematically blowing up
the forts with captured Spanish powder, Vernon sailed away from
Porto Bello with a booty that included about 10,000 Spanish dollars
and a number of brass cannon. Britain had shown the world what
she intended to do in this new war for trade and empire.

On the Georgia-Florida frontier also, hostilities were flaring.
There the British government was relying upon the initiative of
James Oglethorpe, designated commander in chief of all forces in
the southernmost colonies, to provide an adequate defense against
Spanish aggression and, hopefully, seize any opportunity to capture some or all of the Florida peninsula. This meant that the
fortress town of St. Augustine was a principal target, whose fall
would give Britain a base from which to control the strategic Bahama Channel, route of the Spanish treasure fleets and indeed of
most commerce passing from Latin American ports to Spain.
Yet certain difficulties affected Oglethorpe's ability to act. For one
thing, Georgia itself was in the throes of internal dissension caused
by the official policy prohibiting rum and slavery in the colony and
strictly regulating the acquisition of land. Equally troublesome and
dangerous was the problem of Indian relations, especially with the
Creeks, who were showing signs of hearkening to Spanish overtures.
In an attempt to deal with this problem, Oglethorpe made a long
and difficult wilderness journey in July and August of 1739 to the
Indian village of Coweta on the Chattahoochee River, near the
present Phenix City, Alabama. Here he met with the leaders of
the Creek nation, some Choctaws and Chickasaws also being pres-

ent, and induced the Creeks to reaffirm their friendship with the British. This seems to have been a sincere expression of intent, which offered a necessary measure of security for the interior flank of any Georgia expedition moving down against Florida, and cleared the way for the kind of offensive operation Oglethorpe was eager to begin.[9]

Scarcely had Oglethorpe accomplished his mission to the Creeks, when a party of Spaniards reconnoitering on Amelia Island killed two unarmed Georgians.[10] In retaliation, Oglethorpe got together a small expeditionary force of Creek, Chickasaw, and Yuchi Indians, together with some Scottish rangers of his own regiment, and·proceeded up the St. Johns River toward St. Augustine, ravaging as he went. Small Spanish outpost forces took to their heels, leaving the Georgians free to advance speedily to Forts San Francisco de Popa and Picolata on opposite banks of the St. Johns, only 16 miles west of St. Augustine. These small but strategically located forts were easily taken, so that the British now found themselves in control of "the very back door" of the Spanish capital.[11] Even with this success, however, Oglethorpe knew better than to push his luck too far. The complete conquest to which he aspired would require a far stronger expeditionary force with naval support. Accordingly, after burning down Fort Picolata on the east bank, nearest to St. Augustine, Oglethorpe withdrew to home territory.

Manuel de Montiano, Governor of Florida, had good cause for apprehension, especially after the British with their Indian allies had demonstrated how fragile the outer defenses of St. Augustine really were. Like Oglethorpe, Montiano was a man of no little military experience, having campaigned in both North Africa and Central America prior to assuming his present difficult assignment. Soon after his arrival in 1737, he had inspected the Castillo de San Marcos and found it woefully weak in many respects. Montiano then set about improving this situation as best he could with extremely limited resources.[12] By the end of 1739, significant improvements had been made, including the construction of bombproof shelters within ˉthe walls and the building of some outworks to impede any hostile approach. In addition, a considerable reinforcement had been brought in from Cuba, giving Montiano a garrison capable of providing stout resistance.[13] Possibly the greatest weakness yet remaining was the shortage of supplies, including provisions to feed the more than 2,000 soldiers and civilians inhabiting the town.

Early in 1740 Oglethorpe, determined to succeed where Moore had failed a generation earlier, journeyed up to Charleston in quest of aid from the government of South Carolina. He found that colony deeply troubled by its own problems—a recent bloody insurrection of slaves, believed incited by the Spaniards, and tragic gaps in the population caused by an epidemic of yellow fever. So there was much hesitancy and reluctance for Oglethorpe to overcome, but the eager commander finally succeeded in obtaining the promise of an infantry regiment, some troopers, and a number of transport vessels. Important Indian support, especially from the Cherokees, also became available, and a small number of British warships based at Charleston received orders to cooperate in the undertaking. The combined forces were to rendezvous at the mouth of the St. Johns River that spring.

In April, the Royal Navy began patrolling the Florida coast to prevent supplies and reinforcements from reaching St. Augustine. There were three possible approaches by which Havana might funnel seaborne strength in to the threatened fortress—the St. Johns River to the north, a route already pre-empted by the British; the principal entrance to the harbor at St. Augustine; and the auxiliary entrance of Matanzas Inlet, about 13 miles to the south. These were effectively watched and blocked, and St. Augustine was sealed off from the outside world. An ordinarily dull blockade was enlivened with an occasional flash of action. On 10 April the watch on a British frigate lying becalmed while on patrol just outside the bar at St. Augustine suddenly spotted a tiny flotilla of Spanish galliots and launches emerging from the entrance and heading directly for them. It was a daring sortie for the purpose of boarding and capturing the guard ship—one might almost speak of mice pouring out of their hole in the wall to attack an immobilized cat. The British captain hurriedly put his seamen to work in the boats to tow the becalmed frigate out to sea. After a running fight of about two hours, the courageous Spaniards drew off, frustrated, and the frigate resumed its vigil, while Montiano and his garrison anxiously awaited the next move.[14]

Oglethorpe, obviously impatient for action, made a preliminary foray into the enemy's country prior to the rendezvous of the full

expeditionary force, presumably to test enemy strength and clear
away any outlying defenses that might slow the army's advance.
Fort San Francisco on the St. Johns was readily reoccupied, and
Fort Diego, which really was nothing but a crudely fortified
cowpen between the St. Johns and the ocean some 25 miles above
St. Augustine, was seized and held. Then the commander returned
north to the mouth of the St. Johns to meet the main force of
Georgians and Carolinians. Whatever advantage had been gained
by this preliminary foray was thrown away when Oglethorpe decided
to advance upon St. Augustine not by the easy route of the St. Johns
River to the point of debarkation only 16 miles west of the objective,
but by the hot and difficult overland route between the St. Johns
and the sea. This march, which took place in May, proved to be
prodigal of time and energy, wearying the army before it ever
saw the battlements of San Marcos. Oglethorpe's intention was to
approach from the north, investing the town on that side and the
west, while the fleet stood by just off the bar. When all was ready,
barges with men and artillery from the ships would enter the
harbor, land on Anastasia Island, and bombard the fortress from
the east, while Oglethorpe and his troops made the main assault
on the opposite side. The fortifications were to be taken with a
rush, "sword in hand." Obviously this scheme required almost
perfect coordination between land and sea forces, sometimes
difficult under the best of conditions. Unfortunately for the British,
the Spaniards had their own ideas, which were quite good. Station-
ing a number of heavily armed, shallow-draft vessels inside the
bar in shallow water where they could not be approached by the
British warships, the defenders were in a position to deny entrance
to the incoming barges. This prevented the navy from carrying
out its assignment, forcing Oglethorpe to abandon the plan for a
direct assault and to resort instead to an improvised siege.

Two miles north of St. Augustine, within view of the sentinels
on the ramparts, was a small outpost called Fort Moosa. In taking
possession of this minor fortification the British had destroyed the
gates and made several breaches in the walls, thereby rendering
the place virtually indefensible. Nevertheless, a patrol force of
about 135 British and Indians took their ease in this battered relic
during several successive nights when they should have been in
concealment elsewhere. Their laxity offered an unusual opportunity
to the Spaniards, who needed every break they could obtain. During

the evening of 14 June, a daring party of Spaniards led by Captain Antonio Salgado slipped out of St. Augustine and made their way to the dark shape of Fort Moosa. Attacking with zeal, they quickly overwhelmed the surprised defenders and gained full control. Montiano later recorded that Salgado and his men had killed seventy-two of the enemy and taken thirty-four prisoners, but the total casualties may have been even more.[15] It was a very sharp setback for the British.

In the meantime, Oglethorpe had been shifting his forces around to the east, occupying Point Quartell and the northern part of Anastasia Island, where batteries were readied. It was the thirteenth of June when the British artillery began a systematic bombardment designed to force a capitulation. For days the balls went arching across the sky to explode above the ramparts or smash into the parapets and walls. According to Montiano, however, who certainly was in a position to know, Oglethorpe's gunners were not distinguished by their accuracy.[16] The truth of the matter was that the British never were able to advance their artillery close enough to be really effective, and the Spaniards never wavered in their determination to hold their position. After being forced to abandon the plan of taking St. Augustine by storm, Oglethorpe seemed unable to devise a satisfactory alternative, and just kept on pounding from a distance, hoping that eventually the enemy would break.

As the days went by and the futile bombardment continued, heat and humidity sapped the strength of the besiegers and intensified quarrels between the Carolinians and the Georgians. Fever, too, began to take its toll, killing some and weakening others. Morale was slipping badly. On top of all this, about the twenty-third of June seven Spanish ships carrying supplies from Havana managed to slip past the blockading warships into Matanzas Inlet to replenish the dwindling stocks in the fortress.[17] Oglethorpe was brought to the unpleasant realization that Montiano could hold out almost indefinitely, while his own forces were growing weaker with every passing day. It was at this point that the would-be conqueror accepted defeat. In considerable disorder the British dismantled their batteries, packed up their movables, and headed for home. Once again St. Augustine had shown its capacity for survival.

The aftermath of this failure was an unseemly squabble between Georgia and Carolina, each seeking to shift the burden of blame to the other. Oglethorpe made no secret of his opinion that Charleston had been niggardly in its support of the operation, and charged the Carolina contingent with unsoldierlike conduct. The retort from South Carolina was as sharp as any sword—Oglethorpe's own incompetence as a military commander, rather than any alleged shortcomings of the Carolinians, was the real cause of the defeat. This judgment, tinged as it was with partisan anger and frustration, lies uncomfortably close to the truth, and the only possible extenuation is the fact that Oglethorpe was a sick man during the latter part of the siege. He had shown little grasp of military administration, and at best a weak command of strategy and tactics. When his original plan was found to be impractical, Oglethorpe had not contrived an adequate replacement.[18] Blame also fell upon the navy for failing to prevent the Spaniards from passing supplies through the blockade, and there can be no doubt that the timely arrival of ships from Cuba was an important factor in the outcome. All in all, the futile siege of 1740 was a sad lesson in the difficulties of joint operations involving land and sea forces of several governments, under overall command that falls far below the mark of genius. Manuel de Montiano, sitting now securely in his capital, had considerable cause for inward satisfaction. Having proven himself more than a match for the British adversary, he was able to send off a report to his government reflecting credit on himself and his soldiers. Perhaps the Spanish hope of reestablishing a sound frontier above the St. Johns would yet be realized.

The true nature of the warfare in America may best be understood against the backdrop of a royal proclamation issued at the Court of St. James on 9 April 1740. In accordance with legislation already passed by Parliament, the king announced his intention of granting commissions from time to time either to individuals or organized groups who wished to undertake military expeditions against Spanish possessions in America. By the terms of such commissions, it was promised, the successful entrepreneur and those who assisted him would gain title to the territory, goods, settlements, harbors, and fortifications captured.[19] War could hardly be placed on a more mercenary basis. Two months later, another proclamation, issued by the lords justices, set the ratios by which Spanish prizes taken by ships of the Royal Navy and condemned by courts of admiralty were to be divided among the personnel serving on the victorious vessels. The captain was to receive three-eighths of the proceeds, truly a magnificent award which explains why naval officers were so eager to gain their own commands and why captains at sea were so intent upon pursuing any enemy vessel of value. One-eighth was to be shared by the ship's master and all marine and army captains and naval lieutenants aboard. The remainder, one-half of the proceeds, was to be divided among all other personnel down to the lowliest privates and sailors.[20] In effect, then, every man who signed on to "singe the king of Spain's beard" in America, whether officer or mere private, had before his eyes the glittering prospect of wealth through conquest. Truly, it was a war not only for national honor and security and not only for trade, but for personal enrichment as well.

In the autumn of 1740 numerous merchant ships from New England, Pennsylvania, and other mainland colonies set their courses for the Windward Passage and Jamaica, as they had been doing for many years. This time, however, they were heavily laden not with the usual cargoes of lumber, fish, grain, and salt meat, but with troops and military supplies. Altogether, they carried some 3,600 colonial soldiers specially enlisted according to instructions issued from London for service outside their own colonies, a total of thirty-six companies under Governor William Gooch of Virginia, and known collectively as "Gooch's American Foot."[21] Many of these soldiers were servant lads and ordinary laborers, glad of a chance to exchange the broom and the hoe for the fancied rewards of military conquest, even though their ultimate objective, Cartagena, was not revealed to them. Arriving at Port Royal on the south coast of Jamaica, their temporary base, they discovered only too quickly that the authorities in London, with a neglect that seems incredible to those not familiar with eighteenth-century imperial administration, had failed to make adequate provision for their maintenance. Makeshift measures organized by colonial officers on the spot prevented a near breakdown and perhaps demoralization of the regiment. Pending the arrival of large-scale naval reinforcements to bolster the small fleet of Admiral Vernon, and a number of regular regiments from Britain to provide the backbone for an army, there was little for the Americans to do but wait and wonder. Inevitably, as the weeks went by, disease invaded the camp and fresh graves began to appear amidst the lush tropical vegetation.[22]

It was winter before the expected reinforcements from Britain arrived: twenty-five ships of the line commanded by Sir Chaloner Ogle and a veritable swarm of transports carrying more than 5,000 regular troops under the command of General Thomas Wentworth. As soon as possible, the motley and ill-disciplined regiment of colonists was integrated with Wentworth's army, while Vernon took command of the greatly enlarged fleet. The British commanders probably were not surprised at the unmilitary quality of the Americans, when even their own men from the homeland gave little cause for rejoicing. Why not use some of the Americans, they thought, to fill vacancies among the deck force on the various ships, where they could be more useful (and perhaps less disastrous) than serving as soldiers. Before long, many of the colonial troops, to their disgust, found themselves assigned to duty on board the king's ships and subjected to more misery and abuse than they had ever bargained for. Although the armada arrived near Cartagena on 4 March 1740/41, the principal part of the landing force was not ashore until some days later.[23]

The men established a camp in the fever-ridden lowlands near the Spanish base, began encountering the enemy, and wondered why their commanders did not push on with the operation more expeditiously. As the days passed, more and more troops were rendered useless either as a result of combat or, more commonly, as victims of tropical disease. They died by the dozens. At last, in April, Vernon and Wentworth were forced to admit that Cartagena was beyond their grasp, and accordingly the surviving troops were reembarked. More days passed, while the fleet lay at anchor with the sick and wounded lying helpless and the commanders pondering what to do next. Daily the newly dead were lugged to the ships' sides and dropped overboard. Even after the fleet at last put out to sea, the wholesale mortality continued, so that when the American contingent eventually was released to go home it was a tragically small remnant of the thousands who originally had gone so confidently off to war.[24]

Cartagena soon became a tradition in the American colonies, and those who had been there and returned were looked upon as heroes. (It was the Cartagena campaign that indirectly provided a name for what was to be one of the most famous plantations in America, Mount Vernon, named in honor of the admiral by Lawrence Washington, one of the survivors.[25]) Cartagena also provided a solid basis for American antagonism toward the British military establishment. The condescension and even contempt for colonists displayed by British officers had not gone unnoticed by the Americans who served under them, nor were the colonial troops quick to forget the sarcasm and abuse dealt out by British sergeants and boatswain's mates. This was the time, it seems, when there first began to emerge "an increasingly articulate distrust between the Englishmen of Europe and the Englishmen of continental America," accompanied by the rise of a conscious "Americanism" among the colonists, a development whose long-range significance would be difficult to exaggerate.[26]

Following Vernon's attacks in 1739–41, the Spanish government breathed new life into its old plan for driving the British out of Georgia. After Oglethorpe's failure at St. Augustine in 1740, Georgia was little more than a feeble symbol of British intrusion, but its downfall would do much to restore Spanish pride and bolster the morale of the colonists in Florida. Furthermore, such a victory would have a powerful impact upon the Indians of the southern frontier, undoubtedly inclining the important tribes once again toward Spanish interests. If the ravaging of South Carolina could be accomplished in the same operation, an enormous amount of booty would be acquired, while Britain's imperial position in North America would be significantly weakened. These considerations led Philip V to issue orders in the fall of 1741 for a major attack upon Georgia and South Carolina.[27]

The task of organizing and supervising this hopeful project was assigned to Don Juan Francisco Guemes y Horcasitas, governor of Cuba, who in turn appointed Governor Montiano of Florida as the actual commander in chief of the expedition.[28] Montiano was to advance against coastal Georgia with a large fleet of minor warships, transports, and shallow-draft coastal craft carrying an army consisting of units drawn from both Cuba and Florida and totaling about 1,800 troops. The first objective was to smash the defenses of Georgia, if possible trapping and destroying Oglethorpe's regiment on St. Simons Island. Having achieved this, Montiano then would advance toward South Carolina along the inland waterway, ravaging the British settlements as he went. At the proper time he was to arouse the Negro slaves in South Carolina by sending Spanish Negroes up into that colony with a promise of freedom and land for those who would come over to the Spanish side. If this appeal proved successful, the Carolinians would find themselves in dire straits, beset within and without, thus enabling the Spanish forces to invade the colony with ease. "It is of the greatest consequence and importance to raze and destroy Carolina and its plantations," admonished the governor of Cuba in an advisory dispatch to Montiano.[29] With South Carolina a smoking ruin, the British would have to abandon Georgia completely, and Spanish Florida would begin to enjoy a degree of security unknown for many years.

A number of factors seemed to favor the enterprise. First, British sea power still was heavily occupied in the Caribbean, and presumably would not be able to shift northward in time to rescue the continental colonies. The population of Georgia was well under 5,000, scattered through a number of isolated settlements and badly divided by the issue of proprietary policy. Moreover, as a result of Oglethorpe's failure at St. Augustine in 1740, there still was much bad feeling between Georgians and Carolinians, jeopardizing any future attempt to act in concert. South Carolina was further weakened by the presence of its large slave population, which might take advantage of a Spanish invasion by committing acts of sabotage and rebellion. Finally, the Spaniards had the advantage of the initiative, and coming by way of the sea could prevent the British from concentrating their defensive strength until after the initial blow had fallen.

St. Augustine became the advance base for the expedition. Here the invasion fleet assembled early in June 1742 to take on water, embark the Florida contingent, and go over the final plans. Oglethorpe received early warning that something was in the wind when a small advance convoy of Spanish ships en route from Havana to St. Augustine was sighted by a British patrol vessel. From Frederica, Oglethorpe's garrison town on the west side of St. Simons Island, an alert was sent to Savannah and Charleston, notifying them of the extraordinary concentration of shipping now assembling at the Spanish base.[30] Ten days later Oglethorpe sent a message to Charleston requesting that the navy ships in that port be dispatched for the defense of the Georgia coast.

On 20 June the main body of the invasion fleet departed from St. Augustine and headed north. After weathering a violent sou'wester that scattered the ships, the determined Spaniards pulled themselves together again and sailed boldly to an anchorage between Jekyl and St. Simons islands, arriving there on the twenty-ninth. Unfortunately, the shallow-draft coastal craft which they had intended to use for advancing up the inland waterway to Frederica and other shallow inlets along the coast had not rejoined the fleet after the storm, a failure that might prove a severe handicap for Montiano. At present, however, his immediate task was to get his army ashore at the southern end of St. Simons, seize the minor fortifications confronting him there, and then quickly advance seven miles north to envelop Frederica. The purpose of this drive was to destroy Oglethorpe's garrison of regulars on St. Simons Island, Georgia's principal defense, after which the invaders might proceed with relative ease against the British settlements on the lower Altamaha and Savannah rivers.

Not until 5 July was the weather favorable for the warships and transports to enter the harbor at St. Simons and disgorge their troops upon the beach. During that interval of waiting, Oglethorpe did what he could to prepare his own few small craft and the local garrison for resistance. When the Spaniards did make their major move on 5 July they sailed in with guns blazing, brushed aside the opposition, and began to unload their troops. Later, one of Oglethorpe's rangers recalled how, as the Spanish ships entered the harbor one after the other, "I sat on my horse up to the Saddle in Water and kept loading and firing my Peice at them. . . ." [31] By dawn of the sixth, most of the army was safely ashore. There was nothing for Oglethorpe to do but abandon his positions, spiking his guns and destroying what vessels and supplies he could not carry off. Then he led the bulk of his defensive force back to Frederica, leaving a scattering of rangers and Indians to keep an eye on Spanish movements. So far, Montiano had almost complete control of the adjacent waters, a situation that would change only if sufficient naval strength were hurried down from Charleston.

After taking possession of the nearby earthen fortifications, the Spaniards established a camp with outposts, and prepared to exploit their opportunities. Both sides were using Indians as scouts, and there was occasional skirmishing between hostile parties. The climax came on 7 July when Montiano sent reconnoitering parties northward to explore the approaches to Frederica. During that day the Spaniards apparently advanced to within a mile or two of the town, only to be repulsed by Oglethorpe and his men. This marked the beginning of a series of skirmishes along the one narrow road from Frederica to the Spanish camp. At one place where the route passed between a thick, brushy wood and a swampy savannah, the British surprised a large detachment of Spanish troops. Yelling Highlanders, wildly brandishing their claymores, drove the terrified Spaniards into the morass where they did terrible execution.[32] This action, later known as the Battle of Bloody Marsh, seemed to drain the offensive spirit from Montiano's army, much as the massacre at Fort Moosa two years before had done to the British at St. Augustine. The Spaniards recoiled into their beachhead positions at the south end of the island where they could defend themselves against further British attacks.

Savannah, in the meantime, having learned of the actual invasion, was approaching a state of panic. The secretary of the province, William Stephens, fearing that the capital might soon fall, packed the colony's important records in a chest which he sent upriver to the settlement of Ebenezer. Among the populace, there was a growing clamor for escape before the supposedly ruthless Spaniards should appear. "Now the panick prevailed among the Women, thro the whole Town," wrote Stephens, "so suddenly, that nothing, was heard but an Outcry how to carry off them and their Children, which occasion'd great disorder; tho all was done that could be, to pacify them, by getting boats of any kind, where we could find them, or any Conveyance for that purpose." [33] Some people fled upriver to Abercorn or Ebenezer; others sought safety across the border in South Carolina.

After the disheartening setback of 7 July, Montiano and his officers decided that the only feasible approach to Frederica was by the winding water route up the west side of the island. Accordingly, three galleys were sent to explore this route and to find, if possible, a suitable landing place near the town. When these vessels appeared at Frederica they were brought under fire by the British guns and driven back down to their own fleet. The captains having found no place clearly suitable for a landing, Montiano again consulted his principal officers. Shortly before this council of war began, the Spanish lookouts reported strange vessels approaching, a report which, when added to all the other discouraging factors, helped the high command reach a decision to withdraw and forego any further attempt to conquer Georgia. As a matter of fact, the sails sighted were not those of any powerful British squadron. Indeed, not until Montiano and his fleet had hoisted anchor and

headed for home did the naval aid for which Oglethorpe had
pleaded many days earlier actually depart from Charleston harbor.
Lieutenant Governor William Bull of South Carolina had not
been dilatory in raising men and gathering ships to go against the
enemy, but Captain Charles Hardy of H.M.S. *Rye* seems to have
felt no urgency in the crisis. As a result, the relief force did not
appear at St. Simons Island until 26 July, long after the last of
the Spanish vessels had disappeared over the southern horizon.
Hardy's foray was almost totally useless.[34]

Montiano arrived safely at St. Augustine, where he soon undertook the unpleasant duty of reporting his failure to the king.
With a bit more luck, especially in the weather, he might have
scored a decisive victory, indeed, might have seized and held
Savannah, but he clearly lacked the kind of drive that somehow
manages to overcome handicaps. Oglethorpe had lacked it, too,
at St. Augustine, but in the defense of his own colony he proved
himself the better soldier. So far in this war of seaborne expeditions, the laurels had gone almost entirely to the defense, largely
because the extraordinarily difficult problems of coordinating the
movements of sailing vessels, communicating with scattered units
on unfamiliar terrain, and providing adequate supplies of the right
kind at the right place at the right time, had not been mastered
in terms of amphibious warfare. The apparent futility of these
successive advances and withdrawals, resembling the measured
pattern of a country dance or the alternations of a nursery game,
was satirized by *Poor Richard* in 1743:

> From Georgia t'Augustine the General goes;
> From Augustine to Georgia come our Foes;
> Hardy from Charlestown to St. Simons hies,
> Again from thence to Charlestown back he flies.
> Forth from St. Simons then the Spaniards creep;
> Say, Children, is not this your Play, *Bo-peep?* [35]

At St. Augustine the Spaniards, having shot their bolt in 1742,
settled back into a posture of defense. Oglethorpe, in contrast,
continued to exploit the offensive as much as he could with his
limited resources. Using Indians as well as colonial militia, he
harassed the Spaniards almost to the very gates of their capital,
but without decisive effect. In 1743 Oglethorpe went back to
England, never again to see the colony he had founded and

saved. After his departure Georgia seemed to become less aggressive, not only in the conflict with Spain but also in the complicated field of Indian relations, and South Carolina was able to reassert its dominance. Governor James Glen, a self-important and rather touchy Scot, arrived at Charleston in December of 1743 as the new governor of South Carolina, and quickly assumed the role of leadership in the Southeast that Oglethorpe had vacated. At the same time, fortunately, the festering quarrel between the two British colonies was abating.[36] Certainly by the beginning of 1744 the war in the American theater had settled into a condition of virtual stalemate, with the indefatigable privateers providing most of whatever action took place.

Walpole's longstanding policy of peaceful accommodation had been dealt a mortal blow by the politically motivated decision for war in 1739; its burial was completed early in 1742 when Walpole finally resigned. A year later his French counterpart, Cardinal Fleury, who also had been a strong restraining influence, departed from the scene. For some time now Britain, with her Hanoverian monarch, had been involving herself unofficially in the swirling international conflicts comprising the War of the Austrian Succession, especially by subsidizing the forces of Hanover and Hesse which, as allies of Austria, were fighting against France. By 1743, British troops were active on the continent north of France, even though their government was at war only with Spain. In October of that year France and Spain signed the Treaty of Fontainebleau, in effect a revival of the old Family Compact. France promised to help her Bourbon colleague recover Minorca and Gibraltar from Britain, and in addition to help force the British to abandon the colony of Georgia and all forts built on Spanish territory in America.[37] The great international rivalries once again impelling Britain and France toward war more clearly than ever were rooted not only in the old dynastic and territorial concerns of continental Europe but increasingly in the broader considerations of worldwide commerce and empire. Bourbon France and Bourbon Spain were again joining forces against Britain to maintain their mutual interests in the New World as well as in the Old.

A French declaration of war against Britain was issued on 4 March 1744; George II made a counterdeclaration on 29 March. News of this fateful development was hurried across the Atlantic from France, reaching Louisbourg before the end of April. New

England, as yet, had no clear intimation that war with France had begun.[38] The governor of Cape Breton Island hastened to get in the first blow by sending a well-armed expedition against Canso, a small British fishing station located at the extreme northeast corner of Nova Scotia. With no difficulty, the French expedition surprised and overawed the little garrison, forcing its surrender on 13 May. Among those captured and taken back to Louisbourg as prisoners was a Nova Scotian named John Bradstreet, a lieutenant in the British Army. This was Bradstreet's third visit to the French fortress town on Cape Breton Island—he was beginning to feel that he knew the place well. Some of the merchants in Louisbourg, watching the British prisoners as they disembarked, were inclined to regret the outbreak of hostilities in America which could only disrupt the flourishing trade of their town. One called the attack on Canso a "foolish enterprise," breaking a peace which might have been maintained on this side of the Atlantic to mutual advantage, despite the declaration of war in Europe.[39] If so, the harm had been done; New England was aroused.

About the middle of May ships began arriving at Boston from British ports with unofficial news of the royal declaration, whereupon the authorities took the precaution of confining several Frenchmen then visiting in the capital.[40] Soon an official dispatch removed all doubt. Some of the frontier people began withdrawing to places of greater safety, and from one harried frontier leader came the plaintive report that "they have filled this fort and block house with lamenting wives and crying children. . . ."[41] "Should there be any considerable Delay in providing for the safety of the People," warned another, "we shall soon loose half our Inhabitants, several are gone already, and a large Number, and that the Men of the best substance among us, declare they must go, for they are not able to watch and ward, and at the same Time do their Business, without help."[42] Talk such as this naturally caused great uneasiness among land speculators, whose anticipated profits depended upon the continued growth and prosperity of frontier areas. Communities in exposed locations tried to hold together as best they could, while improving their own defenses and appealing to the colony government for additional support. It was a time of wavering confidence, especially in northern New England.

The attack on Canso gave clear warning that the French remained actively interested in Nova Scotia, their former Acadia, and the several thousand French-speaking *habitants* still residing there under British rule. At Annapolis Royal, on the west side of the peninsula, the able and clear-headed Lieutenant Governor Paul Mascarene presided over a feeble and divided colony, trying to uphold British right and authority without unduly antagonizing an alien population. It was no easy task, rendered all the more difficult by the patent animosity of French-stimulated Indians. A few weeks after the fall of Canso, there appeared at the outskirts of Annapolis Royal a large and obviously hostile band of Indians who quickly invested the place. The garrison of about a hundred men took stations in the patched-up earthen fort and prepared to defend themselves. As usual, however, the Indians were not keen to attack a fortified position, and when a detachment of seventy additional soldiers sent from Massachusetts arrived on the scene, they gave up their siege and disappeared.[43] In August the siege was renewed, this time by a combined French and Indian expedition from Louisbourg. The Indians prowled ominously through the vicinity, while the French busily prepared combustibles and scaling ladders for the final assault. Under great apprehension, the defenders began to negotiate with the French commander; there is evidence that Mascarene's officers would have been glad to surrender on honorable terms, but Mascarene himself stoutly held out and finally broke off the negotiations. With the subsequent arrival of still more reinforcements from Boston, the French gave up their attempt and withdrew, not because they lacked the courage for a showdown but in obedience to new orders received from Louisbourg.[44]

During these trying weeks, Mascarene had enjoyed excellent cooperation from Governor William Shirley of Massachusetts, a shrewd, ambitious, and generally able lawyer-turned-administrator. Shirley was an imperialist with a New Englander's special concern for the security of frontier holdings, overseas commerce, and the fisheries. Moreover, he clearly perceived the importance of Nova Scotia as a sort of outworks for New England, potentially profitable in British hands, a menace in French. As a means of deterring the enemy from renewing his attempts against Annapolis Royal, Shirley began leaking to the French the rumor that New England was laying plans for an expedition to capture Louisbourg.[45] Actually, there probably was no serious intention of mounting an attack on so formidable an objective, certainly not without powerful military and naval aid from England. The colonies, after all, had no standing army of their own, and no navy worthy of the name. Yet Louisbourg, as a target, did possess for New England an extraordinary attraction, and many New Englanders had begun to relish the idea of playing Joshua to the French Jericho. This was especially true of the men who made their living by fishing and commerce. As a base for fishing vessels, Louisbourg was in peacetime a major competitor of the New England fishermen; as a base for armed raiders, it threatened all of Nova Scotia, the colonial fishing vessels going to and from the banks of the North Atlantic, and the cargo vessels following the sea lanes between New England and the British Isles. After being badly stung by Louisbourg privateers during the late spring and early summer of 1744, New England shipping interests began sending out armed vessels to retaliate. These fighting ships not only made it too hot for the French marauders along the coast, but also began to interfere with Louisbourg's own vital lines of supply and commerce. Soon the armed raiders were cruising off Cape Breton itself and even within the Gulf of St. Lawrence, intercepting shipping between Quebec and Louisbourg.[46]

The arguments favoring an attack upon Cape Breton Island had been well presented in a memorandum submitted by Robert Auchmuty, Massachusetts' agent in London, to the British government shortly after the declaration of war against France. Starting from the proposition that Louisbourg was a "formidable seminary of seamen" because of its great success in the fisheries, Auchmuty went on to enumerate the advantages that would accrue from its capture by Britain. For one thing, he pointed out, the entire fishery would come under British domination. And because Louisbourg stood at the entrance to the St. Lawrence River, Britain could easily choke off supplies to Quebec, thereby making the Indians of the interior wholly dependent upon the British, who would inevitably become "entirely masters of the rich and profitable fur trade. . . ."[47] No longer would British commerce be threatened by warships and privateers swarming out of Louisbourg; rather, the British themselves would have a valuable new base for servicing their own vessels. Auchmuty, having assembled this impressive bundle of compelling reasons, then proceeded to a specific proposal: that a powerful Anglo-American expedition be organized to capture Louisbourg in 1745.

Was such an operation feasible? Shirley and other colonial leaders had a fairly clear mental image of Louisbourg because so many perceptive New Englanders had been there on business. A ship seeking shelter in Louisbourg's commodious harbor would have to pass through the mile-wide entrance, following a fairly narrow channel. Close on the starboard side, to the north, rose the rocky promontory known as Lighthouse Point, while on the port side, toward Louisbourg itself, were three low, rocky islets, the innermost containing a fort with some thirty-nine cannon sited to blast any unwelcome intruder. Directly ahead, on the western shore of the harbor, stood the Grand or Royal Battery, a fortified position mounting approximately thirty cannon, some of them 42-pounders. Around the periphery of the harbor could be seen some scattered dwellings and outbuildings used by the local fishermen and farmers, but a large part of the population lived within the town, which was located on the south shore of the harbor just inside the entrance. It was a sizable town, consisting of government buildings, warehouses, shops, and dwellings, arranged in a regular pattern of streets. The fortifications, consisting in the main of a series of bastions connected by earthen ramparts faced with stone, had been designed by a disciple of Vauban and constructed over a period of years starting in 1720. They completely enclosed Louisbourg on the land side, offering protection against any overland intrusion from the west. In view of these facts, it was reasonable to suppose that only a major expedition, including a large force of British regulars with plenty of artillery and supported by a powerful fleet, would stand a chance of breaking into this fortress, a view apparently well substantiated by the recent failures at Cartagena and St. Augustine. There was an assumption prevalent at Louisbourg that any attack in force would come by way of the harbor entrance, which was heavily guarded. Only in the sheltered waters of the harbor, it was thought, would an enemy fleet dare put ashore an army to invest the fortress, and this was not likely to occur because of the Island Battery and the Grand Battery. True, just a mile to the southwest of the great ramparts, beyond White Point, could be seen the gray water of Gabarus Bay bordering the south side of the peninsula. But there the shore was rocky and lashed by surf, and the intervening terrain was marshy and unsuitable for large-scale movements of men and equipment.

Late in 1744 there arrived at Boston a group of exchanged

British prisoners just released from Louisbourg, where they had had some opportunity to talk with the inhabitants and even look around a bit. Among them were Joshua Loring, captain of a ship captured by the French the previous summer, and Lieutenant John Bradstreet, formerly of the garrison at Canso. These men had taken advantage of their stay in Louisbourg by noting carefully the state of the town and its defenses. Bradstreet especially was convinced that the place was ripe for the plucking, and he in turn was able to fire a similar enthusiasm in William Vaughan, an ambitious New Englander with strong economic interests in fish and lumber. Governor Shirley listened carefully to the words of these returned prisoners. Soon the enthusiastic Bradstreet was beginning to convince even the practical-minded governor that New England itself, with a little help from the Royal Navy, could guarantee its glorious future by wresting Louisbourg from the hands of the French. This seemingly foolish optimism was based upon positive information revealing that Louisbourg's defenses were not in full readiness and perfect repair, and that the garrison, which included Swiss as well as French troops, was disaffected and probably would not fight well.[48] Vaughan, in the meantime, was conducting virtually a one-man campaign to arouse popular support for such an enterprise. He too gained the governor's ear, and when Shirley found that real interest in the proposal was growing among the fishing and commercial men of coastal Massachusetts, the case was won. Shirley decided to give the proposal his official backing.

On 9 January 1744/45, at a secret session of the General Court, the governor laid the plan before the astonished legislators. To many it seemed to be a dangerous delusion leading straight toward a disaster far greater than Phips' failure at Quebec in 1690. There, at least, most of the New England army had been withdrawn intact. At Louisbourg, thousands of lives—to say nothing of thousands of pounds sterling—might well be thrown away for nothing. The General Court politely told the governor to forget it. Shirley was willing to accept this decision, which perhaps merely confirmed his own deepest instincts, as final. Not so William Vaughan. This indefatigable entrepreneur only renewed his campaign, circulating petitions among the prominent men involved in fishing and other kinds of maritime business, and persuading them to exert pressure on the General Court. As a result, and with a notable assist from a distinguished businessman and member of the council, William

Pepperrell of Kittery, the legislature reconsidered the matter of the Louisbourg venture. On 25 January, by the narrowest of margins, the previous decision was reversed. Massachusetts would undertake to capture Louisbourg if the other northern colonies would render assistance.[49]

Enthusiastic, Shirley hastened to notify the authorities in London and to solicit the active support of all the New England colonies plus New York, New Jersey, and Pennsylvania. A colonial army totaling 3,000 volunteers was to be raised and assembled, a fleet of colonial fighting vessels and transports was to be gathered, and a large quantity of supplies was to be purchased and put at the disposal of this expeditionary force. In an attempt to keep the preparations concealed from the French, a strict embargo was placed upon colonial ports, but as Shirley previously had taken some pains to make sure that the French did think an invasion was being planned, the status of the secret was somewhat beclouded.[50] From the other colonies came mixed responses. Most New Englanders liked the idea of an attempt against Louisbourg, especially when they understood that after the French base had been taken, the British government would reimburse the colonies for their expenses. Massachusetts and Connecticut were wholehearted in their support of the venture, but Rhode Island showed only minor enthusiasm and at first declined to send any troops. Beyond the borders of New England, the response was much less encouraging. New York required the services of her own men for the defense of her own frontier, but did provide some much-needed cannon, while the most that could be obtained from New Jersey and Pennsylvania were offers of provisions. Equally disheartening was the reply received from Commodore Peter Warren, the senior naval commander in the West Indies, whom Shirley had urgently invited to come with some of his fighting ships. Warren was married to an American and was in sympathy with New England's desire to reduce Louisbourg, but he doubted that his orders permitted him to join an operation not endorsed by London. When Warren's decision became known in Massachusetts preparations already were well underway, and Shirley decided to proceed without the participation of the Royal Navy, a bold decision indeed!

One of the most important problems was settled early and well: Whom should the governor designate as supreme commander of the expedition? Several men vied for the honor, but Shirley chose instead a man who was at first sincerely reluctant. This was William Pepperrell, the forty-eight-year-old commander of the Maine militia, who had done so much to win the legislature's endorsement of the plan. Although lacking in significant command experience, Pepperrell was intelligent, enterprising, widely known in northern New England, and above all, popular. A popular figure such as this was needed to attract large numbers of volunteers into the enterprise. Pepperrell and the prospect of plunder turned the trick, and recruiting went on more briskly than in many other campaigns during the colonial wars. In addition, it must be noted, military planning held tightly to the hand of business and politics. There can be no doubt that, as one historian has put it, Shirley was "very much the politician in making arrangements for commissions and contracts," a gross form of political patronage.[51]

During February and the first three weeks of March, the New England colonies were alive with activity, aided by unusually favorable weather.[52] Thousands of volunteer soldiers began converging on the seaports, especially Boston, where they found great quantities of supplies being accumulated for loading into the motley fleet of colonial ships riding at anchor in the harbor. Armed vessels were dispatched to cruise off Louisbourg, with instructions to watch for French ships that might be bringing supplies or reinforcements for the garrison, noting also the condition of the winter ice along the coast. Finally, on the twenty-fourth of March, the fleet of fifty-one transports crammed with 2,800 Massachusetts troops got underway from Nantasket Road under escort of the colony warship *Shirley*. Contingents from New Hampshire and Connecticut, bringing the total troop strength to well over 3,000, were to proceed separately and join the main force at Canso.[53] After Pepperrell and his army had sailed, Governor Shirley received word from Commodore Warren that he was on his way with a squadron of royal warships to cooperate fully in the venture. The British government had given its approval. This good news, an unexpected reversal of a previous disappointment, seemed to provide the seal of success. Yet despite the impressive array of strength that had been brought together, many a common soldier, watching the angry curling of the gray waves whipped by the raw wind of late March, must have thought back to Cartagena and all the Americans who never returned from there. At best the Louisbourg operation was a gigantic gamble.

The voyage north past Nova Scotia to Canso was a hard one for many of the troops, especially those fresh off the farms who had no acquaintance with the boisterous ways of the sea. Sometimes it was a difficult choice between a wet and windswept deck with fresh air, and shelter in a cramped and fetid hold. Wrote one unhappy sufferer, "wee kept Upon Deck Good part of this Night To prevent our being Sick." A little farther along he reported, "our Vessel was A Very Hospital, wee were all Sick, in a Greater or lesser Degree. . . . wee Could not be Upon Deck, as the Night before—But was Shut down in the hold; and a Long, Dark and Teadious night wee had, Such a one I Never See before: Wee was also Much Crouded, even So as to Lay, one on Another. Sick etc." [54] It was an experience only too common for soldiers at sea, causing them to long fiercely for the stable land even though they must go through gunfire to gain it.

Arriving at the bleak island of Canso on 4 April, the Massachusetts troops found the small contingent from New Hampshire already on the scene. Once ashore the men viewed with great curiosity the blackened ruins left by the French in their attack of the previous year. Soon, however, willing hands erected a prefabricated blockhouse to defend this advance staging base, in case the French should pay another call. Then the military companies settled down to drilling and other preparation for the great assault, while Pepperrell and his officers anxiously awaited favorable reports from the ships off Louisbourg. The weather was raw, with frequent rain and even some snow adding to the discomfort, but as much as possible the men were kept at their duties. On the first Sunday at Canso one New Englander recorded in his diary, "Several Sorts of Bisneses Going on to Day Som a Exersiseing Som a Heareing Preaching So the Day Ends—" [55] The air rang with the hoarse commands of militia captains hastily trying to transform ordinary militiamen into competent assault troops, while what seemed like hordes of enthusiastic musicians—drummers, trumpeters, and even fiddlers—created a vaguely martial din. Nor was this cacophony limited to the hours of drill. "After Exersise was Over," complained one long-suffering soldier, "there was a Vast Deal More Drumming and Trumpiting than was needful Which I Trust Displeased a great many, while others Tollarated it." [56]

On 22 April, H.M.S. *Eltham,* the welcome herald of British sea power, arrived and the following morning Warren himself in

H.M.S. *Superbe,* with *Launceston* and *Mermaid,* joined the party. In a message to Pepperrell dated the same day, the commodore assured his colonial colleague that "nothing shall be wanting, on our parts to promote the Success of this Expedition, which I think of the utmost Consequence, to our King and Country." [57] Then, having fired off this encouraging salute, Warren hastened off with his ships to clamp an even tighter blockade on Cape Breton Island. From that station on 25 April he sent down word confirming that Gabarus Bay, the place chosen for the amphibious landing, was free of ice. "Give me leave to Recommend dispatch," he concluded tactfully in this second letter to Pepperrell, "for delays may frustrate all our hopes." [58] Perhaps he too had been thinking about Cartagena, or perhaps almost any number of other military ventures in the colonies.

It was just at this time that the Connecticut contingent of about 500 men made its appearance, with a tale of hazard and escape at sea. Their convoy of seven transports guarded by a Connecticut sloop and Rhode Island's main contribution to the enterprise, the sloop *Tartar,* while proceeding toward Canso had been accosted by the French frigate *Renommée.* This could have been a disaster, but the *Tartar* managed to lure the Frenchman after her in single chase while the other vessels with their precious cargoes of troops and supplies escaped. After dark the *Tartar* too evaded the enemy frigate, and all safely joined the expedition. At the head of this welcome contingent came Major General Roger Wolcott, Connecticut's deputy governor, designated Pepperrell's second-in-command.

The acting governor at Louisbourg, Louis Du Chambon, was becoming increasingly concerned by the growing numbers of British warships hovering off the coast of Cape Breton Island, cutting off his supplies and possible reinforcements, but he seems to have had no knowledge of the army that now was poised for the attack. If the British should strike, he thought, the attack would come in the form of a naval assault against the harbor itself, and that he was quite confident of repelling. In general, the number of troops under Du Chambon's command seemed adequate —nearly 600 regular soldiers together with about 900 militiamen. Their quality, on the other hand, was something under the best. The previous winter there had been a near mutiny among the regular troops, but at least so far as one could now tell they seemed

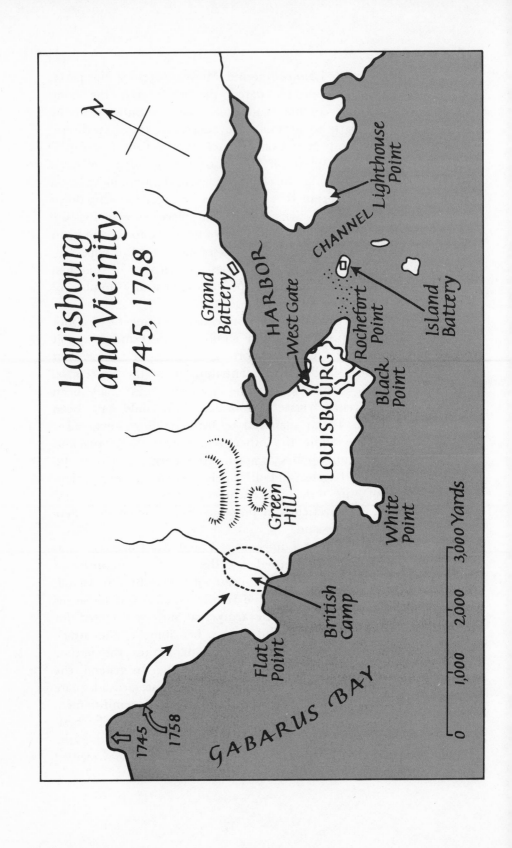

Louisbourg and Vicinity, 1745, 1758

Grand Battery

West Gate

HARBOR

CHANNEL

Lighthouse Point

Rochefort Point

Black Point

Island Battery

LOUISBOURG

Green Hill

White Point

British Camp

Flat Point

1745

1758

GABARUS BAY

0   1,000   2,000   3,000 Yards

ready to do their duty. As for the militiamen, only time and actual combat would provide proof. The town was fairly well stocked with food, and although the quantities of cannon and munitions available were not all that could be desired, they seemed adequate to beat off any likely assault. Du Chambon confidently expected that the guns of Louisbourg, including those of the Grand Battery and the Island Battery, would make kindling of any British ships trying to force their way into the harbor.[59]

Pepperrell, sure now that the time had come, took his fleet of about a hundred sail out of the harbor at Canso on the morning of 29 April. Twenty-four hours later they were moving majestically into Gabarus Bay, southwest of Louisbourg, and Du Chambon was standing agape. Never had he imagined an attack coming from that direction. Now he found it difficult to formulate a plan of resistance. The British showed no such hesitation and proceeded to prepare for their landing with an air of determination. Although the north shore of Gabarus Bay was very rocky, there were several coves where boats could be run close in to the beach without undue difficulty, especially as the weather was favorable and the surf fairly gentle at this particular time. In came the ships' boats, those carrying Colonel John Gorham and his company of Indian rangers in the lead, heading for Flat Point Cove. Suddenly the men in the lead boats sighted an enemy patrol on shore, whereupon the stream of boats changed course, heading for another landing place 2 miles to the west. Thanks to this maneuver, the landing was made virtually without opposition, only one brief skirmish occurring after the first troops were already ashore. Soon hundreds of excited New Englanders, muskets held high out of the water, were "landing fast one upon the back of another." [60] By the time darkness began to close in, Pepperrell had about 2,000 of his men on the beachhead. Disembarkation was completed successfully the next day.

As the amateur general with his amateur army looked across the boggy terrain toward the forbidding ramparts of Louisbourg, he must have felt a deep sense of elation from having carried off the difficult first step so extremely well, and at the same time a certain sense of apprehension in view of the obvious difficulties and dangers just ahead. What Pepperrell intended was to place the town under formal siege, and either force a surrender or take the place by storm. Siegecraft, as developed in Europe over many cen-

turies, involved fairly precise and complicated procedures sometimes extending over a period of many weeks. Pepperrell and his
New Englanders could only aspire to a rough approximation, hoping the outcome would be just as favorable. What they had to
accomplish first, with the invaluable assistance of the navy, was to
seal off Louisbourg from any outside help, after which they would
dig a system of trenches within artillery range of the walls, prepare
battery sites, and haul up their cannon. Then the battering would
begin. Hopefully, as the defense weakened, the siege artillery and
supporting infantry would find it possible to establish even closer
positions, permitting more concentrated fire, until sufficient
breaches were made in the walls to allow the attackers to charge in
through the smoking gaps and overwhelm the demoralized garrison.

To begin, the New Englanders established a crude camp just
above the shore about 2 miles southwest of Louisbourg at a place
where a running brook provided fresh water. Details of men
labored hour after hour, landing supplies through the surf and
lugging them to the camp. In the meantime, roving patrols were
exploring the environs between the camp and the fortress and up
the west shore of the harbor, plundering and burning as they went.
Occasional shots from the ramparts kept them from venturing too
close to the great looming walls. While Pepperrell's army was thus
getting the feel of the terrain and establishing its mastery of the
environs, Warren's fleet was maintaining its tight blockade off the
harbor entrance, making sure that no reinforcements or supplies
reached the French garrison. Artillery was of the utmost importance, and Pepperrell had been able to bring only a few heavy guns
with him. It was no easy task to ferry these ashore and haul them,
under cover of darkness, across the marshy plain to the higher
ground within range of the fortress. This task was accomplished by
strong-backed New Englanders

> with almost incredible labour and fatigue. For all the roads over which
> they were drawn, saving here and there small patches of rocky Hills,
> was a deep Morass, in which whilst the Cannon were upon Wheels,
> they several times sunk, so as to bury not only the Carriages, but the
> whole Body of the Cannon likewise. Horses and oxen could not be
> employed in this Service, but the whole was to be done by the Men,
> themselves up to the knees in Mud at the same time; the nights in
> which the Work was done cold and for the most part foggy.[61]

As soon as they could, the artillerymen began siting their cannon and mortars on the high ground, principally opposite the citadel and the West Gate.

All the colonies from New England south were watching the daring venture with keen interest, for much was at stake. From Philadelphia, Benjamin Franklin wrote to his brother in Boston, "Our people are extremely impatient to hear of your success at Cape Breton. My shop is filled with thirty inquiries at the coming in of every post. Some wonder the place is not yet taken." Here Franklin displayed his good common sense: "I tell them I shall be glad to hear that news three months hence. Fortified towns are hard nuts to crack; and your teeth have not been accustomed to it. Taking strong places is a particular trade, which you have taken up without serving an apprenticeship to it. . . . But some seem to think forts are as easy taken as snuff." [62]

Pepperrell knew that the keys to the defense of Louisbourg were the Island Battery and the Grand Battery, and once it became clear that the town itself could not be taken immediately by a sudden rush, his intention was to gain control of both important outworks. Bradstreet, the former prisoner at Louisbourg and now a colonel in Pepperrell's army, had insisted that the Grand Battery was in bad repair and could easily be taken at the outset. Here, it was hoped, some French cannon might be obtained for use against the town. Pepperrell's luck was with him. The French, deciding that the Grand Battery was indefensible, abandoned it; shortly afterward, on the third day ashore, a party of Americans cautiously approached the fortification and to their astonishment found it unguarded. The thirty guns were still there, hastily spiked but not ruined. This was an acquisition of immense importance to the attackers. Experts were quickly put to work drilling out the blocked touch holes, and by noon of 3 May one cannon was in operating condition. Its first shot whistling in toward the beleaguered town was a terrifying portent for the inhabitants sheltered there.[63] As soon as they could be made ready, the other guns joined in, either from their positions in the Grand Battery or from new positions elsewhere in the American lines. Pepperrell now had the artillery he needed. Had the French been able to hold the Grand Battery, they might have used it as a fortified base from which to raid the rear of the American lines, in addition to preventing the New Englanders from acquiring the additional firepower they needed so badly. But now, as more and more guns came into play, the people of Louisbourg came to know only too well the blast and shock of artillery fire.

As early as the fourth of May, Warren began urging Pepperrell to get on with the capture, which the naval commander envisioned in the form of a simultaneous assault by land and by sea, with the warships forcing their way into the harbor as the army advanced against the walls on the opposite side. Before such an assault could be safely attempted, however, the formidable Island Battery would have to be put out of action. This meant a difficult and exceedingly dangerous amphibious attack by men in small boats advancing upon a closely guarded island. There were several false starts and one abortive attempt, the latter occurring on the night of 23 May. A succinct entry in one man's diary tells the story from his point of view: "This Night about Eight hundred of us went to Tak the Iseland But our head offiser Being a Couard we Rowd a Bout all Night and Never Landed—" [64] Another try was made on the night of 26 May. This time, about an hour after midnight, the lead boats made it to the dark looming objective without arousing the French, but once the cheering troops started pouring onto the rocky strand, guns began to flash from the embrasures above, and there commenced a fierce three-hour battle in which the Americans were cut to pieces. Nearly 200 of the attackers were either killed or taken prisoner. Later that day, Pepperrell's disheartened army found numerous bodies washed up along the shore, some with arms, legs, and even heads missing. On the day following this disaster, Pepperrell wrote a letter to Commodore Warren summarizing the accomplishments and the condition of his men.

We have erected five fascine batteries, . . . with 16 pieces of cannon, and our mortars mounted at said batteries, and with our cannon from the royal [grand] battery, we have been playing on the town, by which we have greatly distrest the inhabitants, made some breaches in the wall, especially at the west gate, which we have beat down, and made a considerable breach there, and doubt not but shall soon reduce the circular battery. . . . We have made five unsuccessful attempts upon the island battery, in the last of which we lost about 189 men, and many of our boats were shot to pieces, and many of our men drowned before they could land. . . . We have also kept out scouts to destroy any settlements of the enemy near us, and prevent a surprise in our camp . . . By the services aforesaid and the constant guards kept night and day round the camp, at our batteries, the army is very much fatigued, and sickness prevails among us, to that degree that we now have but about 2100 effective men. . . .[65]

Warren's blockading ships had no easy task either, especially with the fog so prevalent in that area, but on the whole the naval blockade of Louisbourg was extremely effective; only one French vessel of any size managed to slip into the harbor.[66] The importance of the blockade was clearly shown on 19 May when the new 64-gun French ship of the line *Vigilant* hove into view. Manned by a crew numbering more than 500, this fighting ship was bringing to Louisbourg forty cannon and a thousand barrels of gunpowder as a contribution to the defense, a choice prize. The *Vigilant* was at once lured into action with His Majesty's ships *Mermaid, Superbe, Launceston,* and *Eltham,* and the New England men-of-war *Shirley* and *Massachusetts.* Watchers in Louisbourg could see the rapid flashing of many guns and hear the delayed *thuds* as the running fight continued for some four or five hours in the evening. Finally the French commander, after suffering a number of casualties, was forced to surrender, and the next morning the victorious British boarded and took command.[67] If the *Vigilant* had been able to reach Louisbourg safely, the cannon and gunpowder she brought, together with the additional manpower of her crew, would have enabled the beleaguered town to fight on for many more days, perhaps until relieved. The capture of the *Vigilant,* formally announced to the French by Warren on 8 June, further depressed French morale even as it lifted the spirits of the New England army.

By the tenth of June the army had solved the problem of the Island Battery by emplacing cannon on the undefended Lighthouse Point at the north side of the entrance. From there a hot fire was poured onto the exposed island position, rendering it virtually untenable. The bombardment of the town itself continued, causing the women and children to huddle in fortified casemates while the British shells lazily arched across the sky and blasted their houses to ruins. During the second week in June, three more powerful ships of the line joined Warren's squadron, bringing the total to eleven, not counting the smaller warships from the New England colonies. Command of the sea at Louisbourg was complete.

In the meantime, Warren had been growing increasingly impatient with the slow progress of the siege. Naturally Pepperrell, the self-conscious amateur who knew only too well the limitations of his amateur army, bristled whenever his professional British colleague urged him on to more decisive action. The two commanders, fortunately, were able to keep such tension between themselves well below the point of danger where it might seriously threaten the success of the operation. Pepperrell especially remembered the admonition he had received from Shirley earlier that spring: "It is a general observation, that the land and sea forces, when joined upon the same expedition, seldom or never agree, but I am persuaded it will not be so between you and Commodore Warren, as any misunderstanding between you might prove fatal to his Majesty's service in the expedition." [68] Both commanders had their eyes steadily fixed on Louisbourg, one from the land, one from the sea, and both intended to bring the affair to a victorious conclusion.

On 10 June Warren made two moves designed to speed the desired result. First he sent one of his officers into Louisbourg under a flag of truce with the suggestion that since Du Chambon was approaching the end of his resources he might consider surrendering to the navy rather than to Pepperrell, in order to receive better treatment.[69] This sly move was a patent attempt to grab the glory, but it didn't work. Warren's second step was to lay before Pepperrell a definite proposal for a full-scale, coordinated assault on Louisbourg by sea and by land, to be carried out in the very near future. To this the general, seeing nothing better in the offing, agreed. In the siege lines and on board the ships, special preparations began. Some of the men on shore were put to work gathering piles of moss and making faggots to help protect Warren's warships when they attempted to enter the harbor under fire. Others built ladders to be used in scaling the damaged ramparts, or repaired boats for use in landings on the water side. The batteries, which had been advanced closer and closer to the walls, now intensified their effort both to discourage the enemy and make breaches for the infantry to enter. On 12 June, recorded one artilleryman, "we had a very hott fire more than any before which continued all Day and Broak Down much of their Walls." [70]

Du Chambon was rapidly coming to view his plight as virtually hopeless, with his supply of gunpowder dropping to a dangerously low level and clear signs of mounting discouragement among the garrison troops, to say nothing of the miserable civilian population. Since the beginning of the siege, the town had been battered with some 9,000 cannonballs and 600 explosive shells. One contemporary description speaks of "all the Guns in the Circular Battery except three being dismounted, and the Wall almost wholly broke down; the West Gate demolished, and a large Breach in the Wall adjoining; The West Flank in the King's Bastion almost ruined; all the Houses and other Buildings almost torn to Pieces, but one House in the town being left unhurt. . . ." [71] An officer in Pepperrell's army wrote that "the whole Town is so wreck'd by our Cannon and Bombs, that scarce 3 Houses in it are at this Hour tenantable." [72] It seemed almost certain that the massive assault which the British were about to launch would succeed in overwhelming the defenders, at heavy cost to both sides. Accordingly, on the fifteenth of June, Du Chambon sent out feelers for a cessation of hostilities to which Warren and Pepperrell replied in concert. Serious negotiations took place on the following day, with the result that on 17 June Du Chambon capitulated, after which the victorious British took possession of the town. A French-Canadian historian has called the capture of Louisbourg "a remarkable feat of arms for inexperienced militiamen," adding praise for Pepperrell as a "prudent and skilful general." [73] Clearly, however, the victory belonged also to Warren and the Royal Navy, whose blockade had proved so effective.

Soon after the capitulation, ships were dispatched to Old and New England with the good news. Governor Shirley received the message in the early hours of 3 July, and by five o'clock that morning the bells were ringing all over Boston. Hours later, as darkness again descended, the town glowed with bonfires, fireworks, and the friendly gleam of "Candles in windows in all most Evry house. . . ." [74] Louisbourg had fallen to Pepperrell and his men! From Boston the news spread north and south along the coast, and inland to the farthest frontier. By 6 July it had reached Falmouth in Maine, where it produced "great rejoicing through the country. We fired our cannon five times, and spent the afternoon at the Fort, rejoicing." [75] An express alerted Philadelphia during the evening of 11 July, and the news,

> flying instantly round the Town, upwards of 20 Bonfires were immediately lighted in the Streets. The next Day was spent in Feasting, and drinking the Healths of Governor Shirley, Gen. Pepperel, Com.

Warren, etc. etc. under the Discharge of Cannon from the Wharffs and
Vessels in the River; and the Evening concluded with Bonfires, Illu-
minations, and other Demonstrations of Joy.[76]

Quaker pacifism had prevented Pennsylvania from making any
important contribution to the operation against Louisbourg; doubtless Philadelphia's celebration was in part a taunt directed against
the Quaker leaders by those who opposed their policies. In England, too, there were enthusiastic celebrations. Salutes were fired
by the royal batteries at the Park and the Tower, while the people
of London celebrated the victory with "bonefires and an excess of
all the usual concomitants." [77] But the unexpected victory dumped
in England's lap by a motley army of colonial militiamen and a few
ships of the Royal Navy produced something less than joyful enthusiasm in the highest levels of government. The ministry, headed now
by Henry Pelham and his brother, had been groping for a negotiated
peace with France; the capture of Louisbourg was an upsetting
factor. Political pressure for a more positive war effort began to
develop, and as the Pelhams yielded to this pressure the hopes for
an early peace went glimmering. It is the considered opinion of
one historian that "probably never before had a North American
event exerted such a profound impact upon both the political and
the diplomatic policies of a British government." [78]

At Louisbourg itself the aftermath was anything but pleasant.
The terms of capitulation provided for the repatriation of French
civilians, with their personal possessions, which meant that the victorious New Englanders were not allowed to plunder the town
as they had intended. This unexpected restriction sowed seeds of
resentment that flowered into bitterness. The troops felt that they
had been cheated out of their just reward. This feeling was intensified as they saw the officers and men of Warren's squadron glee-
fully capturing rich prizes simply by leaving the French flag prominently flying above the fortress. Unsuspecting French ships sailed
happily into the harbor only to find themselves in a British trap,
and of course it was the navy who enjoyed the gain. For a time
there was danger of actual mutiny among the New Englanders in
the garrison. In addition, the autumn and winter at Louisbourg
proved to be a time of prolonged discomfort and danger, with
hundreds of men succumbing to disease. Cape Breton's raw coastal
climate was accomplishing what French bombs and bullets had
not. New Englanders in general did find some additional cause for

rejoicing when the British government reimbursed the colonies for their expenses in the Louisbourg campaign, thereby lightening the load being carried by the colonial taxpayers. Special rewards went to the men most responsible for British success: Warren was advanced to the rank of rear admiral, while Pepperrell was made a baronet. Shirley, to his great disappointment, received no greater honor than a colonelcy in the British Army.

Early in 1746, under the prodding of Shirley, Warren, and other aggressive imperialists, the British government laid plans for another expedition, this time to seize Canada itself. Preparations were well underway in both England and the colonies when political and military considerations in Europe caused the cancellation of the venture. As late as October the participating colonies, with their recruited regiments standing in readiness, still awaited the word to proceed, a word which never came. Oldsters shook their heads as they recalled the similar fiasco of 1709.[79] Fortunately for the British colonists, the French fared no better in their plans for revenge. The Duc d'Anville was sent from France to America for the purpose of regaining Louisbourg and Annapolis Royal, and if possible, of destroying Boston. D'Anville commanded a powerful fleet, with a large number of transports carrying an army of more than 3,000 men. But everything went wrong. The fleet was badly battered during an unusually difficult three-month Atlantic crossing, and arrived off the coast of Nova Scotia greatly weakened. Then D'Anville died of apoplexy. His successor attempted suicide, and was in turn succeeded by the Marquis de La Jonquière, the governor-designate of Canada. Fever and smallpox raged through the crowded warships and transports, quickly reducing the army to a feeble remnant incapable of carrying on the offensive operations that had been intended to restore French power in coastal North America. Eventually the wasted fleet limped back to France with nothing to show for its frightful losses.[80]

The renewal of warfare between the French and British along the frontiers of North America in the mid-1740s only intensified the perplexing and tragic dilemma of the Indian tribes. Seeking to survive in a world of diminishing options, they groped uncertainly for some measure of security and trade with one side or the other, or both. No wonder that from the perspective of the European contenders the Indians seemed capricious, unreliable, and even treacherous. The Six Nations of the Iroquois Confederacy were prominent in this regard, and especially important because of their strategic location and their widespread hegemony. Ever since the dark days of King William's War, many of the Iroquois leaders had been inclined toward a policy of neutrality in the apparently endless struggle between France and England. Shifting factional patterns even within the various tribes showed how amorphous the Iroquois position actually was. All through the war the Iroquois wavered, sometimes dabbling in hostilities as allies of the British, sometimes trekking off to Canada to receive the caresses of the French, but most often groping along the narrow and difficult trail of self-interest and neutrality. If allies, they were frustratingly undependable ones. Yet before the war was concluded, the Iroquois' were casting the same charge back at the English. The Reverend Henry Barclay, a missionary among the Iroquois Indians, wrote in 1746 that the Mohawks' attachment to the British interest seemed to be declining, "and it is Impossible It should be Otherwise whilst contradictory messages are sent amongst them, and they are made to Conceive the Meanest opinion of us, by our Indolence, and the Intestine Divisions prevailing amongst us. They plainly see," he continued, "that we Intend to do nothing ourselves to Anoy the Enemy, But endeavour only to Set them on, and Use them like a Pack of Hounds to Hunt them for us." [81] A few months later, another New Yorker recorded much the same sentiment when he called it "a hard matter to prevail on any Indians any more for the future; for they much reflect to me, We only bring them in the Wars to leave them in the Lurch. . . ." [82] Under these circumstances, the French found plenty of opportunity to promote their own interest among the Six Nations, further adding to the difficulties and discomfiture of the British.

Since 1731 the French had maintained a fort at Crown Point, near the south end of Lake Champlain. This outpost was well situated to serve as a base for French and Indian raids into New York and New England, for from that locality the war trails led south along Lake George to the Hudson Valley, and east along Otter Creek to the upper Connecticut.[83] A journal kept by one of the participants in a French and Indian raiding expedition that took its departure from Crown Point on 9 November 1745 enables us to accompany the party as invisible spectators, observing the techniques employed in this kind of warfare.[84] Led by Lieutenant Paul Marin, the striking force totaled more than 520 men including officers, cadets, *habitants*, Iroquois, Nipissings, Hurons, and Abnakis. There was even a surgeon, or at least a practitioner so designated, and a priest. Leaving Crown Point, they proceeded in a fleet of canoes as far south as they could conveniently go by water; then, taking with them only the supplies they could carry on their backs, they began the overland trek toward the upper Hudson. It was a matter of particular concern that no hostile Indian or wandering white discover their presence and give warning to the settlements below; therefore, Marin was careful to proceed with caution, sending out scouts to make sure they were unobserved.

They paused on 14 November to cache a good supply of provisions and utensils which they would recover on their return. Now less heavily laden, they were able to advance more rapidly. Their scouts discovered and captured two Mahican Indians, who assured the French that their approach still was not suspected by the New Yorkers. Nearing the isolated post of the frontier trader John Henry Lydius, near the great bend of the upper Hudson, the raiders approached cautiously, determined to let no person escape and spread the alarm southward. They found the place occupied only by a hired man and Lydius' young son, the remainder of the family and employees having gone to Albany. Marin ordered the two prisoners tied up and left in the house under guard, after which the expedition continued on down the Hudson Valley, some of the men proceeding by water and the others by land. It was quite apparent that in this part of the country the people were anticipating no such intrusion from Canada, assuming, no doubt, that the French would concentrate their efforts against New England. For his target Marin had selected the unsuspecting agricultural settlement of Saratoga, located on the west side of the Hudson not much more than 30 miles above Albany. Here a poorly sited, badly maintained fort stood guard, but without a regular garrison thanks to the parsimony of the New York assembly.[85] The farms themselves were inhabited mostly by Dutch folk with their Negro slaves, people largely indifferent to the Anglo-French war except as it might affect their economic prosperity.

At about midnight the entire striking force assembled quietly just a few miles above Saratoga. The night was bitter cold, and many of the men were wet from wading through streams; but fortunately, the rendezvous was in a low place where they could build small fires without fear of detection, to prevent their wet feet from freezing. After a preliminary reconnaissance, the word to advance was given, and they filed off through the darkness. A good road leading to the village made this last part of the advance easy, and soon the objective was there in front of them, dark, silent, unsuspecting. The plan was to hold the attack until daybreak, but the impulsive Indians headed for the houses at once, yelping as they ran, so the French had no choice but to go it also. As Marin had hoped, the surprise was complete. Smashing doors and windows, the raiders forced their way into the houses and dragged the cowering inhabitants outside. A few residents, apparently hiding in their cellars, died when the houses were put to the torch. The French set fire to everything they could—homes, barns and stables full of grain and livestock, the empty fort, several mills, and a large quantity of lumber.

When all was accomplished, Marin gave the order to withdraw. The triumphant French and Indians, loaded with booty and herding 109 prisoners also heavily laden with the spoils of their own disaster, began a slow retreat back toward Canada. It took them about six days to reach the safety of their base at Crown Point. Approaching it on the twenty-second of November, the returning raiders announced their arrival with three volleys of musketry and three shouts of *"Vive le roi!"* to which the fort replied with three similar volleys and seven cannon salutes. The rejoicing at Crown Point contrasted sharply with the gloom that now had settled upon the people of the upper Hudson Valley. The destruction of Saratoga had come as a great shock, shattering provincial complacency and impelling nearly all the inhabitants along the Hudson above the Mohawk River to abandon their settlements and flee to safer ground. The spreading fear crept even into Albany itself, with the result that some men there began sending their wives, children, and valued possessions to safety in the town of New York.[86]

During the spring of 1746 the exposed settlements between the Kennebec and the Penobscot rivers in Maine came under attack, as the Eastern Indians abandoned their pose of neutrality and joined in the game of plunder. Other Indians tried their luck at Fort Number Four on the Connecticut River in what is now Charlestown, New Hampshire, but were routed by the garrison. In August 1746 one of the heaviest blows was directed at Fort Massachusetts on the upper Hoosick River 25 miles east of Albany, when a large force of French and Indians led by Rigaud de Vaudreuil invested that remote outpost and forced its surrender. The garrison of twenty-one men, together with three women and five children, were made prisoners, and the fort was destroyed by fire.[87] These attacks were typical of many. All along the open frontier of New England the settlers who tried to remain on their property knew the meaning of a precarious existence. Colonial governments, as always, were slow to provide adequate precautions and remedies, both before and after the enemy had shown his hand. Farmers were killed or seized while at work. Much valuable property was destroyed or rendered useless by a kind of warfare against which it was difficult if not absolutely impossible to protect a thinly scattered population.

In Nova Scotia the situation was made especially worrisome for the British by the proximity of French forces in the vicinity of Chignecto Bay as well as by the presence of the neutrality-minded Acadian populace. During the winter of 1746–47, the French Captain Roch de Ramezay with a strong force of troops was in quarters at Beaubassin at the head of Chignecto Bay, while on the British side a garrison of about 500 men under the command of Colonel Arthur Noble had settled in at the Acadian village of Grand Pré, near the southern shore of Minas Basin, 65 miles northeast of Annapolis Royal. Here there was no fort, so a detachment of Noble's soldiers was quartered in a stone dwelling located near the center of the village; the remainder were parceled out among some twenty or more ordinary houses extending over an area about a mile and a half in length. If this arrangement seemed hardly suited for effective defense, it was at least comforting to know that between Grand Pré and the enemy at Beaubassin lay more than 100 miles of sparsely inhabited, winter-lashed terrain. Ramezay, having been thwarted in his attempt to capture Annapolis Royal the previous fall by the default of D'Anville's expedition, was anxious to have another go at the British, winter or not. Unable to lead in person because of an injured knee, he gave command of a winter expedition against Grand Pré to the brave and capable Antoine Coulon de Villiers. Snowshoes and sledges were prepared, for the ground was covered with snow, and only a well-equipped, hardy, and determined party could hope to complete the difficult trek and arrive at the objective ready for combat.

A nucleus of more than 200 Canadians under Villiers' command departed from Beaubassin early in January as winter was entering its fiercest phase. For many days they plodded on with great difficulty, picking up Acadian and Indian recruits as they went. Finally, at the end of the month, they arrived on the outskirts of Grand Pré. Another snowstorm was whipping the bleak countryside, keeping Noble's men close to their firesides, quite oblivious to approaching danger. The French and Indians, after obtaining from local residents helpful information on the distribution of the garrison troops, attacked the separate quarters under cover of darkness. In some places the startled British were quickly overwhelmed and either killed or captured; in others a stout resistance was quickly organized and maintained. Colonel Noble himself was killed at the first onset, and Villiers was disabled by a musket ball. As might have been expected, the most effective defense took place at the stone dwelling, where Noble's men were hemmed in by the attackers. Here the fight continued for a number of hours. At last, with the Canadians and their Indian allies unable to break the British resistance, and the defenders seriously handicapped by a shortage of ammunition, food, and water, both sides agreed to terms. This clearly gave the victory to the French who, compared with the British, had lost few men. By the terms of capitulation, the defeated garrison withdrew to Annapolis Royal, leaving the northern part of Nova Scotia in enemy hands.[88] Soon, however, the victorious French found it expedient to withdraw also, and when spring returned to Grand Pré, so did a strong force of Massachusetts men. The situation in Nova Scotia became stabilized as before.

Privateers of both sides had been extremely active in American waters since the outbreak of the war in 1739, capturing hundreds of vessels with valuable cargoes, and sometimes even making raids upon coastal settlements. One American marauder from Rhode Island boldly sacked a Spanish community on the north coast of Cuba. Not to be outdone, Spanish ships occasionally raided tidewater plantations in Georgia and South Carolina. So effective at times were the Spaniards that American coastal commerce was badly disrupted, with heavy losses to the economy. Insurance rates and shipping charges mounted, while considerable expenditures had to be made for establishing and maintaining lookout posts and forts along the coasts.[89] Every rumor of a mysterious ship hovering just over the horizon, every tale of vessels accosted and confiscated, added to the fears of those who traveled and traded by sea. "Much Talk of two Privateers from Augustine Cruizing on the Coast," reported one Georgian in the spring of 1745, "and that they had snapped lately two or three Small Vessells . . . soon after they were over the Barr; but the Pilots that were in them they had sent on shore again, in their own Boats and gave them Orders to tell any of our Men in Charles Town Harbour, that if they pleased to come out they were ready to receive them." [90] In 1747 a Spanish raiding party plundered the small settlement of Beaufort, near Cape Lookout in North Carolina, and the following year another Spanish force actually seized and held for a short time the town of Brunswick on the lower Cape Fear River. These were freebooting expeditions, not official military invasions.[91]

The year 1747 brought similar trouble to Pennsylvania and Delaware. French and Spanish privateers hovered just off the Capes, waiting for choice victims either going to or coming from Philadelphia. In July one group of marauders entered the Delaware River, penetrated to within about 60 miles of Philadelphia, and came boldly ashore. They robbed at gunpoint the frightened inhabitants of several farms, taking household valuables and Negro slaves.[92] Pennsylvanians began to fear that the enemy, learning of their colony's complete lack of defenses resulting from the long-standing policy of the Quaker-dominated assembly, would take the opportunity to ravage the capital itself. Despite this clear threat and the rising popular demand for protection, the assembly still refused to act. On 2 June 1748 the *Pennsylvania Gazette* reported glumly that "All foreign trade is now at a stand, and the port as much shut up, as if the river was frozen." [93]

While the American colonies were trying to cope with the persistent menace of enemy privateers and at the same time doing some successful privateering of their own, the Royal Navy was busy elsewhere battering French and Spanish sea power at every opportunity. The enemy suffered a great attrition in naval vessels during this conflict; before the war had ended, France found herself virtually stripped of her navy. One authority on naval history has gone so far as to insist that "the main gain to Great Britain by the war was the reduction of the French navy to proportions which, for the time, were no longer formidable." [94] Spain, too, was rendered largely impotent at sea, leaving the Royal Navy clearly dominant. This, in turn, meant that the enemy powers found themselves unable to transfer armies and large quantities of materiel by maritime routes, which boded ill for the French and

Spanish colonies in America. Even though, as Professor Gerald S. Graham has said, in the eyes of the French government the empire was little more than "an important side-show," and France was not likely to collapse merely from the effects of a British naval blockade, the loss of sea power in the latter years of the war was an ominous sign for the future.[95] No nation, it is safe to say, was likely to remain for long an imperial power if unable to make its own way at sea.

On the continent of Europe the situation was far less encouraging for Britain. The Dutch nation, a keystone in the traditional British system of security in western Europe, was near collapse, while the armies of France had largely gained control of the Austrian Netherlands. Although the Jacobite uprising in Scotland had come to a disastrous end at Culloden in 1746, releasing many British regiments for service elsewhere, there seemed little prospect of rolling back the French military tide. In India, the French now held the important trading station of Madras on the Coromandel coast, depriving the British East India Company of large revenues. Indeed, economic considerations clearly rivaled military considerations in the urge for peace. Britain's national debt was now passing the £78 million mark, with no sign of a pause.[96] Some government leaders in London even whispered of bankruptcy. For all these reasons, Britain now was as ready as Spain and France to seek a settlement of international differences.

Negotiations began in April 1748 at the Rhineland city of Aix-la-Chapelle. Within a matter of weeks the diplomats had agreed upon preliminary terms, and the peace was formally concluded the following eighteenth of October. The terms which Britain accepted, not without a degree of reluctance, represented a victory not for France or Spain, but for those political leaders in the British ministry and Parliament who still saw their country's interests as primarily Continental. Others, such as William Pitt and the Duke of Bedford, who already were beginning to glimpse the new imperial vision oriented toward the west, were less well satisfied with what was done at Aix-la-Chapelle. The *asiento*, together with the annual trading ship, was renewed by Spain as a British privilege. Beyond this, however, the Spaniards made no further concession with respect to their closed commercial system. Curiously, the disputed issue of the *guardacostas* was not even mentioned in the terms of peace; Captain Jenkins and his severed ear apparently had long since dropped from public view. What caused the Continentalists to rejoice was France's agreement to withdraw from the Flemish barrier towns and the Austrian Netherlands, yielding by negotiation what never could have been gained by British arms. In addition, the French restored Madras to British control. For these concessions there was a price, far too heavy in the view of many Americans and some leaders in England, but nevertheless paid—the restoration of Louisbourg and Cape Breton Island to France.[97] In general, all captured territory in America was to be relinquished, thereby restoring the *status quo ante bellum*. Disputed boundaries, such as those of Nova Scotia and New France, or Georgia and Florida, were left as much in dispute as before.

Public sentiment in America concerning these terms so deftly made by European politicians was mixed. Even the reversion of Louisbourg was viewed with satisfaction in some quarters, particularly by merchants who looked forward to a renewal of a previously profitable trade. But among many of the common folk and their imperialistic-minded leaders, especially in New England, there arose a feeling of baffled resentment. It seemed that England for her own selfish gain had thrown away New England's security, won so gloriously and at such great subsequent cost only three years earlier. France remained strong in North America and still intent upon gaining the vast interior region beyond the Appalachian Mountains. Viewing this situation, some Americans feared that the mother country had failed to appreciate the full potentiality of the American future and the ominous possibility that such a glorious future well might be destroyed by the rising power of New France. Nearly a year before the opening of negotiations at Aix-la-Chapelle, a Pennsylvania merchant revealed this deep concern in a letter to a business acquaintance in London when he wrote:

I wish your ministry could be brought to judge rightly of the value and consequence North America is to Great Britain and the danger of the French gaining some settlements in some part of what is now possessed by the English. If they should once get masters in America, England could never hold the balance again according to my present apprehensions. Less than half a century may enable North America, if no uncommon accident happens, to become very formidable—I mean the English part of it—as they are capable to furnish within themselves everything necessary for naval armaments of the growth and manufacture of those countries, gunpowder excepted and for this nothing but saltpetre is wanting. And as the people increase greatly their number, in time to come will furnish great quantities of all things necessary without being obliged to call on Europe for them. This is at a great distance, but I think thoughts of this sort should have some weight with our great folks so that they should not part with us tamely; and at present our settlements are of so great an extent of seacoast from Carolina to Newfoundland that trade is very liable to great interruption as well as the ports open to privateers or greater force making descents if not gaining settlements. And should Cape Breton be given up, which we fear will be the case, the French on any rupture may from thence destroy all our trade.[98]

This kind of wordy but clear-sighted complaint from America as yet would have little influence upon the attitude of tradition-bound ministries, but the new younger school of statesmen was rising fast and would be heard from decisively in the future.

Looking back over the record of military campaigning in the American theater during the War of the 1740s, one is immediately struck by the high incidence of failure and is drawn inevitably to the conclusion that military leadership was weak and ineffective. Why was this so? The obvious answer is that the most experienced, most able commanders available to the belligerent powers were utilized in Europe, the principal theater of the war. Men sent out to command in the American theater generally proved to be less than first-rate, and within the colonies themselves no thoroughly competent commanders were likely to be found. Wentworth showed at Cartagena that he lacked the cold courage and the forceful drive of a great general, and Montiano displayed at St. Augustine only a sort of dogged steadfastness that was helpful in defending a besieged fortress but no substitute for the fast, hard-driving kind of leadership needed for the conquest of Georgia. Likewise, Oglethorpe proved to be little more than a mediocre commander, whose great weakness lay in the vital realm of planning, organizing, and administering. At the head of a body of troops in the field he could be superb, but that was not sufficient for the broad responsibility he bore. Du Chambon, the unfortunate defender of Louisbourg, was notably lacking in experience as well as judgment, deficiencies that even the great walls of the fortress could not conceal. Equally true is the fact that Pepperrell's conduct of the siege was anything but exemplary. His command was loose and often indecisive; indeed, one hardly could have expected more from a man with no previous experience in leading a large army in combat. Pepperrell's redeeming qualities were his patience, determination, and good sense which, coupled with his good fortune in having overwhelming numbers of men and the important advantage of naval support, enabled him to win at last the greatest victory of the American theater.

The apparent ineffectiveness of military leadership in America, however, goes far deeper than the personal qualities of the commanders themselves. Observing one of these military operations being planned and carried out is somewhat like watching a film in slow motion. "Dilatory" was the word for colonial military activity. The process of gathering supplies, or recruiting an army, or sending off a fleet seemed almost interminable. Often by the time the necessary preliminaries had been accomplished, a good opportunity for success was already gone. The reasons for this are numerous. One, certainly, was the conservatism of colonial legislatures, jealous of their prerogatives, suspicious of the executive, and wary of extraordinary expense. This condition was aggravated when the operation was intercolonial, involving two or more governments. Communications could be extremely slow over great distances, making coordination difficult. Sometimes, too, the weather was a controlling factor, and a ready expedition might be held up for days by adverse winds or scattered by a storm at sea. Such delays, in turn, partially consumed the store of provisions needed for the campaign.

Commanders in the American theater were inclined to be hesitant and cautious because they were operating at such great distances from the center of power. Lines of supply usually were stretched very thin, and the commander knew that if he took a risk and suffered heavy losses there was no likelihood of rapid support and reinforcement. One bad mistake could mean total failure, even disaster. This was a heavy burden of responsibility, really greater than that generally borne by most commanders in Europe, and it does much to explain such apparent timidity. It is easy in retrospect to assume that more aggressiveness would have produced more and better victories. It might also have caused some terrible defeats. In addition, the quality of personnel at the lower levels was an important contributing factor. Some of the best military leadership in the war was being developed among relatively junior officers who, in the actual experience of combat command, were displaying imagination and boldness. This was especially true in the cases of certain frontier leaders on both sides, but most notably among the French, who were mastering the techniques of wilderness warfare, often in conjunction with Indian allies. In general, however, the troops left much to be desired. Hastily recruited regiments sent over from Europe were not fully trained and disciplined; colonial regiments recruited from the militia were likely to be even more of a problem, and one could never be certain of their behavior under fire. Pepperrell's militia army at Louisbourg consisted of men who were essentially civilians and deeply attached to the democratic tradition of New England—they thought of their officers as being responsible to them! What this could mean to a commanding general in the face of the enemy is shown by what happened on 9 May when the troops learned of Pepperrell's decision to storm the fortress that very night. So unfavorable and so vocal was the reaction in the ranks that the high command found it expedient to reconsider the matter, and the plan was dropped. This kind of problem with colonial troops did not go unnoticed by professional British officers, and only reinforced their rather contemptuous opinion of Americans in arms.

The commander in chief, who in the midst of a difficult operation began to feel that the risk was too great to sustain, characteristically found an escape through his council of war. This body of advisers, the equivalent of a modern staff, included the senior commanders of various units engaged in the operation. Its function was to consider any problems the commander in chief wished to submit, giving him the benefit of various individual opinions. This system made it relatively easy for a commander to give up an operation without himself carrying the full burden of blame, if his council of war concurred, and of course concurrence usually was not difficult to obtain. Admiral Walker, we recall, utilized this technique in 1711. Various discouraged commanders found it useful in the War of the 1740s. Thus, Governor Montiano could write to his king after his failure against Georgia in 1742 that he had held a council composed of

Colonel Don Francisco Rubiani, of Lieutenant Colonel Don Antonio Salgado, and of the Chief of Staff Don Antonio de Arredondo. These all agreed that we should bend all our energies to retreat, that our fear lest Oglethorpe should attack by land while his ships did the same by sea was normal. . . . I do not know, Sir, whether my conduct of affairs will meet with the royal approbation of Your Majesty. . . . Nevertheless, I expect of the royal magnanimity of Your Majesty, that it will deign to regard itself as having been well served in the operations under question, and that I shall have the satisfaction of receiving honors. . . .[99]

This was the way of politics in the 1740s; it was not the way of military greatness or success.

Be that as it may, the war was now over, and a peace reasonably satisfactory to the rival powers had been achieved. The various empires remained intact; the colonies resumed their normal affairs. And if the shrewd ones among the colonists realized only too well how temporary this happy condition was likely to be, most were satisfied to take each day as it came and hoped for the best.

NOTES

1. Walter Louis Dorn, *Competition for Empire, 1740–1763* (New York, 1940), chap. 4, provides a helpful discussion of international relations during this period, with especial attention to the war in Europe.

2. Gerald S. Graham, "The Naval Defence of British North America, 1739–1763," in Transactions of the Royal Historical Society, Ser. 4, XXX (1948), 95–110.

3. Francis L. Berkeley, Jr., "The War of Jenkins' Ear," in Darrett B. Rutman, ed., *The Old Dominion: Essays for Thomas Perkins Abernethy* (Charlottesville, Va., 1964), pp. 42–43.

4. For an authoritative account of the futile negotiations between Britain and Spain in the spring and early summer of 1739, see John Tate Lanning, *The Diplomatic History of Georgia: A Study of the Epoch of Jenkins' Ear* (Chapel Hill, 1936), chap. 7.

5. This acquisitive, optimistic mood was reflected quite clearly in the rise of stocks immediately after war was declared (Dorothy Marshall, *Eighteenth Century England* [New York, 1962], p. 178).

6. Lanning, *Diplomatic History of Georgia,* pp. 188–189. The Duke of Newcastle's instructions of 15 June 1739, mislabeled a "Declaration of War," may be found in Francis Russell Hart, "Struggle for Control of America," *Journal of American History,* II (1908), 330. Some modern accounts still erroneously state that war was declared at that time.

7. Quoted in Daniel A. Baugh, *British Naval Administration in the Age of Walpole* (Princeton, 1965), p. 20.

8. William Laird Clowes, *The Royal Navy: A History from the Earliest Times to the Present* (7 vols.; London, 1897–1903), III, 54–57; Berkeley, "War of Jenkins' Ear," pp. 50–51. The terms of surrender are given in Hart, "Struggle for Control of America," p. 331.

9. An eyewitness account of the mission to Coweta has been published in Newton D. Mereness, ed., *Travels in the American Colonies* (New York, 1916), pp. 218–222. See also Lanning, *Diplomatic History of Georgia*, pp. 221–222; John Pitts Corry, *Indian Affairs in Georgia, 1732–1756* (Philadelphia, 1936), pp. 72–73, 122; David H. Corkran, *The Creek Frontier, 1540–1783* (Norman, Okla., 1967), pp. 100–101.

10. Allen D. Candler, ed., *Journal of the Earl of Egmont, First President of the Board of Trustees, from June 14, 1738, to May 25, 1744* (Colonial Records of Georgia, V, [Atlanta, 1909]), p. 255; Mereness, *Travels in the American Colonies*, pp. 223–224; Lanning, *Diplomatic History of Georgia*, pp. 222–223.

11. Herbert E. Bolton, ed., *Arredondo's Historical Proof of Spain's Title to Georgia* (Berkeley, 1925), p. 86. See also Mereness, *Travels in the American Colonies*, pp. 224–226; Lanning, *Diplomatic History of Georgia*, p. 223; John Jay TePaske, *The Governorship of Spanish Florida, 1700–1763* (Durham, 1964), p. 140.

12. On one occasion the impatient governor reported that the improvements were being effected only with "great slowness, a source to me of the greatest anxiety" (Don Manuel de Montiano, *Letters of Montiano, Siege of St. Augustine* in Collections of the Georgia Historical Society, VII, Part 1 [Savannah, Ga., 1909], pp. 9, 21, 24). See also TePaske, *Governorship of Spanish Florida*, p. 17.

13. Edward McCrady, *The History of South Carolina under the Royal Government, 1719–1776* (New York, 1901), p. 201; Verne E. Chatelain, *The Defenses of Spanish Florida, 1565 to 1763* (Washington, D.C., 1941), p. 92; TePaske, *Governorship of Spanish Florida*, pp. 140–141.

14. Montiano, *Letters*, pp. 49–50.

15. Montiano, *Letters*, pp. 56, 58, 63. See also TePaske, *Governorship of Spanish Florida*, p. 143.

16. Montiano, *Letters*, p. 62.

17. Montiano, *Letters*, p. 59; TePaske, *Governorship of Spanish Florida*, p. 144.

18. Amos A. Ettinger, *James Edward Oglethorpe, Imperial Idealist* (Oxford and New York, 1936), pp. 235–237; Robert L. Meriwether, *The Expansion of South Carolina, 1729–1765* (Kingsport, Tenn., 1940), p. 189; M. Eugene Sirmans, *Colonial South Carolina: A Political History, 1663–1763* (Chapel Hill, 1966), pp. 211–212. For a petition expressing the disillusionment of the authorities in South Carolina after the failure at St. Augustine see J. H. Easterby, ed., *The Colonial Records of South Carolina. The Journal of the Commons House of Assembly, September 12, 1739–March 26, 1741* (Columbia, S.C., 1952), pp. 364–367.

19. Clarence S. Brigham, ed., *British Royal Proclamations Relating to America, 1603–1783* (Worcester, Mass., 1911), pp. 188–189.

20. Brigham, *British Royal Proclamations*, pp. 189–193. Before Cartagena, on 6 March 1740/41, Admiral Vernon notified the men in his expedition "that the Whole of all Booty to be made upon the Enemies at Land, is graciously granted by his Majesty, to be distributed among his Sea and Land Forces, as shall be agreed on by a Council of War of Sea and Land Officers, which have accordingly met and regulated the Distribution thereof, and have

allotted a double Share to any Non-Commission or Warrant Officer, and private Man, that may happen to be wounded in the Service; and to assure of a further Reward from me, out of my Share, all who shall eminently distinguish themselves by any extraordinary actions of Prudence and Resolution, besides a secured Advancement proportionable to their Zeal and Resolution, exerted on so signal an Occasion, for the Honour of the Crown and future Prosperity of our Country" (Hart, "Struggle for Control of America," pp. 337–338).

21. Lanning, *Diplomatic History of Georgia*, p. 206n. The problems encountered and progress made in raising this force may be followed in the published records of the various colonies. See, for example, *Journals of the House of Representatives of Massachusetts, 1740–1741* (Boston, 1942), *passim*, and *The Acts and Resolves, Public and Private, of the Province of the Massachusetts Bay* (21 vols.; Boston, 1869–1922), II, 1037.

22. John W. Fortescue, *A History of the British Army* (13 vols. and 6 atlases; London, 1889–1930), II, 62; Lanning, *Diplomatic History of Georgia*, pp. 191–206.

23. The motivation of plunder is clearly reflected in a statement published in the *South Carolina Gazette* for 9 to 16 July 1741: "It's said, that the Report of there being so much Riches in the Town of Carthagena, greatly animates the Sailors and Land Forces to be within the Walls of the same."

24. Fortescue, *History of the British Army*, II, 66–76; William A. Foote, "The Pennsylvania Men of the American Regiment," *Pennsylvania Magazine of History and Biography*, LXXXVII (January, 1963), 37. Few of these men now would have written, as did another veteran of the Cartagena fiasco, "I Delight in war . . ." (Michael Tyrrell's letter of 28 May 1741, in William Johnson, *The Papers of Sir William Johnson*, James Sullivan and Alexander C. Flick, eds. [13 vols.; Albany, 1921–1962], I, 13).

25. Douglas Southall Freeman, *George Washington, A Biography* (7 vols.; New York, 1948–1957), I, 77.

26. Albert Harkness, Jr., "Americanism and Jenkins' Ear," *MVHR*, XXXVII (June, 1950), 61, 88. See also Richard L. Merritt, *Symbols of American Community, 1735–1775* (New Haven, 1966), pp. 148–157, an interesting analysis of fluctuating "Americanism" during the colonial wars from 1739 to 1763, and Foote, "The Pennsylvania Men of the American Regiment," pp. 36–37.

27. *The Spanish Official Account of the Attack on the Colony of Georgia, in America, and of Its Defeat on St. Simons Island by General James Oglethorpe*, in Collections of the Georgia Historical Society, VII, Part 3 (Savannah, Ga., 1913), pp. 20–24; TePaske, *Governorship of Spanish Florida*, p. 146.

28. This narrative of the operation is based primarily upon Oglethorpe's letters published in the Collections of the Georgia Historical Society, III (Savannah, Ga., 1873), and *The Spanish Official Account*. These and other sources are extremely difficult to reconcile at many points; a careful attempt has been made here to construct an account that conforms to the probable facts and conveys an accurate impression of the operation.

29. *The Spanish Official Account*, p. 30.

30. Oglethorpe's letter to Savannah, dated 8 June, somehow was diverted and did not reach its destination until nearly a month later! By that time Savannah had received another report of impending danger. (See William Stephens, *The Journal of William Stephens, 1741–1743*, E. Merton Coulter, ed. [Athens, Ga., 1958], pp. 100, 103.)

31. Mereness, *Travels in the American Colonies*, p. 233.

32. A description of the terrain, with helpful maps, may be found in *The Spanish Official Account*, pp. 110–111. For contemporary accounts of these actions see the *South Carolina Gazette* for 12 to 19 July 1742, and Mereness, *Travels in the American Colonies*, pp. 234–235.

33. Stephens, *Journal, 1741–1743*, p. 107.

34. W. Roy Smith, *South Carolina as a Royal Province, 1719–1776* (New York, 1903), pp. 189–190; Ettinger, *James Edward Oglethorpe*, pp. 243–244; Sirmans, *Colonial South Carolina*, p. 214.

35. Benjamin Franklin, *The Papers of Benjamin Franklin*, Leonard W. Labaree et al., eds. (14 vols. to date; New Haven, 1959 to present), II, 367.

36. McCrady, *History of South Carolina under the Royal Government*, p. 250; Sirmans, *Colonial South Carolina*, pp. 216, 221.

37. Frances Gardiner Davenport (continued by Charles Oscar Paullin), ed., *European Treaties Bearing on the History of the United States and Its Dependencies* (4 vols.; Washington, D.C., 1917–1937), IV, 66.

38. Brigham, *British Royal Proclamations*, pp. 196–199; John Bartlet Brebner, *New England's Outpost: Acadia before the Conquest of Canada* (New York, 1927), pp. 110–111; J. S. McLennan, *Louisbourg from Its Foundation to Its Fall* (London, 1918), p. 109.

39. George M. Wrong, ed., *The Anonymous Lettre d'un Habitant de Louisbourg* (Toronto, 1897), pp. 15–16.

40. Nathaniel Mountfort to Samuel Waldo, 18 May 1744, Samuel Waldo Papers (Massachusetts Historical Society). See also in the same collection Captain Cutler's letter to Waldo dated 18 May 1744 at Saco Falls.

41. Robert Rutherford to Samuel Waldo, St. George's, 26 May 1744, Samuel Waldo Papers (Massachusetts Historical Society).

42. Enoch Freeman to Samuel Waldo, Falmouth, 6 June 1744, Samuel Waldo Papers (Massachusetts Historical Society).

43. Brebner, *New England's Outpost*, pp. 111–112; McLennan, *Louisbourg*, pp. 112–113.

44. Brebner, *New England's Outpost*, pp. 112–113; McLennan, *Louisbourg*, pp. 114–115. A French account of this affair may be found in Wrong, *Anonymous Lettre*, pp. 19–22.

45. G. A. Rawlyk, *Yankees at Louisbourg* (Orono, Me., 1967), pp. 27–28.

46. McLennan, *Louisbourg*, pp. 118–122; Rawlyk, *Yankees at Louisbourg*, pp. 20–21.

47. 1 *MHC*, V, 203. Auchmuty's memorandum is dated 9 April 1744.

48. Louis Effingham De Forest, ed., *Louisbourg Journals, 1745* (New York, 1932), p. 171; McLennan, *Louisbourg*, pp. 123–124; John A. Schutz, *William Shirley: King's Governor of Massachusetts* (Chapel Hill, 1961), pp. 88–89; Rawlyk, *Yankees at Louisbourg*, pp. 33–34.

49. McLennan, *Louisbourg*, p. 133; Schutz, *William Shirley*, p. 90; Rawlyk, *Yankees at Louisbourg*, pp. 35–40.

50. One resident of Louisbourg later remarked that "for a long time we were not unaware that a secret enterprise against us was in preparation in New England" (Wrong, *Anonymous Lettre*, p. 11).

51. Schutz, *William Shirley*, p. 92.

52. Thomas Hutchinson, *The History of the Colony and Province of Massachusetts-Bay*, Lawrence Shaw Mayo, ed. (3 vols.; Cambridge, Mass., 1936), II, 314.

53. Observers at Louisbourg sighted the first British patrol vessels on 3 March and more continued to appear (Wrong, *Anonymous Lettre*, p. 36). The account of this important operation presented here relies heavily on McLennan, *Louisbourg*, and Rawlyk, *Yankees at Louisbourg*. Also still very useful, and vivid as always, is Francis Parkman's narrative in *A Half-Century of Conflict* (2 vols.; Boston, 1892).

54. De Forest, *Louisbourg Journals*, p. 3.

55. *Ibid.*, p. 82.

56. *Ibid.*, p. 6.

57. *Ibid.*, p. 185.

58. *Ibid.*, p. 186.

59. Wrong, *Anonymous Lettre*, pp. 31–32; McLennan, *Louisbourg*, p. 165n.; George F. G. Stanley, *Canada's Soldiers, 1604–1954: The Military History of an Unmilitary People* (Toronto, 1954), pp. 52–54.

60. Hutchinson, *History of the Colony and Province of Massachusetts-Bay*, II, 317.

61. De Forest, *Louisbourg Journals*, p. 115. The same letter appears also in William Shirley, *Correspondence of William Shirley, Governor of Massachusetts and Military Commander in America, 1731–1760*, Charles H. Lincoln, ed. (2 vols.; New York, 1912), I, 273–279.

62. Franklin, *Papers*, III, 26.

63. Wrong, *Anonymous Lettre*, pp. 30, 39–41; De Forest, *Louisbourg Journals*, p. 174.

64. De Forest, *Louisbourg Journals*, p. 87.

65. Quoted in McLennan, *Louisbourg*, p. 160.

66. Gerald S. Graham, *Empire of the North Atlantic: The Maritime Struggle for North America* (Toronto, 1950), p. 125.

67. Wrong, *Anonymous Lettre*, pp. 46–49; McLennan, *Louisbourg*, pp. 156–157, 177–178.

68. Shirley, *Correspondence*, I, 205.

69. Wrong, *Anonymous Lettre*, pp. 57–58.

70. De Forest, *Louisbourg Journals*, p. 59. A description of the technique employed by artillery in attempting to create a breach is provided in Albert Manucy, *Artillery through the Ages: A Short Illustrated History of Cannon, Emphasizing Types Used in America* (Washington, D.C., 1949), p. 65.

71. Quoted in McLennan, *Louisbourg*, p. 162.

72. De Forest, *Louisbourg Journals*, p. 212.

73. Gustave Lanctot, *A History of Canada. Volume III: From the Treaty of*

Utrecht to the Treaty of Paris, 1713–1763, M. M. Cameron, trans. (Cambridge, Mass., 1965), p. 65. The seven-week siege had caused a surprisingly small number of casualties on both sides, not counting the effects of disease among the New England troops. Probably the number of combat and accidental deaths in Pepperrell's army was not much more than a hundred, the greater part of those occurring in the futile attack on the Island Battery. Among the Swiss and French units defending Louisbourg, fatalities totaled about half that number. Casualties among the civilian population added considerably to the French total, of course. (See De Forest, *Louisbourg Journals*, p. 120; McLennan, *Louisbourg*, pp. 165–166n.; Rawlyk, *Yankees at Louisbourg*, p. 152.)

74. De Forest, *Louisbourg Journals*, p. 98. See also *ibid.*, pp. 214–215; *Boston Gazette*, 9 July 1745; Hutchinson, *History of the Colony and Province of Massachusetts-Bay*, II, 321.

75. William Willis, ed., *Journals of the Rev. Thomas Smith, and the Rev. Samuel Deane, Pastors of the First Church in Portland* (2d ed.; Portland, Me., 1849), p. 119.

76. Franklin, *Papers*, III, 57.

77. Chris Kilby to William Pepperrell, 10 August 1745, Pepperrell Papers, No. 2 (Maine Historical Society).

78. Rawlyk, *Yankees at Louisbourg*, p. 155.

79. J. H. Trumbull and C. J. Hoadly, eds., *The Public Records of the Colony of Connecticut* (15 vols.; Hartford, Conn., 1850–1890), IX, 257–258; Arthur H. Buffinton, "The Canadian Expedition of 1746; Its Relation to British Politics," *AHR*, XLV (April, 1940), 552–580.

80. Clowes, *Royal Navy*, III, 117; Graham, *Empire of the North Atlantic*, pp. 132–134; Lanctot, *History of Canada*, III, 66–68.

81. Rev. Henry Barclay to Daniel Horsmanden, 10 April 1746, Horsmanden Papers (New York Historical Society).

82. John H. Lydius to Col. Stoddard, 20 November 1746 (New York Historical Society). See also William Johnson to Gov. Clinton, 15 March 1747/48, in *Johnson Papers*, I, 146–149.

83. Guy Omeron Coolidge, *The French Occupation of the Champlain Valley from 1609 to 1759* (Brattleboro, Vt., 1938), Appendix A, lists the various routes used.

84. Marin's Journal of the Campaign of Saratoga, 1745 (New York Public Library). In addition to the original (or a nearly contemporary copy) there is a nineteenth-century translation.

85. John Rutherfurd to Cadwallader Colden, 25 January 1745/46, in *Collections of the New-York Historical Society for the Year 1919* (New York, 1920), pp. 192–193.

86. *Johnson Papers*, I, 43.

87. Willis, *Journals of the Rev. Thomas Smith*, pp. 122–123; Benjamin Doolittle, *A Short Narrative of Mischief Done by the French and Indian Enemy, on the Western Frontiers of the Province of the Massachusetts-Bay* (Boston, 1750), pp. 8–9; Lanctot, *History of Canada*, III, 71. A colorful account of

the siege of Fort Massachusetts is found in Parkman, *Half-Century of Conflict,* II, 251–263.

88. Parkman called this raid "one of the most gallant exploits in French-Canadian annals" (*Half-Century of Conflict,* II, 215). See also Brebner, *New England's Outpost,* pp. 117–118.

89. Bolton, *Arredondo's Historical Proof,* p. 90; John Tate Lanning, "The American Colonies in the Preliminaries of the War of Jenkins' Ear," *Georgia Historical Quarterly,* XI (June, 1927), 140–144.

90. William Stephens, *The Journal of William Stephens, 1743–1745,* E. Merton Coulter, ed. (Athens, Ga., 1959), pp. 219–220.

91. Hugh T. Lefler and Albert R. Newsome, *North Carolina: The History of a Southern State* (Rev. ed., Chapel Hill, 1963), pp. 154–155. In the case of Brunswick the Spaniards apparently were after Negroes as well as other plunder. The English who eventually drove away the marauders reported that "the negroes (whom they came to take) were of great service to us, and so exasperated, that they would have given no quarter had they not been stopt" (*South Carolina Gazette* for 24 to 31 October 1748).

92. *Minutes of the Provincial Council of Pennsylvania, from the Organization to the Termination of the Proprietary Government* (10 vols.; Philadelphia and Harrisburg, 1851–1852), V, 89–90, 117–119; Franklin, *Papers,* III, 180–182.

93. Franklin, *Papers,* III, 314.

94. Clowes, *Royal Navy,* III, 138.

95. Graham, *Empire of the North Atlantic,* pp. 141–142.

96. Dorn, *Competition for Empire,* p. 173; Marshall, *Eighteenth Century England,* p. 219.

97. Jack M. Sosin argues convincingly that if there was a *quid pro quo* in these terms it was not Madras for Louisbourg, but rather Flanders for Louisbourg ("Louisburg and the Peace of Aix-la-Chapelle," *WMQ,* XIV [October, 1957], 516–535).

98. Quoted in Anne Bezanson, R. D. Gray, and M. Hussey, *Prices in Colonial Pennsylvania* (Philadelphia, 1935), pp. 275–276.

99. *The Spanish Official Account,* pp. 94–96.

CHAPTER 7

Problems of a Military Era

Wᴀʀ, ᴡʜɪᴄʜ ɪs much more than the sum total of battles on land and sea, may well be described as a ravaging disease in the body of human society, a disease whose destructive course is revealed by many grievous symptoms: Communications are interrupted, the complex flow of goods and services in the economy is deranged, delicate interrelationships among all parts of the structure are disturbed. Sometimes too a society at war experiences a marked intensification of inner turmoil, strain, and debilitation. Inevitably, under such abnormal conditions so disturbing and unpredictable, some men who are either shrewd or lucky or both gain and prosper. But many others, perhaps not so shrewd and not so lucky, suffer heavy loss and ruin. To greater or lesser degree, nearly all civilians in a wartime society suffer a measure of disruption of personal relationships, loss of property and wealth, and psychological damage. The more complex the society, the more diverse and intricate will these problems be; but this does not mean that a simply organized society is immune. American colonial society was much less complex than the societies of modern industrial nations, yet in many ways it was extremely vulnerable to the effects of war, being saved from major disruption only by its remoteness from the principal locale of European warfare and its relative insignificance in the eyes of European governments. For most of the colonial period, America was on the periphery of the great international struggles, although it was understandably hard for the colonists themselves to view their situation in that perspective.

Chapters 1 through 6 have examined the development of military and naval warfare in the American colonies during the seventeenth and early eighteenth centuries. Chapter 7 will reexamine this period in terms of the effects of war upon the colonial population. Attention will focus upon a number of problems facing the wartime colonies, including the disruption of the economy; internal tensions, especially within the structure of colony governments; tensions between and among the British colonies; the tragic problems of wartime captivity, principally as it concerns those persons held prisoner by hostile Indians and their French allies; the perplexing problem of religious pacifism; and finally the question of aid and compensation for combat veterans. Although their major dimensions are well known, most of these aspects of war need further close investigation. Indeed, the student of military history will find here one of his greatest challenges and opportunities in exploring, mapping, and assaying the many important ways in which human society has been and is affected by the phenomenon of war.[1]

Most individuals in early America subsisted within a complex of relationships which at all times was subject to a multitude of disturbing factors, but especially so in wartime. Thus, it was in the colonial economy that the impact of war was felt early and heavily. For one thing, in the continental colonies there were few permanent garrisons of professional soldiers to bear the brunt of combat. This meant that every outbreak required the raising of forces from among the civilian population, with the colonial militia serving as the reservoir of trained manpower. The uprooting of civilians from their normal occupations to serve even briefly as soldiers or sailors created serious problems not only for their families, but also for their communities. Labor was usually in short supply, so that whenever men were called away from their jobs, agriculture and industry were soon affected. Crops cannot wait upon the convenience of men, and farming families often found themselves faced with the herculean task of trying to reap a full harvest without the assistance of sons, servants, and hired men—or sometimes even the head of the household himself. The fisheries too often were neglected while skilled hands served on privateers and other vessels of war or perhaps even lugged a musket into the back country. Merchants and other businessmen found it necessary to rearrange or curtail their usual activities, as clerks, craftsmen, and laborers went off to follow the drum. Said one colonist, commenting ruefully on the wide-reaching and long-ranging effects of a major campaign in 1745, "We almost made ourselves bankrupts, not only with respect to money, but also with regard to labor, the worst bankruptcy that a community can suffer; for we expended some thousands of lives . . . who were some of the flower of the people." [2] Often the wartime shortage of labor was intensified by a simultaneous decrease in the flow of free and indentured immigrants from Europe, and slave immigrants from Africa or the West Indies.

Civil and military authorities sometimes intensified the distress of the populace by impressing not only men and boys, but also provisions, horses, wagons, and other goods needed by the armed forces. The usual practice was to give the unhappy owner a receipt for whatever was taken so that later he might obtain reimbursement from the government, there being little likelihood of the exact property itself ever being returned. Sometimes the authorities were faithful to their bills of promise, but all too often the compensation was neither certain nor, when at last tendered, satisfactory. In the meantime, the inconvenience and hardship caused might be very serious for the deprived individual. During the summer of 1692, when Massachusetts was preparing an expedition against the French, the government created a special four-man committee that was charged with the responsibility of procuring needed supplies. Because some items were not obtainable in the open market, an auxiliary committee was appointed and given authority by warrant to enter any storehouse and impress the needed goods wherever they might be found, giving appropriate receipts for the supplies taken.[3] Customarily, however, most supplies were purchased outright; impressment was usually a last resort. The Massachusetts council ordered on 21 July 1692 that

> the Committee for war do forthwith cause to be Laden on Board the severall Vessells taken up for embarqueing of the Souldiers . . . a sufficient quantity of Provisions for the subsistance of Eight hundred Men, during the space of two Months, with supplies of Clothing and other necessary Stores, taking Bills of Lading or Receipts for what they shall soe Ship. And to draw Notes upon the Treasurer to make pay-

ment for what Provisions, Clothing and other necessarys which they shall purchase of any person or persons for the said service. The said Committee keeping a distinct and particular Accompt of the same. And all Constables are ordered to be aiding and assisting of the said Committee as occasion shall require, for the Impressing of Carts, Labourers, Boats etc. necessary for the speedy dispatch of the said Vessells.[4]

Here, obviously, was ample scope for private profit as well as private loss; but whatever the balance, the community as a whole must have felt the strain. Methods of acquisition did not change appreciably during the next half-century as is clearly revealed in Thomas Hutchinson's account of the 1745 expedition against Louisbourg:

The committee of war were . . . convinced that a sufficiency of provisions, cloathing and warlike stores could not be procured within the province. Whosoever was possessed of any of these articles, by an act or order of government his property was subjected to the committee, who set such price as they judged equitable, and upon refusal to deliver, entered warehouses, cellars, etc. by a warrant for that purpose to the sheriff, and took possession.[5]

Such methods were common throughout the colonies.

Troops in camp or on the move sometimes were unconscionably careless with private property, to the great anger and anguish of the local inhabitants. More often than not, appropriate compensation proved difficult to obtain from tight-fisted colony treasurers. This kind of loss is indignantly enumerated in the petition of one Samuel Bill, who owned land on Spectacle Island in Boston Harbor. The petitioner claimed that two companies of soldiers and sixty seamen who had been stationed on his property for several months burned up as many sleepers of timber as would make a barn floor 60 feet long, cut down several trees, spoiled the grass so that it was ungrazable, milked the cows, killed sixteen fat sheep, and erected "severall little houses upon the said Island." [6] The total loss was estimated to be at least £14. Here one has no difficulty discerning the harsh and immediate impact of military activity upon a single man. Multiply this a thousandfold, in an almost infinite variety of forms, and the extent of disruption among the colonial population is perhaps more clearly seen.

In the world of trade and commerce the larger effects are imme-

diately obvious. Some forms of business activity, of course, actually
were invigorated by wartime conditions, which meant gain for those
men favorably situated in the colonial economy. The interruption
of shipping and other transport created abnormal shortages of
goods, with consequent profiteering by the farsighted or fortunate
few. Likewise, the presence of large military forces invariably placed
a strain upon local sources of supply, causing prices to rise and
enabling some merchants to turn the situation to their own advantage. Sometimes, however, it was a local contractor for army supplies
who suffered the heaviest loss, for if his contract specified prices that
prevailed before the shortage occurred, he sometimes found himself
buying dear and selling cheap, an activity in which no businessman
likes to engage. In some instances, war even breathed new life into
faltering enterprises or gave birth to new ones, usually because
the normal sources were now restricted or blocked. A notable
example is the production of naval stores in several of the colonies,
including New York and the Carolinas. Beginning in 1705 during
Queen Anne's War, the British government established a bounty
for these forest products which greatly stimulated the local industry
and provided it with basic support for the remainder of the
colonial period.[7]

One historian came to the conclusion some years ago that the
adverse effects of the colonial wars upon the industry and commerce
of the British colonies were minimal. "Such a struggle as Queen
Anne's War or the French and Indian War," he wrote,

> if it were to occur to-day, when industry is organized with reference
> to a world market, and when the commercial interests of nations are
> so integrated and so sensitive as to cause every part of commerce to
> feel the shock of a blow received by any portion or section of the
> world's industry and trade, would have temporarily crippled Ameri-
> can commerce; but the effect of these wars upon the industrial welfare
> of the colonies was in reality relatively slight. Production was carried
> on mainly to supply local markets; and although their commerce,
> which was largely maritime, was subjected to special dangers while the
> great commercial nations of Europe were at war, yet the colonial
> merchants continued to take the risks and to carry on an extensive
> trade, not only at friendly ports, but, either directly or indirectly, with
> the necessitous merchants of hostile countries.[8]

This view is only partially correct. It not only underestimates the complexity and sensitivity of commercial relationships in colonial times, but also fails to take account of diverse industries, particular business organizations, and individual entrepreneurs or employees. The abnormal and rapidly fluctuating conditions of wartime were constantly trapping and injuring, even ruining, numbers of well-meaning but bewildered and hapless people. If some businesses grew prosperous and fat, others faltered and collapsed; fortunes were lost; wage earners and their families went hungry. The shifting patterns of success and failure are far too complicated to be traced out here; indeed, a generation of diligent research aided by computers may be needed to reconstruct the complex picture of war's multitudinous effects upon the colonial economy. Only after this has been done can we draw firm conclusions. But there seems little reason to doubt that vaunted wartime prosperity is only a mask. Beneath lie the more far-reaching and tragic effects caused by the abnormal costs of government, increased taxation, interrupted lines of supply, lost markets, and shortages of goods and labor. A simple example shows clearly both the impact of war upon a single small business and, in turn, its effect on the community. The frontier town of Hadley, Massachusetts, was the site of a gristmill that regularly produced considerable revenue for the support of the local school. During King Philip's War the Indians destroyed this mill, depriving the school of its much-needed revenue. As a result, the school began to decline. Four years later the effects were still being lamented, for although the mill had now been rebuilt, the revenue was no longer available to the school.[9]

Farms and plantations, especially if located on exposed frontiers or near the coast, were extremely vulnerable to enemy raiders, who delighted in slaughtering cattle, ravaging crops, seizing slaves, and destroying houses and barns. The principal purpose of such raids was to weaken the economy and discourage those whose skill, labor, and investments were so vital to its health. At one time during King George's War when the threat of French naval raiders loomed suddenly over a certain British sugar island, a contemporary observer reported that "the private insurance offices were seen crowded with planters endeavouring to insure their plantations for 6 months, but some, that had policies to insure £10,000 could not get above £800 underwrote at £10.10 per Ct. premio. It's said by an insurance broker of our acquaintance . . ." he added, "that the insurers would have wrote much more than they did but for the dismal countenances of the planters, which made them afraid to write. . . ." [10]

Whenever Indians were involved in the colonial wars (and it's difficult to think of a time when they were not), the fur trade was almost certain to be affected. The Indians were the principal obtainers and suppliers of peltry, so that in times when they took to the warpath instead of the hunting trail the available stocks of furs diminished appreciably. Also, forest warfare made forest transport even more difficult and dangerous than usual, with raiding parties infesting the long lines of communication and supply. Often under these conditions the flow of peltry from American warehouses to European markets was reduced to a trickle. In New England the fur trade never fully recovered from the effects of King Philip's War, except in the more remote northern areas. The Yamassee War in South Carolina cut the annual export of deerskins from that colony down almost to zero. In the peak year of 1707 the figure had stood at more than 120,000 skins; in 1716 it was less than 5,000. With the restoration of peace, there began a slow recovery; but even as late as 1722 the volume of exports had not risen beyond the halfway mark toward the previous high.[11]

Men who owned or manned the ships engaged in overseas trade or who had any stake in that essential traffic knew full well the additional hazards and burdens imposed by war. On balance, the disadvantages of war frequently outweighed the advantages, and for the consumer this was almost invariably the case. Privateers and enemy warships preyed upon mercantile commerce, destroying or seizing unlucky vessels with their valuable cargoes and personnel. Under such conditions, seamen's wages, the hire of cargo space, and the price of maritime insurance all mounted to abnormal heights, increasing the cost of trading and, accordingly, the cost of living.[12] Many ships now found it expedient to travel in convoy, shepherded by the many-gunned watchdogs of the Royal Navy, but that meant costly delays while waiting for convoys to assemble and slower passages because of the laggards. Furthermore, the simultaneous arrival of many ships at one destination could mean a glutted market and depressed prices, at the expense of the shippers. Equally damaging could be a glut of exports caused by a shortage of shipping, an embargo imposed to prevent goods or intelligence from falling into enemy hands, or simply the inaccessibility of the usual markets.

Prices fluctuated in accordance with a great variety of shifting conditions. The enlarged hazards of venturing on the high seas in wartime, shortages of ships and seamen, and the loss of familiar markets tended to lower the value of colonial exports and raise the cost of imported goods. Likewise, military activity by regular British forces in colonial areas often provided an artificial stimulus for the economy, causing an appreciable rise in local prices. South Carolina, whose economic prosperity rested heavily upon the export of rice, suffered severely during the War of the 1740s as a result of Spanish and French privateering activity against the rice ships. An investigating committee of the assembly reported late in 1744 that they had "enquired into the Causes of the Decay of the RICE Trade, and find the same chiefly owing to the great Freights, high Insurance, Scarcity of Shipping, and other extraordinary Charges on Trade, occasioned by the present War. . . ." These conditions, said the committee, have "reduced the Price of Rice so low, that it will not pay the Expence of raising and manufacturing it. . . ." [13] A similar effect was felt by Pennsylvania when enemy activity at sea depressed the prices obtainable for flaxseed, grain, and naval stores.[14]

Many American merchants and shipowners found opportunities to surmount these difficulties, and kept up their profits by engaging in a clandestine trade with the enemy, especially in the islands of the West Indies. The Royal Navy, already thoroughly occupied in attempting to deal with enemy forces, was saddled with the extra burden of trying to prevent this illegitimate commerce. Success was never more than partial, and the trade continued. Sometimes one or more of the colony governments attempted to choke off the flow of American foodstuffs and other products to the enemy islands by imposing a temporary embargo on exports. The effect of this was to clog colonial storage bins and warehouses with export products, depriving both the producers and the handlers of their normal income, while increasing the difficulty of paying for necessary imports. Often neighboring colonies were none too cooperative in maintaining a corresponding embargo, and before long the whole effort would break down. In the meantime a sizable portion of the mercantile population found work and profits elsewhere, perhaps involving frequent visits to enemy ports. However, evidence suggests that the economic advantages of the clandestine trade with the enemy, at least in the last and greatest of the colonial wars, were not sufficient in themselves to overcome the depressing effect of the embargoes.[15]

Inevitably the medium of exchange in the various colonies, principally currency of various sorts, was greatly affected. Whenever British forces entered a colonial area to engage in military operations or simply to remain on guard, they poured hard cash or bills of exchange into the local economy. The general effect almost always was inflationary. Between 1711 and 1713, for example, the British dispensed bills of exchange to the amount of at least £44,230 at New York and at least £57,100 at Boston.[16] Such bills passed quite freely as currency, augmenting the local medium. So long as Britain's credit was good they were accepted readily by all hands, although perhaps not always at face value. Colonies invariably welcomed this kind of stimulation for prosperity, forgetting that the subsequent withdrawal of the visitors and sudden cessation of income was likely to throw the local economy into a severe recession.

Extraordinary wartime expenditures not only required heavier taxation but also produced a mounting popular clamor for the colonial governments to issue bills of credit and other forms of paper currency. Once begun, this practice proved difficult to restrain. Currency inflation, especially in wartime, became a common problem in colonial America. Cotton Mather, in his biography of Sir William Phips, described the process as it first began in Massachusetts. The futile expedition of 1690 against Quebec left the Bay Colony uncomfortably shouldering a debt of some £40,000. Much of this was money owed to the sailors and soldiers who had served in the expedition and who now were angrily demanding their pay. The government decided to print paper money for the purpose, basing the issue on the anticipated revenue from taxes, and soon the new bills were passing through the hands of the veterans into the general economy. Before long, however, a growing uncertainty about the status of the government, which really was an interim authority cast up by the Glorious Revolution, began to undermine public confidence in the currency, with the result that the bills started to depreciate. This meant inflation.[17] Mather was no economist, but he told the story clearly and with obvious concern for the welfare of the colony. He thought the scheme a good one, and perhaps it was; but it demonstrates only too well the dangers inherent in such issues.

The practice of issuing bills of credit in wartime made a significant new beginning during the troubled years of Queen Anne's War, when several of the colonies found themselves financially hard pressed. Usually these certificates were issued against anticipated taxes, with the expectation of an early redemption. In other words, they were intended only as a temporary emergency measure. South Carolina, for example, found itself saddled with a debt of some £26,000 as a result of Governor Moore's adventure at St. Augustine in 1702. To help liquidate this debt the assembly in 1703 authorized the emission of £6,000 in bills of credit, as legal tender, bearing an annual interest of 12 percent until retirement. The original enactment provided for retirement in two years on the basis of taxes levied on real and personal estates, but the term soon was extended to three years. These provisions, including the one relating to interest, were not faithfully carried out because of the continued financial burden of the war. Instead, still more bills were issued from time to time, until by November 1711 there had been some seven issues totaling £29,000, of which £20,000 was still in circulation. Up to now there had been little or no depreciation. Then in 1712 South Carolina, still pressed for more funds, passed a bank act providing for the emission of £52,000 additional paper, part of which was to be loaned to individuals, with land as security. This, in effect, launched America's first experiment in land banking. The new act made it clear that total redemption was being postponed indefinitely, and before long the bills began to depreciate. Within four years their market value was down to about one-half their face value.[18] North Carolina followed a somewhat similar course with comparable results. In 1712 the assembly began with an emission of £4,000 to be redeemed by the proceeds from a poll tax. The following year this amount was joined by twice as much. Depreciation set in as public confidence weakened, and quickly cut the value of the bills by 40 percent or more. Continued expenses and debts led to a further issue of £24,000 in 1714–15, again in anticipation of a poll tax.[19] Seemingly, an almost painless way to finance colonial warfare, including expeditions against recalcitrant Indians, had been developed. But those colonists who found themselves paying the additional taxes and fingering the depreciated bits of paper must have come to some realization of the cost. What the actual price was in terms of economic instability is very difficult to measure.

During the War of the 1740s various colonies resorted to the printing press as a means of meeting their financial obligations. Compared with some, Massachusetts was extravagant. In that colony issue followed issue, with the total passing the £1,000,000 mark, and the inevitable depreciation began.[20] The joy of capturing Louisbourg quickly dissolved in the gray aftermath of mortality, taxes, and debts. Not only in Massachusetts but everywhere in the colonies, wartime finance as well as the immediate impact of inflation or deflation, prosperity or bankruptcy, high wages or unemployment, helped drive home to the people of colonial America the unsettling, disruptive, sometimes agonizing consequences of international conflict.

In time of war, the military element in government tends to grow in importance and power at the expense of civil authority. This inevitable shift frequently produced tension in a society habituated by long tradition to distrust and fear military rule. A pervading belief in the British colonies, as in England, was that the military power should always be kept subordinate to civil authority, undoubtedly one of Britain's most important legacies to future generations. The tension over this issue runs through much of early American history like an unbroken thread, prominent in the evolving pattern of colonial government. Frequently it took the form of a struggle between the London-appointed governor and the locally elected lower house of the legislature for control of military appropriations and even the administration of military policy. Whenever possible the elected representatives exerted their power (generally that of the purse) to prevent the governor from acting as a military dictator or even a full-fledged commander in chief.

One common cause of civil-military tension, found in every age and place where troops are quartered in close proximity to a civilian community, was friction between the soldiers and the local populace. This resulted from many possible causes—rudeness and insults on either side, profiteering by local merchants, pilfering by military personnel, jealousy over women, to name only a few. Men and boys who at home in their own communities might have been quite docile and unassuming sometimes behaved very differently as soldiers among strangers in a new environment, boasting, larking, showing off before their comrades, getting drunk to forget their loneliness and fear. Such behavior easily gives rise to resentment and trouble. Nor was it uncommon for civilians to take unfair advantage of the soldiers in their midst. One rather curious case, with special overtones of Anglo-Dutch antagonism, occurred at the Hudson River town of Esopus not long after the English had seized control of New Netherland. Acts of violence between members of the English garrison at Esopus and the Dutch townspeople escalated so swiftly and steeply as to produce what contemporary witnesses described as "mutineys," with fatal results for one or more of the civilians. From the recorded testimony it is difficult now to apportion the blame, but there must have been provocation on both sides. On one occasion, we are told, a soldier entered a Dutchman's barn "and findinge there *Dirck Hendrix* . . . tooke his sword and thrusted the same threww the said *Dirck Hendrixes* Breeches." [21] One gathers that perhaps the ample fullness of the Dutch garment was here an advantage, sparing the flesh if not the dignity of the wearer.

Even in situations where garrison and town were of the same national background, unpleasant relations easily developed. Wise commanders tried to anticipate such difficulty and sought to avoid it by keeping their men in close check, but even the best of intentions were not always sufficient. In general, the age-old rule prevailed: When actual danger was near, the civilians welcomed the troops and treated them like honored guests; when danger receded, the civilians resented the burdensome presence of the military. Then it was that friction was most likely to occur.

Military units temporarily stationed in a community lacking barracks customarily were quartered in taverns, churches, barns, or vacant houses. English experience in the seventeenth century had contributed heavily to a widespread popular aversion against the practice of quartering soldiers in occupied dwellings, where they not only caused overcrowding but sometimes made themselves a nuisance in other ways as well. The Petition of Right, forced upon a reluctant Charles I in 1628, forbade the billeting of troops in civilian dwellings, a prohibition that henceforth was considered a major safeguard for the rights of the subject.[22] In the American colonies, however, where houses sometimes served also as forts in areas exposed to enemy attack, it was not uncommon to find soldiers under the same roof with civilians. The problem of quartering

regular troops first became serious in the 1750s, at the time when
the Earl of Loudoun was serving as commander in chief in the
culminating war against the French. Loudoun found this an
exasperating issue, in which the American civilian population displayed what seemed astonishing effrontery not only by their stinginess but also in their base ingratitude toward the king and his
soldiers. The first major confrontation occurred at Albany. As
regular barracks were lacking, Loudoun simply asked that his men
be given shelter in privately owned buildings. This seemingly
necessary and reasonable request, however, opened a bitter controversy with the mayor and other citizens, who considered such
an imposition unconstitutional. When Albany stood fast on its
rights, Loudoun lost his patience and announced his intention
of ordering additional regiments of redcoats into the community,
to take quarters by force if necessary. That turned the trick; doors
were opened, albeit grudgingly. "I have an officer and 6 private
men Billeted upon me," one unhappy resident later wrote. "We
are not Master of our own houses, so that itt is Very hard Living
here at present. . . ." [23]

Just a few months later, when the army was looking for winter
quarters, a similar problem arose at Philadelphia. Loudoun had
sent Colonel Henry Bouquet with a battalion of the Royal American
Regiment to Philadelphia for the winter, only to discover that
the Pennsylvanians too were unwilling hosts. The assembly, it seems,
was agreeable to having the soldiers housed in Philadelphia's 117
licensed taverns but not in private dwellings. If some of Bouquet's
men were inclined to look upon this arrangement as eminently
suitable, their commander was not; and of course in terms of the
comfort, health, and morale of his battalion he was correct. Both
Bouquet and the governor, who was at loggerheads with his
assembly, therefore insisted that better quarters be provided, especially for the officers and the sick. As smallpox was known to be
present among the troops, the townspeople remained reluctant;
and the assembly's commissioners, of whom Benjamin Franklin was
one, continued to fight a delaying action while the soldiers shivered
in makeshift quarters. When Loudoun in New York learned of the
controversy, he recognized a familiar battleground and resorted to
the same tactic that had worked so well at Albany, threatening to
send in additional units until the local authorities saw their duty
and did it. The blunt message from Loudoun reached Philadelphia

on Christmas night, whereupon Franklin convinced his fellow commissioners that the time for conciliation had come, and a satisfactory accommodation was reached.[24] Similar difficulties were experienced by the regulars in other colonies, including Massachusetts and South Carolina.[25] The redcoats were not quick to forget the inhospitable attitude of American civilians, who seemed so ungrateful to the very men who had come to save them from their enemies, nor did the colonists in their eventual grudging acquiescence readily forget what seemed to them a grievous imposition. In short, little love was lost between provincials and the British regular army.

In almost every colony, the elected assembly was inclined to utilize military necessity as an opportunity to grasp a larger share of governmental power, especially in the shaping and administration of military policy, at the expense of the governor and often the council. Because the lower house controlled the purse strings of taxation, its support was essential for nearly all measures of defense. By building certain stipulations into appropriation bills, the assembly could gain a significant role in the appointment of commanding officers, the planning of military operations, and the actual employment of forces. If a governor balked at thus sharing his royal prerogative, he soon found himself without the funds necessary to carry on his policy and program. Prolonged deadlocks sometimes occurred, and usually ended with important concessions on the part of the executive branch. Such maneuvering and skirmishing in the field of military policy and administration contributed heavily to the growing strength of the lower houses, a development of great significance for imperial relations.[26]

One bone of contention was the question of whether the militia could be required by the governor to serve beyond the boundaries of its own county or colony. A longstanding English tradition viewed the militia as an organization primarily for local defense, a tradition now revived by the colonists' objections to distant service. From the governor's point of view, such a restriction was a serious handicap in overall defense, especially when remote frontiers or neighboring colonies were in desperate need of immediate help. Sometimes the representatives could be persuaded that the public interest required that the governor have special authority, as when the Massachusetts General Court decreed during King William's War that

Forasmuch as in this time of war there may be occasion for the raising of souldiers, and transporting or marching of them out of the limits of this province into the neighbouring provinces and colonies of New Hampshire, Rhode Island, Connecticut, Narragansett, or New York for the prosecution of the French or Indian enemy and the defence of their majesties' subjects and interests,—

Be it enacted and ordained . . .

That in the vacancy of the general assembly it shall be in the liberty of His Excellency the present Governour, by and with the advice and consent of the Council, to raise and transport such part of the militia of this province as they shall find needful, or oblige them to march into any of the before-named provinces or colonies. . . .[27]

The authorization was limited to a period of six months, clearly reflecting the popular antipathy toward such executive power. When Governor Moore of South Carolina was preparing for his campaign against St. Augustine in 1702 he found the militia quite unwilling to admit that it could be obliged by the governor to serve outside its own locality. Nor was the legislature willing to pass an enabling act, but ruled instead that only under a condition of martial law could a militiaman be required to march beyond the county line. Moore was forced to work within this rule.[28] In 1759 militia troops of North Carolina refused to obey an order to advance against the Cherokees, because this would mean service outside the colony.[29]

Samuel Shute, governor of Massachusetts in 1722, found himself confronted by a suspicious and obstinate house of representatives unwilling to accept his claim that the terms of the governor's commission endowed him with full authority in matters military. On the contrary, the legislators were determined to have a dominant voice in the conduct of military affairs through their own committees. That the lower house enjoyed support even in the governor's council is indicated by Samuel Sewall's jottings of a council meeting on 1 December 1722:

His Excellency Order'd Mr. Secretary to read the former part of the Clause in the Charter expressing his Excel's power in ordering the Militia, etc. and then read a paper drawn up for him, in these words, to wit,

"His Excellency demands the Opinion of the Honorable Council.

"Whether this clause in the Royal Charter, does not invest His

Majesties Capt. General [the governor], with the Sole Power and Direction of all the Forces in this Government?"

Judge Davenport desired Time; Col Cushing apprehended the Council were properly to advise in the administration of the Government not in interpretation of the Charter.

Here the governor complained with some bitterness that he was "made a Foot-boy."

At last Judge Dudley drew up this question: "Whether the Clause in the Royal Charter, relating to the Governour's Commanding the Militia, doth not invest His Majesty's Capt. General of this Province, with the full power and Government of the Militia or Forces in this Government; under the Limitation, and Restriction in the said Charter, and the Laws of this Province?"

This was Voted in the Affirmative. Court was Adjourn'd. . . .[30]

Later, after Shute had taken his leave of the troublesome Bay Colony, the legislature requested his successor to dismiss certain military officers then in service, and boldly threatened to "draw off part of the forces" if he did not comply.[31]

In New Hampshire during both King George's War and the subsequent conflict of 1755–63, the assembly utilized military necessity to gain Governor Benning Wentworth's reluctant consent to bills providing for the emission of paper money.[32] Had the governor not yielded in 1745, there might have been few if any soldiers from New Hampshire at the siege of Louisbourg. At about the same time, Governor George Clinton of New York was having his own problems with a balky legislature that was determined to limit his control of military administration. The assembly drew up its appropriation bills in such a way as to force Clinton to yield if he wanted the use of the money. This wrung from the outraged governor the complaint that even "Provisions for the Army are not subject to the Orders of the General." [33] At the height of the quarrel Clinton actually was using his own personal funds in sustaining the war effort because adequate grants were being withheld by the legislature. Part of the trouble, it seems, was New York's reluctance to commit its own resources to the defense of neighboring colonies. The legislature, said one observer, "seems resolved to leave all affairs as they found them showing no less indifference about provideing for their own defence than in assisting their Neibours; Nay they wont so much as Consult with, or act in Concert with The other Provinces. . . ." [34] Later the harassed governor complained that the assembly had

> not only in effect assumed to themselves the executive power in Civil Affairs but likewise in the Military so far that they by Act direct the Officers of the Militia, as to places of Rendezvous and times on which they are to call their Regiments and Companies together, and thereby with private Discourse among the people persuade them the King has no other power over the Militia, but what is granted by Act of Assembly.[35]

In Maryland, where there was a long record of tension and strife between the lower house and the proprietary interest as represented by the governor and council, the stress of war played directly into the hands of the popular party. For many years the colony had levied a tax of threepence per hogshead of tobacco exported, for the purpose of acquiring and maintaining the government's stock of arms and ammunition. Not long before the outbreak of war with Spain in 1739, the tax was about to expire, and for obvious reasons the proprietary government was anxious to have it timely renewed by the assembly. The lower house, intent upon increasing its own power at the expense of the governor and his party, alleged that some of the funds previously collected for defense were not adequately accounted for; therefore it declined to act. At this, Governor Samuel Ogle prorogued the assembly.[36] Beneath the surface of this unfortunate impasse smouldered widespread popular resentment of proprietary power and policy, as exercised by the governor and his council of privileged men. The representatives of the people spoke darkly of grievances that cried to be remedied. After the Maryland assembly reconvened in 1740, with war now confronting the colony, the representatives sent to the council for its approval some bills giving the lower house greater control in the disbursement of government funds. The council delayed action on these measures, further irritating the representatives, who now made it clear that they in turn would not approve the disputed bill for renewing the defense duty until the council yielded on the other bills. This bitter quarrel in wartime carried over into the following session, with each side accusing the other of trying to gain legislation by extortion. The governor was in a veritable sweat to resolve the impasse, but his rather sharp lectures to the lower house did little to soothe the ruffled tempers. In fact, the representatives saw clearly that now they had a foot in the stirrup, and were not easily to be put off.[37]

The Maryland case and others like it demonstrate how a determined lower house, resentful of prerogative power, could make use of a crisis to undermine that power and grasp a larger share of authority for itself. Again and again, legislatures in the various colonies found ways to diminish the governors' control of military policy and practice. Granting appropriations, they established committees of their own to oversee the spending; sometimes they even were able to nominate commanders and help shape military planning. What Professor Jack P. Greene has said of the lower houses in the southern colonies is undoubtedly true of the northern ones as well: they "wielded greater authority over military affairs in their respective colonies than did the House of Commons in England."[38] The techniques evolved to achieve this result represent a clear foreshadowing of the later Revolutionary crisis.

In addition to internal tension, wartime conditions also bred tension between and among the various British colonies at a time when they should have been cooperating closely for mutual security. Indeed, until fairly recent times faint lingering echoes of these old colonial antagonisms still could be heard in a few of our present states, especially when local antiquarians crossed paths. In the decades of the colonial wars, longstanding jealousy, antagonism, and rivalry repeatedly broke into the open under the strain of crisis; selfish interests prompted individual colonies to hold back men, supplies, and money needed in the overall war effort. No colony wanted to contribute more than its share, especially when the actual danger was not close to home territory. "Let others defend themselves," became an unspoken but often-thought slogan. The Swedish traveler Peter Kalm, viewing the colonial scene from New York at the midpoint of the eighteenth century, sized up the situation clearly. "In time of war things go on very slowly and irregularly here," he said,

> for not only the opinion of one province is sometimes directly opposite to that of another, but frequently the views of the governor and those of the assembly of the same province are quite different; so that it is easy to see that, while the people are quarrelling about the best and cheapest manner of carrying on the war, an enemy has it in his power to take one place after another. It has usually happened that while

some provinces have been suffering from their enemies, the neighboring ones have been quiet and inactive, as if it did not in the least concern them. They have frequently taken up two or three years in considering whether or not they should give assistance to an oppressed sister colony, and sometimes they have expressly declared themselves against it. There are instances of provinces which were not only neutral in such circumstances, but which even carry on a great trade with the power which at that very time is attacking and laying waste some other provinces.[39]

The first war revealing serious intercolonial tensions was New England's struggle with the hostile Algonquins in 1675–76. King Philip's War was carried on by the three orthodox Puritan colonies of Massachusetts Bay, Connecticut, and Plymouth without the active support and participation of heretical Rhode Island, a fact that in itself bred tension, especially as some of the important campaigning was done by Puritan forces on territory then in dispute between Rhode Island and Connecticut. But that is not the sum of the problem; serious tensions also developed among the Puritan confederates. Efforts at joint operations under a supreme commander provided almost endless opportunities for quarrels over the behavior and employment of the various contingents. At one point an intercolonial force under the command of a Massachusetts officer was cast into a "broken posture" and rendered "uncapable of any great action" when a portion of the Connecticut contingent, contrary to the commander's will, was withdrawn from the area.[40] At the same time, Connecticut was charging that Massachusetts had not provided her fair share of soldiers to the army. Further disputes over contributions of men erupted during a subsequent campaign, resulting in the complete withdrawal of Connecticut's troops and recriminations from Massachusetts directed not only at Connecticut but also at the sister colony of Plymouth, which had made no contribution of manpower to the expedition.[41] Compounding the difficulty was, first, the fact that during most of King Philip's War, Connecticut was in controversy with New York over their mutual boundary and, second, the bitter charges that Albany merchants were supplying the enemy with munitions. Fortunately for the English, their differences never completely overcame their awareness of a common cause, so that cooperation in the war effort outweighed their divisions and they were able to go on to victory.

During the subsequent wars against the French and Indians

starting in 1689, Connecticut troops occasionally were sent north-ward into the back country of Massachusetts to help form a barrier against enemy raiders coming down from Lake Champlain. Garri-soned in Massachusetts frontier towns, these soldiers sometimes irritated the local inhabitants and the Massachusetts troops or felt themselves wronged by their hosts. As late as the 1740s, the inter-colonial antagonism that had erupted so forcefully during King Philip's War still was causing recrimination. Colonel Israel Williams of Massachusetts, writing from Hatfield on 5 August 1748 to the authorities in Connecticut, informed them that "We have a Sharp and Cruel war here, and expect nothing but fighting and Shedding of Blood for the Present," and then went on to complain that Connecticut officers had refused to commit their men to any service other than the defense of two particular towns, saying that they were not subject to orders from the government of Massachusetts.[42] A fortnight later Williams had more of which to complain—the Connecticut troops had suddenly been withdrawn altogether. And so it went. The same kind of problem cropped up once again with the outbreak of the last great colonial war in 1755.[43]

Sometimes personalities were a key factor in such intercolonial quarrels. During King William's War, for example, ill feeling be-tween Governor William Phips of Massachusetts and Governor Benjamin Fletcher of New York helps to explain why the Bay Colony was not more forward in coming to the aid of its neighbor in the Hudson Valley.[44] Every colony tended to apply a magnifying glass to its own dangers and its own expenditures of men and other resources, while deprecating the efforts of its neighbors. Quite typical was the assertion of Governor Joseph Dudley of Massa-chusetts in 1710 that recent military measures and campaigning "have cost this province Sixty thousand pounds which added to their debts for the defence of the Fronteirs will leavee them greatly in arrear whilst Virginia, Maryland, pensilvania, Jersyes and Newyork are covered by these Northern provinces, and sit quiet from losses, or charges. . . ." At this situation, Dudley concluded, "the people here take the Umbrage of dissatisfaction. . . ."[45] A short while later, the Massachusetts agent in London poured much the same complaint into the ears of Lord Dartmouth, criticizing New York for "main-taining a Criminal Neutrality with the French Indians."[46] It was a common technique to boast to the English government about one's own sacrifices while condemning the indifference of other colonies, in the hope of inducing Whitehall to ease future demands upon the diligent and require greater contributions from the dilatory.

Actually, without the aid of a series of careful economic studies on this problem, no one can be certain of the relative weight of the burden carried by each colony. Researchers will have to comb the records for reliable data, collate this mass of information, compare the gains with the losses, and then determine as nearly as possible what portion of a colony's wealth was actually sacrificed in the cause of victory. Such studies, when completed, probably will confirm an impression long held by historians that a colony's zeal in war was very closely related to two factors: the immediacy of danger to itself, and the degree to which it was forced to rely upon its own efforts without assistance from England or other colonies. In general, the flank colonies—New England and New York in the North, South Carolina and Georgia in the South—were the ones most deeply concerned about defense and most inclined to believe that the safer colonies in the middle were profiting by their sacrifices. More often than not, however, legislators everywhere were slow to overcome their natural reluctance to increase taxes even for military appropriations. As one exasperated colonial governor complained, "Fond hopes that Dangers, yet a Distance, may vanish of themselves, are excuses sufficient with many to save Expence." [47] This widespread attitude meant that a sense of common obligation in the face of any but the most immediate danger was difficult to develop.

Only a few imperial-minded Americans really grasped the concept of unity. One such was Colonel Caleb Heathcote of New York who in 1715, when French advances and Indian hostility again appeared threatening, spoke of the colonies as "one family," and argued that "all our interests are the same, and what number soever is wounded or hurt, the whole ought to reckon themselves agrieved, and not carelessly suffer the French to angle us away, province by province, till at last all will be gon." [48] He went on to warn that "if the old rules are still put in practice, and those who are not imeadiately concerned will, like sheep, only stand gazing on, while the wolff is murthering and distroying other parts of the flock, it will come to every ones turn at last." Some years later a New Englander, speaking to the chiefs of the Iroquois Confederacy, laid stress on the positive side of the same argument. "In former times," he said, "the weight of the war has fallen more heavily upon one part and sometimes on another and our unhapiness has been that we have acted too Independantly on Each Other we are all in one Intrest and should we Closely unite and Vigorously Pursue proper methods we might soon Render Our selves formidable to our Common Enemy." [49] He then drove home the point with the prophetic pronouncement: "Our Union is Our strength." Unfortunately, it required the whole of the colonial period and four major wars for the provincial governments to learn that lesson.

Another serious problem in colonial America was the fate of wartime captives. Some of the most fascinating documents to emerge from the colonial period are the memoirs written by prisoners or former prisoners, personal narratives teeming with details of hardship and danger, perseverance and courage. In the warfare at sea, many sailors fell into enemy hands and were packed into vile dungeons for the duration or until exchanged. Along the frontiers, where raiding expeditions were a common feature of international conflict, considerable numbers of civilians, including women and children, were seized as prisoners, especially by the marauding Indians allied with the French.

A typical case begins when a British frontier family is rudely awakened just before a wintry dawn by the blood-chilling sounds of enemy raiders bursting in upon their village. Wild yells, the pounding of gunbutts and hatchets upon splintering doors and shutters, gunshots, muffled screams, are soon joined by the mounting crackle and roar of flames as violated dwellings and outbuildings begin to blaze. There is no time for either defense or flight, and soon the surviving villagers are cowering in the rough grasp of painted Indians highly elated by success and triumphing over their victims. Parents must try to stifle their own terror and quiet the wailing of their smallest children lest the savages turn and kill them on the spot. The gathering together of all the captives in one place, perhaps a barn on the edge of the village, is a time of extreme tension. When the raiders are satisfied that their work is complete, they herd their captives out into the open, assign them a portion of the plunder to carry or drag, and the long, agonizing march toward Canada begins. For the first few days of the retreat into the northern wilderness, the entire party of captors and their prisoners remains together, until the danger of being overtaken by a pursuing force has ended. The dazed captives, in many cases inadequately clothed, must plod along through the snow, mile after weary mile, farther and farther from help and rescue. At this stage the great question is survival. Prisoners who falter and prove unable to keep up with the fast-moving Indian band may expect to be killed out of hand, for if any of them are left alive beside the trail they might provide useful intelligence to any pursuing force. Perhaps the Indians also consider such killing an act of mercy, substituting a quick death for a slow and lonely one.[50]

In this cruel, brutality-breeding kind of frontier warfare, captives —whether Indians in the hands of whites or whites in the hands of Indians—enjoyed no protection under any mutually recognized code. Customarily, Indian captors considered a prisoner they themselves had taken as their own personal property, to be disposed of as they chose. Sometimes the prisoner was killed; sometimes he was sold to another Indian or a Frenchman; sometimes he was retained as a slave. Thus, a captured family might be separated, some being dragged off in one direction by one Indian, and others elsewhere by another. It was a heartbreaking experience for husbands, wives, and children, an experience in which ordinarily free whites actually shared some of the anguish long known to black slaves. On some occasions, Frenchmen leading or accompanying a party of Indian raiders were able to intercede for English captives whose lives were endangered, but generally the Indians insisted on having their own way concerning the fate of their victims.

The records reveal some cases in which Indian captors showed a rough sort of compassion and kindness toward weakened prisoners, allowing them to ride on horseback or carrying small children for many miles. But at best it was a hard experience. When the retreating Indians were short of food, their captives suffered excessively, being less well adapted than their captors to the rigors of a forest diet. Sometimes they had to keep going for days on end along snow-clogged trails and across frozen, windswept lakes on a diet consisting of little more than a pittance of parched corn, acorns, and water. One woman captive subsisted for a time on strips cut from old beaverskin coats, roasted on an open fire until the hair was singed off. At another time she managed to gulp down the "Guts and Garbage" of a beaver, unwashed.[51] Mrs. John Smeed was far along in her pregnancy when taken prisoner by French and Indians at Fort Massachusetts in 1746. Nevertheless, she somehow managed to keep up with the party; and when her time had come, her understanding captors lingered long enough for her to give birth to a baby girl, whom she named "Captivity." Then, we are told by another one of the prisoners, the French "made a frame like a bier, and laid a buck skin and bear skin upon it, and laid Mrs. Smeed, with her infant, thereon; and so two men at a time carried them." [52]

When a returning war party and their weary captives approached an Indian village they customarily announced their arrival by the *"dead Shout,"* a signal of triumph indicating the numbers of scalps they were bringing with them. Scarcely had the echoes of these yells ceased reverberating in the hills before the excited villagers would come pouring out to see the scalps and the prisoners. It was at this very time that the apprehensive captives might experience their first serious abuse at the hands of vengeful squaws and children, perhaps being forced to run the gauntlet while villagers wielding sticks rained blows upon them. One prisoner later told how he was pelted with dirt and stones by a large crowd of Indian boys, although the squaws treated him more kindly.[53] Another described a peculiar form of abuse suffered at the hands of Micmac squaws:

Taking us prisoners by the armes, one Squaw on Each Side of a prisoner, they Led us up to their Village and placed themselves In a Large Circle Round us, after they had Gat all prepared for their Dance, they made us Set Down In a Small Circle, about 18 Inches assunder and began their frolick, Dancing Round us and Striking of us in the face with English Scalps, that Caused the Blood to Issue from our mouths and Noses, In a Verey Great and plentifull manner, and Tangled their hands in our hair, and knocked our heads Togather with all their Strength and Vehemence, and when they was Tired of this Exercise, they would take us by [the] hair and Some by the Ears, and Standing behind us, ablige us to keep our Necks Strong So as to bear their weight, then Raise themselves, their feet off the Ground and their weight hanging by our hair and Ears, In this manner, they thumped us In the Back and Sides, with their knees and feet, and Twitched our hair and Ears to Such a Degree, that I am Incapable to Express it. . . .[54]

After the first welcome, if it can be so described, the prisoner's fate rested with the warrior to whom he belonged, or else with the village leaders. He might be turned over to the widow of a slain warrior, who then had the choice of adopting him to replace the deceased or keeping him as a slave or presiding over his death by torture. Ritual torture and cannibalism were practiced by some of the tribes, and all prisoners stood in danger of violent death

at almost any time.[55] The captive who survived as a slave with an
Indian master was likely to learn the full measure of hardship
and humiliation. A hewer of wood and a drawer of water, he was
at his master's beck and call, and in some cases fortunate if allowed
to shelter in the wigwam and dip into the common pot at mealtime.
Captives who held to their scruples about laboring on the Sabbath
sometimes had to endure severe beatings.[56]

Why is the record of Indian behavior toward white captives, or
for that matter the behavior of whites toward Indian prisoners, so
replete with harshness and even fiendish cruelty? What was there
about this interracial frontier warfare that so readily dissolved the
elements of humanity which otherwise might have served to promote
compassion? Is there any explanation except that human nature
at its worst is very bad indeed? Perhaps a partial answer can come
from the psychologists and the anthropologists. One immediately
suspects a racial-cultural backlash such as that displayed by the
Japanese in their treatment of British and American prisoners
after the fall of Singapore and Bataan in 1942. How satisfying it
can be for one whose people and culture have been scorned as
inferior or even subhuman to gain absolute mastery over one of
the scorners and make him drink the dregs of humiliation. Conversely, a self-styled master race can reinforce its own vaunted self-
image by treating like an animal any member of the despised
inferior group, especially when that group has dared challenge the
superiority of the master race. For either side, the slogan might
well have been, "Make them know their place by putting them
in it!"

Fortunately, there is another side to the story. Some Indians as
well as some whites did display compassion toward helpless prisoners. It is gratifying to learn from a number of colonial writers that
white female captives seldom were molested sexually by Indian
males. The exceptional cases usually were a consequence of Indian
drunkenness.[57] It is also true that some British captives, principally
children and young people, found life among the Indians so
satisfying that they lost all desire to return to their former way of
life. This strongly suggests the effect of Indian hospitality and
kindness, at least to those whites who were adopted into the tribe.
Child prisoners, it was said, readily forgot the niceties of English
manners, displaying a tendency to "turn savages in a little time,"
and often became "more brutish, boisterous in their Behaviour and

loose in their Manners than the Indians." [58] Young Samuel Allen of Deerfield, after spending less than two years among the Canadian Indians, was so attached to his new companions and their way of life that when at last his uncle came to redeem him, the boy was quite unwilling to go and had to be taken home by force.[59]

The experience of the Reverend John Williams and his family, taken captive at Deerfield early in 1704, is revealing in many ways. When the town was assaulted by a party of French and Indians, the minister's six-year-old son and his newborn infant were slain, along with a Negro servant of the family. The surviving members, including Mr. Williams, his wife, and five of their children, were among the shocked group of 111 prisoners who began the long forced march through the winter snow toward Canada.[60] During the next few weeks of misery, about eighteen of the prisoners, generally the weak and faltering, were deliberately killed by their Indian captors. Among these was the mother of the five Williams children. Eventually the surviving captives were divided, as various groups of the Indians broke off to return to their own villages; in this way the members of the Williams family were separated. The Indians sold some of their Deerfield prisoners to French people living in or near Montreal, but others they retained. Among the latter was the minister's daughter Eunice, a seven-year-old girl when her adventure began. Somehow Eunice adapted well to her new situation in the wilderness. As the months and years went by, others of the captives were redeemed and made their way back to New England, but Eunice remained and grew to womanhood. She, the daughter of a Puritan preacher, had become a Roman Catholic and had made the Indian way of life her own. Eventually she married an Indian, and together they raised three children. On several occasions Eunice journeyed down into New England to visit her Protestant relatives and perhaps view the site of her childhood home, but she showed no desire to resume a way of life that obviously had become for her unattractively foreign. She was by choice a Canadian squaw.

One major reason why the Indians took and held white prisoners during the colonial wars was the prospect of extracting ransom for their release. Knowing the sometimes terrible hardships and dangers of such captivity, relatives and friends of the prisoners often made great financial sacrifices for this purpose. Humane Canadians sometimes bought English captives from the Indians, taking them into their own homes as servants and laborers, but of course requiring subsequent compensation from British sources before releasing them to their own people. In general, English prisoners in French households were treated reasonably well. Even the arch-Puritan Cotton Mather had to concede that New Englanders among the French "met with many Instances of *Humanity*, more or less, according to the Humour of those, in whose *Families* they became *Servants* or *Sojourners*." [61]

Almost inevitably one of the unpleasant by-products of such sojourning was a clash of religions. Prisoners who had been reared from infancy in an atmosphere of urgent Calvinism brought to Canada a strong, sometimes even violent prejudice against all the words and works of Rome. This attitude is revealed with stark clarity in the words of one captive when he speaks of a priest who offered him a kindness:

> The Jesuit gave me a Bisket, which I put into my Pocket, and dare not eat; but buried it under a Log, fearing that he had put something in it to make me Love him: for I was very Young, and had heard much of the Papists torturing the Protestants etc. so that I hated the sight of a Jesuit. When my Mother heard the talk of my being Sold to a Jesuit, she said to me, Oh! my dear Child! if it were GOD's Will, I had rather follow you to your Grave! or never see you more in this World, than you should be Sold to a Jesuit: for a Jesuit will ruin you Body and Soul! [62]

In turn, the priests and nuns of Canada viewed all English Protestants as lost heretics and saw an opportunity among the prisoners to regain at least a few souls for God. Some took unfair advantage of weakened and frightened people, especially children, cast into a strange environment without the support and counsel of their former mentors. It was a common practice among the French to place English children acquired from the Indians in the care of the religious orders, whose priests and nuns were eager to win converts. Contemporary English accounts charge that heavy pressure, including corporal punishment, was sometimes exerted against young and impressionable prisoners for the purpose of inducing conversion. It is now virtually impossible to prove or disprove these charges, but evidence strongly indicates the probability of some intimidation on the part of overzealous Catholics. New England churchmen were deeply disturbed by this threat to the integrity of their people. In 1707 Cotton Mather published a tract designed to bolster the will of Protestants who might be so unfortunate as to come under the influence of the French, concluding with a catechism in refutation of Roman Catholic doctrine and practice.[63]

During King George's War, many British prisoners of both sexes were confined in a special prison at Quebec, a long, narrow, stone building two stories high with heavily barred windows. Extending out from the front of the prison was a high palisade enclosing a yard some 30 feet wide and as long as the building itself, where the prisoners were allowed to exercise in the fresh air from nine until noon and from three until five. The interior was divided into eight large compartments occupied by a variety of persons, some of them greatly weakened by previous hardships among the Indians. One group of newly arrived men counted 127 other prisoners, mostly New Englanders, already there. The jailers provided the newcomers with "a Bed Stuff'd with Straw, a Blanket of Bethlem Broad Cloath; then left us with bread and water to our Private Meditations." Later, "the French gave to those who wanted an Indian drest Deer Skin an ozinbridge Shirt and a Jacket but no Stockings nor Shoes." To small mercies were added others— "they gave us Several Packs of Cards to pass away the time with: which hung heavy upon our hands."[64] On 30 September 1746 a count of the prisoners was taken, "and our Number amounted to 259 all in one house, and the Greatest part of us, in a miserable Lowsey Condition."[65] Disease played a large part in the daily struggle for survival, and death was a frequent visitor. For a time the sick and the well were all confined in the one building, but later the French provided separate facilities where the more seriously ill could be segregated. Even though death came frequently, his sway did not go unchallenged. At four o'clock on a chilly afternoon in November the gloom was briefly lightened by a simple wedding ceremony. The clergyman was the Reverend John Norton, captured at Fort Massachusetts; the groom was a prisoner who had been taken at sea; the bride was a New England woman whose husband and four children had been killed by the Indians. Whatever brave hopes this couple may have had for a more happy future together were dashed a few months later when the bride succumbed.[66]

It is not suggested that the government of New France or of any other colony—English, Spanish, or French—was deliberately and extraordinarily harsh in its treatment of enemy prisoners. Accord-

ing to the practices of the time, the authorities generally felt that
they were doing all that was necessary when they provided prisoners a place to sleep, enough food to keep body and soul together,
and a small supply of fuel. Sometimes even the last item was
neglected, as in the case of some French prisoners confined at
Boston in 1696. It took a petition to the General Court from the
sympathetic jailer to obtain for the shivering captives enough wood
to stave off the chill of late November.[67] At Quebec and Montreal
during the colonial wars, sustenance for the entire population was
sometimes in short supply because of the British blockade, so it is
no wonder if prisoners found themselves living on a rather mean
diet. Nehemiah How, a prisoner at Quebec in 1746 who later published an account of his experiences, thought himself treated quite
well, under the circumstances.[68]

Special missions to negotiate for the release of English prisoners
held by the French or Indians were sometimes sent north from
New England and Albany. For the emissaries this could be a
dangerous undertaking, especially if their route lay through Indian
country. Lengthy, complicated negotiations for the mutual release
of prisoners were carried on between Governor Vaudreuil and
Governor Dudley during 1705–07, with brave men such as
Captain Courtemanche, Samuel Vetch, and Deacon John Sheldon
of Deerfield serving as emissaries. The latter, whose own wife had
been shot to death and several of his children taken captive during
the raid on Deerfield, made three difficult, hazardous journeys to
Canada for this purpose. A considerable number of prisoners, both
French and English, regained their freedom as a result of these
efforts.[69] However, returning prisoners sometimes arrived home destitute, only to find their families dispersed or obliterated, their
dwellings in ruins. Compassionate neighbors and other compatriots
usually were able to help with money and other gifts, and in certain
cases the colony government provided some form of compensation.
Presumably one reason why so many former captives published
memoirs of their adventures, replete with pious thoughts as well as
the lurid details of atrocities, was to acquire needed funds. It was a
form of literature that sold very well in colonial America and
England.

A totally different kind of problem affecting the American
colonies, and one that intensified with the years, was pacifism, or
conscientious objection to the support of war. The great majority of

settlers in colonial America were Christians but not pacifists and quite willing, if necessary, to take up arms in defense of their new lands and homes. By the midseventeenth century there began to appear a few settlers of different persuasion who said they would refuse to participate in the violence of war, even in self-defense. Many of them rejected not only actual military service but all forms of preparation for war including training in the militia and the payment of taxes known to be for military purposes. In a society living under a very real and often immediate threat of attack, such pacifism threatened to create serious difficulties for the government, which was responsible for the security of the entire population.

To be sure, orthodox Anglicans and Puritans alike were not oblivious to the pacifism that permeated the teachings of Jesus, especially in the Sermon on the Mount, but their leaders had no difficulty arguing the lawfulness of defensive and even offensive warfare in a just cause, and the common people readily accepted this view because it was in perfect harmony with their own instincts. "*Self-preservation* is a fundamental Law of humane Nature," argued one preacher, "and *Christianity* does not overthrow any such Laws but establish them." [70] But what if a war is not defensive and not even just? What, then, must the individual subject do? The usual answer to this problem of conscience was that the individual should do his duty. As a soldier he had no right to question "the Merits of the Cause, and judge whether the War be lawful or unlawful, for that is an Affair intrusted with the Prince and Councils of a Nation; and the Soldier is to presume that the Government have good Reasons to justify their proclaiming and engaging in a War." [71] Such an easy answer could not long satisfy a probing and sensitive mind, however, so that even Cotton Mather was known to say that if the injustice of a particular war was "notoriously Evident," the citizen should refuse to participate.[72] In 1737 another Massachusetts clergyman expressed much the same conviction when he wrote that a Christian should

> engage in War, only in a just Cause. Not to gratify Pride, Avarice and Ambition, to increase and enlarge our Possessions by the Ruins of those who might dwell *securely* by us. But for the vindication of our own just Rights and Properties, when incroach'd upon and invaded or threatned by the unreasonable and injurious, and this after Terms of Peace and Accommodation are rejected by them. Tho' every good Soldier is not fit to be a *Casuist*, and Causes of *War* may be sometimes

*so complicated and perplexed, as that they may not have ability to
dive thereinto; yet it seems reasonable, that as it is expected, they
should play the Men for the Cities of their God, they should be some
way convinced and satisfied of the justice of the Cause.*[73]

Such arguments vindicating war failed to convince the sincere
doubters, especially among such pacifistic religious sects as the
Anabaptists, Mennonites, Moravians, and most important, the Society of Friends, or Quakers. The latter began entering the colonies
in the 1650s, and although their "peace testimony" was not at first
the principal cause of the opposition they encountered, it grew to
become such as war crises began to occur and the Quakers stead-
fastly refused to make any contribution to military endeavors.
American Quakers refused to drill with the militia or go on military campaigns. Generally, they also refused to pay the fines imposed for these delinquencies and accordingly suffered distraint of
property sometimes worth far more than the fine. Likewise they
would not serve as armed guards, or even labor in the construction
of fortifications. Many refused to pay taxes for military expenditures. Prosecution at law was of little avail. The most extreme
Quakers showed themselves willing to suffer imprisonment, flogging, and even death rather than betray their convictions.[74]

What often appeared to the authorities as infuriating stubbornness on the part of Quaker citizens was a disciplined and often
courageous determination to be right in the eyes of God. Naturally,
governors and other leaders charged with the heavy responsibility
of safeguarding the colonies in time of war were inclined to be
intolerant of the Quaker view, especially when powerful enemies
were pounding at the gates. Governor Alexander Spotswood of
Virginia, confronted in 1711 with an uprising of the Tuscarora
Indians while war with France was still underway, was greatly
exasperated when he learned that the Quakers in his colony not
only would not themselves labor or permit their servants to labor
on the fortifications, but had even affirmed that in good conscience
they could not lend provisions for feeding other men who did
perform such labor. Yet, according to the enraged governor, these
same pacifists were saying that, being obliged by their religion to
feed their enemies, they would freely give provisions to an invading
French army. This to Spotswood was nothing but arrogant non-
sense, and he felt no qualms in prosecuting the sect.[75]

Prosecution usually served only to strengthen Quaker determination, for the Friends believed that in the long run their most grievous sufferings would help convince the world that they were not only sincere but right. This faith is well demonstrated in an excerpt from the minutes of the Henrico Monthly Meeting:

> Our Friend Tarlton Woodson having related to this Meeting his case of having had a horse wrongfully seazed by the sheriff for a Melishey [militia] fine, for not bearing arms according as the Law directs, and desires of this Meeting advice whather he may sew [sue] the sd. auficer for not acting according to Law. This Meeting after deliberate concideration think it may redound more to the honour of Truth to suffer wrong patiently than to take a remedy at Law.[76]

In Rhode Island the Friends constituted a large segment of the population, and at times during the latter part of the seventeenth century even controlled the government of the colony. A Rhode Island law of 1673 actually excused all conscientious objectors from military service, while stipulating that in time of emergency they might be required to perform watch duty unarmed and help lead aged persons to places of safety. Thereafter for many years the question of exemption and special consideration for pacifists was a lively issue in Rhode Island politics, with the legal requirements shifting as the currents of war and Quaker political strength ebbed and flowed.[77]

A large-scale influx of German pacifists began about 1710, and continued for several decades. The most prominent sects were the Mennonites (including the Amish), the Brethren (or Dunkers), the Schwenkfelders, and the Moravians. Although these various groups differed to some degree in their rejection of violence, all were inclined toward pacifism and most were committed to the belief that a Christian must not engage in war.[78] Some of the Moravians settled at first in the new colony of Georgia, in the very front lines of international conflict, as it were. The local authorities resented their stubborn refusal to cooperate in military preparedness, and before long the dispute was being aired before the trustees in England. "Bad Subjects for a frontier Colony," was the terse judgment of one trustee who left his thoughts on record.[79] The upshot was that the Moravians, good folk who only wanted to be left alone, removed themselves to Pennsylvania.

William Penn's proprietary province, founded under Quaker auspices in 1682 just seven years before the start of the great international struggle for America, was the only colony that from

its beginning actually attempted to maintain the "peace testimony"
as official policy. No wonder that the great majority of pacifist
immigrants, Quakers and others, preferred to settle in Pennsylvania. In the early years of the colony's history, the Quakers comprised a very large portion of the population, and enjoyed unchallenged control of the government. Later, under the proprietors'
open-door policy, more and more non-Quakers came in. Many
were German pietists inclined to support Quaker policies in government, but large numbers of other immigrants held no brief
for the pacifist position. Prominent among the latter were the
notoriously combative Scotch-Irish, who quickly made their way
out to the wilderness frontier. Eventually, too, with the passing of
the benevolent William Penn, the proprietorship fell to heirs who
were less firmly committed to the Quaker view of war. Pennsylvania represents a fascinating case of a young state politically
dominated by an idealistic elite group committed to pacifism as
an official policy, in a world permeated with organized violence,
while the growing population for whose security the elite group
supposedly was responsible came to include an increasingly large
nonpacifistic majority. This meant that official pacifism was subject to increasing challenge, becoming a hot political issue and
remaining a focal point of dispute well beyond the seventeenth
and mideighteenth centuries.

As early as 1689, with a war against France impending, the
young Quaker colony was reminded that it was a part of the
British world and not exempt from attack. On this occasion the
Quaker members of the governor's council reluctantly admitted
that nonpacifistic Pennsylvanians had a right to defend the province if they felt so inclined, but made it clear that such persons
would be given no encouragement or help from the government.
Quakers "can neither offensively nor defensively take Armes," explained one councilor. Yet "We would not be understood to tye
others' hands; they may do every One what they please. We do not
take upon us to hinder any.' [80] This being the official attitude, it
is obvious that Pennsylvanians would not be able to contrive any
satisfactory system of defense. How long could such a policy prevail
in a state that was increasingly tempting as a target for Britain's
enemies, and whose population was increasingly out of sympathy
with the "peace testimony"? This was the Quaker dilemma. For

the individual pacifist, wholeheartedly committed to his faith, there was no problem; he knew how to maintain his witness as an individual Friend even at the cost of his life. His position was unshakable. But what of a pacifist in a position of civil authority, responsible for the physical security of a community of people, many of whom considered the defense of themselves and their property a natural right? Could the Quaker justifiably impose his personal commitment and policy upon the entire community by refusing to make any provisions for defense, and thereby perhaps condemn the people to grievous suffering and loss? Must he not either compromise his own scruples in order to satisfy the community, or else relinquish his public authority and responsibility? Frederick B. Tolles, the Quaker historian, leads us straight to the heart of this problem. "From the beginning of the Quaker movement," he writes, "some Friends have felt impelled to go into politics in order to strike down artificial obstacles to human equality and eliminate the causes of war. But . . . politics inevitably involves the manipulation of power, which is foreign to the Quaker way. And to be successful in politics . . . one must be adept at compromise, which is contrary to the Quaker insistence on fidelity to a perfectionist ethic." [81] The dilemma could be an agonizing one for the sincere Quaker magistrate—and for the whole community looking up to him for guidance and protection.

By the 1740s the threat of war was coming very close to Quaker-ruled Pennsylvania, causing louder and louder cries among its people for some kind of military preparation. Even some of the Friends themselves, particularly those who were involved with the proprietary interest and British imperial concerns, were beginning to waver, sounding more and more like Anglicans and Congregationalists as they explored the possible merits of defensive warfare. At the same time, under great pressure the Quaker-dominated legislature was making significant compromises, as indeed it had been doing for several decades. Long since, writes the most recent historian of American pacifism,

> it had become clear that the "religious persuasions" of the Quaker politicians . . . though undoubtedly genuine, were somewhat elastic. They might be stretched on occasion to meet the exigencies of practical politics: hope for a political concession, perhaps, . . . or anxiety over the possible curtailment of their rights if they remained adamant in refusing all compromise.[82]

Their most common form of compromise was voting appropriations, when demanded, that would help support the British imperial war effort. This proved to be a slippery road, and once taken
there was no turning back. By the 1740s it would seem that a
majority of the Friends who were actively involved in government
had "virtually ceased . . . to regard pacifism as of relevance in the
political realm." [83] Indeed, one of them plainly admitted, "I have
clearly seen that government without arms is an inconsistency." [84]
Yet because the official Quaker testimony remained unchanged
and still enjoyed the support of so many Friends and German
pacifists in Pennsylvania, the colony continued to have no militia
organization, no system of compulsory or even voluntary training
for combat. In fact, it lay virtually defenseless, its long frontier and
its widemouthed river open to any foe.

Doctrinaire Quakers continued to insist that the "peace testimony" itself was a sufficient shield. Had it not protected their
colony from Indian trouble ever since the days of William Penn?
If the Indians along the frontier were now showing signs of belligerence, they said, that was only the result of mistreatment at the
hands of unscrupulous colonists and agents of the proprietor. Restore benevolence and all would once again be well. Men who
argued in this fashion seemed unable to grasp the fundamental
fact that the various tribes, like the various colonies, were being
sucked into the roiling whirlpool of international rivalry. French
power and persuasion as well as British perfidy were responsible
for the mounting antagonism being shown by the Indians. Moreover, the French themselves would not be deterred from trying to
seize Pennsylvania if their strength and policy should lead them
to make the attempt. It was this apparent blindness on the part of
many pacifists that so disturbed their exposed and fearful fellow
colonists, as well as a few deeply concerned imperialists who postu-
lated a French plan for the eventual conquest of British North
America. And yet, their cries for military preparedness still went
largely unheeded in the council chamber at Philadelphia.

In 1740 the proprietary governor George Thomas, in accordance
with instructions from the crown, began recruiting eight companies
in Pennsylvania and Delaware for service in the Caribbean. The
recruiting proceeded briskly, and among those Pennsylvanians attracted to the drum were several hundred indentured servants,
many of whom were legally ·obligated to pacifistic masters. The

latter, angered at this loss of valuable labor as well as the unwelcome intrusion of militarism, complained to the assembly, which in turn raised the issue with the governor.[85] This produced a direct confrontation between the antiproprietary, Quaker-dominated assembly and the imperialist-minded proprietary governor who had no doubt as to his duty. Provoked, Governor Thomas stung the Quaker politicians with a barbed question:

> If your Principles are inconsistent with the End of Government at a Time when his Majesty is put under a necessity of procuring Reparation for his injured Subjects by Arms, why did not your Consciences restrain you from soliciting for a Station which your Consciences will not allow you to discharge for the Honour of his Majesty, and the Interest of those you represent.

And he drove home his point by reminding the Quaker legislators that "it is a piece of Injustice to involve a People of which you are not above one-third in Number, in the ill Consequences that must attend a Government under such a Direction." [86] An impasse was reached when the exasperated governor, backed by the proprietor, insisted that he could not discharge the servants in question, and the assembly stubbornly refused to appropriate any funds for defense until he did so. In the following year James Logan, one of the foremost antipacifist Quakers, picked up the governor's pointed question and used it again, urging his pacifist brethren to refrain from accepting political office so that the government might take adequate steps for the colony's protection in a time of great danger. But for that great act of abnegation the Quaker politicians were not yet ready.[87]

When French privateers actually entered the Delaware River and raided some farms along the bank in 1747, the extreme vulnerability of defenseless Pennsylvania was made obvious. Soon there were rumors that next year the enemy would return in much greater strength to fall upon Philadelphia itself. Unmoved, the assembly refused to authorize the formation of a militia, despite the mounting clamor.[88] Among the most spirited leaders of the thousands who now were crying for military preparedness was the Philadelphia publisher Benjamin Franklin. Anonymously he wrote and published a pamphlet entitled *Plain Truth: Or, Serious Considerations on the Present State of the City of Philadelphia, and Province of Pennsylvania*, in which he painted a grim picture of the colony's present danger and condemned the Quakers for their continuing stand against appropriate defensive measures. "The Way to secure Peace is to be prepared for War," he lectured. "They that are on their Guard, and appear ready to receive their Adversaries, are in much less Danger of being attack'd, than the supine, secure and negligent." [89] To remedy the obvious deficiency caused by the assembly's blind pacifism, Franklin promised to bring forward in the near future a plan of voluntary private defense, together with a scheme for raising the necessary funds. What Franklin's fertile mind had envisioned was revealed to the public on 21 November 1747. There was to be a volunteer citizens' militia, known simply as the Association. Volunteers who signed the agreement were to form themselves into companies of from fifty to a hundred men, choosing their own officers (subject to later official approval by the governor). Also to be elected by the members was a General Military Council, which would then provide the organization with any needed regulations. The only penalties, however, were to be in the form of small fines levied at the discretion of each company. Franklin proposed that the cost of this organization be met by means of a lottery.[90]

Pennsylvanians received the proposal with enthusiasm, and began signing up by the hundreds. On 3 December 1747 the *Pennsylvania Gazette* (Franklin's own newspaper) exulted in the spectacle of "all Hands being busy in providing Arms, putting them in Order, and improving themselves in military Discipline." [91] Even some of the Quakers viewed the Association as a sensible answer to the great dilemma; it provided a way for men who believed in defense to take positive action, without compelling the pacifists to join them or even contribute through public taxation. Possibly the most prevalent judgment to be heard in Philadelphia was expressed in the words of the revivalistic preacher Gilbert Tennent, who said that the Association was, "considering the Posture of our Affairs, the best *Expedient* that could be concerted, and of the last *Necessity* to promote the Security and Advantage of this City and Province." [92] As it happened, the ending of the war in 1748 removed the immediate need for further military preparations, and Franklin's brainchild was allowed to die. Once again the Quaker colony lapsed into total unpreparedness. The supreme challenge to the pacifist position in Pennsylvania and elsewhere was yet to come, in the last and greatest of the colonial wars.

One additional problem eventually had to be faced by every

colony that sent its men into combat: What, if any, special assistance or compensation should be granted to military veterans after their return from war? England's notorious ingratitude to its veterans was widely imitated by American taxpayers, who tended to feel that society's debt to a soldier, especially one who had suffered no permanent injury, was fully paid when he was handed his last wage and sent on his homeward way. Yet as one war succeeded another, involving ever larger numbers of men, the veteran element in the colonial population became increasingly strong, with interests and claims that could not be ignored.

The veteran problem first assumed significant proportions in King Philip's War, when hundreds of New England colonists became engaged in extensive operations against the hostile Indians. After the fighting had been underway for nearly a year, the General Court of Massachusetts, confronted with a growing pile of individual petitions from wounded soldiers asking for financial assistance, named a special committee to consider each case and make recommendations.[93] Sometimes many years passed before the disabled veteran or his family brought his plight to the attention of the colony government, or was granted the needed assistance. As late as 1699, for example, one disabled veteran of King Philip's War petitioned the General Court, stating that his resources now were almost exhausted and he and his wife decrepit. In this case the court granted an annual pension of £4, approximately the amount a common laborer could expect to earn in about seven weeks.[94] Plymouth Colony settled accounts with one of its former soldiers by granting him the lump sum of £15 plus the right to collect and retain all fines assessed in the town of Yarmouth for violations of the liquor laws.[95] One can easily imagine this old veteran spending his declining years snooping among his neighbors and making more enemies than he had ever slain in his days of soldiering.

For America, though, the truly significant innovation was the concept that unwounded veterans, too, were entitled to special postwar favors. Shortly after the end of King Philip's War, groups of these men in various localities began making their claims known, and what they demanded in particular was land. Some towns which still had undivided land to distribute readily gave part of it to their own veterans, but such minor grants were not enough to still the clamor. Many of the young, able veterans, having failed to

prosper in the older established towns, were looking toward large
unsettled tracts along the frontier, land which they themselves had
helped wrest from the Indians. It was the colony government, not
the towns, that had authority to grant such land, and accordingly
the veterans began organizing themselves to approach the legislature. For the first time in American history veterans' pressure
groups were formed for the purpose of extracting special benefits
from the government. For many years the veterans pecked away
at their objective, but enjoyed only limited success. Then at· last
in the 1730s, more than half a century after their war had ended,
the surviving veterans and the heirs of deceased veterans prevailed
with the General Court of Massachusetts when the legislature decided to grant a new township on the frontier to every 120 eligible
claimants on the basis of service in King Philip's War.[96]

In the meantime, other great wars had produced more and more
veterans with more and more demands. The problem of how these
men organized themselves, what demands they formulated, and in
what ways the various colony governments responded to their needs
invites exploration. One fact already is clear. The concept of the
soldier as a self-sacrificing hero deserving the unending gratitude of
society had not yet developed and would not develop until the
American Revolution created a pantheon of national heroes. In
colonial times the soldier, unless locally known or a commissioned
officer, frequently was considered to be something of a ruffian or, at
best, an expensive nuisance. Once the war was over, the less heard
of him the better. So it is not surprising that until the veterans
began organizing themselves into real pressure groups able to influence political-minded legislators, their requests were treated in
rather cursory fashion by governments already hard pressed to meet
their ordinary financial obligations and the growing demands of new
wars.

NOTES

1. The author's unpublished doctoral dissertation, "The Causes and Effects
   of King Philip's War" (Harvard University, 1952), is in part an attempt to
   explore the extensive effects on colonial society of one major Indian war.
2. Quoted in Victor S. Clark, *History of Manufactures in the United States*
   (3 vols.; New York, 1929), I, 134.
3. Massachusetts Council Records, pp. 182–183 (Massachusetts Archives).
4. *Ibid.*, p. 187.

5. Thomas Hutchinson, *The History of the Colony and Province of Massa-chusetts-Bay*, Lawrence Shaw Mayo, ed. (3 vols.; Cambridge, Mass., 1936), II, 315. In South Carolina not only the governor but even a captain of militia had the right, in time of emergency, to impress needed provisions, goods, ships, and seamen. (See David William Cole, "The Organization and Administration of the South Carolina Militia System, 1670–1783" [Unpublished Ph.D. dissertation, University of South Carolina, 1953], p. 40.) Of course, in any major emergency in any of the colonies a commanding officer might assume this power.

6. Massachusetts Archives, LXX, 223.

7. Merrill Jensen, ed., *English Historical Documents: American Colonial Documents to 1776* (New York, 1955), pp. 417–418; M. Eugene Sirmans, *Colonial South Carolina: A Political History, 1663–1763* (Chapel Hill, 1966), pp. 73–74.

8. Emory R. Johnson *et al., History of Domestic and Foreign Commerce of the United States* (2 vols.; Washington, D.C., 1915), I, 85.

9. Hampshire County Court Records, I, 38 (Hampshire County Courthouse, Northampton, Mass.).

10. Quoted in Richard Pares, *War and Trade in the West Indies, 1739–1763* (New York, 1936), p. 228.

11. John Pitts Corry, *Indian Affairs in Georgia, 1732–1756* (Philadelphia, 1936), pp. 27–28; Robert L. Meriwether, *The Expansion of South Carolina, 1729–1765* (Kingsport, Tenn., 1940), p. 192.

12. Pares, *War and Trade in the West Indies*, pp. 495–498, indicates that the cost of maritime insurance was "vastly higher" in wartime than in peacetime. For a voyage from Jamaica to England the wartime rate sometimes exceeded 12 percent, compared with a normal peacetime rate of 5 percent to 8 percent.

13. *South Carolina Gazette*, 10 December 1744. See also Sirmans, *Colonial South Carolina*, pp. 269–271. I am grateful for the use of an unpublished essay by one of my students, George Thomas Fox, entitled "The Effect of War on the Civilian Population of the Carolinas and Georgia, 1739–1761," which presents much informative material on this subject.

14. Anne Bezanson, R. D. Gray, and M. Hussey, *Prices in Colonial Pennsylvania* (Philadelphia, 1935), pp. 29, 32–35, 61, 68, 74, 142–144. In contrast, the prices of meat tended to increase. See also Benjamin Franklin, *The Papers of Benjamin Franklin*, Leonard W. Labaree *et al.*, eds. (14 vols. to date; New Haven, 1959 to present), II, 414.

15. Walton E. Bean, "War and the British Colonial Farmer: A Reëvaluation in the Light of New Statistical Records," *Pacific Historical Review*, XI (December, 1942), 439–447.

16. Curtis Nettels, *The Money Supply of the American Colonies before 1720* (Madison, 1934), p. 93. Professor Nettels notes that during the period 1708–11, "Great Britain spent £414,000 on the defense of the commerce and coasts of the mainland colonies" (*ibid.*, p. 195). A considerable part of this amount must have found its way into the American economy in one form or another.

17. Cotton Mather, *The Life of Sir William Phips,* Mark Van Doren, ed. (New York, 1929), pp. 86–90.

18. David Duncan Wallace, *South Carolina, A Short History, 1520–1948* (Chapel Hill, 1951), pp. 69, 134; Sirmans, *Colonial South Carolina,* pp. 109–110.

19. Hugh T. Lefler and Albert R. Newsome, *North Carolina: The History of a Southern State* (Rev. ed., Chapel Hill, 1963), p. 146.

20. John A. Schutz, *William Shirley: King's Governor of Massachusetts* (Chapel Hill, 1961), p. 125.

21. *NYCD,* XIII, 407.

22. Carl Stephenson and Frederick G. Marcham, eds., *Sources of English Constitutional History: A Selection of Documents from A.D. 600 to the Present* (New York and London, 1937), pp. 450–452.

23. Cornelis Cuyler to Philip Cuyler, 7 September 1756, Cornelis Cuyler Letterbook (American Antiquarian Society).

24. Franklin, *Papers,* VII, 38–49, 53, 96–97; Stanley Pargellis, ed., *Military Affairs in North America, 1748–1765: Selected Documents from the Cumberland Papers in Windsor Castle* (New York, 1936), pp. 272–274; Theodore Thayer, *Pennsylvania Politics and the Growth of Democracy, 1740–1776* (Harrisburg, 1953), p. 60.

25. Sirmans, *Colonial South Carolina,* pp. 320–324; Jack P. Greene, "The South Carolina Quartering Dispute, 1757–1758," *South Carolina Historical Magazine,* LX (October, 1959), 193–204.

26. Jack P. Greene, *The Quest for Power: The Lower Houses of Assembly in the Southern Royal Colonies, 1689–1776* (Chapel Hill, 1963); Jack P. Greene, "The Role of the Lower Houses of Assembly in Eighteenth-Century Politics," *JSH,* XXVII (November, 1961), 451–474.

27. *The Acts and Resolves, Public and Private, of the Province of the Massachusetts Bay* (21 vols.; Boston, 1869–1922), I, 36. See also *ibid.,* pp. 99–100, 176–177.

28. Cole, "Organization and Administration of the South Carolina Militia System," pp. 39–40.

29. E. Milton Wheeler, "Development and Organization of the North Carolina Militia," *North Carolina Historical Review,* XLI (July, 1964), 315–316.

30. Samuel Sewall's Diary, in 5 *MHC,* VII, 312–313.

31. John F. Burns, *Controversies between Royal Governors and Their Assemblies in the Northern American Colonies* (Boston, 1923), pp. 65–66, 73. The tension in Massachusetts is discussed at length in Hutchinson, *History of the Colony and Province of Massachusetts-Bay,* II, 163–217. See also Francis Parkman, *A Half-Century of Conflict* (2 vols.; Boston, 1892), I, 230–234.

32. Burns, *Controversies between Royal Governors and Their Assemblies,* pp. 270–272; G. A. Rawlyk, *Yankees at Louisbourg* (Orono, Me., 1967), pp. 52–54.

33. Quoted in Burns, *Controversies between Royal Governors and Their Assemblies,* p. 333.

34. John Rutherfurd to Cadwallader Colden, 22 April 1745, in *Collections of the New-York Historical Society for the Year 1919* (New York, 1920), p. 112.

35. *NYCD,* VI, 522.
36. Newton D. Mereness, *Maryland as a Proprietary Province* (New York, 1901), pp. 292–295.
37. William H. Browne *et al.,* eds., *Archives of Maryland* (71 vols. to date; Baltimore, 1883 to present), XXVIII, 228–233, XL, 423–578, XLII, 1–126.
38. Greene, *Quest for Power,* p. 309.
39. *Peter Kalm's Travels in North America,* Adolph B. Benson, ed. (2 vols., New York, 1937), I, 138–139.
40. Massachusetts Archives, LXVIII, 2. For an extended discussion of the problem of intercolonial relations in King Philip's War, see Leach, "Causes and Effects of King Philip's War," chap. 8. A briefer summary may be found in Douglas Edward Leach, *Flintlock and Tomahawk: New England in King Philip's War* (New York, 1958), pp. 59–62, 96–100, 109, 177, 244–245.
41. Connecticut Archives, War, I, 45*b,* 60; Massachusetts Archives, LXVIII, 157, 196, CCXI, 279; 3 *MHC,* I, 69; J. H. Trumbull and C. J. Hoadly, eds., *The Public Records of the Colony of Connecticut* (15 vols.; Hartford, Conn., 1850–1890), II, 434.
42. Israel Williams Papers (Massachusetts Historical Society), I, 34. See also *ibid.,* pp. 35–37.
43. Israel Williams Papers, I, 66–67, 97, 111, 112.
44. Jerome R. Reich, *Leisler's Rebellion: A Study of Democracy in New York, 1664–1720* (Chicago, 1953), p. 135; Rand Burnette, "The Quest for Union in the American Colonies, 1689–1701" (Unpublished Ph.D. dissertation, Indiana University, 1967), pp. 85–94.
45. Dudley's letter of 15 November 1710, Gay Transcripts, State Papers, X, 70–73 (Massachusetts Historical Society).
46. Jeremy Dummer's memorial, March 1711, *ibid.,* pp. 73–74.
47. Alexander Spotswood, *The Official Letters of Alexander Spotswood . . . ,* R. A. Brock, ed. (2 vols.; Richmond, Va., 1882–1885), II, 124.
48. *NYCD,* V, 430–431.
49. Connecticut Archives, Indians, I, 259.
50. These explanations in extenuation were offered by a colonist who was more judicious than most of his compatriots, Thomas Hutchinson. See his *History of the Colony and Province of Massachusetts-Bay,* II, 104*n.*
51. Elizabeth Hanson, *God's Mercy Surmounting Man's Cruelty, Exemplified in the Captivity and Redemption of Elizabeth Hanson* (Philadelphia, 1728), pp. 9–13.
52. John Norton, *The Redeemed Captive, Being a Narrative of the Taken [sic] and Carrying into Captivity the Reverend Mr. John Norton, When Fort-Massachusetts Surrendered to a Large Body of French and Indians, August 20th 1746* (Boston, 1748), pp. 20–21.
53. Robert Eastburn, *A Faithful Narrative of the Many Dangers and Sufferings . . . of Robert Eastburn, during His Late Captivity among the Indians* (Philadelphia and Boston, 1758), pp. 10, 15. See also Thomas Brown, *A Plain Narrative of the Uncommon Sufferings, and Remarkable Deliverance of Thomas Brown, of Charlestown, in New-England . . .* (Boston, 1760), p. 17.

54. William Pote, Jr., *The Journal of Captain William Pote, Jr. during His Captivity in the French and Indian War from May, 1745, to August, 1747* (New York, 1896), pp. 57–58.

55. Nathaniel Knowles, "The Torture of Captives by the Indians of Eastern North America," *Proceedings of the American Philosophical Society,* LXXXII (March, 1940), pp. 151–225; Raymond Lewis Scheele, "The Treatment of Captives among the North East Indians of North America" (Unpublished M.A. thesis, Columbia University, 1947).

56. Jean Lowry, *A Journal of the Captivity of Jean Lowry and Her Children* . . . (Philadelphia, 1760), pp. 10–11.

57. Samuel Bownas, *An Account of the Captivity of Elizabeth Hanson, Now or Late of Kachecky, in New-England* (2d ed.; London, 1760), p. 24; Jeremy Belknap, *The History of New-Hampshire* (Dover, N.H., 1831), pp. 147–148.

58. John Williams, *The Redeemed Captive Returning to Zion* (Springfield, Mass., 1908), p. 141; Sylvester K. Stevens and Donald H. Kent, eds., *Wilderness Chronicles of Northwestern Pennsylvania* (Harrisburg, 1941), p. 117. See also Kalm, *Travels in North America,* II, 456–457.

59. Williams, *Redeemed Captive Returning to Zion,* p. 188n.

60. Mr. Williams' own account of his experience, *The Redeemed Captive Returning to Zion,* is a New England classic. For additional details, consult Emma Lewis Coleman, *New England Captives Carried to Canada between 1677 and 1760 during the French and Indian Wars* (2 vols.; Portland, Me., 1925), II, 33–64.

61. *Good Fetch'd out of Evil* (Boston, 1706), p. 4.

62. John Gyles, *Memoirs of Odd Adventures, Strange Deliverances, &c. in the Captivity of John Gyles, Esq; Commander of the Garrison on St. George's River* (Boston, 1736), p. 5.

63. *Frontiers Well-Defended. An Essay, to Direct the Frontiers of a Countrey Exposed unto the Incursions of a Barbarous Enemy, How to Behave Themselves in Their Uneasy Station?* (Boston, 1707). For a biased but revealing account of theological disputations between a Calvinist female captive and various French Roman Catholics, see Lowry, *Journal,* pp. 18–31.

64. Isabel M. Calder, ed., *Colonial Captivities, Marches, and Journeys* (New York, 1935), pp. 28–29.

65. Pote, *Journal,* pp. 97–98. On 16 October the count was "267 men women and Children."

66. Pote, *Journal,* pp. 103–104, 128.

67. Massachusetts Archives, LXX, 317. See also p. 257 of the same volume, where on another occasion the authorities at Boston, seeking to gain the release of New Englanders held in Canada, employed the argument that French prisoners were receiving good treatment, even being permitted to earn money if they wished to do so.

68. Nehemiah How, *A Narrative of the Captivity of Nehemiah How, Who Was Taken by the Indians at the Great-Meadow Fort above Fort-Dummer, Where He Was an Inhabitant, October 11th 1745* (Boston, 1748).

69. John Marshall, Diary (Massachusetts Historical Society); [Mather], *Good*

Fetch'd out of Evil, pp. 4–5; C. Alice Baker, "Ensign John Sheldon," *History and Proceedings of the Pocumtuck Valley Memorial Association,. 1870–1879*, I (1890), 405–431. Documents revealing the difficulties and successes experienced by a New England grandfather who went to Canada in 1761 to attempt the recovery of prisoners, including his own grandchildren, have been published in James P. Baxter, ed., *Documentary History of the State of Maine*, XXIV (Portland, Me., 1916), 105–113.

70. William Williams, *Martial Wisdom Recommended* (Boston, 1737), p. 5. The revivalistic preacher Gilbert Tennent likewise drew upon Natural Law as well as Scripture to justify defensive violence. Indeed, "WAR is no doubt lawful, and consequently approved by God," he argued, "when undertaken by the Magistrate, for the Punishment of some great injury or wrong which much affects the Credit and Interest of a Nation or People, after all other softer Means for redress fail of success" (*The Late Association for Defence Encourag'd, or The Lawfulness of a Defensive War* [Philadelphia, 1748], p. 7). See also Arthur H. Buffinton, "The Puritan View of War," in Publications of the Colonial Society of Massachusetts, XXVIII (1935), 67–86.

71. Nathaniel Appleton, *The Origin of War Examin'd and Applied . . .* (Boston, 1733), quoted in Buffinton, "Puritan View of War," p. 79.

72. Quoted in Buffinton, "Puritan View of War," p. 79.

73. Williams, *Martial Wisdom Recommended*, p. 16.

74. Charles H. Lincoln, ed., *Narratives of the Indian Wars, 1675–1699* (New York, 1913), p. 44; Peter Brock, *Pacifism in the United States, from the Colonial Era to the First World War* (Princeton, 1968), pp. 30, 69–70, 72. The Quaker itinerant Thomas Chalkley told of a frontier family of Friends who, living in an area threatened by Indian warfare, wrestled with the problem of whether to flee or stay. The wife, a woman of great faith, believed that to flee would have the effect of weakening their "peace testimony," but her husband and her mother argued that to remain might mean a futile death. Ironically the mother, while en route to another house, was slain by an Indian, and it was the wife who lived to tell the tale (Thomas Chalkley, *A Journal or Historical Account of the Life, Travels and Christian Experiences of . . . Thomas Chalkley* [2d ed.; London, 1751], pp. 40–45). If Chalkley is correct, hostile Indians generally respected the pacifism of the Quakers (even though they did not understand it) and refrained from killing known Friends. A number of contrary cases, however, may be cited.

75. Governor Spotswood to the Board of Trade, 15 October 1711, in William L. Saunders, ed., *The Colonial Records of North Carolina* (10 vols.; Raleigh, N.C., 1886–1890), I, 812. See also William Byrd, *The Secret Diary of William Byrd of Westover, 1709–1712*, Louis B. Wright and Marion Tinling, eds. (Richmond, Va., 1941), pp. 409, 415–416, 419, for examples of how a Virginia official actually dealt with Quakers at this time.

76. Quoted in Rufus M. Jones, *The Quakers in the American Colonies* (New York, 1962), p. 319.

77. John Russell Bartlett, ed., *Records of the Colony of Rhode Island, and Providence Plantations, in New England* (10 vols.; Providence, 1856–1865),

II, 495–499, 549, 567–572, III, 433; General Court of Trials, Record 1, p. 27 (Superior Court, Newport, R.I.); Selective Service System, *Backgrounds of Selective Service*, II, Part 12, pp. 61, 65–66.

78. Brock, *Pacifism in the United States,* chap. 4. As Brock points out, the Schwenkfelders, unlike some pacifists, felt free to lend their horses and wagons to the army even though they themselves, or at least most of them, would not take up arms.

79. Robert G. McPherson, ed., *The Journal of the Earl of Egmont: Abstract of the Trustees Proceedings for Establishing the Colony of Georgia, 1732–1738* (Athens, Ga., 1962), p. 277. See also Amos A. Ettinger, *James Edward Oglethorpe, Imperial Idealist* (Oxford and New York, 1936), pp. 218–219; E. Merton Coulter, *Georgia: A Short History* (Rev. ed., Chapel Hill, 1947), pp. 28–30.

80. *Minutes of the Provincial Council of Pennsylvania, from the Organization to the Termination of the Proprietary Government* (10 vols.; Philadelphia and Harrisburg, 1851–1852), I, 309. See also Jones, *Quakers in the American Colonies,* pp. 480–481.

81. *Quakers and the Atlantic Culture* (New York, 1960), p. 36.

82. Brock, *Pacifism in the United States,* p. 101.

83. Brock, *Pacifism in the United States,* p. 112.

84. James Logan to Benjamin Franklin, 3 December 1747, in Franklin, *Papers,* III, 219.

85. *Minutes of the Provincial Council of Pennsylvania,* IV, 435–438; Franklin, *Papers,* II, 288–289.

86. *Minutes of the Provincial Council of Pennsylvania,* IV, 442.

87. *Pennsylvania Magazine of History and Biography,* VI (1882), 403–411.

88. Franklin, *Papers,* III, 180–188.

89. *Ibid.,* p. 203.

90. *Ibid.,* pp. 184–185, 205–212, 220–224.

91. *Ibid.,* p. 239.

92. *Late Association for Defence Encourag'd,* p. 35.

93. *MCR,* V, 80, 226–227. See also Trumbull and Hoadly, *Public Records of the Colony of Connecticut,* II, 288. For a more extensive discussion of the veteran problem during and after King Philip's War consult Leach, "Causes and Effects of King Philip's War," pp. 473–481.

94. Massachusetts Archives, LXX, 405.

95. Nathaniel B. Shurtleff, ed., *Records of the Colony of New Plymouth in New England* (12 vols.; Boston, 1855–1861), VI, 65.

96. George M. Bodge, *Soldiers in King Philip's War* (3d ed.; Boston, 1906), pp. 406–412.

CHAPTER 8

Dangerous Interlude, 1748–1754

From the vantage point of 1748 one could look back over the preceding sixty years with a growing realization that several significant developments were converging toward some kind of major climax at the midpoint of the eighteenth century. For one thing, it was becoming more clear than ever that the old hope of a "peace beyond the line"—that is, the possibility of preventing the wars of Europe from involving the American colonies—was futile. At the same time, the danger that quarrels between rival blocs of colonies in the New World eventually would draw their respective mother countries into another major war was greater than ever. The modern concept of empire was beginning to take definite form, binding nation-states and their overseas dependencies together against the common threat of rival imperial systems. No longer could the colonies expect to be exempted from the burden of Europe's ancient quarrels nor could the various imperial powers, if they wished to retain their colonies, escape the responsibility of supporting them against their enemies. This inescapable condition of modern imperialism underlay a period of increasing danger in the affairs of nations and empires.

Considering the many potentially dangerous issues left unresolved by the Peace of Aix-la-Chapelle in 1748, there was reason to suppose that the hour of renewed conflict would soon strike. Austria, bitterly resenting the recent Prussian acquisition of Silesia, licked her wounds and awaited her opportunity for revenge. The status of the strategically located Netherlands remained an irritating issue between Britain and France, while the whole vast field of overseas commerce and colonies seethed with their continuing rivalry. India was a bone of contention; Africa, with its important trade in slaves believed to be so vital to the development of the plantation colonies, another. In fact, the helter-skelter race for colonial territory and resources in which the various maritime states of Europe had been engaged since the sixteenth century now was narrowing down to a decisive contest between Britain and France. The other, earlier contenders, such as Portugal, Sweden, Holland, and even Spain, were falling farther and farther behind, finding themselves less and less able to exercise any really decisive influence in the Western Hemisphere. Some of these nation-states had concentrated their efforts elsewhere. Others simply had failed to meet the difficult conditions for successful imperialism in the eighteenth century, including that most important of achievements, the effective linking of a modernized, partly industrialized domestic economy with a diversified, expanding colonial economy by means of commercially oriented sea power. Only Britain and France still qualified in the intensifying contest for imperial supremacy in North America.

After 1748, both countries trod warily, anxious to avoid a decisive confrontation, at least for the present. Both needed time to recover past losses, regain the strength that had been so severely drained by long years of debilitating war, consolidate political power amidst domestic difficulties, and plot a course toward future success. France, governed still by an authoritarian but increasingly irresponsible Louis XV. and his "almost-queen," the Marquise de Pompadour, was displaying a healthy caution. So too was Britain, under the ministry of Henry Pelham and his brother, the Duke of Newcastle. True, more aggressive sentiments were felt and sometimes expressed by imperialist-minded politicians such as William Pitt, but Pitt was strongly disliked by the aging George II and remained excluded from the highest echelon of power. So the current watchword for foreign policy in both London and Paris was caution, in order to avoid a renewal of warfare that neither side was yet ready to undertake.

It was a time for backstairs diplomacy, often as decisive in the affairs of nations as the more open, formal kind. Indeed, scarcely had the quills of Aix-la-Chapelle been laid down than the ambassadors and agents of the various powers began a new series of diplomatic maneuvers that were to prove highly unsettling to the established structure of international alliances. It was as though everything were becoming "unglued," a situation most unnerving to rulers and statesmen in a period of great peril. Eventually this would produce a diplomatic revolution, a major realignment of the contending powers; but such a startling consummation was not yet visible and would not become fully exposed until a new war had begun. One thing did seem certain, however: Regardless of how other nations might shift their policies and alliances, Britain and France would remain deadly rivals. This is not to say that these two major powers were unaffected by the diplomatic maneuvering of others—quite the contrary. Spain, for example, shocked her Bourbon cousin France in 1750 by concluding a commercial treaty with Britain, a clear sign of Spanish displeasure with the rather cavalier attitude of the French government. This set France to scrambling for renewed Spanish esteem and loyalty, to the obvious advantage of Spain and the corresponding discomfort of Britain.[1]

Both Britain and France had been impressed during the recent war by the high degree of competence displayed by the Prussian Army of Frederick the Great, an army in which discipline, mobility, artillery support, and close-order attack had been developed to a new peak of achievement. Like the French and other European military powers, the British responded to this challenge by adopting Prussian practices for their own army. Prussian precision became the standard against which every Continental army was to be measured for the remainder of the century. Even though the British government found it economically necessary to pare down its army to about 18,000 men, a fairly high level of professional competence was preserved under the effective administration of the commander in chief, the Duke of Cumberland, third son of George II. The navy was less fortunate. Reduced to scarcely 10,000 men, Britain's traditional first line of defense was dangerously weakened, as fighting ships were allowed to deteriorate at their moorings. Conversely, the French began pouring money and skill into a major program of rebuilding the sea arm that had been so badly shattered in the recent war. As the years passed, more and more brand-new ships of war slid down the ways of French ship-yards to challenge British supremacy. Here, especially, did the far-flung colonies of the British Empire have cause for concern.

International tension with respect to North America certainly was not ended by the Peace of Aix-la-Chapelle, as was demonstrated by the extreme difficulty encountered in the attempt to obtain the repatriation of all prisoners. Probably as late as 1750, some captives still were retained for the purpose of leverage, as the two sides argued and maneuvered for advantage.[2] Moreover, the Anglo-French commission charged with determining the boundaries be-tween British and French territory in America—William Mildmay and William Shirley for Britain and the Marquis de la Galissonière and Étienne de Silhouette for France—made little progress over a period of many months.[3] Shirley was an ardent expansionist, deter-mined to seek maximum territorial gain. While his French op-ponents favored a boundary that would limit Nova Scotia to the actual peninsula, leaving under the fleur-de-lys the isthmus and the adjacent territory to the west and south, possibly even down to the Kennebec River, Shirley attempted to claim for Britain the entire area between the Kennebec and the St. Lawrence.[4] This was a voracious claim, not actively supported even by the other British commissioner or the ministry in London; nevertheless, Shirley con-tinued to play for all. With so much at stake here and in the other areas under dispute, especially the Ohio Valley, agreement was minimal. Both sides attempted to prove their territorial claims by citing past events and previous agreements, but they might as well have been jousting with rubber lances. "Memorial followed memo-rial and *pièces justificatives* followed *pièces justificatives*," sighed one historian, "without softening in the slightest the inflexibility of either side."[5] Early in 1755, a new British secretary of state proposed that a neutral zone be established between the recognized British and French territories, but this too came to nothing.

Clearly, by the middle of the eighteenth century both the British and the French in America had come to view each other as arch-competitors. Indeed, each side now envisioned the other in the form of a scheming, implacable aggressor, determined to end the game at last by gaining all. By this time, too, colonial societies were so firmly rooted and so well developed that the intensifying con-flict between the two blocs was beginning to show signs of becoming total, an irrepressible struggle between two rival and incompatible ways of life. No longer was it "merely territorial, or commercial, or directed at the control of Indians, or political," writes Professor Max Savelle. "It was religious and cultural, the very basis of civilization itself now seeming to be at stake." [6] Every advance, or even potential advance, by one side aroused instant suspicion and fear on the part of the other, who saw this as fresh evidence of a nefarious scheme of conquest. There was a great temptation to try advances here and there because the zone of disputed territory lying between the respective areas of actual occupation lay largely vacant except for the Indians.

British entrepreneurs continued to promote the Indian trade most vigorously, taking advantage of the superior quality and low cost of their goods to extend their contacts with the western tribes. Ambitious, profit-seeking land companies also were active, making haste to plant actual settlers on disputed land. The French lacked the advantage of cheap trading goods and hordes of potential pioneers, but they did have compensating resources, most notably a degree of central direction almost totally lacking in the British system. When the authorities at Quebec or New Orleans made a decision and issued an order, some corresponding action was likely to follow in rather quick time. A force would assemble and depart, a destination would be reached, a fort would be built. All this might actually be accomplished while several British colonies were spending weeks or even months arguing about what they ought to do and who would pay for it when they did it. In the meantime, private enterprise on the British side pursued its own interests on the frontier, winning the allegiance of the Indians and perhaps even negating some of the advantages that otherwise would have gone to the French as the fruits of their decisive action.

Shirley returned to Massachusetts and resumed his duties as governor in 1753, more determined than ever to undermine the French threat along New England's frontier. After his experience on the joint international commission, he was especially concerned for the future of Nova Scotia, still separated from New England by intervening territory in dispute between Britain and France. Shirley's failure to attain the extreme boundaries he had advocated meant that the French presence wedged in between New England and Nova Scotia would continue to endanger the frontiers of both areas. Moreover, the Acadian peasant population of Nova Scotia,

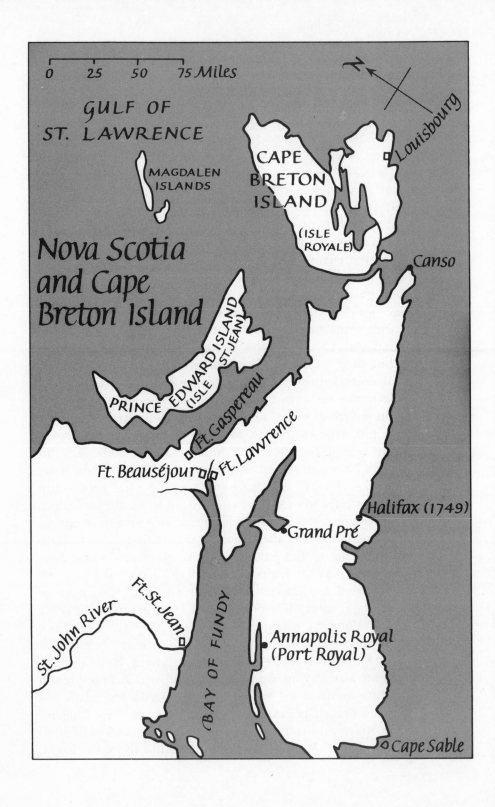

Nova Scotia and Cape Breton Island

French speaking and Roman Catholic, remained stubbornly neutral or, as the British suspected, secretly hoped for a French conquest. Superimposed on this deeply rooted Gallic population was a British population of soldiers and settlers mainly concentrated in the vicinity of Annapolis Royal and the newly established base at Halifax, all under the governorship of Colonel Edward Cornwallis.

The irregular isthmus of Chignecto, which connected the peninsula with the mainland, was of great strategic importance in this situation and was claimed by both sides. Running across part of the disputed isthmus and into Chignecto Bay was a sluggish little stream known as the Missaguash. On opposite sides of this natural but quite unofficial boundary, the French and their British rivals erected small forts, French Fort Beauséjour on the west and British Fort Lawrence on the east. In effect, then, the Missaguash had become the *de facto* boundary of Nova Scotia by virtue of military confrontation. Fortunately, despite occasional shows of force and even acts of violence, the responsible commanders on the scene did not overstep the bounds of prudence. Indeed, as time went on they even permitted some demonstrations of mutual regard and a surreptitious trade between the two garrisons, for the area was bleak and lonely, and the duty boring. Nevertheless, the sharply conflicting territorial claims and the continued activity of the French priest Le Loutre, who incited the nearby Micmac Indians to harass British settlers, left no doubt that Nova Scotia presented a problem of truly serious proportions.[7]

The burden of imperial defense in the province of New York was borne by Governor George Clinton, like his counterpart in New France a naval officer of high rank. Since 1743 Clinton had carried this heavy responsibility, often handicapped by the penurious policy of his own legislature which seemed more determined to diminish the governor's power than to save the province from the French. The struggle between Clinton and his assembly was especially intense during the period from 1746 to 1750, with the legislative branch habitually withholding funds desperately needed for New York's defense and the furtherance of good relations with the Six Nations. Although Clinton lacked the important qualities of a first-class political leader, he saw more clearly than many the critical importance of New York's traditional tie with the Iroquois, the role of the fur trade in that relationship, and the urgency of securing the frontiers by building forts at strategic points to forestall the French. No doubt Clinton's awareness of these important matters was largely the result of the tutelage he received from knowledgeable men in the colony, Cadwallader Colden and William Johnson in particular. The former was a longtime councilor, scientist, and student of Indian affairs; the latter a tall, handsome Mohawk Valley trader, land speculator, and trusted friend of the Iroquois. Since 1746 Johnson had been New York's principal agent in dealing with the Six Nations, a position of crucial importance in view of the inroads of French Catholic influence among those tribes and the strategic necessity for keeping them attached to the British interest.

As Governor Clinton viewed the northern frontier, he was painfully aware of danger from two directions: the Champlain Valley and Lake Ontario. The former gave great concern to New England as well, for the French continued to hold Fort St. Frédéric at Crown Point near the southern end of Lake Champlain, a base of operations which permitted them to strike eastward into New England and southward toward the Hudson Valley. Crown Point controlled the strategic Champlain Valley route between Montreal and Albany, important in peacetime for the flow of furs and trading goods and in wartime for the advance of invading armies. Lake Ontario was at least of equal importance, for it not only gave the French a backdoor approach to the Mohawk Valley fur route and the lands of the Iroquois Confederacy, but also served as a vital link in the French chain of communication with the distant West and Louisiana. It is no exaggeration to say that whoever controlled Lake Ontario would eventually dominate the Six Nations, gain the lion's share of the western fur trade, and in all probability win supremacy in much of the vast region north of the Ohio River.

After 1748, the French vigorously embarked upon a program of fort building and the complementary activity of seducing important groups of Indians from their ties with the British. This gave cause for deep concern to Clinton, who had his own hands partially tied by his recalcitrant legislature. As William Johnson observed in 1749, it was "a standing Maxim" with the French "to be before hand—Those that fortify first in the Indian Country are not molested unless in war time. . . ." [8] Although writing nearly two years later, Cadwallader Colden seemed to be completing Johnson's rueful line of thought when he commented, "The English only complain and expostulate with the Governor of Canada or the Court of France; The French give amusing or evasive answers, but still go on with their works, and in pursuing their grand design, till they shall have brought their work to such perfection, that they can without fear avow their Intention." [9]

Fort Frontenac, at the northeastern corner of Lake Ontario near the entrance to the upper St. Lawrence, was complemented in 1750 and 1751 by the construction of a French fort 150 miles farther west, where the trade routes from Lake Huron and Georgian Bay emerged on the western shore of Lake Ontario. This new post, known as Fort Toronto, was well situated to block at least some of the flow of western peltry toward the British post at Oswego.[10] Even more important in French long-range strategic thinking was their fortification of Niagara, guarding the vital water route and portage between Lake Ontario and Lake Erie. Facilities for trading had existed here for many years, guarded by log palisades. Now the French, hoping to prevent the British and hostile Iroquois from ever taking over that most advantageous location, built what one contemporary described as "a strong and regular Fortification of Stone." [11] Thus was secured an essential gateway for the further expansion of French influence in the West as well as continued communication between New France and Louisiana. In June of 1751, Governor Clinton took pains to inform Governor La Jonquière of New France that Niagara was Iroquois territory and therefore British; but the French governor simply restated what his predecessors had been insisting for many years, that the Six Nations were not subjects of the British crown. "A Peice of unparalled Effronteree" was what Clinton labeled this routine denial, but there was little he could do to erase what seemed to him and many others a mounting threat to British interests in the West.[12]

Clinton's apprehension as he looked toward the frontiers of his province was fed also by the extremely unsettled state of Indian relations. When the Pennsylvania frontiersman Conrad Weiser paid a visit to the Iroquois country in 1750 he found the pro-French faction clearly in the ascendance, especially among the three westernmost tribes.[13] There was no doubt that the Iroquois were being deeply affected by the dual pressure of intimidation and enticement being exerted upon them by French officials and missionaries. In 1749 a Sulpician priest, François Picquet, had founded a new Indian mission called La Présentation where the Oswegatchie River flows north into the St. Lawrence. This was just above

Iroquois country, and clearly intended to draw disaffected Iroquois into the French orbit, as the mission at Caughnawaga had been doing for many years. Father Picquet was an ardent promoter not only of the Roman faith but of French imperial interests as well, a fact which Governor Duquesne, La Jonquière's successor, doubtless had in mind when he wrote that "the mission of M. l'Abbé Picquet succeeds admirably. This is to be attributed to the talent of that missionary in civilizing the Indians and molding them to his ends." [14]

Clinton's feud with his legislature had severely restricted the flow of public funds so necessary if the Indians were to be kept contented and their lands adequately protected against hostile Indians, the French, and New York's own greedy land speculators. Disgusted with such a handicap, William Johnson had resigned as principal agent for Indian affairs, and there was no one fully qualified to take his place. Certainly no other New Yorker would be quite so acceptable to the chiefs of the Six Nations, who favored Johnson because, as they said, "he has large Ears and heareth a great deal, and what he hears he tells to us; he also has Large Eyes and sees a great way, and conceals nothing from us." [15] In short, they trusted him, and he more than any other man stood a chance of preventing the Iroquois from drifting into the French camp. Facing the Indian problem squarely, Clinton in 1751 sought to convene an intercolonial conference of Indians and whites for the purpose of seeking remedies to their mutual problems. New York's own legislature gave little practical support, and the response from other colonies also was disappointing. Only three—Massachusetts, Connecticut, and South Carolina—sent delegates to meet with Clinton, the leaders of the Six Nations, and a half-dozen Catawba chiefs. The principal achievement was a patched-up peace between the Iroquois and the Catawbas, hopefully bringing to an end the Iroquois war raids into the South that had been so disturbing to the Carolina frontier. Unfortunately, this proved illusory. By the summer of 1753 hostile raiders from the North were again active along the southern frontier, revealing both the extent of French influence among these Indians and the futility of British endeavors to weld a solid phalanx of friendly tribes.[16]

This failure was of direct concern to Governor James Glen of South Carolina, who bore much of the heavy responsibility of promoting British imperial interests throughout a vast wilderness area extending from the southern ridges of the Appalachians to French Louisiana and Spanish Florida. Having wrestled since 1743 with complicated problems of frontier advance, the fur trade, and relations with the various tribes of the Southeast, this conscientious, rather legalistic Scot considered himself an expert in such matters and was inclined to be resentful when other men tried to intervene, especially in the affairs of South Carolina's own Indians. With almost brutal frankness Glen once informed another British governor, whom he considered a rival, that South Carolina was "jealous of any other Colonies intermedling [with] our Indians," concluding with the observation that the other governor still had much to learn about Indian affairs.[17] There is no doubt of Glen's diligence as a governor and his sincere concern for the British cause in America. Like Shirley and Clinton, he recognized the danger of French intrigue and expansion, to which was added, in Glen's area, the lingering heritage of Spanish hostility.

The problem of rival imperialism and Indian relations on the southern frontier was every bit as complicated as the corresponding situation in the North, so that Glen had little occasion for ease. One of his major objectives, comparable to Clinton's unrealized goal, was to bring into harmonious relations all tribes considered to be pro-British by ending their seemingly endless squabbles. Of particular concern was the continuing warfare between the two major tribes of the Southeast—the Creeks and the Cherokees. The French in Louisiana, of course, were not averse to fishing in these troubled waters. Having regained effective domination over the faction-ridden Choctaws in 1750, they proceeded to extend their influence eastward the next year by rebuilding Fort Toulouse. Soon the French, and the Spaniards as well, were enjoying increased success in their dealings with the Creeks. Although the Cherokees, like the Six Nations in the North, were traditionally aligned with the British, this pattern too was beginning to crack under the combined pressure of the French advance, the hostility of the Creeks, and continuing difficulties with Carolina. Glen did his best to hold the loyalty of the Cherokee chiefs, but the Indians themselves were divided, with some definitely leaning toward the French. As a means of increasing its influence, South Carolina in 1753 constructed Fort Prince George on the Keowee River near the Cherokee country. This may have been helpful to the traders, but it seemed to have little effect in slowing the advance of French influence. The Cherokees as well as the Creeks remained divided, and Glen's hope for Indian unity in the British interest appeared to be as ill founded as the similar hope cherished by Clinton.[18]

And what of the great central region of the Appalachian West, the extensive, attractive frontier area of Pennsylvania and Virginia? Here the crucial factor was the intensifying three-way rivalry among the French, the Pennsylvanians, and the Virginians for predominant influence among the Indians of that area, for domination of the fur trade, for control of the strategic water and forest routes, and for the land itself. Just west of the Appalachian barrier the Monongahela River glides slowly northward to meet the waters of the turbulent Allegheny River flowing swiftly down from the land of the Senecas. They join at what is known as the Forks of the Ohio, from which point their mingled waters run west and southwest as the Ohio River, eventually to pour themselves into the great Mississippi. Although potentially an important connecting route between New France and Louisiana, the Allegheny-Ohio waterway had been relatively neglected by the French, who generally followed the more western routes, especially those of the Wabash and the Illinois. Fur traders from Pennsylvania, on the other hand, had been increasingly active along the Allegheny and upper Ohio, and Virginians too were contending now for the economic advantages of that area.[19]

Much of this same central region was claimed by the Six Nations of the Iroquois Confederacy who, through the agency of a sort of vicegerent known as the Half King, exercised a fatherly authority over the various groups of Indians residing there. The latter for the most part were recent migrants from other areas—Mingos, Delawares, and Shawnees. Their principal village, known to the English as "Logstown," was located on the north bank of the Ohio River approximately 18 miles below the Forks. Here in this important trading center were congregated Indians of all three groups. Other villages of Mingos and Delawares were found along the banks of the river for miles below, while the greater part of the Shawnee people dwelled along the lower reaches of the Scioto River farther to the west. Like the Iroquois and the Cherokees, the tribes of the upper Ohio knew the tension of internal pro-French and pro-British factionalism. Fortunately for the British cause, however, the Half King himself was strongly inclined against the French, and the groups under his jurisdiction in general were enjoying the material advantages of British trade.[20]

With no international boundary agreements, both the French and the British sought to claim and exercise jurisdiction over the entire central West. French claims rested primarily upon the explorations of La Salle in the 1670s. British claims were more diverse, deriving from royal grants in the charters of several colonies, which in turn depended upon the royal claim to a large segment of North America by virtue of the Cabot voyages. In addition, the British argued that the Six Nations were subjects of the crown, as France had admitted in the Treaty of Utrecht, and that much of the Ohio Valley had come under Iroquois jurisdiction by conquest, with the Six Nations in turn conveying large portions of the region to certain British colonies and companies in a series of treaties. Both the British and the French insisted that their people had been active in the area for many years, mostly engaged in peaceful commerce with the Indians. Theoretically, it should have been possible to settle the dispute by negotiation, but in actuality such agreement was highly unlikely. There was no meaningful or justifiable natural boundary anywhere between the Appalachian Mountains and the Mississippi River, for the entire West was a vast unitary drainage basin all of whose water routes led inexorably to French territory along the lower Mississippi and the Gulf. Geography demanded that the whole region belong to one people or the other; if unnaturally divided between them, there was little possibility of peace.

Obviously, whoever managed to gain firm control of the area at the Forks of the Ohio would be in a position to dominate the central West. Each of the principal contenders—New France, Pennsylvania, Virginia—had direct access to a route leading to the Forks, New France by way of Lake Erie and the Allegheny River, Pennsylvania by a system of trading paths across the Appalachian Mountains, Virginia by way of the Potomac River and either a trading path or the Youghiogheny River. These three rival routes converged on the Forks from the north, the east, and the southeast respectively. In 1748, none of the contenders was effectively established at the junction of the Allegheny and Monongahela rivers; the only settlement there was an Indian village known as Shannopins Town frequented by the rival traders. By this time, however, the French were coming to the painful realization that if either Virginia or Pennsylvania made good its claim and effectively occupied the Forks, the British would have driven a sharpened wedge into the weak midsection of France's North American empire. Conversely, effective French occupation would seriously disrupt the extensive British fur trade and block further British westward expansion.

There is ample evidence to illustrate the growing concern of both sides as they contemplated the power vacuum in the upper Ohio Valley. "This country," wrote one British imperialist,

> lying in the middle space between their settlements in *Canada* and *Louisiana* . . . and at the back also of our middle colonies, would give them an opportunity not only of joining their two very distant plantations . . . but also of preventing us from extending our settlements backward beyond the great mountains towards the *Mississippi,* and of attacking them on that side. It would farther strengthen them and weaken us, by putting it in their power to gain the *Indians* of that large country over to their interest, some of whom . . . are very numerous and warlike.[21]

"The river Ohio and the rivers which fall into it unquestionably belong to France," insisted the French minister of marine. "It was discovered by M. de la Salle; since then we have always had trading posts there, and our possession of it has been all the more continuous since it is the most used communication between Canada and Louisiana." [22] Another concerned French official pointed out that "if the English were to establish themselves there it would give them entry into all our posts and would open to them the way to Mexico." [23] Summarizing the official French view, a memorandum of 1751 notes that "It is not a question of acting against the Indians. It is a question of checking illicit trade carried on by the English in a country that belongs to us, and which they had not ventured to dispute with us before the last war, and of discouraging at the same time any notions they may have of making settlements there."[24] Thus an area that in 1748 was inhabited only by Indians and a few roaming traders had become the prime objective for the converging expansionist ambitions of three rival states.

One other Indian tribe not yet mentioned was adding to French concern—the Miamis (or Twightwees, as they often were called by the British). In 1748 a large segment of this western tribe, under the leadership of a strongly pro-British chief known as La Demoiselle or Old Briton, had migrated southward down the Miami River, away from French influence, to establish on the west bank of the river a new village called Pickawillany. Old Briton was eager to welcome British traders to his new settlement, and soon the Pennsylvanians were frequenting Pickawillany, trading with the Miamis for peltry, even constructing their own huts and store-houses there. This meant a strong upsurge of British influence some 250 miles west of the Appalachian barrier, deep in country which the French strongly claimed and considered vital to their own interests.[25] To make matters worse, from the French point of view, it was reported that Old Briton was "doing everything pos-sible at the solicitation of the English to draw to his side the tribes of the Wabash. . . ." still farther west. "If the post on Great Miami River [Pickawillany] remains for only a little longer," was the gloomy prediction, "the English will succeed in winning over the Wabash tribes . . . and little by little those of the Missouri, which would occasion . . . the loss of the trade of Canada and the com-munication by way of the Mississippi River." [26]

There was yet another reason for the French to be uneasy about their future in the West. About the time that Old Briton was founding Pickawillany, a small group of Virginia investors was in the process of organizing the Ohio Company for the purpose of acquiring and settling a tract in the vicinity of the Forks. In larger perspective, this represented an attempt to wrest the fur trade from Pennsylvania and make good Virginia's claim to the Ohio Valley. The crown was favorably inclined, with the result that in 1749 the company was authorized to receive from the colony of Virginia a tract of 200,000 acres in the disputed area. On the upper Potomac River at the mouth of Wills Creek, the new company established a small advance post from which a route could be cut through the mountain passes to the Forks of the Ohio.

Already the French had begun to react. In June 1749 a force of some 200 French and 30 Indians commanded by Captain Pierre-Joseph Céloron de Blainville headed west from Lachine, its destina-tion the Ohio Valley. Céloron's mission was to reaffirm French sovereignty in the area, chase off any British interlopers including the enterprising traders from Pennsylvania, and if possible win the local Indians away from their alignment with the British colonies.[27] Following the portage route from Lake Erie to Lake Chautauqua, the French force made its way by canoe to the Allegheny and thence down to the Ohio, burying at the mouth of various important streams lead markers with an inscription setting forth in no uncertain terms the claim of France.[28] As Céloron proceeded along his predetermined route, he could see that the French had much opposition to overcome, thanks to the powerful influence of the British traders in the area. Many of the local Indians, fearing French reprisals, fled at the approach of Céloron's force, while others who remained to parley displayed a disturbing truculence. As he conferred with Indian leaders at various points along his route down the Ohio and up the Miami River, Céloron found them obviously reluctant to abandon their advantageous trade relations with the British. Encountering some of these traders, the French commander peremptorily ordered them out of the country, and because of the temporary presence of French military power the traders had no choice but to obey. Céloron then continued back to the Great Lakes by way of the Maumee River, and so to Montreal.[29] Having taken the measure of the problem in this way, the French authorities now were convinced that if their claim was to be upheld it would have to be done through forceful policing of the Ohio Valley.

The year after Céloron's expedition, the French began foreclosing on the warning they had given by actually arresting and confining British traders found west of the Appalachians. These traders, it was charged, were not only trespassing on territory belonging to the French crown, but also subverting the Indians of the area.[30] Indian sentiment was made clear at the Logstown conference of May 1751, when delegations from the Iroquois tribes, the Delawares, the Shawnees, the Hurons and the Miamis gathered to hear the rival appeals and proposals of French and British colonial agents. Speaking for the French was Philippe Thomas Joncaire (sometimes known to the British as Jean Cour), a Canadian half-breed who had long been developing a powerful influence among the Senecas. Representing Pennsylvania were the experienced trader and frontiersman George Croghan and the interpreter Andrew Montour. It was a dramatic confrontation, requiring courage and skill on the part of the white contenders. From the beginning the advantage seems to have been all with the British. When Joncaire pressed the assembled Indian leaders for a commitment to exclude the British traders from the Ohio Valley, as Céloron had previously requested, an Iroquois chief gave an unequivocal answer that was not of the kind the Frenchman had hoped to hear. "I now tell you from our Hearts we will not," were his words as Croghan later reported them, "for we ourselves brought them here to trade with us, and they shall live among us as long as there is one of us alive. . . . Our Brothers are the People we will trade with and not you." [31] Later the Indians even went so far as to request that a British fort be constructed on the Ohio River for their protection. This was an opportunity that was declined by the Pennsylvania assembly, whereupon the initiative in the Ohio Valley began to shift rapidly from Pennsylvania to Virginia. Fearing the threat of French retaliation and recognizing that little or no actual protection would be forthcoming from pacifistic Pennsylvania, the Indians were coming to rely more and more upon the strength of Virginia. In June of 1752, the Six Nations granted that colony the right not only to construct fortified trading posts in the upper Ohio Valley, but also to plant settlements in the area south of the river.[32]

Versailles, in the meantime, anxious to avoid a disastrous conflict with the western Indians, had formulated a new policy embodied in the official instructions issued to the Marquis Duquesne, who was preparing to sail for Canada as La Jonquière's successor. Duquesne was to cancel the old program of trying to intimidate the tribes; instead, he was to concentrate on further discouraging the British traders, while at the same time enlarging the French presence in the area and doing everything possible to entice the Indians into the French orbit.[33] Unfortunately, the new governor arrived in the colony too late to prevent an act of open aggression apparently authorized by La Jonquière. Céloron and other French leaders had recommended the destruction of Pickawillany as a means of weakening British influence among the western tribes and recovering some measure of prestige for France.[34] Accordingly, in June of 1752, long before Duquesne arrived with the new instructions, a war party of about 240 Miami-hating Chippewas and Ottawas was gathered at Detroit under the command of the half-breed trader Charles Michel de Langlade. Proceeding southward, they arrived near Pickawillany at a time when most of the able-bodied Miami warriors were away on the hunt acquiring more peltry to trade with their British friends. Langlade's determined party attacked the fortified village on 21 June 1752, surprised the hapless inhabitants, and soon was in full control. Among those

who died in this affair were Old Briton himself and one of the
British traders; five other white men were taken captive. Not satisfied with gloating over the sachem's corpse, Langlade's warriors
celebrated their triumph by preparing a cannibal feast with Old
Briton himself cooked to suit their taste. They also slaughtered the
traders' packhorses and burned down the traders' huts before
heading back north with their British prisoners and a large quantity of plunder.[35]

The successful blow against Pickawillany had far-ranging repercussions. Thoroughly cowed, the Miami survivors abandoned their
village, many of them migrating up to the Maumee River where
they placed themselves again under French influence. Pickawillany,
which had burgeoned so amazingly in only four years under the
stimulus of British trade, now lay a deserted ruin, while the trade
itself sank into decay through a large part of the upper Ohio
Valley. Pennsylvania and Virginia traders understandably were
extremely hesitant to risk valuable stocks of goods, to say nothing
of their lives, within striking range of the revitalized French and
their fierce Indian allies. The surprise destruction of Pickawillany
in June 1752 was a major turning point in the Anglo-French struggle for domination of the West, and now, it seemed, the advantage
was shifting definitely toward New France.

Any lingering complacency among the British colonists was
obliterated in 1753 when Quebec set in motion a definite program
for seizing and fortifying the line of communication from Lake
Erie to the upper Ohio. Although apparently not designed at
Versailles, this program was in accord with new official policy as
laid down in the instructions given to Governor Duquesne. The
endeavor of Céloron in 1749 was to be completed by finally expell-
ing all British traders from the Ohio Valley. A large expeditionary
force was to seize and hold the Lake Erie portage route to the
Allegheny River, fortifying that vital approach to the upper Ohio.
Then an advance was-to be made to the Ohio itself, "La Belle
Rivière," with another fort being constructed at Logstown below
the Forks, and still another at the mouth of the Scioto River.
French garrisons stationed at all these posts would keep the English
out of the area and, hopefully, regain the allegiance of the Indians
by protecting a renewed French trade.[36]

The first units of the expeditionary force, some 250 troops under
Lieutenant Charles Deschamps de Boishébert, started west "by

Land and Ice" on 1 February 1753, with the assignment of gaining a firm foothold at the Lake Erie end of the portage route to the Ohio.[37] They proceeded by way of Fort Frontenac, Fort Toronto, and Niagara, following a route that kept them well clear of Oswego. Other units began their westward journey in April when the weather was more favorable, and these did not escape observation. At midnight on 19 April, a band of "whooping and hollowing" Iroquois aroused William Johnson at his dwelling in the Mohawk Valley to tell him of a large French force, "about twelve Hundred, besides the Battoe Men," with "a great many officers and young gentlemen . . ." proceeding up the St. Lawrence toward the Great Lakes.[38] Once it became certain that this ominous movement of French power was not directed against the homeland of the Six Nations, as the Iroquois at first feared, colonial leaders realized that what was about to occur was a French occupation of the upper Ohio Valley, where the British had as yet not a single fortified post to block the menacing tide.[39]

Commanding the hundreds of French and Canadian soldiers, bateaumen, and Indians was the Sieur de Marin, assisted by other chosen officers including the Chevalier François Le Mercier, an engineer whose principal assignment was to supervise the siting and construction of the proposed forts. The first of these forts, Presqu'île, was erected at a small bay on the south shore of Lake Erie where the city of Erie, Pennsylvania, now stands. Then, leaving a garrison to hold this new post, Marin proceeded to clear a wagon road south to the Rivière aux Boeufs, a tributary of the Allegheny River. Near the former, in what is now Waterford, Pennsylvania, the army began the construction of Fort Le Boeuf. While this work was in progress, an advance detachment of about fifty men was sent forward some 50 miles to the junction of the Rivière aux Boeufs and the Allegheny where, at a place called Venango, they found and occupied the trading post of the Pennsylvania trader John Frazier. The wagon road south from Presqu'île was completed to Fort Le Boeuf, but from there to Venango and beyond, the French were forced to rely upon the natural water route and forest trails.

Watching these developments with the utmost concern was the royal governor of Virginia, Robert Dinwiddie, a portly Scot and a veteran of many years in the colonial service. Dinwiddie's concern was both official and personal, for not only was he chief executive of a royal colony but also a stockholder of the Ohio Company and therefore financially interested in the future of the Forks.[40] At this very time he was awaiting approval by the Board of Trade of a plan he had submitted for the construction of several Virginia forts in the upper Ohio Valley, and the Ohio Company itself had intentions of building one fort in the vicinity of the Forks.[41] In contrast with what Marin was actually accomplishing, this represented nothing more than wishful thinking—too little and too late. On 11 August 1753, William Trent, one of Virginia's agents in the West, advised Dinwiddie that

> The Eyes of all the Indians are fixed upon you[.] you have it now in your Power with a small Expense to save this whole Country for his Majesty, but if the Opportunity is missed it will never be in the Power of the English to recover it but by a great Expence and the United Force of all the Colonies. The French have already built a Fort on Lake Erie, and another is partly finished on a little Lake, which is at the Head of French or Venango Creek [Rivière aux Boeufs]. . . . From Venango They propose to proceed down the Ohio, to build a Fort in the Fork, made by that River and the Monongehela. They tell the Indians in all their Speeches that they will drive the English over the Allegany [sic] Mountains.[42]

Fortunately for the British colonies, even as Trent was writing his letter of warning the French advance was beginning to lose its frightening momentum, and Marin himself was losing his confidence. Vital supplies were running low and many of the men were becoming seriously, even fatally ill as a result of their inadequate diet and forced labor in the heat of summer. Altogether several hundred of them died, and large numbers of those remaining were rendered unfit for strenuous duty.[43] A badly needed shipment of provisions was sent from the Illinois country under military escort in September, but was never seen by the army. The escorting detachment, encountering difficulties of its own, had cached it in the wilderness. Adding to Marin's problems was the declining depth of water in the streams as the result of sparse rainfall, an important factor in any further advance.[44] In what must have been an agonizing reappraisal of plans and intentions, the leaders of the expedition finally decided not to proceed to the Forks in 1753, but to leave garrisons at Venango, Fort Le Boeuf, and Fort Presqu'île to hold open the route already won by such hard labor. The majority of the men in the expedition would return to Montreal. By the time this decision was reached, Marin himself was approaching his own end. The man to whom New France had entrusted its great hope for the Ohio Valley died at lonely Fort Le Boeuf on 29 October 1753.[45]

When the French failed to exploit their newfound advantage to the full by occupying and fortifying the Forks, they gave the British one last chance to forestall a complete French takeover. Presumably that chance would expire sometime during the late spring of 1754. As it happened, certain developments on the British side were just now approaching maturity, so that action at last was becoming possible. Of greatest importance was the fact that the ministry in London, stimulated by the cries of alarm pouring from the American colonies, finally was moved to endorse some positive action even at the risk of war. On 28 August 1753, the secretary of state for the Southern Department issued a set of guidelines for colonial governors attempting to confront the French advance. After detecting an intrusion upon British territory by the French, a governor first was "to represent the injustice of such proceeding, and to require them forthwith to desist from any such unlawful undertaking." However, if this formal warning did not suffice to prevent the intruders from occupying and holding British territory, then the governor whose colony was being invaded was to "draw forth the armed Force of the Province, and . . . repell force by force."[46] Other colonies were expected to provide help in such a situation. These official instructions are noteworthy for their insistence upon a defensive response. The governors were required to avoid all semblance of aggression on their part, confining their military activity to a defense of territory clearly within the boundaries of a British colony. In actuality, this included much valuable territory which France, with equal firmness, was claiming as her own.

It was late in October when the royal instructions came to the hand of Governor Dinwiddie in Williamsburg. Time was now more precious than ever. The first thing to do was give the French, now established on the Allegheny River, their formal warning, so that the way would be clear for more forceful measures if necessary. Certainly Dinwiddie cannot have entertained for a moment any serious hope that a word of rebuke from him would send the French army scurrying back to Canada. Rather, the letter of warning that he addressed to the French commandant on 31 October

1753 was a diplomatic gesture, a required prelude to the inevitable moves and countermoves, perhaps even skirmishes and battles, that almost certainly would follow.[47] The task of carrying this important letter from Williamsburg to the Allegheny and then returning with the French reply, a 900-mile journey through a wintry wilderness, required a messenger of undoubted stamina and steadfast courage as well as reliability. An ordinary rough-and-ready frontiersman would hardly do, as the mission involved not only dealing with Indians both friendly and hostile, but also possible face-to-face discussions with shrewd and experienced French officers. The ability to influence Indians favorably was a much-needed qualification, for a secondary purpose of the mission was to prevent, if possible, the further spread of pro-French sentiment among the Indians of the disputed area. Finally, too, the messenger should have a soldier's eye for noting geographical features of strategic importance as well as the actual location and strength of any French fortifications. The volunteer to whom Dinwiddie confided the heavy responsibility of such a mission was a tall, slender, twenty-one-year-old major in the Virginia militia, George Washington.[48]

Leaving Williamsburg on 31 October, Washington formed his party as he went. His own knowledge of the French language being totally inadequate, he secured the services of an interpreter, Jacob Van Braam. At Wills Creek he added the experienced woodsman Christopher Gist and four servants. The group was slowed by soggy, snow-covered ground, and did not reach the first trading post, Frazier's on the Monongahela River, until 22 November. Here they learned of Marin's death and the withdrawal of the greater part of his army. At the Forks, Washington paused to assess the terrain and was favorably impressed. The angle of land formed by the conjunction of the Allegheny River flowing in from the northeast and the Monongahela from the southeast he described as "extremely well situated for a Fort, as it has the absolute Command of both Rivers. The Land at the Point is 20 or 25 Feet above the common Surface of the Water, and a considerable Bottom of flat, well-timbered Land all around it, very convenient for Building." [49] Next the party proceeded to the Indian settlement of Logstown. Here Washington had a conference with the Half King who, having himself gone to Fort Le Boeuf only a few weeks earlier to protest against the French intrusion and been treated with contempt, was glad to tell the Virginian all he knew about the location and nature of the French works.

On the morning of 30 November, after an unavoidable delay of several days, Washington resumed his northward journey, this time with the Half King and several other friendly Indians in company. The party reached Venango on 4 December and found the old trading post occupied by Joncaire and two other French officers, who indicated that their commander was at Fort Le Boeuf 50 miles farther upriver. With admirable courtesy Joncaire invited Washington to dinner; the invitation was more than welcome after the days and nights of rough living along the trail. Washington later recalled that his hosts resorted rather freely to the bottle, which little by little dissolved their discretion until at last they bluntly asserted "That it was their absolute Design to take Possession of the *Ohio,* and by G— they would do it." [50] The English, they explained to their properly self-restrained and dignified young guest, simply were too slow to do anything about it. From Washington's point of view, it must have been quite an evening. For the next two days Joncaire strove to subvert the Half King and the other Indians in Washington's party, causing the Virginian no little concern, for the clever half-breed's reputation for influence among the Indians was well known. Washington was glad when he was able to resume his journey on 7 December.

Again there was much foul weather, rain and snow, which mired the way. Arriving at Fort Le Boeuf on the eleventh, Washington delivered Dinwiddie's letter to the French commander, Le Gardeur de Saint-Pierre, the following day. Then for two days Washington found himself at leisure while awaiting the reply, during which time he was able to examine the fortification and ascertain the approximate number of canoes and boats available for the use of a French army the following spring. On the evening of the fourteenth, he was given the commander's written answer. It was a cool reply, formally courteous and firm. Dinwiddie's letter, Saint-Pierre promised, would be transmitted to Governor Duquesne. "As to the Summons you send me to retire," continued the commander of Fort Le Boeuf, "I do not think myself obliged to obey it; whatever may be your Instructions, I am here by Virtue of the Orders of my General; and . . . am determin'd to conform myself to them with all the Exactness and Resolution which can be expected from the best Officer." [51] This, of course, was exactly what any competent French officer would have said and exactly what Dinwiddie must have anticipated. But at least the royal insistence upon a warning to the French prior to any hostile counteraction had been obeyed. Now Virginia was free to act whenever the threat from the north reappeared.

At Fort Le Boeuf the French again exerted themselves in various ways to undermine the loyalty of the Half King and the other Indians, while Washington sought desperately to counteract this influence. His mind was not easy on this account until at last on 16 December he and his party embarked in canoes for the first leg of the homeward journey. On the day after Christmas Washington, impatient with the slow progress being made through the wintry wilderness and exceedingly anxious to deliver Saint-Pierre's reply to Dinwiddie, divided the party. He and Christopher Gist would push on alone by the quickest route, while the others came along as best they could. During the next few days Washington and his staunch companion twice came close to death, the first time when an Indian suddenly fired on them, and again while trying to cross the ice-clogged Allegheny River on a hastily constructed raft. Finally on 16 January, completing "as fatiguing a Journey as it is possible to conceive," Washington arrived back in Williamsburg, where he hurried to the governor with news of his experience and the reply from Saint-Pierre.[52]

Even before Washington's return, the Ohio Company had dispatched men and supplies for the construction of an outpost at the Forks of the Ohio.[53] Obviously this was an attempt to be the first in actual occupation of the area, feeble though the gesture might be. When Washington returned with clear evidence that the French intended to advance to the Forks and beyond the following spring, Dinwiddie realized that something more than a feeble gesture was urgently required. He decided to get the House of Burgesses into session as quickly as possible, so that the funds necessary for sustained military activity on the distant frontier might be forthcoming. What the aroused governor now had in mind was a full-scale intercolonial expedition to meet the impending French thrust, in accordance with the royal instructions. To his fellow governors from New England to the Carolinas, he sent letters announcing his plan for a rendezvous at Wills Creek early in March. "It certainly is of the last Consequence to be as expeditious as possible," Dinwiddie prodded, "especially, as the French design to be at Ohio early in the Spring with a more considerable Number than they had there in the Fall, which then Amounted to 1500." [54] Impetuously, without waiting for the approval of Governor Glen of South Carolina, he approached the Catawbas and Cherokees directly, asking them to send warriors for the expedition.

The most immediate problem, however, was the possibility that an armed force of French and Indians might arrive at the Forks before Virginia's little fort could be completed. To meet this contingency, Dinwiddie authorized William Trent, an experienced trader and frontiersman then in the West, to recruit immediately a company of troops from among the trading fraternity. This company was to assemble as soon as possible at the Forks in order to give protection to the men working on the fort. In the meantime, George Washington began raising a second company in Frederick and Augusta counties, with the intention of hastening to Trent's support. Apathetic Virginians showed little enthusiasm for these almost frantic preparations. The militia as such could not be used because the question of whether the area of the Forks lay within Virginia's boundaries remained undetermined, a question which Dinwiddie apparently had chosen to ignore when he embarked upon his program for blocking the French advance. Volunteers were hard to find, and Washington had great difficulty raising his authorized company of a hundred men. "You may, with almost equal success, attempt to raise the dead," he complained.[55] Even the House of Burgesses was hesitant to support the governor's belligerent program. Some members were inclined to believe, not without cause, that he was acting primarily in the interests of the Ohio Company which, after all, was only the most prominent among several organized groups speculating in western lands. The financial backing finally provided was accordingly stinted.[56] Nor was the response from the other British colonies any more heartening. As usual, colonial particularism frustrated the hope for united action, so that with the significant exception of several independent companies of regulars dispatched from South Carolina and New York, the burden of defending the region immediately threatened by the French advance fell almost entirely on Virginia.

The volunteers raised in Virginia for the expedition were organized as a regiment under Colonel Joshua Fry with Washington, now commissioned a lieutenant colonel, as second-in-command. Not until 2 April 1754, was Washington able to lead his little body of troops out of Alexandria and west toward the Ohio Company's base at Wills Creek. Arriving at Winchester about eight days later, they were joined by an additional company which brought the total strength to approximately 160 men. Washington made every effort to impress wagons and teams in sufficient quantities to meet the supply problem of the growing expedition, but his success was minimal. The animals he did obtain were old and tired and the wagons too few. Again the populace had demonstrated its unwillingness to make heavy sacrifices in a dubious cause. When at last Washington resumed his westward advance about the eighteenth of April, only a dozen wagons creaking under their loads of provisions, tools, ammunition, and miscellaneous gear went along with his three companies.[57]

In the meantime, work on the fort at the Forks was proceeding under the protection of Trent's understrength company of less than three dozen men. Trent himself journeyed east to Wills Creek for additional supplies, leaving his brother-in-law, Ensign Edward Ward, in command at the Forks. On 13 April, Ward received the dreaded information that a French force was coming down the river toward his position. The next day he sent this intelligence along to Trent, and went himself to seek the assistance of his immediate superior, Lieutenant John Frazier, who then was in residence at Turtle Creek, some 8 or 10 miles away. When Frazier declined to return to the Forks and take command of the defense, Ward did so, but his hasty preparations were hopeless in the face of overwhelming strength.[58] A large French force commanded by Captain Claude-Pierre Pécaudy de Contrecoeur arrived in the vicinity of the uncompleted fort on 17 April, and without firing a shot easily forced the Virginians to abandon the site. In this way New France gained possession of the most important strategic location in the upper Ohio Valley, seriously challenging British aspirations for a future in the West. Without delay, the French troops began building a stronghold of their own at the junction of the Allegheny and Monongahela rivers, naming it Fort Duquesne after the governor of their expanding colony.[59] Washington, still en route with reinforcements, learned of the disaster on 20 April. Two days later he heard the sorry story from Ward's own lips. The defeated ensign also conveyed to Washington a significant message from the Half King addressed to the governors of Virginia and Pennsylvania, in which the Indian leader earnestly appealed for assistance against the French. "If you do not come to our aid soon," he warned, "it is all over with us, and I think that we shall never be able to meet together again." [60] The West, with its rich supply of furs and its millions of acres of virgin land, was in imminent danger of being lost by the Ohio Company, by Virginia, and by the British empire.

With Contrecoeur in actual possession of the Forks, the Virginians were forced to redesign their entire plan of operation. The decision reached by Washington and his officers was to advance as far as the junction of Redstone Creek and the Monongahela River, 30 miles south of the Forks, where a base could be established in preparation for a later drive to expel the French. Comparing the weakness of the force available to Washington with the assumed strength and capability of Contrecoeur's army, this involved a very large risk. Not to attempt it, however, would have meant leaving the French completely free to consolidate their positions beyond the mountains, while retaining for Virginia no advantageous ground from which to launch an offensive in the future. So a fateful decision was reached.

The first essential task was to clear a track from Wills Creek across 60 miles of ridged and forested wilderness to the mouth of Redstone Creek, so that wagons and artillery could pass readily to the proposed base. Fortunately, several years earlier a trail traversing this area had been laid out for the use of the Ohio Company. This could now be widened into a wagon road. The army labored as it moved, clearing the trail, pushing and hauling the groaning wagons over the rough places. It was slow going. Rumors of French and Indian reinforcements and movements added to Washington's concern; and although he made some use of scouts and patrols, it was hard to discover the truth about the enemy's location and strength. Continuing forward across successive ridges of the heavily wooded Appalachians, Washington arrived on 24 May at a place known as the Great Meadows. Located about 40 miles west of Wills Creek, on the far side of Laurel Ridge, this was two-thirds of the way to their destination. It was an open vale of grassland well watered by a meandering stream, with a tributary brook joining at nearly right angles. On either side rose low-lying hills sheltering and partially enclosing this attractive spot. Washington decided to establish here a camp that might readily be developed into a way station on the road to Redstone Creek.

The men busied themselves erecting shelters along the bank of the stream, while the draft animals grazed contentedly. But there was little opportunity to enjoy the apparent peacefulness of the pastoral scene. Information derived from friendly Indians gave warning of a French force advancing to attack, and as soon as he could Washington sent out scouts, who discovered nothing. Two days later, on 27 May, Washington's old companion Christopher Gist showed up with more alarming news: The previous day a French detachment had been at his wilderness farm 12 miles north of the camp, just beyond Chestnut Ridge. Worse yet, the tracks of this party had been observed only about 5 miles from Washington's camp. That evening a message from the Half King capped the story —the Indians had discovered the place where the mysterious French force was in bivouac.[61] Now the British camp came alive, as the troops heard the shouted commands of their officers and hurried to obey. They assembled the wagons and ammunition in the most defensible position, in case the French should attack first. Washington selected a detachment of forty men, about half the total available at that time, to proceed with him at once to the Half King's camp 5 miles to the northwest on the slope of Chestnut Ridge. The night was black and rainy, the trail difficult to follow, so that it was nearly sunrise before the Virginians came upon the Indian wigwams. Seven of the men had somehow become lost, so that only thirty-three were available for action. Washington hastily conferred with the Half King, who indicated that the French were encamped in a ravine only a couple of miles to the north. Both the Indian and the Virginia commander felt sure that the enemy force, now so very close, was up to no good. Accordingly, they decided to make a joint strike.[62]

In actuality the mysterious enemy force was a reconnaissance party of about thirty-five men commanded by Ensign Joseph Coulon de Jumonville. They had been sent out from the Forks with instructions to order the Virginians off French territory and at the same time to learn as much as they could about British strength in the area, an assignment quite comparable to that of Washington the previous winter. There was, however, this difference: Jumonville and his men came as an armed force, and they took pains to conceal their movements while lurking on disputed territory. The fact is that both Jumonville and Washington were maneuvering under arms on territory presumably still being discussed by a joint international commission. England and France were not at war, yet an uncompleted British fortification had been seized by a French military force, and Washington was certain that he had official authorization to eject the French by force if he could.[63]

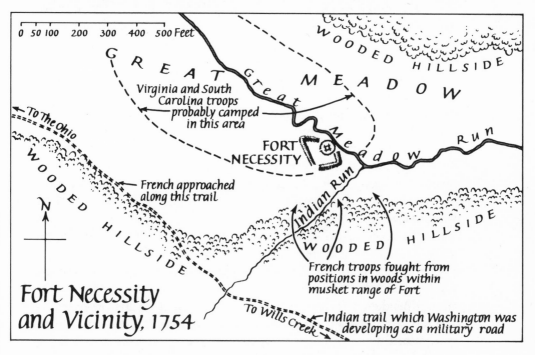

0 50 100 200 300 400 500 Feet

GREAT MEADOW

WOODED HILLSIDE

Virginia and South Carolina troops probably camped in this area

To The Ohio

Great Meadow Run

FORT NECESSITY

French approached along this trail

Run

WOODED HILLSIDE

N

Indian Run

WOODED HILLSIDE

French troops fought from positions in woods within musket range of Fort

Fort Necessity and Vicinity, 1754

To Wills Creek

Indian trail which Washington was developing as a military road

With his thirty-three soldiers and a handful of the Half King's Indians, Washington proceeded to the vicinity of the French bivouac. Approaching cautiously, he found the enemy snugly encamped in a woody glen, their backs to a bare, steep-rising rock ledge. What happened next became a matter of hot dispute. Clearly Jumonville's detachment was completely surprised, becoming aware of danger only when the British were already within musket range. The point of dispute is whether the French then attempted to parley or simply reached for their weapons. In any case, Washington took no chances, but opened fire instantly. For a quarter of an hour the bullets flew in both directions; then the French, trapped and suffering heavily, surrendered. At this, the Indians rushed in to scalp the dead and the wounded; when they had finished their bloody work, Jumonville and nearly a third of his men lay sprawled in death among the rocks and trees. One Frenchman somehow had escaped the trap to carry the news back to Fort Duquesne. All the others were made prisoners by an elated young commander who had just scored his first military victory.[64]

Even in his elation, Washington must have been fully aware of the grave consequences of his decisive action. He was nearly 50 miles away from his principal base, in an exposed position, after having opened hostilities and shed the blood of soldiers owing allegiance to the king of France. A French army believed to number a thousand or more was based only about 50 miles to the northwest, with units possibly operating much closer. Had Washington been more restrained on 28 May, actual hostilities might have been further postponed, giving Virginia more time to assemble adequate forces. Yet even if Washington had recognized Jumonville as an emissary rather than a foe, it is not likely that peace could have been preserved for long. Surely the proud young Virginian would not have obeyed Jumonville's order to withdraw, and Contrecoeur then would have been forced to exercise his option of either sending a powerful force to drive Washington away or waiting to attack the Virginians after they had arrived at Redstone Creek. At it was, Washington's aggressive action against Jumonville gave the French their justification for whatever they found necessary to do. Washington prudently called for reinforcements, sent off his prisoners to the east, and set his troops to fortifying the camp at the Great Meadows. While some of the men went into the nearby forest to secure logs of oak about 9 or 10 feet in length, others labored in the angle formed by the two streams to dig a trench 2 feet deep in the form of a circle with a diameter of 53 feet. The oak logs, split in half, were placed upright in the trench, with thinner unsplit logs interspersed so as to block any irregular gaps, the whole forming a circular palisade about 7 or 8 feet high with an entrance on one side and gun ports at frequent intervals. In the center, the men built a crude log shelter for ammunition and other supplies.[65]

The first week of June brought news of Colonel Fry's death at Wills Creek, which meant that Washington gained a promotion and the full responsibility for commanding the Virginia regiment. Two of the companies were already present and under his direct command; the other three arrived on the ninth of June, about 181 additional men in all, led by Lieutenant Colonel George Muse. With them they brought Washington's only artillery—nine swivel guns. A few days later Captain James Mackay of the British army led in his independent company of regulars from South Carolina, approximately 100 men plus officers, together with a small herd of beef cattle. By the middle of June the British troops on the scene totaled about 400. Mackay brought not only beef on the hoof and firepower but also trouble. Unlike Washington, this punctilious Scot had his commission from the king, which meant that he was not obligated to operate under the orders of a provincial colonel. Mackay insisted upon this point, and as though to emphasize it he ordered his company to set up its own camp separate from that of the Americans and with distinct passwords. Worse yet, Mackay informed Washington that British regulars were not required to perform extra labor, such as road building or the construction of fortifications, without extra pay. Washington had no pay to offer and had no choice but to keep his own weary and ragged troops hard at work, while the redcoats kept to themselves. Inevitably, there was much grumbling among the Virginians of all ranks. The officers from the commander on down were resentful of the way their government was treating them in the matter of pay, while the enlisted men griped about the lazy regulars, the scarcity and poor quality of the food, and their lot in general. Morale had become a serious problem.[66]

Hearing that the once-friendly Delawares and Shawnees now were shifting to the French side, Washington marched with the Virginia companies across Chestnut Ridge to Gist's plantation, where he held a three-day conference with the Indians that did little to increase his optimism. Although the Delawares and Shawnees professed continuing loyalty, it was only too obvious that French strength and determination at the Forks were having their effect. This, coupled with the nonappearance of Catawba and Cherokee allies, meant that Indian support of Washington's endeavor was at best weak and uncertain.[67] During the next few days the commander remained at Gist's, pondering his best course of action, while his men carried on the work of improving the road. Washington also had his scouts out probing in the direction of Redstone Creek and Fort Duquesne, hoping to gain some definite indication of French intentions. Finally the long-expected word came, brought by a loyal Indian. A strong body of French and Indians, possibly 900 or more, was about to leave Fort Duquesne and advance southeastward against Washington. Their purpose, presumably, was to exact vengeance for what the French considered to be the murder of Jumonville.

Once again Washington reacted swiftly, recalling two detachments that were out on special assignments and sending for the independent company that had remained in camp at the Great Meadows. The soldiers already on the scene frantically began throwing up a "hog pen fort" made of fence rails, in case the French should attack at once.[68] When the regulars had arrived after an all-night march, Washington called a council of war to decide what should be done. It was clear that the Half King's Indians had no stomach for a stand at Gist's, nor were the troops there adequately supplied with provisions. Moreover, if the army chose to defend the remote plantation, the enemy could simply bypass them, overwhelm the guard at the Great Meadows, and then roam unhindered through the Virginia backcountry. For these good and sufficient reasons, Washington decided to fall back at once upon his base camp. The hasty withdrawal across Chestnut Ridge probably began on the afternoon of 29 June. Due to the difficulty of the route, the shortage of horses, and the labor of manhandling the swivel guns (a task which the regulars again left entirely to the Virginians), the hungry and bone-weary troops did not finally fling down their burdens at the Great Meadows until sometime on the first of July.[69] It is likely that Washington's tiny army would have continued the withdrawal all the way back to Wills Creek if the shortage of food and draft animals had not been so severe. As it was, the men simply lacked the stamina to lug their artillery and supplies the additional 40 or more miles, with the French and Indians at their heels. The name "Fort Necessity" given to the crude palisade in the meadow seemed peculiarly appropriate.

Washington's plight emphasized how imprudent had been the decision to push as far west as Redstone Creek in the face of superior French strength and without adequate troops, transport, and supplies. Indeed, nearly everything needed to sustain such an effort, except possibly courage, was wanting. Two independent companies from New York and a volunteer force from North Carolina were on their way but had not yet reached the frontier. The service of supply, headed by Major John Carlyle, had proven woefully unable to provide adequate support with a regular flow of provisions to the troops in the field. Hopefully, a large convoy of supplies might reach the Great Meadows at any time, and equally important, there was a good possibility that the two independent companies sent down from New York were now as close as Wills Creek. They too might appear in the very near future to bolster Washington's strength. Accordingly, the decision was made to send an urgent request for supplies and reinforcements, and to improve the defensive works at Fort Necessity so that when the French did attack they might be held off until help from Wills Creek arrived.[70]

The little army, weary and discouraged, spent 2 July taking stock of their situation and obtaining additional logs for the strengthening of their fort. All that night it rained, soaking the ground and forming great puddles in every low place. The men, even most of those who were sick or otherwise incapacitated, were camped in the open and had to cope with the storm as best they could. First priority on space in the tiny log storehouse had been given to the casks of gunpowder. The rain continued the next day. About nine o'clock that morning Washington received definite information that a strong force of French and Indians, estimated to number about 900 men, was approaching the Great Meadows from the direction of Gist's. In general, this intelligence was correct, although the number was somewhat exaggerated. Captain Louis Coulon de Villiers, the elder brother of the slain Jumonville, had departed from Fort Duquesne with about 500 troops and a number of Indian auxiliaries on 28 June. His orders were to find and attack Washington's army in retaliation for the assault against Jumonville's party, or, if the British had retired already, to do what damage he could in some of Virginia's frontier settlements. This was conceived as just punishment for prior misconduct by the Virginians, and Villiers was specifically instructed to make clear to the responsible authorities that the French were not attempting to begin a war.[71]

When Washington learned of the near approach of Villiers' formidable force, he hastened every possible preparation. The principal job now was to complete a simple pair of angled trenches as outworks protecting the circular stockade on the three sides not covered by the stream. These were dug about 2 feet deep, the excavated earth being piled up on the outside to form a parapet. In this way the defended area was enlarged to include about a quarter of an acre of ground for the approximately 400 men. Actually, the number of men fully fit for active duty was less than

300, the remainder being either sick or physically exhausted. All friendly Indians had already slipped away, leaving the British troops to bear the full brunt of the attack.[72]

About 11:00 A.M., one of the sentries sighted the advancing enemy on the high ground to the west and discharged his piece in that direction. This aroused the whole camp, putting a sudden end to the work of fortification as the soldiers dropped tools and grabbed guns. Washington, apparently at first anticipating an encounter in the open field, began to form up his units on the ground outside the earthworks, a maneuver certainly ill-considered in view of the reported strength of the French force. There was some early and quite ineffectual firing, after which the British scrambled for the shelter of their sodden trenches, while the French and Indians speedily deployed within the cover of the forest where it came closest to the British position. This meant that Villiers' men were able to gain positions as close as 60 yards from the southernmost earthworks, and yet retain the advantage of being able to fire from behind trees. They began pouring their fire in upon the defenders, and likewise took the opportunity to pick off the horses and cattle in the adjacent meadow.[73] The French had no artillery, and the British may have had no more than a couple of their swivels in operating position, so it became a contest in musketry. Having a concentrated target, the French and their Indian allies were able to gall the defenders with a converging fire whistling in from various points along the forest's edge. The leaden balls bit deep into the upright stakes of the stockade, and sent splinters of wood flying from the storehouse within. To make matters worse, the rain became exceedingly heavy, causing the muddy water to rise around the ankles of the drenched men crouching in the trenches. Their powder became wet, their firearms increasingly unreliable. Villiers' men, firing from the shelter of the woods, suffered only very light losses as the long afternoon wore on, but in Fort Necessity the toll among the British was staggering. By eight o'clock that evening, approximately one-third of the active defenders were either dead or wounded.[74]

Despite his obvious and growing advantage, Villiers had reason to want a quick end to the affray. His men, too, were seriously hampered by the foul weather, their ammunition was running low, and the Indians with him were becoming increasingly impatient. Furthermore, he could not be certain that strong British reinforcements were not sufficiently close to change the whole complexion of affairs on the morrow. For these reasons, after the fighting had been going on for about nine hours, Villiers offered Washington an opportunity to parley. At first the Virginian was not inclined to accept, but the miserable condition of his men and the apparent hopelessness of his situation were compelling reasons for at least considering a French proposal. Captain Van Braam, who had served Washington as interpreter during his journey to Fort Le Boeuf, was sent out into the open to meet the French, and returned with a written set of terms. By this time, darkness had settled over the sodden meadow, and the colonial officers had only a flickering candle to help them read what Villiers had offered. The scrawl was in French and extraordinarily difficult to read because of the blotting caused by rain. Van Braam provided a verbal interpretation which seemed acceptable; both Mackay and Washington signed the document.

The articles of capitulation signed at Fort Necessity on the evening of 3 July 1754 permitted the British to withdraw with their possessions, artillery excepted. Two hostages, Captain Jacob Van Braam and Captain Robert Stobo, were to be left with the French as guarantors for the early repatriation of the prisoners taken by Washington in the attack on Jumonville. In effect, then, Villiers was wiping out the stain of that defeat and actually forcing the British to retreat beyond the mountains. Significantly, the text of the articles made two additional points that Washington may not have noticed or fully understood when the terms were so hurriedly translated to him that wet, dark evening: Villiers was avenging the "assassination" of Jumonville, and the British were being required to withdraw from territory belonging to France. When Washington hurriedly scrawled his name below the text, he was officially endorsing these potentially damaging claims.[75]

While Washington's pathetic soldiers—unkempt, weary, hungry, beaten—trudged back to the base at Wills Creek, carrying their severely wounded in makeshift litters, the victorious French methodically burned down the stockade and storehouse of Fort Necessity. Villiers was careful to leave nothing that might prove useful to the British should they return. Then the French force headed back toward Fort Duquesne, taking the two hostages with them. At Gist's plantation and again at Redstone Creek they paused to destroy the material remains of former British occupation. When

Villiers finally reported to Contrecoeur at Fort Duquesne, he could avow with little or no exaggeration that every British structure from the Great Meadows to the Forks lay in ruins.[76]

Governor Dinwiddie found it difficult to accept the reality of defeat, and for days afterward he talked and planned as though there could be a renewed British offensive that fall. To Washington, who was striving desperately to hold the little army together in some semblance of readiness, this was sheer madness. Trouble among the troops broke into the open soon after the army came dragging into the post at Wills Creek. As one soldier later recalled,

> Sixteen of the Volunteers of the Virginia Regiment went in a Body to Col[onel] Washington telling him, that as they Came to Settle the Lands, Which now they had no more thoughts of doing, They were determined to Return home. Col[onel] Washington endeavoured to perswade them to Stay, promising to procure them some Gratuity from the Government of Virginia for all their trouble and Losses, But he could not prevail with them, For they went off in a Body. . . .[77]

And they continued slipping away, individually and in small groups. On 20 August Washington complained that "the Soldiers are deserting constantly, and yesterday . . . 25 of them collected and were going off in Face of their Officers, but were stop'd and Imprison'd before the Plot came to its full height. . . . There is scarce a Night, or opportunity, but what some or other are deserting, often two, or three, or 4 at a time."[78] Not only were the men bitterly disappointed at being deprived of new lands in the West; they lacked many of the more immediate and fundamental possessions as well. "The chief part are almost naked," their commander testified, "and scarcely a man has either shoes, stockings, or hat. These things the merchants will not credit them for. . . . There is not a man that has a Blanket to secure him from cold or wet."[79] For the young Virginia colonel, the aftermath of his defeat at Fort Necessity was a bitter foretaste of what he would have to face, and in more serious circumstances, two decades in the future. One thing became increasingly clear—there could be no new British advance beyond the mountains in 1754.

During the month prior to the disaster at Fort Necessity, delegates from seven of the British colonies convened at Albany, New York, for the purpose of promoting unified action in the face of the French menace and, hopefully, to prop up the badly sagging Anglo-Iroquois alliance. The delegates tried to convince the leaders of the Six Nations that the British still had the Indians' own best interests at heart, but even though the Iroquois leaders formally renewed the old alliance there was good reason to doubt the strength of their attachment. To many of the Indians, neutrality and even an advantageous rapprochement with the French seemed a much safer course in the troubled seas of Anglo-French conflict.[80]

The matter of intercolonial cooperation occupied much of the delegates' time at the Albany Conference. James De Lancey, the acting governor of New York, strongly urged what so many of his predecessors had tried and failed to achieve—a jointly financed intercolonial program for the building of needed forts along the New York frontier. As usual, the other colonies found a reason for postponing action on this admittedly important program. The delegates did endorse a report which took note of the danger being created by French advances, and made some positive recommendations for coping with this menace. Most important of all, they debated and finally adopted a proposal for an intercolonial form of government, generally known as the Albany Plan of Union, which would enable the British mainland colonies to act harmoniously and expeditiously in matters of Indian relations and defense. This plan, in its final form largely the work of Benjamin Franklin, one of the delegates from Pennsylvania, was the outgrowth of a deep concern long felt and strongly voiced by imperial-minded colonial leaders such as William Shirley of Massachusetts. It did not originate in England, nor did it enjoy the active support of the British government. Despite the obvious administrative advantages of such a plan, there was an uneasy feeling among many members of Parliament, too strong to be challenged by the ministry, that colonial unity would weaken British authority in America.[81] Nor were the colonial governments themselves any more enthusiastic over the proposal hatched at Albany, fearing the submergence of their own jealously guarded prerogatives. Not a single colony ratified the Albany Plan of Union, and the failure of the ministry to endorse it completed the abortion of an extremely important and promising experiment that might have hastened the defeat of New France and even prevented the American Revolution.[82]

There is no doubt that the French were exerting every effort to exploit their new advantage among the Indians in 1754. While being held at Fort Duquesne as a hostage, Captain Stobo managed

to smuggle out to the British a letter revealing conditions at the
Forks. This extraordinary document, in addition to providing a
plan of the fort, described the way in which the French were successfully undermining Indian confidence in the British by telling them
that after the fall of Fort Necessity the Half King and his people
had been cruelly betrayed by their supposed white friends. The
Indian men, the French said, had been executed by the British,
while the women and children were abandoned to the cruelty of
the Catawbas and Cherokees.[83] What effect such propaganda was
having upon the wavering Indians of the Ohio Valley was a question
of growing concern in the British colonies.

In looking back over the events of 1754, it is essential to remember that Britain and France were not at war, a fact which colonial
leaders on both sides of the frontiers had to consider in all their
planning. This required them to use extraordinary restraint in some
circumstances, while in others it emboldened them under the
assumption that the opposition might be inhibited from extreme
reaction and retaliation. This was a highly dangerous game. Certainly
no colonial leader, whether French or British, actually dared take
upon himself the responsibility of touching off a new international
war, and the respective governments at London and Versailles,
even as they followed these developments in faraway America with
increasing interest and concern, had no intention of allowing their
overeager colonists to drag them into a major conflict. It is interesting to notice how nimbly Governor Dinwiddie acted, once the
fighting had begun with Washington's attack on Jumonville, to
shift the blame elsewhere. "I do assure You," he wrote to Sir
Thomas Robinson, the new secretary of state for the Southern
Department, "I have acted with all possible Precaution in this
Affair, that no Rupture might be chargable on Britain as the
Agressor, the Indians having begun the Action, and we were as
Auxillaries." [84] To the Earl of Albemarle he announced, "We are
now in a State of War, begun very unjustly by the French
Forces. . . ." [85] The argument was dubious at best, but war was a
hot potato that neither Dinwiddie nor his French opposite cared
to be left holding. Duquesne's instructions from the minister of
marine were "to manage on occasions in which there may be acts
of violence, in such a manner as not to appear the aggressor; and
to confine yourself to the adoption of all possible measures to be
in a position to repel force by force." [86] It was the very ambiguity

of the situation in North America, with boundaries unsettled and governors only partly restrained, that so greatly intensified the danger.

NOTES

1. Max Savelle, *The Origins of American Diplomacy: The International History of Angloamerica, 1492–1763* (New York, 1967), pp. 422–423.
2. William Johnson, *The Papers of Sir William Johnson,* James Sullivan and Alexander C. Flick, eds. (13 vols.; Albany, 1921–1962), I, *passim; NYCD,* VI, *passim.*
3. Both Shirley and La Galissonière had been colonial governors; they knew the extreme claims of the rival colonies and the high stakes for which the game was being played.
4. John A. Schutz, *William Shirley: King's Governor of Massachusetts* (Chapel Hill, 1961), pp. 160–161.
5. Savelle, *Origins of American Diplomacy,* p. 395. See also Max Savelle, "Diplomatic Preliminaries of the Seven Years' War in America," *CHR,* XX (March, 1939), 22–25.
6. *Origins of American Diplomacy,* p. 550.
7. John Bartlet Brebner, *New England's Outpost: Acadia before the Conquest of Canada* (New York, 1927), p. 176; Ronald O. MacFarlane, "British Indian Policy in Nova Scotia to 1760," *CHR,* XIX (June, 1938), 160–163.
8. *NYCD,* VI, 541.
9. *NYCD,* VI, 743.
10. Louise P. Kellogg, *The French Régime in Wisconsin and the Northwest* (Madison, 1925), p. 379.
11. Stanley Pargellis, ed., *Military Affairs in North America, 1748–1765: Selected Documents from the Cumberland Papers in Windsor Castle* (New York, 1936), p. 33.
12. *NYCD,* VI, 711–712, 731–736.
13. Weiser Correspondence, I (1741–1756), 28 (Historical Society of Pennsylvania); Theodore Thayer, *Israel Pemberton, King of the Quakers* (Philadelphia, 1943), p. 64.
14. Theodore Calvin Pease and Ernestine Jenison, eds., *Illinois on the Eve of the Seven Years' War, 1747–1755* (Springfield, Ill., 1940), p. 850.
15. *Johnson Papers,* I, 340.
16. *NYCD,* VI, 713–715; Douglas (Summers) Brown, *The Catawba Indians: The People of the River* (Columbia, S.C., 1966), p. 191.
17. Quoted in Brown, *Catawba Indians,* p. 197. See also M. Eugene Sirmans, *Colonial South Carolina: A Political History, 1663–1763* (Chapel Hill, 1966), p. 297.
18. Wilbur R. Jacobs, ed., *Indians of the Southern Colonial Frontier: The Edmund Atkin Report and Plan of 1755* (Columbia, S.C., 1954), p. 54; John Pitts Corry, *Indian Affairs in Georgia, 1732–1756* (Philadelphia, 1936), pp. 136–138; David H. Corkran, *The Cherokee Frontier: Conflict and Survival,*

1740–62 (Norman, Okla., 1962), pp. 19–49; David H. Corkran, *The Creek Frontier, 1540–1783* (Norman, Okla., 1967), pp. 146–150, 160–168; Sirmans, *Colonial South Carolina,* pp. 286–289.

19. W. Neil Franklin, "Pennsylvania-Virginia Rivalry for the Indian Trade of the Ohio Valley," *MVHR,* XX (March, 1934), 464–468.

20. Randolph C. Downes, *Council Fires on the Upper Ohio: A Narrative of Indian Affairs in the Upper Ohio Valley until 1795* (Pittsburgh, 1940), pp. 44–46.

21. *State of the British and French Colonies in North America . . .* (Facsimile ed., [New York], 1967), p. 3.

22. Pease and Jenison, *Illinois on the Eve of the Seven Years' War,* p. 630.

23. Pease and Jenison, *Illinois on the Eve of the Seven Years' War,* p. 97. See also *ibid.,* p. 631; Theodore Calvin Pease, ed., *Anglo-French Boundary Disputes in the West, 1749–1763* (Springfield, Ill., 1936), pp. 13–16.

24. Pease, *Anglo-French Boundary Disputes,* pp. 24–25.

25. Kellogg, *French Régime in Wisconsin and the Northwest,* p. 413; Lawrence H. Gipson, *Zones of International Friction: North America, South of the Great Lakes Region, 1748–1754* (New York, 1939), p. 177.

26. Gov. La Jonquière to Rouillé, 15 October 1750, in Pease and Jenison, *Illinois on the Eve of the Seven Years' War,* p. 241.

27. Pease and Jenison, *Illinois on the Eve of the Seven Years' War,* pp. 97–98. The Reverend Joseph Pierre de Bonnecamps, a Jesuit mathematician, accompanied Céloron as secretary and scientific observer.

28. Downes, *Council Fires on the Upper Ohio,* p. 53, suggests that the reason for burying the markers rather than attaching them to posts or trees was to prevent the hostile Indians from discovering and vandalizing them. One of these plates was brought to William Johnson by some Iroquois Indians late the following year (*NYCD,* VI, 610–611).

29. Gipson, *Zones of International Friction: North America, South of the Great Lakes Region,* pp. 191–202; George A. Wood, "Céloron de Blainville and French Expansion in the Ohio Valley," *MVHR,* IX (March, 1923), 302–319.

30. Christopher Gist's Journal, in Thomas Pownall, *A Topographical Description of the Dominions of the United States of America,* Lois Mulkearn, ed. (Pittsburgh, 1949), Appendix, pp. 176, 182–183; Testimony of Morris Turner, Ralph Kilgore, and John Patton, in Penn Manuscripts, Indian Affairs, I (1687–1753), 63–65 (Historical Society of Pennsylvania); Depositions of John Patton and Thomas Bourke, 8 March 1752, in Pease and Jenison, *Illinois on the Eve of the Seven Years' War,* pp. 490–505; *NYCD,* VI, 731–734; *Johnson Papers,* I, 302–304.

31. Penn Manuscripts, I, 72–74.

32. Gipson, *Zones of International Friction: North America, South of the Great Lakes Region,* pp. 213–216; Douglas Southall Freeman, *George Washington, A Biography* (7 vols.; New York, 1948–1957), I, 271–272.

33. Pease and Jenison, *Illinois on the Eve of the Seven Years' War,* pp. 633–634, 645–646.

34. *Ibid.,* pp. 283–287, 417–422, 904–905.

35. Kellogg, *French Régime in Wisconsin and the Northwest,* pp. 420–422;

Gipson, *Zones of International Friction: North America, South of the Great Lakes Region*, pp. 221–222.

36. William A. Hunter, *Forts on the Pennsylvania Frontier, 1753–1758* (Harrisburg, 1960), pp. 20–23.

37. Deposition of Stephen Coffin, *NYCD*, VI, 835. Coffin was an escapee from French custody who swore that he had been permitted to accompany Boishébert as a common soldier. His account of his experiences does have the ring of truth, although it seems remarkable that a captive Briton should have been allowed to participate in such a crucial military operation.

38. William Johnson to Gov. Clinton, 20 April 1753, *NYCD*, VI, 778–779. The date of this report does not correspond exactly with the known movement of the various French groups. A party of some seventy men did depart from Montreal on 15 April, but the main body of more than 500 men did not leave Montreal until about 26 April. One possible explanation is that the Iroquois had received news of a large force preparing to depart from Montreal for the West, and that when some Indians actually sighted a group on the move it was quickly reported to Johnson as though the whole expedition had been seen in motion. This would have the effect, the Iroquois perhaps hoped, of stimulating a major British response.

39. William Trent to William Logan, [8?] May 1753, Shippen Family Papers, I (Historical Society of Pennsylvania); Captain Stoddard to William Johnson, 15 May 1753, *NYCD*, VI, 779–780.

40. Alfred P. James, *The Ohio Company: Its Inner History* (Pittsburgh, 1959), pp. 54, 56.

41. Savelle, *Origins of American Diplomacy*, pp. 260–261; Lois Mulkearn, "The English Eye the French in North America," *Pennsylvania History*, XXI (October, 1954), 332–333.

42. Kenneth P. Bailey, ed., *The Ohio Company Papers, 1753–1817, Being Primarily Papers of the "Suffering Traders" of Pennsylvania* (Arcata, Calif., 1947), pp. 23–24.

43. W. J. Eccles, *The Canadian Frontier, 1534–1760* (New York, 1969), pp. 161–162.

44. Pease and Jenison, *Illinois on the Eve of the Seven Years' War*, pp. 861–869.

45. Hunter, *Forts on the Pennsylvania Frontier*, pp. 22–23.

46. *NYCD*, VI, 794.

47. Dinwiddie's letter was first published in conjunction with *The Journal of Major George Washington* (Williamsburg, Va., 1754). A facsimile edition of that volume was issued by the University Press of Virginia in 1959.

48. Freeman, *George Washington*, I, 276.

49. Washington, *Journal*, p. 4.

50. *Ibid.*, p. 13.

51. *Ibid.*, p. 27.

52. *Ibid.*, p. 22. Not long after Washington returned to Williamsburg, the Pennsylvania frontiersman John Patton completed a fact-finding mission to the Ohio Valley for Governor James Hamilton, who despite the intransigence of his Quaker assemblymen still was not willing to concede primacy to Virginia in the area of the Forks. (See George A. Cribbs, "The Frontier Policy

of Pennsylvania," *Western Pennsylvania Historical Magazine,* II [July, 1919], 194.)

53. Washington noted in his journal that on 6 January, "we met 17 Horses loaded with Materials and Stores for a Fort at the Forks of *Ohio,* and the Day after some Families going out to settle" (*Journal,* p. 22).

54. Robert Dinwiddie, *The Official Records of Robert Dinwiddie . . . ,* R. A. Brock, ed. (2 vols.; Richmond, Va., 1883–1884), I, 69.

55. Quoted in Hugh Cleland, *George Washington in the Ohio Valley* (Pittsburgh, 1955), p. 63.

56. "With great Application, many Arguments, and with much difficulty they were prevailed on to vote 10,000 [£ in] this Currency for supporting the Expedition. . . ," the governor informed the Earl of Holderness (Dinwiddie, *Official Records,* I, 93; see also *ibid.,* pp. 98, 102). Dinwiddie confided to Governor Hamilton of Pennsylvania that this amount was "not half what I expected . . ." (*ibid.,* p. 120).

57. George Washington, *The Writings of George Washington, from the Original Manuscript Sources, 1745–1799,* John C. Fitzpatrick, ed. (39 vols.; Washington, D.C., 1931–1944), I, 41; Freeman, *George Washington,* I, 343–349.

58. Technically, by the terms of his commission, the trader John Frazier was not obligated to return with Ward to the scene of impending action. Nevertheless, he and Trent subsequently were criticized by Dinwiddie for their apparent negligence and irresponsibility. (See Dinwiddie, *Official Records,* I, 149; Washington, *Writings,* I, 80.)

59. Contrecoeur's summons to Ward has been published in *NYCD,* VI, 841–843. See also James Burd to Edward Shippen, 30 April 1754, Shippen Family Papers, I, 151 (Historical Society of Pennsylvania); Cleland, *George Washington in the Ohio Valley,* p. 69; Gipson, *Zones of International Friction: North America, South of the Great Lakes Region,* pp. 309–310n. Ward believed that Contrecoeur's force totaled a thousand men or more, almost certainly an overestimate. It is an obvious fact, however, that resistance would have been futile.

60. From Washington's Journal, in Cleland, *George Washington in the Ohio Valley,* p. 71.

61. Washington, *Writings,* I, 54–55.

62. Washington, *Writings,* I, 63–64.

63. Governor Dinwiddie's instructions to Washington, based upon the instructions issued the previous year by the ministry, have been published in Dinwiddie, *Official Records,* I, 59.

64. Washington, *Writings,* I, 56, 70; Freeman, *George Washington,* I, 372–373; Hunter, *Forts on the Pennsylvania Frontier,* p. 54; Marcel Trudel, "The Jumonville Affair" (transl. and abridged by Donald H. Kent), *Pennsylvania History,* XXI (October, 1954), 351–381.

65. Archeological investigation of the site, begun in 1952, has provided a fairly clear picture of the fortification. (See J. C. Harrington, *New Light on Washington's Fort Necessity: A Report on the Archeological Explorations at Fort Necessity National Battlefield Site* [Richmond, Va., 1957].)

66. Dinwiddie, *Official Records,* I, 198–199, 221, 223; Washington, *Writings,*

I, 80–84; Freeman, *George Washington,* I, 389–390; Lawrence H. Gipson, *The Great War for the Empire: The Years of Defeat, 1754–1757* (New York, 1946), pp. 29, 33.

67. Washington, *Writings,* I, 84–88; Freeman, *George Washington,* I, 392–394.

68. James Wood Notebook (Winchester-Frederick County Historical Society, Va.), p. 47.

69. James Wood Notebook, p. 47; Landon Carter, *The Diary of Colonel Landon Carter of Sabine Hall, 1752–1778,* Jack P. Greene, ed. (2 vols.; Charlottesville, Va., 1965), I, 110; Cleland, *George Washington in the Ohio Valley,* pp. 94–95; Freeman, *George Washington,* I, 398–400.

70. Cleland, *George Washington in the Ohio Valley,* p. 95.

71. Gipson, *The Great War for the Empire: The Years of Defeat, 1754–1757,* pp. 36–37.

72. James Wood Notebook, p. 48; Harrington, *New Light on Washington's Fort Necessity,* pp. 83–89; Freeman, *George Washington,* I, 403. The trenches may have been started earlier, in which case the hurried labor of 3 July would be an attempt to improve and perhaps extend the line of defense.

73. Details of this engagement are drawn from the contemporary accounts by Villiers, John Shaw, and George Washington, as presented in Cleland, *George Washington in the Ohio Valley,* pp. 91–115. Additional information, including the precipitate withdrawal of the British into the trenches, is provided by the James Wood Notebook, p. 48, and Carter, *Diary,* I, 110–111. See also Dinwiddie, *Official Records,* I, 239–243.

74. Cleland, *George Washington in the Ohio Valley,* p. 111; Freeman, *George Washington,* I, 405, 412n.

75. When these terms became known in the colony, there was an upsurge of indignation. One leading Virginian reached the extreme when he characterized the agreement as "the most disgraceful Capitulation that ever was made . . ." (Carter, *Diary,* I, 111). Some men jumped to the conclusion that Van Braam, a foreign immigrant, had deliberately deceived Washington when he interpreted Villiers' terms. The accusation against Van Braam was not sustained in court, and there now is no good reason to believe that he was unfaithful. As Washington's biographer has suggested, Van Braam's faulty translation probably was due not to treason but to an imperfect knowledge of the English language (Freeman, *George Washington,* I, 548–549). Governor Dinwiddie was one who thought otherwise. (See his letter of 12 February 1755, in Dinwiddie, *Official Records,* I, 497–498.) When William Johnson of New York heard of what had happened at Fort Necessity, he sensed impending disaster. "I can . . . foresee," said Johnson gloomily, "the ruin of this country verry shortly without the imediate interposition of his Majesty and Parliament, which I most earnestly wish, and warmly pray for above all things, as nothing else will save us . . ." (*Johnson Papers,* I, 410). Unlike Johnson, however, most Virginians were not inclined to blame Washington personally. The young colonel, they felt, had performed at least reasonably well under great difficulties. But this did little to lessen the embarrassment and gloom now being felt in all quarters. Washington's

unexpected defeat meant the end of any significant British presence west of the Alleghenies. The French now were in full possession and free to consolidate their position. Furthermore, with the signed admission of murder, inadvertent on Washington's part and not known to be such by Villiers, the French had achieved an important gain in the field of propaganda. Only about two months after the episode, the French minister of foreign affairs explained to a British envoy in Paris that the purpose of Villiers' expedition had been to take revenge for the assassination of Jumonville, and coolly displayed the articles of capitulation in which the damning charge was admitted (Albemarle to Robinson, 18 September 1954, in Pease, *Anglo-French Boundary Disputes*, pp. 52–53).

76. Cleland, *George Washington in the Ohio Valley*, pp. 111–112; James, *Ohio Company*, p. 101.
77. Deposition of John Shaw, in Harrington, *New Light on Washington's Fort Necessity*, p. 132.
78. Dinwiddie, *Official Records*, I, 288–289.
79. Washington, *Writings*, I, 94.
80. See, for example, George Croghan to Governor Robert Hunter Morris, 23 December 1754, Pennsylvania Miscellaneous (Manuscript Division, Library of Congress).
81. Alison Gilbert Olson, "The British Government and Colonial Union, 1754," *WMQ*, XVII (January, 1960), 22–34.
82. The Plan is carefully analyzed in Robert Clifford Newbold, *The Albany Congress and Plan of Union of 1754* (New York, 1955), chap. 6.
83. Copy of Robert Stobo's letter of 28 July 1754, Shippen Family Papers, I, 151.
84. Dinwiddie, *Official Records*, I, 203.
85. Dinwiddie, *Official Records*, I, 209–210.
86. Quoted in Eccles, *Canadian Frontier*, p. 167.

CHAPTER 9

The Climactic Struggle for Empire: First Phase, 1755-1757

WASHINGTON'S DEFEAT AT FORT NECESSITY, which forced the Virginians to withdraw east of the Appalachian Mountains, did much to convince the ministry in London that the threat of French domination in North America was immediate and serious. Neither Britain nor France desired an early resumption of war. However, being well aware of each other's need for a further period of peace, each apparently calculated that in certain ways and within certain limits it was relatively safe to be aggressive in faraway America. Thus, each nation had given its respective colonial governors permission to advance into disputed territory and even to drive out rival forces under the name of territorial integrity. The rival power, it was believed, would prefer to swallow its pride and accept an accomplished fact rather than resume a major international struggle. Such reasoning was especially influential in Whitehall during the late summer of 1754, producing a positive British program for dealing decisively with the French threat.[1]

Since the Americans so obviously were incapable of holding their ground in the West, the ministry, not without some qualms, decided to tilt the balance at this time of crisis by throwing a heavy commitment of regular military power onto the scales. The Forty-fourth and Forty-eighth regiments of foot, together with a train of artillery, were to be conveyed to the colonies by a strong naval squadron. These two regiments would then be further recruited in the colonies to a strength of 700 enlisted men each, while being joined by two brand-new regiments entirely raised in America, one commanded by Sir William Pepperrell and the other by Governor William Shirley. These, supported by some provincial regiments, would constitute a striking force capable of retaking the advanced positions occupied by the French and restoring vast areas with their Indian inhabitants to British control. With more optimism than past experience seemed to justify, the ministry recommended that the colonies help pay for this mutually beneficial enterprise by setting up a joint fund. The man selected as commander in chief was Edward Braddock, a stocky and sometimes blunt career officer with more than forty years of experience. On his broad shoulders now came to rest the destiny of British imperial interests in North America.[2]

Braddock's assignment was to proceed with the Forty-fourth and Forty-eighth regiments to Virginia, where he was to organize and lead an expedition of regulars and provincials against Fort Duquesne at the Forks of the Ohio. Actually, Pennsylvania would have provided a better staging area and an easier route to the objective, but the decision for Virginia was made in London, no doubt at the behest of influential men who would personally benefit by the development of a military road to the Forks by the Virginia route. According to the plan devised in London, Braddock's expedition was to advance through Virginia and across the mountains, while Pepperrell and Shirley with their new regiments commenced operations against French positions on the northern frontier. Then, following the repossession of the vital Forks area, Braddock was to lead his army northward and, with the assistance of Pepperrell and Shirley, proceed to occupy the French positions at Niagara and then Crown Point. In the meantime, to complete the repulse of the French intruders, a separate force under Governor Charles Lawrence of Nova Scotia was to seize Fort Beauséjour, the French outpost on the isthmus of Chignecto.[3] Under this ambitious and daring plan, if all went well, by the end of 1755 Britain not only would have regained a vast extent of territory previously endangered and partially occupied by the French, but at the same time would have cut important French lines of communication and trade running through the Great Lakes and south to Louisiana. To assume that

France would accept such a setback without resorting to war was indeed a gamble, but the ministry was betting that the speed and power of its move would be decisive.

Braddock's two regiments of British soldiers, many of them castoffs from other units of the army, departed from Ireland in the last month of 1754. As the crowded transports and their naval escort butted their way westward through the wintry Atlantic, the top-level diplomats of France and England were busily exchanging proposals and counterproposals hopefully contrived to stave off actual war. The record of these earnest negotiations suggests that both governments were beginning to share a common regret that their respective colonial governors had been quite so aggressive in the recent past. It was as though each power now saw dimly ahead the frightening abyss and sought to draw back, but always without sacrificing any important gains already made. "A little more or a little less territory in North America should not cause a war," chided one French official. "Each nation possesses more than she can use for a long time to come." [4] It was a noble sentiment, little heeded; and Braddock already had his orders. By 17 March 1755, the French minister was beginning to see the futility of continuing the negotiations. "War alone can end our differences, . . ." he wrote. "If they are determined at London to kindle a war, all we can say to forestall that evil will not prevent it." [5] Both sides, determined to yield nothing of real importance in America, were slowly but surely ingesting the idea, distasteful though it might be, that a renewal of international warfare was an acceptable risk. In this increasingly ominous atmosphere, the high-level negotiations continued far into the spring of 1755, while Braddock was pursuing his mission.

Even before Braddock arrived in Virginia, Governor Robert Dinwiddie, enthusiastic over the prospect now that British regulars were on the way, was hard at work making ready for the operation. Indian assistance would be very important, and Dinwiddie not only appealed directly to the Catawbas and Cherokees for their active support, but also urged Governor James Glen of South Carolina to effect the same end.[6] In addition, he began recruiting a Virginia regiment for the expedition, and set about gathering the great quantities of provisions and other supplies that would be required by such a large force on the move. The Ohio Company's post at Wills Creek on the upper Potomac was designated the advance base for the expedition: Here the colony began constructing a fortified base known as Fort Cumberland. When Sir John St. Clair, Braddock's deputy quartermaster general, inspected the new base he found two independent companies from New York and one from South Carolina already on the scene. These were regular units of the British army, but singularly unimpressive nonetheless. In fact, many of the men in the New York companies were time-worn veterans who, as St. Clair remarked incredulously, seemed to have been "draughted out of Chelsea." [7]

At the sleepy little village of Alexandria, located on the Potomac River 150 miles below Fort Cumberland, Braddock's two regiments disembarked in March and established their first camp. Plunging into the work of preparing for both his own westward push and the simultaneous efforts elsewhere, Braddock soon found himself beset with frustrations, especially as he began to encounter the endless problems of colonial particularism and Indian relations. What Dinwiddie had once clumsily described as the "Lethargick Supineness" of the colonies other than his own, principally Pennsylvania and Maryland, quickly became for the British general an infuriating handicap to his important mission.[8] Colonial troops, Indian scouts, huge quantities of provisions and other supplies, together with a large number of draft animals, packhorses, and wagons for transport, were required for the expedition; yet virtually nothing was promptly obtainable. Often the quality and quantity that finally did appear, perhaps after weeks of wheedling or nagging or threatening, fell far below expectations, while the costs mounted to figures that seemed little short of outrageous.

Another difficulty, stemming from a high-level decision made by the British government in the fall of 1754, already was causing some grumbling among colonial military officers. Its long-range effects were to prove seriously corrosive to morale whenever provincial forces found themselves operating with regular units of the king's army. The king had decided that "all Troops serving by Commissions signed by Us, or by Our General Comanding in Chief in North America, shall take Rank before all Troops which may serve by Commission from any of the Governors or Councils of Our Provinces in North America." [9] In effect, this meant that provincial field officers

> shall not roll with the King's Regular Forces, but only have the Inspection, and Direction, of their Provincial Corps.—That, If any of

these Provincial Troops should be employed with Detachments of the King's Regular Troops, Their Captains shall be Junior to all Captains, who have the King's Commission: In like manner, Their Lieutenants to be Junior to all the Lieutenants; And their Ensigns to be Junior to all the Ensigns, who bear the King's Commission.[10]

This discriminatory arrangement was especially galling to colonial officers of some practical experience and merit in an age when commissions in the British Army could be purchased by wealthy young gentlemen whose principal qualifications were money, family, and aristocratic self-assurance.

During the third week of April, the commander in chief convened an important meeting of colonial leaders at Alexandria to coordinate the various military operations of the year and seek solutions to his other nagging problems. In addition to Braddock and his senior naval commander, Admiral Augustus Keppel, those present included Governor Dinwiddie of Virginia, Governor Sharpe of Maryland, Governor Morris of Pennsylvania, Governor De Lancey of New York, Governor Shirley of Massachusetts, and the prominent Mohawk Valley Indian trader William Johnson. To the latter Braddock gave an appointment as sole superintendent of the Six Nations and related tribes, which meant in effect that the man most thoroughly trusted and respected by the Iroquois Confederacy now would enjoy royal backing, including funds, in his administration of Indian affairs along a large portion of the northern frontier.[11] When General Braddock raised the question of a common war chest for financing the campaign against the French, the governors opined that this excellent idea could not be put into effect because the stubborn colonial assemblies would not agree. Americans, it seems, wanted the French expelled, but at the king's expense.

Both Governor Shirley and Superintendent Johnson recommended that Braddock direct his main thrust against Niagara, arguing that the capture of that important outpost would sever the French line of communication to the south and west, so that Fort Duquesne would fall from lack of support. Although Braddock could see the force of this argument, he considered himself already committed to advance directly against Fort Duquesne from his Virginia base, and informed the governors of his intention to move north to the Great Lakes after the area of the Forks was again under British control.[12] It was decided that Shirley's plan for an expedition to seize Fort Beauséjour at Chignecto could be effected by 2,000 volunteers from New England in cooperation with British regulars already stationed in Nova Scotia. This was to be the easternmost prong of the 1755 offensive to restore British territory. Superintendent Johnson, with a temporary commission as major general not from the king but from the colonies of New England and New York, was to lead a provincial army of 4,400 men against Fort St. Frédéric at Crown Point. Shirley himself, designated by Braddock as second-in-command of all British forces in North America and thus Braddock's own immediate subordinate, was to lead a third expedition to strengthen Fort Oswego and then proceed against Niagara. For this mission he was to have his own and Pepperrell's newly raised regiment, plus the independent companies still in New York, some provincial troops, and allied Indians. Braddock himself, with the Forty-fourth and Forty-eighth regiments, various provincial units from the southern colonies, and hopefully some Catawbas and Cherokees, was to advance west across the mountains, building a road as he went, and drive the French from the Forks. Then Braddock's expedition was to drive north to join Shirley and Johnson in a climactic, decisive campaign reaching to the shores of the Great Lakes and Lake Champlain.[13]

Even before Braddock had sailed for America the plans for his expedition were known to the French government, which correctly interpreted the show of force as a real threat to French interests in the Ohio Valley. In response, Versailles made hurried plans for a counterreinforcement of 3,000 regular troops, under the command of the Baron de Dieskau, to sail from France at the earliest possible date. Two of the regiments were destined for Louisbourg to reinforce the garrison of that key fortress, while the other four had orders for Canada. Not since 1665, when the Carignan-Salières regiment was shipped to New France, had a major unit of the *troupes de terre,* France's European regulars, disembarked in Canada. Always the colony had been defended, in the main, by its own militia together with the *troupes de la marine* (the colonial regulars). By 1755, however, both Britain and France had come to realize that well-disciplined regulars from Europe were needed in America to prevent a disastrous tilting of the balance of military power. This significant departure from previous policy was to make the next war different from all that had gone before.[14]

French preparations, in turn, alarmed the British, prodding them into another dangerous decision. A cabinet minute of 10 April 1755, noting the lack of real progress in the current negotiations between the two governments, as well as the French naval and military preparations, recommended

> the Sending, as soon as conveniently can be, a Squadron of seven ships of War to North America; in order to protect and defend His Majesty's Colonies, and to oppose any Force; That may be sent thither by the French, with proper Instructions to the Commander of the said Squadron, for seizing, and securing any French ships of War, or ships having Troops or Warlike Stores on board, which He may meet in those parts; and for Taking and Destroying any such Ships, in case of Opposition to His so Seizing and Securing Them.[15]

Orders to this effect accordingly were issued to Vice Admiral Edward Boscawen, who sailed from Plymouth for American waters on 27 April with a fleet of thirteen warships. Apparently the British government by this time had largely abandoned any expectation of a satisfactory negotiated settlement, and either accepted war as inevitable or remained clinging to the slim hope that France would not fight even after such a bold affront.

Less than a week after Boscawen's departure on his warlike mission, a French convoy carrying Dieskau and his six regiments sailed from Brest. Also on board was an especially important passenger —the Marquis de Vaudreuil, Canada's new governor.[16] Nearing American shores, the French convoy encountered thick fog and gradually became separated into several groups. On 8 June the waiting Boscawen stumbled upon one of these groups, capturing the two 64-gun warships *L'Alcide* and *Le Lys.* Among the prisoners were a number of French engineers and eight companies of regulars who were taken to Halifax. After this exploit, Boscawen continued his patrol off the entrance to the Gulf of St. Lawrence, but bagged no other ships of the French fleet, his successes being limited to the capture of merchantmen laden with much-needed provisions for Canada's population and growing military garrison. In response to Boscawen's capture of *L'Alcide* and *Le Lys,* the French government recalled its minister from London, and formal negotiations for the avoidance of open war came to an end.[17]

During the month of May, Braddock's expeditionary force slowly assembled at Fort Cumberland, transforming that hastily developed frontier outpost into a scene of bustling activity—a rendezvous for troops, wagonloads of supplies, lumbering artillery, and beef on the hoof. Provincials mingled with redcoats, each group sizing up the other, and it would be difficult to say which was the more successful in showing or concealing disdain. Understandably the colonial officers were not happy with the royal order concerning rank, especially when they discovered how blind the regular officers could be to the difficult problems of warfare in the deep wilderness. Prominent among these colonial officers, and one especially favored by the British general, was George Washington, who was taken into Braddock's official family as an aide-de-camp.

The principal problem faced by the army was that of transport. To storm Fort Duquesne without first battering down the palisades with artillery could be very costly in lives, so Braddock intended to take with him a number of heavy cannon. These ponderous guns, drawn by horses or oxen, were the very core of the general's problem. If the artillery was to be successfully moved across the mountains to Fort Duquesne, the wilderness trail would have to be transformed into a road. Gangs of laborers would have to work ahead of the advancing troops, cutting down trees and brush, building bridges, blasting rocks, and grading the worst of the inclines. This meant that the advance would be slow, at best a few miles each day. The slowness, in turn, compounded the problem, for the army would require provisions and other supplies in huge quantities, and these would have to be carried with the troops in a long train of farm wagons and packhorses. The large number of horses required provender, although to some extent this could be supplemented with pasturage if the expedition did not proceed too early in the season. All in all, it was a baffling problem in logistics as well as engineering, made even more difficult by the infuriating reluctance of colonial assemblies to appropriate funds or supplies for the venture and of colonial farmers to risk their teams and wagons with the army. Despite these difficulties, however, Braddock persisted, and at last the necessary supplies and transport began to arrive at Fort Cumberland. This was mostly the result of Dinwiddie's energetic pleading and prodding · and the insistent demands of lesser officials who scoured the countryside for whatever could be obtained. In Pennsylvania, truly a breadbasket colony, the public-spirited Benjamin Franklin of Philadelphia managed to persuade a large number of farmers to send off their wagons and horses to the army, an invaluable contribution.[18]

Equally baffling and disturbing to Braddock was the Indian problem, and he was wise enough to realize the importance of

Indian support for all the expeditions. Johnson wrote gloomily from New York that the Six Nations were showing the effects of French enticement and could not be depended upon at this juncture. Perhaps the best that could be hoped for was Iroquois neutrality.[19] This was bad news indeed. On the southern frontier the Catawbas and Cherokees, whose help Braddock greatly needed for his own expedition, were subject to French influence emanating from Fort Toulouse. Unfortunately, British counterinfluence was weakened by the usual intercolonial jealousies. Governor Glen of South Carolina deeply resented the fact that Dinwiddie had by-passed him in appealing directly to the tribes under South Carolina's supervision, and half suspected that the Virginians were exaggerating the threat of French aggression in the Ohio Valley as a justification for their own expansionism.[20] Entertaining ideas of his own as to what should be done to further British interests, Glen scheduled an Indian conference to be held at Saluda Old Town about the end of June. This drew the Catawba and Cherokee leaders like a magnet, at the very time when Dinwiddie and Braddock needed the warriors for the expedition against Fort Duquesne. Bitterly the Virginia governor complained that "Mr. Glen appears to do every Thing in his Power to obstruct the Expedition." [21] Actually, the southern Indians had reason for not being eager to join the British drive to the Ohio. Earlier that year they had been visited by a delegation of Shawnees and Mingos who told of growing French strength, the dangerous enmity of Canadian Indians, and the intended neutrality of the Six Nations.[22] So it seems that for many of the Catawba and Cherokee chiefs Glen's invitation to the Saluda conference provided a welcome excuse for not making Braddock's acquaintance.

With or without Indian support, the British leaders pushed ahead with their preparations for all four expeditions. Officers enlisted and trained their men,[23] workmen busily constructed bateaus for river transport, and commissaries assembled stockpiles of supplies, while the commanders conferred with their subordinates and pored over their maps. With the excitement of preparation and the appearance of increasing numbers of troops actually in arms, some of the usual colonial apathy and antagonism seemed to abate. At Albany, the principal staging area for both Shirley's and Johnson's expeditions, a New England soldier was frank enough to confess that he liked the local inhabitants better than he had expected, finding them to be apparently "as hearty in the present Expedition as Any of us." This, he added generously, was "Contrary to Common fame." [24] Johnson himself was less enthusiastic, especially about the troops under his command. "Officers and Men with very few Exceptions are not only Strangers to Military Life but show an averseness to Discipline and Regularity which gives me no small trouble and uneasiness," he confided.[25]

All this hurry and bustle of preparation from New England to Virginia could hardly be concealed from the French. Indians coming and going between Canada and the back areas of the British colonies picked up scraps of information which helped fill in part of the picture for Vaudreuil and his colleagues. To this were added the fragmentary reports derived from sailors and traders. By mid-June the authorities at Louisbourg had received a letter, secretly transmitted from someone in Virginia, confirming that British forces, including large numbers of regulars, were preparing to attack Chignecto, Crown Point, and the French posts on the upper Ohio.[26] The question was, would the French be ready in time? Fortunately for them, the continuing difficulties experienced by the British commanders, and the consequent delays, gave them some of the time they needed.

Neither Johnson nor Shirley was an experienced soldier, to say nothing of commander. To make matters worse, there developed between them a personal antagonism reflecting the political and economic factionalism so rife in the British colonies, in this case the longstanding, almost traditional hostility between New England and New York. The immediate cause of trouble in 1755 seems to have been Shirley's understandable desire to shift some troops from Johnson's army to his own, thereby achieving a better balance. But this would weaken the force available for the capture of Fort St. Frédéric, and Johnson obviously could not relish that. To some extent Johnson was already the victim of his own self-doubts, faced as he was with the awesome responsibility of leading an army against the French fortifications in the Champlain Valley. Furthermore, as sole superintendent of Indian affairs, the New Yorker resented the New Englander's attempts to recruit Iroquois warriors for his own army. Iroquois assistance was hard enough to come by as it was, without two commanders bidding against each other! At a deeper level, the quarrel spread broadly through the social, economic, and political arteries of several colonies. Certainly the acting governor of New York, James De Lancey, and his brother Oliver disliked having the shrewd and ambitious Shirley, New England's principal spokesman and promoter, intrude into the affairs of their province. There was bitter rivalry for the profits to be made in supplying the armies, and Shirley was in a position to favor New England and Pennsylvania contractors. The De Lanceys, in turn, did little to smooth Shirley's way as he worked to organize and equip his army for the assault on Niagara. Such factional in-fighting, made all the more intense by the fact that both armies were assembling in the same general area of upper New York, unquestionably was having an adverse effect upon the overall effort.[27]

The first of the four British expeditions to get underway was the combined New England–Nova Scotia venture against Chignecto. By 2 June a force of 2,000 New Englanders under Lieutenant Colonel John Winslow augmented by about 280 regulars, all under the command of Colonel Robert Monckton of the Nova Scotia garrison, was assembled at Fort Lawrence on the east side of the Missaguash River. Less than 2 miles to the west, beyond the stream, lay their principal objective, the pentagonal Fort Beauséjour, defended by a garrison of French regulars with twenty-six cannon. Augmenting the defense were a considerable number of *habitants* from the nearby village, and some Indians. On 4 June the British offensive began when Monckton's attacking column, with four brass 6-pounders in tow, marched several miles upstream to a potential crossing point. On the opposite bank several hundred *habitants* and Indians, sheltered in prepared positions, were ready to contest the crossing, but despite enemy fire the British managed to throw a crude bridge across the stream and gain the other side. Thereupon the French, as one New Englander put it, "Sot all thare Buildings on Fire and Fled" toward Fort Beauséjour, followed by Monckton and his men.[28] During the next few days, the British established a camp a short distance above the French fort, engaged in occasional minor skirmishes with parties of the enemy, and brought up more guns. French cannon firing from the walls were answered by the British guns, while working parties from the camp began digging approach trenches. Finally on 16 June, before the British were fully ready to make their bid, the defenders offered to surrender, and before dark that night Monckton's men were in command of Fort Beauséjour, with some 450 prisoners, about one-third of them French regulars. Monckton gave the stronghold a new name—Fort Cumberland—honoring the supreme commander of the British army.

Fifteen miles to the north on the far shore of the isthmus stood Fort Gaspereau, important mainly as a supply base for the French and Indians of the Chignecto area. The commander of this small fort quickly recognized the futility of resistance in the face of such overwhelming strength and yielded his post to Colonel Winslow on 18 June. Within the fort was found an accumulation of provisions and military supplies, a welcome form of plunder.[29] To complete the operation, British ships proceeded to the mouth of the St. John River on the western side of the Bay of Fundy, where they destroyed an abandoned French fortification. The Chignecto campaign must be reckoned an unqualified success, cutting the last threads of French control over the strategic isthmus that links Nova Scotia with the mainland. From Baie Verte to the Bay of Fundy, the military power of Britain was now without serious challenge.

Three days after Monckton's men fought their way across the Missaguash River, the main body of Braddock's powerful expedition began its slow, plodding march from the other Fort Cumberland, on the upper Potomac, toward Fort Duquesne at the Forks of the Ohio. Although the much-desired contingent of Catawbas and Cherokees had not appeared, Braddock and his officers, both English and provincial, were confident. By every calculation, Britain at last had in America the power to win and to win readily. The immediate objective, under the command of the Sieur de Contrecoeur, was nothing more than a palisaded, wilderness fort with a garrison probably numbering fewer than 300 regulars and militiamen, together with some undisciplined Indians encamped outside the walls. Once Braddock's artillery was in position, Fort Duquesne would be doomed.

Washington must have reflected often upon his bitter experience of the previous summer as he retraced the old familiar route. What a contrast this new army made with the contemptible little force he had led. This time, two Irish regiments and three independent companies of regulars brought the pride and prestige of the king's uniform to the untamed wilderness, while companies of Virginians, small contingents from Maryland and North Carolina, numerous woodsmen, wagoners, and even a few loyal Indians,

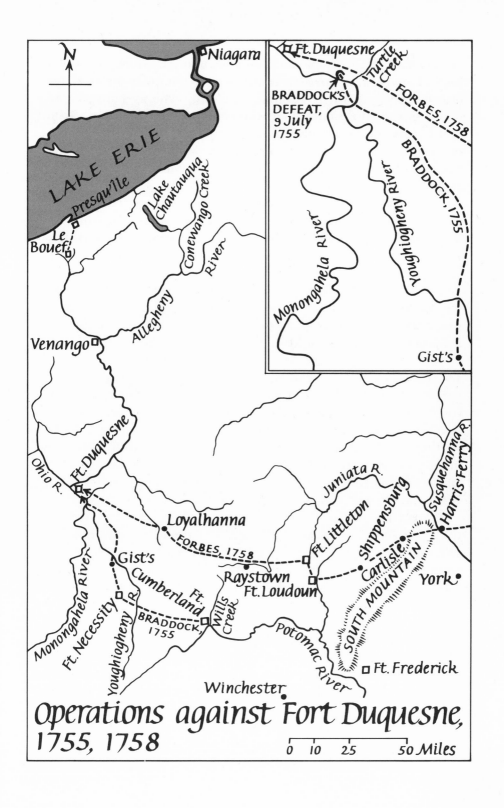

Operations against Fort Duquesne, 1755, 1758

0 10 25 50 Miles

added more strength. Braddock was no fool and took reasonable precautions against surprise, sending small groups of scouts ahead of the army and, where feasible, deploying flanking parties along either side of the route. The woodsmen labored in gangs, axing down trees, clearing brush, building bridges, and either prizing or blasting away obstructive rocks. In the worst swamps and on the steepest grades, sweating wagoners and soldiers had to aid the straining horses by putting their own shoulders to the wheels. Every night was spent in a huge wilderness encampment, with sentries stationed along the dark perimeter and with only the flickering light of the campfires and perhaps an occasional lantern or candle to hold back the encompassing blackness and its terror.

Averaging little more than 2 miles a day, the army had gone no farther than the Little Meadows by 16 June. This was too slow for Braddock, who feared that if given enough time the French would be able to pour additional men and supplies into Fort Duquesne. It was the wagon train with its weakening, faltering horses that was the main drag on the army; and so, following the advice of Washington, the impatient general now made an important change in the disposition of his force.[30] The slow-moving train with a sufficient escort of troops, under the command of Colonel Thomas Dunbar of the Forty-eighth Regiment, was to continue on as best it could, while an advance striking force of more than 1,400 officers and men, drawn from the various units and commanded by Braddock himself, forged ahead to invest the French fort at the earliest possible opportunity.

Toward the end of June, when the advance force had reached the Great Crossing of the Youghiogheny beyond Gist's plantation, two raiding parties of hostile Indians demonstrated their elusive mobility by appearing far to the rear. They struck at British settlements only a few miles from Fort Cumberland, murdering members of nine families, which sent a flock of refugees scurrying into Fort Cumberland for shelter.[31] Presumably these raids were intended to draw off some of Braddock's strength, but the general sent no detachments in pursuit. He had his eye fixed firmly on one target only—Fort Duquesne. During the first week of July, as Braddock pushed ever closer to his objective, groups of French Indians from the fort prowled along the army's flanks without being able to slow its progress or shake its determination; the British precautions were quite effective. By the evening of 8 July, the advance force lay near

the Monongahela between the Youghiogheny and the mouth of
Turtle Creek, while Colonel Dunbar and the train were com-
fortably encamped some 40 miles to the rear. Ahead for the next
day was the double crossing of the Monongahela, first above the
mouth of Turtle Creek and then back again just below, thereby
avoiding a dangerous pass known as the Narrows. Once the two
crossings were completed, the striking force would find itself
within 8 miles of its objective, unhindered by any other geographical barrier.

Early on the morning of 9 July Lieutenant Colonel Thomas
Gage, commanding an advance party of more than 300 regulars
supported by two 6-pounders, moved out of camp to secure the
fords. Then the remainder of the advance force broke camp and
began to make the crossings under the protection of Gage's men.
That same morning Contrecoeur dispatched from Fort Duquesne
a blocking force consisting of 108 French regulars, 146 Canadian
militiamen, and about 650 Indians, all under the command of
Captain Daniel Liénard de Beaujeu, leaving the fort itself guarded
by only a few dozen men. It was a gigantic gamble, but Contrecoeur knew full well that his only hope was to stop the approaching army before it came close enough to site its artillery.[32]

Sometime after 1:00 P.M., the last of Braddock's troops sloshed
up onto the right bank of the river after completing the second
crossing, and the order was given to resume the advance upon the
fort. Again the scouts moved on ahead followed by Gage's detachment and a working party under St. Clair, while flanking parties
advanced along either side of the route. They crossed a ravine and
continued on through thick woods. On their right they passed a
wooded slope, and had gone a short distance beyond when the
foremost men suddenly sighted part of Beaujeu's force in the trail
just ahead. Firing commenced almost at once, with the British
wheeling their two cannon into position on the left. Blasts of grape
from these guns together with the musketry of the redcoats jolted
the enemy, and many of the Canadian militia ran away in terror.
Beaujeu himself was mortally wounded, leaving Captain Dumas
in command. Whether or not the French were as surprised as the
British by the sudden encounter remains unclear, but at least they
reacted more effectively after the opening volleys. Quickly they and
their Indian allies split like a stream of water, running along both
flanks of the British column, flitting through the woods unseen,

engulfing or driving in the flanking parties. Before the startled British knew what was happening, the enemy had seized all the advantageous positions in the ravines and on the high ground, including the wooded hill that Gage had neglected to secure while passing and which now dominated the right flank.

Under heavy fire Gage and his redcoats gave ground, abandoning their artillery and moving back along the trail toward the main body, even as Braddock, hearing the sudden outbreak of firing ahead, sent forward a detachment to lend support. This detachment jammed into Gage's party, compounding the confusion, and as the rest of the column lurched forward it too became entangled in disaster. The enemy, well concealed in the woods and further shielded by the thickening pall of gunsmoke now enveloping the scene on all sides, kept pouring a hot fire into the masses of redcoats that formed and broke and tried to form again under the deadly lash of bullets. Repeatedly the British officers attempted to rally their men and storm the hill now held by the French and Indians, but the officers were falling even faster than the privates, and all was in vain. The Virginians instinctively headed for the flanks on either side to take shelter behind trees and fight Indian fashion. In taking such positions, however, they remained fully exposed to flying bullets coming from their rear, whether from the wild-firing redcoats or enemies on the opposite flank. The Virginians, and the redcoats too, suffered appalling losses. Braddock had five horses shot from under him and was critically wounded through his arm and side, the bullet penetrating to the lungs. Sir Peter Halkett, the commanding officer of the Forty-fourth Regiment, was killed; St. Clair was wounded, as were Braddock's aides-de-camp Robert Orme and Roger Morris, and Lieutenant Colonels Gage and Burton. It was a near miracle that George Washington, although in the very thick of the action, remained uninjured.[33] There was heroism and panic mixed together, and no one in effective control. After more than two hours of such confusion and terror, Braddock's men broke and began fleeing back along the way they had come, back across the Monongahela, leaving their artillery, their wagons, and their dead on the field of battle, while the general, critically wounded but still nominally in command, was carted from the scene by his faithful subordinates. Realizing that the lives of the shocked survivors were in jeopardy, he hastily summoned relief from the main force 40 miles away. Fortunately for the

British, the victorious French and Indians did not pursue far, but quickly busied themselves scalping the fallen, securing prisoners, and gathering booty.

The inglorious retreat of this broken army can be described quickly. Most of the walking survivors, supporting their wounded comrades, dragged themselves into Gist's plantation as darkness settled over the forest; they had plodded more than thirty agonizing miles in little over twenty-four hours. There they spent a dreadful night, tormented by hunger and their fear of enemy pursuit. About eleven o'clock the next morning, on 11 July, they were overjoyed to see a column of wagons approaching from the direction of Dunbar's camp, the relief that had been summoned. Food brought renewed strength, so that the withdrawal could be resumed, and later that day most of the army arrived at the camp.[34] The re-united forces spent the next day systematically destroying artillery, wagons, and excess supplies to prevent their falling into enemy hands. Nearly everything an army would need for an expedition was consigned to the flames or otherwise destroyed. On the thirteenth the final withdrawal was begun, with Braddock now declining fast. That night he died and was buried in the road about a mile north of the ruins of Fort Necessity, leaving Dunbar in command. A few days later the miserable, dispirited, broken remnants of a once-powerful striking force began hobbling in to the welcome refuge of Fort Cumberland.

The French had little difficulty reckoning their losses in the battle. They were listed as three officers, two soldiers, three Canadians, and fifteen Indians killed. Sixteen men were known to have been wounded. On the battlefield the victors found hundreds of British dead and wounded, a large number of horses and cattle, fifteen pieces of artillery with quantities of ammunition, numerous muskets, and personal effects of all kinds. Dinwiddie later reported that British losses included about 600 men killed or wounded, plus many officers. A more precise tally specified that of 86 officers involved in the action, 63 were casualties; while 914 out of the 1,373 enlisted men were either killed or wounded. In addition to the mounds of weapons and other equipment, the enemy recoverd from the battlefield a totally unexpected prize—a set of official papers, Braddock's own, containing detailed information about the impending British operations farther north. Soon the Baron de Dieskau, deploying his regular regiments along the northern frontier, had the tremendous advantage of knowing almost exactly what Shirley and Johnson intended to do in the next few weeks.[35] Shirley, who had never commanded so much as a company in action, succeeded to the supreme command.

The news of the disaster on the Monongahela spread through the colonies like the shock wave from an earthquake. Such a sudden drastic reversal of fortunes on the very threshold of a confidently expected victory was of course followed by a heated debate, principally to lay the blame. Braddock was immediately criticized, and ever since in American tradition has been viewed as an arrogant drillbook commander who ignored American advice and paraded his soldiers through the wilderness to disaster. It is true that Braddock was inexperienced in wilderness warfare, but he did listen to advice and he did take precautions against surprise. Given his extremely difficult route and the shortage of friendly Indian auxiliaries, Braddock turned in a generally creditable performance up until the very day of his defeat. Of his personal bravery there can be no question. The most serious mistakes of 9 July were made by other officers when it was too late to correct them, most importantly Gage's failure to secure the dominating hill before he passed it, and then, when attacked, his failure either to push forward to more open ground or else stand fast and wait for support to arrive. There is no reason to suppose that if the regulars like the Virginians had broken ranks and tried to fight individually in the forest they would have avoided an even greater massacre.

Colonial officers such as George Washington praised the behavior of the Virginia troops and condemned the regular soldiers as cowards. In his previous military venture, Washington had developed almost a contempt for slipshod militiamen, but now he testified that they had "behav'd like Men and died like Soldiers." On the other hand, ". . . the dastardly behaviour of the English Soldier's expos'd all those who were inclin'd to do their duty to almost certain Death." [36] Regular officers who had survived the disaster were strongly inclined to agree in denouncing the behavior of their men. But why such a miserable performance by supposedly well-trained regular troops? One theory voiced at the time was that during the weeks of preparation and advance, the provincials had so impressed the redcoats with their descriptions of Indian ferocity and the terrors of the deep forest and had so deprecated the effectiveness of formal British tactics under wilderness conditions, that the regular troops had lost confidence in themselves.[37] Possibly, though, the basic quality of those troops may be the real key to the problem, many of the men being either castoffs from other regiments or fairly new recruits inveigled into the king's service. Yet it seems likely that the training and discipline under Braddock had been fairly rigorous, and that the men who comprised the advance striking force were the best of the various units from which they were drawn. Perhaps the most charitable judgment is that the shock of surprise, the consequent confusion in the British command, the disadvantages of the terrain, and the excellent use that the enemy made of his own advantages were a combination that might have shaken the best units in any army.

One significant consequence of the defeat was a quickened interest among Anglo-American military leaders in a reevaluation and modification of standard British tactics. Although the fact had been known for nearly a hundred years, it was now more obvious than ever that the conditions of warfare in the vast and dense American forest required special techniques and practices unfamiliar to European troops. Down through the years since the early Indian wars, Americans had been gradually developing a new style of warfare, actually a blend of Indian tactics, colonial improvisations, and the most useful of the formations and tactics prescribed in the standard military manuals.[38] Even before the fatal ninth of July in 1755, one observer of the colonial scene had argued that regular troops trained in orthodox tactics would be ineffective against Indians. "They are only of use to defend a fort, or to support *Indian* forces against regular troops," he said.

> Besides, being used to fire from walls, they scorn to shoot from behind trees; and would rather die than go out of their own road to practise such a low kind of military art. Not considering that the nature of the country, which is, as it were, one continued wood, requires that way of going to war, and that of all the methods of fighting that is best which is safest.[39]

It was the natural environment that made the difference, it seems. "The plain truth is," reasoned another commentator,

> *Regular troops,* in this *Wilderness-country,* are just the same that *irregular ones* would be in *Flanders. American irregulars* would easily

be confounded by *regular troops* in the *open fields* of *Europe;* and *regular troops* would be as easily reduced to the like confusion by *American irregulars* in the *woods here.*[40]

A Pennsylvanian thought that both methods of fighting could be retained and utilized according to circumstances by having "one Company of English and one of Indians always together that they may learn from each other and fight either after the English or Indian fashion." [41] No doubt that was expecting too much of both groups, but certainly there was a growing concern that colonial troops as well as regulars be trained to cope more effectively with the enemy in the wilderness environment.

One political leader who began urging this was Governor Dinwiddie. "I cannot expect You can do much this fall," he wrote to Colonel Washington, "but to keep the People [provincial troops] together, to have them taught their Exercises, and to teach them as much as possible Bush fighting." [42] What Dinwiddie was advocating here was to retain the best of the old while introducing the new, and this was the pattern most commonly followed by colonial military leaders. Two developments in particular showed the strength of the trend. In 1756 Parliament ordered that a new regular regiment, the Royal Americans, be formed in the colonies, mainly with American personnel.[43] This major unit of the British forces in America, officered in part by foreigners such as Henry Bouquet and Frederick Haldimand, developed its proficiency in forest warfare to a degree far surpassing the usual regiment of the line by applying the lessons learned during the previous hundred years of American experience. It was also in 1756 that a New Hampshire frontiersman named Robert Rogers began organizing and training a special corps of American rangers, schooling them in the ways of the woods and Indian tactics. Rogers' rangers were to become an invaluable asset to the British forces in the later campaigning along the northern frontier.[44]

The capture of Fort Beauséjour and Fort Gaspereau had greatly strengthened the British position in Nova Scotia without doing much to solve the problem of the recalcitrant Acadians, who still declined to swear allegiance. Governor Lawrence feared, understandably, that whenever France began a counteroffensive, from Louisbourg these people would become a dangerous fifth column. One drastic solution, which Lawrence apparently was considering during the early summer of 1755, was mass deportation. This was very much in line with the thinking of Shirley and other New Englanders, who had long resented the Acadians and coveted their rich farmlands. What helped Lawrence make up his mind was the shocking news of Braddock's defeat, portending a resurgence of the French menace and greater danger for Nova Scotia. Without authorization from the ministry, the governor and his council began issuing the necessary deportation orders, while concealing from the Acadians their impending fate. A fleet of vessels was chartered and assigned the task of removing the entire Acadian population to the various other British colonies as far south as Georgia, where they were expected to be absorbed.[45]

Then, early in September, the Acadians were assembled under military supervision and informed of the official decree that "your Lands and Tennements, Cattle of all Kinds and Live Stock of all Sortes are Forfitted to the Crown with all other your Effects Saving your money and Household Goods and you your Selves to be removed from this . . . Province." [46] Having been given this stunning piece of news, the people were kept thereafter under guard until the transports were ready to take them on board, while New England troops systematically burned down their dwellings and barns. On 8 October the main embarkation began, the poor inhabitants going off, as one officer noted, very unwillingly, "the women in Great Distress Carrying off Their Children In their arms. Others Carrying their Decript Parents in their Carts and all their Goods Moving in Great Confussion . . . a Sceen of woe and Distres." [47] Sailings continued through the fall of that year, until virtually all the Acadians, except a few who managed to escape and conceal themselves, were gone. It was one of the great human tragedies of history, never forgotten in French America.[48]

At the time of Braddock's defeat, nearly 5,000 troops were assembling in the Albany-Schenectady staging area for the expedition under Shirley against Niagara and that under Johnson against Crown Point. Both expeditions would have to advance along difficult wilderness routes, but unlike Braddock's army, they could follow streams and lakes much of the way, enabling them to rely upon water transport. But this too presented difficulties. Hundreds of water craft had to be constructed and assembled at the appropriate places, and after being carefully loaded with troops, equipment, supplies, and artillery, navigated by experienced boatmen. The type of craft most commonly employed on rivers was the bateau, "a light flat-bottomed boat, widest in the middle, and at each end sharp pointed, of about 1500 weight burden, and managed by two men, with paddles and setting-poles." [49] In more open waters, such as Lake Ontario, whaleboats and various kinds of small sailing vessels were preferred.

The two armies departed and went their separate ways during the latter part of July, each hoping to gain some victory to offset the disaster in Virginia. Shirley proceeded west from Schenectady with about 1,750 men, following the difficult Mohawk-Oswego water route; Johnson with his army of more than 3,000 men headed north up the Hudson Valley toward Lake George. Each expedition was strung out over many miles, with scouts and gangs of woodsmen moving far in advance to prepare the way, while details of sweating soldiers, boatmen, and wagoners labored along behind them in the endless task of maintaining the vital flow of supplies. At about the same time, Dieskau's regiments from France, strongly supported by units of *troupes de la marine* and Canadian militia, were being deployed from Quebec and Montreal. Some moved southward to defend the Champlain Valley toward which Johnson was advancing, while others moved westward to defend Fort Frontenac and the upper St. Lawrence now presumably threatened by Shirley. Thus each side had chosen to divide its main force in the northern theater, with the greater part of its strength directed toward the impending confrontation at Crown Point.

Shirley and Johnson proved alike in one respect—both were cautious fortifiers, unwilling to venture against a remote enemy until essential bases were made secure. For Johnson this meant the construction of a fort, which he named Edward in honor of the prince, at the Carrying Place on the upper Hudson, a site long occupied by the trading post of John Henry Lydius. Troops were detailed to carry on this extensive task, while others worked farther along improving the 14-mile road that led northwestward to the near end of Lake George.[50] There, on rising ground about a quarter of a mile from the water's edge, Johnson's army also began work on another fortification to be known as Fort George. Not until this advance base was in a defensible condition would Johnson embark his army and proceed down Lake George toward Crown Point. Meanwhile, Shirley had arrived at Oswego on 18 August only to discover serious weaknesses in the fortifications there. He dared not go on to Niagara without first strengthening Oswego, lest a French force descend from Fort Frontenac in his absence and occupy the essential base. Accordingly, he put his men to work making needed improvements, while sending scouts to the vicinity of both Fort Frontenac and Niagara.[51] The precautions being taken by Shirley and Johnson to safeguard their bases meant long delays while precious summer days and weeks slipped by.

Vaudreuil, who had the great advantage of the intelligence derived from Braddock's captured papers, intended that Dieskau should first defeat Johnson and then proceed with the bulk of his army as rapidly as possible to Lake Ontario for the struggle with Shirley.[52] By the first of September, only four days after Johnson had arrived at the southern end of Lake George, Dieskau's army of more than 3,000 regulars, militia, and Indians was in position at Fort St. Frédéric, "all in the best dispositions to treat the English as well as they had been treated at Fort du Quesne." Indeed, it was said by a colleague that Dieskau envied the glory achieved by Contrecoeur at the Monongahela and yearned to "efface it by something more brilliant." [53] His chance came, it seemed, when a British prisoner (who may have been deceiving his captors deliberately) informed Dieskau that the defenses of Fort Edward still were weak and the garrison small.[54] The baron decided to strike fast and hard.

A striking force of about 200 grenadiers together with some 700 Canadians and 600 Indians, under Dieskau's personal command, proceeded by boat up Wood Creek to South Bay, where they disembarked. Leaving about a hundred men to guard the boats, on 6 September the French advanced southward along a wilderness trail leading to Fort Edward. The following day both sides gained important information. Mohawk scouts with the British army informed Johnson, who was encamped with the main body of his force at the southern end of Lake George, that they had discovered tracks of a large body of French and Indians advancing from South Bay toward Fort Edward. Immediately Johnson sent a courier down to warn the threatened post, but the rider was waylaid and killed by some of Dieskau's Indians.[55] When the French commander, who now controlled a section of the connecting road several miles above Fort Edward, learned that Johnson actually was encamped not at Fort Edward but at Lake George a dozen miles to the north, he faced a dilemma. Which should he now attack, his original target only a short distance below him, or the main army in his rear? The decision was for the latter.[56]

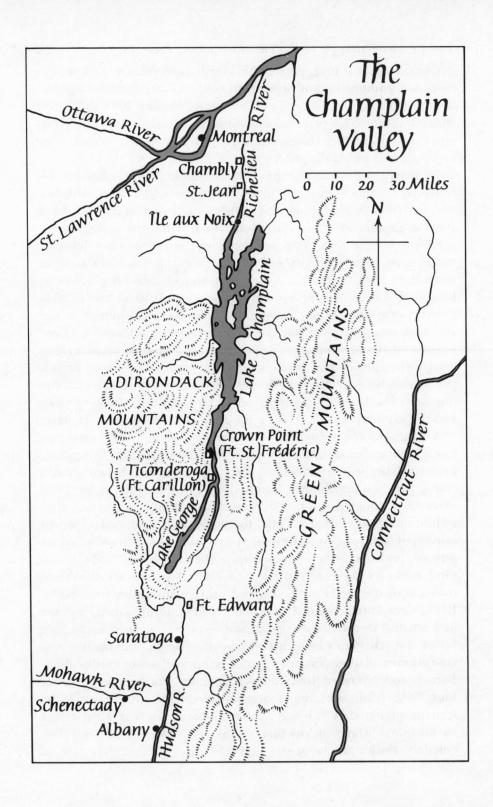

The Champlain Valley

0 10 20 30 Miles

N

Ottawa River

Montreal

Chambly

St. Jean

Île aux Noix

St. Lawrence River

Richelieu River

ADIRONDACK

MOUNTAINS

Lake Champlain

Crown Point
(Ft. St. Frédéric)

Ticonderoga
(Ft. Carillon)

Lake George

GREEN MOUNTAINS

Connecticut River

Ft. Edward

Saratoga

Mohawk River

Schenectady

Albany

Hudson R.

On the morning of the eighth, Dieskau headed north up the road, his striking force disposed in five parallel columns—regulars in the center, Canadians 30 paces outward on either side, and Indians a similar distance beyond the Canadians. When he had gone perhaps 6 or 7 miles and was approaching the defile at the south end of French Mountain, Dieskau received warning of a large body of troops and Indians coming down the road toward him. This was a force commanded by Colonel Ephraim Williams of Massachusetts, dispatched by Johnson to block the withdrawal of the French. Under his command Williams had perhaps as many as 1,000 provincials together with some 200 Indians led by Hendrick, the famous Mohawk chief.[57] Quickly the French commander deployed his men to form a trap, the Canadians and Indians lying concealed in advanced positions on either side of the road, with the regulars farther back to serve as bait. Unfortunately for Dieskau, some of his Iroquois warriors revealed themselves to the British too soon, possibly because they believed they were discovered, although Dieskau was convinced of treachery.[58] Nevertheless, the British were caught in a heavy crossfire that inflicted severe casualties on their van, especially among the Indians. Hendrick was killed and so was Williams, who fell before he could get off a single shot in reply. The premature attack on the van served as an alarm to the remainder of the British column. It didn't take them long to decide they could fight more effectively from the shelter of their camp, and so they headed back on the run, leaving the others to extricate themselves as best they could.[59]

Johnson's position at this date was not a fort but only a camp, crudely protected by a trench and a barricade of felled trees, wagons, and overturned bateaus and defended by perhaps a thousand men. As soon as Johnson heard the firing to the south, he ordered his men to the defenses. Soon the panting survivors of Williams' detachment were seen loping toward them along the road and across the cleared ground, dropping at last in the welcome shelter of the waiting camp. There they added to the uncertainty and confusion with their excited reports of a huge army of determined French and ferocious Indians drawing near. For a time Johnson's men were perilously close to panic, sensing how unprepared for a major action they really were, and some, it is said, actually hid themselves or feigned sickness to avoid the coming clash.[60] Fortunately, the respite of a few minutes brought some restoration of confidence, so that by the time the first of Dieskau's men came into view most of the defending troops were steeled for action, infantry spread along behind the barricade with muskets at the ready. There was artillery, too, pointed toward the south with gunners prepared to serve their pieces.

The brief respite was the result of Dieskau's trouble with his Indians who, after the initial skirmish, were loathe to follow close after the fleeing British. This attitude seemed to infect the Canadians too, forcing the exasperated commander to rely almost entirely upon his 200 grenadiers. It was midday when the French appeared before the camp. Without waiting to reconnoitre, Dieskau quickly deployed his force and launched a direct attack, hoping that the confusion and fright caused by the precipitate return of the beaten detachment would enable his regulars to sweep through Johnson's crude defenses, with Canadians and Indians affording some support. "The Regulars Came rank and File about 6 abrest," and began firing by platoons.[61] What Dieskau had not anticipated was the effectiveness of Johnson's artillery at close range. The British guns, as one jubilant defender observed, "made Lanes, Streets and Alleys" through the French formation;[62] the attackers had no cannon of their own with which to reply. When the first daring assault failed, the French were forced to be satisfied with holding what ground they had, while trying to discourage the British with an effective counterfire. They must have done well, with many Canadians and Indians now joining in, for a New England soldier later exclaimed that "the Hailstones from Heaven have not been much thicker than their Bullets came." [63] One of those bullets found lodging in the flesh of Johnson's hip, causing a wound more embarrassing than disabling. Dieskau, who himself had advanced far forward, was hit once and then again. A Canadian who came up to assist him was struck also and tumbled down over the fallen commander. Stubbornly, Dieskau refused to be carried to the rear.

After several hours of hot and futile fighting, the battered assault force finally began a disorderly retreat. Johnson was unable to initiate an organized pursuit; nevertheless, the more aggressive of the smoke- and sweat-begrimed Americans did begin scrambling across the barricade to give chase, and soon turned the French withdrawal into a rout. Excited parties of provincials and allied Indians hounded the fleeing enemy, killing and capturing many.

Braddock's defeat, 9 July 1755, by E. W. Deming. *Courtesy of the State Historical Society of Wisconsin*

The wounded Braddock being lifted into a wagon, 9 July 1755, by Howard Pyle. *Courtesy of Howard P. Brokaw*

Governor Robert Dinwiddie of Virginia.
*Courtesy of the National Portrait Gallery,
London*

Earl of Loudoun.

ATTAQUES DES RETRANCHEMENS DEVANT LE FORT CARILLON
en Amérique

par les anglais commandés par le général Abercrombie contre les français aux ordres du Marquis de Montcalm le 8 Juillet 1758.

RENVOIS.

A Le fort Carillon. B Retranchemens, que les français ont commencé à faire le 7 Juillet, au matin. C Camp de l'armée française, où elle se rendit le 6 & resta sous les armes pendant la nuit du 7 au 8. Le 8 à la pointe du jour elle prit la position D en ordre de bataille derrière les retranchemens. E Les grénadiers & les piquets pour reserve derrière chaque bataillon. F Colonnes des anglais, qui attaquent les retranchemens à midi & demie. G Pelotons de troupes legères & provinciales fusillant entre ces colonnes. H Les canadiens sortent du retranchement, & attaquent une colonne anglaise en flanc. I Chaloupes des anglais, qui parurent pendant l'attaque, & furent repoussées par l'artillerie du fort. K Retraite des colonnes anglaises dans leur premier camp près des moulins à four vers sept heures du soir; leur troupes legères couvrirent cette retraite par leur feu prolongé jusques dans la nuit. L Position des français après la retraite des anglais. M Batteries, redoutes & retranchemens, que les français établirent après le combat.

C.P.S.C.M.

Plan of Abercromby's attack on Fort Carillon (Ticonderoga), 8 July 1758. *Courtesy of The Public Archives of Canada, Manoir Richelieu Collection*

A view of Louisbourg in North America, taken near the Light House
. . . 1758, by Captain Ince. *Courtesy of The Public Archives of Canada*

Sketch of the Siege of Louisbourg, 1758, by Thomas Davies. *Courtesy of The Royal Artillery Institution, Woolwich, London*

The Battle of Rogers' Rock, March 1758, by J. L. G. Ferris. This fierce skirmish between the Rangers and men from a French outpost took place near Lake George. *Courtesy of The Glens Falls Insurance Company*

Montcalm congratulating his victorious troops after the defeat of Abercromby, 8 July 1758, by Harry A. Ogden. *Courtesy of Fort Ticonderoga Museum*

Embarkation of Abercromby's Expedition, Lake George, 5 July 1758,
by F. C. Yohn. *Courtesy of The Glens Falls Insurance Company*

Morning of the Battle of the Plains of Abraham, Quebec, 13 September
1759, by Frederic Remington. The British line is awaiting the arrival of
the French.

Charge of the Black Watch at
Fort Carillon (Ticonderoga), 8
July 1758, by G. R. Embleton.
*Courtesy of Fort Ticonderoga
Museum*

The wounded Montcalm reentering Quebec, 13 September 1759, by
Howard Pyle. *Courtesy of Howard P. Brokaw*

Lieutenant General Jeffrey Amherst, by Joseph Blackburn, 1758. *Courtesy of the Mead Art Building, Amherst College, Sesquicentennial gift of Mrs. Richard K. Webel*

General James Wolfe, by J. S. C. Schaak. *Courtesy of the National Portrait Gallery, London*

Marquis de Montcalm. *Courtesy of The Public Archives of Canada*

Sir William Johnson, Indian Superintendant, by John Wollaston, ca. 1751. *Courtesy of the Albany Institute of History and Art*

General Hames Abercromby. *Courtesy of the New Brunswick Museum, St. John, N.B., Webster Collection*

General Robert Monckton.

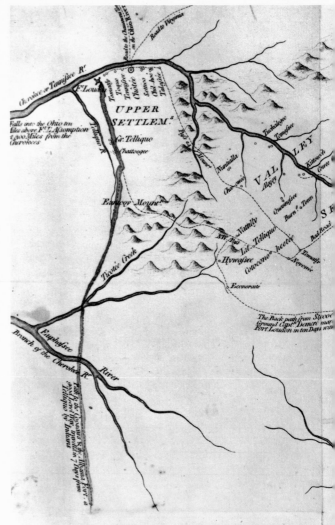

NB. Way pretty Level from Hywassee to Tomassee in the Lower
Settlem.ts Distance about, 90 Miles. The Trading path is 45 Miles
from Keeowee to the Middle Settlem.ts The Pass over the 24 Mount.s
is the nearest Way, but more Difficult even than the North West Pass at Natally.
Euwucoy is the last Mount.n you have after you get over Natally Pass in the Way
to Great Telliquo, Fort Moore Fort Augusta lie about South East from
Fort P. George 150 Miles

A sketch of the Cherokee country. *Courtesy of the Massachusetts Historical Society*

Pontiac's attack on Fort Detroit, 1763, by Frederic Remington.

At the Iroquois Council Fire, by Frederic Remington.

On the War-Path, by Howard Pyle. Indians attacking a colonial farmer.
Courtesy of Howard P. Brokaw

Dieskau, lying critically wounded, was taken prisoner and eventually carried to Johnson's tent. Thus ended the main phase of what an exulting New Englander called, "the greatest Fight that ever was known on the American Shores," the Battle of Lake George on 8 September 1755.[64]

Having left their knapsacks containing necessary rations at the site of the first skirmish near French Mountain, many of the fleeing Canadians and Indians hurried there only to encounter a detachment of more than 200 New Hampshire and New York troops hastening up from Fort Edward. Beaten once, the French now were badly mauled again. There was nothing for the hungry, weary survivors of these various actions to do but make their way as best they could around the lower end of French Mountain and then north to their boats. It was a downcast and bedraggled shadow of a striking force that finally reached Fort St. Frédéric several days later.[65] Total French losses included about a hundred killed or missing and a somewhat greater number wounded; more than 75 of these casualties were regulars. Johnson had about 189 of his men killed or missing and some 90 or more wounded, not counting the more than 30 Indians who died, principally in the first encounter.[66]

Most of Johnson's Indians left him a few days after the battle, disheartened by their grievous losses. Fearing that the enemy would return in greater strength to resume the attack, Johnson tried to prod his weary provincials into improving their defenses, but intercolonial antagonisms were bobbing up again in the wake of victory, and little was accomplished. The frustrated commander, unable to rely upon many of his officers, to say nothing of the unkempt musket-slopers, began to have serious doubts about the feasibility of advancing farther toward Crown Point that year. As for the French on Lake Champlain, they were fully occupied in trying to bring order out of the chaos of defeat, while beginning the construction of a new fort at Carillon, 12 miles south of Crown Point. At that strategic site, where the portage route from Lake George connects with Lake Champlain, would arise the first form of what later was to become Fort Ticonderoga. Prior to the battle of 8 September 1755, Vaudreuil had had designs on Oswego, hoping to gain full control of Lake Ontario, but the severe setback at Lake George convinced the French governor that major offensive activity must be postponed until the following year. In fact, neither side was ready to advance farther. Shirley, enmeshed in difficulties of his own at Oswego and piqued by Johnson's failure to send him a direct account of the recent action, urged the New Yorker to get on with the offensive against Crown Point, but that was like poking a sick dog. Before the end of September, Shirley himself was forced to give up any hope of continuing on to Niagara. So the year's activity came to an end, with the French firmly retaining the Forks of the Ohio, Niagara, and Crown Point. Small garrisons were left to hold the various forts in the wilderness, and the rest of the troops either went into winter quarters or were demobilized.[67]

One immediate by-product of British military failure, evident as early as August of 1755 and continuing on through the fall and winter, was the intensification of Indian raiding activity along the exposed frontiers of the colonies. This only served to complicate the military problem, as threatened areas cried for troops and retaliation. "We are almost every Day receiving News of Indians killing and captivating our Friends in divers Places," wrote a New Englander in August, while another reported that enemy Indians had become so bold as "to Return our watch word In the Night *Sharp— All is Well."* [68] Obviously, with conditions like these spreading along the frontier from Maine to Virginia, all was not well. Dunbar's hasty withdrawal to Philadelphia after Braddock's defeat left the entire task of defending the long, exposed Virginia frontier to George Washington and his provincials, a force quite inadequate for that difficult assignment. In October the terror came to Pennsylvania, the colony without a militia, as disaffected Delawares and Shawnees began attacking pioneer settlements in the Susquehanna Valley. One Pennsylvanian reported that "almost all the women and children over Sasquehannah have left their habitations and the roads are full of starved, naked, indigent multitudes. . . . Not one twentieth man has arms."[69] "You cannot conceive," wrote Governor Morris in mid-November, "what a vast Tract of Country has been depopulated by these merciless Savages." [70] On the first day of 1756, Indian raiders wiped out the Moravian settlement of Gnadenhütten on the Lehigh River, leaving "all silent and desolate the Houses burnt the Inhabitants butchered in the most Shocking Manner their mangled Bodies for want of Funerals exposd to Birds and Beasts of Prey. . . ." [71] It is difficult to discover how much of such raiding was actively promoted by French officials and how much the Indians did solely on their own initiative, but in any case it usually worked to the advantage of the French. Vaudreuil himself set a value on the raids when he said that "nothing is more calculated to disgust the people of those Colonies and to make them desire the return of peace." [72] Random destruction of life and property was a means to an end, terror a part of the official strategy, all of which was no more than a continuation of the pattern developed in the earlier wars and utilized to a greater or lesser degree by both sides.

Shirley, while still at Oswego in September 1755, had begun to turn his energetic mind to the prospects for the following year. Contemplating a series of new offensives, he later gained general approval of his plans from a number of other governors and then, during the early months of 1756, proceeded with the necessary preparations. Four armies were to move simultaneously against important French positions: one up the Kennebec River to threaten the Chaudière Valley and Quebec; a second, utilizing Johnson's old base at Lake George, against Crown Point; a third, based upon Oswego, against Fort Frontenac and Niagara; and a fourth, consisting largely of southern provincial troops, against Fort Duquesne.[73]

Even as Shirley schemed and prepared, however, steps were being taken in London to replace him as commander in chief. His failure to gain control of Lake Ontario in 1755 made it easy for his American enemies, who now had access to important members of the ministry, to impugn his ability. England was crying for a drive to victory in America, and Shirley was deemed not the man to produce what the country demanded. In contrast, William Johnson was shining with new luster. His remarkable rapport with the Iroquois made him almost indispensable. What is more, Johnson's defensive victory at Lake George had been favorably reported in England even as it was being immoderately vaunted in the colonies, with the result that a grateful king awarded him a baronetcy and £5,000.[74] Had the scales been fairly balanced, the same would have come to Shirley, but instead the New Englander lost not only his command but also his post as governor of Massachusetts. Yet it was not the favored Johnson who was to be his successor as commander in chief, for the ministry quite properly placed little faith in amateur generals. The supreme command was given to an experienced officer of the regular army, John Campbell, Earl of Loudoun. France, too, found it necessary to select a new commander, since

Baron Dieskau now was a prisoner of the British. The man chosen
for the job was Louis Joseph, Marquis de Montcalm, a gentleman
and scholar as well as a soldier, at that time in his mid-forties.
Montcalm was sent to Canada in the spring of 1756 with two fresh
regiments, Royal Roussillon and La Sarre, and a group of able,
talented officers among whom was the general's aide, young Louis
Antoine de Bougainville.[75]

Far more important than the shifting of commands in America
were the international developments that had been taking place in
Europe since 1754. The British ministry, headed by the Duke of
Newcastle, was deeply apprehensive about the security of Hanover,
which was threatened by the military power of Prussia and France.
With the ominous developments of 1755, Newcastle began to seek
allies. His advances to France's traditional enemy Austria were
rebuffed, for the Hapsburg state was seeking an advantageous
friendship with France. In the fall of 1755, Britain succeeded in
obtaining an alliance with Russia, and then a few months later, in
January 1756, she concluded the Convention of Westminster with
Frederick II of Prussia, thereby gaining some additional security
for Hanover. France was surprised and indignant that Frederick
had placed himself under such obligation to Britain in a pact so
obviously aimed against herself. Accordingly, the French government became receptive to renewed Austrian wooing, and signed a
defensive alliance with the Hapsburg monarchy early in May 1756.
This completed what historians have called the "Diplomatic Revolution of 1756," a major reversal of alliances, pitting France and
Austria against Britain, Prussia, and Russia. At this time Spain,
a weak and declining power, remained uncommitted.

Sometime before this consummation, the French government had
lost all hope of a peaceful solution to its continuing quarrel with
Britain in Europe, India, and America, and had begun making
serious preparations for war. Newcastle, apparently, still clung to
the hope of peace. The assembling of French naval and military
resources during the early months of 1756 aroused in England
deep fear of a cross-Channel invasion, but the blow, when it came,
actually fell upon the British-held island of Minorca in the western
Mediterranean. A French expedition landed there in April and by
the end of June had made itself master of the important British
base of Mahon. In the meantime, Newcastle's government issued a
declaration of war against France on 17 May 1756, citing a long

record of French aggression in the West Indies and North America and justifying the British countermeasures.[76] Now the conflict, later known in Europe as the Seven Years' War, was open and official, with the contending powers fully committed to the support of their respective colonies.

Shirley, at first not aware of how disastrously his standing in London had been undermined by his political enemies, spent the winter and spring of 1756 in carrying forward as best he could the essential preparations for the year's campaigning. Much of his attention was drawn to Oswego, his base in 1755, where the garrison troops left through the winter had suffered greatly from lack of adequate shelter and supplies. Shirley knew how important it was to safeguard the long, difficult access route from Schenectady to Oswego, as well as to rectify the weaknesses in Oswego's fortifications before the French could arrive in force. If ever the French should capture Oswego and transform it into a power base of their own, the Six Nations and their satellite tribes would be drawn irresistibly into the French orbit, a great part of the fur trade would fall into French hands, and much of the West would be blocked off from future British expansion. French Oswego, like Crown Point, then would be the sharp tip of a dagger aimed at the vitals of the British northern colonies. The French, too, realized full well the strategic importance of Oswego and subscribed to the dictum that "nothing . . . must be omitted for the destruction of this dangerous post. . . ." [77]

Shirley made an excellent appointment when he designated Lieutenant Colonel John Bradstreet to be in full charge of the difficult and often dangerous task of keeping supplies moving from Schenectady to Oswego. Bradstreet was given command of a corps of 2,000 fighting bateaumen organized in forty companies. He was to supervise the construction of hundreds of bateaus and whaleboats for the army's use, the employment of wagons and sledges for moving bulky supplies over the several portages, and the clearing of any obstructions from the shallow waterways.[78] Roughly midway between Schenectady and Oswego was the principal portage, an overland track several miles long which connected the upper Mohawk with Wood Creek. The Mohawk, or eastern, end of this portage was guarded by Fort Williams, while the western terminus, at Wood Creek, was guarded by a small palisaded post known as Fort Bull. On 27 March 1756, a French and Indian raiding force led by Lieutenant Gaspard-Joseph Chaussegros de Léry suddenly appeared at Fort Bull, overwhelmed the garrison, dumped the captured munitions and other supplies in the creek, stove in fifteen bateaus, and demolished the fort. When William Johnson arrived with a strong relief force several days later, the enemy was gone.[79]

Despite this discouraging blow, the essential preparations were continued at Oswego and elsewhere. Bradstreet's corps carried on various projects for improving the supply route and kept the supplies flowing toward Oswego, while ship's carpenters and sailors stationed at the base on Lake Ontario hastened the building of sailing craft and whaleboats to assure naval supremacy. There never seemed to be enough hands, or enough money, to accomplish all that needed to be done. Although the fortifications at Oswego required major improvements to make them secure, priority was given to the program of naval construction. Shirley had high hopes that this time a strong, aggressive army, including four regiments of regulars, would gain the mastery of Lake Ontario and capture the French forts at either end. The naval aspect of the impending struggle was given dramatic emphasis on 26 June when a French convoy encountered several of the small British craft away from their base and managed to capture one of them.[80]

Earlier in the year, Captain Villiers had established an advance base camp at Sackett's Harbor on the eastern shore of Lake Ontario, from which point he and his raiders could easily advance south through the woods to harass Oswego and its long line of communication with Schenectady.[81] On 3 July, Villiers with a force of 600 French and Indians at last encountered Bradstreet himself, less than 12 miles south of Oswego. At the time, Bradstreet was conducting a long convoy of bateaus with several hundred bateaumen en route back to Schenectady, and when the enemy suddenly appeared the British at first were thrown into near confusion. Bradstreet, however, managed to rally his men for "a Sharpe fight . . . in the Indian Way" along the riverbank and through a nearby swamp, until at last Villiers broke off and withdrew. Both sides later claimed victory, with inflated reports of enemy losses, and it is not clear which employed the greater exaggeration. At least Bradstreet and his party did reach Schenectady, to receive the plaudits of their superiors, but some must have wondered how a British army would be able to operate beyond Oswego with a line of supply so vulnerable.[82]

All through June and the first weeks of July, Shirley and the other provincial leaders were anxiously awaiting the arrival of the new commander in chief, Lord Loudoun, for without him the really serious business of despoiling the French could hardly begin. Loudoun was preceded by his two subordinates, Major Generals James Abercromby and Daniel Webb, who arrived at Albany during the last week of June 1756, accompanied by the Thirty-fifth Regiment of foot and the Forty-second Highlanders. Abercromby immediately assumed temporary command, relieving Shirley of his heavy responsibility. For the Massachusetts lawyer, politician, and amateur general, this represented the culmination of personal failure made all the more bitter by his own knowledge of how earnestly he had worked for his country's good. By this time, the two northern armies—one destined for Lake Ontario and the other, under Major General John Winslow of Massachusetts, destined for Lake George—were assembling with all the bustle and confusion, the squabbling and complaining, that colonial leaders had come to recognize as normal. The arrival of the two British regiments raised the question of whether they should be assigned to the Lake George expedition, which up to this time had been conceived of as an all-provincial force. At a council of war on 16 July, Winslow made it clear that his New England troops wanted no part of the regulars, probably because the colonial officers were loathe to take orders from their juniors in the king's service, while the colonial rank and file feared the introduction of British military discipline. Abercromby quickly discovered that it was best not to press the matter too far, and accordingly it was agreed that units of regulars would follow Winslow's army as it advanced, occupying positions vacated by the provincials and ready to provide support if needed.[83]

Loudoun himself stepped ashore at New York on 23 July to be greeted with enthusiastic celebration. Shirley was there for the occasion, as was Benjamin Franklin. After several days of conferences and social gatherings, the new commander in chief sailed for Albany. Shirley's enemies lost no time in regaling His Lordship with highly biased accounts of the deposed commander's delinquencies, until Loudoun became convinced that Shirley was not only incompetent but in all probability guilty of negligence and even dishonesty. The inadequate system of supply that had caused such a heavy mortality at Oswego the previous winter, the confusion in army contracting, the current tension between provincial troops and regulars, the continuing weakness of the fortifications at Oswego, all were laid to Shirley's account. Under this dark cloud the former commander sailed for England, where his hopes for vindication were dashed when his patron, Newcastle, was succeeded by William Pitt.[84]

Meanwhile in New France, Montcalm arrived before the end of July at Fort Frontenac with a strong expeditionary force. There he learned the results of a reconnaissance mission to Oswego just completed by Villiers and a French engineer. On the basis of this report, as well as information gained from deserters, he decided to proceed against the British base.[85] At this time Oswego was a cluster of military and trading facilities on both banks of the Oswego River where it empties into Lake Ontario from the southeast. On the western bank, in the angle formed by the river and lake, stood the old stone trading post, now protected with outworks

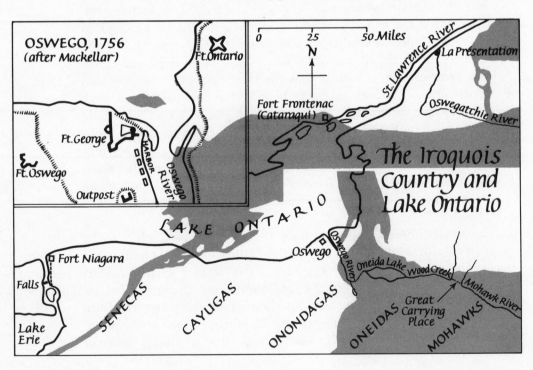

OSWEGO, 1756
(after Mackellar)

Ft. Ontario

Ft. George

HARBOR

Oswego River

Ft. Oswego

Outpost

0   25   50 Miles

N

Fort Frontenac
(Cataraqui)

St. Lawrence River

La Présentation

Oswegatchie River

The Iroquois
Country and
Lake Ontario

LAKE ONTARIO

Fort Niagara

Falls

Lake
Erie

SENECAS

CAYUGAS

ONONDAGAS

Oswego

Oswego River

Oneida Lake

Wood Creek

ONEIDAS

Great
Carrying
Place

Mohawk River

MOHAWKS

facing to the south and west. Just below the trading post was the small harbor where the British kept most of their fleet of whale-boats and the half-dozen combat vessels then available or nearing completion. To the south, strung out along the river's edge, were the huts of the trading village, partially defended by a small forti-fication on high ground just beyond. Unfortunately, the trading post and harbor were overlooked by high land on the east bank of the river only a quarter of a mile away. In order to prevent that dominating position from being occupied by an attacking army, the British had built an outwork called Fort Ontario, walled with a stout palisade surrounded by a ditch. Occupying these positions was a garrison of about 1,135 officers and men of the Fiftieth and Fifty-first regiments, Schuyler's New Jersey regiment, and the Royal Regiment of Artillery, all under the command of Colonel James Mercer, together with a considerable number of sailors, workmen, and traders. The Iroquois, who could provide invaluable assistance should the place be invested, were notably lacking.[86]

Montcalm's expeditionary force, coming down from Sackett's Harbor during the second week of August, totaled about 3,000 men of whom 1,300 were regulars of the regiments of La Sarre, Guyenne, and Béarn; 1,500 were *troupes de la marine* and colonial militia; and the remainder were Indians. The main force, which was transported down the coast in a fleet of boats, was preceded by advance parties of Canadians and Indians on foot to secure a site for landing and keep an eye on the garrison. By the tenth of August, the British were aware of the Indians' presence, though as yet there was no other warning of an impending attack. During the night of 10 August the main body of Montcalm's army dis-embarked without opposition at a cove only a mile or two above Oswego and established a base camp. When Mercer sent a schooner to reconnoiter the coast the next day, the camp was discovered, and the British knew their enemies were upon them. Two armed ves-sels sent to harass the French base came under such hot fire from the shore that they finally drew back to a more comfortable distance and contented themselves with patrolling.[87]

On the afternoon of 11 August an advance force of Canadians and Indians appeared at Fort Ontario and, taking shelter behind trees and stumps began peppering the fort with small-arms fire, which was returned by the defenders. After dark, the British inside the palisade heard the unmistakable sounds of ax-work as the

Canadians set about clearing a road for bringing up their artillery from the camp. The next day both sides resumed firing, and it became increasingly obvious to the British that a full-scale attack was underway. Mercer, realizing how exposed the fortifications on the west side of the river would be if the enemy gained control of the high east bank, pressed his men to continue improving the works by ditching and walling, while Fort Ontario held the French at bay. More manpower was urgently needed to bolster the defense, so two Indian messengers were hurried off with urgent dispatches to Johnson and Abercromby. Unfortunately, the messengers deserted or were seized by French Indians; the papers they carried provided Montcalm with important details concerning the strength and condition of the garrison.[88]

The arrival of the French regulars with their artillery and the digging of a parallel trench only a pistol shot from Fort Ontario, marked the beginning of the actual siege. By 13 August, the artillerymen were nearly ready to open up at close range from positions higher than the top of the palisade. Mercer, on the west bank, was forced to the conclusion that Fort Ontario could not be defended much longer; he therefore sent permission for the garrison to withdraw across the river and help defend the other fortifications. The withdrawal was skillfully executed during the afternoon, apparently without revealing to the enemy what was happening. Once the evacuation was discovered, however, the French quickly took possession of the abandoned fort and became masters of the dominating east bank. Now Montcalm set his men to work preparing artillery positions just west of the captured fort, at the edge of the bluff overlooking the trading post 400 yards across the river. During the night of 13 August, twenty cannon were lugged "in men's arms" to these new positions, and by 6:00 A.M. on the fourteenth the French were ready to commence their bombardment. Now the British were exposed "even to the buckle of their shoe. . . ."[89] The first echoing *booms*, quickly followed by splintering crashes and the rising of dust in the exposed British positions, were manfully answered by Mercer's own artillery, but Montcalm's tremendous advantage was apparent to all. Enfiladed and dominated from higher ground, the garrison found itself bereft of adequate defense or shelter. More and more shots tore into the exposed area, killing some of the seriously ill as they huddled in their tents. Many of the able-bodied men abandoned the walls and cowered in the ditch to escape the devastating fire, while terrified army wives added their screams to the din.

About 8:00 A.M. a large force of Canadians and Indians was sighted crossing the river a mile above the fort, "some swimming, others wading up to the waist or neck. . . ." [90] This was the Sieur de Rigaud's command, hurrying to gain a foothold on the west bank in order to surround the British and prevent any relief or escape. Before a counterforce could be dispatched to oppose this maneuver, Mercer was killed by a cannonball, leaving the command to Lieutenant Colonel Littlehales. The new commander, facing disaster on all sides, consulted with his subordinate officers and decided that further resistance was useless. When the elated Montcalm heard a British drum beat the rappel and saw the white flag go up, he knew Oswego was his. Capitulation the French "had not dared to expect so soon," after only three days of fighting.[91] At about 10:00 A.M., Littlehales sent a flag of truce across the river to arrange terms. It was agreed that the defeated troops were to become prisoners of war, and Montcalm promised them protection against Indian vengeance.[92] When the tally of prisoners was taken, it amounted to more than 1,600, including a considerable number of females. In addition, the French acquired at least 6 vessels of war, some 200 barges or bateaus, numerous cannon, a supply of ammunition, hundreds of barrels of flour and meat, and more than 18,000 *livres* in cash. Montcalm could afford to indulge in a little boasting. "This expedition," he informed Versailles,

is decisive for the Colony. Chouaguen [Oswego] has been the apple of discord. Its position on Lake Ontario—the manner in which the English were fortifying themselves—the facility the Indians experienced at that place, to dispose of their peltries to much better advantage than in our forts; all these reasons created the apprehension that, sooner or later, England would possess the superiority in the trade of the Upper countries. The capture of Chouaguen destroys their projects in this regard.[93]

Unfortunately, Montcalm's perfect victory was tarnished when his Indians slipped out of control and began plundering the terrified British prisoners, killing a number of them before the French troops could restore order. Needless to say, this was extremely distasteful to a professional officer and gentleman of honor such as Montcalm, and he deeply regretted the stain.[94]

Would Montcalm now push on through the Mohawk Valley to

capture Albany and take Winslow's army in the rear? This was a glittering prospect, but the French general knew that it was beyond his capability in 1756. The route was long and difficult, and extremely vulnerable to Iroquois attack. Furthermore, Montcalm's Canadians now were anxious to return home, for the harvest was approaching and families needed food.[95] If no further offensive was possible, then surely the French regulars could transform Oswego into a secure base of their own, since it already was partially fortified and could readily be supplied by water from Fort Frontenac. Oswego in French hands would deny to the British their only good access to Lake Ontario, with the consequent drying up of the Albany fur trade and the almost inevitable shifting of Iroquois interests toward Quebec. Even that undeniably great advantage Montcalm felt constrained to forego. His army, he thought, had done all that he could reasonably demand. Accordingly, after thoroughly demolishing Oswego, the victorious army withdrew from the former British base and began its journey back to Montreal.

The strategic consequences stemming from the destruction of Oswego were far-reaching. Now Loudoun had no advance base from which to launch a British offensive against Fort Frontenac or Niagara, which meant in turn that the French could afford to shift some of their western strength into the Champlain Valley to help stop Winslow's drive toward Crown Point. Sir William Johnson sensed yet another disturbing consequence: "The fate of Oswego," he informed Loudoun, "has I fear involved in it the Attachment of some of our Indians, shaken that of others and alarmed most of them." [96]

At Lake George, Winslow and his army were still struggling with every problem except the French. Fort William Henry, begun by Johnson the previous year and now almost completed, stood at the south end of the lake a short distance west of the remains of old Fort George, but it contributed little or nothing to the offensive spirit of the army. A floundering supply system meant an inadequate diet for the troops, which in turn contributed to a lengthening list of sick and dying soldiers. One officer at Fort Edward wrote that they had been "burying 5 and 6 a day at this place for some days past—not more than 2 thirds of our Army fit for Service, and those extremely dispirited, and disheartned [sic], not half the Men they were when they came from home." [97] It was obvious that the army had lost its spirit and will, especially after hearing of Oswego's fate.

In fairness to Loudoun it must be said that the campaigning of 1756, with all its frustrations and failures climaxed by the disastrous destruction of Oswego, was not his war. He had arrived in the middle of preparations, with no opportunity to shape a viable plan of operations or find early solutions to the host of frustrating administrative problems dumped into his lap. Had the transfer of command occurred in the early spring, Loudoun would have had a reasonable chance to build upon Shirley's basically sound program, and might then have enjoyed a fair measure of success. After the fall of Oswego, the commander in chief clung to the small hope that Winslow's army at Lake George might yet provide some measure of victory. Early in October he went upriver to Fort Edward, only to discover that by that time there was little he or anyone else could do to restore the vigor of the faded regiments. Winslow's army no longer was capable of exertion. As for Montcalm, who had come down to Carillon after receiving the applause of Montreal, he now wisely accepted the dictate of approaching winter and on 26 October began his return journey to the St. Lawrence. Some days later Loudoun, too, retired from the front, leaving only a holding force at Fort William Henry and Fort Edward. By the time the garrisons of both armies had settled into their Spartan quarters, a foot of snow covered the frozen ground.[98]

In Pennsylvania, Maryland, Virginia, and the Carolinas, 1756 was the year of the agonizing defensive, when inadequate forces of rangers and militia strove desperately to cope with the widespread and highly destructive raids of the Indians and French. Fort Duquesne and Indian villages such as Kittanning in the upper Ohio Valley served the enemy well as bases for these raids eastward into the backcountry of the British colonies. The potential weakness of isolated, ill-supported frontier outposts was well demonstrated about the end of July when a party of French and Indians destroyed Fort Granville on the Juniata River in Pennsylvania.[99] This blow occurred just as Governor Robert Morris of Pennsylvania was preparing an offensive strike against Kittanning, a complex of villages on both sides of the Allegheny River less than 50 miles above Fort Duquesne. Morris selected Colonel John Armstrong, a frontier surveyor whose own brother had died in the defense of Fort Granville, to be leader of what now became a retaliatory effort. Armstrong assembled a composite striking force of 300 men, mostly Scotch-Irish frontiersmen, some of whom were experienced traders familiar with the western forest. Their rendezvous was Fort Shirley (Aughwick) on one of the upper branches of the Juniata, about 90 miles from the target.

Taking his departure from Fort Shirley on 30 August, Armstrong pushed rapidly westward along well-established trails leading across the seemingly endless succession of ridges toward the Allegheny. By daybreak of 8 September, the attack force was in position at the edge of Kittanning. The sudden furious assault took the sleeping Indians by surprise. Leaping to their feet, they caught up their muskets and prepared to defend themselves. At least one and perhaps many of the Delaware dwellings were substantial structures built of logs; in these the Indians made their stand, firing at the attackers through loopholes and windows. For several hours the heavy firing continued, with a thickening cloud of gunsmoke accumulating around the embattled cluster of huts. At last the Pennsylvanians resorted to the torch. When the flames began crackling and leaping along the walls and roofs of the dwellings, some of the Indians emerged and ran for the river. Armstrong's men, whenever they could, shot them as they appeared or killed them in the water. Captain Jacobs, a Delaware war chief notorious among the whites, crawled out through a window only to be shot and killed. The frightful din began to be punctuated with the sharp reports of exploding weapons inside the huts as the flames engulfed the interiors, and worse, occasional heavy explosions of stored gunpowder, hurling Indian bodies and debris into the air. By noon, the battle was over, with the victorious Pennsylvanians in control of the main village and the surviving Indians gathering with others in the untouched outlying settlements. It was at best an incomplete victory. Armstrong, himself wounded in the shoulder by a musket ball, was able to rescue eleven white colonists who had been prisoners of the Delawares, but it seems certain that most of the enemy Indians and their captives, as well as a few Frenchmen believed to have been present, eluded the attackers.[100] After finishing the destruction of the main village, Armstrong began a swift withdrawal. In all, the Pennsylvanians had lost seventeen of their own men.

Despite the rather limited success gained by Armstrong and his men, the blow to Kittanning had some lasting effects. It served as a pointed reminder to the French that even after their victory at Oswego the long, thin line of communication and supply stretching from Montreal through the Great Lakes and down to Fort Duquesne was still vulnerable. Morale in the Middle Colonies, hitherto drooping under the almost continuous battering of French and Indian raiding parties, now began to revive a little with the demonstration that Americans could give as well as take punishment. Conversely, the hostile Indians were shaken by the realization that they no longer enjoyed immunity from retaliation for their attacks on pioneer settlements. For the remainder of the year, these Indians were noticeably less aggressive, and Pennsylvania gained additional time to gather its strength and build up its long-delayed defenses.[101]

So far, the war had not imposed great economic strain on the British colonies; in fact, for some sectors of the colonial world, economic opportunities were abnormally favorable. Privateering, as in previous wars, offered attractive possibilities to daring investors and mariners. So did illegal commerce. At Louisbourg and in certain Caribbean ports, British and French merchants continued their profitable exchange of goods, despite official attempts to stamp out the traffic. When American sea captains found it too dangerous to take their cargoes directly to French ports in the West Indies, they began going instead to the neutral Dutch islands of Curaçao and St. Eustatius, where the exchange could take place without undue risk.[102] The enterprising Dutch, seeking to wring maximum advantage from their neutrality, also began carrying cargoes back and forth between France and the French colonies in America, on the supposition that the Royal Navy would not interfere with neutral shipping. France, benefiting from this traffic, was quite willing to overlook the fact that it clearly violated her own mercantile laws. Britain, however, took a different view, and in 1756 issued an official pronouncement asserting that a form of trade illegal in time of peace might not be legitimized in time of war. This so-called "Rule of the War of 1756" provided the justification for a more stringent blockade by the Royal Navy, involving serious interference with neutral shipping.[103]

During 1756, the northern colonies received a more legitimate economic boost when Parliament granted them a subsidy totaling £115,000 as compensation for the sacrifices they had made the previous year and to encourage further endeavors. At first no comparable reward went to the southern colonies, largely because of their former stinginess toward Braddock; but later, in 1757, Parliament did relent and voted £50,000 in compensation to Virginia and the Carolinas.[104] These funds helped to sustain the American economy, as the British government in effect exempted the colonists from carrying a large part of the financial burden of the war. What is more, not even serious price inflation was noted in most areas until 1757 or later, despite a considerable amount of war profiteering on the part of colonial contractors.[105]

Pennsylvania, in the meantime, was being confronted more directly than ever with its own peculiar problem, the question of pacifism or defense. The Quakers themselves now were divided on the issue, with only a diminishing minority still opposing any and all defensive measures. Most had come to recognize that under the circumstances, with the Delawares and Shawnees now active enemies, and marauders from the sea able to enter Delaware Bay almost at will, some steps to protect the province were required. Thus, the government had been enabled to project a chain of forts along the frontier and also to create a volunteer militia.[106] Those Quaker legislators who could not bring themselves to compromise their own standards in the interests of public defense were beginning to realize the extreme awkwardness of their position as supposed representatives of an imperiled people. On 7 June 1756, six of them voluntarily and doubtless with great regret relinquished their seats, thus further reducing the pacifistic influence in government.[107]

In the fall of 1756, Sir William Johnson, as superintendent of Indian affairs, instructed his deputy George Croghan to begin actively exploring the prospects for a rapprochement with the Delawares and Shawnees. This fitted in well with the plans of the strict Quakers in Pennsylvania, who were anxious to continue their campaign for peace. Already some of them, under the determined leadership of Israel Pemberton, had formed the "Friendly Association for Gaining and Preserving Peace with the Indians by Pacific Measures," an organization dedicated to identifying and remedying the specific grievances which the Quakers believed were the actual cause of Indian hostility. Since the alleged grievances were rooted mainly in proprietary purchases of land, especially the notorious "Walking Purchase" of 1737, the efforts of the Friendly Association came to have a strong antiproprietary flavor.[108] Therefore, it is not surprising that the popular party, led by Franklin, readily lent its support to Pemberton's endeavor. From this time the leaders of the Friendly Association participated actively in major negotiations with the Indians, often undermining the government's official spokesmen by stimulating and endorsing Indian complaints. So persistent were these Quakers that before long they not only had laid a foundation for renewed amity between the Delawares and Pennsylvania, but also had gained widespread public acceptance of their charge that proprietary greed and chicanery were the real causes of Indian hostility.[109]

In French Canada, the *habitants* were suffering far more acutely than most of their antagonists to the south. Wartime conditions proved detrimental to agriculture, and near famine became a yearly ordeal for many Canadians. During the long Canadian winters, when the St. Lawrence River was frozen solid for months at a time, no provisions from France could enter, and the people were forced to subsist on whatever had been left over from the previous harvest. One of Montcalm's officers wrote that by November 1756 Canada was facing "the image of a famine," with winter just beginning.[110] Daily at Quebec the hungry *habitants* clustered at a certain wicket, jostling for position, to receive from the authorities a dole of bread made from a mixture of flour and peas. Compounding the general suffering was an unusually severe winter in 1756–57, with the snow accumulating in great drifts 10 to 12 feet deep. As late as April, the river at Montreal still bore the weight of loaded sleighs.[111]

Even though all major campaigning was stopped during the winter months while the opposing armies huddled around fires in their winter quarters, occasional forays were made by small groups to test the enemy's condition and perhaps to grab a prisoner or two for interrogation. Captain Robert Rogers, the leader of the rangers at Fort William Henry, led one such raid to Lake Champlain in the latter part of January 1757.[112] On the nineteenth of that month, Rogers and a party of seventy-three men, heavily armed and bundled against the cold, came to shore a few miles south of Fort Carillon, having advanced over the ice from the southern end of Lake George. Strapping on their snowshoes, they now moved inland to bypass the French fort, and on 21 January, a day of rain, arrived on the western shore of Lake Champlain approximately midway between Fort Carillon and Fort St. Frédéric. At once they sighted a horse-drawn sleigh and an escort of ten soldiers proceeding northward on the ice toward Crown Point. Rogers dispatched a party to intercept, and then headed south with another party to cut off a possible retreat. In doing so he soon discovered a convoy of about eight additional sleighs following the first. As soon as the leader of this second group sighted the rangers coming toward him over the ice, he ordered the sleighs to reverse course and make a run for the safety of Fort Carillon. Rogers' men were quick enough to capture three of the sleighs and seven of the escorting troops, whom they later interrogated for information about French dispositions and plans.[113]

Fort Carillon now would be alerted to the presence of the British raiders, and so it was decided to begin an immediate withdrawal, following approximately the same bypass route used in the advance. After drying their flintlocks at the previous night's campsite, the rangers started south in single file along a narrow trail through the woods. It was about midafternoon, and they had gone less than a mile when they suddenly received a blasting volley at close range, delivered by a strong detachment of French and Indians sent to intercept them.[114] A number of the British were hit, at least two of them mortally. Recovering quickly from the first shock, Rogers' men floundered through the wet snow to a nearby hill, heavily wooded, which afforded them some advantage. Now began a fire-fight that continued until dark, making the sodden forest ring with gunshots. Rogers, who had been grazed on the head at the first French volley, took a bullet through his hand and wrist, so that he found it impossible to load his gun. At intervals the French tried to persuade him to surrender, shouting out threats of a ruthless slaughter when expected reinforcements arrived or, sometimes, promises of good treatment for all prisoners. After darkness settled upon the scene, the firing slackened; and Rogers, with his ammunition now nearly gone, decided to attempt an escape with those of his men still able to walk, although this meant abandoning the dead as well as the seriously wounded. For hours the rangers made their way southward through the dark forest, fighting down the dread of another ambush. Arriving at last on the ice of Lake George, well below the southernmost French outpost, Rogers sent three men ahead to obtain transport for the walking wounded. A sledge thus obtained helped Rogers bring his returning group of forty-eight effectives and six wounded men in to Fort William Henry on the evening of 23 January.[115]

At about this same time, in frozen Canada, Governor Vaudreuil was laying plans for a daring strike that, if successful, would throw

Loudoun off balance and delay the start of the next British campaign on the northern frontier. Thus Canada would gain additional time to receive the desperately needed supplies from France, without which Montcalm could not begin a major offensive of his own. An expedition of 1,500 regulars, Canadians, and Indians was assembled in February, under the command of the governor's own brother, Rigaud. Their target was Fort William Henry. If possible, the fort was to be destroyed, but that failing, they were to wreck the boats and other facilities necessary for British operations in the spring. Montcalm, who was becoming increasingly annoyed by Vaudreuil's habit of making military plans on his own, preferred sending a smaller force commanded by a regular officer in order to conserve supplies, but of course the governor had his way. Early in March, Rigaud and his men arrived at Fort Carillon, where they found scaling ladders already prepared for their use. Setting out on the fifteenth, they advanced along the ice of Lake George in 5 columns, and on the night of 17 March camped on the frozen surface without fires, only about 4 miles from Fort William Henry.[116]

The next day an advance party reconnoitered the objective, studying it carefully from a nearby hill with the aid of a telescope. Fort William Henry itself, located at the edge of the lake, consisted of four bastions connected by earthen walls faced with logs. Within these protecting walls could be seen the roofs of barracks capable of housing several hundred men. Outside were a number of other facilities, including some huts and a sawmill.[117] An unfinished vessel rested on the stocks just under the lakeside wall, while three sloops were observed to be frozen fast in the ice. Nearby, a large number of bateaus had been carefully stacked for later use. Rigaud became convinced that an attempt to take Fort William Henry by storm was too risky, and therefore gave priority to the destruction of the undefended outlying facilities. This task, which had to be accomplished under fire from the fort, was started on 19 March when the troops began setting fire to the huts and bateaus. The British commander, Lieutenant Colonel William Eyre, wisely kept his garrison inside, for he lacked the strength to drive the French away. The next day Rigaud fully invested the fort, and sent some of his Indians to guard the road leading south to Fort Edward. Hoping to intimidate the garrison and perhaps precipitate a surrender, he paraded his army on the lake in full view, with scaling ladders prominently displayed, after which he sent an officer to Eyre with a demand for capitulation. The British commander refused, whereupon the French resumed their work of destruction.

By this time the alarm had reached Albany, where the militia began assembling.[118] For two more days the French remained at Fort William Henry, severely handicapped by unfavorable weather but systematically destroying whatever they could. They burned the sawmill, huts, storehouses, bateaus, and the three sloops in the ice. A daring party of volunteers even succeeded in setting fire to the vessel on the stocks, almost within spitting range of the fort itself. The Indians pillaged at will, making off with "clothing of all sorts, guns, tents, a quantity of kettles, boxes, medicine chests, and barrels of various kinds of liquor, on which they got so drunk that they would have remained around the fort, wrapped in the sleep of drunkenness, had they not been removed. . . ."[119] Then on 23 March, the raiders headed north for their own base, unmolested. Their losses had been very slight, and the damage to the British installation heavy. "General Lawden's [sic] beautiful and immense preparations have been calcined by the flames at a trifling expense," boasted Vaudreuil after learning of his brother's success.[120]

In the meantime, the famine in Canada continued, while all eyes watched for the ice to break. Only with agonizing slowness did the glistening barrier yield to warmer weather, and even then no ships from France were sighted from Quebec's high walls. "Bread is scarce, and what little there is is of the worst quality," wrote Montcalm's aide-de-camp in May. "The lack of provisions prevents us from starting the campaign. All thought of offensive action is impossible for us, and even the defensive, if the enemy comes in force quickly and from several directions is scarcely less so." [121] With the French so desperately short of food and the British so divided, disorganized, and discouraged, the wonder is that a major military campaign for 1757 was even contemplated.

Now that Oswego lay in ruins and the base at Lake George was so heavily damaged, Loudoun's plans for 1757 had come to focus more sharply upon a distant objective. If a major thrust on Lake Ontario was out of the question and campaigning in the Champlain Valley was to be severely handicapped, why not tackle Louisbourg and force open the gateway to the St. Lawrence? Indeed, all previous disasters could be redeemed by a swift advance up the great river of Canada and a successful attack upon Quebec itself. The one absolute essential—a fleet from England—had been promised. In addition, quite early in the year Loudoun took the precaution of imposing a severe embargo at colonial ports, not only to prevent news of his intentions from leaking to the enemy, but also to assure for himself the auxiliary ships and sailors he would need.[122] Could the great feat of 1745 be repeated? Loudoun believed it could, especially by regiments of well-trained regulars and a full application of British sea power. At New York in May, the commander in chief assembled an army of 3,500 men and a large fleet of warships and transports under the command of Admiral Sir Charles Hardy, governor of New York. Additional troops were available at Halifax, which was to serve as the advance staging area for the operation. A supporting fleet from England, commanded by Vice Admiral Francis Holburne, was expected to join Loudoun and Hardy at Halifax, after which the entire force would move against Louisbourg. While Loudoun attacked Louisbourg, garrisons at Fort William Henry, Fort Edward, and the fortified outposts still standing in the Mohawk Valley were to hold Montcalm at bay, wherever he might appear. Once Louisbourg had fallen and Loudoun was in the St. Lawrence, the French would have more than they could do in defending the heartland of Canada.

Despite Loudoun's embargo, news of his intentions had reached Versailles, causing the dispatch of one fleet from France and another from the West Indies to aid in the defense of Louisbourg. While these important movements were taking place, Loudoun and Hardy were lingering at New York, fearful lest their transports fall prey to the French ships known to be coming north from the Caribbean. Day after day the crowded transports rode at anchor, wasting invaluable time needed for the attack on Louisbourg and the subsequent advance to Quebec. Finally, on 20 June Loudoun and Hardy ventured out to begin the operation, arriving safely at Halifax's well-sheltered harbor about the first of July. Here they soon were joined by the fleet and army from England. During the next few weeks, the commander in chief kept his troops occupied with drills in preparation for the assault, while awaiting favorable reports from scout ships patrolling off Louisbourg. In this manner July gave way to August.[123]

Even as Loudoun was assembling his strength at Halifax, Montcalm was making his own preparations for the summer's campaign. In 1756 he had ground Oswego under his heel, making it temporarily useless as a threat against the French West. Now his objective was to complete Rigaud's work at Lake George, so that no attack could be launched against Crown Point and Montreal from that area. Accordingly, in July he gathered the veteran regiments and the Canadian militia at the forts on Lake Champlain, determined that the continuing shortage of food in New France should delay his campaign no longer. The Indians came too, hungry not for food but for scalps and plunder. After his experience at Oswego, Montcalm realized full well what this might mean, but he also knew that no French army could succeed in wilderness warfare without them. The French soon found that the British were alert, maintaining scouts in the woods and boat patrols on the waters of Lake George to prevent any surprise. A major skirmish occurred unexpectedly on 24 July when a fleet of twenty-two boats from Fort William Henry unwarily came within reach of a concealed band of French and Indians on the shore. Springing into action, the warriors easily captured the first six boats, and then went after the remainder in their swift canoes. When they caught up with the desperately paddling militiamen a furious fight occurred, with some of the Indians actually jumping into the water and overturning the British boats. Only two of the craft managed to escape disaster, and the exulting victors returned to Fort Carillon with more than 160 dejected prisoners.[124]

The force available to Montcalm for his operation against Fort William Henry and Fort Edward included 2,570 regulars of the Royal Roussillon, Languedoc, Guyenne, Béarn, La Reine, and La Sarre regiments; 524 men of the *troupes de la marine* led by Rigaud; 188 artillerymen; 2,946 Canadian militiamen and volunteers; and 1,799 Indians. Second-in-command under Montcalm was the Chevalier de Lévis, an officer of wide experience. The regulars alone probably outnumbered the entire garrison of Fort William Henry, which now consisted of about 850 regulars, mostly of the Fiftieth Regiment, but including also men 'from the Sixtieth Regiment and two independent companies; a small detachment of Royal Artillery; 95 rangers; and 1,400 militiamen from New York, New Jersey, New Hampshire, and Massachusetts. Commanding at Fort William Henry was a regular officer, Lieutenant Colonel George Monro of the Thirty-fifth Regiment, who in turn was responsible to General Daniel Webb at Fort Edward.[125] The significant discrepancy in numbers between Montcalm's army and Monro's garrison was without doubt a consequence of Loudoun's venture against Louisbourg, which had drained much of the strength from the frontier garrisons. Loudoun's calculated risk had given the French commander a dangerous but highly attractive opportunity.

Advance units of Montcalm's striking force departed from Fort Carillon on the evening of 29 July and made their way southward along the western shore of Lake George. They were followed three days later by the remainder of the expedition embarked in a fleet of canoes and 247 bateaus. Cannon and mortars needed for the anticipated siege were securely lashed to platforms mounted on paired boats. Steadily the fleet advanced up the long lake until, about 2:00 A.M. on 2 August, the officers made out three separate fires blazing on the dark western shore. This was a prearranged signal made by the advance force to mark the general rendezvous, a bay about 7 miles from the British fort. By nightfall of that same day, a large part of Montcalm's army was bivouacked in the woods, waiting to march the remaining 5 or 6 miles to their objective. During the night two scout boats from the fort blundered into the hands of the Indians, who took three prisoners. When questioned, the terrified captives revealed that Monro expected the attack, and Montcalm knew that his hope for surprise was gone. Victory, then, depended upon superior skill, courage, and strength. Having obtained all the information the three prisoners were able or willing to give, the French left them to the mercy of their captors, who promptly put them to death. Other crewmen of the two boats, having escaped the Indians and made their way back to the fort on foot, told their officers about the "vast Number of French upon the Lake, and some landed." [126]

As soon as possible, Montcalm dispatched scouts to observe the British position at the southern end of the lake. Fort William Henry itself was much as Rigaud had seen it five months before, but now, in addition to the fort itself the British were occupying an entrenched camp about a quarter of a mile southeast of the fort. The road to Fort Edward ran eastward from the fort, following the shore for about 400 yards before turning abruptly inland to pass just to the west of the entrenched camp and then on between the rising hills on either side. Adjacent to the western side of the fort, along the shore of the lake, was a large cleared area being used by the garrison as a garden for raising fresh produce.

During the night of 2 August, the French and Indians began

their final advance, some units proceeding in bateaus toward the head of the lake, while others trudged on foot "through mountains and almost impassable forests." [127] In the first light of dawn on 3 August, the British sentries sighted the fleet of bateaus floating impudently just beyond cannon range. Immediately the alarm guns were fired, and soon the gunners were trying to reach the fleet with their artillery. The French proceeded to establish their camp on the west bank of the lake little more than a quarter of a mile north of Fort William Henry. From there Montcalm directed the positioning of his various units and the laying out of siege lines and batteries. As he lacked sufficient manpower to invest completely the entire British base, Montcalm concentrated his major strength on the west, or garden, side, relying upon Lévis' Canadians and Indians to cover the entrenched camp and the road to Fort Edward. While the French busied themselves erecting shelters, digging trenches, making fascines and gabions, and bringing up their artillery, Monro's men tore the wooden shingles from the roofs of their barracks to lessen the danger of fire, and labored to improve their earthworks. Montcalm felt a great sense of urgency; Monro was anxious to buy all the time he could.

At 6:00 A.M. on 6 August the first French battery, consisting of eight cannon and a mortar, commenced firing, sending projectiles whistling over the corner of the lake into the fort. Twenty-four hours later, a second battery joined in, not only battering the wall of the fort, but also by ricochet reaching the entrenched camp beyond. During daylight hours, the opposing forces exchanged cannon fire supplemented with musketry. At night, Monro had his men light bonfires at regular intervals around the perimeter of the entrenched camp to reveal any surprise approach, while the troops continued laboring on the unfinished breastwork.

General Webb had only about 1,600 men at Fort Edward, and dared not attempt a rescue until reinforced by the militia from Albany. He wrote a dispatch to Monro conveying this information; the messenger was intercepted and killed by Indians, who turned the important letter over to the French. Montcalm, reading correctly its tone of pessimism, sent the captured document in to Monro on 7 August, hoping that this would convince the British commander that further resistance was futile.[128] For two more days Monro pondered his dilemma, while the firing continued and the French extended their trenches ever closer to the west wall of the fort.

It was becoming painfully clear that whenever the final assault came, the defenders would be overwhelmed by superior numbers, including hundreds of rapacious Indians. On 9 August, with some of his artillery now rendered useless and no sign of rescue, Monro finally raised the white flag. Montcalm was not exorbitant in his demands. The two commanders agreed to terms allowing the garrison to march under military escort to Fort Edward and safety, on condition that the officers and men not serve again for a period of eighteen months.[129]

Soon after daybreak on 10 August, the surrendered British troops, who had been assembled in their entrenched camp, were formed into a column guarded by a small detachment of French soldiers for the march down to Fort Edward. As the long column started marching off down the road a group of Abnakis suddenly raised shouts of vengeance and rushed upon the rear. At once all was wild confusion, with other Indians joining in and the British, thrown into panic, trying to protect themselves or escape. Montcalm himself, hearing the uproar, rushed to the scene, but before the French could restore order, about twenty of the helpless prisoners had been slaughtered and many others dragged into captivity. Some of the French actually risked their own lives to save the British and afterward shared their own clothing with men who had been stripped and plundered. Later that same day most of the Indians departed for home, taking with them their captives including a number of Negroes who had been serving with the British. Montcalm was mortified by the episode, and took the unusual step of sending messages to Webb and Loudoun explaining how the massacre had occurred contrary to the terms of surrender and despite the precautions taken. In a way, though, it was the plundered prisoners themselves who had their own revenge when smallpox, contracted from captives and booty, began spreading through the tribes and taking a heavy toll of lives.[130]

Now once again, as in 1756 at Oswego, Montcalm had to decide how to wring the greatest advantage from his conquest. Should he advance to confront Fort Edward? Considering the fatigue of his men, the impatience of the Canadians to return home for the harvest, the departure of the Indians, and the strength of the opposition, Montcalm concluded that the risk was far too great. Could he, then, hold his ground at the southern end of Lake George in order to deny to the British an essential advance base for any future offensive in the Champlain Valley? Again Montcalm's answer was no, and this time his fear was more justified than at Oswego, for at Fort William Henry his supply route was more difficult and insecure, and the British were firmly established in force only a dozen miles distant with an easy line of advance. Any French garrison left at the fort through the winter would live in constant peril, and almost certainly would be overwhelmed in the spring before sufficient reinforcements could be brought down from Canada. So Montcalm had to be satisfied, as in 1756, with an unexploited victory that constituted a severe setback to British aspirations but did little to forward French hopes for the ultimate defeat of Britain in North America. Before leaving the scene of their conquest, the French troops leveled the entrenched camp, razed the fort, and either destroyed or appropriated for their own use any boats found in the vicinity.[131] By 19 August, the victorious army was safely back at its own base on Lake Champlain.

About the time that Fort William Henry came under siege early in August, but before news of that alarming development could reach Halifax, Loudoun was completing the solution of a difficult equation. Naval reconnaissance had determined that the French squadrons which had been converging on Louisbourg were now assembled there in the harbor. Considering the lateness of the season, the limited capabilities of the British forces at Halifax, the defensive strength of Louisbourg itself, and the large number of French warships available to assist in its defense, Loudoun, in consultation with Hardy and Holburne, concluded that the risks inherent in his plan had become unacceptable. The long-delayed operation against Cape Breton Island was accordingly canceled, and the various units were dispersed to their winter quarters.[132] Loudoun's painful decision was the only wise one under the circumstances, but it immediately exposed the unhappy commander to the fire of military and political critics. The utter futility of the whole costly expedition, the single major British offensive of the entire 1757 military season in America, was fully revealed just after Montcalm had succeeded in erasing another key British base, a French victory which would not have happened if Loudoun's army had been available in the vicinity. Actually, the original concept for the operation against Louisbourg followed by an advance up the St. Lawrence was not without merit, and if successful would have rendered Montcalm's victory useless. Had Loudoun gotten underway more expeditiously and been joined earlier by the reinforcements from England, he might have won a significant victory. His failure to make the assault before the French could assemble a powerful naval force at Louisbourg necessitated the unhappy decision he finally had to make. An unpleasant postlude was added in September, when a vicious hurricane slashed its way up the coast and mauled the ships of both navies.[133]

By October 1757 it seemed that another year of indecisive campaigning was nearly over, but the hardy Canadians and their Indian allies had one more blow to strike before settling down to endure another long, lean winter. Early in November, a force of some 300 raiders led by Picoté de Belestre moved eastward from the vicinity of Oneida Lake and advanced stealthily down the Mohawk Valley. Their target was the peaceful Palatine farming community of German Flats, located on the north side of the river 55 miles west of Schenectady. On 12 November the raiders burst upon their objective. Almost directly opposite on the south shore was Fort Herkimer with a garrison of 200 British regulars, but this establishment might as well have been standing in the main square of Albany for all the protection it was able to afford the German farmers. Belestre's men ravaged at will through the surprised and terrified community, and after burning a large number of dwellings and other buildings they departed with about 150 captives including the mayor.[134]

In this way, the year 1757 came to an end in the American colonies, leaving a general feeling of gloom and deep apprehension. The best efforts of Britain's army and navy, as well as the large forces raised by the various colonies themselves, seemed futile against the slashing tactics of the French and their fierce Indian cohorts. Three years of war had produced much heartbreaking loss and little tangible gain. Americans were close to losing faith in themselves, their military leaders, and the mother country.

Up to this time four major military commanders from Europe —two French and two British—had been called to play leading roles in the American struggle. Braddock and Dieskau were very ordinary commanders, technically competent perhaps, but lacking the superior qualities of insight and imagination and a certain flexible strength so essential in meeting the rapidly shifting conditions of warfare in a vast and largely unfamiliar country. Neither showed any great skill or adaptability in dealing with colonists

and Indians. Both concluded their American careers by advancing
boldly into defeat. There is little evidence to suggest that Loudoun
was any more talented as a commander than the ill-starred Braddock. He inherited a parcel of administrative problems that had
grown more difficult since Braddock's time, demanding much of
his attention and frustrating his will to get on with the war. Never
was he able to organize a well-coordinated, timely, and effective
campaign.

Montcalm, too, showed little sign of real distinction. Appalled
and disgusted by the rampant graft he saw in the civil administration of Canada, he was handicapped by his military subordination
to Governor Vaudreuil. Montcalm was not given a free hand in
planning overall strategy or even particular operations, but had
to accept the tasks given him by the governor. In executing his
assignments he did well, producing notable victories at Oswego
and Lake George and thus sparing Canada the serious danger
of British attack from Lake Ontario and Lake Champlain. Certainly these French victories of 1756 and 1757 were in part the
result of steady, methodical leadership on the part of the French
general, who assessed every circumstance carefully and deployed
his available forces to the best advantage. In similar situations,
the British commanders Braddock and Loudoun probably would
have made the same decisions and with comparable results. Montcalm's successes were partly the product of Canadian experience
and skill in wilderness warfare, effective relations with Indian
allies, and the unitary authority of French Canada which could
command persons and resources in the achievement of predetermined goals. The far greater resources of the British colonies had
not yet been effectively mobilized and concerted, a fact which
proved fatal to Braddock and constantly frustrating to Loudoun.

NOTES

1. For a good discussion of Anglo-French diplomacy at this time, see Patrice
   Louis-René Higonnet, "The Origins of the Seven Years' War," *Journal of
   Modern History*, XL (March, 1968), 57–90. "No one wanted to fight this
   war," writes Higonnet. "It would never have occurred if, in their sincere
   efforts to resolve it, the French and English governments had not inad-
   vertently magnified its insignificant original cause into a wider conflict.
   The coming of the Seven Years' War owes more to diplomatic misconcep-

tion efficiently achieved than to 'the course of history' " (*ibid.*, pp. 57–58). See also Max Savelle, *The Origins of American Diplomacy: The International History of Angloamerica, 1492–1763* (New York, 1967), pp. 399–400.

2. Stanley Pargellis, ed., *Military Affairs in North America, 1748–1765: Selected Documents from the Cumberland Papers in Windsor Castle* (New York, 1936), pp. 34–36; *NYCD*, VI, 915–916.

3. Pargellis, *Military Affairs*, pp. 45–48; *NYCD*, VI, 920–922.

4. Theodore Calvin Pease, ed., *Anglo-French Boundary Disputes in the West, 1749–1763* (Springfield, Ill., 1936), pp. 175–176. Important documents relating to the negotiations are assembled in *ibid.*, pp. 60–247; note especially the maps opposite pp. 150, 190. See also Savelle, *Origins of American Diplomacy*, pp. 400–418; Lawrence H. Gipson, "A French Project for Victory Short of a Declaration of War, 1755," *CHR*, XXVI (December, 1945), 361–371.

5. Pease, *Anglo-French Boundary Disputes*, pp. 161–162.

6. Robert Dinwiddie, *The Official Records of Robert Dinwiddie . . .*, R. A. Brock, ed. (2 vols.; Richmond, Va., 1883–1884), I, 391, 399–400.

7. Pargellis, *Military Affairs*, p. 62.

8. Dinwiddie, *Official Records*, I, 474, 476, 525.

9. Pargellis, *Military Affairs*, p. 44. See also William A. Whitehead, ed., *Documents Relating to the Colonial History of the State of New Jersey*, VIII (Newark, 1885), Part 2, pp. 29–30.

10. Pargellis, *Military Affairs*, p. 36.

11. Johnson's commission, dated 15 April 1755, has been published in *The Papers of Sir William Johnson*, James Sullivan and Alexander C. Flick, eds. (13 vols.; Albany, 1921–1962), I, 465–466.

12. James T. Flexner, *Mohawk Baronet: Sir William Johnson of New York* (New York, 1959), p. 126. In a letter of 17 March 1755, Johnson had brought to Braddock's attention the strategic advantage of striking first at Niagara. Shirley, too, recognized the crucial importance of that location, as did every other knowledgeable colonial leader in the northern colonies. Even Dinwiddie, with all his interest in Ohio Company lands below the Forks, agreed that the French fort at Niagara was "of the greatest Consequence." In this connection it is interesting to find Governor Vaudreuil of Canada testifying, in a letter of 10 July 1755, that "the preservation of Niagara is what interests us the most. Were our enemies masters of it, and to retain Choueguin [Oswego], the Upper countries would be lost to us, and we should have no further communication with the river Oyo [Ohio]." (See *Johnson Papers*, I, 458–459; William Shirley, *Correspondence of William Shirley, Governor of Massachusetts and Military Commander in America, 1731–1760*, Charles H. Lincoln, ed. [2 vols.; New York, 1912], II, 144–152; Dinwiddie, *Official Records*, I, 524; *NYCD*, X, 305.)

13. Shirley, *Correspondence*, II, 158–164; Pargellis, *Military Affairs*, pp. 81–82; Lawrence H. Gipson, *The Great War for the Empire: The Years of Defeat, 1754–1757* (New York, 1946), pp. 71–72.

14. Julian S. Corbett, *England in the Seven Years' War: A Study in Combined Strategy* (2d ed., 2 vols.; London, 1918), I, 31; William Laird Clowes, *The*

Royal Navy: A History from the Earliest Times to the Present (7 vols.; London, 1897–1903), III, 140; C. P. Stacey, *Quebec, 1759: The Siege and the Battle* (New York, 1959), p. 13.

15. Pease, *Anglo-French Boundary Disputes*, p. 207.

16. *NYCD*, X, 297–299.

17. *NYCD, X,* 347–348; Corbett, *England in the Seven Years' War*, I, 54–55, 61.

18. Benjamin Franklin, *The Papers of Benjamin Franklin*, Leonard W. Labaree *et al.*, eds. (14 vols. to date; New Haven, 1959 to present), VI, 19–22, 57–59.

19. *Johnson Papers*, I, 514.

20. Robert L. Meriwether, *The Expansion of South Carolina, 1729–1765* (Kingsport, Tenn., 1940), pp. 205–206; Douglas (Summers) Brown, *The Catawba Indians: The People of the River* (Columbia, S.C., 1966), p. 186; M. Eugene Sirmans, *Colonial South Carolina: A Political History, 1663–1763* (Chapel Hill, 1966), pp. 296–298; David H. Corkran, *The Creek Frontier, 1540–1783* (Norman, Okla., 1967), pp. 163–167; P. M. Hamer, "Anglo-French Rivalry in the Cherokee Country, 1754–1757," *North Carolina Historical Review*, II (July, 1925), 306–307.

21. Dinwiddie, *Official Records*, II, 112. See also *ibid.*, 125–126, 202, 225–226; Brown, *Catawba Indians*, pp. 202–203; Hamer, "Anglo-French Rivalry," p. 307.

22. David H. Corkran, *The Cherokee Frontier: Conflict and Survival, 1740–62* (Norman, Okla., 1962), pp. 54–57.

23. Shirley specified that "none, but right good Men . . ." were to be accepted into his regiment, "and not under five feet five Inches without their shoes, unless they are young enough to grow to that Height; and none above forty years old" (Shirley, *Correspondence*, II, 144).

24. Perez Marsh's letter of 7 July 1755, Israel Williams Papers, I, 147 (Massachusetts Historical Society).

25. *Johnson Papers*, IX, 206. A detailed account of general preparations for the various expeditions is given in Shirley, *Correspondence*, II, 195–205.

26. *NYCD*, X, 296.

27. Shirley, *Correspondence*, II, 355–364; John A. Schutz, *William Shirley: King's Governor of Massachusetts* (Chapel Hill, 1961), pp. 198–207, 223.

28. John Thomas, Diary (Collections of the Nova Scotia Historical Society, I [1878]), 123. See also *ibid.*, III, 189–190; Pargellis, *Military Affairs*, pp. 146–148.

29. Thomas Mante, *The History of the Late War in North-America, and the Islands of the West-Indies . . .* (London, 1772), p. 19.

30. George Washington, *The Writings of George Washington, from the Original Manuscript Sources, 1745–1799*, John C. Fitzpatrick, ed. (39 vols.; Washington, 1931–1944), I, 142–143; Gipson, *The Great War for the Empire: The Years of Defeat, 1754–1757*, pp. 82–83, 97–98.

31. Among the refugees was "one poor Boy . . . with his Scalp of[f] . . . [who] liv'd 4 Days" (Isabel M. Calder, ed., *Colonial Captivities, Marches, and*

Journeys [New York, 1935], p. 183). See also Dinwiddie, *Official Records,* II, 85–87, 89.

32. Pargellis, *Military Affairs,* pp. 129–130; Gipson, *The Great War for the Empire: The Years of Defeat, 1754–1757,* pp. 91–92.

33. According to Washington's own account written only nine days after the battle, four bullets passed through his coat and two horses were shot from under him. Officers on horseback made excellent targets above the huddled mass of foot soldiers (Washington, *Writings,* I, 149).

34. Dinwiddie, *Official Records,* II, 221–222.

35. Pargellis, *Military Affairs,* pp. 97, 131–132; *NYCD,* X, 303–304, 311–312; Shirley, *Correspondence,* II, 209; *Johnson Papers,* II, 232–233; Dinwiddie, *Official Records,* II, 223; Gipson, *The Great War for the Empire: The Years of Defeat, 1754–1757,* p. 96. One concerned colonist exclaimed with pardonable exaggeration that "Perhaps, all circumstances considered, history will scarce furnish an instance of such a dreadful carnage" ([Charles Chauncy], *A Letter to a Friend; Giving a Concise, but Just, Account . . . of the Ohio-Defeat* [Boston, 1755], p. 4).

36. Washington, *Writings,* I, 149.

37. Shirley, *Correspondence,* II, 313, 320; [William Livingston], *A Review of the Military Operations in North-America . . .* (Dublin, 1757), p. 55.

38. Benjamin Franklin was one who recognized that "the manual Exercise and Evolutions taught a Militia, are known by Experience to be of little or no Use in our Woodes . . ." (Franklin, *Papers,* VI, 219). It must be remembered, however, that American militia was supposed to be prepared to fight against European troops as well as against Indians.

39. *State of the British and French Colonies in North America . . .* (Facsimile ed., [New York], 1967), p. 70.

40. [Chauncy], *Letter to a Friend,* p. 9.

41. Richard Peters to Conrad Weiser, 18 October 1755, Weiser Correspondence, I, 58 (Historical Society of Pennsylvania).

42. Dinwiddie, *Official Records,* II, 201.

43. Jeffery Amherst, *The Journal of Jeffery Amherst, Recording the Military Career of General Amherst in America from 1758 to 1763,* J. Clarence Webster, ed. (Chicago, 1931), p. 69n.; John W. Fortescue, *A History of the British Army* (13 vols. and 6 atlases; London, 1889–1930), II, 289.

44. John R. Cuneo, *Robert Rogers of the Rangers* (New York, 1959), pp. 32ff. Out of the experience of Braddock's defeat and the ensuing discussion of Old World versus New World ways of fighting there began to emerge in the American mind an image sharply contrasting the stiff and stupid redcoat with the shrewd, woods-wise American bush fighter who had learned his tactics from the Indians. This stereotype was to contribute heavily to American self-esteem and self-confidence during the years of pre-Revolutionary agitation after 1763. During the tea controversy in 1773, for example, a Boston newspaper published the views of a correspondent identified only as "A Ranger." Should Britain ever send regular forces to subdue the colonists, wrote this patriot, the Americans would resort to bush

fighting, pick off the British officers, and gain the victory. That was what happened to Braddock's army, he took pains to remind his readers. (Cited in Benjamin Woods Labaree, *The Boston Tea Party* [New York, 1964], p. 133.)

45. John Winslow, Journal (Collections of the Nova Scotia Historical Society, III), 78–83; John Bartlet Brebner, *New England's Outpost: Acadia before the Conquest of Canada* (New York, 1927), pp. 199–201, 222–224.

46. John Winslow, Journal, p. 94.

47. *Ibid.*, p. 166.

48. Altogether about 7,000 Acadians were deported in 1755. Put ashore in groups in the various British colonies, they were met with suspicion if not open hostility. Colonial assemblies grudgingly appropriated funds for their relief, and some compassionate individuals offered what additional assistance they could, but for most of the exiles the future was very bleak. The greater part of those who survived the early hardships eventually found their way to French-speaking lands.

49. [Livingston], *Review of the Military Operations in North-America* (London, 1757), p. 42n.

50. Elisha Hawley, Journal, Hawley Papers, Box 1, p. 66 (New York Public Library).

51. That Shirley's fear of an attack upon Oswego from Fort Frontenac was not unfounded is shown by Dieskau's letter of 16 August 1755 in *NYCD*, X, 311–312.

52. Vaudreuil's orders to Dieskau, dated at Montreal 15 August 1755, are published in *NYCD*, X, 327–330. These are followed by Dieskau's instructions to his troops (*ibid.*, pp. 330–331). See also *ibid.*, p. 338; *Johnson Papers*, II, 18–19, 72.

53. *NYCD*, X, 338, 367.

54. *NYCD*, X, 316, 331–335.

55. *Johnson Papers*, IX, 228–229.

56. *NYCD*, VI, 1005, X, 317, 321; *Johnson Papers*, II, 72; [Charles Chauncy], *A Second Letter to a Friend* (Boston, 1755), p. 3.

57. *Johnson Papers*, IX, 229; *NYCD*, VI, 1003, X, 317, 353. Johnson obviously had no idea that the French were doing anything but attacking Fort Edward, which of course would have been a most serious threat to his own position.

58. Johnson later recorded that "one of the enemys Musketts by accident went off which allarmed our People and discovered the enemy . . ." (*NYCD*, VI, 1013).

59. *NYCD*, VI, 1010. Those of the van who survived the first enemy fire began a fighting withdrawal, and "a very hansom retreet they made by Continuing there fire and then retreeting a little and then rise and give them a brisk Fire." In this fashion they inflicted a number of casualties on the advancing French and Indians, slowed Dieskau's approach toward Johnson's camp, and in the process managed to avoid being entirely overwhelmed (Seth Pomeroy, *The Journals and Papers of Seth Pomeroy*, L. E. de Forest, ed. [New Haven, 1926], p. 114).

60. Pargellis, *Military Affairs*, p. 139.
61. Pomeroy, *Journals and Papers*, pp. 114, 137-138.
62. *NYCD*, VI, 1005.
63. Seth Pomeroy to his wife, 20 [10?] September 1755, Israel Williams Papers, I, 183 (Massachusetts Historical Society). Pomeroy, who had been at Louisbourg in 1745, also described the exchanges as "the most vilolent [*sic*] Fire Perhaps that Ever was heard of in this Country In any Battle . . ." (Pomeroy, *Journals and Papers*, p. 114).
64. Nathan Fiske, Diary (American Antiquarian Society).
65. *NYCD*, VI, 1004; Pargellis, *Military Affairs*, p. 140. Vaudreuil complained that "the return of the army to Fort St. Frédéric supplied me with more sick, than fighting, men" (*NYCD*, X, 324).
66. *NYCD*, VI, 1003-1004, 1010, X, 323-324, 336, 354, 360-361; *Johnson Papers*, IX, 234-238; Robert Hale, Chronicle (American Antiquarian Society).
67. Shirley, *Correspondence*, II, 270-276, 289-301; *Johnson Papers*, II, 52-53, 73-77; *NYCD*, VI, 1010, X, 324-325, 356.
68. Fiske, Diary (American Antiquarian Society); Ebenezer Hindsdale to Colonel Williams, August 1755, Israel Williams Papers, I, 163 (Massachusetts Historical Society). See also *ibid.*, p. 234.
69. Quoted in Nicholas B. Wainwright, *George Croghan: Wilderness Diplomat* (Chapel Hill, 1959), p. 98.
70. *Johnson Papers*, IX, 310.
71. Franklin, *Papers*, VI, 381. See also *ibid.*, p. 357.
72. *NYCD*, X, 413.
73. Schutz, *William Shirley*, pp. 221-222, 229.
74. Something of the extravagant praise that was lavished on Johnson after the Battle of Lake George may be glimpsed through a poem published in the *Boston Gazette* for 13 October 1755. It reads in part:

> There curst Canadia's motley savage Herd,
> With Hecatom's of faithless *Frenchmen* bled:
> Old Gallic Bands, there made their last Campaign
> And drench'd in Gore, lay welt'ring on the Plain,
> *New-England* Valour, thro' each Bosom spread
> And number'd Myriads, with th'expiring Dead. . . .
>
> Like Autumn Leaves, *French* Victims fell around,
> Curs'd their perfidious Stars, and bit the Ground.
> The dying Chief, groan'd out his latest Word,
> "*Not* Braddock *now—but* Johnson *wields the Sword.*"

75. Montcalm's commission, dated 1 March 1756, has been published in *NYCD*, X, 394-395. See also *ibid.*, pp. 413-414.
76. Clarence S. Brigham, ed., *British Royal Proclamations Relating to America, 1603-1783* (Worcester, Mass., 1911), pp. 203-206.
77. Pease, *Anglo-French Boundary Disputes*, p. 13. See also Shirley, *Correspondence*, II, 229-230.
78. Shirley, *Correspondence*, II, 419-422, 442-445, 567-571. Cape Cod and Nantucket whalers formed two of Bradstreet's companies, while others

came from the coastal towns above Boston (*The Conduct of Major Gen. Shirley, Late General and Commander in Chief of His Majesty's Forces in North America. Briefly Stated* [London, 1758], pp. 72–73).

79. *NYCD*, X, 411, 481; *Johnson Papers*, IX, 414–415. French estimates of the quantity of British gunpowder destroyed ranged up to 45,000 pounds.

80. The captured vessel was variously described as a schooner, shallop, sloop, and even a row galley. Commanded by Captain Jasper Farmer, it was manned by some fourteen to sixteen sailors and soldiers and was armed with swivel guns. Bougainville assessed the capture as "a petty victory . . . but interesting because of the impression of superiority that it gives our Indians" (Louis Antoine de Bougainville, *Adventure in the Wilderness: The American Journals of Louis Antoine de Bougainville, 1756–1760*, Edward P. Hamilton, trans. and ed. [Norman, Okla., 1964], p. 5). See also *NYCD*, X, 428, 434, 477, 482; Shirley, *Correspondence*, II, 442–444, 490, 567, 570; Pargellis, *Military Affairs*, pp. 188, 191, 197, 199, 200, 202–203; *Conduct of Major Gen. Shirley*, pp. 72–74; Extract of a letter from Oswego dated 17 May 1756, in the *Boston Gazette* for 7 June 1756.

81. Extract of a letter from Oswego dated 17 June 1756, in the *Boston Gazette* for 5 July 1756; Pargellis, *Military Affairs*, pp. 195, 205.

82. Shirley, *Correspondence*, II, 489. See also Bougainville, *Adventure in the Wilderness*, p. 6; Pargellis, *Military Affairs*, pp. 200–201; *NYCD*, X, 434, 467, 471, 477, 483; Franklin, *Papers*, VI, 473. One credulous French correspondent actually passed along the report that Bradstreet had lost 800 men and about 500 bateaus, at a cost to Villiers of only ten men. But then, this is the same person who had reported Braddock's loss as more than 1,800 men! (*NYCD*, X, 528–531).

83. *Johnson Papers*, IX, 484–485. The usually perceptive Franklin transmitted a different, less likely, explanation for the provincials' reluctance to serve with regulars: "The Provincials, it seems, apprehend, that Regulars join'd with them, would claim all the Honour of any Success, and charge them with the Blame of every Miscarriage" (Franklin, *Papers*, VI, 473).

84. Shirley, *Correspondence*, II, 491–492; Franklin, *Papers*, VI, 472; Pargellis, *Military Affairs*, p. 226; Schutz, *William Shirley*, pp. 236–243, 248–249; John A. Schutz, *Thomas Pownall, British Defender of American Liberty: A Study of Anglo-American Relations in the Eighteenth Century* (Glendale, Calif., 1951), pp. 59–70, 77.

85. Louis Joseph de Montcalm-Gozon, "Montcalm's Correspondence," *Report of the Public Archives of Canada for the Year 1929* (Ottawa, 1930), pp. 45–47; *NYCD*, X, 433–434, 454, 458, 465, 467, 471–472, 475.

86. Pargellis, *Military Affairs*, pp. 190–192, 210, 218–219; *NYCD*, X, 458, 494; Shirley, *Correspondence*, II, 574–575.

87. Pargellis, *Military Affairs*, pp. 207, 220; *NYCD*, X, 441–442, 455, 462, 465.

88. Pargellis, *Military Affairs*, p. 208; *NYCD*, X, 442, 455–456, 459, 462; Extract of a letter dated 31 December 1756, in the *Boston Gazette* for 23 May 1757.

89. *NYCD*, X, 468. See also *ibid.*, pp. 442, 460.

90. *NYCD*, X, 460.

91. *NYCD*, X, 443.

92. Two versions of the articles may be found in *NYCD*, X, 444 and 474–475. See also Pargellis, *Military Affairs*, pp. 212–213.

93. *NYCD*, X, 463. See also *ibid.*, pp. 443–444, 456, 460–461, 464, 468, 473, 476, 484–485, 520–523; Bougainville, *Adventure in the Wilderness*, pp. 27–28.

94. The massacre was concealed or glossed over in most of the French reports, some of which asserted that some English had been killed while attempting to escape. (See *NYCD*, X, 443, 456, 460, 464, 466, 473, 476.)

95. Jean Elizabeth Lunn, "Agriculture and War in Canada, 1740–1763," *CHR*, XVI (June, 1935), 133.

96. *Johnson Papers*, IX, 515.

97. Thomas Williams to Colonel Israel Williams, 28 August 1756, Israel Williams Papers, I, 245 (Massachusetts Historical Society).

98. Montcalm, "Correspondence," pp. 49–51; Bougainville, *Adventure in the Wilderness*, p. 63; *NYCD*, X, 546–547; Calder, *Colonial Captivities*, p. 197.

99. *NYCD*, X, 489–490; William A. Hunter, *Forts on the Pennsylvania Frontier, 1753–1758* (Harrisburg, 1960), pp. 390–394.

100. Hunter, *Forts on the Pennsylvania Frontier*, p. 408.

101. Wayland F. Dunaway, *The Scotch-Irish of Colonial Pennsylvania* (Chapel Hill, 1944), pp. 150–151.

102. Dinwiddie, *Official Records*, I, 472–473, 476–477; George Louis Beer, *British Colonial Policy, 1754–1765* (New York, 1907), pp. 77–79, 93; Richard Pares, *War and Trade in the West Indies, 1739–1763* (New York, 1936), pp. 433–434.

103. Savelle, *Origins of American Diplomacy*, pp. 223–224. Despite the Rule of the War of 1756, neutral shipping interests found ways to help France move cargoes back and forth across the seas. For example, a French cargo destined for some French port in America might be conveyed first to a neutral seaport near France and there unloaded. Technically, this "neutralized" the cargo. Thereupon the very same goods would be put aboard a neutral vessel which then would resume the interrupted voyage and deliver the "neutral" cargo to a neutral port in America, whence it later could be sent on to its French destination. Theoretically, for that part of the voyage in which the "neutral" cargo was in a neutral ship, it was safe from interference by the British. Britain responded to this subterfuge by announcing the "doctrine of continuous voyage," which stated that enemy goods en route from one enemy port to another did not acquire neutral status by being unloaded at a neutral port and then carried in a neutral vessel. Indeed, the British government insisted, even a neutral ship itself was liable to confiscation if found to be carrying enemy goods.

104. Beer, *British Colonial Policy, 1754–1765*, pp. 53–55.

105. A careful study of prices in Pennsylvania has revealed that the prices of grains and bread in that colony actually dropped during the early years of the war, partly because of the decline in shipping caused by embargoes (Anne Bezanson, R. D. Gray, and M. Hussey, *Prices in Colonial Pennsylvania* [Philadelphia, 1935], *passim*).

106. See earlier, pp. 297–298. During the summer of 1756 the Privy Council, heeding the wishes of the proprietor, disallowed the Pennsylvania Militia Act because it was noncompulsory. When this became known in Pennsylvania, the colony decided to raise instead a force of paid volunteers enlisted under specific terms (Theodore Thayer, *Pennsylvania Politics and the Growth of Democracy, 1740–1776* [Harrisburg, 1953], pp. 54–55).

107. Franklin, *Papers*, VII, 10n.; Sydney V. James, *A People among Peoples: Quaker Benevolence in Eighteenth-Century America* (Cambridge, Mass., 1963), p. 167; Peter Brock, *Pacifism in the United States, from the Colonial Era to the First World War* (Princeton, 1968), pp. 141–147.

108. For a brief discussion of the "Walking Purchase" and its effect on Indian relations, see Douglas Edward Leach, *The Northern Colonial Frontier, 1607–1763* (New York, 1966), pp. 141–143.

109. Albert T. Volwiler, *George Croghan and the Westward Movement, 1741–1782* (Cleveland, 1926), pp. 126–127; Theodore Thayer, *Israel Pemberton, King of the Quakers* (Philadelphia, 1943), pp. 126–135; Theodore Thayer, "The Friendly Association," *Pennsylvania Magazine of History and Biography*, LXVII (October, 1943), 356–376; James, *A People among Peoples*, pp. 178–183.

110. Bougainville, *Adventure in the Wilderness*, p. 72. See also *NYCD*, X, 496–499; Lunn, "Agriculture and War in Canada, 1740–1760."

111. Montcalm, "Correspondence," p. 52; *NYCD*, X, 549, 563.

112. Sources concerning this operation include the following: Robert Rogers, *Journals of Major Robert Rogers*, Howard H. Peckham, ed. (New York, 1961), pp. 28–33; Thomas Brown, *A Plain Narrative of the Uncommon Sufferings, and Remarkable Deliverance of Thomas Brown, of Charlestown, in New-England* . . . (Boston, 1760), pp. 4–12; Bougainville, *Adventure in the Wilderness*, pp. 81–82; *NYCD*, X, 546, 548, 569–570.

113. There is some apparent disagreement among the various sources as to whether the seven men captured were with the advance sleigh or the main convoy. Preference has been given to Rogers' own narrative. Another British participant later spoke of some fifty sleighs, an obvious exaggeration. It is known that the convoy was en route to Fort St. Frédéric to pick up brandy and forage for the garrison at Fort Carillon.

114. One French account says that the rangers walked into the ambush singing. If this is true, which seems unlikely, Rogers' discipline was incredibly lax (*NYCD*, X, 570).

115. Rogers later reckoned his casualties as fourteen killed, six missing, and six wounded. French accounts, however, speak of from thirty-four to forty-two British being found on the ground, which must be an exaggeration if Rogers actually brought as many as fifty-four of his men safely back.

116. French accounts of the operation may be found in Bougainville, *Adventure in the Wilderness*, pp. 85–99; and *NYCD*, X, 542–545, 548–549, 551, 554–555, 563–565, 570–572.

117. This description of the fort is based upon a report dated 22 June 1756, in Pargellis, *Military Affairs*, pp. 177–179.

118. Calder, *Colonial Captivities*, p. 198.

119. *NYCD*, X, 572.

120. *NYCD*, X, 543.

121. Bougainville, *Adventure in the Wilderness*, pp. 108–109.

122. Mante, *History of the Late War*, pp. 85–86; Clowes, *Royal Navy*, III, 166–167.

123. John Knox, *An Historical Journal of the Campaigns in North-America, for the Years 1757, 1758, 1759, and 1760*, Arthur G. Doughty, ed. (3 vols.; Toronto, 1914–1916), I, 31–44.

124. Bougainville, *Adventure in the Wilderness*, pp. 142–143; Montcalm, "Correspondence," p. 98.

125. Bougainville, *Adventure in the Wilderness*, pp. 152–153, 175–177; *NYCD*, X, 585.

126. *Boston Gazette*, 5 September 1757. A contemporary journal mentions the arrival in Albany on 30 July of an express from General Webb warning of the French advance. Since, as we have seen, Montcalm's advance force did not leave Fort Carillon until the evening of 29 July, this alarm may have been based on premature information. (See Calder, *Colonial Captivities*, p. 198.)

127. Bougainville, *Adventure in the Wilderness*, p. 158.

128. Bougainville, *Adventure in the Wilderness*, pp. 162–163, 166–167.

129. This arrangement was far more lenient than the terms at Oswego, under which the entire garrison had been taken to Canada as prisoners of war. Three considerations probably explain the difference: the tenacious resistance offered at Fort William Henry, the known difficulty of protecting prisoners against vengeful Indians, and the severe shortage of food in Canada. Montcalm had won his victory at a relatively light cost to his own army. According to one contemporary account which seems reliable, the French and Canadians had lost twelve of their men killed and twenty-two wounded during the siege, while their Indian allies suffered a total of twenty-three casualties (Bougainville, *Adventure in the Wilderness*, pp. 169–170, 177–178).

130. Louise P. Kellogg, *The French Régime in Wisconsin and the Northwest* (Madison, 1925), pp. 432–433. Smallpox had been a problem in Canada since at least 1756. Common opinion was that it had been introduced by British prisoners and Acadian refugees (Bougainville, *Adventure in the Wilderness*, p. 192).

131. Hale, Chronicle (American Antiquarian Society).

132. Pargellis, *Military Affairs*, pp. 387–397. On 16 August, after the operation against Louisbourg had been canceled, Loudoun received dispatches informing him that Fort William Henry was under siege (Knox, *Journal*, I, 52).

133. Knox, *Journal*, I, 100–101; Clowes, *Royal Navy*, III, 169; J. S. McLennan, *Louisbourg from Its Foundation to Its Fall* (London, 1918), pp. 207–210. A defense of Loudoun was provided in *The Conduct of a Noble Commander in America, Impartially Reviewed* (London, 1758).

134. Bougainville, *Adventure in the Wilderness*, p. 194; William Pitt, *Correspondence of William Pitt with Colonial Governors*, G. S. Kimball, ed.

(2 vols.; New York, 1906), I, 183–185; Wainwright, *George Croghan,* pp. 136–137. The inhabitants of German Flats were known by both sides to be something less than ardent in their enthusiasm for the British cause. Apparently these Palatine farmers had hoped that their indifference would exempt them from molestation, and neglected to take ordinary precautions when warned of danger. (See Walter Allen Knittle, *Early Eighteenth Century Palatine Emigration: A British Government Redemptioner Project to Manufacture Naval Stores* [Philadelphia, 1937], pp. 219–220.)

☆   ☆   ☆   ☆   ☆

CHAPTER 10

The Climactic Struggle for Empire: Second Phase, 1758-1760

LATE IN 1756 England's destiny in the Seven Years' War had been taken in hand by a patriot politician, the forty-eight-year-old Secretary of State William Pitt. From then until 5 October 1761, except for a brief interlude during the spring of 1757, this man was the moving spirit of the British war effort. His task was a hard one. Functioning as chief minister in a coalition government shared with his political rival the Duke of Newcastle, Pitt had to contend almost constantly with several severe handicaps. The king's regard for Pitt was low, and many of the prime minister's colleagues in government disliked and distrusted him as well. It was Newcastle, not Pitt, who controlled the majority in the House of Commons. To make matters worse, the state of Pitt's health was somewhat precarious, due to the early stirrings of the painful gout that later was to incapacitate him. Only the man's immense popularity among the British populace and his own unshakable conviction that he alone could lead the nation to victory enabled him to pursue his course unswerving.

The king (who also was Elector of Hanover), along with New-castle and most of England's political leaders, was primarily concerned for Anglo-Hanoverian interests on the Continent of Europe. These men could see only one logical course—to continue committing the bulk of Britain's available resources to the Continental struggle involving the armies of Russia, Austria, France, Prussia, Hanover, and numerous lesser states. Fearing an amphibious invasion from France, they thought it essential to employ Britain's powerful navy in the monotonous task of guarding the home island. Far-flung naval operations in other seas and border warfare in distant colonies were considered by these Continentalists to be peripheral and relatively inconsequential. From their point of view, it was victory on the Continent that really mattered. In sharp contrast, Pitt was the first European leader to view the continuing struggle among the powers in its full, worldwide dimension. To him it seemed eminently clear that Britain's future depended upon the preservation and growth of her empire. As an island kingdom with limited natural resources and a relatively small population, Britain did not have the capacity to become master of Europe, but her powerful navy and her well-developed merchant marine enabled her to build and sustain an empire which in turn would nourish Britain's own greatness throughout the world. Hanover and other Continental interests should not be abandoned, of course, but they could best be safeguarded by subsidizing the armies of Frederick of Prussia and his allies, while Britain concentrated on winning the war for empire. Pitt was a thoroughgoing mercantile imperialist. For him the main objective was to make the world safe for British commercial expansion, and this meant not only the preservation of colonies and the maintenance of sea lanes, but also the dismembering of rival empires, Spanish and French. He intended to lay France low by breaking her strength in America.

Pitt, because of his widespread popularity and the British yearning for victory, was able to have his own way and became the executor of the new strategy. This meant some significant changes in the British way of doing things. Henceforth, the regular forces, both army and navy, would play a larger role in the American theater of operations. Indeed, Pitt was to turn the old French and Indian War into a contest between regular forces, with provincial troops playing little more than a supporting role. Yet strong provincial support was urgently needed, and the energetic prime minister found ways to gain that essential support. Whenever possible he avoided measures that might give offense to the colonists. He changed the rule subordinating provincial officers to regular officers, so that henceforth the former were to have command over regular officers of lower rank. Also, and this was very important, he continued and even expanded the policy of encouraging colonial participation in the war effort by promising financial compensation. The subsidies he disbursed enabled various colonies to raise contingents of troops and provide needed logistical support without excessive strain on their own economies. England's treasure as well as the blood of her own sons now was being expended to gain a final magnificent victory over the old foe.[1]

Another question of great importance to Pitt was the selection of commanders to carry forward the war in America. The dilatory Loudoun had to be replaced, for in Pitt's eyes he was not the man to lead the bold offensive now envisioned. In the matter of military appointments the prime minister had to reconcile his own wishes with those of the king, which for Pitt was not easy. The officer whom George II preferred as Loudoun's successor was a rather colorless and certainly undistinguished Scot, James Abercromby, already on the scene in America. Pitt was not overly pleased with the choice, but was able to acquiesce.[2] However, Pitt's choices for subcommanders clearly reflected his own willingness to disregard the strong tradition of seniority in his search for real talent. Prominent among these were John Forbes and Jeffery Amherst, both in their forties. The latter was especially honored by the promotion, being advanced above many officers of longer service and higher rank, including Forbes himself.

Actually it was not until 1758 that Pitt's ideas and methods began to have their full impact upon the conduct of the war in America. The defeats and disasters of 1755, 1756, and 1757 were now a matter of record; and although the sting was still felt, the new year marked a fresh beginning. Pitt's plan was a clear reflection of his strategic concept, carefully constructed to achieve his major objective: the conquest of Canada. He had begun with a brilliant alteration of naval policy designed to advance the date when the armies would be able to commence operations. The old practice had been to assemble expeditionary forces in Britain and, when all were together and the winds favorable, to send them across to their American destination as one big fleet. This meant long delay in preparation and an unduly heavy commitment of the Royal Navy to escort duty. When the campaigning of 1757 came to an end following Loudoun's failure, Pitt ordered some of the warships to winter in American ports rather than return to England, so that they would be on hand early for the next year's operations. Furthermore, in 1758 he began to send smaller groups of transports and storeships from Britain to the colonies under the same light convoy protection as was afforded merchant vessels. Whenever ready, such groups could take advantage of the next favorable wind and be on their way. They made the crossing with little escort protection except at the beginning and the end of their journey, where the danger was greatest. This method expedited the assembling of forces at American bases, while freeing the ships of the line for more important tasks.[3]

When the prime minister studied his map of North America, he could see with absolute clarity what so many provincial leaders had long been proclaiming—Quebec must be the principal objective. As one contemporary pointed out, "When the spring is diverted or cutt off, the river must dry up. Such is the position of Quebec that it is absolutely the key of French America, and our possession of it would for ever lock out every Frenchman."[4] But how to get at Quebec? Here there was ample precedent from which to draw. The basic plan had been public property for many years, and indeed had been tried more than once, but never with success. It was this same basic plan that Pitt now adopted and refurbished. New, however, was the extreme care he took to ensure that enough ships, supplies, and trained manpower would be available where and when needed. The principal roles were assigned to units of the regular forces.

Prior to 4 March 1758, when the news that Loudoun had been succeeded by Abercromby reached New York, the former was proceeding with his own plans for the new campaign. Fortunately, these did not differ radically from Pitt's own intentions, so that the change of command caused little or no actual delay.[5] Brigadier General John Forbes was assigned the task of conducting an offensive on the western frontier, to undermine the French position in the West and prevent the garrisons in that area from hastening to the defense of the St. Lawrence Valley. Forbes selected as his principal target the obvious one—Fort Duquesne—and chose to begin his offensive in Pennsylvania. The western operation was an integral part of Pitt's grand strategy but secondary to the double-pronged offensive against Quebec. Abercromby himself was to lead an army of regulars and provincials from Fort Edward north into the Champlain Valley. The diligent Pitt, neglecting no detail within his ken, ordered New York's lieutenant governor to have enough boats constructed by 1 May to carry at least 20,000 men against Fort Carillon (Ticonderoga).[6] After seizing Ticonderoga and Crown Point, Abercromby was to proceed down Lake Champlain and the Richelieu River to the St. Lawrence, snuffing out French resistance as he went. At the same time Amherst, after assembling a powerful fleet and army of regulars at Halifax, was to fall upon Louisbourg in a replay of the 1745 operation. This time, however, the landing and siege would be carried out by the regular forces in a display of professional tactics. Once Louisbourg was in British hands, Amherst was to enter the St. Lawrence, advance to Quebec, and join with Abercromby in conquering the heartland of New France. Then, having achieved these great victories, British forces would deliver a resounding afterstroke in the form of a naval assault against French positions at Mobile and on the lower Mississippi, so that the enemy would suffer confusion and defeat from one end of their great line to the other.[7] In Pitt's mind, 1758 was to be the year of decision in America.

This kind of determined leadership, with Britain's increasing commitment of military and financial resources to the American theater, did much to buoy American morale. Even in the boggy field of Indian relations, some colonial leaders were beginning to see cause for a cautious optimism. Influential chiefs of various tribes hitherto inclined toward the French seemed to be sensing now a shifting of the tide, as evidenced by their increasing receptivity to British appeals. At the same time the French, their supply of trading goods greatly diminished as a result of the British naval blockade, were noticing a new and alarming coolness on the part of wavering Indians. If Sir William Johnson and other British leaders could exploit this apparent defection from the French, there was a good chance that the great military expeditions being planned would have the advantage of considerable Indian support, a matter of no little importance as nearly every British officer now realized.[8]

Preliminary skirmishing, quite independent of Pitt's plans, began early in 1758, in fact, even before the snows of winter had disappeared. The results showed only too well that the path to victory would not be an easy one, for the French and their Indian allies had lost neither their cunning nor their courage. In March, Captain Robert Rogers led a raiding party of about 180 men, mostly rangers, out of Fort Edward for a strike against the garrison at Ticonderoga. His intention was to lay an ambush somewhere in the vicinity of the French fort in the hope of surprising a work detail or scouting party, thereby gaining prisoners and information. Wearing ice creepers on their feet, the raiders made their way cautiously along the frozen surface of Lake George toward their objective. As it happened, hostile Indians discovered their approach and notified the commander at Ticonderoga, who speedily sent out a counterforce consisting mostly of Indians but including some French and Canadian troops. The two parties clashed on 13 March along the snow-clogged bank of Trout Brook about 4 miles west of the French fort, in what became known as the "Battle on Snowshoes." For the rangers it proved a disaster. So heavy and effective was the enemy's fire that Rogers' men, now fighting desperately for their lives, were able to disengage and retreat only after suffering severe losses. Rogers and his remnant began the long agonizing withdrawal to Fort Edward, where they arrived on the fifteenth— fifty-four survivors, less than one-third of the original force. It was a severe setback just as American confidence in the rangers was beginning to rest on a firm foundation.[9]

In the Mohawk Valley, open to easy enemy intrusion since the destruction of Oswego in 1756, inhabitants of the outlying settlements such as German Flats were extremely apprehensive. "I fear unless this part of the Country be protected by a good Body of Troops and proper Rangers verry soon, it will be intirely depopulated," wrote Sir William Johnson from his own fortified manor.[10] As early as March, there were rumors of the enemy's approach on snowshoes, but it was not until the late afternoon of the last day in April that the long-dreaded blow fell upon German Flats. A scalping party of French Indians suddenly appeared, and soon the attack was in full swing. Many of the villagers tried to escape to the shelter of nearby Fort Herkimer; some made it, many did not. Those who failed were scalped. It was a forceful demonstration that the enemy had both the will and the way to continue the kind of devastating hit-and-run raids that had been terrorizing the frontier ever since Braddock's defeat.[11]

Episodes such as these, however, merely masked the increasingly difficult strategic problem confronting the French high command in Canada. Vaudreuil and Montcalm, handicapped by the late arrival of spring and the usual long delay in the arrival of much-needed supplies and reinforcements from France, had little choice but to adopt an essentially defensive strategy. "As far as this year (is concerned) I shall think I am doing a great deal in warding off everything, so do not look for anything brilliant," warned Montcalm. "I prefer to be Fabius, rather than Hannibal, and it is necessary (that I should)." [12] This significant reversion to the defensive, after three years of rather successful offensive operations, showed how limited were the resources available to the French. The defensive strategy now being adopted, although largely dictated by circumstances, was in fact Canada's best hope for thwarting Pitt's great ambition in North America, as the balance of trained manpower shifted ever more heavily to the side of the British. An alert defense might exact such a heavy toll of the attackers that they would at last give up their goal of conquest, leaving Canada to rebuild its strength.

As soon as the weather permitted, Abercromby and Forbes began assembling their expeditionary forces at Albany and Philadelphia respectively. Amherst, charged with the heavy responsibility of capturing Louisbourg, was on his way from England. The enemy was well aware of the "immense preparations" for these offensives, but as late as the last week of May could not be sure where the British would strike the first blows.[13] Rear Admiral Sir Charles Hardy, preceding Amherst, arrived at Halifax as early as 19 March. He was pleased to find the squadron that had wintered there under Pitt's new policy nearly ready to assume patrol and blockade duty off Louisbourg Harbor. As soon as feasible, Hardy established the naval blockade, hoping to prevent further strengthening of the enemy garrison. Abercromby took the precaution of imposing a general embargo at seaports from Nova Scotia all the way down to South Carolina as a means of concealing from the French the vast preparations being made. Regular regiments were shipped to Halifax from Boston, New York, and Philadelphia. Other regiments came from the British Isles, arriving in the staging area on or about 12 May, under convoy of a squadron commanded by Admiral Edward Boscawen, senior naval officer for the Louisbourg operation. When the entire army was assembled at Halifax, it consisted of fourteen regiments of regular infantry, four companies of rangers, and a detachment of artillery, in all more than 13,000 men. This force was organized in three brigades, the first commanded by Brigadier General Edward Whitmore, the second by Governor Charles Lawrence of Nova Scotia, and the third by Brigadier General James Wolfe. The important post of chief engineer, the officer who would be responsible for laying out the siege lines, was occupied by Colonel John Henry Bastide. Assisting this officer was Patrick Mackellar, who had been wounded in Braddock's defeat, captured at Oswego, and released in 1757. Boscawen commanded a naval force of no less than twenty-three ships of the line plus sixteen smaller vessels carrying a total of 1,842 guns and manned by more than 14,000 sailors, excluding the transports and auxiliaries. Counting all troops, regular and otherwise, available to the French for the defense of Louisbourg plus the seamen on the ships in the harbor, the British advantage in manpower would stand at nearly four to one.[14]

While Boscawen awaited the long-expected arrival of Amherst, he drilled the troops in the difficult and dangerous techniques of landing on a hostile shore. In one of these exercises, using all available boats, 5,700 soldiers were successfully landed near Halifax, a feat that helped build confidence in the men who participated.[15] Finally the time came when Boscawen could wait no longer to begin a difficult operation that had to be completed before the onset of the hurricane season in September. So, trusting that the belated Amherst would join him near Louisbourg, on 29 May he set in motion the great fleet of more than 150 sail. Scarcely had the teeming ships set their course when H.M.S. *Dublin* made her appearance, bringing Amherst to assume command. The general lost no time in boarding the admiral's flagship, where a conference of the senior commanders took place. Then, without further delay, the fleet proceeded north toward Cape Breton Island.[16]

Since 1748 the French had regarrisoned Louisbourg, repaired the great walls and bastions, and reestablished the Island Battery, making the base as formidable as ever. Its commander now was Governor Augustin de Drucour, a captain in the French Navy, who rejoiced in the additional strength afforded by ten warships, under the command of Marquis Charry des Gouttes. Remembering 1745, the French were determined to prevent a British landing anywhere along the north shore of Gabarus Bay and had prepared extensive shore defenses. These consisted of a system of trenches and gun emplacements along the crest of land just above the rocky beaches, protected by great masses of felled trees arranged so that their tangled, outward-pointing branches formed a barrier against any intruders from the sea. Every beach lay exposed to the French guns.[17]

Amherst knew that he would have to make his main landing somewhere along that shore; and on 2 June, the very day of his arrival in Gabarus Bay, he took Wolfe with him in a ship's boat to get a closer look at the French defenses. The next day bad weather set in. From 3 to 6 June, the British fleet lay impatiently at anchor off the beaches, unable to begin the assault landing. During this anxious interlude, with the British thus exposed against a lee shore, Des Gouttes had a rare opportunity to sortie from the harbor and fall upon the loaded transports, an extremely risky venture that could have terminated the threat to Louisbourg. This opportunity he let pass, preferring to remain passive under the guns of the fortress, awaiting Amherst's next move.[18]

On 7 June the air cleared, and during the afternoon even the swell of the sea began to diminish noticeably, presaging a lessening of the surf. Amherst, hoping to divert some of the enemy's attention, sent one regiment in sloops eastward around Black Point and past the mouth of the harbor to establish a small base at Lorembec.[19] In the meantime, final preparations were being made for the main assault landing in the face of French shore defenses now manned by more than 2,000 regulars. When the time came, each of the three British brigades, embarked in ships' boats, was to assemble off a designated part of the shore: Wolfe opposite L'Anse à la Coromandière near the western extremity of the French line, Lawrence farther east in the center, and Whitmore beyond that near White Point. Gunfire support ships would be stationed so as to be able to pound the beach and shore defenses ahead of each division. This arrangement, it was hoped, would force the enemy to keep his strength spread along the entire length of the line. Only Wolfe, however, was to move straight in. His assignment was to get his men ashore somehow at L'Anse à la Coromandière, under the covering fire of the frigate *Kennington* and the snow *Halifax,* while Lawrence, followed by Whitmore, sideslipped westward to land in the same area, thereby bringing the full force of the British attack against the westernmost part of the French defenses. Wolfe knew from personal observation that his assigned beach formed a concave arc confined at either end by low rocky headlands, with the French defenses so arranged as to pour a deadly crossfire upon the beach and the zone of felled trees just above it. The landing would be extremely dangerous.[20]

Two hours after midnight on 8 June, signal lights displayed on the flagship gave the order to prepare for the assault. The redcoats scrambled over the ships' sides and down into the waiting boats, each man careful to make his jump as the boat rose to meet him. When filled, the boats proceeded quietly to their assigned assembly points, guided by lanterns displayed on the seaward side of the gunfire support ships. Dawn broke, and the French began shelling the anchorage once again. The weather, fortunately, was favorable for the landing, although the surf on the beaches still was more boisterous than Wolfe would have liked. About 4:00 A.M., as the sun began to rise, the *Kennington* and the *Halifax* opened fire, while off to the east the other support vessels followed suit. The smoke of their guns drifted landward into the enemy positions, providing some concealment for the boats. For about a quarter of an hour the bombardment continued, after which Wolfe's division began rowing toward the beach. At first the French held their fire, but as the wave of troop-laden boats drew near, they opened up with a storm of shot and shell.

Wolfe saw that a frontal landing in the face of such fire would be disastrous, and therefore signaled for his flotilla to draw back. At about the same time, three of the boats veered off to the eastward toward the small rocky headland. This they found undefended and sufficiently high to shield them from enemy fire. Led by three young officers, the men in the three boats braved the surging water and managed to clamber up onto dry rocks. Wolfe, seeing their success, waved on his division to follow. As they came in to the rocks boats were battered and stove; some men, weighted down with their equipment, slipped into the water and drowned, but most managed to gain the land. Impetuously, Wolfe and his men now advanced against the nearby French positions, taking them by surprise on the flank, while Lawrence and Whitmore, seeing Wolfe's success in landing, brought their divisions in also. Thus by a combination of sheer luck and bold enterprise, the British army gained its beachhead. Soon the French all along the line were fleeing toward Louisbourg, with the British infantry hard on their heels. Not until they began to come under cannon fire from the fortress itself did the excited redcoats stop their pursuit, having bagged a total of about six dozen prisoners. Half-amazed at what they had been able to accomplish after such an uncertain beginning, the British began consolidating their newly won position, with advanced units holding ground only about 2 miles from the walls of Louisbourg. Amherst himself now was in command on shore and eager to begin the siege.[21]

The wind was rising ominously, whipping up the sea again and making it impossible to land the artillery. Fortunately, however, tents and light supplies could be ferried ashore, so that within a few days the army was well established in an entrenched camp. On 11 June, during a temporary interval of more favorable weather, some light field artillery was landed, but the heavy cannon essential to the siege had to wait for calmer seas.[22] In the meantime, Amherst proceeded with his preparations, while Boscawen blockaded the port. On 12 June, Wolfe led a detachment of more than 1,200 men around the harbor on foot to establish batteries at Lighthouse Point overlooking the Island Battery. There he received necessary supplies and artillery from the British outpost at Lorembec, where there was sufficient shelter to permit easy landing. By industrious labor in defiance of enemy fire from the Island Battery, Wolfe's men made rapid progress in siting their guns so as to dominate the entrance to the harbor. The main body of British troops, in the meantime, was beginning to lay out siege lines opposite the western, or landward, walls of the fortress, a work which had to be carried on mostly at night because of French gunfire. Enemy cannon boomed almost incessantly from the fortress and the ships in the harbor, harassing the men at work in the trenches and redoubts. The first really good weather came on the sixteenth, more than a week after the landing, and within a few days even the heavy 24-pounders were being landed successfully and dragged forward to await completion of the positions from which they could begin battering the walls.[23] Wolfe's guns at Lighthouse Point opened fire for the first time on the night of 19 June, confirming Drucour in his gloomy conviction that all was indeed lost.

This deadly duel at the gateway to the St. Lawrence nevertheless had its more pleasant aspect, in the finest tradition of old-fashioned chivalric warfare. Amherst, ever the gentleman, sent a pair of pineapples from his well-stocked larder into the town as a gift for Madame Drucour. The governor returned the compliment in the form of good French champagne *en bouteille*. Nor was the hard-working Wolfe neglected. From Louisbourg to Lighthouse

Point went a "Pyramid of Sweetmeats," whose conveyance must
have been a task of some difficulty and perhaps danger. Even in
the eighteenth century such pleasant exchanges were, as one
amused officer remarked, "strange Complaisance between inveterate
Enemies!" [24] For the common folk within the constricting walls—
nearly 4,000 civilians plus the garrison under arms—the siege
brought little but suffering and horror. Night and day they
cowered wherever they could find shelter from the shattering explosions of British shells. Discouragement and desertion began to
sap the garrison's strength, although many of the troops and some
of the civilians conducted themselves with great bravery. Drucour
resorted to Draconian measures against any who evaded their duty;
at one time the British counted sixteen hanged men dangling from
the walls. In the British lines, smallpox made an unwelcome intrusion, striking most fatally in the company of New England carpenters.[25]

Even as Amherst was moving against Louisbourg, Abercromby's
army of 6,300 regulars and 5,900 provincial troops was assembling
at Albany and Schenectady for the attack on Ticonderoga. (Forbes'
campaign in Pennsylvania developed much more slowly, and will
be discussed later in the chapter.) Provincial troops were not raised,
organized, and trained without some difficulty, although one colonist reported that in Massachusetts, at least, "Men chearfully enlist,
and the most are likely, well behav'd Men that seem to march on
with Courage and Resolution. . . ." [26] That is, if they were paid and
fed. In one contingent marching from Massachusetts to Albany
some of the men, believing that their billeting allowance was being
withheld, went on strike and refused to proceed. "About 30 of us
turnd out and cried billitin money and would not go," one of the
protesters wrote in his diary.

> The captain told us wee had beter go along but we said no and the
> Captain went in to the Colonel and the Colonel came out and smil[d]
> and told the Clarck to Set our names down and after that he bid us
> march, and we march along all but 9 and they Said they would not go
> till they had their money and they Stad behind and the ridgiment
> marcht of[f]. . . .[27]

How could one blame common soldiers when even the colony
legislatures did not scruple to take advantage of the extraordinary
need for men and supplies in order to pry concessions from frantic royal governors? In New Hampshire the assembly refused to

raise more than 800 men and limited their period of service to nine months. On top of that, the legislature insisted on having a voice in the selection of officers. Governor Benning Wentworth saw this last demand as an encroachment on the royal prerogative but was forced to yield in the interests of the war effort. "I am hopeing," the embarrassed governor wrote to Pitt, "I shall not Incurr His Majesty's displeasure by this or any other Condescention I may be under a Necessity to make for the good of the Common Cause." [28] Nothing must be allowed to stall the drive against Canada.

The soldiers in their camps and billets experienced the wearing combination of boredom and discomfort that has usually been the lot of troops primed for action but not yet called upon to fight. At Schenectady some of the troops "were forced by the Lice that fought with them to Leave the barucks and betake them Selves to barns[.]" [29] Abercromby finally got his army moving in June, much later than originally planned. Civilians along the route leading north toward the advance base at Lake George did not always take kindly to the ways of troops on the move. A Massachusetts soldier told how, during a long day of rain, "our mess was a Cooking by the side of the orchard and we took Some boards of[f] of the fence of the top boards of[f] to make a Shed and the Dutch man Came out and took up our hatchets and Swore that he would kill us if wee Did not put on the boards again and was agoing to beat our kittle to pieces but we got out of his way. . . ." [30]

Arriving at the south end of Lake George, Abercromby established his advance base and the newcomers in the army had a chance to observe the charred remains of Fort William Henry near the new camp. To the north stretched the blue waters of Lake George, narrowing among the steep green mountains along either shore in the direction of Ticonderoga and the enemy. Abercromby sent out scouts to keep him informed of French dispositions and, with the active assistance of his very able and popular second-in-command, Brigadier General George Augustus Howe, continued training his troops for the important mission they were about to undertake. Howe was an inspiration to the men, regulars and provincials alike, with his sensible informality and his forward-looking appreciation of the new style of combat most effectively demonstrated by the rangers. For Abercromby, however, the principal problem was transport, first of supplies to his main base at Lake George, and then of his troops and artillery to the vicinity of

the French fort. Thanks to the diligence of John Bradstreet, workmen at Albany and Schenectady had made available about 1,500
bateaus, most of which had to be paddled, poled, and hauled to
the advance base.[31] This and other heavy tasks were completed at
last, so that by 4 July the army was ready to make its bid for
victory.

Abercromby's intention was to advance his army down Lake
George, make a landing near the lower end of the lake, advance
through the woods several miles to the vicinity of Fort Carillon,
and then force the French to surrender. The fort stood on a broad
peninsula bounded on the south by La Rivière de la Chute (the
outlet of Lake George), and on the north and east by the waters of
Lake Champlain. Because the fort itself was too small to shelter all
of the eight regular battalions plus the approximately 400 *troupes
de la marine* and militiamen who were present to defend it, most
of Montcalm's men were encamped outside the walls. Moreover,
the French were short of provisions and so had little hope of with-
standing a prolonged siege. Abercromby's striking force of regular
and provincial regiments, with rangers and boatmen, totaled about
15,000, nearly five times the number of defenders.[32]

Early on the morning of 5 July, Abercromby's army, primed for
action, embarked in the greatest flotilla ever seen on Lake George
—800 or more bateaus, at least ninety whaleboats, and a number of
rafts bearing the artillery. As groups of craft were filled with their
allotment of troops and supplies, they moved out from the shore
and formed in columns according to a prearranged plan, until the
whole formation, spread over many acres of water, was complete.
Then they began advancing slowly down the lake, each boat trying
to maintain its proper position in column. One soldier in a boat
near the head of the formation took a moment to drink in the spectacle—hundreds of craft in rank and file, redcoats and splashing
paddles, flags and martial music, the pageantry of an army afloat on
a magnificent wilderness lake. "I think I never beheld so delightful
a prospect," he later recalled.[33]

Notified of Abercromby's advance, Montcalm saw clearly that
his own essential task was to hold off the attackers as long as possible without sacrificing too many of his men and then, if necessary,
evacuate his troops to Crown Point. Better to lose Ticonderoga
than the eight battalions of regulars, who would be sorely needed
for the further defense of Canada. In preparation for their stand,

the French troops hurried to complete a defensive line extending across the peninsula at an extreme distance of approximately 1,400 yards from Fort Carillon. The main part of this line was constructed of large tree trunks laid horizontally one on top of the other and held firmly in place with uprights on either side. Loopholes were cut at convenient heights, and sandbags were laid along the top to a height of seven or more feet, providing excellent protection against small-arms fire. In addition, the branches that had been lopped off in preparing the barricade were laid thickly together a short distance to the fore, sharpened points outward, forming a bristling *abatis.* Tactically, the line was weakest on either flank, but especially on the right, where a fairly broad expanse of lowland sloping down to the waters of Lake Champlain afforded opportunity for an end sweep.

On the morning of 6 July, while the French were frantically making these preparations, Abercromby's army landed unopposed at a small cove near the lower end of Lake George. The easiness of the debarkation, so vastly different from Wolfe's at Gabarus Bay four weeks earlier, gave no forewarning of the difficulties ahead. Abercromby formed his main force in four columns, which he set in motion toward Fort Carillon not by the regular portage route, but instead by a roundabout way through the woods, a circuitous route eliminating the necessity of crossing the river. French outpost detachments retreated quickly before this bold advance, and the British might have marched on without serious difficulty to confront Montcalm's men in their new line, had not an accidental encounter occurred. One of the British columns, with the zealous Lord Howe at its head, suddenly came into contact with a French detachment of several hundred men hastening back toward the fort. In the immediate exchange of fire, Lord Howe, undoubtedly the most popular and in some respects the most able of the senior officers, slumped to the ground dead. The French detachment was defeated and many of its members were made prisoners, but that was small consolation for the loss of a leader so highly regarded throughout the army. To make matters even worse, the British columns now fell into confusion, with various units floundering through unfamiliar wilderness and even exchanging fire with each other. Eventually, at least by the next morning, most of Abercromby's troops regrouped at the landing place, having accomplished nothing.[34]

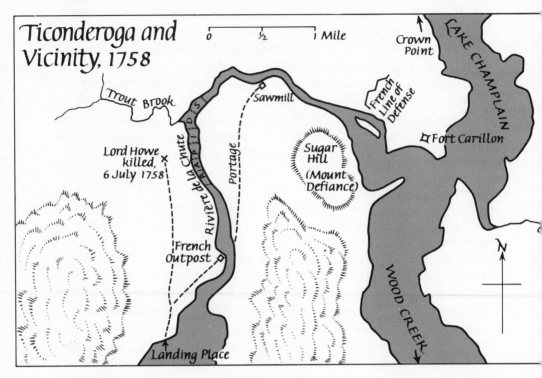

The army made a fresh start on the seventh, again leaving its artillery at the landing place, but this time proceeding by the more direct portage route leading to a sawmill at the second crossing of the river. That night the British camped a short distance beyond the river and only a mile from the French sentries at the barricade, with advance parties even closer.[35] During that same evening, Montcalm received a welcome reinforcement of about 400 troops, which more than made up for the losses of the previous day. Abercromby, too, gained additional strength, although in this case its value proved questionable. On the morning of the eighth, William Johnson appeared at the sawmill with 395 Indian warriors, mostly of the Six Nations. This group proceeded to the slopes of Mount Defiance overlooking the main French positions across the river, where they amused themselves by trying to annoy the enemy with long-range musketry.[36]

Abercromby had never seen Fort Carillon or the peninsula on which it stood, nor did he go forward now to observe the new French line. Instead, he accepted the word of an inexperienced engineering officer who reported after reconnoitering that Montcalm's defenses were susceptible to a frontal attack by infantry without artillery preparation. Two other courses of action, both preferable, could have been chosen instead: First, to circle to the north around Montcalm's weak right flank and establish a strong position on the shore of Lake Champlain between Fort Carillon and Crown Point; or second, simply to dig in all along the front and bring up the artillery before commencing the attack. But Abercromby was in a great hurry because he feared the arrival of strong French reinforcements, and he found the idea of an immediate assault on the hastily erected and not fully completed barricade appealing. Accordingly, he advanced a screen of rangers, light infantry, and provincials toward the French line. Behind that screen, the assault regiments formed and prepared to attack the log barricade, the men being instructed to "march up briskly, rush upon the Enemy's fire, and not to give theirs, untill they were within the Enemie's Breastwork." [37]

Before all units were in position and ready, sharp firing began on one of the wings, precipitating the general assault. Redcoated regiments, formed in line of battle three deep, began advancing through the screen toward the tangle of sharpened branches. Each regiment seemed to be operating independently, maintaining its own formation as it marched forward in its assigned sector; overall there was little coordination or evidence of centralized command. The waiting French, aiming their muskets through the loopholes, began dropping British officers and men all along the line. The *abatis*, as intended, destroyed any semblance of an orderly formation, for once in the tangle of branches every man had to struggle forward as best he could with the balls whistling by on all sides. One soldier later told how "the ground was Clogged up . . . with Logs and trees Intermixed with Brush which greatly Interupted the speedy and Regular march of our troops; and as they marched 3 deep they had Enough to do to fill up the Vecant places made up by With Dead and wounded which fell." [38] About the same time Abercromby, back near the sawmill, sent several barges armed with cannon down the river to help turn Montcalm's left flank. As soon as these clumsy craft appeared, they were taken under fire by the guns of Fort Carillon. Two of the barges were effectively smashed, and the others hastily withdrew.[39]

Throughout most of this hot July afternoon, the British in-

fantry bravely formed and re-formed in successive but always
futile attempts to break into the French line. Their dogged courage
in the face of withering fire was admired even by the well-protected
enemy. Thickening smoke from the heavy musketry and from occasional fires springing up in the heaps of brush before the barricade hung low over the scene of deadly struggle. Increasing numbers of redcoated bodies lay strewn here and there on the open
ground and among the tangle of tree limbs. Abercromby apparently
remained close to his headquarters at the sawmill, listening to the
drumming musketry and refusing to call off his men. If only the
heavy artillery had been available, British gunners almost certainly
could have cleared a way; instead, the whole, terrible burden
rested upon the infantry, whose courage and firepower were simply
insufficient. Even the contagious zeal of the late lamented Lord
Howe could not have made the difference. As evening approached,
Abercromby at last was brought to realize that he was commanding
a disaster and that now his only hope was to end the futile assault.
Far too late, but better late than never, the badly disillusioned
general called back his shredded regiments with as many of the
wounded as they could rescue, leaving the field to the dead and
dying—and the exulting Montcalm.

Unlike Braddock and Dunbar in 1755, Abercromby had the
capability of regrouping and then resuming the offensive. Although
badly battered, his regular regiments still were organized fighting
machines with adequate supplies and equipment, while his provincial troops were scarcely blooded. The latter had suffered approximately 350 casualties out of a total of 9,000 men, whereas the
regulars had lost over 1,600 men including a large number of commissioned officers. In contrast, Montcalm's casualties totaled about
377.[40] If Abercromby had now taken a day or two to rest his weary
troops and bring forward all his artillery, he would have had a
reasonably good chance of smashing through the French defenses
and seizing Fort Carillon. But the British commander had had
enough in one day, and ordered his army back to its base at the
southern end of Lake George. When the defeated army had gone,
a French party, following the line of withdrawal along the portage
to the lake, found "Wounded, provisions, abandoned equipment,
shoes left in miry places, remains of barges and burned pon-
toons," in short, ample evidence of an army in hasty retreat.[41] The
jubilant French were not inclined to minimize their astonishing

victory over an army so much larger than their own. "The glorious day of the 8th will always be an honour to our armies," wrote Montcalm. "Never," added his chief of staff piously, "has a victory been more especially due to the finger of Providence." [42] Now all that the British could do was swallow their bitter medicine and look hopefully toward Louisbourg where Amherst's men were conducting their siege.

By the twenty-sixth of June, Wolfe's artillery at Lighthouse Point had managed to silence the Island Battery, thereby greatly increasing the prospects for a successful intrusion by the navy. In a desperate attempt to forestall this eventuality, Des Gouttes had four of his own ships scuttled in the channel, leaving only five French line of battle ships and a frigate still in action.[43] The month of June closed with Amherst's men laboring to advance their siege lines on the western side of the town, Boscawen's ships patrolling off the coast to prevent the exit or entry of any French vessels, and Drucour's men ashore and afloat employing their cannon to hold the besiegers at arm's length. Day after day in July through fair weather and foul, the cannonading continued on both sides, while the British kept hard at work improving their access roads, extending their trenches, and building their batteries and redoubts ever closer to the massive walls and bastions of Louisbourg. On one occasion, at night, a force of about 725 French troops made a daring raid into the British lines from the vicinity of Black Point. They took a British outpost by surprise, killing the officer in charge and four of his men, and then pushed on to penetrate an important segment of Amherst's line. By this time the alarm was spreading, and hastily assembled reinforcements were hurrying to block the French thrust. When the raiders finally were forced to withdraw, having suffered fairly heavy losses, they took with them as prisoners two British officers and twenty-eight grenadiers. French partisans and Indians roving behind the British lines also posed something of a threat, but were unable to effect any serious damage.[44]

At midday of 21 July, British fortunes took another surge toward victory. A lucky shot from one of the siege guns ignited some powder aboard the French 74-gun *Entreprenant* causing a heavy explosion and conflagration, with flames leaping up into the rigging. The unfortunate ship swung so near to the 64-gun *Capricieux* that that vessel also took fire and in turn set the

Célèbre ablaze. By four o'clock that afternoon "they were all three young Aetna's which had a pretty Effect all Night long." [45] During this holocaust, French boats swarmed busily between the stricken vessels and the town, providing the British gunners an unusual opportunity to employ their grapeshot. By this time the British had as many as twenty mortars and a large number of cannon bombarding the shuddering town, which was rapidly becoming a cluster of ruins. On the morning of the twenty-second, Amherst's batteries set the barracks in the citadel on fire, and as the blaze spread a large part of the citadel was ruined. Some of the civilian inhabitants dared remain within the walls no longer, preferring to take their chances in the ditch or other hiding places outside.

With the Island Battery now "tore all to Pieces," the only serious threat remaining to prevent Boscawen from sailing his own powerful ships into the harbor were the 74-gun *Prudent* and the 64-gun *Bienfaisant*. Both lay close to the town, with most of the sailors ashore assisting in the defense of the fortress. Should any British ships approach to force an entry, the two heavily gunned French ships could be quickly remanned and made ready to rake the intruders. In order to clear a way for the safe entry of the British fleet, Boscawen and Amherst agreed upon a daring plan, carried out on the dark night of 25 July. While Amherst's batteries distracted the French garrison with a heavy bombardment, a large number of well-armed British sailors in about fifty boats slipped quietly into the mouth of the harbor. Some occupied the ruins of the Island Battery to make sure there was no interference from that quarter, while the remainder approached and boarded the *Prudent* and the *Bienfaisant*. The former was hard aground and so, after releasing the twenty British prisoners found on board, Boscawen's men set her afire. The *Bienfaisant* they were able to tow beyond the range of French artillery. During this bold and highly successful exploit, the British took 152 prisoners while losing only seven men killed and nine wounded.[46] That was enough for Drucour and the inhabitants of Louisbourg. Before Boscawen could put into effect his intention of sending a powerful squadron into the harbor, the French governor asked for terms.

The surrender, arranged on 26 July and effected the next day, included all French forces on Cape Breton Island and Prince

Edward Island. At Louisbourg, civilians who had not borne arms were to be shipped to France; the four regiments of regulars and the twenty-four companies of *troupes de la marine* were made prisoners of war. Considering the scope and difficulty of the operation, British losses from 8 June to 26 July had been relatively light, but the French lost the whole garrison and 2,400 seamen as well, to say nothing of many valuable fighting ships.

By the first of August, Amherst and Boscawen had learned of Abercromby's failure and agreed that the projected operation against Quebec would have to be postponed until the following year. Montcalm's successful stand on 8 July and Drucour's tenacious defense of Louisbourg had bought for Canada another twelve months of time. Most of August was spent shipping off the French prisoners and making hurried repairs to damaged buildings so that there would be adequate shelter for a British garrison. Detachments were sent to secure the remainder of Cape Breton Island and Prince Edward Island. In addition, Amherst sought to weaken the enemy and increase the security of Nova Scotia by raiding French installations and settlements in nearby areas. One expedition, commanded by Colonel Robert Monckton, proceeded to burn and destroy along the lower St. John River, and Wolfe with three regiments carried out a similar assignment on the Gaspé Peninsula. Amherst, in the meantime, had sailed for Boston with five regiments, arriving there on 13 September. The enthusiastic town provided a welcome for heroes. Under conditions far more pleasant than anything they had known during the long siege, the redcoats set up camp on the Common. "Thousands of People came to see them and would give them Liquor and make the men Drunk in Spite of all that could be done," Amherst grumbled good-naturedly.[47] Doubtless, many a local veteran of 1745 sought out a willing group of redcoats, offered a bottle, and then plied them with questions about Louisbourg.

Abercromby had been immobilized since his defeat at Ticonderoga but was not unmindful of military needs and opportunities in other areas, especially the Mohawk Valley and Lake Ontario. Soon after his return to base, he had sent Bradstreet with a force of provincial troops to increase British strength at the Great Carrying Place of the Mohawk River, where Brigadier General John Stanwix was constructing a new fort. His purpose was not entirely defensive. Bradstreet was authorized to take 3,600 men and attempt to capture Fort Frontenac, a project he had long cherished.[48] Strategically, the destruction of Fort Frontenac would be of great importance, for the lines of communication and supply for most of the important French installations in the West had a common origin where the St. Lawrence River takes its leave of Lake Ontario. If only Bradstreet could seize Fort Frontenac and turn it into a British base, Fort Duquesne, Niagara, and other French forts to the south and west would wither on the vine. Montcalm saw the danger, but fearing that Abercromby might make a second attempt against Ticonderoga, dared not divert any of his own strength to help save Fort Frontenac.[49]

It was 14 August when Bradstreet took his leave of Stanwix at the Great Carrying Place and headed for Oswego. With him he had an army of more than 3,000 men, all provincials except for about 150 regular soldiers. The forts at Oswego still lay in ruins, much as Montcalm had left them two years before, and Bradstreet lingered there only overnight before setting out on the broad lake in his fleet of bateaus.[50] On 25 August he arrived at his objective, landing late in the evening within about a mile of the fort. There was no immediate opposition. Although the stone walls and bastions of Fort Frontenac supported a large number of cannon, many of these guns remained unmounted and unready for action, while the garrison was outnumbered by Bradstreet's men by more than twenty to one.[51] In yet another way fortune favored the eager provincials. Nine French vessels, some of them recently arrived with valuable cargoes, rode at anchor in the harbor.

The British landed their cannon early the next morning, approached the fort, and spread their lines for a siege. Both sides commenced firing, which continued throughout the day without any great damage to either side. Already, however, the commander of the fort could see only too clearly how hopeless it was to resist such an overwhelming force. On the morning of 27 August, after only about twenty-four hours of bombardment, he agreed to capitulate. According to the terms agreed upon, the garrison was permitted to withdraw to Montreal on condition that a similar number of British prisoners, including Colonel Schuyler, be repatriated.[52] A great amount of plunder fell to the victors, there being "scarce a Millitary or Naval Store which this Place did not abound with." The quantity of goods found in the fort was simply "uncrediable," wrote one exulting victor.[53] So Bradstreet found himself in command of a fort that was virtually intact, with an army of 3,000 men to guard it, and a small fleet of captured sailing craft that could be armed and sent out to sever the main French lines of communication with the West. It was sweet revenge for the destruction of Oswego. Yet apparently Bradstreet gave little thought to the possibility of turning Frontenac into a British base which, if utilized effectively not only to break the French grip on the West but also as a staging point for a major invasion of the St. Lawrence Valley, might have shortened the war by a year. Instead, the victorious troops hastily demolished the French installations, burned seven of the vessels in the harbor, and loaded their plunder, including furs and trading goods, on the remaining brig and schooner. When all was ready, the fleet of two vessels and more than a hundred bateaus got underway for Oswego. Later one of the officers described how the plunder was assembled and divided at the Oneida Carrying Place: "As our Battoas Came up they were Stricktley Serched and also the mens Packs and Colected ower Plonder together and after gethering it Divide it to Each Regiment their proportion . . . and Leut Bass and Ensigns Dorr and Ensign Fisk Devided ower Company's Plonder amongest the men." [54] This dry-land privateering, for such it really was, goes far to explain why Bradstreet and his men had shown so little interest in the possibility of remaining at the fort. What good is plunder to a man stationed at a wilderness outpost? Nevertheless, the destruction of Fort Frontenac, following so closely upon the loss of Louisbourg, was a severe blow to Canadian morale, and Montcalm himself now considered the military situation "critical." [55]

All this while, Abercromby was toying with the idea of joining Amherst's Louisbourg veterans to his own army at Lake George for a second attempt against Fort Carillon. Answering his summons, the regiments at Boston packed their gear and marched to Albany, where they set up camp. Amherst himself continued on to Lake George. There he was greeted by the commander in chief on 5 October, and the two generals prudently decided that it would be unwise to take an army to Ticonderoga so late in the year. Just as Amherst had found it necessary to forego his intended sail up the St. Lawrence, so Abercromby now lost his chance to redeem his reputation at Ticonderoga. Indeed, it was his last chance, for already Pitt's orders relieving him of his command were en route from England. Abercromby the defeated was to be replaced by Amherst the victorious.[56]

As early as 17 October, Abercromby began sending his heavy artillery, excess ammunition, and bateaus back to the Hudson for greater security during the winter. He had a sloop dismasted and then carefully sunk so as to be available the following year, and some of the whaleboats hidden in the forest. Then, leaving a garrison to hold Fort Edward, he took most of the army down to winter quarters. Montcalm, too, withdrew from his wilderness strongholds after arranging for the security of Ticonderoga and Crown Point. By 14 November, he and most of his troops were at Montreal. On Cape Breton Island the recently appointed British governor, Brigadier General Edward Whitmore, remained at Louisbourg with a garrison force.[57]

Many miles to the south, in the mountainous country between the Susquehanna River and the Forks of the Ohio, the third major prong of Pitt's 1758 offensive, under the command of General Forbes, had been slowly advancing toward Fort Duquesne. Like Abercromby's army at Lake George, that of Forbes was built around a strong nucleus of regulars, some 1,600 altogether, principally of the Highland regiment commanded by Lieutenant Colonel Archibald Montgomery together with four companies of the Royal Americans under the very able Swiss, Colonel Henry Bouquet. Pennsylvania, its government no longer dominated by Quaker pacifists, was able to provide a respectable contingent of 2,700 troops commanded by Colonel John Armstrong, while Virginia contributed Colonel George Washington and a force of 2,600 provincials. All told, the army consisted of nearly 7,000 troops plus a large number of civilian wagoners and sutlers. Bouquet was given great responsibility in making advance preparations along the army's route from Philadelphia toward the mountains.[58]

As soon as Forbes reached Philadelphia from New York in mid-April 1758, he began to encounter frustrating problems that were to hamper his campaign for the next five or six months. To begin with, the degree of cooperation afforded by the Pennsylvania assembly was directly tied to its continuing struggle with Governor William Denny over the taxation of proprietary lands. Even more disturbing to Forbes was the fact that the Maryland assembly coolly adjourned "without giving one man or one Sixpence" for the support of the expedition.[59] Moreover, the British general soon came to the unhappy conclusion that the provincial troops, officers and men alike, were slovenly and unreliable. With few exceptions, he wrote angrily, they were "an extream bad Collection of broken Innkeepers, Horse Jockeys, and Indian traders . . . a gathering from the scum of the worst of people. . . ." As for the civilians in the countryside, Forbes discovered to his cost that almost to a man they seemed "rather bent upon our ruin, and destruction, than give the smallest assistance, which if at last extorted is so infamously charged as shews the disposition of the people in its full Glare." [60] Bouquet found the farmers extremely reluctant to lease their wagons and draft animals to the army, apparently on the grounds that adequate compensation had not been paid for previous losses. "I know of none except, perhaps, one horse that was drowned last year, and not paid for," responded the baffled Swiss officer. "I hope that for a Dead Horse, the People . . . will not Distress the Service in such urging Circumstances, and Load themselves with the Consequences of such undutiful Behaviour towards their King and Country." To the commanding general Bouquet sent an earnest plea: "I cannot avoid recommending a trifle," he wrote, "which is to find some way of paying . . . the cost of that cursed horse which was drowned last year. . . . That will have a very good effect, and will smooth over many difficulties." [61] It is not known whether the aggrieved owner ever was given compensation, but somehow by a combination of cajolery and threats a barely adequate number of teams and wagons gradually was obtained.

Another almost constant problem concerned the Indian allies, mainly Catawbas and Cherokees. Forbes knew what the absence of such auxiliaries had meant to Braddock, but after a few months' experience with the impatience, caprice, unreliability, and greed of those warriors who drifted into and later drifted out of his army, he sometimes was tempted to wish them all away—except for the inescapable fact that he needed them so badly as scouts. Groups of them were induced, from time to time, to trek out to the vicinity of Fort Duquesne, where they supposedly studied the state of the French defenses and then reported what they had discovered. Yet Forbes never felt that he had an accurate picture of the situation. "The Indians I cannot mention . . . with any manner of patience," he once wrote to Abercromby, who was in a position to sympathize. ". . . I look upon them, their Interpreters, their Superintendents, and every creature any ways connected or attached to them, as the most imposing Rogues that I have ever had to deal with." [62] The trouble was that the Cherokees and others were in the campaign for what they could carry away from it, and all too often what Forbes and his subordinates could offer them was not sufficient. "I think it would be easier to make Indians of our White men, than to coax that damned Tanny Race," snorted Bouquet.[63] Perhaps so. Some officers, it seems, were not above making the attempt. As in the case of Rogers' rangers, so now on the middle frontier, unsuspected virtue was being discovered in the rough buckskin costume of the true woodsman. Forbes assured Bouquet that he had

> been long in your opinion of equiping Numbers of our men like the Saveges and I fancy Col: Byrd of Virginia has most of his best people equipt in that manner . . . I was resolved upon getting some of the best people in every Corps to go out a Scouting in that stile for as you justly observe, the Shadow may be often taken for the reality, And I must confess in this country, wee must comply and learn the Art of Warr, from Ennemy Indians or anything else who have seen the Country and Warr carried on in itt.[64]

These astonishing words from a British professional soldier are a measure of how greatly Braddock's defeat and other actual experiences in America had affected the once-rigid views of the best British commanders.

Forbes planned to advance slowly by the most advantageous route, taking time to build an adequate road along which the heavy wagonloads of supplies as well as the artillery could move. At appropriate intervals the advancing army would establish fortified supply depots which would be held by garrison troops safeguarding the lengthening line of communication and supply. Basic to the conduct of this campaign was the choice to be made between two alternative routes leading to the principal objective, Fort Duquesne. The question of which route to follow opened the door to intercolonial politics, with economic rivalry threatening to trample upon strategic considerations. Obviously, after the French had been ousted from the Ohio Valley, the colony through which Forbes had built his road would have a great advantage over rival colonies in being able to utilize the military road for general access and trade. The British general quickly found himself under pressure from Virginia and Pennsylvania, the two principal rivals, each wanting the road. Through most of the spring while the expedition was forming, Forbes' initial intention had been to proceed to Fort Cumberland by way of Fort Frederick in Maryland. At Fort Cumberland he would be joined by the Virginia contingent, after which the entire expedition would follow Braddock's road to Fort Duquesne. Toward the end of May, however, the commander was persuaded to alter this plan. Now he decided to advance west as far as Raystown, a frontier outpost at the junction of several Indian trails and trading routes. From Raystown, the army could either cut a road south to Fort Cumberland or else—and this was the intriguing possibility—open an altogether new road west across the mountains directly to the Forks.[65]

For nearly two months the question remained unresolved, as the rival parties maneuvered and connived in their own interests. The Virginians argued that Braddock's road was already open and known, while the proposed Pennsylvania route would have to be laboriously constructed over a succession of steep mountain ridges. The Pennsylvanians, on the other hand, argued that their route was more direct and hence many miles shorter. Braddock's road, they said, was now overgrown and had the further disadvantage of difficult river crossings and wooded defiles where the French could prepare ambuscades. These conflicting arguments swirled through the upper levels of the army even as the troops advanced from Carlisle and established their new base at Raystown. By the end of July, Forbes had decided in favor of the Pennsylvania route all the way. An officer sent forward to reconnoiter this route found at Loyalhanna Creek on the far side of Laurel Ridge a spot eminently suitable for a new advance base. It was, he reported, a very pretty place, with ample water and pasturage, "and what makes it more desirable is the Westeren breeses carrying with them the Smell of the French Brandy." [66] Loyalhanna was less than 50 miles southeast of Fort Duquesne.

While the army was pushing forward slowly, Forbes also was cooperating with the government of Pennsylvania in a diplomatic offensive to regain the allegiance of the Delaware and Shawnee Indians, and if possible detach other Indians of the Ohio Valley from the French. A courageous Moravian missionary, Christian Frederick Post, was sent west with an invitation for these Indians to attend a new conference at Easton in September. When it became clear that many of the western Indians were planning to appear, Forbes very wisely delayed his offensive still further to avoid alienating Indians who hopefully might soon be counted as friends or at least neutrals.[67]

Major James Grant of Montgomery's Highlanders unexpectedly broke the temporary lull. Sent to the vicinity of Fort Duquesne with a body of more than 800 Virginians and Highlanders, under orders to reconnoiter and if possible obtain some prisoners for interrogation, Grant arrived undetected on a hill not far from the French fort on the night of 13 September. Believing that the garrison was weak, he was tempted by the possibility of presenting Fort Duquesne to his commander on a silver platter. After dividing his force with the intention of drawing the enemy into an ambush, at break of day on the fourteenth Grant ordered the drums to beat. What happened next came as a great surprise to the major. The French and their Indian allies, aroused by the unexpected affront, emerged in great strength and launched an immediate attack which soon split the British into desperately fighting segments. Grant himself was captured, as were several other officers. Altogether the British lost about 270 men, or approximately one-third of their number. This made it clear that the French at Fort Duquesne still had some fight left and, worse, that many of the Ohio Indians still thirsted for British blood. Forbes was quick to blame the unhappy Grant and rebuke Bouquet for this distressing incident, fearing that it might undermine Pennsylvania's hopeful diplomatic offensive.[68]

Actually, Grant's ill-advised gamble at Fort Duquesne had little effect on the Easton conference, which occupied most of October. Attending were the governors of Pennsylvania and New Jersey, Israel Pemberton of the Friendly Association, Conrad Weiser, George Croghan in the capacity of Johnson's deputy, and more than 500 Indians from some fifteen tribes. Among the latter were Teedyuscung, the self-proclaimed spokesman for the Delawares, and important leaders of the Six Nations. Two important developments occurred, both favorable to British imperial interests. The leaders of the Six Nations belittled Teedyuscung, informing the Delawares in no uncertain terms that they must accept Iroquois hegemony and put an end to their prolonged quarrel with the British. Pennsylvania, in turn, promised to restore to the Iroquois those lands west of the Allegheny Ridge that had been purchased by proprietary agents at the time of the Albany Congress. The Delawares and Shawnees now found it expedient to conform by resuming their former peaceful relationship with Pennsylvania, even though their principal grievances were not fully resolved. When the conference closed on the twenty-fifth of October, the British had more reason than in 1757 to feel optimistic about their future relations with the Indians of the western frontier. Again Christian Frederick Post started toward the Ohio Valley to inform the Indians there of what had transpired and to urge them to refrain from giving any further support to the French. The success of the conference at Easton and of Post's subsequent mission was to have an important bearing on the military offensive which Forbes now was free to resume.[69]

By 2 November the entire expedition, including Colonel Washington and the Virginians, was congregated at Loyalhanna, with small but effective garrisons holding the line of supply depots stretching back to the east. The season was now late, and once again a British offensive that had been painfully slow in developing seemed threatened by the approach of winter. Forbes knew that his army was not equipped to survive a winter in the wilderness; yet at this point, after so much painful preparation, it was maddening to think of abandoning the attempt against Fort Duquesne. On 12 November a party of enemy Indians made a raid upon the army's cattle and horses at Loyalhanna, whereupon Forbes sent two parties of 500 men each to intercept the marauders. Most of the raiders escaped, but the troops did bag one important captive, a British subject who had been living and moving with the Indians. This man revealed the actual weakness of Fort Duquesne. Apparently by this time, too, many of the Ohio Valley Indians, influenced by the Treaty of Easton as well as the approach of British military power, had moved away from Fort Duquesne so as not to be caught in the impending showdown. Forbes made his decision accordingly. The final attack must not be postponed until the spring—it must be launched immediately wtih 2,500 men.[70] The remaining miles to Fort Duquesne could be covered fairly quickly, for the slopes were gradual and the forest quite open, with little underbrush. Forbes ordered his three brigades, under Bouquet, Montgomery, and Washington, to proceed by parallel routes, with flanking parties deployed to guard against any repetition of the disaster on the Monongahela. The general himself, suffering from a painful and exhausting malady, rocked along in a litter slung between a pair of horses. On the evening of 24 November, when the army was encamped only about 15 miles short of its objective, Indian scouts returned with the electrifying news that the French had burned and abandoned Fort Duquesne. At once Forbes dispatched a troop of horse to the scene. By daylight on the twenty-fifth, the eager commander had his army underway again, without the wagons, everyone straining forward to catch a first view of what promised to be a memorable sight. About six o'clock in the evening they emerged from the forest and saw before them, in the confluence of the two rivers, a cluster of blackened chimney stacks standing gaunt amidst the charred ruins of fort and village. The French, having dumped their cannon in the river and burned their installations, had departed. For the first time since May of 1754 the Forks of the Ohio was under the British flag, and that without a battle. Later, early in December, Post arrived at the Forks with the good news that the Indians of the Ohio Valley had decided for peace.[71]

With winter treading hard on his heels, Forbes left a garrison holed up at the Forks and took the rest of his victorious army back across the mountains along the road they had recently constructed. Soon a new village to be known as Pittsburgh would spring up near the ruins of Fort Duquesne, while traders and speculators from Virginia and Pennsylvania renewed their old rivalry for economic advantage at the Forks. Thanks to Forbes' insistence on following the more direct route to the Forks, the advantage now lay with Pennsylvania. The ailing general, however, had only a short time to reflect upon these matters and the acclaim that his success would surely win for him in London. On 11 March 1759 he died in Philadelphia, and was buried in the chancel of Christ Church.[72] It was a somber last note of the 1758 campaign, which in reality was the pivotal campaign of the entire war in North America.

Surging British power had swept away great portions of New France's outer ring of defenses, most notably Louisbourg and Fort Duquesne. The fall of Louisbourg opened the way to the St. Lawrence from the east; the fall of Fort Duquesne opened the way to Lake Erie from the south, and in addition turned the Indians of the Ohio Valley back toward an alignment with the British. Fort Frontenac, although still in French hands, had been seriously damaged, so that the entrance to the St. Lawrence from the west no longer was effectively guarded, nor was French shipping so predominant on Lake Ontario along the lifeline to Niagara. Still under French control were Ticonderoga and Crown Point, blocking the route down the Champlain Valley; Niagara, guarding the portage between Lake Ontario and Lake Erie; and Fort Toulouse on the southern frontier. In all likelihood, these would be important targets for the British in 1759, with Montreal and Quebec as the ultimate objectives.

Montcalm's trusted aide Bougainville sailed from Canada to France with news of the northern colony's plight, in order to plead for additional aid. The defensive force still available in Canada—eight battalions of regulars plus the *troupes de la marine* and the Canadian militia—was greatly inferior to the overwhelming numbers of British regulars and provincial troops available to Amherst for the next year's campaigns. How, then, could Canada be saved without a major infusion of new military resources? Versailles demonstrated its continued confidence in Montcalm by promoting him to the rank of lieutenant general and ordering Governor Vaudreuil to consult with him on all military matters; that, at least, gave Montcalm somewhat freer play for his own expert knowledge. Beyond that, however, the French government decided not to attempt any large-scale military reinforcement of Canada. This, in effect, left Montcalm no choice but to remain on the defensive in 1759, in a desperate attempt to hold off the surging tide of British military power rolling in from east, south, and west. Burdened with this discouraging assignment, the French commander rightly wondered how long New France could survive. All around him during the winter of 1758–59 were alarming signs of weakness. The shortage of food was severe, while profiteering flourished. From top to bottom, the official bureaucracy seemed rotten with self-seeking, a condition that cannot have gone unnoticed and unresented by the common people.

From the British perspective, 1759 was the year of great opportunity. Thanks to Amherst's and Forbes' victories of the previous year, conditions now were right for the often-discussed but long-delayed thrust into the heartland of Canada, the St. Lawrence Valley between Montreal and Quebec. Strategic routes had been laid open, ample military and naval forces were available, and the Indians were responding more favorably to British diplomacy as they sensed

the growing weakness of New France. Finally, Pitt had discovered
the military leaders for the job. Amherst, the commander in chief,
was known as a steady, methodical officer who had demonstrated
his ability to win. Unlike Loudoun or Abercromby, this man was
not likely to waste his army. He would enjoy the assistance of young
James Wolfe, whom Pitt had rewarded with the temporary rank
of major general in recognition of his aggressive leadership at
Louisbourg. The new commander of naval forces in North American waters was to be Vice Admiral Charles Saunders, a protégé of
the famous Anson.

In letters dated 9 and 29 December 1758, the hard-driving prime
minister carefully outlined the main features of his plan for the
1759 campaign to his military commanders and colonial governors.
Amherst was to lead a large army of regulars and provincials from
the Hudson Valley to the upper St. Lawrence by way of the
Champlain Valley or Lake Ontario or both. Wolfe, after assembling
a 12,000-man army at Louisbourg under cover of a general embargo
at the colonial seaports, was to advance up the St. Lawrence River
to Quebec and operate there in cooperation with Amherst to effect
the fall of Quebec or Montreal or both. To prevent supplies and
reinforcements from reaching Canada before these two armies could
move, a naval squadron commanded by Rear Admiral Philip
Durrell was assigned the task of patrolling the wide mouth of the
St. Lawrence River in the spring. In addition to the Amherst-
Wolfe operation, Pitt authorized an expedition against Niagara,
if Amherst desired it, and likewise encouraged the southern colonies
to make preparations for a drive against French and Indian centers
of resistance farther south. Governor William Henry Lyttelton
of South Carolina had even recommended that an expedition be
sent against Fort Toulouse while seaborne forces attacked the
French settlements at Mobile and on the lower Mississippi River,
but this ambitious project was deferred.[73] It was expected that
New England, New York, and New Jersey would raise large provincial forces to participate in Amherst's advance, while Pennsylvania and the southern colonies provided manpower for any
military activities that might develop along the western or southern
frontiers. Pitt promised to provide the provincial troops with necessary arms, ammunition, tents, and provisions at royal expense.
The colonies themselves were to clothe and pay their own men,

but the prime minister wisely added the inducement of possible financial reimbursement by Parliament. With the help of these concessions, the governors found it possible to secure the cooperation of their legislatures and people.

While Amherst's North American regulars were in winter quarters, rolling cartridges and sharpening their marksmanship for the 1759 campaign, Pitt sent a British amphibious force against the French sugar island of Martinique. The main purpose was to grab a valuable piece of territory that in subsequent negotiations for peace might be exchanged for Minorca, thereby avoiding a second restoration of Cape Breton Island.[74] On 16 January 1759 the troops were landed, but the extremely difficult terrain they encountered on the island soon persuaded their commanders to call them back and direct their attempt at the island of Guadeloupe instead. After sailing to the latter, 100 miles farther north, the ships bombarded the town of Basseterre on 23 January, causing it to burn like a torch, "being full of Sugars and Rum." [75] Troops were put ashore the next day, and for the next three months they struggled against tropical disease as well as French resistance, until the island finally capitulated on the first of May. The terms of surrender were lenient, allowing the French landowners to continue their production of sugar, but now with the advantage of the protected British market. Guadeloupe actually climbed out of depression into prosperity as a result of the conquest.[76]

The fleet bringing Saunders, Wolfe, and a large force of fresh regulars from Britain was prevented by ice from entering the harbor at Louisbourg, the designated rendezvous, and proceeded instead to Halifax, where the anchors were dropped on the last day of April. At Halifax, Saunders found Durrell, who was supposed to be long since on patrol in the St. Lawrence, awaiting a favorable report on ice conditions. Saunders ordered him to sail at the first opportunity, and by 5 May Durrell was on his way north with ten ships of the line. Fortunately for the French, he was too late to intercept most of the relief ships from France, some twenty in all, and Vaudreuil received the much-needed provisions that would enable him to conduct a more prolonged and effective defense. One of the French ships reached Quebec on 10 May, bringing Bougainville back to Canada after his unsuccessful attempt to obtain strong military reinforcements. Instead of more troops, Bougainville brought a copy of one of Amherst's letters which had fallen into French hands, disclosing in considerable detail the British plan of operations.[77]

Amherst had decided to drive north down the Champlain Valley to Montreal, taking Forts Carillon and St. Frédéric as he went. To Colonel John Prideaux of the Fifty-fifth Regiment he gave the important subsidiary assignment of leading an expedition to seize the French fort at Niagara. In this way, while Amherst was threatening Montreal, Prideaux would be severing the lifeline of the French garrisons south of Lake Erie. Both expeditions had need of Indian support, and so the commander in chief, whose contempt for the natives was exceeded only by his distrust, traveled to Schenectady for consultation with Sir William Johnson. He received a comforting assurance of Indian support for the campaign, but was careful not to share with Johnson the details of his plan lest the information pass to the Iroquois and from the Iroquois to the enemy.[78]

During May, the colonial contingents were arriving at Albany, often with fewer men than Amherst had been led to expect. These provincial troops were given additional training to bring them as close as possible to the standards of the regulars. Amherst also displayed a good general's concern for the health of his men, although one of his innovations was not calculated to increase his popularity with the troops. Instead of liquor he encouraged the soldiers to quaff a "wholesome beverage" consisting of "melasses and the tops of the spruce fir, boiled together in a proper quantity of water." This "spruce beer," it was said, had been found to be "a most excellent antiscorbutic, and even an antidote against those distempers frequently occasioned by the excessive drinking of spirituous liquors."[79] There was some desertion, probably not related to the campaign against intoxicating beverages. Units of regulars and provincials were sent north as needed, to labor at the seemingly endless task of conveying supplies and guarding the way stations along the military route that extended from Albany to the southern end of Lake George. Gangs of men worked to improve the roads and fortifications at various points along this vital route. Amherst himself left his second-in-command, Thomas Gage, at Albany to complete the provincial forces, and proceeded to Fort Edward, where he arrived on 6 June. The bustle of preparation at this advance base and along the road leading to Lake George fed his impatience. "I wish the Regts. were up," Amherst exclaimed. "'Tis time I should get forward." [80] By 22 June Amherst and the bulk of his army, well over 6,000 men, were at Lake George preparing to construct a new fort. Bateaus, whaleboats, and supplies were being transported daily up the road from the base on the Hudson, while other equipment that had been cached the previous year was being recovered and prepared for use.

The expedition against Niagara, under Prideaux, had assembled along the Mohawk River during the latter part of May and early June. Included were the Forty-fourth and Forty-sixth regiments of regulars, plus two companies of the Royal Americans, artillery, and more than 2,600 New York provincials. Also available were about 600 Indians recruited by Johnson, who was second-in-command under Prideaux. As the army advanced to Oswego the numbers declined considerably, for garrisons had to be provided for several important bases along the line of advance, lest the French and Indians from Canada cut in behind the main body and sever its lifeline. By the end of June, Prideaux's expedition was poised at Oswego, where Amherst had ordered a new fort constructed, and was ready to move west toward Niagara.[81]

Assembling at Louisbourg, the army that Wolfe was to lead up the St. Lawrence consisted of ten regiments of foot, a provisional battalion made up of three grenadier companies from three regular regiments that were to remain for the defense of Louisbourg, three companies of artillerymen, and six companies of American rangers —altogether, about 8,500 men. This force was organized in three brigades commanded by Brigadier Generals Robert Monckton, James Murray, and George Townshend. Wolfe had hoped to have the 12,000 men originally intended, but as usual the demands of a worldwide war upon a limited military establishment had necessitated a reduction. Remaining at Louisbourg with the three regular regiments were approximately a thousand Massachusetts militiamen whose great contribution was to release a large number of regulars for combat duty with Wolfe. So the three British armies under Wolfe, Amherst, and Prideaux stood ready to undertake the downfall of New France in the early summer of 1759.

Bougainville's arrival from France with intelligence of British designs against Quebec produced a massive shift of French strength from the Montreal area to the threatened town 150 miles below, for Wolfe's expedition from Louisbourg was correctly seen to be

more immediately dangerous than the necessarily slow advance of
Amherst's army down the Champlain Valley. Both Vaudreuil and
Montcalm went to Quebec to lead the defense. In addition to the
units of regulars from Montreal, there poured into the Quebec area
thousands of Canadian militiamen from the surrounding country.
Altogether the defenders of Quebec included five battalions of
regulars plus between 5,000 and 6,000 militiamen, while other
men sprang to arms in the downriver villages toward Gaspé. Without an effective French naval force in the river, however, there
was little chance of stopping the British fleet short of Quebec itself.
At Ticonderoga and Crown Point, Colonel François de Bourlamaque
stood ready with more than 3,000 troops, of whom better than half
were regulars. It was realized that even a sizable and well-disciplined
force such as this could not hold Fort Carillon and Fort St. Frédéric
for long against a large British expedition which gained naval
supremacy on Lake Champlain. A futile defense of these forts,
culminating in the entrapment of thousands of troops who might
be needed for the defense of Montreal and Quebec, was to be
avoided if possible. Therefore, Bourlamaque had been ordered to
delay Amherst's advance as long as he could and then, if necessary,
abandon Ticonderoga and even Crown Point in order to preserve
his army. Although this would mean the loss of Lake Champlain,
it would result in the consolidation of French strength much closer
to the threatened heartland.[82]

Quebec itself was endowed by nature with an unusually strong
defensive position. First, there was the great river itself, whose
persistent fogs, treacherous currents, and rocky shoreline were
notorious. Small groups of merchant vessels and an occasional
frigate, directed by experienced local pilots, navigated the river
fairly easily during the ice-free months, but a great battle fleet
with deep-draft ships of the line and crowded transports was another
matter. Even if such a fleet did manage, with good luck, to make
its way 400 miles upriver to Quebec, there were yet more of
nature's defenses to be confronted. The town was situated just
above the broad Île d'Orléans, in the angle formed by the
St. Charles River as it flows into the St. Lawrence from the west.
Here the great river is less than a mile wide. To the northeast,
between the St. Charles and the Montmorency rivers, stretched the
Beauport shore whose tidal flats and beaches were backed by low
bluffs suitable for entrenchments and redoubts commanding any

potential landing sites. It was here that Phips' ill-prepared army had come to grief in 1690, not even able to force its way across the St. Charles, to say nothing of storming the heights of Quebec. This entire Beauport sector was protected on the north, at a distance of about 6 miles from the town, by the natural moat of the Montmorency River, whose spectacular fall almost at its very mouth roared a constant warning to any intruders.

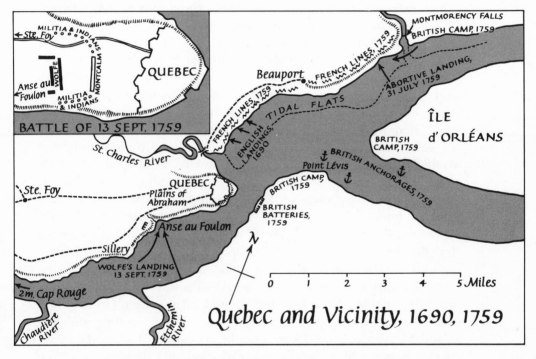

Quebec and Vicinity, 1690, 1759

As for the town itself, in a sense there were two Quebecs—*basse ville* and *haute ville*. The lower town was a cluster of shops, dwellings, and warehouses crammed into the small lowlying area between the St. Lawrence and the 350-foot precipice of Cape Diamond. Perched atop the cliff was the principal part of the town containing the major governmental buildings, churches, and residences. A steep access road on the less formidable north side led from *basse ville* to *haute ville*. Southwestward from Cape Diamond, a chain of steep cliffs ranging from 150 to 250 feet in height ran for some distance fairly close to the river's edge, leaving only a narrow strip of lowland where an invading army might land. A landing here was considered unlikely, for the transports first would have to run the severe gauntlet of Quebec's well-sited batteries, after which the troops would be confronted with the problem of landing in the face of hostile fire from mobile forces operating along the top edge of the cliffs. No army could form and maneuver effectively under those conditions. The defenders, on the other hand, would have complete freedom of movement on the broad, open reaches of the plateau known as the Plains of Abraham, which extended all along the top edge of these cliffs west of Quebec. To Vaudreuil and Montcalm, therefore, it seemed certain that any major landing force coming up the St. Lawrence against Quebec would have to make its attempt somewhere along the Beauport shore. For this reason the French dug a line of trenches and redoubts all along the crest of the Beauport shore from the St. Charles to the Montmorency. The recently arrived supply ships, still laden with precious provisions, were sent to an anchorage at Batiscan, more than 60 miles above Quebec. From there the supplies could be brought down the river in convoys of boats as needed.[83]

In the meantime, Saunders' great fleet carrying Wolfe and his army, preceded by some of Durrell's ships, was carefully making its way upriver from the sea. Advance vessels, such as Captain James Cook's *Pembroke,* explored and buoyed the difficult passages for the three squadrons of transports which followed. Thanks to this careful work and the skill of British mariners aided by captured French pilots, not a single ship was lost.[84] By 26 June, the first division of the fleet had arrived off the Île d'Orléans, and next day, without opposition, the army began landing on that island. Hardly had this debarkation been completed when the broad river was swept by a violent storm of wind that drove some of the transports into others and caused the loss of numerous ships' boats and anchors. It seemed a bad omen, yet fortunately not one of the ships was wrecked. Wolfe himself, once ashore, hurried to the point of the island nearest Quebec and began to study his difficult problem of topography.[85] His search for a military solution of that problem is the story of the next eleven weeks.

Shortly after midnight on 29 June the French made their first move against the anchored British fleet. Saunders' sailors on watch suddenly saw flames begin to leap simultaneously on seven French vessels in the river above them, and soon these seven fireships, blazing ever higher, were drifting down upon the British vessels. Immediately sailors were ordered into the boats, and with great courage and skill they were able to get lines aboard the drifting incendiaries in time to tow them clear. It was a spectacular show while it lasted, undoubtedly watched by every eye afloat and ashore, French and British, but it was totally unsuccessful. The seven fireships finally either sank or ran harmlessly aground.[86] That same day Monckton's brigade of four regiments began landing on the south shore of the St. Lawrence a short distance below Quebec, and soon the troops were busy building batteries in the vicinity of Point Lévis within artillery range of the town. The French were about to pay the price of neglecting to fortify and defend this strategic area. On 12 July, in the evening, the first flashes and booms from six 32-pounders and five 13-inch mortars signaled the start of a bombardment that was to pound Quebec for weeks on end. It was part of Wolfe's attempt to break the morale of the civilian population and possibly force Montcalm out of his strong defensive lines in order to challenge the British in the open.

Several days earlier, on 9 July, Wolfe had taken a landing force of grenadiers ashore just below the mouth of the Montmorency, beyond the farthest extent of the French lines. There was no opposition. From their new vantage point the British could admire the 274-foot falls near the river's mouth, and look beyond to the nearest French defenses. Soon Townshend's brigade and most of Murray's joined Wolfe, in preparation for an offensive across the Montmorency to roll back the French left flank and, hopefully, approach Quebec itself. During the next two weeks Wolfe continued to consolidate his position and study the problem before him, while British artillery at Point Lévis hurled shells into Quebec, and six of Saunders' ships successfully passed upriver beyond the town under cover of darkness. Momentarily Wolfe pondered the advantages of landing above Quebec if more ships could duplicate the feat, but quickly returned to his present plan. On 26 July, he led two of his regiments up the Montmorency to the first ford above the falls. The fierce resistance to this probe left no doubt that Montcalm's screen of Indians was fully alert. As yet there appeared no serious flaw in the French defenses.[87]

In the meantime, Vaudreuil had ordered a second desperate attempt to demoralize the British fleet at anchor below Quebec. The French chained together a number of rafts and boats loaded with combustibles, and on the night of 27 July they sent the monster drifting silently toward the anchorage. Not until they were within 500 yards of the nearest British ship did the daring French sailors set their strange craft ablaze and then abandon it. Once again, the British navy moved quickly to avert disaster. Aroused sailors piled into ships' boats, boldly approached the flaming fire-craft, and towed it off to one side where it could do no harm. After this, the British maintained a nightly patrol of small boats very close to Quebec itself to deal with any further attempts of this kind.[88]

Wolfe, having been rebuffed once, decided to try a frontal assault against a French redoubt located in the Beauport line just above the Montmorency River. This, perhaps, would bring on a more general engagement advantageous to the British, or at least give Wolfe a vantage point from which to study the main enemy defenses. Accordingly, on the morning of 31 July thirteen companies of grenadiers and a part of Monckton's brigade from Point Lévis were embarked in boats preparatory to a landing on the beach before the redoubt. Townshend's and Murray's brigades plus the light infantry commanded by Lieutenant Colonel William Howe, brother of the late Lord Howe, remained on the far side of the Montmorency, ready to wade across the shallow mouth of the river at low tide to join in the attack. Fire support was provided by about fifty cannon sited along the Montmorency, as well as the guns of H.M.S. *Centurion* and two shallow-draft transports, or "cats," which were deliberately run aground off the beach as close as possible to the enemy lines. "We were all in our Flat Bottom Boats at Noon," one officer of the main landing force later recalled, "rowing backwards and forwards, in sight of the Enemy, and exposed to their shells for six hours, waiting I believe till the Batterys were silenced, (which the ships could not Effect) and till the Water was low enough to Cross at the Falls. . . ."[89] During part of this time of extreme tension, Wolfe was observing the situation from one of the grounded cats. To his amazement he discovered what had not been apparent previously from the British positions —the redoubt that he intended to take and hold was dominated by other nearby French works and therefore would be untenable. Instead of canceling the operation, which he well might have done under the circumstances, Wolfe decided to proceed even farther and make an assault upon the main line of entrenchments beyond the redoubt, utilizing the same plan of attack.

Toward evening the troop-laden boats drove for the beach and, after considerable difficulty with the shoals, put the landing force ashore. For some reason the grenadiers failed to form up properly and await the arrival of the other brigades, but instead rushed immediately toward the redoubt. Seeing them coming pell-mell, the defenders abandoned the position. Having gained this first objective, the grenadiers now were forced to seek whatever shelter they could find as the French in the nearby works above them, as well as parties of Indians in concealment all over the adjacent slopes, began to pour in heavy fire. Other British troops were landing and forming in good order on the beach, while the Montmorency force began crossing below the falls. Even with this additional strength, Wolfe's men found it impossible to attain the higher positions, and their losses were increasing. Adding to the confusion was the sudden approach of a violent thunderstorm and the dimming of daylight, so that soon it became necessary for the disappointed Wolfe to order a general withdrawal. Clearly, Montcalm had scored a victory. At a loss of only about five dozen of their own men, the French had inflicted nearly 450 casualties, to which must be added the total loss of the two cats. Montcalm's lines remained intact. For five weeks now Wolfe had maneuvered and probed, and although he held important ground at Point Lévis, on the Île d'Orléans, and below the Montmorency River, and even had a few ships in the upper St. Lawrence, he had failed to discover any likely route to his objective. Baffled, he nevertheless remained firm in his determination.[90]

If Wolfe had known what had occurred 400 miles southwest of Quebec, he might have felt more cheerful. On 1 July, Prideaux's army of nearly 3,000 men took its departure from Oswego in a fleet of bateaus and whaleboats, heading west toward Niagara. For six days Prideaux's men paddled by day and camped by night, finally arriving near their destination undetected on the evening of 6 July. Early the next morning Captain Pierre Pouchot, holding Niagara with a garrison of only about 600 regulars and militiamen, found his fort invested and a siege about to begin. By the eleventh, Prideaux had two batteries pounding the French works, while the usual trenches were being dug and extended toward the enemy fort. Significantly, there were few if any French Indians in the vicinity to harass Prideaux's men. This time, as a result of waning Indian confidence, the French had been left to their own resources. On 20 July, however, within a space of three hours the British suffered two major losses. First the colonel of the New York regiment was mortally wounded by a musket ball. Then Prideaux himself was accidentally killed by a shell from one of his own guns. Command of the expedition thereupon fell to Sir William Johnson, who continued the siege with resolution.[91]

The French had only one trump to play, and upon that depended all. A relief force of about 1,200 French and Indians, fabricated from the garrisons of Detroit, Venango, Fort Le Boeuf, and Fort Presqu'île, now was approaching Niagara from the direction of Lake Erie. The British, however, received advance warning, probably from Indian scouts, and Johnson was able to prepare a proper reception. He deployed his light infantry, two companies of grenadiers, and part of the Forty-sixth Regiment athwart the road leading down along the right bank of the river, along which the relief force would come, while his Indians concealed themselves on the flank. At 9:30 A.M. on 24 July, the French walked into the trap, and within an hour the relief force had been shredded. This disaster convinced Pouchot that further defense of Fort Niagara was hopeless, and he surrendered the next day. At a cost of fewer than 250 casualties, most of them wounded, the British now sat directly astride the main French route to the Mississippi Valley. Johnson next sent three whaleboats north to reconnoiter the vicinity of Fort Toronto. They returned on the night of 30 July with the report that the French had burned and abandoned that fort; with them came a Chippewa sachem to confer with the victors. Johnson, superbly equipped by experience for such an opportunity, opened wide the door to future friendship and trade. Taking from the sachem's neck a large medal given by the French, he replaced it with an English medal and a silver gorget. Then he sent the sachem back to his own people to spread the message of Pax Britannica and the advantages of British trade.[92]

Meanwhile, during the first three weeks of July, Amherst's army of regulars and provincials had remained in camp at the southern end of Lake George, busy with the usual elaborate preparations for a major advance through the wilderness. Supplies were still being accumulated; bateaus, whaleboats, and a raft for artillery were being readied; craft sunk at the end of the previous campaign to conceal them from the enemy were being raised and refurbished. In addition, Amherst saw that his troops were given intensive training, with attention to the special military skills now known to be vitally important in woods fighting. It was a strong, aggressive, well-prepared army of more than 11,000 men, including nearly 6,000 regulars, that finally embarked on the morning of 21 July, four days before Johnson captured Niagara and ten days before Wolfe's futile assault on the Beauport line.[93] Moving steadily down Lake George, the four long parallel columns of boats would have made a magnificent sight for any observer looking down from one of the summits. Doubtless their approach toward the landing place at the far end of the lake was noted and reported by some of Bourlamaque's scouts. Nevertheless, Amherst landed the next day without serious opposition, and the army's advance toward Fort Carillon was challenged only by small parties of skirmishers, readily brushed aside. One French prisoner gave the British the exciting news that Wolfe had landed on the Île d'Orléans. On the morning of 23 July, as Amherst's advance units approached the main French lines, which extended along much the same ground as those that had proved so deadly to Abercromby's men the previous year, the defenders fell back to the fort itself without attempting to hold their positions. Soon the British could see that many of the French had embarked in boats and were withdrawing northward toward Crown Point, although the booming of cannon from the walls of the fort announced that a garrison was still on duty and ready to resist. Apparently, then, it would be a matter of siegecraft, as at Louisbourg, and Amherst began to prepare accordingly.[94]

Firing continued for the next three days, while the British troops labored to move their artillery and supplies along the portage from Lake George, and dug their approaches before the fort. During the afternoon of the twenty-sixth, the French fire slackened noticeably. That evening a deserter made his way into the British lines and informed Amherst that Fort Carillon was to be abandoned and destroyed by explosives. It was no lie, for late that evening the magazine blew up with a tremendous, earth-shaking roar. Bourlamaque had carried out his assignment of delaying the British advance and now was making sure that even as he preserved his army for later action, he left Amherst as little as possible that could be turned to advantage. Early the next morning, despite the fire that now was raging in the deserted stronghold, British volunteers entered Fort Carillon to assess the situation and begin taking what measures they could. Although the fire was not completely extinguished for several days, the British found that the French fort still was usable. Amherst had gained Ticonderoga at a cost of fewer than a hundred casualties.[95]

Remembering that Wolfe would need his help to complete the conquest of Canada, Amherst was eager to continue his northward push without losing momentum. "I am trying all I can to get forward," he wrote on the very day of Wolfe's attack on the Beauport line, lamenting that some of his officers were "always pulling different ways." [96] While the troops established a camp at Ticonderoga and transferred boats and supplies to the shore of Lake Champlain, scouts were sent to observe the situation at Crown Point. On 1 August they returned with the exhilarating report that Fort St. Frédéric with its stone walls and citadel also had been abandoned, the French apparently withdrawing still farther down the lake to their Richelieu River bases. At last on 4 August, Amherst was able to embark a portion of his army, and reached Crown Point that same evening. The place was indeed abandoned, the fort partly destroyed. Soon Amherst received more good news when a messenger arrived to tell of Johnson's victory at Niagara. In daylight the general surveyed the remains of Fort St. Frédéric with the eye of a professional. This had been the principal bastion of French power in the Champlain Valley since the 1730s. Now its ruins echoed to the excited exclamations of British voices. Crown Point under British control meant the final end of any French potential for a sustained offensive against either the western frontier of New England or the Hudson Valley. Now it was the British who would be able to utilize Crown Point and the waters of Lake Champlain for launching their last great drive north into Canada.

While Amherst was relishing this prospect, his junior colleague at Quebec continued wrestling with the seemingly impossible problem of how to break Montcalm's defenses. The daily bombardment was ruining the town without gaining for the British any likely opportunity for a successful assault. Wolfe, angered by the partisan warfare being carried on against his army by groups of armed *habitants* along the great river, kept some of his men busy ravaging French villages in retaliation. Hundreds of Canadian' farmhouses and barns were destroyed in this systematic campaign of reprisal, leaving some of Canada's choicest farming and fishing regions devastated.[97]

Once Saunders had demonstrated the feasibility of slipping ships past the guns of Quebec and into the upper river, Montcalm realized that the town might be seriously threatened from that side as well. Early in August he assigned additional troops to the upriver defenses, and gave Bougainville the task of preventing the British from gaining any foothold on the north shore between Quebec and the French supply ships at Batiscan. Occasional British raids in this sector further emphasized the danger and wearied Bougainville's mobile force by making it hurry from one threatened area to another; nevertheless, the French high command continued to believe that Wolfe's main thrust would occur somewhere along the Beauport shore.[98]

On the night of 27 August, five more British vessels braved the heavy fire from the walls of Quebec and made their way into the upper river. Four nights later another group of like size duplicated the feat. In the meantime Wolfe, recovering slowly from a fever, was conferring with his three brigadiers about a future course of action. The approach of September with its promise of colder weather was a reminder to all that something must be accomplished soon or the campaign would end in failure. Wolfe still talked about ways of breaking into Montcalm's Beauport defenses, to the growing exasperation of Monckton, Murray, and Townshend, who were convinced that the only feasible way to get at Quebec was by landing somewhere above the town. Even if the army should succeed in getting a foothold at Beauport, the St. Charles would have to be crossed before a final assault on Quebec itself could begin. And should the town be overrun, the French would still be free to retreat upriver toward Montreal, where they could regroup and fight on indefinitely. On the other hand, once the army was ashore *above* Quebec Montcalm would be cut off from all supplies and reinforcements. In fact, soon after his line of supply from Batiscan had been severed, he would be forced to come out of his defenses and attack the British or else surrender for lack of sustenance. Every one of Wolfe's schemes for breaking into the Beauport lines required that the attacking force be divided, whereas, if the camp at the Montmorency River were abandoned and only a holding force retained at the Île d'Orléans and Point Lévis, the army might be concentrated for one decisive effort above Quebec. This essentially was the plan that the three brigadiers, after consultation with Saunders, now forcefully proposed to Wolfe. Somewhat reluctantly he accepted their basic thesis as the foundation for future action in the few weeks that remained.[99]

By this time Quebec was in sad condition, with provisions running very low. Yet the French will to resist remained unbroken. Wolfe himself now was doubtful of success, but was determined to make one more major attempt, this time in accordance with the basic proposal of his subordinates. On 3 September, the British troops evacuated their long-held camp on the Montmorency and concentrated on the south shore opposite Quebec. Montcalm interpreted the move not so much as a threat to the upriver sector as an indication that Wolfe was contemplating an assault just below the mouth of the St. Charles or possibly even directly upon the lower town. Starting on 5 September, Wolfe marched his regiments upriver from Point Lévis toward the little fleet of waiting transports and warships above. His intention now, it seems, was to make a landing on the north bank somewhere west of the Cap Rouge River, at least 8 miles above Quebec. However, upon examining the terrain along the north shore through a glass, Wolfe became impressed with the possibility of landing much closer to the town at a place known as the Anse au Foulon, scarcely 2 miles from the outer walls. Above this little cove loomed formidable heights, but what had aroused Wolfe's keenest attention was a steep, narrow path climbing diagonally from the beach to the top. This path, although blocked and guarded, could be climbed by a determined body of agile men who, once they had surprised and overcome the weak outpost at the top, would have opened the way to the Plains of Abraham for any force that could be assembled on the beach below.[100]

By the evening of 12 September, a large part of Wolfe's army was poised on board the warships and transports now grouped in the vicinity of Cap Rouge, approximately 6 miles above the Anse au Foulon. Bougainville and his mobile defense force were on the north shore nearby, while Vaudreuil and Montcalm remained in the vicinity of the Beauport line, below Quebec, with the bulk of the French army. Wolfe and his brigadiers, together with Saunders, had devised a landing plan which they hoped would enable the army to attain a position on the open Plains of Abraham and form in battle array before the sun was well above the horizon on 13 September. Surprise was virtually essential for success. One outrageously lucky circumstance helped to make that surprise possible—the French had planned to move some supplies downriver by boat to Quebec that very night and then had canceled the movement without notifying their own outposts of the change. This meant that the French sentries along the shore were denied the advantage of knowing that any boats in motion on the river were almost certain to be British.[101]

In the middle of the night the British assault force of light infantry and other units, totaling 1,800 men under the command of Howe, clambered over the ships' sides into waiting boats. About 2:00 A.M. these boats began to move silently downriver with the tide, leaving the ships to follow along three-quarters of an hour later with additional troops. This major movement from Cap Rouge was successfully executed without giving alarm to Bougainville. At the same time, other boats from the ships still stationed below Quebec were making a demonstration off the Beauport shore, maneuvering as though preparing for a landing. This occupied Montcalm's attention until nearly daylight. The long column of boats carrying Howe's men toward the landing place could not possibly have escaped detection altogether, but the shouted "Qui vive?" of a sleepy French sentry on a beach or point of land was answered with "La France!" and the bluff worked. After two very tense hours, the Anse au Foulon came into view under the dark, looming ramparts of the cliffs, with the great forbidding mass of Cape Diamond and Quebec just below. Now was the moment when every soldier and seaman held his breath. Were the French ready and waiting for them?

Sometime between 4:00 and 4:30 A.M., the first boats scraped the sand and the light infantry began jumping into the shallow water and wading onto the beach. The tide had carried them a little below the place where the path began to ascend; directly before them loomed a steep, bush-covered slope. While a small party of volunteers moved off to the left to find the path, Howe and the rest of the attack force climbed directly up, scrambling for footing, hauling themselves by brush and branches. Already the small French force on duty above had heard them and opened fire, not only with muskets but also with a battery of four guns located off to the left of the path. Nevertheless, in short order the attacking units overwhelmed the French outpost, cleared the path of major obstructions, and gained a firm foothold on the high ground. A detachment sent to deal with the battery on the left speedily put it out of action. Now the ships were arriving on the scene, and the boats were clustering around them to take on the second wave of troops, while a third wave waited to be ferried from the south shore. As darkness gradually gave way to dawn and dawn to the full light of day, the apparently endless stream of redcoated figures continued to climb slowly but steadily up the steep, narrow path to the Plains. Wolfe himself ascended to take command and begin forming his line of battle. Sweating gunners strained to haul two 6-pounders up the same difficult route, providing the army with its only available artillery until the path could be improved to accommodate the heavier pieces. Altogether some 4,500 men were landed before the day had scarcely begun, and with very little loss. Coordination between army and navy, and among the various units involved, had been close to perfection, despite darkness and the presence of the enemy. Says one modern authority, "This night's work fully supports the reputation of the enterprise as a classic of combined operations. It was a professional triumph." [102] As a result, the extraordinarily difficult problem of topography had been overcome.

By this time, news of the British landing had reached French army headquarters in the Beauport lines, and a massive shift of French strength was getting underway as Vaudreuil and Montcalm, surprised and shocked at the report, prepared to face their foe where he now threatened in earnest. French units in their white uniforms, accompanied by Canadian militia and Indians in rougher dress, were hurrying across the St. Charles to the Plains of Abraham. Wolfe could see their increasing numbers as they formed and deployed between him and the walls of the town. The British commander coolly arranged his own regiments in line of battle, with his right anchored at the edge of the cliff some distance beyond the place of ascent, and his left well around to the west in order to guard against interference by Bougainville's mobile force. Sharp firing began as Canadian and Indian irregulars took positions in a birch coppice near the British left flank. Their galling musketry caused increasing casualties among the exposed regiments, but the troops never wavered and Wolfe bided his time, hoping for the arrival of additional artillery. Montcalm, on horseback, directed the disposition of his regulars, forming them in a three-column front opposite the main section of the British line which faced toward the town.[103]

For some time the preparatory maneuvers continued, Wolfe extending and adjusting his formation as new units arrived, Montcalm likewise getting his hastily formed array in order. Erratic, excited bursts of musketry and the booming of cannon echoed over the river as each side sought to unnerve the other. The two opposing forces were now about equal in size, numbering approximately 4,500 men each, but the British were all regulars, while even Montcalm's regular regiments contained considerable numbers of newly recruited Canadians. Yet despite any possible inferiority, Montcalm had little choice but to come out in the open and fight where Wolfe had gained his foothold and selected his ground. The fortifications of Quebec, at least on the southwest side facing the Plains of Abraham, were too weak to withstand a siege, and supplies of provisions in the town were dangerously low. If Montcalm could not smash the army that faced him now on 13 September, Quebec was doomed. In a sense, many a professional officer on both sides must have felt a gratifying sense of returning to the familiar after all those many decades of bewildering, frustrating warfare in a dark, encumbering wilderness of forests and swamps. Here it was daylight, and two disciplined armies were facing each other on an open field, according to the European practice. This was what war was supposed to be.

About 10:00 A.M., a grimly determined Montcalm gave the order for his columns to advance. The men lurched forward, walking rapidly or even trotting, straight toward the long red line that stood in perfect order impassively waiting. Montcalm, high on his mount, was conspicuous above the heads of his advancing regiments, and Wolfe, although afoot, was almost reckless in exposing himself to inspire his men. For this bravery in command there was a price to pay, and the time of reckoning was very near. The British regiments held their fire as the three French columns hurried directly toward them across the open plain. Only the two British cannon spoke decisively, sending clouds of grape whistling through the enemy ranks. When Montcalm's men were only about fifty paces from the British line, they paused in their advance to deliver one ragged volley. Even yet the redcoats held their fire, as ordered, although the enemy's volley had opened numerous gaps in that

disciplined line. Once more the French resumed their advance, ten
or so rapid steps, coming very close to the waiting British line
standing now with muskets leveled. Suddenly, all up and down
the length of the red line came the awaited command, followed
almost instantaneously by the terrible blast of platoon fire. It was
a staggering volley that in one awful moment shredded Montcalm's
formations and stopped them in their tracks. When the great cloud
of gunsmoke slowly thinned, the demoralized French troops were
seen in reverse motion, running helter-skelter back toward Quebec
in a scene of wild confusion. The British were quick to seize their
advantage, and rushed forward in hot pursuit, sword in hand or
bayonet to the fore. Fiercely exultant, they pressed their pursuit
of the disorganized French "quite to the walls, and killed many
of them upon the glacis and in the ditch." [104] Only Bougainville
with his mobile force in the British rear was in a position to change
the fortune of the day, but he did not arrive from Cap Rouge
until after the British victory had been won.

During the brief but decisive encounter, both Wolfe and Montcalm had been hit. Wolfe first received a wound on his wrist and
soon afterwards was struck in the chest by a musket ball. The second
wound proved fatal within a matter of minutes, but Wolfe died
on what he knew to be a field of victory. Montcalm, too, had
been seriously wounded. He was able to remain astride his horse,
carried along in the confused rout of his army, and entered the
shelter of the walled town. There he succumbed early the next day.
The abrupt and nearly simultaneous downfall of Montcalm and
Wolfe in the climactic battle on the Plains of Abraham has always
endowed this encounter with a special element of drama. No
doubt the luster that in retrospect has accumulated about the name
and fame of each is in part due to this accident of history. Each
brought to the culminating battle a growing reputation that might
have been envied by any rising young officer. Montcalm was
famous, at least in Canada, as the victor of Oswego, Fort William
Henry, and Ticonderoga. Wolfe had become widely admired in
British North America as the bold, aggressive leader of the assault
landing at Louisbourg and a major contributor to Amherst's victory
there. In comparison with the string of mediocre commanders who
had preceded them, both men seemed the very embodiment of
military competence if not actual genius. Yet careful analysis of the
Quebec campaign through the fatal thirteenth of September does

little to support the reputation of either. Montcalm's conduct of the defense, for which Vaudreuil must share the blame, was unimaginative and extraordinarily inflexible. Wolfe wasted much precious time and actually did not seize the key to success until it was virtually thrust upon him by his brigadiers. On the day of the battle, although Montcalm did find it necessary to leave the protection of Quebec's walls and fight Wolfe on the open field, he was not compelled to begin his attack as soon as he did. Had he delayed for a few hours, his army would have been more nearly ready for battle, with a decided advantage in artillery, and Bougainville might have been able to create a diversion by attacking the British left flank or rear. Wolfe, in a sense, redeemed his own reputation by his masterful landing and stunning victory on 13 September. As Machiavelli once wrote, "A single battle that you win cancels all your other bad actions." [105] Montcalm was not so fortunate.

Despite heavy French losses in the battle and subsequent rout, the British regiments were unable to complete the destruction of Vaudreuil's army, to say nothing of forcing their way into the town. Therefore the French troops safely regrouped beyond the St. Charles River, after which they made a wide swing to the west, bypassing Quebec and the encamped British, and took station in the area of the Jacques Cartier River between the British and Montreal. The fact was that Quebec was doomed, and Vaudreuil knew it. Consequently he had preserved his army intact to fight later in the defense of Montreal, leaving only a garrison force in Quebec with little or no expectation of retaining the town.

The British, with Townshend in temporary command after the death of Wolfe and the wounding of Monckton, undertook the usual preparations for a siege, while Saunders began moving his heavy-gunned ships closer to the town for effective bombardment. At noon on the seventeenth, however, the French commander sent out a flag of truce, and the next morning articles of capitulation were signed. Advance parties of British troops and seamen then entered the battered town to preserve order pending the formal entry of Townshend's regiments on 19 September.[106]

Amherst, far from threatening Montreal as he had hoped to do in support of Wolfe's effort, was still consolidating his position on Lake Champlain. The principal bar to his advance from Crown Point was not a well-entrenched French army farther up the lake, but a few armed vessels capable of creating havoc in an unprotected covey of bateaus and whaleboats. Having no way of bringing needed naval escorts to Lake Champlain, Amherst resorted to the time-consuming expedient of having a brig and a sloop built by his carpenters. In addition, he put other men to work constructing a huge raft, or radeau, capable of carrying six 24-pounders. "No likelihood of the Enemys coming but I cant be too secure," reasoned the cautious Amherst, and saw to it that his troops were well occupied in repairing Fort Carillon and building a new fort at Crown Point. To make doubly sure that an impossible French counteroffensive did not take him by surprise, the commander in chief sent scouting parties of rangers and Indians to reconnoiter in the direction of Canada.[107]

About the middle of September, before Amherst knew of Wolfe's victory at Quebec, Major Rogers led a mixed force of fewer than 200 rangers, regulars, and Indians out of Crown Point for a diversionary raid against the French Indian village of St. Francis, located near the south bank of the St. Lawrence about 100 miles above Quebec. Just before dawn on 6 October he attacked, achieving complete surprise. The rangers burned nearly all the dwellings and slaughtered a large number of the inhabitants before disappearing into the wilderness with five prisoners and a similar number of rescued British captives. This blow greatly weakened the protective shield of Indian strength which had long stood between the St. Lawrence settlements and British invaders.[108]

Brigadier General Gage, who had gone to take command at Oswego and lead the western thrust into the upper St. Lawrence Valley, notified Amherst in September that the Oswego force would not be able to carry out its mission.[109] Amherst himself could see clear signs of declining morale among his own provincial troops, yet clung to the hope of making some further advance toward Montreal before the season ended. On 11 October he and his army, embarked in the usual fleet of small craft reinforced with a brig and a sloop, started north down the lake from Crown Point. The next day the brig and sloop had the excitement of chasing three enemy sloops into a bay where they were abandoned by their crews; but soon after this victory a violent storm forced the army to huddle in a makeshift camp on the shore for five days. Then on 18 October came the news that Quebec had surrendered and Wolfe was dead. To Amherst this meant that the French would shift the bulk of their forces back to Montreal, and since freezing weather now was so obviously at hand, he too relinquished his hope of further conquest in 1759. After dismissing his Indians and near-mutinous provincials at Crown Point and leaving small garrisons to hold that post as well as Ticonderoga, the disappointed general proceeded to New York for the winter.[110]

It was disappointing, of course, not to have been able to complete the destruction of Canada in 1759 as planned, especially when a little better coordination and cooperation, a little more speed and drive, might have made the conquest possible. Gage and Amherst both had weighed the risks of precipitate action and had judged them too great. Yet even rash advances in the fall of 1759 might have been crowned with success if Wolfe's victorious army had been able to trap the broken but still sizable army of French and Canadians at Quebec. Once Vaudreuil's men had broken free of the closing ring and reestablished themselves on the Jacques Cartier River under the command of Lévis, the chance of a major British conquest before 1760 was gone.

Yet who in England or the British colonies could fail to thrill at the victories actually won during the past year? There was Niagara, Ticonderoga, Crown Point, and above all Quebec! "The country is all in ecstacy upon the surprising news of the conquest of Quebec," exclaimed one colonist.[111] More eloquent but no less heartfelt was the comment made by a prominent Massachusetts preacher in one of his sermons: "Quebec, after repeated struggles and efforts is at length reduced: QUEBEC, I had almost called it that Pandora's box, from whence unnumber'd plagues have issued for more than an hundred years, to distress, to enfeeble, to lay waste, these northern colonies; and which might, perhaps in the end have proved fatal to them!"[112] Crowds in faraway English villages, too, sensed the magnitude of what had been accomplished, and set the sky aglow from the Irish Sea to the English Channel with triumphal bonfires, while the aged George II, soon to pass from history's stage, proclaimed a public thanksgiving to God.[113]

At Quebec, the immediate concern of the victorious British army was not so much how to complete the destruction of the enemy as how to survive the coming winter. Not only were the town walls inadequate protection against a strong force having ready access to the Plains of Abraham, but the long, heavy bombardment preceding Wolfe's victory had left nearly one-third of the houses in ruins while many other buildings in the town were seriously damaged. With a bitter winter already fast approaching, it was necessary to speed repairs and new construction so that both the civilian population and the troops would have adequate shelter. Saunders felt obliged to hurry out of the river with his fleet before the ice locked him in; thus, by the end of October the navy was gone, leaving behind only two sloops and three other small armed vessels to pass the winter with the garrison. Townshend sailed for England. The wounded Monckton also retired to a warmer clime after turning over the command to Murray, who became governor of Quebec.[114]

As long as the weather permitted, the troops were kept hard at work improving the defenses, storing provisions, repairing quarters, and making other preparations for a difficult sojourn. Fortunately, the French civilian population was cooperative. In fact, for a considerable distance above and below Quebec there was a general acceptance of the British victory and an earnest attempt to make the necessary adjustments. The *habitants* took the required oath of fidelity, turned in their firearms, accepted British protection, and in many instances helped perform the army's tasks.[115] One of the most pressing requirements was fuel to stave off the deadly cold. According to one contemporary report, at the time of the fleet's departure Quebec had enough firewood to last only about fifteen to twenty days. It was estimated that some 16,000 cords were needed to see the men safely through the winter. Yet most of the land in the immediate vicinity of the town was open, the nearest forest being at Ste. Foy, several miles distant. A great wood-cutting campaign was organized, with working parties of soldiers and civilians going out to wherever fuel could be found, cutting it in convenient lengths, and transporting it to Quebec on sledges. This involved a certain amount of danger as well as discomfort and fatigue, for French raiding parties sometimes lurked in the vicinity, seeking cattle or careless redcoats. Another hazard was frostbite, especially in the coldest days after November. Inevitably, under these conditions, sickness invaded the barracks, seriously reducing the number of men available for duty. An officer of the Royal Americans reported that as many as a thousand men of the garrison perished during that winter, probably more than five times the number who lost their lives in the great battle of 13 September.[116]

Always it was necessary to be alert against a French attack. In

February, the enemy actually attempted to establish a position at Point Lévis, but British detachments sent across the frozen river were able to drive the French away and hold the ground themselves. The aggressive activity of Lévis' men was simply a foretaste of what Murray might expect in the spring, when his army had been further reduced and weakened by disease and a shortage of provisions. There was some further skirmishing south of Quebec in March and April. Murray, finding that the enemy was trying to rekindle the hopes of the local population by spreading reports of reinforcements coming from France, adopted a counterstratagem that not only served to intimidate the *habitants* but raised the spirits of his own enfeebled troops. He had a party of five rangers secretly cross to the south shore and then present themselves to a British outpost as having come with an "important message" from General Amherst.[117] The implication was that a powerful army was on its way to relieve Quebec and complete the destruction of Canada. Actually, Amherst was just beginning to bestir himself in preparation for the decisive campaign of 1760, and it would be many weeks yet before there could be a conjunction of forces on the Canadian front.

Sometime in April, Murray dispatched his light infantry to establish blocking positions at Cap Rouge. Hardly had this detachment begun hacking at the frozen ground when, on 23 April, the great river finally shattered its icy bonds and once again lay open to navigation. Lévis was ready with thousands of men—regulars, Canadians, and Indians—alerted to go into action against Murray's greatly weakened army. The six French frigates that had wintered safely in the upper river were loaded with troops and sent down to St. Augustin, about 15 miles above Quebec, where the attack force was landed on 26 April.[118] To avoid capture, the British outposts at Cap Rouge, Lorette, and Ste. Foy withdrew into Quebec, leaving the whole area west of the town open to the French. On the night of 27 April, Lévis' main force was firmly established at Ste. Foy, with advance units probing almost to the very walls of Quebec. The French commander had probably about 7,000 troops on hand, including eight regiments of regulars, while Murray's effectives were fewer than 4,000.[119]

At 9:00 A.M. on 28 April, Murray led out the greater part of his army, with twenty field guns, to dig a line of defense across the Plains of Abraham. Suddenly they sighted the French army on the move along the Ste. Foy road. Murray decided to seize the initiative before Lévis could form up, and swung his units into battle formation. It was a decision made on impulse, without careful consideration of the probable ˙consequences. Advance British units surged forward and drove back the first French parties encountered, but Murray failed to exploit this early advantage, and before long the enemy began enveloping both British flanks. When this happened, the main line quickly crumbled; Murray's ill-advised attack was transformed into a precipitate retreat toward Quebec, with the artillery being left. on the field as trophies for the victorious French. British casualties were surprisingly heavy—far more numerous than in the battle of the previous September, totaling a thousand or more, nearly one out of every three soldiers involved. The French, too, suffered severely, but Lévis' advantage in manpower instead of diminishing was growing. On the evening of his unexpected victory, the French commander established his camp on the Plains of Abraham above the Anse au Foulon, and his six frigates came to anchor in the river not far from the place where Wolfe had landed. The previous roles had been totally reversed.[120]

It is doubtful that the number of able-bodied men available to defend the walled town was as much as 2,500. Thus, the ambulatory sick and wounded were pressed into helping with the almost desperate preparations, filling sandbags and making cartridges for the cannon on the ramparts. It seemed almost certain that only the arrival of major reinforcements by land or by sea could save Quebec for the British. Murray sent a messenger downriver by ship with instructions to get word of the army's plight to Amherst in New York, but two weeks passed before the messenger reached his destination.[121] In the meantime, on 9 May, a ray of hope broke through the dark clouds when a frigate was sighted coming up past the Île d'Orléans. Was it French or British? Murray had his colors hoisted at the citadel, and in response to that signal the unknown frigate likewise displayed a British flag. It is not difficult to hear, in imagination, the jubilant shout that went up from 2,000 watchers on the walls. The newcomer proved to be H.M.S. *Lowestoft*. Six days later, with the French bombardment of Quebec already well underway, a great ship of the line accompanied by a second frigate arrived to aid in the defense. On the morning of 16 May, the two British frigates sailed past the town and attacked the six French frigates above, driving them aground and effectively erasing all of Lévis' naval support. The French commander immediately gave up all thought of continuing the siege and withdrew his army to the vicinity of Montreal, leaving behind a large part of his artillery and stores. Not until later was it known that a relief convoy of French ships had arrived at the mouth of the St. Lawrence on 14 May, losing the race with the British by less than a week.[122]

In the spring of 1760 Pitt, determined to cripple France as a major imperial power, knew that time was against him. The longer the French were able to hold a few strategic positions in America, the smaller the chance that they would suffer a total loss; for in England the yearning for peace was growing, and to many influential people a negotiated settlement seemed increasingly desirable and possible. For this reason, Pitt and his generals were eager to strike the mortal blow in North America while the opportunity was still available. Amherst understood the urgency of the situation and was making his preparations for an early and, it was hoped, decisive campaign against Canada. The strategic plan followed the pattern of the past few years except that now the target was single —Montreal, the last remaining center of French strength. According to this plan, Murray was to advance with his army upriver from Quebec, Lieutenant Colonel William Haviland was to lead a second army north from Crown Point, and Amherst was to proceed with a third army from Oswego into the upper St. Lawrence in order to approach Montreal from the west. There was always the possibility, especially if the movement of the three armies was not well coordinated, that Lévis' still-potent defensive forces might be able to meet and defeat them separately.

One great bonus produced by the British victories of 1758 and 1759 was clearly evident in the spring of 1760. The Indian support on which the French had depended so heavily in the past now was rapidly melting away under the intense heat of British success. From Nova Scotia to the Ohio Valley, British officials hastened to take advantage of this opportunity by offering the prospect of peace and prosperity to those Indians who would lay down the French tomahawk and lend assistance to their new British friends. With British traders already busily reconstructing the network of Anglo-Indian commerce in much of the transappalachian West, the Indians were falling into line in order to share in the advantages of the new order. Only the most adamant of the French tribes

still were eating at the French cooking pots, and even they were
beginning to hunger for more hearty and satisfying fare. As a
consequence, Vaudreuil no longer could count on massive Indian
support in the last-ditch defense of the Canadian heartland.[123]

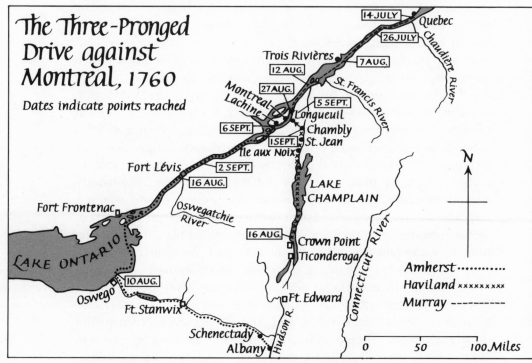

The Three-Pronged
Drive against
Montreal, 1760

Dates indicate points reached

14 JULY | Quebec
26 JULY
Trois Rivières | 7 AUG.
12 AUG.
Montreal | 27 AUG.
Lachine | 5 SEPT. | Longueuil
6 SEPT. | Chambly
1 SEPT. | St. Jean
Île aux Noix
Fort Lévis | 2 SEPT.
16 AUG.
Fort Frontenac | LAKE CHAMPLAIN
Oswegatchie River
16 AUG. | Crown Point
LAKE ONTARIO | Ticonderoga
10 AUG. | Ft. Edward
Oswego
Ft. Stanwix
Schenectady
Albany

St. Francis River
Chaudière River
Connecticut River
Hudson R.

N

Amherst ···········
Haviland xxxxxxxxx
Murray ‒‒‒‒‒‒‒‒‒

0   50   100 Miles

Montreal was situated on the south shore of a large island in
the St. Lawrence River 150 miles above Quebec and nearly 200
miles from Lake Ontario. Unlike Quebec, its geographical location provided no great defensive advantages except that any
approach would have to be made on the waters of a river liberally
endowed with rapids. The main part of the town was enclosed
by a ditch and wall, but as most of the houses within the wall were
built of wood, the place could easily be set ablaze by artillery.
In fact, Montreal's only hope for survival was to prevent an invading
army from approaching the vicinity and gaining a foothold anywhere on the island. Bougainville now was in command of the
outlying defenses to the south, consisting principally of a chain of
fortified posts along the Richelieu River. The southernmost of
these was located on the Île aux Noix, backed up by Fort St. Jean
and Fort Chambly closer to Montreal. The approach downriver

from Lake Ontario was blocked by Fort Lévis on a small island in the river not far below the mouth of the Oswegatchie. Should these outer defenses fall, there remained only Lévis' army at Montreal itself to stave off the conquest.[124]

Of the three British armies ordered to converge on Montreal, Murray's was the first to get underway. Some 2,500 troops began embarking at Quebec on 14 July 1760, for the slow voyage upriver along shores inhabited by a potentially hostile population. The advance was made with care and caution. At Trois Rivières, a possible trouble spot, Murray directed his boats along the south shore beyond the range of French cannon in the town. But in general, the *habitants* of the small villages along the way readily submitted to British authority and openly traded provisions to Murray's men. When the army finally reached the mouth of the Richelieu River on 12 August, only about 40 miles remained between Murray and his objective, and Bougainville was in danger of being trapped between Murray's army and that of Haviland advancing north from Crown Point.[125] Indeed, for many weeks Bougainville had been made to understand how precarious his situation really was. Toward the end of May Amherst, not yet informed that Quebec had been relieved by the arrival of British reinforcements, had ordered Rogers to take a strong detachment of rangers and light infantry to the vicinity of the Richelieu River in order to create a diversion. On 16 June this force was lurking on the outskirts of the little village of Ste. Thérèse, between St. Jean and Chambly, where the French had a small stockaded fort. Rogers divided his men into parties to surprise the various dwellings nearby and took a group to seize the fort itself. Observing a cartload of hay approaching the gate, Rogers awaited his opportunity and ran in after it, taking the garrison by surprise. In a matter of moments the rangers found themselves masters of the whole village. Sparing his prisoners, Rogers systematically destroyed or confiscated everything of value, including fort, houses, cattle, and boats, after which he withdrew to Lake Champlain.[126] Harassment such as this, in the very midst of the French line of defense, did much to undermine the morale of civilians and soldiers under Bougainville's command, paving the way for Haviland's advance.

The army at Crown Point began its northward voyage toward Île aux Noix and Montreal on 16 August. Bougainville, who was under orders to retreat rather than risk being enveloped, evacuated the fort on Île aux Noix and drew farther back. Several days later, Rogers and his rangers arrived at St. Jean, a dozen miles downriver, where they found the fort in flames. Again Bougainville had retreated to avoid a disastrous engagement. Proceeding past the ruins of Ste. Thérèse to Chambly, the British accepted Chambly's surrender on 1 September. All along the way, the *habitants* were quick to yield their weapons and take the oath of allegiance, recognizing as had so many of their compatriots along the St. Lawrence River that French dominion was crumbling fast. Bougainville prudently fell back on Montreal, where he joined Lévis and Vaudreuil. Now there was nothing to stop Haviland's advance to the south bank of the great river; and on the morning of 5 September, Rogers reached Longueuil, almost directly opposite Montreal. The next day contact was established with Murray, who had arrived at Île Ste. Thérèse a short distance below the town.

But meanwhile, what of Amherst and his powerful expedition on Lake Ontario? In the forenoon of 10 August, Amherst's troops had begun their departure from Oswego, heading north in two snows, five row galleys, and a great number of smaller craft. Once in the upper St. Lawrence, this great force of 10,000 men found its way blocked by Captain Pouchot and his garrison of only 300 men in Fort Lévis. No further advance was possible until this strongpoint was reduced, for the fort was located on an island commanding the river passage. Therefore, Amherst established batteries on nearby terrain, and on 23 August began battering the enemy position with gunfire. After two days of this bombardment Pouchot, having put up a stout resistance which now appeared futile, surrendered; the way to Montreal lay open.[127] Indeed, the only obstacles now remaining between Amherst and his objective were the dangerous rapids below. On 4 September, at a place where the river coursed wildly, many British bateaus and other craft laden with artillery and supplies were lost, and with them at least eighty-four lives, before the dangerous passage was completed.[128] Two days later, on 6 September, Amherst's army began landing at Lachine on the south side of the very island on which Montreal was situated. In contrast to the passage of the rapids, the unopposed landing at Lachine, only about 7 miles from the enemy center, seemed like a picnic. At this time, as noted, Haviland and Murray also were newly arrived. "So, like the striking of a clock, Amherst's wide-flung movements chimed together at the appointed hour. . . .

One of the most perfect and astonishing bits of work which the annals of British warfare can show." [129] A combined host of 15,000 men now stood ready to challenge Vaudreuil and Lévis for all that was left of Canada.

As Amherst's troops advanced on Montreal that September day, bayonets fixed, colors flying, drums beating, the French offered little opposition. Lévis held the bulk of his defensive force within the walls, waiting for the final assault. In the afternoon the British units moved into battle positions before the walls, and then spent the night on the alert. At daybreak on the seventh, the troops were again in formation under arms, ready for whatever Vaudreuil might choose to do. About 8:00 A.M. there emerged from one of the town gates an officer with a flag of truce. It was Bougainville with a message from Vaudreuil requesting a cease-fire pending the arrival of a courier, imminently expected, who would be able to confirm or deny a report of peace between England and France. This request, so obviously a delaying tactic, Amherst flatly refused, stating that he had come to take Canada and "did not intend to take anything less." [130] Bougainville then asked for a cessation until noon, which was granted with the understanding that Murray's and Haviland's armies might continue their movements, involving further landings on the island. Hostages were exchanged as a sign of good faith. At noon Vaudreuil sent out a set of proposals which Amherst altered and returned, and it was not until the morning of 8 September that the two sides came to full agreement. The victorious commander signed the fifty-five articles of the capitulation that afternoon, after which a British column of grenadiers, light infantry, and royal artillery marched into Montreal with drums beating and colors flying. Next day a smaller procession marched out of the town. It consisted of a British military band and a detachment of grenadiers escorting the colors of Shirley's and Pepperrell's regiments which the French had captured at Oswego in 1756.[131]

The terms of capitulation provided for the end of all French military resistance throughout Canada and the assumption of control by British military authorities, pending a final disposition by the home governments. In effect, Canada was out of the war, and the British colonies were released from the age-old peril of raids and conquest. The intrepid leader of the rangers, groping for words to express the significance of the victory, called it a conquest perhaps of the greatest importance that is to be met with in the British annals, whether we consider the prodigious extent of country we are hereby made masters of, the vast addition it must make to trade and navigation, . . . the security it must afford to the northern provinces of America, . . . the irretrievable loss France sustains hereby, and the importance it must give the British crown among the several states of Europe. . . .[132]

As usual, Rogers was not far from the mark.

Amherst sent away his provincial regiments shortly after the surrender, wisely preferring to have the occupation of the St. Lawrence Valley conducted by disciplined regulars, who had no long-standing animosity toward the Canadians. For purposes of administration and control, he appointed three of his subordinates as military governors—Colonel Ralph Burton at Trois Rivières, Brigadier General Murray at Quebec, and Brigadier General Gage at Montreal. British officers were sent to the outlying villages, where they tendered the oath of allegiance and collected weapons from the *habitants*. The transition to British control was made with little difficulty, partly because Amherst was shrewd enough not to tamper unnecessarily with the routine of Canadian agricultural and religious life. In Montreal, compassionate Sisters willingly assumed the task of nursing sick British soldiers, and won the sincere thanks of the conqueror, who showed his gratitude by presenting them with 200 crowns and two dozen bottles of Madeira. On at least one occasion, Amherst and Vaudreuil sat down together over a good meal with pleasant conversation.[133]

There now remained the task of removing the French garrisons from the remote western posts and convincing the more recalcitrant tribes that they must conform to the new order in North America. This task was assigned to Rogers, together with Lieutenant Dietrich Brehm and two companies of rangers. As a means of authenticating the mission, Rogers carried a letter from Vaudreuil announcing the surrender of New France. Leaving Montreal on 13 September, Rogers proceeded to Presqu'île, where he was joined by a company of Royal Americans and the deputy Indian superintendent, George Croghan. On 4 November they set out for Detroit.[134] The French commander at Detroit, Captain Picoté de Belestre, after perusing Vaudreuil's letter readily relinquished his post on 29 November. Likewise the French garrisons at Forts Miami and Ouiatenon on the Maumee and upper Wabash rivers submitted to Rogers' orders.

Croghan met with leaders of the Ottawa, Potawatomi, and Huron tribes, informing them that henceforth all Indian trade would pass through British-controlled channels in a system that could prove advantageous to the Indian participants. The effect of this important conference, along with others previously held elsewhere, was to confirm the new and momentous fact of British hegemony throughout the length of the Ohio Valley as far west as the Wabash.[135] With ice already beginning to clog Lake Huron, Rogers gave up his intention of obtaining the surrender of Fort Michilimackinac, leaving that remote outpost to be scooped into the British pocket the following year.

Amherst had taken his departure from Montreal on 27 September, proceeding first to Quebec, then to Crown Point, Albany, and New York. At Albany he saw provincial troops streaming in from Oswego and the Mohawk Valley, thankful to be escaping a winter of garrison duty, glad to be heading for home. In February, at New York, he received from Rogers himself a report on the surrender of the western posts. Amherst may perhaps be forgiven if, in reviewing in his own mind the highly successful campaign he had conducted in 1760, resulting in the downfall of a vast colony which the French had been laboriously building for a century and a half, he took deep pride in what he himself was able to report to his sovereign.

NOTES

1. George Louis Beer, *British Colonial Policy, 1754–1765* (New York, 1907), pp. 55–58; Dorothy Marshall, *Eighteenth Century England* (New York, 1962), pp. 302–303.
2. O. A. Sherrard, *Lord Chatham: Pitt and the Seven Years' War* (London, 1955), pp. 284–285.
3. Julian S. Corbett, *England in the Seven Years' War, A Study in Combined Strategy* (2d ed., 2 vols.; London, 1918), I, 310–311; Sherrard, *Lord Chatham*, pp. 256–257.
4. Quoted in Hubert Hall, "Chatham's Colonial Policy," *AHR*, V (July, 1900), 669.
5. John Forbes, *Writings of General John Forbes Relating to His Service in North America*, Alfred P. James, ed. (Menasha, Wis., 1938), pp. 54–55; William Pitt, *Correspondence of William Pitt with Colonial Governors*, G. S. Kimball, ed. (2 vols.; New York, 1906), I, 363.
6. Pitt, *Correspondence*, I, 152.
7. Pitt, *Correspondence*, I, 170–171.

8. William Johnson, *The Papers of Sir William Johnson,* James Sullivan and Alexander C. Flick, eds. (13 vols.; Albany, 1921–1962), IX, 879–886; Louis Antoine de Bougainville, *Adventure in the Wilderness: The American Journals of Louis Antoine de Bougainville, 1756–1760,* Edward P. Hamilton, trans. and ed. (Norman, Okla., 1964), pp. 201, 204; James Thomas Flexner, *Mohawk Baronet: Sir William Johnson of New York* (New York, 1959), p. 188.

9. Robert Rogers, *Journals of Major Robert Rogers,* Howard H. Peckham, ed. (New York, 1961), pp. 58–74; Bougainville, *Adventure in the Wilderness,* pp. 198–199; Louis Joseph de Montcalm-Gozon, "Montcalm's Correspondence," *Report of the Public Archives of Canada for the Year 1929* (Ottawa, 1930), pp. 64–65; Forbes, *Writings,* pp. 58–59; John R. Cuneo, *Robert Rogers of the Rangers* (New York, 1959), pp. 74–79.

10. *Johnson Papers,* II, 809.

11. *Johnson Papers,* II, 835–836; Pitt, *Correspondence,* I, 255.

12. Montcalm, "Correspondence," pp. 70–71.

13. Bougainville, *Adventure in the Wilderness,* p. 207.

14. Pitt, *Correspondence,* I, 231, 242, 257; Corbett, *England in the Seven Years' War,* I, 320; J. S. McLennan, *Louisbourg from Its Foundation to Its Fall* (London, 1918), pp. 236–242, 262–263.

15. J. Mackay Hitsman, with C. C. J. Bond, "The Assault Landing at Louisbourg, 1758," *CHR,* XXXV (December, 1954), 321–322.

16. Jeffery Amherst, *The Journal of Jeffery Amherst, Recording the Military Career of General Amherst in America from 1758 to 1763,* J. Clarence Webster, ed. (Chicago, 1931), pp. 46–47; Stanley Pargellis, ed., *Military Affairs in North America, 1748–1765: Selected Documents from the Cumberland Papers in Windsor Castle* (New York, 1936), p. 416; McLennan, *Louisbourg,* p. 242.

17. McLennan, *Louisbourg,* pp. 246–248.

18. *Ibid.,* p. 301.

19. Amherst, *Journal,* p. 49; Pitt, *Correspondence,* I, 272.

20. The description of the operation is based upon McLennan, *Louisbourg,* chaps. 13–15, as well as contemporary accounts.

21. Letter from an officer at Louisbourg, 4 August 1758, *Boston Gazette,* 18 September 1758.

22. Amherst, *Journal,* p. 51.

23. By 24 June the British artillery park contained thirteen 24-pounders and seven 12-pounders (Pitt, *Correspondence,* I, 282–284, 291).

24. Extract of a letter from an officer at Louisbourg, 24 June 1758, *Boston Gazette,* 14 August 1758.

25. Pitt, *Correspondence,* I, 284, 292.

26. Nathan Fiske, Diary (American Antiquarian Society).

27. Carr Huse, Diary (New York Historical Society).

28. Pitt, *Correspondence,* I, 216.

29. Huse, Diary.

30. *Ibid.*

31. [Bradstreet] to [Abercromby], 13 and 24 March 1758, and note of 31 De-

cember 1758, John Bradstreet Papers (American Antiquarian Society); Pitt, *Correspondence*, I, 232, 253.

32. Pargellis, *Military Affairs*, p. 418; Thomas Mante, *The History of the Late War in North-America, and the Islands of the West-Indies* . . . (London, 1772), p. 145. The French battalions at Ticonderoga were La Reine, La Sarre, Royal Roussillon, Languedoc, Guyenne, First and Second Berry, and Béarn (Montcalm, "Correspondence," pp. 72, 83). See also Edward P. Hamilton, *The French and Indian Wars: The Story of Battles and Forts in the Wilderness* (New York, 1962), p. 222.

33. Quoted in S. H. P. Pell, *Fort Ticonderoga: A Short History* (Reprinted for the Fort Ticonderoga Museum, New York, 1968), p. 41. See also Pitt, *Correspondence*, I, 297; Hamilton, *French and Indian Wars*, p. 217.

34. Pitt, *Correspondence*, I, 297–298; Montcalm, "Correspondence," p. 73; Bougainville, *Adventure in the Wilderness*, pp. 228–229; Rogers, *Journals*, pp. 81–82. The confusion of movement is well reflected in contemporary accounts such as the Huse Diary. Bougainville considered the twenty-four hour delay a godsend to the French (*Adventure in the Wilderness*, p. 229). At least one competent observer noted that the British regulars seemed to have improved but little since Braddock's day. "I observed the fire round them, tho' at some distance, seem'd to Alarm them," wrote Lieutenant Colonel William Eyre. "In the Wood, where nothing can be Seen, but what is near, the men fancy is [*sic*] worse, or the Enemy more Numerous than they Are; our own fire they Are Apt some times to think is the Enemy's Our Irregulers Yelling is believed by those who Are not engaged, to be the Enemy; in short Sir, I am more than ever convinced that numbers of our People cannot hear a great deal of firing round them coolly. I mean when they hear and do not See" (Eyre to Robert Napier, 10 July 1758, in Pargellis, *Military Affairs*, pp. 418–419).

35. John Bremner, Journal, 1756–1764 (New York Historical Society); Pargellis, *Military Affairs*, p. 419; Hamilton, *French and Indian Wars*, p. 220.

36. According to Bougainville, on 8 July the French force totaled 3,526 men, including fifteen Indians (*Adventure in the Wilderness*, p. 231). See also *Johnson Papers*, IX, 936–939, 944–945; Rogers, *Journals*, p. 83; "Account of the Victory Won By the Royal Troops at Carillon on the 8th Day of July, 1758," in Pell, *Fort Ticonderoga*, p. 37.

37. Pitt, *Correspondence*, I, 299–300; Hamilton, *French and Indian Wars*, pp. 222–223.

38. Bremner, Journal. At one point, this same combatant reported, the French employed a ruse, striking their own colors and hoisting an English flag. Some British troops, interpreting this as a sign of surrender, drew close to the French position, whereupon "The Enemy gave them a smart Volly and Hove a great Numbr of Grenads chells among them. . . ." No other such report has come to the author's attention.

39. Bougainville, *Adventure in the Wilderness*, p. 233.

40. Pitt, *Correspondence*, I, 300–301; Bremner, Journal; Montcalm, "Correspondence," p. 73; "Account of the Victory," in Pell, *Fort Ticonderoga*, p. 40.

41. Bougainville, *Adventure in the Wilderness,* p. 235.

42. Montcalm, "Correspondence," p. 73; Bougainville, *Adventure in the Wilderness,* p. 242.

43. Amherst, *Journal,* p. 60; Pitt, *Correspondence,* I, 292, 308.

44. Pitt, *Correspondence,* I, 302–304; Amherst, *Journal,* pp. 63–64, 67–68.

45. *Boston Gazette,* 28 August 1758. For additional details see the issue for 14 August 1758; Pitt, *Correspondence,* I, 308; and McLennan, *Louisbourg,* p. 280. The sources vary in giving the order in which the French ships took fire. Preference has been given to Boscawen as presumably authoritative.

46. Extract of a letter from Gabarus Bay, 24 July 1758, *Boston Gazette,* 14 August 1758. See also the issue for 28 August 1758; Pitt, *Correspondence,* I, 306–308; Amherst, *Journal,* p. 71; Bougainville, *Adventure in the Wilderness,* p. 312.

47. Amherst, *Journal,* p. 86.

48. Pitt, *Correspondence,* I, 301.

49. Occasional raids and skirmishes in the area between Fort Edward and Lake George during July and August gave evidence of Montcalm's determination to keep Abercromby off balance as much as possible. One skirmish near the headwaters of Wood Creek resulted in the capture of Israel Putnam, the able and respected Massachusetts frontier leader (Pitt, *Correspondence,* I, 316–322; Rogers, *Journals,* pp. 85–86).

50. Benjamin Bass, "Account of the Capture of Fort Frontenac by the Detachment under the Command of Col. Bradstreet," *New York History,* XVI (October, 1935), 449–451.

51. The size of the garrison differs in various accounts, ranging from 70 to more than 120. (See Montcalm, "Correspondence," p. 75; *Johnson Papers,* II, 889–890, 895; *Boston Gazette,* 25 September 1758.)

52. One report stated that some of the garrison (actually, perhaps, traders or boatmen) managed to escape by boat as the colors were struck (*Boston Gazette,* 25 September 1758). Schuyler and a number of other British prisoners were released by the French in November (Pitt, *Correspondence,* I, 404–406).

53. Captain Thomas Sowers' Account, in Richard A. Preston and Leopold Lamontagne, eds., *Royal Fort Frontenac* (Toronto, 1958), p. 268; *Johnson Papers,* II, 889.

54. Bass, "Account of the Capture of Fort Frontenac," p. 451.

55. Montcalm, "Correspondence," p. 75.

56. Amherst, *Journal,* pp. 92–98; Pitt, *Correspondence,* I, 354–355, 365, 399–402, 430–431.

57. Pitt, *Correspondence,* I, 401–402; Montcalm, "Correspondence," pp. 76–78.

58. Forbes, *Writings,* pp. 76–78 (Also in Pitt, *Correspondence,* I, 235–238); Henry Bouquet, *The Papers of Henry Bouquet.* Vol. II: *The Forbes Expedition,* S. K. Stevens, D. H. Kent, and A. L. Leonard, eds. (Harrisburg, 1951), pp. 226–227; Benjamin Franklin, *The Papers of Benjamin Franklin,* Leonard W. Labaree *et al.,* eds. (14 vols. to date; New Haven, 1959 to present), VIII, 107*n.;* E. Douglas Branch, "Henry Bouquet: Pro-

fessional Soldier," *Pennsylvania Magazine of History and Biography*, LXII (January, 1938), 44–45.

59. Forbes, *Writings*, pp. 68, 103.

60. Forbes, *Writings*, p. 205 (Also in Pitt, *Correspondence*, I, 342); Forbes, *Writings*, pp. 224–225.

61. Bouquet, *Papers*, II, 28, 50.

62. Forbes, *Writings*, p. 226.

63. Bouquet, *Papers*, II, 206.

64. Forbes, *Writings*, p. 125.

65. Forbes, *Writings*, p. 103; Niles Anderson, "The General Chooses a Road: The Forbes Campaign of 1758 to Capture Fort Duquesne," *Western Pennsylvania Historical Magazine*, XLII (June, 1959), 110–114, 120–124.

66. Bouquet, *Papers*, II, 283.

67. Forbes, *Writings*, pp. 197–199.

68. Forbes, *Writings*, pp. 215–220, 225, 237–241; Solon J. Buck and Elizabeth H. Buck, *The Planting of Civilization in Western Pennsylvania* (Pittsburgh, 1939), p. 92.

69. Henry F. DePuy, comp., *A Bibliography of the English Colonial Treaties with the American Indians, Including a Synopsis of Each Treaty* (New York, 1917), p. 44; Buck and Buck, *Planting of Civilization in Western Pennsylvania*, p. 88; Flexner, *Mohawk Baronet*, p. 196; Theodore Thayer, *Israel Pemberton, King of the Quakers* (Philadelphia, 1943), chap. 12; Nicholas B. Wainwright, *George Croghan: Wilderness Diplomat* (Chapel Hill, 1959), pp. 145–151.

70. Forbes, *Writings*, p. 255; Marie Le Roy, "The Narrative of Marie Le Roy and Barbara Leininger, for Three Years Captives among the Indians," Edmund de Schweinitz, trans., *Pennsylvania Magazine of History and Biography*, XXIX (October, 1905), 412; Anderson, "The General Chooses a Road," pp. 391–393.

71. The victorious commander was reminded of the terrible ninth of July 1755, and on 28 November he sent a large detachment along the bank of the Monongahela to find and bury the strewn bones of Braddock's men (*Boston Gazette*, 25 December 1758). See also Forbes, *Writings*, pp. 262, 264; Christian Frederick Post, *The Second Journal of Christian Frederick Post, on a Message from the Governor of Pensilvania to the Indians on the Ohio* (London, 1759), pp. 31–62; Randolph C. Downes, *Council Fires on the Upper Ohio: A Narrative of Indian Affairs in the Upper Ohio Valley until 1795* (Pittsburgh, 1940), pp. 93–95; Harold A. Thomas, "The Last Two Campsites of Forbes' Army," *Western Pennsylvania Historical Magazine*, XLVI (January, 1963), 54–55.

72. Lawrence H. Gipson, *The Great War for the Empire: The Victorious Years, 1758–1760* (New York, 1949), p. 332.

73. Pitt, *Correspondence*, I, 387–392.

74. Corbett, *England in the Seven Years' War*, I, 371–376.

75. Pitt, *Correspondence*, II, 29.

76. Pitt, *Correspondence*, II, 20–31, 45–50, 100–105; Mante, *History of the*

Late War, Book IV; Corbett, *England in the Seven Years' War,* I, 371–387; William Laird Clowes, *The Royal Navy: A History from the Earliest Times to the Present* (7 vols.; London, 1897–1903), III, 201–203; Richard Pares, *War and Trade in the West Indies, 1739–1763* (New York, 1936), pp. 186–193.

77. Bougainville, *Adventure in the Wilderness,* p. 324; Pitt, *Correspondence,* II, 92–93, 110, 115, 162; Corbett, *England in the Seven Years' War,* I, 402–410, 415; C. P. Stacey, *Quebec, 1759: The Siege and the Battle* (New York, 1959), p. 8.

78. Amherst, *Journal,* pp. 107, 109; Pitt, *Correspondence,* II, 121.

79. Mante, *History of the Late War,* p. 206.

80. Amherst, *Journal,* p. 117.

81. *Johnson Papers,* III, 31–32, 42–43; Pitt, *Correspondence,* II, 123–125; Flexner, *Mohawk Baronet,* pp. 200–201; Wilfred B. Kerr, "Fort Niagara, 1759–1763," *New York History,* XV (July, 1934), 281–282.

82. Stacey, *Quebec, 1759,* p. 43.

83. Corbett, *England in the Seven Years' War,* I, 419–420, 434, 443–444; Stacey, *Quebec, 1759,* pp. 41–42.

84. Clowes, *Royal Navy,* III, 206; Corbett, *England in the Seven Years' War,* I, 411, 416; Stacey, *Quebec, 1759,* pp. 49–51.

85. Pitt, *Correspondence,* II, 159; Pargellis, *Military Affairs,* p. 433; Stacey, *Quebec, 1759,* pp. 51–52.

86. Ashley Bowen, "Journal Kept on the Quebec Expedition, 1759, by Ashley Bowen of Marblehead," *Essex Institute Historical Collections,* LXX (July, 1934), 243.

87. Pitt, *Correspondence,* II, 151–152; Pargellis, *Military Affairs,* p. 435; Stacey, *Quebec, 1759,* pp. 60, 68–72.

88. Pargellis, *Military Affairs,* p. 436; Stacey, *Quebec, 1759,* p. 73. According to one report, the French attempted to discourage the boat patrol by constructing a floating booby trap, which did inflict some casualties when a zealous midshipman from H.M.S. *Dublin* jumped aboard it. The idea of employing a huge fireraft against a British fleet at Quebec was not new in 1759. Such a device apparently was constructed in 1709, but never used. (See Gerald S. Graham, ed., *The Walker Expedition to Quebec, 1711* [Toronto, 1953], pp. 265, 320.)

89. Pargellis, *Military Affairs,* p. 434.

90. Pargellis, *Military Affairs,* pp. 434–435; Pitt, *Correspondence,* II, 153–155; Bougainville, *Adventure in the Wilderness,* p. 318; Stacey, *Quebec, 1759,* pp. 73–80.

91. *Johnson Papers,* III, 61–63, 106–107, 111–114; Pitt, *Correspondence,* II, 146; Flexner, *Mohawk Baronet,* pp. 201–204.

92. *Johnson Papers,* III, 108–110, 112–115, 131–132, 139–140, XIII, 114–119, 125; Mante, *History of the Late War,* pp. 224–230.

93. Amherst, *Journal,* pp. 131–139; Mante, *History of the Late War,* p. 210; Sigmund Samuel, comp., *The Seven Years War in Canada, 1756–1763* (Toronto, 1934), pp. 49–55.

94. Amherst, *Journal*, pp. 142–143; Samuel, *Seven Years War in Canada*, pp. 59–61.

95. Amherst, *Journal*, p. 146; Pitt, *Correspondence*, II, 143; Samuel, *Seven Years War in Canada*, pp. 62–64.

96. Amherst, *Journal*, p. 148.

97. Stacey, *Quebec, 1759*, pp. 88–93. Possibly as many as 8,000 Canadians were left homeless. A version of this cruel warfare is given by a participant, in David Perry, *Recollections of an Old Soldier* (Cottonport, La., 1971), pp. 18–22, 26–31.

98. Bougainville, *Adventure in the Wilderness*, pp. 319–320.

99. Stacey, *Quebec, 1759*, pp. 93–100. Amherst, after gaining control of Crown Point, had sent word of his success through the wilderness toward Quebec by two separate parties. One group encountered hostile Indians en route and never arrived at Wolfe's camp. The other party, led by Ensign Hutchins of the rangers, reached the vicinity of Quebec during the first week of September. Pondering the information brought him by Hutchins, Wolfe realized that Amherst could not arrive in time to help him take Quebec. The responsibility for success or failure remained his alone. (See Amherst, *Journal*, pp. 153, 178; Pitt, *Correspondence*, II, 187, 194, 198.)

100. Pitt, *Correspondence*, II, 164; Stacey, *Quebec, 1759*, pp. 102–117. French observers across the river had noticed Wolfe intently surveying the terrain through his glass, and although they had no way of knowing his identity reported the incident to their superiors. Had this warning been correctly interpreted, Bougainville could have rushed more manpower to guard the beach and the heights about the Anse au Foulon while Montcalm was shifting some of his strength from the Beauport lines to the Plains of Abraham. However, the French high command clung to the belief that any British activity above Quebec was nothing more than a feint designed to divert attention away from a major attack somewhere along the Beauport shore. Accordingly, the warning was largely ignored and nothing was done to reinforce the little camp at the head of the path manned by only about a hundred Canadians, most of whom were home on leave harvesting their crops. One is reminded of Pearl Harbor. (See Corbett, *England in the Seven Years' War*, I, 463–464; George F. G. Stanley, *Canada's Soldiers, 1604–1954: The Military History of an Unmilitary People* [Toronto, 1954], p. 89.)

101. Stacey, *Quebec, 1759*, p. 120.

102. Stacey, *Quebec, 1759*, p. 133. See also Pargellis, *Military Affairs*, pp. 437–438.

103. Christopher Lloyd, *The Capture of Quebec* (New York, 1959), p. 133.

104. Samuel, *Seven Years War in Canada*, p. 123.

105. Niccolò Machiavelli, *The Chief Works and Others*, Allan Gilbert, trans. (3 vols.; Durham, 1965), II, 581.

106. Bowen, "Journal," p. 263; Pitt, *Correspondence*, II, 168.

107. Amherst, *Journal*, p. 153. In September a small party of Amherst's men made a daring attempt to burn one of the French warships at Île aux Noix, but failed. (See Amherst, *Journal*, p. 168; Pitt, *Correspondence*, II, 195.)

108. Rogers, *Journals,* pp. 104–115; Amherst, *Journal,* p. 168; Pitt, *Correspondence,* II, 195–196, 198; Cuneo, *Robert Rogers,* chap. 9; Thomas M. Charland, "The Lake Champlain Army and the Fall of Montreal," *Vermont History,* New Series, XXVIII (October, 1960), 296–299.

109. Amherst, *Journal,* p. 171; Pitt, *Correspondence,* II, 196. According to Amherst, Gage's letter reached him on 18 or 19 September. Yet not until 10 October did Gage authorize Johnson to inform the Indians of the decision. (See *Johnson Papers,* XIII, 136–138, 147–148, 154–155.)

110. Amherst, *Journal,* pp. 179ff.; Pitt, *Correspondence,* II, 199–204.

111. William Willis, ed., *Journals of the Rev. Thomas Smith, and the Rev. Samuel Deane, Pastors of the First Church in Portland* (2d ed.; Portland, Me., 1849), p. 182.

112. The Reverend Jonathan Mayhew, quoted in Arthur H. Buffinton, "The Policy of the Northern Colonies towards the French to the Peace of Utrecht" (Unpublished Ph.D. dissertation, Harvard University, 1925), p. 11n.

113. Clarence S. Brigham, ed., *British Royal Proclamations Relating to America, 1603–1783* (Worcester, Mass., 1911), pp. 207–209.

114. Pargellis, *Military Affairs,* p. 440; Pitt, *Correspondence,* II, 214–215; Alfred L. Burt, *The Old Province of Quebec* (Minneapolis, 1933), p. 13; Stacey, *Quebec, 1759,* p. 161.

115. Pitt, *Correspondence,* II, 178; James Murray, *Governor Murray's Journal of the Siege of Quebec, from 18th September, 1759, to 25th May, 1760* (Toronto, 1939), p. 15; Burt, *Old Province of Quebec,* pp. 16–19, 21. The British garrison provided Quebec with its first effective system of street lights when the tinsmiths in the various regiments manufactured a large number of lanterns to be hung in appropriate places.

116. Pargellis, *Military Affairs,* pp. 440–441, 445–446; Corbett, *England in the Seven Years' War,* II, 109; Burt, *Old Province of Quebec,* p. 15.

117. Murray, *Journal,* p. 23.

118. According to a statement later made by the French commander, he brought his army down to the vicinity of Quebec anticipating the arrival of reinforcements from France and hoping for some opportunity to engage the British in the open. A siege of Quebec itself was not a part of the plan. (See Amherst, *Journal,* p. 252.)

119. Pargellis, *Military Affairs,* p. 443; Murray, *Journal,* pp. 25–26; Stacey, *Quebec, 1759,* pp. 162–163.

120. Pargellis, *Military Affairs,* pp. 443–445; Murray, *Journal,* pp. 26–27; Amherst, *Journal,* p. 252.

121. Murray, *Journal,* p. 28; Amherst, *Journal,* pp. 201–202; Mante, *History of the Late War,* pp. 281–282.

122. Murray, *Journal,* pp. 30–34; Pargellis, *Military Affairs,* p. 445; Corbett, *England in the Seven Years' War,* II, 112–113.

123. *Johnson Papers,* III, 208–217; Downes, *Council Fires on the Upper Ohio,* pp. 102–103; Ronald O. MacFarlane, "British Indian Policy in Nova Scotia to 1760," *CHR,* XIX (June, 1938), 166–167.

124. *NYCD,* X, 454; "Journal of Captain Phineas Stevens' Journey to Canada,

1752," in Newton D. Mereness, ed., *Travels in the American Colonies, 1690–1783* (New York, 1916), pp. 321–322; Burt, *Old Province of Quebec,* p. 6.

125. Hamilton, *French and Indian Wars,* p. 299.
126. Rogers, *Journals,* pp. 124–135; Amherst, *Journal,* pp. 208–209; *Johnson Papers,* III, 260.
127. Amherst, *Journal,* pp. 227, 232–239; Bremner, Journal; *Johnson Papers,* XIII, 169–170.
128. Amherst, *Journal,* p. 244; Bremner, Journal.
129. Corbett, *England in the Seven Years' War,* II, 117. Amherst himself, of course, was justly proud of the achievement: "I believe never three Armys, setting out from different and very distant Parts from each other joyned in the Center, as was intended, better than we did" (Amherst, *Journal,* p. 247).
130. Amherst, *Journal,* p. 246.
131. Bremner, Journal; Rogers, *Journals,* p. 141.
132. Rogers, *Journals,* p. 142.
133. Amherst, *Journal,* pp. 247-248, 252–255.
134. Amherst, *Journal,* p. 251; Rogers, *Journals,* pp. 142–155.
135. Amherst, *Journal,* pp. 264–265; Rogers, *Journals,* pp. 157–166; Burt, *Old Province of Quebec,* p. 62; Downes, *Council Fires on the Upper Ohio,* pp. 103–105.

CHAPTER 11

The Transition to Peace
and Revolution

SOME WARS COME to a fairly tidy conclusion—a final decisive battle and then a treaty of peace. Not so the last of the colonial wars in America. After the fall of Canada in September 1760 came twenty-nine months of strain and violence before peace was officially proclaimed. In Europe, the Prussia of Frederick II fought to hold off a powerful coalition led by France, Austria, and Russia, while Britain sought to bolster Frederick in order to save Hanover and other British interests on the Continent. At the same time, France and Britain continued their naval warfare in the Caribbean and along the important sea lanes of the world. Nor did the fall of Canada in 1760 immediately deprive the French of their other extensive North American colony, Louisiana, and there too an active French resistance, including intrigue with the Indians against the British, continued. In fact, even the conclusive Peace of Paris of 1763 came too late to prevent the outbreak of a serious Indian uprising which was to last several years. During this same period of time, the British colonists also found themselves unhappily involved in a portentous Anglo-American political crisis that opened the way for the American Revolution. So it was that the great war of the 1750s evolved into the turbulence of the 1760s without any clean break.

486

True, the British military government of Canada, starting in 1760, had little difficulty securing the cooperation of the civilian population and managed to hold the colony in a gentle grip without destroying the traditional structure of law and authority at the local level. This meant that when British civil administration succeeded the military in 1764 the transition was easy, with the inhabitants already accustomed to a pattern of mutual cooperation.[1] In 1761, British forces completed their takeover of the western posts, establishing small garrisons at such remote wilderness trading posts and forts as Michilimackinac and St. Joseph. The main centers of British strength in the West were those forts which commanded the most important water routes—Niagara, Detroit, and the new Fort Pitt at the Forks of the Ohio. Hardly had the smoke of battle dissipated along the frontiers than the British traders began pushing forward again to barter with the Indians for peltry; and despite all official attempts to regulate the rapidly reviving trade, the old abuses soon were rampant once more. Land speculators and pioneering farmers, too, were again becoming active, with the result that settlements destroyed during the war were reoccupied, new dwellings arose near the ruins of the old, and the more enterprising of the colonists even began pushing into areas previously unsettled. In short, the westward movement of population was again underway, seeking to take full advantage of British military success and the downfall of the old enemy. This was potentially dangerous, because the Indians were still there and already becoming thoroughly alarmed as the advancing tide of whites began seeping into their hunting grounds.

Indeed, on the southern frontier a serious new Indian war had broken out as early as 1759. It was serious because the tribe involved was the Cherokee—numerous, powerful, near neighbor to South Carolina, and traditionally aligned with the British. One hundred and sixty miles northwest of Charleston, on a branch of the Saluda River, stood the frontier settlement known as Ninety-Six, an important way station on the path leading into the Cherokee country. Beyond that the British had constructed two wilderness strongholds—Fort Prince George, just across the Keowee River from the Indian town of that name, about 65 miles northwest of Ninety-Six, and Fort Loudoun at the junction of the Tellico and Little Tennessee rivers deep in the mountainous Cherokee country, 100 miles northwest of Fort Prince George. These forts

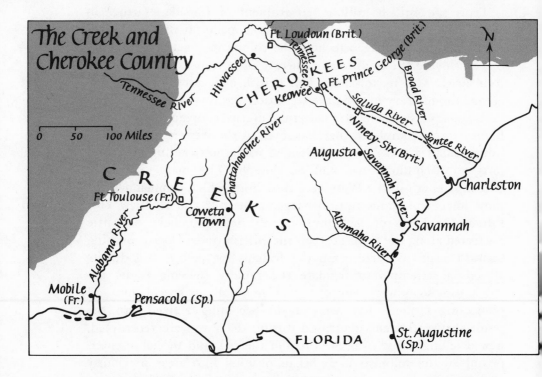

The Creek and Cherokee Country

were intended to protect the Cherokees against enemy Indians and the French, but inevitably they also came to symbolize the deepening intrusion of the British traders and settlers upon Cherokee lands. By 1758, more and more of the Cherokees were becoming resentful and hostile.[2]

Trouble began when Cherokee warriors en route to Virginia in 1758 to join the Forbes expedition provided themselves with horses by stealing them from white settlers. The frontiersmen retaliated, with the result that blood was shed and hatred increased. Further depredations occurred in 1759, the Indians now raiding frontier settlements in North Carolina and threatening whites in or near the Cherokee towns. Angry warriors prowled the trading paths, cutting off communication between Forts Loudoun and Prince George. Without doubt the French, working through certain elements in the Creek nation, were actively trying to promote a general war between the Cherokees and the British, which would work greatly to their advantage, but it is equally clear that in 1759 neither the Creeks nor the Cherokees were united in support of the French. In fact, the Creeks wisely declined to abandon their traditional neutrality, while Cherokee hostility toward the British was centered mostly in the eastern portion of the nation. The Catawbas remained faithful to the British.

Governor William Henry Lyttelton of South Carolina, determined to punish the offending Cherokees and reassert British authority, led a military expedition to Fort Prince George during the fall of 1759. Demanding that the Cherokees deliver to him a certain number of their people to be punished for the murders committed on the frontier, Lyttelton held an equivalent number of Indian leaders as hostages in the fort. On 26 December, spokesmen for the nation accepted the governor's terms and Lyttelton withdrew, leaving the Cherokee hostages as prisoners in Fort Prince George pending the actual delivery of the guilty ones. That all Cherokees were not so submissive soon became apparent when raiders resumed their vicious attacks along the frontier in January 1760. Dozens of terrified settlers were massacred or taken prisoner, and on 3 February Ninety-Six itself was attacked. At Fort Prince George, a band of Cherokees lured the British commander outside the walls for a parley and then shot him from ambush. This so infuriated the garrison that the Indian hostages, fearing for their lives, refused to come out of their quarters when summoned, whereupon a fight began, the hostages attempting to defend themselves with weapons they had previously concealed. When the fray was over, every one of the hostages lay dead.[3]

At this time General Amherst was in New York making plans for his climactic campaign against Montreal. Having been informed of the mounting trouble on the southern frontier, he dispatched an expedition of 1,300 Highlanders and Royal Scots under the command of Colonel Archibald Montgomery to chastise the Cherokees. Montgomery's second-in-command was Major James Grant, who had learned about Indian fighting the hard way near Fort Duquesne and subsequently had been exchanged by the French. Their orders were to suppress the uprising and then return to New York as promptly as possible in order to participate in the offensive against Canada.

The transports carrying Montgomery and his men arrived at Charleston about the first of April. Bolstering his force of regulars with rangers and a party of Catawbas, the British commander proceeded up the long trading path toward Fort Prince George.

On 2 June he plundered and burned several Indian villages and then led his weary troops into bivouac under the protecting guns of the fort. He lingered there for nearly three weeks, vainly trying to lure the Cherokees into negotiations for peace before resuming the offensive on 24 June. The army crossed the Keowee River and headed northwest toward isolated Fort Loudoun. On 27 June, while advancing down the west bank of the Little Tennessee, Montgomery suddenly ran into strong Cherokee opposition about 5 miles from his next objective, the Indian village of Etchoe. This precipitated a battle which lasted for several hours before the Cherokees were driven off. When Montgomery finally reached the village, he found it deserted. With more than half a hundred wounded in his ranks, he concluded that it would be unwise to advance farther into hostile country with a weary and depleted army. The transports were waiting at Charleston, and Amherst would be impatient for his return. Therefore, considering that he had achieved all that could reasonably be expected under the circumstances, Montgomery began a hasty withdrawal to the coast.

By the time Montgomery's men were safely aboard their transports, the condition of Captain Paul Demere's garrison at Fort Loudoun, under siege for many weeks and cut off from regular contact with the outside world, was approaching desperation. Governor Francis Fauquier of Virginia had answered South Carolina's call for help by sending Colonel William Byrd with a relief expedition to approach the beleaguered fort from the north by way of the interior valleys. Unfortunately, Byrd's expedition advanced slowly and never reached its destination. Montgomery's almost precipitate withdrawal at the end of June and Byrd's failure to arrive during July sealed the fate of Captain Demere and his starving people. Officers from the fort met with Cherokee leaders on 7 August and arrived at terms which were accepted by both sides. The victorious Indians, elated at one of their greatest triumphs, agreed to let the garrison withdraw in safety to a British settlement. On 9 August those men able to walk, together with a number of women and children who had been living in the fort, began their march toward Fort Prince George, leaving their sick to be cared for by the Indians, who had promised them good treatment. En route the next day they were ambushed by vengeful warriors. Demere himself was scalped; most of his officers and a large number of his men also were killed and the remainder taken captive. This presumably was revenge for the Cherokee hostages previously slain inside Fort Prince George.

After this the Cherokees seemed at least partially satisfied, and the influence of the peace faction began to increase, especially as the Indians were suffering greatly from the stoppage of trade. The government of South Carolina, however, had been deeply offended by what it considered the perfidious, savage behavior of the Indians and would not consider a peace without punishment. Amherst, believing it important to drive home the lesson of white supremacy, sent a second expedition of regulars to crush the Cherokee uprising. Command of this force was given to Grant, who had been promoted to the rank of lieutenant colonel. Like Montgomery before him, Grant advanced inland from Charleston to Fort Prince George, and on 7 June 1761 crossed the Keowee River to begin his offensive deep in the Cherokee country. Grant's force at this time consisted of regulars, rangers, provincials, wagoners, and friendly Indians, possibly more than 2,500 men altogether, in a column stretching out for 2 miles. Proceeding much as Montgomery had done, on 10 June he was only about 2 miles short of the place where the previous battle had been fought when again the Cherokees struck. The opening assault was ineffectual, and Grant deliberately pushed on across a ford in the river to take a stand on more open ground. Here, although the Indians kept up their fire for several hours, the disciplined regulars stood firm and held the field until the enemy withdrew. British losses in this battle were remarkably light. That evening the army arrived in good order at the deserted village of Etchoe. During the remainder of June, the British force rampaged through the Middle Settlements of the Cherokee country, systematically destroying dwellings, cutting down orchards, and ruining crops in the fields. In fifteen Cherokee towns the destruction was almost total. Having accomplished all this, Grant reckoned that he had amply completed his assignment and led his army back to Fort Prince George, arriving on 9 July.

There can be no doubt that the ravaging was effective, but it may not have been necessary for the achievement of a satisfactory peace. The Cherokee leaders already knew that further hostilities were useless, especially since other tribes had not come to their assistance. About the first of July they decided to seek terms with the British.[4] The leader of the peace faction among the Cherokees, Attakullaculla, or the Little Carpenter, approached Grant in August to begin negotiations. Out of this and subsequent discussions carried on near Charleston in September emerged a treaty that finally was ratified by the leaders of both sides in December 1761. The Cherokees were required to relinquish Fort Loudoun and return all prisoners. When this had been done, it was agreed, the Indian trade would be reopened. The territorial settlement, at least in theory, was fairly advantageous for the Cherokees, involving as it did a considerable concession on the part of South Carolina. A line of demarcation separating white territory from Indian territory was to be drawn 40 miles east of Keowee. Under these terms peace was restored to the southern frontier, leaving the Cherokees chastened but temporarily secure again in their alignment with the British.

France, in the meantime, was continuing her long struggle with Britain and her other enemies in Europe and elsewhere around the globe, but with diminishing hopes. Not only was the French national debt approaching the staggering total of 2,000,000,000 livres carried at extraordinarily high rates of interest; the financial sacrifice, to say nothing of the loss of human lives, apparently was not going to produce a commensurate victory.[5] At best France was struggling to stave off a disastrous defeat, hoping that the mounting war weariness among the British people and the military difficulties of Prussia on the Continent would make possible a negotiated peace preserving France's vital interests.

The last almost desperate French bid for a decisive victory had developed and then collapsed in 1759, coincidental with Wolfe's campaign against Quebec, when France made extensive preparations for a cross-Channel invasion of England. The French had the army for such a venture, but sea power was even more important, and that was where the French fell short. It was necessary for the Toulon fleet under M. de la Clue to enter the Atlantic and proceed to Brest in order to join the French Channel fleet commanded by Admiral Conflans. La Clue's fleet succeeded in passing through the Strait of Gibraltar, but off Lagos on the south coast of Portugal it was intercepted by Admiral Boscawen's fleet and decisively smashed on 18–19 August. Almost exactly three months later, Admiral Edward Hawke pounced upon Conflans' fleet in Quiberon Bay and, despite gale winds and heavy seas, administered a crushing defeat. The two British victories at sea on 18–19 August and 20–21 November put an end to the French scheme for invading England.[6] By the end of the following year the French Navy had been largely destroyed, with only a scattering of fighting ships still in condition to venture out on occasional missions.

On 25 October 1760 the elderly George II died at Kensington and was succeeded by his grandson George III, a young man little concerned with the fate of Hanover and highly suspicious of Pitt, the dynamo of the British war effort. The Cabinet itself was divided on the question of war policy, with Newcastle and others far less determined than Pitt to prolong the war until France's maritime and imperial power was thoroughly dissipated. Indeed, among the British public in general there was a swelling desire for peace, even though the people took great pride in their conquests of the past three years and relished the thought of complete victory. To Pitt, the most popular figure in the government, the essential goal was to deprive France of Canada, exclude her from the Newfoundland fisheries, and terminate her role as a serious maritime competitor of the British Empire. That would require more fighting and more expense—perhaps a great deal more.

The Duc de Choiseul, principal minister of Louis XV, knew how badly France needed peace, and in March 1761, through a communication to Pitt, initiated negotiations with the British government. Choiseul had one strong card to play, the possibility that Spain, which hitherto had remained neutral, might come to France's assistance in the war. The death of Spain's King Ferdinand VI in 1759 had brought to the throne his half-brother Charles, a man not inclined to view with complacency the excessive growth of British imperial power. Spain had a number of causes for anger and alarm, including the continuing activity of British logwood cutters on the coast of Central America, the highhanded interference of British privateers with Spanish merchant vessels, and Britain's attempt to monopolize the Newfoundland fisheries. British military and naval victories in North America and the Caribbean seemed to Charles III a growing threat to Spain's own imperial interests, for if Britain became dominant in America what other world empire would be secure? Therefore Choiseul, even while negotiating with the British for an end to the war, was able to create with Spain the so-called *Pacte de Famille,* an alliance signed on 15 August 1761. Attached to this important international agreement was a secret convention by which Spain bound herself to enter the war against Britain no later than 1 May 1762, unless prior to that date Britain had agreed to a peace satisfactory to both France and Spain.[7]

The signing of the Bourbon Family Compact gave Choiseul a greater option for continuing the war if, as was actually the case, Pitt's terms remained excessively high. In September Pitt, suspecting the impending belligerence of Spain, broke off the negotiations with France and sought a British declaration of war against Spain. When the Cabinet insisted on waiting until Spain's actual intentions were clarified, the exasperated prime minister resigned on 4 October. Subsequently, the Spanish government was unable to give sufficient reassurance to the British government, with the result that exactly three months after Pitt's resignation Britain issued her declaration of war. The next day, on 5 January 1762, occurred the death of one of Frederick II's most implacable foes, the Tsarina Elizabeth of Russia, after which the anti-Prussian coalition collapsed. Frederick was safe again, and Britain was able to devote her attention to the pursuit of peace through victory over the French and Spanish empires.

There were a number of choice targets for attack and conquest. In the West Indies, Britain already held the sugar island of Guadeloupe. Dominica came under British control in June 1761. The following winter saw a British fleet and army under Rear Admiral George Rodney and Major General Robert Monckton assembled for an attack on the major French sugar island of Martinique. In February the island was conquered, and then allowed to enter the British commercial system under much the same favorable terms as had been granted Guadeloupe three years earlier.[8] The islands of St. Lucia, Grenada, and St. Vincent also were swept into the British bag. Clearly, the ministry now was engaged in a process of gathering pawns for later trading during the eventual negotiations for a treaty. There was general agreement at the highest levels of government that Canada and Cape Breton Island were to be retained, and so the game was to collect additional pieces of territory which later could be exchanged for Minorca, the British Mediterranean base lost to the French in 1756.[9]

During the late spring of 1762, a small French expedition under Comte D'Haussonville managed to slip across the Atlantic from Brest to Newfoundland where, in late June, it forced the surrender of St. John's. Next the French, thoroughly enjoying their little taste of victory, moved from place to place on the large island destroying the boats and facilities used by the British fishing industry. Apparently the British command in North America had been taken by surprise, not anticipating such a bold intrusion into an area supposedly protected by the Royal Navy. When Amherst learned of the thrust, he assigned his brother, Lieutenant Colonel William Amherst, the task of driving off the enemy. Colonel Amherst joined forces with Lord Colville, then commanding the North American squadron based at Halifax, and landed at Torbay, a short distance north of St. John's, on 13 September. As Amherst approached the town, the small French fleet prudently departed, leaving D'Haussonville to surrender his force of more than 750 men. When this was done on 18 September, Newfoundland was again secure.[10]

That same summer the British mounted a much greater and more important offensive directed against the Spanish base of Havana on the north coast of Cuba. It was anticipated that after the fall of Havana an army of 8,000 troops under General Amherst would effect the conquest of French Louisiana. The first landing was made early in June a few miles east of Havana, and on 30 July the British troops seized El Morro, the principal fortification at the entrance to the harbor. Two weeks later Havana surrendered. This great Spanish base was a major prize in the war, for it was the principal rendezvous and haven for all Spanish convoys en route from the colonies to Spain. In yielding this key base, Spain not only gave up control of the principal route used by her homeward-bound vessels, but in addition lost a significant portion of her navy which had been trapped in the harbor, including six ships of seventy guns each, one of sixty-four guns, and five of sixty guns.[11] The expedition against Louisiana had to be canceled; but two months after the fall of Havana and halfway around the world, Manila in the Philippines fell to a British expedition from Madras, India. At the time when this expedition appeared at the entrance to Manila Bay, the Spaniards there had not yet learned of Britain's declaration of war against their country. Manila in British hands could be another extremely useful pawn at the bargaining table.[12]

As it happened, however, between the surrender of Havana and the surrender of Manila serious international negotiations for peace had been resumed at Paris, and because of the great distance between the Philippines and western Europe the diplomats came to agreement before they were aware that Manila had fallen. The preliminary articles were signed on 3 November 1762. Pitt rose in the House of Commons to denounce the settlement, which he con-

sidered far too lenient and quite incommensurate with the glorious
naval and military victories he had engineered. But the British
public and the government were weary of a long, expensive war
and welcomed the peace.[13] The Treaty of Paris in its final form
was signed by the spokesmen for Britain, France, and Spain at Paris
on 10 February 1763. Five days later, at Hubertusburg, Austria and
Prussia signed a treaty settling their territorial differences. So ended
one of the truly decisive wars of Western history.[14]

France gave up all claims to territory in India acquired by her
since the beginning of 1749, and in addition relinquished Senegal
on the coast of Africa and Minorca in the Mediterranean. Britain
restored to the French their slaving base of Goree in Africa. Reluctantly France agreed to drop her claims to compensation for the
many French ships seized by the British prior to the formal declaration of war. In the Caribbean the various islands were reassigned:
of the four so-called Neutral Islands, France received St. Lucia,
while St. Vincent, Dominica, and Tobago went under the British
flag. Also assigned to Britain were Grenada and the Grenadines.
France regained Mariegalante, Guadeloupe, and Martinique; Spain
recovered Cuba.[15] The British logwood cutters on the Bay of Hon-
duras were given official assurances that henceforth they would not
be molested by Spanish authorities.

One of Pitt's most insistent requirements had been that France
be totally excluded from the cod fisheries of Newfoundland and
the Gulf of St. Lawrence, a recognized source of major economic
and maritime strength. In the final treaty, however, the French
retained an important handhold. They were given the small, rocky
islands of St. Pierre and Miquelon off the south coast of Newfoundland as fishing bases; France also retained the right to fish
in the Gulf of St. Lawrence within 3 leagues of the shore and the
right to cure fish on the northern and western coasts of Newfoundland. It was Spain that was forced to yield all claims to the right of
participating in the Newfoundland fisheries.

The most momentous changes occurred on the continent of
North America. France was required to cede to Britain not only
all of Canada, Cape Breton Island, and whatever was left of Acadia,
but also all of Louisiana east of the Mississippi River excepting New
Orleans. After learning that Canada had been lost forever, Voltaire
wrote to Choiseul, "Permit me to compliment you. I am like the
public; I like peace better than Canada and I think that France

can be happy without Quebec." [16] The French sage was not being sarcastic. Most of France was thoroughly tired of the Canadian burden and almost glad to see it go. Britain completed her territories east of the Mississippi River by taking Florida from Spain as part of the price exacted from the unhappy Charles III for entering the war on the losing side. Nevertheless, for Spain there was some compensation. In addition to regaining Cuba from Britain, she inherited from France New Orleans and all French territorial claims west of the Mississippi River.[17] In short, except for two tiny islands in the Gulf of St. Lawrence, France after 1763 was without territory anywhere on the continent of North America. The Mississippi River was established as the dividing line between British and Spanish territory, and British subjects were guaranteed the right of free navigation along the entire length of that great artery.

In 1763, as a result of major conquests around the world, Britain had reached a high peak of glory and power. Her navy ruled the seas and her greatly enlarged empire gave clear promise of further strength and wealth to keep the nation first among all nations. Yet as Pitt had taken pains to point out, France was not driven completely from the field of maritime and imperial rivalry, even though greatly weakened by her losses in the war. Retaining her important island possessions in the West Indies and her firm handhold in the Newfoundland fisheries, France had the means for rebuilding her naval and commercial strength, to become once again a serious rival.

Britain's North American colonists saw great reason to rejoice in the elimination of the French and Spanish menace along their extended frontiers. Presumably now the Indians who formerly were incited by the enemy would remain docile, making it possible for the British to reap all the profits of the fur trade, and in time also to convert large areas of transappalachian wilderness into prosperous farmland. What they didn't realize was that the agony and bloodshed of the frontier experience was not yet over, not for them, not for the Indians.

After the British victories of 1758 to 1760, the Indian tribes of the West found increasing cause for discontent and dismay. They had hoped that the victorious British armies, having defeated the French, would withdraw to the East and leave the great interior free for Indian use. Instead, the conquerors established fortified positions as centers of trade at such places as the Forks of the Ohio,

Niagara, and Detroit. To these centers flocked the old corps of
British traders with their usual greed and their all-too-familiar
tactics. Efforts by the authorities to regulate the trade were, as
usual, something less than successful. Worse still, prospective settlers were beginning to cross the mountains, congregating in the
vicinity of the fortified posts, seeking out fertile land for farming.
This the Indians readily recognized as the licking edge of a great
tide. What affected the Indians most immediately, however, was
the policy laid down by the commander in chief, General Amherst,
whose attitude toward Indians in general bordered on contempt.
Not appreciating the niceties of Indian diplomacy, Amherst fostered
economy—and Indian resentment—by his official disapproval of the
customary gift-giving in the process of negotiation. He placed stringent limitations on the old practice of providing the Indians with
gunpowder, which they desperately needed for hunting. And he
thought he knew exactly how to deal with any Indian trouble-
makers. "Services must be rewarded; it has ever been a maxim with
me," Amherst lectured the knowledgeable Johnson with lofty self-
assurance, "but as to purchasing the good behavior either of Indians, or any Others, is what I do not understand; when men of
what race soever behave ill, they must be punished but not
bribed." [18] As the Indians compared the way they now were being
treated by the British with the way they formerly had been treated
by the French, they had serious reason to be concerned about the
future. Their apprehensions gave opportunity to insinuating French
traders and officials still residing in the West, who whispered to
them of new French armies coming to regain Canada and free the
Indians from the harsh grasp of the British.

Among the Delawares there had risen up a leader called the
"Prophet," who preached a new religion that was finding a widespread reception among the disgruntled Indians of the West. The
Indians should break free of the white man's insidious influence, he
said, and regain their integrity by returning to the ways of their
ancestors, the old, self-sufficient, forest ways of the happy time before
the Europeans began to intrude. This meant a rejection of firearms, liquor, and other products obtainable only from the whites,
and a withdrawal from entangling alliances that led only to war and
the further sapping of Indian strength. The preaching of the Delaware Prophet was the potential beginning of a pan-Indian movement that could produce serious trouble for the British, even

though he apparently stressed racial and cultural integrity rather than war. Among the Indians who were coming under the influence of this new preaching was an Ottawa war chief known as Pontiac. A stirring orator as well as a man of action, Pontiac exercised great influence over the groups of Ottawas, Chippewas, and Potawatomis in the vicinity of the British post at Detroit. Early in May 1763, nearly three months after the establishment of peace between France and Britain, Pontiac aroused the Indians around Detroit to begin a war against the British.

At first, it seems, Pontiac had only a fairly limited objective, that is, to capture the fort at Detroit and drive the British out of that region. Presumably he could count on the help or at least the passive support of most if not all of the local French inhabitants who had long been traders and farmers in the area. The fort itself, located on the western shore of the Detroit River about 7 miles below Lake St. Clair, was garrisoned by British regulars under the command of Major Henry Gladwin, who had been wounded in Braddock's defeat eight years before. At the outset Pontiac tried to gain control of the fort by a ruse, but Gladwin, whom a modern historian has called "a block of granite," had been forewarned and was able to thwart the attempt.[19] Once the heavy wooden gates had been slammed shut, Pontiac's Indians placed the fort under siege. In addition, war parties were sent off to attack the fort at Sandusky on the south shore of Lake Erie and Fort St. Joseph on the St. Joseph River near the present Niles, Michigan. These as well as a number of other outposts in the transappalachian West were held by small garrisons of British troops quite unprepared for a major Indian uprising.

Surprise and treachery were Pontiac's ace cards, as violence swept with frightening speed across much of the upper West. Sandusky fell on 16 May, with only the commanding officer, Ensign Christopher Pauli, surviving the Indians' fury and taken back to Detroit as a prisoner. Nine days later, Fort St. Joseph was captured and most of the garrison killed. When the Miami Indians learned of the uprising they readily joined with some Frenchmen to seize Fort Miami on the Maumee River. In this episode the faithless Indian mistress of the fort's commanding officer effected the downfall on 27 May. Fort Ouiatenon on the upper Wabash was taken on the first of June, and the next day, nearly 400 miles to the north, the fort at Michilimackinac fell to a band of Chippewas. During the

first month of the sudden uprising, five British posts had been overwhelmed while Detroit was kept under siege. The Delawares and
Mingos had joined the Ottawas, Chippewas, Potawatomis, and
Miamis, followed early in June by the Senecas and Shawnees. At
Fort Pitt, where Captain Simeon Ecuyer commanded a strong garrison, frightened settlers were brought inside the protecting walls,
and soon the Indians in the vicinity were creating unmistakable
evidence of their hostility. About the middle of June, the small post
at Venango was overcome, on 18 June Fort Le Boeuf fell, and approximately three days later Fort Presqu'île shared the same fate.
All in all, the first six weeks of Pontiac's Uprising constituted a
stunning demonstration of British weakness and Indian strength in
the West. There was imminent danger, or so it seemed to many
alarmed Americans, that the victory of 1760 would be transformed
into the defeat of 1763.

Amherst, when first notified of the violence in the West, was
inclined to minimize the seriousness of the situation. His attitude
changed rather abruptly on 16 June, however, when he learned
that a detachment of 96 men under Lieutenant Abraham Cuyler
had been surprised and routed by Indians at Point Pelee on the
north shore of Lake Erie, with heavy losses.[20] At last the British
high command began to initiate countermeasures proportionate to
the mounting threat. The principal task was given to Colonel
Henry Bouquet, designated to lead a relief expedition west from
Carlisle, Pennsylvania, to Fort Pitt. Bouquet marched out of Carlisle on 18 July with two understrength Scottish regiments, a battalion of Royal Americans, and some rangers. Considering the
disaster on the Monongahela in 1755, this seems a daring thrust
indeed, for Bouquet's force totaled only about 460 troops. By this
time, however, British regulars had become far more accustomed to
wilderness warfare and thus more confident in their ability to out-
fight the undisciplined enemy.

Toward the end of July, while Bouquet was en route, the Indians
began an attack on Fort Pitt that lasted about five days and then
ended as the warriors moved off toward the east to encounter the
approaching British army. Bouquet plodded on after leaving one
of his companies to strengthen Fort Bedford. Early in the afternoon
of 5 August, at Edge Hill 26 miles east of Fort Pitt, the waiting
Indians attacked the advancing column. Although the regulars kept
their heads and repeatedly drove off the attacking enemy, they were

unable to prevent the Indians from sweeping around the flanks, completing the encirclement, and attacking the pack train at the rear. The action continued until darkness enveloped the hills. All that night Bouquet's men huddled in a circular formation on high ground, protecting their wounded and the packhorses carrying provisions for the fort. Next morning, when the battle was resumed, Bouquet feigned a retreat, and as the Indians advanced to seize their advantage two companies of light infantry hit them from an unexpected quarter. Completely surprised by this sudden maneuver, and suffering heavy losses, the enemy warriors broke and fled, their rout being hastened by two other companies who also had been advantageously placed. This ended the Battle of Bushy Run, a clear vindication of British military discipline and valor when properly sustained in the wilderness by modified tactics based on experience. Although Bouquet had lost about fifty men killed, five missing, and sixty wounded, he had held the field and now was able to continue on to relieve Fort Pitt, while the morale of the Delawares and Shawnees plummeted.[21]

Niagara, which had been sustaining Detroit whenever possible with reinforcements and provisions sent by water, was yet to witness a disaster. On 14 September, a guarded convoy of supply wagons was rumbling along the Niagara portage route about 4 miles below the Falls when it was suddenly attacked by several hundred Senecas. The Indians, fighting furiously against desperately resisting soldiers and wagoners, overwhelmed the convoy, forcing some of the wagons—drivers, oxen, and all—over a precipice. Two companies of troops which hastened to the rescue also were ambushed, with heavy losses. Altogether the British lost five officers and at least sixty-seven men killed in this bloody affray, their "worst drubbing of the war," as the leading historian of Pontiac's Uprising has well said.[22]

Nevertheless, Pontiac's inability to force Gladwin to surrender the fort at Detroit and the relief of Fort Pitt by Bouquet were clear signs that the far-spread Indian resistance movement had passed its peak. If the mystical ideas of the Prophet coupled with the bold war schemes of Pontiac had ever had a chance to fuse into a real pan-Indian rebellion, that chance now lay in the receding past, as Amherst rallied his military resources for the showdown. By October 1763, five months after the outbreak, the tribes were beginning to waver in their support for Pontiac's cause. When, about the end of the month, the Ottawa war chief finally received definite

word from the French commander at Fort de Chartres that the war
between the French and the British really was over and that the
French would not give any further support to Indian hostilities, he
broke off the siege of Detroit.

The Indians of the southern frontier, in the meantime, had remained generally quiescent since the suppression of the Cherokee
uprising, but were potentially susceptible to the contagion from the
north. In November 1763 more than 800 Catawbas, Choctaws,
Chickasaws, Cherokees, and Creeks converged on Augusta, Georgia,
for a major conference with John Stuart, superintendent of Indian
affairs for the southern district, and the royal governors of Georgia,
South Carolina, North Carolina, and Virginia. The purpose was to
establish a general peace and arrange for the resumption of normal
trade, thereby insulating the southern frontier against the influence
of Pontiac and his followers. Lasting less than a week, the conference was a great success for the British, who gained further ces-
sions of Indian land and promises of security for the existing white
settlements along the frontier.[23] That same month Amherst relinquished his post as commander in chief to General Thomas Gage
who, like Gladwin, had learned about Indian fighting with Braddock.

Pontiac spent the winter of 1763–64 on the Maumee River,
not yet willing to admit that all was lost. In 1764 Gage sent out two
expeditions for the purpose of pacifying the offending tribes in the
West. Colonel John Bradstreet, accompanied by Sir William Johnson, first proceeded to Niagara. There during the month of July
Johnson received delegations from a number of tribes, mostly ones
which had not been actively hostile. In coming and offering assurances of their loyalty, these Indians were testifying to their need
for trade and acknowledging the futility of further Indian resistance
against the British. Early in August, Bradstreet continued on to
Presqu'île and then Detroit with an army of about 1,200 men. At
Detroit during the first week of September, he obtained formal
commitments to peace from leaders of various tribes including the
Ottawas, Chippewas, Hurons, Miamis, and Potawatomis. The second expedition, consisting of approximately 1,500 men under
Bouquet, took its departure from Fort Pitt early in October. Proceeding west, Bouquet advanced through the valley of the upper
Muskingum River, serving notice on the Delawares and other Indians that they had better submit without equivocation or delay. An

essential aspect of submission was the releasing of white captives, of whom the Indians held a considerable number. By 12 November, Bouquet had obtained the release of more than 200 captives, together with promises that the remainder would be freed the following spring.[24] Having in effect pacified the region between Lake Erie and the Ohio River, Bouquet returned to Fort Pitt, arriving there on 28 November.

Pontiac, ever seeking further help for his dying cause, saw more and more of his support crumbling away. While his war had been petering out, the British government, spurred by the Indian uprising, had announced its new policy for the West in a royal proclamation dated 7 October 1763. The entire area between the Appalachian Mountains and the Mississippi River, from the Great Lakes to the boundary of the Floridas, was declared an Indian reservation where no new white settlers were to intrude and where only licensed traders would be allowed to do business with the tribes. It was a heroic attempt to buy more time by protecting the Indians against the tidal wave of westward-moving pioneers.[25] This, together with the rising supremacy of British military power, was rapidly undermining the basis for further Indian resistance. One by one the various groups made their submission, and in July 1765 Pontiac himself, meeting with George Croghan at Fort Ouiatenon, agreed to preliminary terms. Then he accompanied Croghan to Detroit, where he participated in the peace-making process with the Ottawas, Chippewas, Hurons, and Potawatomis. Finally, in July of 1766, Pontiac's Uprising was fully liquidated when Pontiac and other chiefs reached full accord with Johnson at Oswego, in terms that left no doubt of British supremacy. Now at long last the colonial wars had reached their termination under the royal banner of George III.

In history every conclusion is also an introduction. What happened between Britain and her American mainland colonies during the troubled decades of the 1760s and 1770s was in large measure a result of the colonial wars. It seems obvious, for example, that the removal of the French and Spanish menace from the near vicinity of the British colonies made the Americans less dependent upon the mother country for security and more willing to strike out on their own. Even before that, however, the economy and indeed the very war effort of Britain, especially during the last great war against the French, had been seen to be at cross-purposes with the commercial needs of at least some of the colonies. The illicit trade which the Americans carried on with the French obviously was detrimental to British interests in general. Because the mother country needed colonial support for its American campaigns and dared not offend the colonies by severe repression, Pitt at first was very cautious in his approach to the problem. Once the tide had turned, however, he became increasingly impatient with the unpatriotic traffic, which undoubtedly was helping to sustain French resistance in North America. On 23 August 1760, he ordered the colonial governors to stop it.[26] The repression never was fully successful, but the attempt not only greatly annoyed the colonial maritime communities, especially in New England, but led directly into the controversy over writs of assistance.

From 1755 to 1763 Britain had carried the financial burden of an extensive warfare whose principal objective was to guarantee the future security and prosperity of her American colonies, and hence of Britain herself. During that period, the national debt increased from £75,000,000 to nearly £130,000,000.[27] As a consequence, the English taxpayer was heavily assessed, while the colonial taxpayer emerged nearly scot free, beginning in the later stages of the war when Pitt was subsidizing the colonies so generously. Soon, too, the decision was made to maintain a military establishment of some 10,000 regular troops in America for the future protection of the colonies. This, in turn, would lead the ministry to the conclusion that the Americans would have to be taxed to help pay the costs of their own defense. The fact that regular troops were near at hand and available when the colonists began to balk at the unprecedented taxation in 1764 and 1765 was the consequence of the heavy British military commitment during the previous war and Pontiac's Uprising. All this is well known.

What has not been so widely recognized is that the growth of mutual antagonism between Britons and Americans began long before the last of the colonial wars; indeed, it can be traced deep into the military history of the seventeenth century. The fact is that nearly all the colonial wars from earliest times contributed something to the creation of attitudes leading directly toward the American Revolution. Anglo-American friction began to develop at an early date between British regular forces serving in the colonies, on the one hand, and American provincial troops and civilians on the other. Basic attitudes undoubtedly were involved. The colonist, it should be remembered, was a person who had left his homeland in order to make a fresh start in a new environment. In effect, he had stepped quite deliberately across a significant line dividing old from new, traditional from innovative, an action that seemed to imply a prior dissatisfaction with the homeland and a preference for the outland. Once counted among those who had crossed that line, the colonist felt a strong need to justify his action by making obvious his willing identification with and his preference for the colony. In similar fashion the homelander, now enrolled in His Majesty's forces serving in America, felt compelled to justify his continuing attachment to the old country by flaunting the superiority of its people and its way of life. It was easy and natural for the colonist to view with a certain disdain those who appeared to be willing adherents of that which he himself had abandoned. Similarly, the true Briton was inclined to scorn the colonist as one who, having failed to measure up at home, had opted out for a crude existence in the wilderness.

Further, there can be no doubt that nearly a hundred years before the Declaration of Independence, British regular forces began to be viewed by Americans as the arm of repressive authority. When in 1677 Colonel Herbert Jeffreys led more than 1,000 British troops into Virginia to restore royal authority after Bacon's Rebellion, he was introducing one soldier for every forty inhabitants, the equivalent of bringing more than 116,000 armed troops into the present state of Virginia. Thereafter in America, redcoats represented authority and a distant authority at that. One notes that in 1689 when the despised Andros regime was toppled by a popular uprising in Boston, the companies of local militia were active participants against the royal forces in the town, showing that their deepest loyalty was to their own people and not the regular military establishment.

After such episodes related to the Glorious Revolution in England, the role of repression tended to be obscured by the more urgent requirements of the colonial wars. Theoretically, this should have meant a harmonious relationship between the British armed forces and the American colonists, for their immediate objectives now seemed to coincide. Instead, the mutual antipathy continued to develop, although along somewhat different lines. Here two major elements can be distinguished—a conflict of attitudes related to differing standards of military behavior and a conflict of material interests. Both, embedded in the matrix of psychological hostility, further poisoned the relations between Britons and Americans.

The aristocratic professional officers from Britain tended to look down upon the provincials as something of an inferior breed— crude, uncultured, undisciplined, and largely untrained in the science of civilized warfare. Their disdain often extended beyond the obviously unprofessional rank and file to include colonial officers, who were amateurs at war and largely self-taught. Even the British private, one suspects, entertained a certain contempt for his provincial counterpart, he of the unkempt locks, the drooping stocking, and the bastard musket. While the professionals prided themselves on the smartness of their appearance, the quality and uniformity of their weapons, and their mastery of complex evolutions, the provincials, unable to achieve such standards, sometimes may even have flaunted a certain casualness of military style that to the regular soldier was simply a mark of inferiority. Quite naturally the provincials, both officers and common soldiers, resented every manifestation of the regulars' contempt.

British commanders attempting to organize military operations during the colonial wars frequently were baffled and disgusted by stubborn noncooperation on the part of colonial legislatures. Usually the legislature's attitude was a manifestation of intercolonial rivalry or an internal power struggle with the royal executive; but an impatient British general was in no position to appreciate these facts of colonial politics when the effect was to deprive him of the resources necessary for an impending expedition. To all this was added the factor of individual reluctance on the part of colonial civilians to risk either body or goods in a dangerous venture, coupled with their obvious eagerness to profit at the expense of remote government. Not only were funds withheld and galling restrictions imposed by stubborn legislatures; the population in general was inclined to hoard goods and services, or else provide them only at inflated prices. Under these conditions, British regulars naturally concluded that noncooperation was being developed by the Americans to the level of a fine art. Occasionally they spoke even of rampant obstructionism. It is a well-known fact that the dire needs of executive and military authorities during the colonial wars served as the stirrup by which the colonial assemblies mounted to the saddle.

Braddock's staggering defeat in 1755 released an idea that American soldiers had been nourishing secretly for many years. This was that Americans, through long experience in fighting both the stealthy Indians and the shrewd French in the wilderness, had developed a special expertise that was neither possessed nor appreciated by the regulars, who supposedly were trained only for open, European-style warfare. This idea led slowly but inexorably to another—that under certain favorable conditions a small force of well-armed and woods-wise colonists could rout a much larger, more ponderous formation of professional soldiers. It was an intriguing proposition, not easily forgotten. When, during the later stages of the last French war and Pontiac's Uprising, the regulars proved that they too could fight in the wilderness with good effect, this idea went underground again only to emerge once more in the 1770s at the very brink of revolution. In the meantime, however, the provincials seemed quite content to let the regulars do all the hard, dirty fighting, especially against Pontiac's Indians. And the redcoats, fighting and dying for the American West, did not easily forget the colonial towns that had sought to deny them comfortable quarters during past winters or the colonial farmers who had concealed horses, wagons, and other necessary supplies lest they be expended in the march to victory.

Long before the explosive developments of the 1770s, then, uncomplimentary and usually exaggerated or distorted images were being established on both sides of the line. Aristocratic regular officers came to think of provincial officers as crude amateurs, incompetent in a demanding profession, ineffective in disciplining and leading their slovenly, unreliable troops. That image was to have importance later as British authorities prepared to cope with rising disobedience in the colonies. Provincial troops tended to view British officers as aristocratic snobs and their men as mere puppets who marched impressively at the word of command but had little feel for the kind of fighting that prevailed in the deep wilderness of North America. That view, too, was to be important as Americans contemplated the prospect of armed resistance to the mother country. Mutual distrust between colonies and mother country, long nourished during the colonial wars, had become rampant. The colonists had come to believe, partly as a result of past experiences with British military personnel, that royal authority was inclined to be overbearing, careless of civil rights, and oblivious to the real interests of America. On both sides of the quarrel, the old exaggerated images and ideas rose again to the fore. It is not difficult to discover in such firmly shaped impressions, born of the colonial wars, living seeds of revolution and separation.

NOTES

1. Alfred L. Burt, *The Old Province of Quebec* (Minneapolis, 1933), pp. 32–56.
2. Good accounts of the Cherokee War, 1759–1761, are found in Robert L. Meriwether, *The Expansion of South Carolina, 1729–1765* (Kingsport, Tenn., 1940), chap. 15, and David H. Corkran, *The Cherokee Frontier: Conflict and Survival, 1740–62* (Norman, Okla., 1962), chaps. 11–18.
3. William L. McDowell, Jr., ed., *Documents Relating to Indian Affairs, 1754–1765* (Colonial Records of South Carolina, Columbia, S.C., 1970), pp. 497–500.
4. Corkran, *Cherokee Frontier,* pp. 250–255.
5. Lee Kennett, *The French Armies in the Seven Years' War: A Study in Military Organization and Administration* (Durham, 1967), pp. 93–94. Toward the end of the war France actually tried to borrow money in England, *sub rosa* of course, at 11.5 percent.
6. William Laird Clowes, *The Royal Navy: A History from the Earliest Times to the Present* (7 vols.; London, 1897–1903), III, 218–222; Walter L. Dorn, *Competition for Empire, 1740–1763* (New York, 1940), pp. 354–357.
7. Dorn, *Competition for Empire,* p. 373; Lawrence H. Gipson, *The Great War for the Empire: The Culmination, 1760–1763* (New York, 1954), pp. 249–250; Jack M. Sosin, *Whitehall and the Wilderness: The Middle West in British Colonial Policy, 1760–1775* (Lincoln, Neb., 1961), pp. 15–16.
8. Jeffery Amherst, *The Journal of Jeffery Amherst, Recording the Military Career of General Amherst in America from 1758 to 1763,* J. Clarence Webster, ed. (Chicago, 1931), p. 280; Stanley Pargellis, ed., *Military Affairs in North America, 1748–1765: Selected Documents from the Cumberland Papers in Windsor Castle* (New York, 1936), pp. 450–455; Julian S. Corbett, *England in the Seven Years' War, A Study in Combined Strategy* (2d ed., 2 vols.; London, 1918), II, 218–225.
9. Richard Pares, *War and Trade in the West Indies, 1739–1763* (New York, 1936), p. 185.
10. Amherst, *Journal,* pp. 288n., 294–295; David Perry, *Recollections of an Old Soldier* (Cottonport, La., 1971), pp. 41–50; Gipson, *The Great War for the Empire: The Culmination, 1760–1763,* pp. 270–273.
11. Clowes, *Royal Navy,* III, 245–249; Gipson, *The Great War for the Empire: The Culmination, 1760–1763,* pp. 260–268.
12. Gipson, *The Great War for the Empire: The Culmination, 1760–1763,* pp. 275–282.
13. On 3 December, a packet bearing the royal proclamation for a cessation of hostilities sailed from England, arriving at New York on 21 January. Three days later the proclamation was officially published there, and before long

the joyous news was known throughout the colonies. (See Amherst, *Journal*, pp. 299–300.)

14. The text of the Treaty of Paris has been published in Charles Jenkinson, comp., *A Collection of All the Treaties of Peace, Alliance, and Commerce, between Great-Britain and Other Powers, from the Treaty Signed at Munster in 1648, to the Treaties Signed at Paris in 1783* (3 vols.; London, 1785), III, 177–202; Sigmund Samuel, comp., *The Seven Years War in Canada, 1756–1763* (Toronto, 1934), pp. 210–226; and Fred L. Israel, ed., *Major Peace Treaties of Modern History, 1648–1967* (4 vols.; New York, 1967), I, 305–328.

15. There is a large body of sources, both primary and secondary, dealing with the hotly disputed question of whether Britain should retain Canada or Guadeloupe. Pitt understood that the former must be retained for the future security of the British North American colonies, and as early as 1761 the ministry had decided that way. (See Sosin, *Whitehall and the Wilderness*, pp. 9–10.)

16. Quoted in Sigmund Diamond, "An Experiment in 'Feudalism': French Canada in the Seventeenth Century," in Paul Goodman, ed., *Essays in American Colonial History* (New York, 1967), p. 93.

17. The Treaty of Paris also provided that territory not specifically mentioned should not change hands as a result of the war. Because the capture of Manila was not known in Paris when the treaty was arranged, no mention of it was made, and so this provision had the effect of restoring the Philippines to Spanish jurisdiction.

18. William Johnson, *The Papers of Sir William Johnson*, James Sullivan and Alexander C. Flick, eds. (13 vols.; Albany, 1921–1962), III, 345.

19. Howard H. Peckham, *Pontiac and the Indian Uprising* (Princeton, 1947), p. 129. The account of the war in this chapter is based largely upon Peckham's excellent work. Parkman's interpretation in his *Conspiracy of Pontiac and the Indian War after the Conquest of Canada*, first published in 1851, is now dated.

20. Amherst, *Journal*, pp. 305–307.

21. Amherst, *Journal*, pp. 316–319; Peckham, *Pontiac and the Indian Uprising*, pp. 212–213; Lawrence H. Gipson, *The Triumphant Empire: New Responsibilities within the Enlarged Empire, 1763–1766* (New York, 1956), pp. 111–112; Niles Anderson, "Bushy Run: Decisive Battle in the Wilderness: Pennsylvania and the Indian Rebellion of 1763," *Western Pennsylvania Historical Magazine*, XLVI (July, 1963), 211–245.

22. Peckham, *Pontiac and the Indian Uprising*, p. 226.

23. Hugh T. Lefler and Albert R. Newsome, *North Carolina: The History of a Southern State* (Rev. ed.; Chapel Hill, 1963), p. 159; M. Eugene Sirmans, *Colonial South Carolina: A Political History, 1663–1763* (Chapel Hill, 1966), p. 345; David H. Corkran, *The Creek Frontier, 1540–1783* (Norman, Okla., 1967), pp. 237–240.

24. Randolph C. Downes, *Council Fires on the Upper Ohio: A Narrative of Indian Affairs in the Upper Ohio Valley until 1795* (Pittsburgh, 1940), p.

121; Gipson, *The Triumphant Empire: New Responsibilities within the Enlarged Empire, 1763–1766*, p. 125.

25. Clarence S. Brigham, ed., *British Royal Proclamations Relating to America, 1603–1783* (Worcester, Mass., 1911), pp. 212–218.

26. George Louis Beer, *British Colonial Policy, 1754–1765* (New York, 1907), chap. 6; Pares, *War and Trade in the West Indies*, pp. 445–446; Max Savelle, *The Origins of American Diplomacy: The International History of Angloamerica, 1492–1763* (New York, 1967), pp. 302–305.

27. Lawrence H. Gipson, *The Coming of the Revolution, 1763–1775* (New York, 1954), pp. 55–56; Merrill Jensen, *The Founding of a Nation: A History of the American Revolution, 1763–1776* (New York, 1968), p. 60.

GLOSSARY OF MILITARY AND NAVAL TERMS

abatis	A defensive barrier consisting of felled trees laid together with sharpened branches pointing toward the enemy.
bandolier	A leather shoulder strap from which hung about a dozen wooden cylinders each containing one charge for a musket. Prevalent in the first half of the seventeenth century, the bandolier later was replaced by the powder flask and shot pouch, which in turn were superseded by the cartridge box.
bar shot	An artillery projectile consisting of a metal bar with a solid half-sphere at each end.
bastion	A strongpoint in the perimeter of a fortress, angled out beyond the main line of walls to permit enfilade fire.
battalion	A body of foot soldiers, subdivided into companies, sometimes identical with a regiment.
battery	A protected position designed as a firing place for one or more pieces of artillery. The term also may include the pieces in such a position.
bayonet	A sharp-pointed stabbing weapon, invented about 1640, designed to be attachable to the muzzle of a musket.
blockhouse	A thick-walled building usually constructed of logs, with loopholes for muskets, designed as a center for defense.
bomb (or *shell*)	An explosive projectile made of cast iron, detonated in flight or after penetrating the target by means of a fuse.
bore	The interior diameter of a gun barrel.
brigade	A military force consisting of two or more regiments.
camp follower	A civilian, often a woman, who accompanies an army and performs various services for the troops.
carbine	A light flintlock musket with a relatively short barrel.
cartridge	A prepared package, cylindrical in shape, containing both the propelling charge and the projectile for a gun.
casemate	In a fortress, an enclosed space or chamber in which cannon may be sited to fire through embrasures.
case shot	An artillery projectile consisting of a cylindrical tin container holding many balls. When fired, the canister burst and the balls continued toward the target in a spreading pattern.
chain shot	An artillery projectile consisting of two iron spheres or half-spheres connected with a short length of chain.

cock	On a flintlock, the metal arm which holds the flint.
company	A unit of infantry, typically consisting of about eighty officers and men under the command of a captain. The British army had some "independent companies" not incorporated in any regiment.
curtain	In a fortification, a length of outer wall connecting two bastions.
cutlass	A cutting sword with a broad, slightly curved blade, sharp along one edge.
ditch	A moat protecting a defensive wall.
enfilade	To fire into a formation of troops from a position approximately on the extension of its principal axis. A projecting bastion permits enfilade fire along the outer face of the adjacent curtain against a line of troops attempting to scale the wall.
ensign	The most junior officer in a company of infantry. Traditionally the ensign carried the colors in battle.
fascine	A bound bundle or fagot of green sticks, approximately 1 foot in diameter and 6 feet in length, used to strengthen earthworks, build up parapets, or fill in a moat.
field piece	A piece of artillery mounted on a wheeled carriage for use in the field.
firelock	A mechanism on a pistol or shoulder gun which when activated creates a spark to detonate the propelling charge.
fireship	A vessel loaded with combustibles, deliberately set afire and sent drifting down upon a group of enemy ships.
flintlock	On a musket or pistol, a firing mechanism which, when activated by the trigger, causes a piece of flint to strike sparks from a steel plate (battery or frizzen).
foot	Foot soldiers, or infantry.
forlorn hope	A body of troops, sometimes volunteers, assigned the mission of leading an attack.
frigate	A type of warship developed in the eighteenth century, mounting from approximately twenty to as many as fifty guns, mostly 6- , 9- , and 12-pounders.
fusil	A type of flintlock musket.
gabion	A very large wattle basket open at both ends. When set upright it could be filled with earth and used to protect guns and troops from enemy fire.
glacis	In a fortified area, the elevated slope just outside the ditch.
grenade	A small, hand-thrown bomb detonated by means of a fuse.
grenadier	A soldier specially trained and equipped for throwing grenades. One company of grenadiers generally was included in every British regiment, and in battle was stationed on one of the flanks. Grenadiers, "the tallest and briskest Fellows" in the

regiment, could be identified by their mitre-style headgear which, lacking a brim, did not interfere with their hurling.

howitzer	A type of artillery that came into British service about 1720. It was a short-barreled, short-range piece, with relatively low muzzle velocity, capable of being fired horizontally but also able to throw an explosive shell along a fairly high trajectory.
mortar	An extremely short-barreled piece of artillery usually mounted on a heavy oaken base, used to hurl shells along a high trajectory and down into fortified positions.
musket	A smooth-bore shoulder gun, after the middle of the seventeenth century usually of the flintlock type.
outwork	A fortified position located outside or in advance of a principal fortification.
palisade	In wooded country, a defensive wall consisting of pointed stakes set upright in the ground. Also known as a *stockade*.
pan	In the firing mechanism of a firelock, the small receptacle into which the priming powder is placed to receive the spark.
parallel	In a siege operation, a trench or system of trenches dug by the besieging army roughly parallel to the enemy's ramparts as a line from which to begin a further advance.
pike	A thrusting weapon consisting of a pointed head of iron or steel mounted on a long wooden pole.
pioneer	A civilian or soldier employed in laboring on roads or fortifications.
press	The system by which governmental authority commandeered men, equipment, and supplies for military or naval service. The process was known as *impressment*.
priming powder	Gunpowder placed in the pan or touch hole of a firearm to receive the spark and ignite the propelling charge in the barrel.
quoin	A wooden wedge inserted beneath the breech of a cannon to control the elevation of the muzzle.
rammer	A long tool used by artillerymen to press the charge firmly down into the barrel. The corresponding implement for the musket was the *ramrod*.
rampart	The principal outer wall of a fortress, usually consisting of a broad, steep-sided embankment.
redoubt	A small fortification.
regiment	A body of soldiers, subdivided into battalions and companies, commanded by a colonel. Sometimes a regiment included only one battalion, so that the two terms often may be used interchangeably, and are so used in this book. The actual size of regiments varied considerably. A typical regiment in the field might number roughly 850 men.

shell (or *bomb*)   An explosive projectile made of cast iron, detonated in flight or after penetrating the target by means of a fuse.

ship of the line   A warship mounting from fifty guns (fourth-rate ship) to as many as 100 guns (first-rate ship), sufficiently powerful to fight in the line of battle.

snaphance   The earliest type of flint-fired gun.

sutler   A civilian storekeeper who accompanies an army and sells liquor, provisions, and other supplies to the troops.

swivel gun   A small cannon designed to be mounted by means of a vertical rod or pivot upon the gunwale of a ship or the top of a parapet, and capable of being traversed by hand.

tomahawk   A type of hatchet used as a weapon.

touch hole   The narrow hole through the breech of a gun by means of which the propelling charge in the barrel was ignited. Also called a *vent*. Cannon could be rendered temporarily useless by driving a spike into the touch hole and cutting it off level with the outer surface of the breech.

troop   A company of mounted soldiers or cavalry.

wad   A packing of straw or other material pressed down upon the charge of powder in a cannon to keep it securely in place until fired. A small patch of cloth sometimes served the same purpose in a musket.

BIBLIOGRAPHY

This bibliography is designed to serve as a helpful guide for beginning research. It should not be considered exhaustive, nor is it an accurate gauge of research completed. While most of the sources listed have been consulted, some have not and are included for their potential utility. If the reader wishes to trace the author's lines of investigation, especially in the use of primary sources, he is referred to the footnotes. Within the major categories or divisions below, bibliographic aids and primary sources generally are grouped ahead of secondary works. The capitalization of words in titles is in accordance with modern usage.

Recommended as guides to collections of documents are *The National Union Catalog of Manuscript Collections;* Henry P. Beers, ed., *The French in North America: A Bibliographical Guide to French Archives, Reproductions, and Research Missions* (Baton Rouge, 1957); Philip M. Hamer, ed., *A Guide to Archives and Manuscripts in the United States* (New Haven, 1961); and the catalogs or guides provided by the repositories themselves. The extensive published records of governments, both European and colonial, are introduced in Oscar Handlin *et al.,* eds., *Harvard Guide to American History* (Cambridge, Mass., 1954). Here and in *The American Historical Association's Guide to Historical Literature* (New York, 1961), also may be found extensive bibliographies of secondary sources. For help in locating personal narratives and other literature specifically relating to the frontier, the student should consult R. W. G. Vail, ed., *The Voice of the Old Frontier* (Philadelphia, 1949). Also useful for the period 1677–1768 is Henry F. DePuy, comp., *A Bibliography of the English Colonial Treaties with the American Indians, Including a Synopsis of Each Treaty* (New York, 1917). The standard guide to early American newspapers is Clarence S. Brigham, comp., *History and Bibliography of American Newspapers, 1690-1820* (2 vols.; Worcester, Mass., 1947). Helpful maps will be found in James T. Adams, ed., *Atlas of American History* (New York, 1943); Vincent J. Esposito, ed., *The West Point Atlas of American Wars* (2 vols.; New York, 1959); and *The American Heritage Pictorial Atlas of United States History* (New York, 1966).

Primary Sources (General)

Brigham, Clarence S., ed. *British Royal Proclamations Relating to America, 1603-1783* (Transactions and Collections of the American Antiquarian Society, XII). Worcester, Mass., 1911.

Colden, Cadwallader. *The Letters and Papers of Cadwallader Colden, 1711–*

1775 (Collections of the New York Historical Society, L–LVI, LXVII–LXVIII). New York, 1918–1937.

Davenport, Frances Gardiner, ed. *European Treaties Bearing on the History of the United States and Its Dependencies* (Carnegie Institution of Washington, Publication No. 254). 4 vols. Washington, D.C., 1917–1937.

Franklin, Benjamin. *The Papers of Benjamin Franklin,* ed. Leonard W. Labaree *et al.* 14 vols. to date. New Haven, 1959 to present.

Hutchinson, Thomas, comp. *Collection of Original Papers Relative to the History of the Colony of Massachusetts Bay.* Boston, 1769. (Reprinted by the Prince Society under the title *Hutchinson Papers.* Albany, 1865.)

Indian Treaties Printed by Benjamin Franklin, 1736–1762. With an Introduction by Carl Van Doren, and Historical and Bibliographical Notes by Julian P. Boyd. Philadelphia, 1938.

Israel, Fred L., ed. *Major Peace Treaties of Modern History, 1648–1967.* 4 vols. New York, 1967.

Johnson, William. *The Papers of Sir William Johnson,* ed. James Sullivan and Alexander C. Flick. 13 vols. Albany, 1921–1962.

Labaree, Leonard Woods, ed. *Royal Instructions to British Colonial Governors, 1670–1776.* 2 vols. New York, 1935.

Laurens, Henry. *The Papers of Henry Laurens,* ed. Philip M. Hamer *et al.* 2 vols. to date. Columbia, S.C., 1968 to present.

O'Callaghan, Edmund B., ed. *The Documentary History of the State of New-York.* 4 vols. Albany, 1849–1851.

O'Callaghan, Edmund B., and Fernow, Berthold, eds. *Documents Relative to the Colonial History of the State of New-York.* 15 vols. Albany, 1856–1887.

Pargellis, Stanley, ed. *Military Affairs in North America, 1748–1765: Selected Documents from the Cumberland Papers in Windsor Castle.* New York, 1936.

Pownall, Thomas. *A Topographical Description of the Dominions of the United States of America,* ed. Lois Mulkearn. Pittsburgh, 1949.

Randolph, Edward. *Edward Randolph; Including His Letters and Official Papers from the New England, Middle, and Southern Colonies in America, with Other Documents Relating Chiefly to the Vacating of the Royal Charter of the Colony of Massachusetts Bay, 1676–1703* (Publications of the Prince Society, XXIV–XXVIII, XXX–XXXI, ed. Robert N. Toppan and Alfred T. S. Goodrick). Boston, 1898–1909.

Sewall, Samuel. Diary [1674–1729] (Collections of the Massachusetts Historical Society, Ser. 5, V–VII). Boston, 1878–1882.

Shirley, William. *Correspondence of William Shirley, Governor of Massachusetts and Military Commander in America, 1731–1760,* ed. Charles H. Lincoln. 2 vols. New York, 1912.

Stevens, Sylvester K., and Kent, Donald H., eds. *Wilderness Chronicles of Northwestern Pennsylvania.* Harrisburg, 1941.

Stock, Leo Francis, ed. *Proceedings and Debates of the British Parliaments Respecting North America* (Carnegie Institution of Washington, Publication No. 338). 5 vols. Washington, 1924–1941.

Washington, George. *The Diaries of George Washington,* ed. John C. Fitzpatrick. 4 vols. Boston and New York, 1925.

——. *The Writings of George Washington, from the Original Manuscript Sources, 1745–1799,* ed. John C. Fitzpatrick. 39 vols. Washington, D.C., 1931–1944.

GENERAL ACCOUNTS

Adams, James Truslow. *Provincial Society, 1690–1763.* New York, 1927.

Alvord, Clarence W. *The Illinois Country, 1673–1818.* Springfield, Ill., 1920.

Andrews, Charles McLean. *Colonial Self-Government, 1652–1689.* New York, 1904.

Belknap, Jeremy. *The History of New-Hampshire.* 3 vols. Boston, 1784–1792.

Beverley, Robert. *The History and Present State of Virginia.* . . . London, 1705. (New edition edited by Louis B. Wright [Chapel Hill, 1947].)

Bolton, H. E., and Ross, Mary. *The Debatable Land.* Berkeley, 1925.

Boorstin, Daniel J. *The Americans: The Colonial Experience.* New York, 1958.

Brebner, John Bartlet. *New England's Outpost: Acadia before the Conquest of Canada.* New York, 1927.

Buck, Solon J., and Buck, Elizabeth H. *The Planting of Civilization in Western Pennsylvania.* Pittsburgh, 1939.

Buffinton, Arthur H. "The Policy of the Northern Colonies towards the French to the Peace of Utrecht." Unpublished Ph.D. dissertation, Harvard University, 1925.

Clark, Andrew Hill. *Acadia: The Geography of Early Nova Scotia to 1760.* Madison, 1968.

Clark, Charles E. *The Eastern Frontier: The Settlement of Northern New England, 1610–1763.* New York, 1970.

Cook, Roy Bird. "Virginia Frontier Defenses, 1719–1795," *West Virginia History,* I (January, 1940), 119–130.

Coolidge, Guy Omeron. *The French Occupation of the Champlain Valley from 1609 to 1759* (Proceedings of the Vermont Historical Society, New Series, VI). Brattleboro, 1938.

Corry, John Pitts. *Indian Affairs in Georgia, 1732–1756.* Philadelphia, 1936.

Crane, Verner W. *The Southern Frontier, 1670–1732.* Durham, 1928.

Craven, Wesley Frank. *The Colonies in Transition, 1660–1713.* New York, 1968.

——. *The Southern Colonies in the Seventeenth Century.* Baton Rouge, 1949.

Crouse, Nellis M. *The French Struggle for the West Indies, 1665–1713.* New York, 1943.

Douglass, William. *A Summary, Historical and Political, of the* . . . *British Settlements in North-America.* 2 vols. Boston, 1749–1751.

Downes, Randolph C. *Council Fires on the Upper Ohio: A Narrative of Indian Affairs in the Upper Ohio Valley until 1795.* Pittsburgh, 1940.

Fiske, John. *New France and New England.* Cambridge, Mass., 1902.

Fox, Dixon Ryan. *Yankees and Yorkers.* New York, 1940.

Gipson, Lawrence H. *The British Empire before the American Revolution.* 15 vols. Caldwell, Idaho, and New York, 1936–1970.

Graham, Gerald S. *Empire of the North Atlantic: The Maritime Struggle for North America.* Toronto, 1950.

Greene, E. B. *Provincial America, 1690–1740.* New York, 1905.

Hamilton, Edward P. *The French and Indian Wars: The Story of Battles and Forts in the Wilderness.* New York, 1962.

Higgins, Ruth L. *Expansion in New York, with Especial Reference to the Eighteenth Century.* Columbus, Ohio, 1931.

Hutchinson, Thomas. *The History of the Colony and Province of Massachusetts-Bay,* ed. Lawrence Shaw Mayo. 3 vols. Cambridge, Mass., 1936.

Jacobs, Wilbur R. *Diplomacy and Indian Gifts: Anglo-French Rivalry along the Ohio and Northwest Frontiers, 1748–1763.* Stanford, 1950.

Johnson, James Guyton. "The Colonial Southeast, 1732–1763; An International Contest for Territorial and Economic Control," *University of Colorado Studies,* XIX, No. 3 (1932), 163–225.

Labaree, Leonard W. *Royal Government in America.* New Haven, 1930.

Leach, Douglas Edward. *The Northern Colonial Frontier, 1607–1763* (Histories of the American Frontier Series). New York, 1966.

McCorison, Marcus A. "Colonial Defence of the Upper Connecticut Valley," *Vermont History,* XXX (January, 1962), 50–62.

MacFarlane, Ronald O. "British Indian Policy in Nova Scotia to 1760," *Canadian Historical Review,* XIX (June, 1938), 154–167.

———. "Indian Relations in New England, 1620–1760: A Study of a Regulated Frontier." Unpublished Ph.D. dissertation, Harvard University, 1933.

Mathews, Lois K. *The Expansion of New England.* Boston, 1909.

Means, Philip Ainsworth. *The Spanish Main, Focus of Envy, 1492–1700.* New York, 1935.

Meriwether, Robert L. *The Expansion of South Carolina, 1729–1765.* Kingsport, Tenn., 1940.

Morgan, William Thomas. "English Fear of 'Encirclement' in the Seventeenth Century," *Canadian Historical Review,* X (March, 1929), 4–22.

Mulkearn, Lois. "The English Eye the French in North America," *Pennsylvania History,* XXI (October, 1954), 316–337.

Nammack, Georgiana C. *Fraud, Politics, and the Dispossession of the Indians: The Iroquois Land Frontier in the Colonial Period.* Norman, Okla., 1969.

Newton, Arthur Percival. *The European Nations in the West Indies, 1493–1688.* London and New York, 1933.

O'Neil, Emmett Francis. "English Fear of French Encirclement in North America, 1680–1763." Unpublished Ph.D. dissertation, University of Michigan, 1941.

Osgood, Herbert L. *The American Colonies in the Eighteenth Century.* 4 vols. New York, 1924–1925.

———. *The American Colonies in the Seventeenth Century.* 3 vols. New York, 1904–1907.

Pares, Richard. "American Versus Continental Warfare, 1739–1763," *English Historical Review,* LI (July, 1936), 429–465. (Also in Richard Pares, *The Historian's Business and Other Essays* [Oxford, 1961], pp. 130–172.)

———. *Colonial Blockade and Neutral Rights, 1739–1763.* Oxford, 1938.

————. *War and Trade in the West Indies, 1739–1763*. New York, 1936.

Parkman, Francis. *France and England in North America.* 9 vols. Boston, 1865–1892.

Peckham, Howard H. *The Colonial Wars, 1689–1762*. Chicago, 1964.

————. "Speculations on the Colonial Wars," *William and Mary Quarterly,* Ser. 3, XVII (October, 1960), 463–472.

Penhallow, Samuel. *The History of the Wars of New-England with the Eastern Indians.* Boston, 1726. (Republished in the Collection of the New Hampshire Historical Society, I [Concord, 1824], 14–133.)

Phillips, Paul Chrisler. *The Fur Trade.* 2 vols. Norman, Okla., 1961.

Pomfret, John E., with Shumway, Floyd M. *Founding the American Colonies, 1583–1660.* New York, 1970.

Raymond, W. O. "Nova Scotia under English Rule . . . 1710–1760" (Transactions of the Royal Society of Canada, Ser. 3, IV [1910], 55–84).

Reese, Trevor Richard. *Colonial Georgia: A Study in British Imperial Policy in the Eighteenth Century.* Athens, Ga., 1963.

Robinson, W. Stitt. "Virginia and the Cherokees: Indian Policy from Spotswood to Dinwiddie," in Darrett B. Rutman, ed., *The Old Dominion: Essays for Thomas Perkins Abernethy* (Charlottesville, Va., 1964), pp. 21–40.

Savelle, Max. "The American Balance of Power and European Diplomacy, 1713–78," in Richard B. Morris, ed., *The Era of the American Revolution: Studies Inscribed to Evarts Boutell Greene* (New York, 1939), pp. 140–169.

————. *The Diplomatic History of the Canadian Boundary, 1749–1763.* New Haven, 1940.

————. *The Origins of American Diplomacy: The International History of Angloamerica, 1492–1763.* New York, 1967.

Sawtelle, William Otis. "Acadia: The Pre-Loyalist Migration and the Philadelphia Plantation," *Pennsylvania Magazine of History and Biography,* LI (1927), 244–285.

Sheehan, Bernard W. "Indian-White Relations in Early America: A Review Essay," *William and Mary Quarterly,* Ser. 3, XXVI (April, 1969), 267–286.

Smith, William. *The History of the Province of New-York, from the First Discovery to the Year 1732.* London, 1757.

Sylvester, Herbert M. *Indian Wars of New England.* 3 vols. Boston, 1910.

Tyler, L. G. *England in America, 1580–1652.* New York, 1904.

Van Alstyne, Richard W. *The American Empire: Its Historical Pattern and Evolution.* [London], 1960.

Webster, J. Clarence. *The Forts of Chignecto; A Study of the Eighteenth Century Conflict between France and Great Britain in Acadia.* St. John, N.B., 1930.

Wertenbaker, Thomas J. *The First Americans, 1607–1690.* New York, 1927.

Williamson, James A. *A Short History of British Expansion.* Third ed., London, 1947.

Winsor, Justin, ed. *A Narrative and Critical History of America.* 8 vols. Boston, 1884–1889.

Wright, J. Leitch. *Anglo-Spanish Rivalry in North America.* Athens, Ga., 1971.

ARMED FORCES AND WARFARE

In the Manuscript Room of the New York Public Library are four volumes of Sir Charles Frederick's record books, containing "records and letters concerning the military establishment and its equipment in Europe and America, 1642–1766." Sir Charles was Surveyor of the Ordnance.

Jameson, John Franklin, ed. *Privateering and Piracy in the Colonial Period: Illustrative Documents.* New York, 1923.

Secondary Sources

Albion, Robert G. *Forests and Sea Power: The Timber Problem of the Royal Navy, 1652–1862* (Harvard Economic Studies, XXIX). Cambridge, Mass., 1926.

————. *Introduction to Military History.* New York, 1929.

Archibald, E. H. H. *The Wooden Fighting Ship in the Royal Navy, AD 897–1860.* London, 1968.

Baugh, Daniel A. *British Naval Administration in the Age of Walpole.* Princeton, 1965.

Chapin, Howard Millar. *Privateer Ships and Sailors: The First Century of American Colonial Privateering, 1625–1725.* Toulon, France, 1926.

Clark, Dora Mae. "The Impressment of Seamen in the American Colonies," in *Essays in Colonial History Presented to Charles McLean Andrews by His Students* (New Haven, 1931), pp. 198–224.

Clowes, William Laird. *The Royal Navy: A History from the Earliest Times to the Present.* 7 vols. London, 1897–1903.

Cruickshank, C. G. *Elizabeth's Army.* London, 1946.

De Watteville, Herman G. *The British Soldier: His Daily Life from Tudor to Modern Times.* London, 1954.

Earle, Edward Mead. *Makers of Modern Strategy: Military Thought from Machiavelli to Hitler.* Princeton, 1944.

Falls, Cyril, ed. *Great Military Battles.* New York, 1964.

Firth, Charles Harding. *Cromwell's Army: A History of the English Soldier during the Civil Wars, the Commonwealth and the Protectorate.* Third ed. Reprinted, London and New York, 1962.

Fortescue, John W. *A History of the British Army.* 13 vols. and 6 atlases. London, 1889–1930.

Graham, Gerald S. "The Naval Defence of British North America, 1739–1763," in Transactions of the Royal Historical Society, Ser. 4, XXX (1948), 95–110.

Grose, Francis. *Military Antiquities Respecting a History of the English Army, from the Conquest to the Present Time.* 2 vols. London, 1786–1788.

Hall, A. R. *Ballistics in the Seventeenth Century: A Study in the Relations of Science and War with Reference Principally to England.* Cambridge, 1952.

Hamilton, Edward Pierce. "Colonial Warfare in North America," in Proceedings of the Massachusetts Historical Society, LXXX (1969), 3–15.

Hayward, John F. *The Art of the Gunmaker.* Vol. II: *Europe and America, 1660–1830.* New York, 1963.

Hughes, B. P. *British Smooth-Bore Artillery: The Muzzle Loading Artillery of the 18th and 19th Centuries.* Harrisburg, 1969.

Irvine, Dallas. "The First British Regulars in North America," *Military Affairs,* IX (Winter, 1945), 337–354.

Ivers, Larry E. *Colonial Forts of South Carolina, 1670–1775.* Columbia, S.C., 1970.

Kennett, Lee. *The French Armies in the Seven Years' War: A Study in Military Organization and Administration.* Durham, 1967.

Lawson, Cecil C. P. *A History of the Uniforms of the British Army.* 2 vols. London, 1940–1941.

Lewis, Michael. *The Navy of Britain, a Historical Portrait.* London, 1948.

Mahan, Alfred T. *The Influence of Sea Power upon History, 1660–1783.* Boston, 1890.

Mahon, John K. "Anglo-American Methods of Indian Warfare, 1676–1794," *Mississippi Valley Historical Review,* XLV (September, 1958), 254–275.

Manucy, Albert. *Artillery through the Ages: A Short Illustrated History of Cannon, Emphasizing Types Used in America.* (National Park Service Interpretive Series, History No. 3). Washington, D.C., 1949.

Montross, Lynn. *War through the Ages.* Revised and enlarged ed., New York and London, 1946.

Pargellis, Stanley. "The Four Independent Companies of New York," in *Essays in Colonial History Presented to Charles McLean Andrews by His Students* (New Haven, 1931), pp. 96–123.

Peterson, Harold L. *Round Shot and Rammers.* Harrisburg, 1969.

Richmond, Herbert. *The Navy as an Instrument of Policy, 1558–1727,* ed. E. A. Hughes. Cambridge and New York, 1953.

Robson, Eric. "British Light Infantry in the Mid-Eighteenth Century: The Effect of American Conditions," *Army Quarterly,* LXIII (January, 1952), 209–222.

Russell, Carl P. *Guns on the Early Frontiers: A History of Firearms from Colonial Times through the Years of the Western Fur Trade.* Berkeley, 1957.

Sawyer, Charles W. *Firearms in American History.* 3 vols. Boston, 1910–1920.

Scouller, R. E. *The Armies of Queen Anne.* Oxford, 1966.

Western, J. R. "Professionalism in Armies, Navies and Diplomacy," in Alfred Cobban, ed., *The Eighteenth Century: Europe in the Age of Enlightenment* (New York, 1969), pp. 181–216.

Wintringham, Thomas H. *The Story of Weapons and Tactics from Troy to Stalingrad.* Boston, 1943.

MILITARY BOOKS AND MANUALS

Cockle, Maurice J. D. *A Bibliography of Military Books up to 1642.* London, 1900. (Reprinted in 1957.)

Stanley, John Henry. "Preliminary Investigation of Military Manuals of Amer-

ican Imprint Prior to 1800." Unpublished M.A. thesis, Brown University, 1964.
Webb, Henry J. *Elizabethan Military Science: The Books and the Practice.* Madison, 1965.

Primary Sources

Barret, Robert. *The Theorike and Practike of Moderne Warres, Discoursed in Dialogue Wise.* London, 1598.
Barriffe, William. *Military Discipline: or The Young Artillery-Man.* Third ed., London, 1643.
[Blakeney, William]. *The New Manual Exercise.* Philadelphia, 1746.
Bland, Humphrey. *An Abstract of Military Discipline; More Particularly with Regard to the Manual Exercise, Evolutions, and Firings of the Foot, from Col. Bland.* Boston, 1743.
————. *A Treatise of Military Discipline.* Second ed., London, 1727.
[Boone, Nicholas]. *Military Discipline. The Compleat Souldier, or Expert Artillery-Man.* Boston, 1701.
[————]. *Military Discipline. The Newest Way and Method of Exercising Horse & Foot.* Boston, 1718. [A reduced version of the editions of 1701 and 1706.]
Brattle, William. *Sundry Rules and Directions for Drawing up a Regiment. . . . for the Use and Benefit of the First Regiment in the County of Middlesex.* Boston, 1733.
[Breton, William]. *Militia Discipline. The Words of Command, and Directions for Exercising the Musket, Bayonet, & Carthridge.* Boston, 1733.
Elton, Richard. *The Compleat Body of the Art Military.* London, 1650.
The Gentleman's Compleat Military Dictionary. Containing The Military Art; Explaining the Terms and Phrases Us'd in the Field or Garrison. Eighteenth ed., Boston, 1759.
Hexham, Henry. *The Principles of the Art Militarie.* London, 1637.
The New Exercise of Firelocks and Bayonets: With Instructions How to Perform Every Motion by Body, Foot and Hand; Together with the Number of Operations in Performing the Several Words of Command. New London, 1717.
[Scott, James Fitzroy] (Duke of Monmouth). *An Abridgment of the English Military Discipline.* Boston, 1690.
Smythe, Sir John. *Certain Discourses.* London, 1590. (New edition edited by J. R. Hale, Ithaca, 1964.)
Webb, Thomas. *A Military Treatise on the Appointments of the Army . . . Proposing Some New Regulations in the Army, Which Will Be Particularly Useful in Carrying on the War in North-America. . . .* Philadelphia, 1759.

MILITIA (ENGLISH AND AMERICAN)

Marshall, John. Diary, 1689–1711. Massachusetts Historical Society.
Peabody, Oliver. *An Essay to Revive and Encourage Military Exercises, Skills and Valour among the Sons. . . .* Boston, 1732.

True, Capt. Henry. Memorandum and Account Book, 1696–1719. New York Public Library.

Secondary Sources

Barnes, Thomas Garden. *Somerset 1625–1640: A County's Government during the "Personal Rule."* Cambridge, Mass., 1961.

Boynton, Lindsay. *The Elizabethan Militia, 1558–1638.* Toronto, 1967.

Bruce, Philip Alexander. *Institutional History of Virginia in the Seventeenth Century*, II. New York and London, 1910.

Cole, David. "A Brief Outline of the South Carolina Colonial Militia System," in Proceedings of the South Carolina Historical Association, 1954 (Columbia, S.C., 1955), pp. 14–23.

——. "The Organization and Administration of the South Carolina Militia System, 1670–1783." Unpublished Ph.D. dissertation, University of South Carolina, 1953.

French, Allen. "The Arms and Military Training of Our Colonizing Ancestors," in Proceedings of the Massachusetts Historical Society, LXVII (1945), 3–21.

Kenny, Robert W. "The Beginnings of the Rhode Island Train Bands," *Rhode Island Historical Society Collections*, XXXIII (April, 1940), 25–38.

Leach, Douglas Edward. "The Military System of Plymouth Colony," *New England Quarterly*, XXIV (September, 1951), 342–364.

Mook, H. Telfer. "Training Day in New England," *New England Quarterly*, XI (December, 1938), 675–697.

Morton, Louis. "The Origins of American Military Policy," *Military Affairs*, XXII (Summer, 1958), 75–82. (Reprinted in Raymond G. O'Connor, ed., *American Defense Policy in Perspective: From Colonial Times to the Present* [New York, 1965], pp. 9–15.)

Peterson, Harold L. *Arms and Armor in Colonial America, 1526–1783.* New York, 1956.

——. "The Military Equipment of the Plymouth and Bay Colonies, 1620–1690," *New England Quarterly*, XX (June, 1947), 197–208.

Powicke, Michael. *Military Obligation in Medieval England: A Study in Liberty and Duty.* New York, 1962.

Quarles, Benjamin. "The Colonial Militia and Negro Manpower," *Mississippi Valley Historical Review*, XLV (March, 1959), 643–652.

Radabaugh, Jack S. "The Militia of Colonial Massachusetts," *Military Affairs*, XVIII (Spring, 1954), 1–18.

Rutman, Darrett B. "The Virginia Company and Its Military Regime," in Darrett B. Rutman, ed., *The Old Dominion: Essays for Thomas Perkins Abernethy* (Charlottesville, Va., 1964), pp. 1–20.

Scisco, Louis Dow. "Evolution of Colonial Militia in Maryland," *Maryland Historical Magazine*, XXXV (June, 1940), 166–177.

Sharp, Morrison. "Leadership and Democracy in the Early New England System of Defense," *American Historical Review*, L (January, 1945), 224–260.

——. "The New England Trainbands in the Seventeenth Century." Unpublished Ph.D. dissertation, Harvard University, 1938.

Shy, John W. "A New Look at Colonial Militia," *William and Mary Quarterly,*
    Ser. 3, XX (April, 1963), 175–185.
Thomson, Gladys Scott. *Lords Lieutenants in the Sixteenth Century: A Study
    in Tudor Local Administration.* London, 1923.
United States, Selective Service System. *Backgrounds of Selective Service.* Wash-
    ington, 1947. (Includes a compilation of pertinent legislation from all of
    the thirteen colonies.)
Weigley, Russell F. *History of the United States Army* (Wars of the United
    States Series). New York, 1967.
Wheeler, E. Milton. "Development and Organization of the North Carolina
    Militia," *North Carolina Historical Review,* XLI (July, 1964), 307–323.

                                            INDIANS

Dockstader, Frederick J., comp. *The American Indian in Graduate Studies:
    A Bibliography of Theses and Dissertations* (Contributions from the
    Museum of the American Indian Heye Foundation, XV). New York, 1957.

                                    Primary Sources

Colden, Cadwallader. *The History of the Five Indian Nations Depending on
    the Province of New-York in America.* New York, 1727, 1747. (Repub-
    lished, Ithaca, 1958.)
Leder, Lawrence H., ed. *The Livingston Indian Records, 1666–1723.* Gettys-
    burg, Pa., 1956.
McDowell, William L., Jr., ed. *Colonial Records of South Carolina: Documents
    Relating to Indian Affairs, May 21, 1750–August 7, 1754.* Columbia, S.C.,
    1958; *Documents Relating to Indian Affairs, 1754–1765.* Columbia, S.C.,
    1970.
[Thomson, Charles]. *An Enquiry into the Causes of the Alienation of the
    Delaware and Shawanese Indians from the British Interest.* London, 1759.
Washburn, Wilcomb E., ed. *The Indian and the White Man.* New York, 1964.
Wraxall, Peter. *An Abridgment of the Indian Affairs . . . of New York, From
    the Year 1678 to the Year 1751,* ed. Charles H. McIlwain (Harvard His-
    torical Studies, XXI). Cambridge, Mass., 1915.

                                   Secondary Sources

Brown, Douglas (Summers). *The Catawba Indians: The People of the River.*
    Columbia, S.C., 1966.
Corkran, David H. *The Cherokee Frontier: Conflict and Survival, 1740–62.*
    Norman, Okla., 1962.
———. *The Creek Frontier, 1540–1783.* Norman, Okla., 1967.
Hadlock, Wendell Stanwood. "War among the Northeastern Woodland In-
    dians," *American Anthropologist,* XLIX (April–June, 1947), 204–221.
Hunt, George T. *The Wars of the Iroquois: A Study in Intertribal Trade
    Relations.* Madison, 1940.
Jacobs, Wilbur R. "British-Colonial Attitudes and Policies toward the Indian
    in the American Colonies," in Howard Peckham and Charles Gibson, eds.,

Attitudes of Colonial Powers toward the American Indian (Salt Lake City, 1969), pp. 81–106.

Lydekker, John W. *The Faithful Mohawks*. New York, 1938.

[Pargellis, Stanley]. "The Problem of American Indian History," *Newberry Library Bulletin*, IV (March, 1957), 129–138.

Phelps, Dawson A. "The Chickasaw, the English, and the French, 1699–1744," *Tennessee Historical Quarterly*, XVI (June, 1957), 117–133.

Smoyer, Stanley C. "Indians as Allies in the Intercolonial Wars," *New York History*, XVII (October, 1936), 411–422.

[Snyderman, George S.] "Behind the Tree of Peace: A Sociological Analysis of Iroquois Warfare," *Pennsylvania Archaeologist*, XVIII (1948), 2–93.

Trelease, Allen W. *Indian Affairs in Colonial New York: The Seventeenth Century*. Ithaca, 1960.

———. "The Iroquois and the Western Fur Trade: A Problem in Interpretation," *Mississippi Valley Historical Review*, XLIX (June, 1962), 32–51.

SPANISH, FRENCH, AND DUTCH COLONIES

Arnade, Charles W. "The Failure of Spanish Florida," *The Americas*, XVI (January, 1960), 271–281.

Chatelain, Verne E. *The Defenses of Spanish Florida, 1565 to 1763* (Carnegie Institution of Washington, Publication No. 511). Washington, D.C., 1941.

Diamond, Sigmund. "An Experiment in 'Feudalism': French Canada in the Seventeenth Century," in Paul Goodman, ed., *Essays in American Colonial History* (New York, 1967), pp. 68–94.

Eccles, W. J. *Canada Under Louis XIV, 1663–1701* (Canadian Centenary Series, III). New York, 1964.

———. *The Canadian Frontier, 1534–1760* (Histories of the American Frontier Series). New York, 1969.

———. "Frontenac and the Iroquois, 1672–1682," *Canadian Historical Review*, XXXVI (March, 1955), 1–16.

———. "The Social, Economic, and Political Significance of the Military Establishment in New France," *Canadian Historical Review*, LII (March, 1971), 1–22.

Folmer, Henry. *Franco-Spanish Rivalry in North America, 1524–1763*. Glendale, Calif., 1953.

Gallardo, José Miguel. "The Spaniards and the English Settlement in Charles Town," *South Carolina Historical and Genealogical Magazine*, XXXVII (April, July, October, 1936), 49–64, 91–99, 131–141.

Goldstein, Robert A. *French-Iroquois Diplomatic and Military Relations, 1609–1701*. The Hague, 1969.

Haring, C. H. *The Spanish Empire in America*. New York, 1947.

Harman, Joyce Elizabeth. *Trade and Privateering in Spanish Florida, 1732–1763*. St. Augustine, Fla., 1969.

Johnson, Amandus. *The Swedes on the Delaware, 1638–1664*. Philadelphia, 1915.

Kellogg, Louise P. "France and the Mississippi Valley: A Résumé," *Mississippi Valley Historical Review*, XVIII (June, 1931), 3–22.

————. *The French Régime in Wisconsin and the Northwest*. Madison, 1925.

Lanctot, Gustave. *A History of Canada. Volume One: From Its Origins to the Royal Régime, 1663*. Cambridge, Mass., 1963; *Volume Two: From the Royal Régime to the Treaty of Utrecht, 1663–1713*. Cambridge, Mass., 1964; *Volume III: From the Treaty of Utrecht to the Treaty of Paris, 1713–1763*. Cambridge, Mass., 1965.

Lunn, Jean Elizabeth. "Agriculture and War in Canada, 1740–1760," *Canadian Historical Review*, XVI (June, 1935), 123–136.

McDermott, John Francis, ed. *The French in the Mississippi Valley*. Urbana, Ill., 1965.

McLennan, J. S. *Louisbourg from Its Foundation to Its Fall*. London, 1918.

O'Neill, Charles Edwards. *Church and State in French Colonial Louisiana: Policy and Politics to 1732*. New Haven, 1966.

Parkman, Francis. *La Salle and the Discovery of the Great West*. Twelfth ed., Boston, 1893.

————. *The Old Régime in Canada*. Twenty-ninth ed., Boston, 1893.

Parkman, Dr. Francis. "French Policy in the Lower Mississippi Valley, 1697–1712," in *Publications of the Colonial Society of Massachusetts*, XXVIII (Boston, 1935), 225–238.

Preston, Richard A., and Lamontagne, Leopold, eds. *Royal Fort Frontenac*. Toronto, 1958.

Priestley, Herbert I. *The Coming of the White Man, 1492–1848*. New York, 1929.

————. *France Overseas through the Old Régime*. New York, 1939.

Raesly, Ellis Lawrence. *Portrait of New Netherland*. New York, 1945.

Robinson, Percy J. *Toronto during the French Régime: A History of the Toronto Region from Brûlé to Simcoe, 1615–1793*. Toronto, 1965.

Stanley, George F. G. *Canada's Soldiers, 1604–1954: The Military History of an Unmilitary People*. Toronto, 1954.

TePaske, John Jay. *The Governorship of Spanish Florida, 1700–1763*. Durham, 1964.

Thomas, Daniel H. "Fort Toulouse—in Tradition and Fact," *Alabama Review*, XIII (October, 1960), 243–257.

————. "Fort Toulouse: The French Outpost at the Alibamos on the Coosa," *Alabama Historical Quarterly*, XXII (Fall, 1960), 135–230.

Ward, Christopher. *The Dutch & Swedes on the Delaware, 1609–64*. Philadelphia, 1930.

————. *New Sweden on the Delaware*. Philadelphia, 1938.

Wrong, G. M. *The Rise and Fall of New France*. 2 vols. New York, 1928.

BIOGRAPHICAL STUDIES

Johnson, Allen, and Malone, Dumas, eds. *Dictionary of American Biography*. 22 vols. New York, 1928–1944.

Stephen, Leslie, and Lee, Sidney, eds. *Dictionary of National Biography*. Revised ed., 22 vols. London and New York, 1908–1909.

Secondary Sources

Alberts, Robert C. *The Most Extraordinary Adventures of Major Robert Stobo.* Boston, 1965.

Alden, John Richard. *General Gage in America.* Baton Rouge, 1948.

------. *John Stuart and the Southern Colonial Frontier: A Study of Indian Relations, War, Trade, and Land Problems in the Southern Wilderness, 1754–1775.* Ann Arbor, 1944.

Ambler, Charles H. *George Washington and the West.* Chapel Hill, 1936.

Clarke, Desmond. *Arthur Dobbs, Esquire, 1689–1765, Surveyor-General of Ireland, Prospector and Governor of North Carolina.* Chapel Hill, 1957.

Cleland, Hugh. *George Washington in the Ohio Valley.* Pittsburgh, 1955.

Cognets, Louis des, Jr. *Amherst and Canada.* Princeton, 1962.

Crouse, Nellis M. *Lemoyne d'Iberville: Soldier of New France.* Ithaca, 1954.

Cuneo, John R. *Robert Rogers of the Rangers.* New York, 1959.

Dodson, Leonidas. *Alexander Spotswood, Governor of Colonial Virginia, 1710–1722.* Philadelphia, 1932.

Eccles, W. J. *Frontenac: The Courtier Governor.* Toronto, 1959.

Ettinger, Amos A. *James Edward Oglethorpe, Imperial Idealist.* Oxford and New York, 1936.

Fairchild, Byron. *Messrs. William Pepperrell: Merchants at Piscataqua.* Ithaca, 1954.

Flexner, James T. *George Washington: The Forge of Experience (1732–1775).* Boston, 1965.

------. *Mohawk Baronet: Sir William Johnson of New York.* New York, 1959.

Freeman, Douglas Southall. *George Washington, A Biography.* 7 vols. New York, 1948–1957.

Graeff, Arthur D. *Conrad Weiser, Pennsylvania Peacemaker.* Fogelsville, Pa., 1945.

Hall, Michael Garibaldi. *Edward Randolph and the American Colonies, 1676–1703.* Chapel Hill, 1960.

Hanna, William S. *Benjamin Franklin and Pennsylvania Politics.* Stanford, 1964.

Kennedy, John H. *Thomas Dongan, Governor of New York (1682–1688).* Washington, D.C., 1930.

Kessler, Henry H., and Rachlis, Eugene. *Peter Stuyvesant and His New York.* New York, 1959.

Knollenberg, Bernhard. *George Washington: The Virginia Period, 1732–1775.* Durham, 1964.

Koontz, Louis K. *Robert Dinwiddie: His Career in American Colonial Government and Westward Expansion.* Glendale, Calif., 1941.

Leder, Lawrence H. *Robert Livingston, 1654–1728, and the Politics of Colonial New York.* Chapel Hill, 1961.

Long, John C. *Lord Jeffery Amherst, a Soldier of the King.* New York, 1933.

------. *Mr. Pitt and America's Birthright: A Biography of William Pitt the Earl of Chatham, 1708–1778.* New York, 1940.

Lounsberry, Alice. *William Phips.* New York, 1941.

McCardell, Lee. *Ill-Starred General: Braddock of the Coldstream Guards.* Pittsburgh, 1958.
Mather, Cotton. *The Life of Sir William Phips,* ed. Mark Van Doren. New York, 1929.
Nixon, Lily L. *James Burd, Frontier Defender.* Philadelphia, 1941.
Nolan, J. Bennett. *General Benjamin Franklin: The Military Career of a Philosopher.* Philadelphia, 1936.
Pargellis, Stanley McCrory. *Lord Loudoun in North America, 1756–1758.* New Haven, 1933.
Parkman, Francis. *Count Frontenac and New France under Louis XIV.* Boston, 1877.
Pound, Arthur, in collaboration with Day, R. E. *Johnson of the Mohawks: A Biography of Sir William Johnson, Irish Immigrant, Mohawk War Chief, American Soldier, Empire Builder.* New York, 1930.
Schutz, John A. *Thomas Pownall, British Defender of American Liberty: A Study of Anglo-American Relations in the Eighteenth Century.* Glendale, Calif., 1951.
————. *William Shirley: King's Governor of Massachusetts.* Chapel Hill, 1961.
Sherman, Richard P. *Robert Johnson: Proprietary & Royal Governor of South Carolina.* Columbia, S.C., 1966.
Slick, Sewell E. *William Trent and the West.* Harrisburg, 1947.
Thayer, Theodore. *Israel Pemberton, King of the Quakers.* Philadelphia, 1943.
Van Doren, Carl C. *Benjamin Franklin.* New York, 1938.
Volwiler, Albert T. *George Croghan and the Westward Movement, 1741–1782.* Cleveland, 1926.
Wainwright, Nicholas B. *George Croghan: Wilderness Diplomat.* Chapel Hill, 1959.
Wallace, Anthony F. C. *King of the Delawares: Teedyuscung, 1700–1763.* Philadelphia, 1949.
Wallace, Paul A. W. *Conrad Weiser, 1696–1760: Friend of Colonist and Mohawk.* Philadelphia, 1945.
Waller, G. M. *Samuel Vetch: Colonial Enterpriser.* Chapel Hill, 1960.
Waugh, W. T. *James Wolfe, Man and Soldier.* Montreal and New York, 1928.
Whitton, F. E. *Wolfe and North America.* Boston, 1929.
Willson, Beckles. *The Life and Letters of James Wolfe.* London, 1909.

WARS PRIOR TO 1675

Bradford, William. *Of Plymouth Plantation, 1620–1647,* ed. Samuel Eliot Morison. New York, 1952.
Jameson, J. Franklin, ed. *Narratives of New Netherland, 1609–1664.* New York, 1909.
[Johnson, Edward]. *Johnson's Wonder-Working Providence, 1628–1651,* ed. J. Franklin Jameson. New York, 1910.
Kregier, Martin. Journal of the Esopus War, in E. B. O'Callaghan and B. Fernow, eds., *Documents Relative to the Colonial History of the State of New York* (15 vols.; Albany, 1856–1887), XIII, 323–354.

Mather, Increase. *Early History of New England* . . . , ed. Samuel G. Drake. Boston, 1864.

Morton, Nathaniel. *New Englands Memoriall.* Cambridge, Mass., 1669. (Facsimile edition, ed. Howard J. Hall, New York, 1937.)

Orr, Charles, ed. *History of the Pequot War.* Cleveland, 1897. (Contains the accounts by Lion Gardiner, John Mason, John Underhill, and Philip Vincent.)

A Perfect Description of Virginia. London, 1649. (Reprinted in the Collections of the Massachusetts Historical Society, Ser. 2, IX [Boston, 1832], 105–122.)

Smith, John. *The Generall Historie of Virginia, New-England, and the Summer Isles.* . . . London, 1624.

Stith, William. *The History of the First Discovery and Settlement of Virginia.* . . . Williamsburg, Va., 1747.

Winthrop, John. *Winthrop's Journal "History of New England," 1630–1649,* ed. J. K. Hosmer. 2 vols. New York, 1908.

Secondary Sources

Bradstreet, Howard. *The Story of the War with the Pequots, Re-Told.* New Haven, 1933.

Bushnell, David. "The Treatment of the Indians in Plymouth Colony," *New England Quarterly,* XXVI (June, 1953), 193–218.

Craven, Wesley Frank. "Indian Policy in Early Virginia," *William and Mary Quarterly,* Ser. 3, I (January, 1944), 65–82.

Eisinger, Chester E. "The Puritans' Justification for Taking the Land," *Essex Institute Historical Collections,* LXXXIV (April, 1948), 131–143.

Powell, William S. "Aftermath of the Massacre: The First Indian War, 1622–1632," *Virginia Magazine of History and Biography,* LXVI (January, 1958), 44–75.

Vaughan, Alden T. *New England Frontier: Puritans and Indians, 1620–1675.* Boston, 1965.

———. "Pequots and Puritans: The Causes of the War of 1637," *William and Mary Quarterly,* Ser. 3, XXI (April, 1964), 256–269.

Ward, Harry M. *The United Colonies of New England—1643–90.* New York, 1961.

WARS, 1675–1688

A Brief and True Narration of the Late Wars Risen in New-England. London, 1675.

Church, Thomas. *The History of King Philip's War,* ed. Henry Martyn Dexter. Boston, 1865.

"A Discription of the Fight between the English and the Indians, in May 1676," *William and Mary College Quarterly Historical Magazine,* IX (July, 1900), 1–4.

A Farther Brief and True Narration of the Late Wars Risen in New-England. . . . London, 1676.

Harris, William. Letter to Sir Joseph Williamson, 12 August 1676, in Collections of the Rhode Island Historical Society, X (Providence, 1902), 162–179.

———. *A Rhode Islander Reports on King Philip's War: The Second William Harris Letter of August, 1676,* ed. Douglas Edward Leach. Providence, 1963.

"The History of Bacon's and Ingram's Rebellion, 1676," in C. M. Andrews, ed., *Narratives of the Insurrections, 1675–1690* (New York, 1915), pp. 47–98.

Hubbard, William. *The History of the Indian Wars in New England from the First Settlement to the Termination of the War with King Philip, in 1677,* ed. Samuel G. Drake. Roxbury, Mass., 1865.

Lincoln, Charles H., ed. *Narratives of the Indian Wars, 1675–1699.* New York, 1913. (Includes "A Relacion of the Indyan Warre," "The Present State of New England," "A Continuation of the State of New England," "A New and Further Narrative of the State of New England," and "The Warr in New England Visibly Ended.")

Mather, Increase. *The History of King Philip's War, By the Rev. Increase Mather, D. D. Also, A History of the Same War, By the Rev. Cotton Mather, D. D.,* ed. Samuel G. Drake. Boston, 1862.

Mathew, Thomas. "The Beginning, Progress, and Conclusion of Bacon's Rebellion, 1675–1676," in C. M. Andrews, ed., *Narratives of the Insurrections, 1675–1690* (New York, 1915), pp. 15–41.

News from New-England, Being a True and Last Account of the Present Bloody Wars. London, 1676.

A True Account of the Most Considerable Occurrences That Have Hapned in the Warre between the English and the Indians in New-England. . . . London, 1676.

"A True Narrative of the Rise, Progresse, and Cessation of the Late Rebellion in Virginia . . . ," in C. M. Andrews, ed., *Narratives of the Insurrections, 1675–1690* (New York, 1915), pp. 105–141.

[Wharton, Edward]. *New-England's Present Sufferings, under Their Cruel Neighbouring Indians.* London, 1675.

Wheeler, Thomas. *A Thankefull Remembrance of Gods Mercy to Several Persons at Quabaug or Brookfield.* Cambridge, Mass., 1676.

Secondary Sources

Bodge, George M. *Soldiers in King Philip's War.* Third ed., Boston, 1906.

Ellis, G. W., and Morris, J. E. *King Philip's War.* New York, 1906.

Leach, Douglas Edward. "Benjamin Batten and the *London Gazette* Report on King Philip's War," *New England Quarterly,* XXXVI (December, 1963), 502–517.

———. *Flintlock and Tomahawk: New England in King Philip's War.* New York, 1958.

———. "A New View of the Declaration of War against the Narragansetts, November, 1675," *Rhode Island History,* XV (April, 1956), 33–41.

———. "The Question of French Involvement in King Philip's War," in Publications of the Colonial Society of Massachusetts, XXXVIII (1959), 414–421.

———. "The 'Whens' of Mary Rowlandson's Captivity," *New England Quarterly*, XXXIV (September, 1961), 352–363.

Washburn, Wilcomb E. "Governor Berkeley and King Philip's War," *New England Quarterly*, XXX (September, 1957), 363–377.

———. *The Governor and the Rebel: A History of Bacon's Rebellion in Virginia*. Chapel Hill, 1957.

Wertenbaker, Thomas Jefferson. *Torchbearer of the Revolution: The Story of Bacon's Rebellion and Its Leader*. Princeton, 1940.

KING WILLIAM'S WAR, 1689–1697

Church, Thomas. *The History of the Eastern Expeditions of 1689, 1690, 1692, 1696, and 1704 against the Indians and French*, ed. Henry Martyn Dexter. Boston, 1867.

Davis, Sylvanus. "The Declaration of Sylvanus Davis," in Collections of the Massachusetts Historical Society, Ser. 3, I (1825), 101–112.

Fitzhugh, William. *William Fitzhugh and His Chesapeake World, 1676–1701: The Fitzhugh Letters and Other Documents*, ed. R. B. Davis. Chapel Hill, 1963.

Hall, Michael G., Leder, L. H., and Kammen, M. G., eds. *The Glorious Revolution in America: Documents on the Colonial Crisis of 1689*. Chapel Hill, 1964.

A Journal of the Proceedings in the Late Expedition To Port-Royal. Boston, 1690.

[Mather, Cotton]. *Decennium Luctuosum: An History of Remarkable Occurrences in the Long War, Which New-England Hath Had with the Indian Salvages . . .* , in Charles H. Lincoln, ed., *Narratives of the Indian Wars, 1675–1699* (New York, 1913), pp. 179–300.

———. Diary (Collections of the Massachusetts Historical Society, Ser. 7, VII, VIII). Boston, 1911–1912.

———. *The Present State of New-England. Considered in a Discourse on the Necessities and Advantages of a Public Spirit in Every Man*. Boston, 1690.

———. *The Short History of New-England*. Boston, 1694.

A Narrative of an Attempt Made by the French of Canada upon the Mahaques Country Being Indians under the Protection of Their Majesties Government of New-York. [New York], 1693.

Savage, Thomas. *An Account of the Late Action of the New-Englanders, under the Command of Sir William Phips, against the French at Canada*. London, 1691.

Walley, John. "Major Walley's Journal in the Expedition against Canada in 1690," in Thomas Hutchinson, *The History of the Colony and Province of Massachusetts-Bay*, ed. Lawrence Shaw Mayo (3 vols.; Cambridge, Mass., 1936), I, 459–467.

Secondary Sources

Barnes, Viola F. *The Dominion of New England: A Study in British Colonial Policy*. New Haven, 1923.

Bennett, C. E. "The Burning of Schenectady," *New York History,* XIII (October, 1932), 413–419.

Biggar, H. P. "Frontenac's Projected Attempt on New York in 1689," *New York Historical Association Quarterly Journal,* V (April, 1924), 139–147.

Broshar, Helen. "The First Push Westward of the Albany Traders," *Mississippi Valley Historical Review,* VII (December, 1920), 228–241.

Burnette, Rand. "The Quest for Union in the American Colonies, 1689–1701." Unpublished Ph.D. dissertation, Indiana University, 1967.

Eccles, W. J. "Frontenac's Military Policies, 1689–1698: A Reassessment," *Canadian Historical Review,* XXXVII (September, 1956), 201–224.

Ehrman, John. *The Navy in the War of William III, 1689–1697: Its State and Direction.* Cambridge, 1953.

Leamon, James S. "Governor Fletcher's Recall," *William and Mary Quarterly,* Ser. 3, XX (October, 1963), 527–542.

Morgan, William T. "The British West Indies during King William's War (1689–97)," *Journal of Modern History,* II (September, 1930), 378–409.

———. "Economic Aspects of the Negotiations at Ryswick," in Transactions of the Royal Historical Society, Ser. 4, XIV (1931), 225–249.

Reich, Jerome R. *Leisler's Rebellion: A Study of Democracy in New York, 1664–1720.* Chicago, 1953.

Selden, George B., Jr. "The Expedition of the Marquis de Denonville against the Seneca Indians: 1687," in Rochester Historical Society Publication Fund Series, IV (1925), 1–82.

QUEEN ANNE'S WAR, 1702–1713

Barnwell, John. "The Tuscarora Expedition: Letters of Colonel John Barnwell," *South Carolina Historical and Genealogical Magazine,* IX (1908), 28–54. (Reprinted from the *Virginia Magazine of History and Biography,* V and VI [1898], 391–402, 42–55.)

Buckingham, Thomas. *The Private Journals Kept by Rev. John [i.e., Thomas] Buckingham, of the Expedition against Canada, in the Years 1710 & 1711.* New York, 1825.

Byrd, William, II. *The Secret Diary of William Byrd of Westover, 1709–1712,* ed. L. B. Wright and Marion Tinling. Richmond, 1941.

"The Deplorable State of New-England, by Reason of a Covetous and Treacherous Governour and Pusillanimous Counsellors," in Collections of the Massachusetts Historical Society, Ser. 5, VI (1879), 97–131.

Dummer, Jeremiah. *A Letter to a Noble Lord, Concerning the Late Expedition to Canada.* London, 1712.

Graham, Gerald S., ed. *The Walker Expedition to Quebec, 1711* (Publications of the Champlain Society, XXXII). Toronto, 1953. (Includes the journals of Admiral Walker, General Hill, and Colonel King.)

"A Memorial of the Present Deplorable State of New-England . . . ," in Collections of the Massachusetts Historical Society, Ser. 5, VI (1879), 31–64.

"A Modest Enquiry into the Grounds and Occasions of a Late Pamphlet,

Intituled, A Memorial of the Present Deplorable State of New-England," in Collections of the Massachusetts Historical Society, Ser. 5, VI (1879), 65–95.

Moore, James. "An Account of What the Army Did under the Command of Colonel Moore in his Expedition Last Winter, against the Spaniards and Spanish Indians," in B. R. Carroll, comp., Historical Collections of South Carolina, II (New York, 1836), 573–576.

Salley, Alexander S., Jr., ed. *Narratives of Early Carolina, 1650–1708.* New York, 1911.

Secondary Sources

Arnade, Charles W. "The English Invasion of Spanish Florida, 1700–1706," *Florida Historical Quarterly,* XLI (July, 1962), 29–37.

————. *The Siege of St. Augustine in 1702.* Gainesville, Fla., 1959.

Barnwell, Joseph W. "The Second Tuscarora Expedition," *South Carolina Historical and Genealogical Magazine,* X (January, 1909), 33–48.

Bond, Richmond P. *Queen Anne's American Kings.* Oxford, 1952.

McCully, Bruce T. "Catastrophe in the Wilderness: New Light on the Canada Expedition of 1709," *William and Mary Quarterly,* Ser. 3, XI (July, 1954), 440–456.

Morgan, William Thomas. "The Five Nations and Queen Anne," *Mississippi Valley Historical Review,* XIII (September, 1926), 169–189.

————. "Queen Anne's Canadian Expedition of 1711," *Queen's University Bulletin,* No. 56 (1928).

————. "The South Sea Company and the Canadian Expedition in the Reign of Queen Anne," *Hispanic American Historical Review,* VIII (May, 1928), 143–166.

Wallace, Anthony F. C. "Origins of Iroquois Neutrality: The Grand Settlement of 1701," *Pennsylvania History,* XXIV (July, 1957), 223–235.

Waller, G. M. "New York's Role in Queen Anne's War, 1702–1713," *New York History,* XXXIII (January, 1952), 40–53.

Zóltvany, Yves F. "New France and the West, 1701–1713," *Canadian Historical Review,* XLVI (December, 1965), 301–322.

WARS, 1714–1738

Baxter, James Phinney. *The Pioneers of New France in New England.* Albany, 1894.

Eckstorm, Fannie Hardy. "The Attack on Norridgewock: 1724," *New England Quarterly,* VII (September, 1934), 541–578.

Hildner, Ernest G., Jr. "The Role of the South Sea Company in the Diplomacy Leading to the War of Jenkins' Ear, 1729–1739," *Hispanic American Historical Review,* XVIII (August, 1938), 322–341.

Logan, James. "Of the State of the British Plantations in America: A Memorial," ed. Joseph E. Johnson, *Pennsylvania Magazine of History and Biography,* LX (April, 1936), 113–130.

Pennington, Edgar L. "The South Carolina Indian War of 1715, as Seen by the

Clergymen," *South Carolina Historical and Genealogical Magazine,*
XXXII (October, 1931), 251–267.

Symmes, Thomas. *Historical Memoirs of the Late Fight at Piggwacket, with a
Sermon Occasion'd by the Fall of the Brave Capt John Lovewell and
Several of His Valiant Company.* . . . Second ed., Boston, 1725.

Trask, William B., ed. *Letters of Colonel Thomas Westbrook and Others
Relative to Indian Affairs in Maine, 1722–1726.* Boston, 1901.

PRISONERS OF WAR

Bownas, Samuel. *An Account of the Captivity of Elizabeth Hanson, Now or Late
of Kachecky, in New-England.* Second ed., London, 1760.

Brown, Thomas. *A Plain Narrative of the Uncommon Sufferings, and Remarkable Deliverance of Thomas Brown, of Charlestown, in New-England.* . . .
Boston, 1760.

Calder, Isabel M., ed. *Colonial Captivities, Marches, and Journeys.* New York,
1935.

Eastburn, Robert. *A Faithful Narrative of the Many Dangers and Sufferings ...
of Robert Eastburn, during His Late Captivity among the Indians.*
Philadelphia and Boston, 1758.

Fleming, William and Elizabeth. *A Narrative of the Sufferings and Surprizing
Deliverances of William and Elizabeth Fleming.* Boston, 1756.

Gist, Thomas. "Thomas Gist's Indian Captivity, 1758–1759," ed. Howard H.
Peckham, *Pennsylvania Magazine of History and Biography,* LXXX (July,
1956), 285–311.

Gyles, John. *Memoirs of Odd Adventures, Strange Deliverances, &c. in the
Captivity of John Gyles, Esq; Commander of the Garrison on St. George's
River.* Boston, 1736.

Hanson, Elizabeth. *God's Mercy Surmounting Man's Cruelty, Exemplified in
the Captivity and Redemption of Elizabeth Hanson.* Philadelphia, 1728.

How, Nehemiah. *A Narrative of the Captivity of Nehemiah How, Who Was
Taken by the Indians at the Great-Meadow Fort above Fort-Dummer,
Where He Was an Inhabitant, October 11th 1745.* Boston, 1748.

Jogues, Isaac. *Narrative of a Captivity among the Mohawk Indians, and a
Description of New Netherland in 1642–3.* New York, 1856.

Le Roy, Marie. "The Narrative of Marie Le Roy and Barbara Leininger, for
Three Years Captives among the Indians," ·trans. Edmund de Schweinitz,
Pennsylvania Magazine of History and Biography, XXIX (October, 1905),
407–420.

Lowry, Jean. *A Journal of the Captivity of Jean Lowry and Her Children.* . . .
Philadelphia, 1760.

[Mather, Cotton]. *Frontiers Well-Defended. An Essay, to Direct the Frontiers
of a Countrey Exposed unto the Incursions of a Barbarous Enemy, How
to Behave Themselves in Their Uneasy Station?* Boston, 1707.

[————]. *Good Fetch'd out of Evil.* Boston, 1706.

Norton, John. *The Redeemed Captive, Being a Narrative of the Taken* [sic]
and Carrying into Captivity the Reverend Mr. John Norton, When Fort-

Massachusetts Surrendered to a Large Body of French and Indians, August 20th 1746. Boston, 1748.

Pote, William, Jr. *The Journal of Captain William Pote, Jr. during His Captivity in the French and Indian War from May, 1745, to August, 1747.* New York, 1896.

Rowlandson, Mary. *Narrative of the Captivity of Mrs. Mary Rowlandson, 1682,* in Charles H. Lincoln, ed., *Narratives of the Indian Wars, 1675–1699* (New York, 1913), pp. 112–167.

Williams, John. *The Redeemed Captive Returning to Zion.* Springfield, Mass., 1908.

Williamson, Peter. *French and Indian Cruelty; Exemplified in the Life and Various Vicissitudes of Fortune, of Peter Williamson.* Third ed., Glasgow, 1758.

Secondary Sources

Baker, C. Alice. "Ensign John Sheldon," in History and Proceedings of the Pocumtuck Valley Memorial Association, 1870–1879, I (1890), 405–431.

Coleman, Emma Lewis. *New England Captives Carried to Canada between 1677 and 1760 during the French and Indian Wars.* 2 vols. Portland, Me., 1925.

Knowles, Nathaniel. "The Torture of Captives by the Indians of Eastern North America," *Proceedings of the American Philosophical Society,* LXXXII (March, 1940), 151–225.

Scheele, Raymond Lewis. "The Treatment of Captives among the North East Indians of North America." Unpublished M.A. thesis, Columbia University, 1947.

Vail, Robert W. G. "Certain Indian Captives of New England," in Proceedings of the Massachusetts Historical Society, LXVIII (1952), 113–131.

PACIFISM

Chalkley, Thomas. *A Journal or Historical Account of the Life, Travels and Christian Experiences of . . . Thomas Chalkley.* Second ed., London, 1751.

[Franklin, Benjamin]. "Plain Truth: Or, Serious Considerations on the Present State of the City of Philadelphia, and Province of Pennsylvania," in Leonard W. Labaree *et al.,* eds. *The Papers of Benjamin Franklin* (14 vols. to date; New Haven, 1959 to present), III, 188–204.

[Galloway, Joseph]. *A True and Impartial State of the Province of Pennsylvania.* Philadelphia, 1759.

Keith, George. *A Journal of Travels from New-Hampshire to Caratuck, on the Continent of North-America.* London, 1706.

Philalethes (pseudonym) [Thomas Maule?]. *Tribute to Caesar, How Paid by the Best Christians, and to What Purpose. With Some Remarks on the Late Vigorous Expedition against Canada.* [Philadelphia?] [1712?].

Smith, John. *The Doctrine of Christianity, As Held by the People Called Quakers, Vindicated: In Answer to Gilbert Tennent's Sermon on the Lawfulness of War. . . .* Philadelphia, 1748.

[Smith, William]. *A Brief State of the Province of Pennsylvania, in Which the*

Conduct of Their Assemblies for Several Years Past Is Impartially Examined. London, 1755.

[————]. *A Brief View of the Conduct of Pennsylvania, for the Year 1755.* London, 1756.

Tennent, Gilbert. *The Late Association for Defence Encourag'd, or the Lawfulness of a Defensive War.* Philadelphia, 1748.

Williams, William. *Martial Wisdom Recommended.* Boston, 1737.

Woolman, John. *The Journal of John Woolman,* ed. Janet Whitney. Chicago, 1950.

Secondary Sources

Brock, Peter. *Pacifism in the United States, from the Colonial Era to the First World War.* Princeton, 1968.

Buffinton, Arthur H. "The Puritan View of War," in Publications of the Colonial Society of Massachusetts, XXVIII (1935), 67–86.

Cribbs, George A. "The Frontier Policy of Pennsylvania," *Western Pennsylvania Historical Magazine,* II (January, April, July, 1919), 5–35, 72–106, 174–198.

Hershberger, Guy F. "The Pennsylvania Quaker Experiment in Politics, 1682–1756," *Mennonite Quarterly Review,* X (October, 1936), 187–221.

James, Sydney V. *A People among Peoples: Quaker Benevolence in Eighteenth-Century America.* Cambridge, Mass., 1963.

Jones, Rufus M. *The Quakers in the American Colonies.* London, 1911.

Ketcham, Ralph L. "Conscience, War, and Politics in Pennsylvania, 1755–1757," *William and Mary Quarterly,* Ser. 3, XX (July, 1963), 416–439.

Marietta, Jack D. "Conscience, the Quaker Community, and the French and Indian War," *Pennsylvania Magazine of History and Biography,* XCV (January, 1971), 3–27.

Root, Winfred Trexler. *The Relations of Pennsylvania with the British Government, 1696–1765.* New York, 1912.

Stillé, Charles J. "The Attitude of the Quakers in the Provincial Wars," *Pennsylvania Magazine of History and Biography,* X (1886), 283–315.

Thayer, Theodore. "The Friendly Association," *Pennsylvania Magazine of History and Biography,* LXVII (October, 1943), 356–376.

Tolles, Frederick B. *Meeting House and Counting House: The Quaker Merchants of Colonial Philadelphia, 1682–1763.* Chapel Hill, 1948.

————. "Nonviolent Contact: The Quakers and the Indians," in Proceedings of the American Philosophical Society, CVII (April, 1963), 93–101.

————. *Quakers and the Atlantic Culture.* New York, 1960.

Wenger, John C. "Franconia Mennonites and Military Service, 1683–1923," *Mennonite Quarterly Review,* X (October, 1936), 222–245.

Zimmerman, John J. "Benjamin Franklin and the Quaker Party, 1755–1756," *William and Mary Quarterly,* Ser. 3, XVII (July, 1960), 291–313.

INTERNAL STRAINS, POLITICAL AND ECONOMIC

Bean, Walton E. "War and the British Colonial Farmer: A Reevaluation in the Light of New Statistical Records," *Pacific Historical Review,* XI (December, 1942), 439–447.

Bezanson, Anne, Gray, R. D., and Hussey, M. *Prices in Colonial Pennsylvania.* Philadelphia, 1935.

Burns, John F. *Controversies between Royal Governors and Their Assemblies in the Northern American Colonies.* Boston, 1923.

Franklin, W. Neil. "Pennsylvania-Virginia Rivalry for the Indian Trade of the Ohio Valley," *Mississippi Valley Historical Review,* XX (March, 1934), 463–480.

Greene, Jack P. *The Quest for Power: The Lower Houses of Assembly in the Southern Royal Colonies, 1689–1776.* Chapel Hill, 1963.

——. "The Role of the Lower Houses of Assembly in Eighteenth-Century Politics," *Journal of Southern History,* XXVII (November, 1961), 451–474.

Johnson, Emory R. *et al. History of Domestic and Foreign Commerce of the United States.* 2 vols. Washington, 1915.

Nettels, Curtis. *The Money Supply of the American Colonies before 1720.* Madison, 1934.

Sachs, William S. "Agricultural Conditions in the Northern Colonies before the Revolution," *Journal of Economic History,* XIII (Summer, 1953), 274–290.

The War of the 1740s

Bidwell, Adonijah. Journal, in *New England Historical and Genealogical Register,* XXVII (1873), 153–160.

Bradstreet, Dudley. Diary (Proceedings of the Massachusetts Historical Society, Ser. 2, XI [June, 1897], 423–446).

Cadogan, George. *The Spanish Hireling Detected: Being a Refutation of the Several Calumnies and Falshoods in a Late Pamphlet, Entitul'd An Impartial Account of the Late Expedition against St. Augustine under General Oglethorpe.* London, 1743.

Cleaves, Benjamin. "Benjamin Cleaves's Journal," *New England Historical and Genealogical Register,* LXVI (1912), 113–124.

Craft, Benjamin. "Craft's Journal of the Siege of Louisbourg," *Essex Institute Historical Collections,* VI (October, 1864), 181–194.

De Forest, Louis Effingham, ed. *Louisbourg Journals, 1745.* New York, 1932.

Doolittle, Benjamin. *A Short Narrative of Mischief Done by the French and Indian Enemy, on the Western Frontiers of the Province of the Massachusetts-Bay.* Boston, 1750.

Easterby, J. H., ed. *The St. Augustine Expedition of 1740: A Report to the South Carolina Assembly. . . .* Columbia, S.C., 1954.

A Full Reply to Lieut. Cadogan's Spanish Hireling, &c. and Lieut. Mackay's Letter, Concerning the Action at Moosa. London, 1743.

Gibson, James. *A Journal of the Late Siege . . . at Cape Breton, the City of Louisbourg. . . .* London, 1745.

Giddings, Daniel. "Journal Kept by Lieut. Daniel Giddings of Ipswich during the Expedition against Cape Breton in 1744–5," *Essex Institute Historical Collections,* XLVIII (October, 1912), 293–304.

An Impartial Account of the Late Expedition against St. Augustine under General Oglethorpe. London, 1742.

Montiano, Don Manuel de. *Letters of Montiano, Siege of St. Augustine* (Collections of the Georgia Historical Society, VII, Part 1). Savannah, Ga., 1909.

Pepperrell, William. "The Journal of Sir William Pepperrell Kept during the Expedition against Louisbourg, Mar. 24–Aug. 22, 1745," ed. C. H. Lincoln, in American Antiquarian Society Proceedings, New Series, XX (1909–1910), 139–176.

Pomeroy, Seth. *The Journals and Papers of Seth Pomeroy,* ed. L. E. de Forest. New Haven, 1926.

Pote, William, Jr. *The Journal of Captain William Pote, Jr., during His Captivity.* . . . New York, 1896.

"A Ranger's Report of Travels with General Oglethorpe, 1739–1742," in N. D. Mereness, ed., *Travels in the American Colonies* (New York, 1916), pp. 218–236.

Shirley, William. *A Letter . . . to . . . the Duke of Newcastle, with a Journal of the Siege of Louisbourg, and Other Operations of the Forces during the Expedition against the French Settlements of Cape Breton.* London, 1746.

The Spanish Official Account of the Attack on the Colony of Georgia, in America, and of Its Defeat on St. Simons Island by General James Oglethorpe (Collections of the Georgia Historical Society, VII, Part 3). Savannah, Ga., 1913.

Stephens, William. *The Journal of William Stephens, 1741–1743,* ed. E. Merton Coulter. Athens, Ga., 1958.

———. *The Journal of William Stephens, 1743–1745,* ed. E. Merton Coulter. Athens, Ga., 1959.

Tailfer, Pat[rick] et al. *A True and Historical Narrative of the Colony of Georgia . . . with Comments by the Earl of Egmont,* ed. Clarence L. Ver Steeg. Athens, Ga., 1960.

Wolcott, Roger. "Journal of Roger Wolcott at the Siege of Louisbourg," in Collections of the Connecticut Historical Society, I (1860), 131–162.

Wrong, George M., ed. *The Anonymous Lettre d'un Habitant de Louisbourg.* Toronto, 1897.

Secondary Sources

Berkeley, Francis L., Jr. "The War of Jenkins' Ear," in Darrett B. Rutman, ed., *The Old Dominion: Essays for Thomas Perkins Abernethy* (Charlottesville, Va., 1964), pp. 41–61.

Buffinton, Arthur H. "The Canadian Expedition of 1746: Its Relation to British Politics," *American Historical Review,* XLV (April, 1940), 552–580.

Caldwell, Norman W. *The French in the Mississippi Valley, 1740–1750.* Urbana, Ill., 1941.

———. "The Southern Frontier during King George's War," *Journal of Southern History,* VII (February, 1941), 37–54.

Chapin, Howard M. *Privateering in King George's War, 1739–1748.* Providence, 1928.

Foote, William A. "The Pennsylvania Men of the American Regiment," *Pennsylvania Magazine of History and Biography,* LXXXVII (January, 1963), 31–38.

Lanning, John Tate. "The American Colonies in the Preliminaries of the War of Jenkins' Ear," *Georgia Historical Quarterly,* XI (June, 1927), 129–155.

———. "American Participation in the War of Jenkins' Ear," *Georgia Historical Quarterly,* XI (September, 1927), 191–215.

———. *The Diplomatic History of Georgia: A Study of the Epoch of Jenkins' Ear.* Chapel Hill, 1936.

Parkman, Francis. *A Half-Century of Conflict.* 2 vols. Boston, 1892.

Rawlyk, G. A. *Yankees at Louisbourg.* Orono, Me., 1967.

Reese, Trevor R. "Britain's Military Support of Georgia in the War of 1739–1748," *Georgia Historical Quarterly,* XLIII (March, 1959), 1–10.

Richmond, Herbert W. *The Navy in the War of 1739–48.* 3 vols. Cambridge, 1920.

Sosin, Jack M. "Louisburg and the Peace of Aix-la-Chapelle," *William and Mary Quarterly,* Ser. 3, XIV (October, 1957), 516–535.

Wainwright, Nicholas B. "George Croghan and the Indian Uprising of 1747," *Pennsylvania History,* XXI (January, 1954), 21–31.

Wall, Robert Emmet, Jr. "Louisbourg, 1745," *New England Quarterly,* XXXVII (March, 1964), 64–83.

Dangerous Interlude, 1748–1754

Clarke, William. *Observations on the Late and Present Conduct of the French, with Regard to Their Encroachments upon the British Colonies in North America.* Boston, 1755.

Dinwiddie, Robert. *The Official Records of Robert Dinwiddie . . .* (Collections of the Virginia Historical Society, III, IV, ed. R. A. Brock). Richmond, 1883–1884.

Gist, Christopher. *Christopher Gist's Journals . . . ,* ed. William M. Darlington. Pittsburgh, 1893.

[Huske, John]. *The Present State of North America.* Second ed., London, 1755.

Jacobs, Wilbur R., ed. *Indians of the Southern Colonial Frontier: The Edmund Atkin Report and Plan of 1755.* Columbia, S.C., 1954.

[Jefferys, Thomas]. *The Conduct of the French, with Regard to Nova Scotia; From Its First Settlement to the Present Time.* London, 1754.

Kalm, Peter. *Peter Kalm's Travels in North America,* ed. Adolph B. Benson. 2 vols. New York, 1937.

[Kennedy, Archibald]. *The Importance of Gaining and Preserving the Friendship of the Indians to the British Interest, Considered.* New York, 1751.

[———]. *Observations on the Importance of the Northern Colonies under Proper Regulations.* New York, 1750.

[———]. *Serious Considerations on the Present State of the Affairs of the Northern Colonies.* New York, 1754.

Pease, Theodore Calvin, ed. *Anglo-French Boundary Disputes in the West, 1749–1763.* Springfield, Ill., 1936.

——, and Jenison, Ernestine, eds. *Illinois on the Eve of the Seven Years' War, 1747–1755.* Springfield, Ill., 1940.

State of the British and French Colonies in North America. . . . London, 1755. (Facsimile edition, New York, 1967.)

Stevens, Phineas. "Journal of Capt. Phineas Stevens to and from Canada— 1749," in Collections of the New Hampshire Historical Society, V (1837), 199–205.

Washington, George. *The Journal of Major George Washington.* London and Williamsburg, 1754. (Facsimile edition, Charlottesville, Va., 1959.)

Weiser, Conrad. "The Journal of Conrad Weiser, Esqr., Indian Interpreter, to the Ohio," in R. G. Thwaites, ed., *Early Western Travels, 1748–1846* (32 vols.; Cleveland, 1904–1907), I, 21–44.

Secondary Sources

Abernethy, Thomas P. *Western Lands and the American Revolution.* New York, 1937.

Alvord, Clarence W. *The Mississippi Valley in British Politics.* 2 vols. Cleveland, 1917.

Bailey, Kenneth P. *The Ohio Company of Virginia and the Westward Movement, 1748–1792.* Glendale, Calif., 1939.

Baker-Crothers, Hayes, and Hudnut, Ruth A. "A Private Soldier's Account of Washington's First Battles in the West: A Study in Historical Criticism," *Journal of Southern History,* VIII (February, 1942), 23–62.

Cowan, John P. "George Washington at Fort Necessity," *Western Pennsylvania Historical Magazine,* XXXVII (Fall–Winter, 1954–1955), 153–180.

Everett, Edward G. "Pennsylvania's Indian Diplomacy, 1747–1753," *Western Pennsylvania Historical Magazine,* XLIV (September, 1961), 241–256.

Gipson, Lawrence Henry. "British Diplomacy in the Light of Anglo-Spanish New World Issues, 1750–1757," *American Historical Review,* LI (July, 1946), 627–648.

——. "Thomas Hutchinson and the Framing of the Albany Plan of Union, 1754," *Pennsylvania Magazine of History and Biography,* LXXIV (January, 1950), 5–35.

Harrington, J. C. *New Light on Washington's Fort Necessity: A Report on the Archeological Explorations at Fort Necessity National Battlefield Site.* Richmond, 1957.

James, Alfred P. *The Ohio Company: Its Inner History.* Pittsburgh, 1959.

Kent, Donald H. "The French Advance into the Ohio Country," *Western Pennsylvania Historical Magazine,* XXXVII (Fall–Winter, 1954–1955), 135– 151.

——. "The French Occupy the Ohio Country," *Pennsylvania History,* XXI (October, 1954), 301–315.

Mulkearn, Lois. "Why the Treaty of Logstown, 1752," *Virginia Magazine of History and Biography,* LIX (January, 1951), 3–20.

Newbold, Robert Clifford. *The Albany Congress and Plan of Union of 1754.* New York, 1955.

Olson, Alison Gilbert. "The British Government and Colonial Union, 1754," *William and Mary Quarterly,* Ser. 3, XVII (January, 1960), 22–34.

O'Meara, Walter. *Guns at the Forks.* Englewood Cliffs, N.J., 1965.

Phelps, Dawson A. "The Vaudreuil Expedition, 1752," *William and Mary Quarterly,* Ser. 3, XV (October, 1958), 483–493.

Savelle, Max. "Diplomatic Preliminaries of the Seven Years' War in America," *Canadian Historical Review,* XX (March, 1939), 17–36.

Schlicksup, Edward Joseph. "William Johnson and the British-Iroquois Alliance, 1746–54." Unpublished M.A. thesis, Vanderbilt University, 1971.

Trudel, Marcel. "The Jumonville Affair," trans. and abridged by Donald H. Kent, *Pennsylvania History,* XXI (October, 1954), 351–381.

Wood, George A. "Céloron de Blainville and French Expansion in the Ohio Valley," *Mississippi Valley Historical Review,* IX (March, 1923), 302–319.

The Great War for the Empire, 1755–1763

Amherst, Jeffery. *The Journal of Jeffery Amherst, Recording the Military Career of General Amherst in America from 1758 to 1763,* ed. J. Clarence Webster. Chicago, 1931.

Bass, Benjamin. "Account of the Capture of Fort Frontenac by the Detachment under the Command of Col. Bradstreet," *New York History,* XVI (October, 1935), 449–451.

Bolling, John. "A Private Report of General Braddock's Defeat," ed. John A. Schutz, *Pennsylvania Magazine of History and Biography,* LXXIX (July, 1955), 374–377.

Bougainville, Louis Antoine de. *Adventure in the Wilderness: The American Journals of Louis Antoine de Bougainville, 1756–1760,* trans. and ed. Edward P. Hamilton. Norman, Okla., 1964.

Bouquet, Henry. *The Papers of Henry Bouquet.* Vol. II: *The Forbes Expedition,* ed. S. K. Stevens, D. H. Kent, and A. L. Leonard. Harrisburg, 1951.

Bowen, Ashley. "Journal Kept on the Quebec Expedition, 1759, by Ashley Bowen of Marblehead," *Essex Institute Historical Collections,* LXX (July, 1934), 227–266.

Bremner, John. Journal, 1756–1764. New York Historical Society.

[Burke, William?]. *An Examination of the Commercial Principles of the Late Negotiation.* London, 1762.

[———]. *Remarks on the Letter Address'd to Two Great Men.* London, [1760].

Burnaby, Andrew. *Travels through the Middle Settlements in North-America. In the Years 1759 and 1760.* Second ed., London, 1775. (Reprinted, Ithaca, 1960.)

[Chauncy, Charles]. *A Letter to a Friend; Giving a Concise, but Just, Account . . . of the Ohio-Defeat.* Boston, 1755.

[———]. *A Second Letter to a Friend; Giving a More Particular Narrative of the Defeat of the French Army at Lake-George, by the New-England Troops, Than Has Yet Been Published.* Boston, 1755.

Clark, David Sanders, comp. "Journals and Orderly Books Kept by Massachusetts Soldiers during the French and Indian War," *New England Historical and Genealogical Register*, XCV (April, 1941), 118–121.

The Conduct of a Noble Commander in America, Impartially Reviewed. London, 1758.

The Conduct of Major Gen. Shirley, Late General and Commander in Chief of His Majesty's Forces in North America. Briefly Stated. London, 1758.

Cross, Stephen. "Journal of Stephen Cross of Newburyport. . . ." *Essex Institute Historical Collections*, LXXV (October, 1939), 334–357, LXXVI (January, 1940), 14–42.

Dorr, Moses. "A Journal of an Expedition against Canaday," *New York History*, XVI (October, 1935), 452–464.

Entick, John. *The General History of the Late War: Containing It's Rise, Progress, and Event, in Europe, Asia, Africa, and America.* Third ed., 5 vols. London, 1766–1772.

Eyre, William. "Colonel Eyre's Journal of His Trip from New York to Pittsburgh, 1762," ed. Frances R. Reece, *Western Pennsylvania Historical Magazine*, XXVII (March–June, 1944), 37–50.

"The Fall of Quebec," *Canadian Historical Review*, XXXIII (June, 1952), 165–167.

Forbes, John. *Writings of General John Forbes Relating to His Service in North America*, ed. Alfred P. James. Menasha, Wis., 1938.

[Franklin, Benjamin]. "The Interest of Great Britain Considered, with Regard to Her Colonies, and the Acquisitions of Canada and Guadaloupe," in Leonard W. Labaree, *et al.*, eds., *The Papers of Benjamin Franklin* (14 vols. to date; New Haven, 1959 to present), IX, 59–100.

A Full and Free Inquiry into the Merits of the Peace. . . . London, 1765.

Gordon, Harry. "A Letter from Will's Creek: Harry Gordon's Account of Braddock's Defeat," ed. Charles M. Stotz, *Western Pennsylvania Historical Magazine*, XLIV (June, 1961), 129–136.

Hamilton, Charles, ed. *Braddock's Defeat: The Journal of Captain Robert Cholmley's Batman. The Journal of a British Officer. Halkett's Orderly Book.* Norman, Okla., 1959.

Holden, David. "Journal of Sergeant Holden," in Proceedings of the Massachusetts Historical Society, Ser. 2, IV (1889), 387–409.

"The Importance of the Upper Ohio Country in 1758—A Contemporary View," *Western Pennsylvania Historical Magazine*, XVII (June, 1934), 123–125.

Knox, John. *An Historical Journal of the Campaigns in North-America, for the Years 1757, 1758, 1759, and 1760.* 2 vols. London, 1769.

La Chapelle, Passerat de. "La Chapelle's Remarkable Retreat through the Mississippi Valley, 1760–61," trans. and ed. Louise P. Kellogg, *Mississippi Valley Historical Review*, XXII (June, 1935), 63–81.

A Letter Addressed to Two Great Men, on the Prospect of Peace; And on the Terms Necessary to be Insisted upon in the Negociation. Boston, 1760.

[Livingston, William]. *A Review of the Military Operations in North-America.* . . . London and Dublin, 1757.

Mante, Thomas. *The History of the Late War in North-America, and the Is-lands of the West-Indies. . . .* London, 1772.

[Mitchell, John]. *The Contest in America between Great Britain and France, with Its Consequences and Importance.* London, 1757.

"The Moneypenny Orderly Book," *Bulletin of the Fort Ticonderoga Museum,* XII (December, 1969), 328–357, and subsequent issues.

Montcalm-Gozon, Louis Joseph de. "Montcalm's Correspondence," (*Report of the Public Archives of Canada for the Year 1929* [Ottawa, 1930], pp. 31–108).

Murray, James. *Governor Murray's Journal of the Siege of Quebec, from 18th September, 1759, to 25th May, 1760.* Toronto, 1939.

Perry, David. *Recollections of an Old Soldier.* Cottonport, La., 1971.

Pitt, William. *Correspondence of William Pitt with Colonial Governors,* ed. G. S. Kimball. 2 vols. New York, 1906.

Post, Christian Frederick. *The Second Journal of Christian Frederick Post, on a Message from the Governor of Pensilvania to the Indians on the Ohio.* London, 1759.

Pownall, Thomas. *Considerations towards a General Plan of Measures for the English Provinces.* New York, 1756.

Procter, Jonathan. "Diary Kept at Louisburg, 1759–1760, by Jonathan Procter of Danvers," *Essex Institute Historical Collections,* LXX (January, 1934), 31–57.

Rogers, Robert. *Journals of Major Robert Rogers,* ed. Howard H. Peckham. New York, 1961.

Samuel, Sigmund, comp. *The Seven Years War in Canada, 1756–1763.* Toronto, 1934.

Smith, James. *An Account of the Remarkable Occurrences in the Life and Travels of Col. James Smith. . . .* Lexington, Ky., 1799.

Thomas, John. Diary (Collections of the Nova Scotia Historical Society, I [1878], 119–140).

Williams, Joshua. Orderly Book. New York Public Library.

Williamson, Peter. *A Brief Account of the War in N. America.* Edinburgh, [1760].

———. *Some Considerations on the Present State of Affairs.* York, 1758.

Winslow, John. Journal (Collections of the Nova Scotia Historical Society, III [1882–1883], 71–196, IV [1884], 113–246).

Wood, William, ed. *The Logs of the Conquest of Canada.* Toronto, 1909.

Secondary Sources

Abbott, Raymond B. "Braddock's War Supplies and Dunbar's Camp," *Western Pennsylvania Historical Magazine,* XVII (March, 1934), 49–52.

Anderson, Niles. "The General Chooses a Road: The Forbes Campaign of 1758 to Capture Fort Duquesne," *Western Pennsylvania Historical Magazine,* XLII (June, September, December, 1959), 109–138, 241–258, 383–401.

Baker-Crothers, Hayes. *Virginia and the French and Indian War.* Chicago, 1928.

Beer, George Louis. *British Colonial Policy, 1754–1765.* New York, 1907.

Burt, Alfred L. *The Old Province of Quebec.* Minneapolis, 1933.

Charland, Thomas M. "The Lake Champlain Army and the Fall of Montreal," *Vermont History,* New Series, XXVIII (October, 1960), 293–301.

Corbett, Julian S. *England in the Seven Years' War, A Study in Combined Strategy.* Second ed., 2 vols. London, 1918.

Coulter, E. Merton. "The Acadians in Georgia," *Georgia Historical Quarterly,* XLVII (March, 1963), 68–75.

Doughty, Arthur G. *The Siege of Quebec and the Battle of the Plains of Abraham.* 6 vols. Quebec, 1901.

Fisher, John S. "Colonel Armstrong's Expedition against Kittanning," *Pennsylvania Magazine of History and Biography,* LI (January, 1927), 1–14.

Frégault, Guy. *Canada: The War of the Conquest,* trans. Margaret M. Cameron. Toronto, 1969.

Gipson, Lawrence Henry. "A French Project for Victory Short of a Declaration of War, 1755," *Canadian Historical Review,* XXVI (December, 1945), 361–371.

Gold, Robert L. *Borderland Empires in Transition: The Triple-Nation Transfer of Florida.* Carbondale, Ill., 1969.

Graham, Dominick. "The Planning of the Beauséjour Operation and the Approaches to War in 1755," *New England Quarterly,* XLI (December, 1968), 551–566.

Grant, William L. "Canada Versus Guadeloupe, an Episode of the Seven Years' War," *American Historical Review,* XVII (July, 1912), 735–743.

Hall, Hubert. "Chatham's Colonial Policy," *American Historical Review,* V (July, 1900), 659–675.

Hamer, Marguerite B. "The Fate of the Exiled Acadians in South Carolina," *Journal of Southern History,* IV (May, 1938), 199–208.

Hamer, P. M. "Anglo-French Rivalry in the Cherokee Country, 1754–1757," *North Carolina Historical Review,* II (July, 1925), 303–322.

Hamilton, Edward Pierce. *Fort Ticonderoga: Key to a Continent.* Boston, 1964.

Hibbert, Christopher. *Wolfe at Quebec.* London, 1959.

Higonnet, Patrice Louis-René. "The Origins of the Seven Years' War," *Journal of Modern History,* XL (March, 1968), 57–90.

Hitsman, J. Mackay. "Order before Landing at Louisbourg, 1758," *Military Affairs,* XXII (Fall, 1958), 146–148.

————, with Bond, C. C. J. "The Assault Landing at Louisbourg, 1758," *Canadian Historical Review,* XXXV (December, 1954), 314–330.

Hotblack, Kate. "The Peace of Paris, 1763," in *Transactions of the Royal Historical Society,* Ser. 3, II (1908), 235–267.

Howard, C. N. "The Military Occupation of British West Florida, 1763," *Florida Historical Quarterly,* XVII (January, 1939), 181–199.

Hudnut, Ruth Allison, and Baker-Crothers, Hayes. "Acadian Transients in South Carolina," *American Historical Review,* XLIII (April, 1938), 500–513.

Hunter, William A. *Forts on the Pennsylvania Frontier, 1753–1758.* Harrisburg, 1960.

————. "Provincial Negotiations with the Western Indians, 1754–58," *Pennsylvania History*, XVIII (July, 1951), 213–219.

Jacobs, Wilbur R. "A Message to Fort William Henry: An Incident in the French and Indian War," *Huntington Library Quarterly*, XVI (August, 1953), 371–381.

James, Alfred P., and Stotz, Charles M. "Drums in the Forest," *Western Pennsylvania Historical Magazine*, XLI (Autumn, 1958), 3–227.

Kerr, Wilfred B. "Fort Niagara, 1759–1763," *New York History*, XV (July, 1934), 281–301.

Klein, Milton M. "William Livingston's *A Review of the Military Operations in North-America*," in Lawrence H. Leder, ed., *The Colonial Legacy.* Vol. II; *Some Eighteenth-Century Commentators* (New York, 1971), pp. 107–140.

Koontz, Louis K. *The Virginia Frontier, 1754–63.* Baltimore, 1925.

Labaree, Leonard W. "Benjamin Franklin and the Defense of Pennsylvania, 1754–1757," *Pennsylvania History*, XXIX (January, 1962), 7–23.

Lloyd, Christopher. *The Capture of Quebec.* New York, 1959.

Lowe, Richard G. "Massachusetts and the Acadians," *William and Mary Quarterly*, Ser. 3, XXV (April, 1968), 212–229.

Millard, Clifford. "The Acadians in Virginia," *Virginia Magazine of History and Biography*, XL (July, 1932), 241–258.

Mullett, Charles F. "James Abercromby and French Encroachments in America," *Canadian Historical Review*, XXVI (March, 1945), 48–59.

Nichols, Franklin Thayer. "The Organization of Braddock's Army," *William and Mary Quarterly*, Ser. 3, IV (April, 1947), 125–147.

Nixon, Lily Lee. "Colonel James Burd in the Campaign of 1759," *Western Pennsylvania Historical Magazine*, XVIII (June, 1935), 109–124.

————. "Colonel James Burd in the Forbes Campaign," *Pennsylvania Magazine of History and Biography*, LIX (April, 1935), 106–133.

Norkus, Nellie. "Virginia's Role in the Capture of Fort Duquesne, 1758," *Western Pennsylvania Historical Magazine*, XLV (December, 1962), 291–308.

Pargellis, Stanley. "Braddock's Defeat," *American Historical Review*, XLI (January, 1936), 253–269.

Parkman, Francis. *Montcalm and Wolfe.* 2 vols. Boston, 1884.

Pease, Theodore C. "The Mississippi Boundary of 1763: A Reappraisal of Responsibility," *American Historical Review*, XL (January, 1935), 278–286.

Rashed, Zenab Esmat. *The Peace of Paris, 1763.* Liverpool, 1951.

Rice, Otis K. "The French and Indian War in West Virginia," *West Virginia History*, XXIV (January, 1963), 134–146.

————. "The Sandy Creek Expedition of 1756," *West Virginia History*, XIII (October, 1951), 5–19.

Riker, Thad W. "The Politics behind Braddock's Expedition," *American Historical Review*, XIII (July, 1908), 742–752.

Salay, David Lewis. "The William Johnson-William Shirley Dispute: Origins, Course, and Consequences," Unpublished M.A. thesis, Vanderbilt University, 1972.

Schutz, John A. "The Disaster of Fort Ticonderoga: The Shortage of Muskets during the Mobilization of 1758," *Huntington Library Quarterly*, XIV (May, 1951), 307–315.

Shaw, Helen Louise. *British Administration of the Southern Indians, 1756–1783.* Lancaster, Pa., 1931.

Sherrard, O. A. *Lord Chatham: Pitt and the Seven Years' War.* London, 1955.

Siebert, Wilbur H. "How the Spaniards Evacuated Pensacola in 1763," *Florida Historical Society Quarterly*, XI (October, 1932), 48–57.

———. "Spanish and French Privateering in Southern Waters, July, 1762, to March, 1763," *Georgia Historical Quarterly*, XVI (September, 1932), 163–178.

Smelser, Marshall. *The Campaign for the Sugar Islands, 1759: A Study of Amphibious Warfare.* Chapel Hill, 1955.

Stacey, C. P. "The Anse au Foulon, 1759: Montcalm and Vaudreuil," *Canadian Historical Review*, XL (March, 1959), 27–37.

———. "Quebec, 1759: Some New Documents," *Canadian Historical Review*, XLVII (December, 1966), 344–355.

———. *Quebec, 1759: The Siege and the Battle.* New York, 1959.

Thayer, Theodore. "The Army Contractors for the Niagara Campaign, 1755–1756," *William and Mary Quarterly*, Ser. 3, XIV (January, 1957), 31–46.

Thomas, Harold A. "The Last Two Campsites of Forbes' Army," *Western Pennsylvania Historical Magazine*, XLVI (January, 1963), 45–5(

Trimble, David B. "Christopher Gist and the Indian Service in Virginia, 1757–1759," *Virginia Magazine of History and Biography*, LXV (April, 1956), 143–165.

Wallace, Paul A. W. " 'Blunder Camp': A Note on the Braddock Road," *Pennsylvania Magazine of History and Biography*, LXXXVII (January, 1963), 21–30.

Young, Chester Raymond. "The Effects of the French and Indian War on Civilian Life in the Frontier Counties of Virginia, 1754–1763." Unpublished Ph.D. dissertation, Vanderbilt University, 1969.

THE CHEROKEE WAR AND PONTIAC'S UPRISING

Anderson, Niles. "Bushy Run: Decisive Battle in the Wilderness: Pennsylvania and the Indian Rebellion of 1763," *Western Pennsylvania Historical Magazine*, XLVI (July, 1963), 211–245.

Grant, Charles S. "Pontiac's Rebellion and the British Troop Moves of 1763," *Mississippi Valley Historical Review*, XL (June, 1953), 75–88.

Hamer, P. M. "Fort Loudoun in the Cherokee War 1758–1761," *North Carolina Historical Review*, II (October, 1925), 442–458.

Henry, Alexander. *Massacre at Mackinac: Alexander Henry's Travels and Adventures in Canada and the Indian Territories between the Years 1760 and 1764,* ed. David A. Armour. Mackinac Island, Mich., 1966.

Jacobs, Wilbur R. "Presents to Indians as a Factor in the Conspiracy of Pontiac," *Michigan History*, XXXIII (December, 1949), 314–322.

Kellogg, Louise Phelps. *The British Régime in Wisconsin and the Northwest.* Madison, 1935.

Parkman, Francis. *The Conspiracy of Pontiac and the Indian War after the Conquest of Canada*. Tenth ed., 2 vols. Boston, 1893.

Peckham, Howard H. *Pontiac and the Indian Uprising*. Princeton, 1947.

Sosin, Jack M. *Whitehall and the Wilderness: The Middle West in British Colonial Policy, 1760–1775*. Lincoln, Neb., 1961.

Anglo-American Tension

Gipson, Lawrence Henry. "The American Revolution as an Aftermath of the Great War for the Empire, 1754–1763," *Political Science Quarterly*, LXV (March, 1950), 86–104.

Greene, Jack P. "The South Carolina Quartering Dispute, 1757–1758," *South Carolina Historical Magazine*, LX (October, 1959), 193–204.

Harkness, Albert, Jr. "Americanism and Jenkins' Ear," *Mississippi Valley Historical Review*, XXXVII (June, 1950), 61–90.

McCormac, E. I. *Colonial Opposition to Imperial Authority during the French and Indian War*. Berkeley, 1911.

Merritt, Richard L. *Symbols of American Community, 1735–1775*. New Haven, 1966.

Savelle, Max. "The Appearance of an American Attitude toward External Affairs, 1750–1775," *American Historical Review*, LII (July, 1947), 655–666.

Shy, John. *Toward Lexington: The Role of the British Army in the Coming of the American Revolution*. Princeton, 1965.

INDEX

Index